THE TWO GERMANIES

A Modern Geography
Roy E.H. Mellor

Harper & Row, Publishers

London   NewYork   Hagerstown   SanFrancisco   Sydney

First published 1978
Harper & Row Ltd
28 Tavistock Street
London WC2E 7PN

British Library Cataloguing in Publication Data
Mellor, Roy Egerton Henderson
    The Two Germanies.
    1. Germany – Economic conditions – 1945 –
    I. Title
    330.9'43'087   HC286.6

ISBN 0-06-318066-9
ISBN 0-06-318081-2 Pbk

Designed by Richard Dewing 'Millions', London
Phototypeset by Tradespools Ltd, Frome, Somerset
Printed by The Pitman Press, Bath, Avon

CONTENTS

PREFACE

My interest in Germany began in the years of the Third *Reich* and has remained through the great changes that have followed. Over such a span of time, an observer like myself becomes much impressed by the importance of the events, personalities and attitudes that comprise history in influencing the contemporary: it is this experience that has coloured the pattern of this text.

It would be difficult to list all the kind people in Britain and in Germany who have tolerated my inquiry and have tried to provide the answers I sought over the years – to them all I say a heartfelt thank you. I am also grateful for help received from the British Council and from the Carnegie Trust for Scotland as well as for the opportunity to spend terms in the Universities of Münster in Westfalen and Bochum.

For secretarial assistance in preparing the manuscript I greatly appreciate the help of Mrs. Jane Calder, Miss Christina Morrison, Miss Lily Findlay and Miss Elizabeth Weir. I have also received valuable assistance from Dr. Sheila Bain and Mrs. Irene Greig. The maps have been prepared and drawn by Mr. L. McLean, Mrs. Alison Sandison and Mr. Philip Glennie – their efforts are much appreciated. The work would never have been finished without the untiring assistance of my wife, who has done so many of the more tedious tasks.

R.E.H.M.

We still speak of *Germany* without usually qualifying to which *Germany* we are referring. Indeed, among the countries of Europe, Germany has been very much a fluctuating political–geographical unit with a changing pattern of territorial organization. So great have been the upsets and changes of the last hundred and fifty years that it is important to appreciate the historical dimension in the contemporary German scene. The great territorial upheavals of Napoleonic times were followed by faltering progress towards political-geographical unity in the Second *Reich* of 1871: a truly unitary and centralized German state appeared for a mere twelve years in the Third *Reich*. The Second World War has been followed by the emergence, in an abbreviated overall territorial framework, of two dimensionally and ideologically contrasting German states under outside sponsorship.

The nineteenth century, revolutionary in a political, social, economic, and technological sense, witnessed not only a changing political–geographical framework in Germany, but also laid the foundation of social and economic spatial patterns within the borders as drawn in 1815, later modified by both addition and loss. The dislocation caused by territorial loss after the First World War brought subsequent adjustments to and compromises with the new situation, hardly fully assimilated by the spatial structure of society and economy before the outbreak of the Second World War in 1939. Unconditional surrender in 1945, again followed by substantial territorial loss, brought a radical reordering of the nation's remaining political space. The victorious powers, despite their original aspiration to treat Germany as a unit, quickly separated, with the three Western allies confronting the Soviet Union in a tense interface of the Cold War that divided Germany in the 1950s, a line particularly disruptive because it cut through some of the most intensively developed parts of Germany. This ideological conflict between the Western and Eastern *blocs* hastened the recreation of German sovereignty, even if constrained, not as one state territory but as two, despite the single national identity of the German people. For over twenty-five years these two states have coexisted, each modelled on the ideology, values, and systems of its sponsors, and broadly attached to the wider spatial patterns of the *bloc* in which it finds itself. To the several interwoven patterns arising from past events, another has been added to complicate further the understanding of the palimpsest of space relationships that is Germany.

Thus the two German states provide, through their complex inter-relationships, a particularly interesting subject for regional geographical study, for they have each striven to disentangle the patterns of their territorial space inherited from the past and to establish new ones suited to their contemporary needs and to the pressures exerted from outside. Despite their present apparently cool and low-key relations, it seems unreal to study one in isolation from the other. First, two separate spatial organisms of society and economy have emerged from one integrated and closely knit complex system that culminated in the Third *Reich*. Second, the different political and economic systems erected in these states have faced similar inherited problems of their territorial space but by different paths have produced their own distinctive solutions through the generation of new spatial patterns. Third, these new structures have been engineered without completely removing the possibility that one day there may again be one and not two Germanies: neither wishes to see a final and irreparable break. Fourth, spatial patterns in the economy and society of the two states have been increasingly affected by the growing contact with neighbours within the large new inter- and supranational organizations that have grown in their respective *blocs* and have generated significant large-scale patterns of circulation and economic activity within their respective spheres.

Despite all their contrasts and comparisons, each state has in its own way been a postwar 'economic miracle' and both rank among the top ten of the world's industrial powers. While it is germane to stress the problems and difficulties faced by these states in adjusting to their new territorial and ideological structures, the magnitude and challenge of these problems may in themselves have acted as a stimulus to generate the 'economic miracle syndrome'. While influential external forces unquestionably have played a significant role – for example, the economic stimulant injected into West Germany by the involvement of the British and American economies in the Korean War or the Soviet spur to selected sections of the Central German economy to contribute to the strengthening of the Soviet home economy – there was a strong internal determination arising after 1945 from the suddenly impoverished German people, including large numbers forced to flee into the much reduced territory, to overcome the enormity of the damage and disruption caused by war and to reestablish what they felt to be a reasonable standard of living within the constraints of the times and within the political and economic systems in which they arbitrarily found themselves.

Some observers have pointed to the emergence of contrasts between landscapes of Eastern and Western Europe arising from the differences in policy generated by the ideological systems of the two *blocs*. In Western Europe, the landscape is said to bear the imprint of a modestly regulated free market economy in which market forces within broad limits dictate change; in Eastern Europe, the imprint in the landscape is that of change directed by centrally planned economic systems. Whereas before 1945 the German landscape was everywhere moulded by the same factors and economic philosophies, particularly a type of neomercantilism, this has been changed by the operation of strikingly different systems in the two contemporary German states. Since both began from a similar base landscape, an examination of this change in the two states is of particular value. Nevertheless, the divergences already apparent are perhaps less than might have been expected, and some of the change has been generated by the need to rectify imbalances in the economic structure, arising from the split of the formerly integrated system as much as through the differences generated by contrasting ideologies.

PART ONE
THE FOUNDATIONS

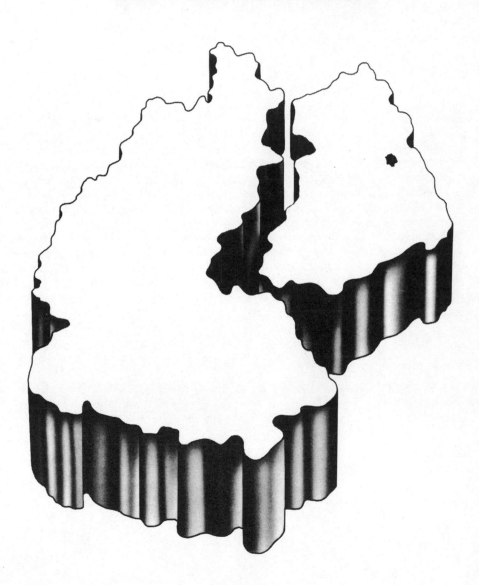

CHAPTER 1

THE GERMAN LANDS
THE GEOGRAPHICAL SETTING

Embedded in the core of Europe, the German peoples, identified by language and culture, but with varied religious and political affiliations, occupy a realm whose limits have varied considerably over time. German language and culture had spread (though not without setbacks) through colonization and migration from early mediaeval times until the nineteenth century, when – in the words of *Deutschland über Alles* – they extended from 'the Maas to the Memel, from the Adige to the Belt'. Twentieth-century events have, however, brought a contraction of this settlement area, but together the German peoples in the broadest ethnic sense still comprise about 90 million, almost one-fifth of Europe's population outside the Soviet Union. In modern times, the German peoples have been divided between the German nation state in its several forms; the Austrian nation state (until 1918 a component of a vast polyglot Habsburg empire); and the German-speaking cantons of the Swiss Confederation. Until the late 1940s, large numbers of German communities were found scattered beyond the bounds of the German states, though some remain on a much diminished scale.

Mediaeval Germany was simply a name across the map where people spoke German; Metternich in 1815 still regarded it as no more than 'a mere geographical expression'. The fragmented collection of principalities and lesser orders had been given some semblance of unity for nearly a millennium by the Holy Roman Empire of the German Nation (the first *Reich*), a vague and ineffectual body, whose emperor, supposedly guardian of Roman

Christianity, was seldom able to exert his will over the dissident secular and ecclesiastical lands of his fluctuating imperium, which in any case contained many non-Germans. The remarkable territorial fragmentation and the competition for leadership by the major dynasties bedevilled the search for political unity in a German nation state, though Prussian drive ultimately created the Second *Reich* in 1871, a congery of principalities welded unenthusiastically into a powerful state under the Prussian king in the role of emperor (*kaiser*). After territorial losses in the First World War and subsequent political upheavals, the Third *Reich*, a fully centralized state, sought after 1933 to draw all Germans into the first reputedly truly 'national state', an aim nearly achieved between 1942–1945 in *Grossdeutschland*. The dramatic political upheaval after 1945 divided remaining German territory into four occupation zones between the Allied powers, pledged to treat Germany after surrender as a unit, but the ideological abyss between the *blocs* quickly eroded this intent and instead two German states emerged – the western Federal Republic, sponsored by the British, Americans, and French, and the eastern Democratic Republic, tutored by the Soviet Union.

The German's nodal position within Europe was particularly important in the nineteenth and twentieth centuries when Germany lay as the eccentrically placed core of a nebulously defined but recognizably existing macroregional concept of *Mitteleuropa*. The reorganization of political space after the First World War weakened but did not destroy *Mitteleuropa*, and the final disintegration came only after 1945 in its division between two contrasting and mutually suspicious political spheres. The void left by its collapse is an important part of the overall contemporary German problem. Nevertheless, the nodality of the position remains, and the German political-territorial organism – whether one state or two – continues to lie as a bridge or barrier across the corelands of Europe. There is thus clearly an important political–geographical undertone in any regional study of Germany, however we may define it. First, there is the long search for unity among the German people and yet their striking reluctance to surrender strong regional distinctions and allegiances that impress a powerful parochialism into everyday life. Second, there are the territorial issues long outstanding between Germany and its neighbours, and even between its component parts. Third, events in Germany are seldom without repercussions elsewhere in Europe, and this latter impact remains particularly strong through the association of the Federal Republic with the European Community and of the Democratic Republic with the Council for Mutual Economic Aid (COMECON).

Clear lines of demarcation – 'natural frontiers' – for the German state (or states) are hard to find. The southern frontier has lain with remarkable stability in the northern fringes of the eastern Alps and along the upper Rhine, though physical features provide no clue, and the line is marked only by the

5

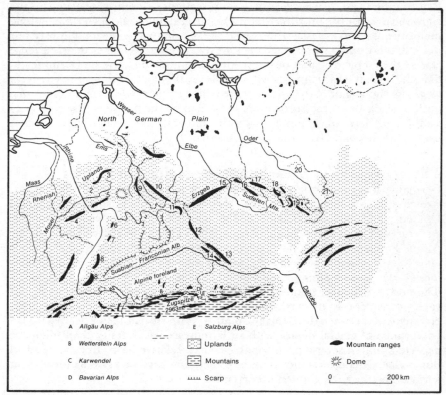

Figure 1.1 Relief

subtle sense of national association. Long stability has also marked the southeastern frontier, based on historic provinces strengthened by dynastic associations around the upland rim of Bohemia (though until 1945 German settlement extended well into the Bohemian interior). On the west, the frontier – a moderately shifting divide in modern times – represents in great measure the balance between the German view of the Rhine as a traditional axis and the French belief in the river as their strategically acceptable eastern limit. Further north, between Germany and the Benelux countries, the subjectivity of national identity has played a major role in the definition of the frontier, though in the extreme north it bisects the homeland of the Frisian people, while ethnic criteria finally decided the frontier in the Jutland Peninsula after Denmark for long held territories that would now be regarded as indisputably German. On the east, mediaeval German colonization spread along the better soils of the Silesian lands and the more attractive morainic country of the

The German Lands: The Geographical Setting

Baltic littoral to generate fretted and complex ethnic borders. In the eighteenth century, much country in the east without a German ethnic majority passed to Prussia, which set about 'Germanizing' its inhabitants; but in 1918, this frontier was pushed back westwards into Germany to define more closely the ethnic distributions in the important divide between German and Slav. In 1945, it was again pushed westwards, though this time ethnic criteria were less significant in the minds of the Allied leaders, while the whole ethnic pattern of East Central Europe was simplified by the mass expulsion of long-established German communities, both from annexed German territory and from lands beyond Germany's 1937 borders.

The geographical backcloth – the major landscapes

Germany, never coterminous with the major physiographic units of Europe, stretches across part of the North European Plain, part of the Central Uplands, and also across some of the scarps and vales that overlie older structures east and west of the Rhine Rift Valley, while it abuts on to the Alpine Foreland and the northernmost flanks of the eastern Alps.

The North German Plain

The northern Plain extends across North Germany from east to west, but varies considerably in north-south width, as it has outliers forming great embayments between the Central Uplands. With surface forms derived from a wide range of glacial deposits, there is more relief diversity than might be expected, and in several parts 'plain' seems a relative term. But the depth of fluvio-glacial deposits is such that the underlying hard rocks break the present surface only in a few limited occurrences.

Relative changes in land and sea levels since the retreat of the ice have shaped the features of the German North Sea and Baltic coasts. In the German Bight, the East Frisian Islands are dune islands on the seaward edge of coastal mudflats, which, under longshore drift, gradually shifted eastwards until modern counter measures were undertaken. The broad coastal mudflats reflect the slow encroachment of the sea upon the land since late glacial times, although the modern coast bears much witness of land reclamation. The North Frisian Islands, the sea-fretted edge of old morainic country, suffered dramatic losses to the sea in mediaeval times, but have also been extensively reclaimed in modern times, while the red sandstone cliffs of Helgoland are surrounded by a wide marine abrasion platform, mute testimony to the erosive power of the sea. Landwards of the fertile coastal marsh lie wide, almost imperceptibly undulating plains between the lower reaches of the main rivers, forming *Geest* – nearly featureless spreads of glacial outwash broken by low morainic remnants, markedly sandy country, with patches of moorland, swamp or peaty fens. Through suitable manuring, the dry *Geest* has been developed agriculturally, while reclamation has turned wet moor into pastureland and, on the sandiest areas, afforestation (mostly with conifers) has been widely practised.

The root of the Jutland Peninsula is a microcosm of the northern lowlands. Its western flank is coastal marsh and offshore islands backed by a sharp break of

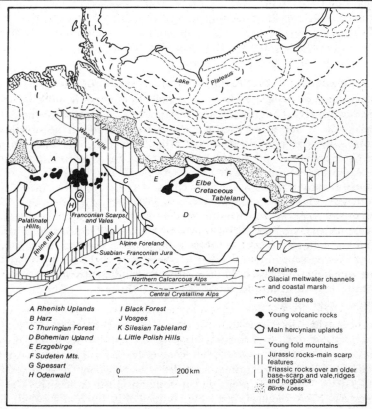

Figure 1.2 Landscape and morphology

slope representing an ancient coastline above which lies *Geest*. The dry country of the older western morainic plateau, largely arable country, merges eastwards into clearly marked young moraines that die away towards the Baltic into fertile clayey spreads. Among the moraines lie innumerable lakes and marshy hollows, while the Baltic coast has long and relatively deep drowned estuaries (*Föhrden*). The Lake Plateau of Mecklenburg lies north of the main meltwater valleys of Brandenburg and comprises two almost parallel

The German Lands: The Geographical Setting

moraine complexes forming an east-west belt of confused glacial country, with numerous lakes, many small but some of significant proportions, including long fingerlike channels. The climax vegetation of beech forest has been largely cleared to provide fertile farming country on the slightly leached soils, while drained marshy hollows provide pastures, with sandy outwash used for rye, potatoes or coniferous woods. The coastal clay plain, broadening eastwards, is also generally fertile, while the coast has been smoothed by bars built by an easterly longshore drift behind which lie shallow lagoons (*Bodden*). But in some places, clays or outcrops of solid rocks have been eroded into low cliffs, most striking in the rocky outcrop at Kap Arkona, and drowning of the coast has created islands like Rügen and Usedom.

The central east-west belt of the North German Plain is formed by five great meltwater channels separated by low interfluves of geest or morainic ridges. The modern rivers, though considerable in size, are clearly misfits in their immense shallow valleys, but wherever they have cut through the interfluves to follow the natural grain of the country to the Baltic, the courses are restricted between steeper valley sides. The confluence of meltwater channels in the Province of Brandenburg is particularly striking, where the landscape of lake, river, and forest contributes much to Berlin and its environs. The interfluves in the south are mostly sandy outwash comprising extensive heathland, but to the north they comprise clay ground moraine and jumbled knots of morainic hills. The remains of the older southern moraines form a broad tract of heathland or light pine forest and the westernmost of these sandy plateaulike interfluves is the Lüneburger Heide; further east lies the Altmark, an early marchland against the Slavs, while east of the Elbe, heathlands extend from the Fläming eastwards into Lusatia, a focus of industrial development around rich resources of lignite.

Where the northern lowlands abut onto the edge of the central uplands, a cover of fine windblown dust, *loess*, forms a fertile landscape of wide, farmed horizons broken only by small tree-clad hills, known as *Börde*. These rich soils are underlain by considerable mineral wealth – brown coal, iron ore, oil and mineral salts – with consequent sharp competition in land use. The most southwesterly *Börde*, the grain-growing country of Zülpich and Jülich, lies in the broad embayment around Köln, though further north the vast dissected Rhine-Maas gravel outwash fan is less fertile, so that along the Lower Rhine there is meadow in moist hollows and woodland on low hills of material pushed up by ice-age glacier snouts (*Stauchmoränen*). The large embayment between the Sauerland and Teutoburger Wald, the Münsterland, is mostly covered by heavy clays and loams (with patches of sandier heath), but *loess* occurs in the south in the fertile Soester *Börde*. The large bituminous coal resources that underlie the Münsterland have brought the slow march of coal mining from the Ruhr valley to the north bank of the Lippe, just as the

Vorgebirge horst landscape west of Köln has been changed by opencast brown coal mines and their aftermath. Another valuable *Börde* lies around Hannover, where again there is competition for land between mining, industry, and farming; but the classic *Börde* occurs around Magdeburg, Halle and between Leipzig and Gera, as well as in the more sheltered parts of the Thuringian Basin, notably in the *Goldene Aue*. Fertile loessic soils also continue eastwards into Lower Silesia.

The Central German Uplands

The Central Uplands, one of the most varied landscapes, consist largely of remains of older fold mountains, where in the vast deltaic swamps of rivers draining from them millenia ago were laid down sediments that now form the great bituminous coalfields. Reduced later to rolling hills and peneplains, seas flooded across their flanks depositing sediments from Triassic to Cretaceous age, but the orogenic forces that built the Alps shattered this older country into great blocks – some forced upwards to form massifs, others depressed and covered by younger sediments – accompanied by volcanic activity. The shattering took place along diagonal lines of weakness – from southeast to northwest and intersected from northeast to southwest – reflected in the shape of the massifs and their drainage. An important modern corridor of movement is provided by the striking structural weakness forming the lower country of the Hessian Corridor (in part blocked by the extinct 'Hawaian'-type volcano, the Vogelsberg), the Rhine Rift Valley and the Burgundian Gate to the Rhône. Other routeways are formed by deeply incised valleys, many of meandering character as the rivers, like the Mosel and Lahn, on the old peneplain surface gradually cut down to a new base level as the country was uplifted.

The Rhenish Uplands – *Rheinisches Schiefergebirge* – are divided into landscapes with subtle differences in physical form and human geography: on the west are the Eifel and Hunsrück, whereas east of the Rhine are the Taunus, Westerwald, Siegerland, Siebengebirge, Bergisches Land, Sauerland and Rothaargebirge. They comprise, however, a massive block of country, with a large, gently undulating surface about 400 metres above sea level, deeply incised by canyonlike valleys and broken by higher ridges and great knolls rising to roughly twice the height, while broad depressions represent the remains of ancient valleys. In the Eifel, round lakes (*Maare*) mark one-time explosive volcanic vents and ancient volcanoes provide the wooded domes of the Siebengebirge, whereas there are also basaltic cupolas and numerous mineral springs. Distinctive broad subsidence basins occur, like the Neuwied Basin with its valuable cover of granulated pumice (*Bims*), the Goldener Grund around Limburg, or the fertile Wittlicher Senke. The higher surfaces in the west are generally wetter than those east of the Rhine, trapping moisture from the inflow of humid Atlantic air, easily seen in the moors of the Schneifel and Hohes Venn. Everywhere are large forests, particularly on steep slopes and poorer soils, while farming has a strong livestock element. But in the basins, grain growing, fruit farming or early potatoes are important, as is lead ore in the Eifel, iron ore in the Lahn-Dill country and Siegerland, and ceramic clay in the *Kannenbäcker Ländchen* (Montabaur-Höhr-Grenzhausen) attracted settlement. Along deeply incised valleys, wherever aspect is suitable, vineyards are found, whereas the unsuitable northerly valleys of the Eifel and Sauerland contain large reservoirs to serve nearby industrial districts.

The Uplands of Hessen, ridges and hills amid broad depressions or narrower river valleys, reach to over 700 metres but lower country at 200–350 metres forms the Hessian Corridor that makes possible easier north-south movement. The landscape is a colourful contrast of farmland and forest, of favoured and unfavoured areas, with a diversity lacking in the massiveness and monotony of the Rhenish Uplands or the Harz, and infertile hills, either rather tabular blocks or volcanic domes, are separated by fertile north-south depressions. The largest volcanic areas are the Rhön, Knüll, and the Meissner, while the 2500 square kilometres of the low rounded cupola of the Vogelsberg is the largest continuous basalt area in Europe. These cool and moist uplands, mostly devoted to livestock, have much abandoned marginal land, now returned to forest, and small resources of brown coal occur in some basins; but the Werra basin contains a large potash deposit.

The Weser and Westphalian Hills are extensively folded and warped sedimentary structures reminiscent of the English Weald, with the scarps of the Teutoburger Wald and the Wiehengebirge separated by a lowland floored by clays. The Weser breaks through the southern scarp in the imposing *Porta Westfalica* and east of the river the landscapes of the Leine (or Lower Saxon) Hills arise from forms eroded into various hardnesses of sedimentary strata. The southern part is a landscape of broad and monotonous plateaus, with extensive forest, where the Weser flows in a deeply incised and narrow winding valley, but the Leine, occupying a broad north-south riftlike structure up to 8 kilometres wide, is the more important routeway. The north is far more diverse, with the folded rocks etched into escarpments of resistant sandstones and limestones, separated by intervening vales of less resistant materials, where a wide spread of fertile loessic soils occurs and the landscape has been modified by subsurface salt domes, while oil, natural gas and iron deposits, as well as some coal and mineral salts have given considerable economic importance.

The Harz, the most northerly of the old massifs of the Central Uplands, stands distinctively above the lower and younger materials on its flanks, from which it looks like roughly dissected hills. To fly over it shows the classical horstlike form, 190 kilometres long and 30 kilometres wide, with flanks deeply scored by incised valleys and comprising broad steplike erosion surfaces with a few residual masses (notably the Brocken, 1142 metres) rising above them. The Harz is still largely forest, with oak and beech on the lower surfaces and spruce above, but the highest parts are often bare moor, and early colonization was to work its wealth of lead, zinc, copper, and even silver.

The Thuringian Basin, separating the Harz from the structurally similar Thüringer Wald to the south, and surrounded by low, forested sandstone plateaus, is a basin-shaped extent of limestone, the edge of which is a forested scarp, whose dip slope is mostly arable land, whereas clays in the centre of the Basin are overlain by fertile blackish soil. The climate, warm but rather dry in summer, is well reflected in the extensive grain country of the Goldene Aue. The Thüringer Wald projects northwestwards from the Bohemian Massif as a ridgelike block, with the highest part (rising to almost 1000 metres) of resistant porphyry, though mostly slate, granite, conglomerate, and metamorphic rocks. Not particularly fertile, settlement began about AD 1000, attracted by iron and copper ores and by water power and charcoal. Between the Thüringer Wald and the Bohemian Massif, the Frankenwald and Vogtland, lower and more easily passable country, form an important historical routeway, although the latter is really a knot of hills among more prominent adjacent massifs, while the Frankenwald forms a rough fringe to the poor country of northeastern Bavaria. Both remains of old massifs, they are more extensively cleared and farmed than the Thüringer Wald, and ceramic clays have attracted industry. The remaining landscapes of the central uplands are really the fringes of the Bohemian Massif. The northwestern edge is the vast block of the Erzgebirge, tilted like a desk top to overlook from a steep fault scarp the Czech valley of the Ohře, while the northern dip slope drops in broad steps to the Saxon lowlands, with numerous north-flowing streams cutting the surface into broad interfluves. The forested Erzgebirge rises in places to over 1200 metres, and settlement penetrating from the north reaches 750 metres, with a few small hamlets in clearings up to 1000 metres. The name – Ore Mountains – suggests the mediaeval attraction to settlers: silver, lead, and iron; later nickel and cobalt; even recently radioactive minerals. The eastern Erzgebirge merges into the landscape of the Saxon Switzerland – the Elbe Sandstone Hills – horizontally bedded sandstones in a downfaulted zone through which the Elbe valley narrows in a striking gorge, leaving large flat-topped buttes (*Lilienstein, Königstein*), rock towers, and columns, making a popular tourist area. The foreland of clays has been hollowed out by the Elbe into a broad warm loess-covered basin, with Dresden as its centre, where high quality clay gave rise to the porcelain industry of Meissen. Further east lie the Upper Lusatian Hills extending to the Görlitzer Neisse, a landscape of gently undulating ridges and domes, many granite or basalt, with extensive tracts of hard sandstone. The higher parts generally remain forested, but *loess* over the lower areas makes them important agriculturally, and some brown coal occurs in subsidence basins around Zittau.

In the former German territories east of the Görlitzer Neisse, the physiographic pattern is similar to Saxony – in the south, a mountain or hill country dipping northwards to a broad foreland merging into the glacial northern plains. The Sudeten mountains rising to 1603 metres comprise a number of mountain groups and blocks of country, notably the Riesengebirge and the Glatz Hills. Between the main uplands are useful routeways, and two tectonic depressions are better settled patches of country – in the northwest around Hirschberg (Jelenia Góra) and in the southeast around Glatz (Kłodzko) – while important coal deposits occur near Waldenburg (Wałbrzych).

The southern flank of the Bohemian Massif in German territory is mostly infertile, forested country, where the Fichtelgebirge is a complex of forested hills and low plateaus, of generally hard crystalline rocks with poor soils and a raw, moist climate. But high-quality ceramic clays make Selb well known for porcelain. To the south, the Cham-Fürth depression is a major routeway into Bohemia and the Oberpfälzer Wald, lower country rising towards the Bohemian border, forms arable and meadowland. The Bayrischer Wald (and in part, the Böhmerwald), rolling country of seemingly endless forest, broken by a few small lakes of glacial origin, wet moorland and patches of large granite blocks from tor formation, has small industries using local raw materials for glass, pottery, and pencil making, but it is thoroughly inhospitable for the farmer.

The South German landscapes
Much of South Germany comprises distinctive landscapes of scarps, vales, and benches; but the core of this physiographic region is the rift valley of the upper Rhine, flanked on the east by the Odenwald and Schwarzwald and on the west by the Hardt and French Vosges. Away from the rift, gently dipping strata of sediments of varying thickness slope away from these uplands, but disruption of the ancient basement when the Alps were forming dislocated the great depth of overlying younger sedimentary materials, so that subsequent erosion produced scarps where harder sandstones and calcareous rocks occur, and broad terraces or vales in softer clays and mudstones, while rivers cut these scarps and vales into well-defined units.

The massifs flanking the Rhine are probably part of a vast uplifted dome where the central section cracked and subsided to form the rift valley, some 40 kilometres wide and 300 kilometres long, whose floor is covered by an immense depth of younger sedimentary deposits topped by riverine gravels. In the south, where the force of the orogenic thrust was greatest, the massifs are

The Two Germanies

highest; whereas in the north, the levels are irregular and the older crystalline rocks are partially covered by younger materials. Steep scarp faces along the rift give it a troughlike character, though the flat floor is broken by 'foothills' caused by splinter faults and by the volcanic Kaiserstuhl, while the scarp face is marked by 'embayments' (e.g., Breisgau). The rift continues northwards into the rich Rhine-Hessen and into the Burgundian Gate in the south. The once meandering Rhine was regulated in the nineteenth century and large areas of rich alluvium were reclaimed for farming, which also flourishes on the gravel terraces and the 'foothills', where there is a partly loessic cover. The Saar-Nahe lands comprise an old depression filled by Carboniferous and Permian sediments and volcanic materials subsequently diversely eroded. Nearer the Rhine, the *plateaulike* Hardt, remains of a broken dome structure and an area of hard sandstone overlooking the rift in a forested scarp, drops on the west to the Saar-Nahe depression and the Gutland of the edge of the Lorraine Plateau, while in the extreme southwest lies the Saar coalfield. Most northerly of the eastern Rhine Massifs, the forested Spessart has its western part of crystalline rocks but its eastern of resistant sandstones. On the southwest, across the deeply incised meandering valley of the Main, lies the slightly higher Odenwald, of similar structure and character, where on the east a dusting of *loess* has made good farmland. The Odenwald is separated from the Schwarzwald by the Kraichgau, a broad depression and a downwarp of the old basement, forming a wide farming landscape without much forest and a key routeway from the Rhine into the scarplands proper, though the Neckar surprisingly ignores this obvious route and cuts a deep, narrow valley through the southern Odenwald. The Schwarzwald or Black Forest, a massive asymmetrically tilted block, comprises granite and gneiss in the southwest (rising to 1500 metres), but to the north has a cover of older sedimentary rocks. The eastern flank is modestly dissected by headwaters of the Danube, but Rhine tributaries, deeply incised in the west and south, have cut across the massif to capture the upper Kinzig, a one-time Danube tributary. Remarkably even skylines arise from a series of erosion surfaces, while a small glacier has also left its impress on the landscape. Everywhere altitude and aspect are important influences on settlement, and much of the landscape is literally 'black forest'.

Travelling east from the massifs, a remarkable change takes place as the true scarp and vale country is reached, one of the oldest settled parts of South Germany, where a series of scarps and plateaus cut into limestone and clays extend from the Rhine near Schaffhausen across the Kraichgau and northwards to the headwaters of the Werra. From the Rhine above Basel, varied sedimentary rocks radiate out towards the north, becoming less tilted but broader in extent, so that gradually broad plateaus of the component rocks appear in place of a compact scarp and vale landscape. In the north, this

The German Lands: The Geographical Setting

country of the *Gäuland* is monotonous and undulating with many dry, shallow valleys and an absence of surface water. Largely without forest, it forms good farming country, particularly where there is a veneer of *loess*, but towards the south, however, there are stony soils. In the south, where dissection is more intense, altitude makes the land more suited to grazing (Klettgau), and between the Schwarzwald and the Suabian Alb, the Baar is a high, raw country. From the Neckar Basin in Schwaben, the *Gäu* plateaus – widening from east to west as one goes northwards – extend right across historical Franconia: the western part is a Calcareous plateau, dry, stony and poor, rising to over 400 metres in a western scarp, whereas, eastwards, sandstones, shales, and clays overlain by *loess* form an even plateau landscape of open arable lands dotted by tightly nucleated villages in depressions around springs or wells. The deep, warm, and lively valley of the Main in the north contrasts with the quiet plateau, and along its steep limestone sides the vine is found on sunny slopes. The eastern boundary of the *Gäu* plateaus is a distinct scarp rising to over 500 metres, whose lower slopes in the south are grassland or fruit gardens, though the sandstone cap is forest – once deciduous, but now mostly conifers – while wherever aspect is suitable vines appear. Further north, this scarp has three distinct sections: the Frankenhöhe, the Steigerwald, and the Hassberge, where generally poor sandy soils and a cool climate are unattractive to farmers and much forest remains. In Franconia, the lower western sandstone scarp stands at a greater distance from the high limestone scarp than in Suabia, and between them lies the broad Nürnberg Basin, with much heath and pine forest, though careful farming has enriched the light, easily warmed, sandy soils.

The great Suabian-Franconian Alb concave to the north, the highest and most clearly defined of the scarps, marks the eastern and southern boundary of the South German Scarplands. Rising to 1000 metres, it runs in a massive bow from the Rhine above Basel to the Frankenwald, some 400 kilometres, and for most of its extent some 40 kilometres wide, separating many small comblike scarps on the north from the open Alpine Foreland on the south. What appears to be a substantial obstacle to north-south movement is in fact crossed by many easy routes following valleys and gaps, though the most obvious are not necessarily the most commonly used. The Suabian Alb – the southwestern sector – has gentle lower slopes cut in clay, whose brown soils are well watered by springs from the overlying limestone, while steep beech-covered slopes rise some 350 metres above the surrounding country. Streams have fretted the scarp face, leaving isolated and commonly castle-crowned outliers, and provide easy access to the summit. The limestone dip slope forms a high rolling surface with dry valleys, karstic phenomena and small forested hills. The major routeway is the Geislinger Steige, followed by the main railway from Stuttgart to München. This sector of the Alb ends in the great circular depression of the Ries around Nördlingen, floored by younger rocks mantled by *loess*, for which both volcanic and meteorite origins have been postulated. East of the Ries, the Franconian Alb begins and is crossed by the Altmühl that rises in the Frankenhöhe and flows through the scarp in a spectacular gorge to the Danube which has cut into the lower flanks of the dip slope by its northwards deflection. After swinging to a roughly southwest-northeast alignment, the Alb changes character – the west-facing scarp becomes less impressive, broken by an intermediate break of slope in a bench of hard ferruginous sandstone, while the woods change from beech to mostly spruce. The dip slope has also been uplifted and fractured by movement of the Bohemian Massif, so that a minor east-facing scarp has formed to create an extremely dry and sparsely populated northern plateau. Between the Alb and the Bohemian Massif lie the Upper Palatinate Hills, a basinlike area of hills of varied rocks broken by basaltic knolls, whose nickname, 'Potato Palatinate' (Kartoffelpfalz) reflects local farming practice.

The German Alps and their foreland
The southernmost physiographic province is the Alpine Foreland and the German part of the eastern Alps. The Foreland, roughly triangular between the Alps, the Alb, and the Bohemian Massif, is a trough deeply filled by sediments eroded from the Alps and covered by materials deposited from the alpine glaciers. These materials have been cut and terraced into isolated segments by tributaries flowing north to the Danube, so that, apart from the gentle hills of Lower Bavaria in the northeast, it is a landscape of broad plateaulike gravel terraces, whose surface drops from 750 metres in the south to about 400 metres in the north. From west to east, climatic conditions become more continental, though soil quality improves, forming good arable country, with meadowland in the valleys, but wherever clays occur there is wet moor (Dachauer, Freisinger, Erdinger Moos), now largely drained and settled. The southern gravel plateaus carry moraines left by the retreat of the alpine valley glaciers, giving a green and forested landscape of rolling country with small lakes and peaty hollows, most striking in the moraines of the Rhine glacier north of the Bodensee. The Bodensee itself is a zone of subsidence hollowed out by ice and probably associated with the volcanic landscape of the Hegau to the west. Heavily laden tributaries from the Alps have pushed the Danube to the northern edge of the Foreland along the foot of the Alb dip slope to form a sluggish, braided stream clogged by sediments, with patches of marshland and peaty moor. In its upper reaches, where it flows across the limestone of the Alb dip slope, consequently losing much water by seepage to the Rhine, its course is often dry.

The Alps form an essential part of the popular image of Germany and yet are one of the least representative landscapes. Though constituting a psychological barrier between the German lands and the European South, they are no real barrier to communication, with many routes across them, with the most important gateways into the inner valleys from the German side through the Inn valley via Kufstein and the Schnarnitzer Klause (*Porta Claudia*) via Mittenwald. On German territory, the alpine zone extends only from the pre-alpine hills to the northern Calcareous Alps, with elevations all below 3000 metres so that, despite high rainfall and winter snow, only three small glaciers and some snowfields exist on the Zugspitze and Watzmann. Sandstones, clays, conglomerates, Cretaceous limestones, and early Tertiary sediments flank the older limestones of the High Alps, everywhere carved by Quaternary ice. Forest reaches to 1800 metres, above which rise alpine pastures (most extensive in the Allgäu Alps) and even bare pointed peaks. Slope and aspect are major influences on settlement along the long, broad, overdeepened U-shaped valleys, whose floors are strewn by moraines, lakes, and wet patches, and the outwash cones along the valley sides are favoured for settlement above the likely flood level.

Climate

The German lands have a climate transitional between the western maritime conditions and the continentality of the eastern marchlands. Except in unusual years, although the annual variation is considerable, it is without great extremes of heat or cold, nor is it excessively dry or unbearably moist; but day-to-day variation is sufficiently great to make 'weather' in the real sense, while year-to-year variation is such as to allow years to be designated as wet, dry, hot, cold, etc. No major relief obstacles prevent deep penetration by westerly air masses so characteristic of Europe's temperate climates (though southerly influences are generally restricted by the barrier of the Alps), but penetration by boreal conditions across the northern plains and the central uplands of modest elevation is frequent. The general synoptic situation has over three quarters of the days with marked westerly circulation, the influence of the Azores high pressure system. Nevertheless, the build-up of a large cold air mass extending from Asia into central Europe generally marks winter, strengthened by the outflow of its own cold air that tends to ward off the cyclones of milder westerly air. Along the contact between the differing air masses there is commonly disturbance, with rain or snow showers, and wide day-to-day fluctuations in temperature. But the further east one travels, the stronger does the continental cold air mass become and the more stable winter conditions. If this cold continental air mass develops particularly strongly, then extremely cold winters are experienced (1946–1947); whereas when it fails to develop its usual vigour over the high-pressure axis along the 50°N line, conversely mild winters occur (1973–1974). The breakdown of the high-pressure system in spring is usually rapid and temperatures rise quickly, particularly in the east, so that depressions from the Atlantic and even the Mediterranean penetrate further inland. As the land warms more quickly than the sea, summer pressure conditions are the reverse of winter and the great low-pressure system over northern Asia extends into eastern Europe; but shallow depressions bring turbulence, with thundery conditions giving sharp, short showers and providing a summer precipitation maximum that distinguishes the interior from the maritime west. If the Azores high-pressure system penetrates into South Germany, long hot spells are experienced, sometimes lasting into September, though this system flags in late summer, when depressions from the Atlantic carry in unsettled rainy weather. Only in the far southeast is autumn drier than spring, while in the far northwest (where maritime influence is strongest) there is an autumn–winter precipitation maximum. Temperatures drop quickly from late September, again most markedly in the east, and snow may occur by late October. Autumn is shorter than in the extreme west of Europe and grows less pronounced towards the east.

The long daily insolation and lower elevation in the north balance substantially the higher intensity of insolation but greater elevation in the south, so average summer temperatures are consequently remarkably even everywhere. Thunder downpours from rapid heating make summer usually the wettest part of the year, though greater evaporation tends to keep down humidity. Winter temperatures are lower away from the northwest towards the east and southeast, but everywhere February is the driest month. Though winter precipitation declines towards the east, snow becomes more important as it lies longer, though it is seldom deep, and rivers are frozen longer. The east shows more 'continental' features, with greater annual and diurnal variations in temperature: it is also drier and less humid, while the mild clammy weather of winter in West Germany is seldom experienced, and long periods of settled weather occur although, in the lee of uplands, drought is common.

Five climatic regions bear close relationship to the major physiographic provinces. The open lowland of North Germany allows air masses from all directions easy access. Friesland, the Lower Elbe, and the Jutland Peninsula are markedly maritime in character: winter is mild and moist, with freezing of rivers rare; January temperatures are generally above freezing level, with much drizzly rain in winter (though the precipitation maximum remains in summer) and mists and fog are common. Spring and autumn last long by German standards, while summer is often very warm, though thunder is less common than further east. Eastern Schleswig-Holstein shows a more truly Baltic régime, with colder winters and more snow; inland winter is drier and cooler, while summer is warmer and thunder common. In the far west, in the Lower Rhine and the Münsterland as well as in the coastal lands, snow falls on more days than it lies, often melting as it reaches the ground, but heavy falls that thaw suddenly produce exceptionally bad conditions for transport. East of the Elbe is more continental, but the more severe winter is offset by plenty of settled weather when the sun shines from clear skies over a snow-decked landscape. Snow lies on more days than on which it falls, lakes and rivers freeze, and ice may occur even along the Baltic coast. A short spring gives way to a very warm summer – though the contrast between summer temperatures east to west across the plain is less than for winter temperatures. Summer precipitation comes notably from thunderstorms, though the total is lower than in the west, particularly in the lee of uplands.

Of great climatic diversity are the Central Uplands, where aspect and elevation play important roles. The maximum vertical temperature contrast occurs in spring, when the hollows and valleys are warming up but snow remains on the tops. Minimum vertical contrast is in winter, when cold air seeps into hollows and temperature inversion results. Precipitation is also clearly related

Table 1.1
Climate of selected German stations

Station	Elevation	Months/Temperature			
	m	<0°C	Jan. °C	July °C	Precipitation mm
G.D.R.					
Schwerin	59	1	−0.1	17.5	627
Wüstrow	7	2	−0.2	17.0	569
Greifswald	5	1	−0.4	17.3	604
Magdeburg	56	0	0.3	18.8	506
Potsdam	81	1	−0.7	18.1	585
Cottbus	70	1	−0.6	18.3	586
Erfurt	217	1	−0.7	17.6	500
Leipzig	113	0	0.2	18.7	545
Dresden	112	0	0.3	18.9	661
Zittau	245	2	−1.1	17.9	664
Meiningen	308	2	−1.1	16.5	644
Geisingberg	823	3	−3.8	14.1	818
Brocken	1142	3	−4.8	10.5	1483
Inselsberg	914	3	−4.1	12.9	1269
Fichtelberg	1214	3	−5.3	11.3	1094
Brotterode	580	2	−2.5	14.8	1082

Station	m	<0°C	Jan. °C	July °C	Precipitation mm
G.F.R.					
Flensburg	41	0	0.2	16.6	804
Hamburg	13	0	0.0	17.3	740
Aachen	202	0	1.8	17.5	840
Essen	154	0	1.5	17.5	897
Hannover	53	0	0.2	17.6	637
Berlin–Dahlem	51	1	−0.7	18.7	587
Kassel	158	1	−0.1	17.9	595
Saarbrücken	191	0	0.9	18.2	786
Geisenheim/Rheingau	109	0	0.7	18.8	517
Frankfurt am Main	125	0	0.8	19.4	604
Stuttgart	305	0	0.8	19.0	662
Würzburg	259	1	−0.7	18.4	560
Nürnberg	310	2	−1.4	18.2	592
Ulm	522	3	−1.8	17.7	702
München– Nymphenburg	515	3	−2.1	17.5	886
Oberstdorf	810	3	−3.4	15.3	1722

Source: Statistical yearbooks of the two German republics

to elevation, with most on west-facing slopes, while valleys and basins are relatively dry, particularly if in lee of a large upland. The western uplands at 600–700 metres are as wet as the more easterly mountains at 1000 metres. In general, the higher areas have more precipitation in winter and the basins more in summer. Snow cover expectedly lies longest on the higher surfaces and generally longer but less deeply towards the east, where winter is also colder and longer and spring shorter. Precipitation in the uplands provides water for the German rivers, and valley reservoirs store water needed by the growing demand from lowland industries.

Along the Rhine, winter is generally mild, while spring comes early, particularly in the rift valley, and though precipitation is generally low, it is often hazy or misty in spring and summer. Autumn also lasts late, with frequent warm sunny days in October in good years, vital for vine cultivation. In the rift valley, January temperatures are usually well above freezing, while summers have a July average well over 18°C. Relief is important, so that the central rift valley receives moisture penetrating through the Saverne Gap,

The German Lands: The Geographical Setting

while summer instability conditions give thundery rain; but it is the least snowy part of Central Europe. Elevational contrasts are particularly clearly seen in the Rhine gorge, where cold air flowing down tributary valleys can bring treacherous ice in winter.

The basins and valleys of the scarplands of South Germany are especially warm in summer, though often cold air traps in winter, which, because of their position and elevation, is as long and as great as in the eastern part of the northern plains. The large expanses of calcareous rock give a dry aspect to the country which it hardly deserves, but the scarp edges, mostly west or north facing, trap moisture and show higher precipitation than the dip slope. The southwest corner in the lee of the Black Forest is relatively dry, but cold air drainage makes the Baar one of the most frost-threatened parts of Central Europe. Position and elevation also result in snow lying as long as in the higher Central Uplands.

The Alpine Foreland has a marked continentality, but the summers are cooler than in the Rhine rift valley, and the winters are cold from the general elevation (400–500 metres) and from cold air drainage from adjacent higher lands, with January temperatures generally below −2°C. Autumn is long, clear, and still, but usually with frost at night (even by early September), while spring is short. The locally modified climate of the Bodensee makes the Insel Mainau mild enough to support many subtropical and Mediterranean plants. Along the foot of the Alps, precipitation rises sharply, with heavy thundery rain in summer, and the *föhn* wind in spring may raise temperatures 10°C in a day.

The Alps have an annual precipitation over 1500 millimetres, much coming as snow, which lies long and makes the area important for winter sports (e.g., Garmisch-Partenkirchen, Oberstdorf). Like many inland areas of Germany, dry and powdery snow usually falls in still air without consequent drifting. Thus it is less of a hazard to transport than the wet and drifting snow typical of the more maritime parts. While summer in the highest mountains is singularly cool, valleys and basins have warm and oppressive summer conditions, whereas, in contrast, due to cold air drainage, winter is outstandingly raw and cold. Great cold is experienced at great height: the Zugspitze observatory (2964 metres) has an average of −11°C in January, with permanent snow all the year. On north-facing slopes, direct sunlight is hardly experienced in winter, so settlement seeks the warmer and brighter south-facing aspect away from possible avalanche tracks that are peculiarly dangerous when the *föhn* wind blows.

The resource endowment of the German lands

The general picture of resource endowment in the German states is of little in plenty but a wide variety, though presence of a mineral does not assure its use:

deposits must be large and easy enough to work to make possible their exploitation at given price levels (but 'uneconomic' working has taken place under strategic necessity), and this condition accounts for the German lands having been major producers of metals in the Middle Ages compared to more recent times.

Industrial development in the nineteenth-century steam age was closely linked to generous deposits of bituminous and brown coal. Of the major bituminous coalfields along the northern edge of the Central Uplands, the westernmost lies in two distinct basins near Aachen, geologically related to the deposits of Dutch Limburg and the Belgian Kempenland. Coal is no longer worked from exposed seams in the Inde Basin, and the main centre is now the deeply buried coal measures of the Wurm Basin around Alsdorf, with an anthracite deposit in the Erkelenz Horst north of Jülich. Annual production is around seven million tons, mostly coking quality, despite thin seams and structural problems. The large Ruhr or Rhenish-Westphalian coalfield, contributing about 75–80 percent of total German production, extends over 3300 square kilometres in the shaft and borehole zone; but the proven area is twice as great, extending away northwards under an increasing thickness of younger sediments. To a depth of 1200 metres, some 50 workable and about 30 conditionally workable seams are known, with the reserves measured to this depth sufficient for a yearly production of 100 million tons for 350 years. Between 1200–1500 metres another 30–42 thousand million tons are estimated. Several mines already work below the 1200-metre level. Annual production averages about 90–100 million tons (record 127 million tons in 1938), with about 70 percent in coking coal. The exposed coalfield in the south has been worked out and mining has moved north; but as the seams are folded into broad saddles and basins, often dislocated by transverse faults, mines tend to seek out the crests of the saddles. Despite the wetness and structural difficulties in the seams, the excellence of the coking coal makes this one of the most important European fields. Structurally probably a part of the Rhenish-Westphalian coal seams, deposits on the northwest flank of the Teutoburger Wald near Ibbenbüren are worked in a field 15 kilometres long by 6 kilometres wide. Annual output is about 2.3 million tons, 30 percent sold for domestic use, while 20 percent is good industrial coal. Other small deposits have been formerly worked in the Bückeberge and the Deister (Barsinghausen) southwest of Hannover.

Between the French and Luxemburg frontiers lies the Saar coalfield, which to a depth of 1200 metres, contains a thousand million tons of exploitable coal, extending over an area of about 525 square kilometres; but the seams are folded and dislocated by transverse faults. West of the Saar river the seams are covered by a considerable depth of barren rocks, but large accessible reserves exist, while part of the field lies across the French frontier in the Rosselle valley. On the southeast, a thrust fault buries the seams at unworkable depth, whereas, on the north and northeast, they dip away under barren deposits. Seams averaging 2 metres are currently worked (the 55 seams contain together about 60 metres of coal) and output averages about 11 million tons, three fifths in coking coal; but although low in sulphur, Saar coals do not make high quality metallurgical coke. Small deposits of mostly indifferent bituminous coal exist in South Germany, and in Upper Bavaria between the Lech and the Inn 'tar coals' (*Pechkohle*) of Tertiary date occur, where a heavy overburden accelerated metamorphism into a shiny black coal with a high heating value. At Peissenberg, down to a depth of 1400 metres, are about 40 million tons of exploitable coal in two seams, but working of the last mine ceased in 1971, though six pits operated in the 1930s.

The German Democratic Republic has only limited bituminous coal resources; of the 200 million tons reserves, only a small part is exploitable, with the most likely future source in the Doberlug-Kirchhain district (west of Finsterwalde). It is unlikely that large deposits reputed to exist in the deeply buried basement of the North German Plain will ever be exploitable. Before 1945, output comprised only 2 percent of German production, mostly steam and locomotive coal; after the Second World War, production rose to about 3 million tons and then fell back. Mining is now limited to the Zwickau district (some coal of coking quality), with abandonment of the Freital-Dresden, Plötz and Lugau-Ölsnitz deposits.

In prewar Germany, Upper Silesia, one of the largest coal reserves in Europe, was the second major producer, when only 10 percent of the reserves then lay in German territory, although German mines produced over half the total output. The seams are little disturbed and not deeply buried, but the coals are of inferior coking quality. The field suffered from political geographical problems in the interwar years and it was lost completely to Germany in 1945. The Lower Silesian field is much disturbed and difficult to mine, though the bulk of the field lay in German territory, worked around Waldenburg (Wałb-rzych) for coals of good coking quality.

About a third of world production of brown coal (lignite) comes from the German Democratic Republic and a little over 10 percent from the Federal Republic, while the former state holds the bulk of the German reserves exploitable by opencast mining (23,000 million tons), extending over about 300,000 hectares. In the G.D.R., a large part of the brown coal west of the Elbe has a high salt content, but between the Saale and the Elbe are significant resources of good quality coal, well suited for use in the chemicals industry. Intensive working has, however, nearly exhausted some good seams, for example, in the Geiseltal. With shallower seams nearing exhaustion, deeper seams are now being exploited, and the tendency is to concentrate on the more accessible

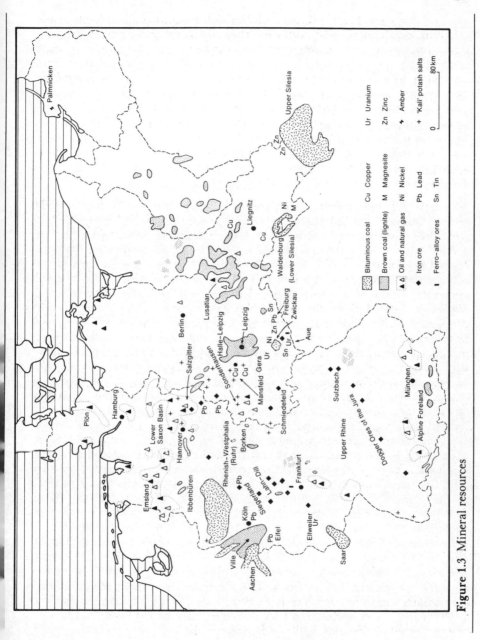

Figure 1.3 Mineral resources

The German Lands: The Geographical Setting

deposits in Lower Lusatia, where 60 percent of the opencast resources lie, mostly between Senftenberg and the Neisse river. Brown coal output in the Federal Republic is almost 95 percent from the Ville (Vorgebirge) horst west of Köln, but mining is moving northwards as the southern deposits are exhausted. Large reserves are also known to the west and north in the Lower Rhine, but mostly at depths presently uneconomic to work, though opencast working is already generally deeper than in the Elbian and Lusatian fields. Some small workings lie near Aachen. The workings on the western end of the Magdeburg field within West Germany near Helmstedt are less significant as are other deposits such as Schwandorf in Bavaria, Wölfersheim north of Frankfurt am Main, and Borken near Kassel, while small unworked deposits lie scattered in the Westerwald and in the Hessian Corridor.

Although oil seepages were first tapped near Celle in 1859, the German lands remain limited producers of oil and natural gas, despite promising geological structures, mostly associated with salt dome structures. Modern methods of survey have, however, led to increased reserves being mapped in the 1960s, in many cases in areas where deposits have been known since the turn of the century – for example, in the Ems and Weser basins, in Schleswig-Holstein, and in the Alpine Foreland and Rhine Rift Valley. During the interwar years, Nienhagen near Hannover became the main producing centre, when domestic production covered about 10 percent of requirements. The Federal Republic now covers under one-fifth of its greatly increased home needs, with about 45 percent of production presently from the Lower Ems (Bentheim-Lingen-Emlichheim); the older workings in the Aller basin supply about 30 percent; while Schleswig-Holstein and the Rhine Rift Valley as well as the Bavarian Alpine Foreland supply the remainder. The German sector of the North Sea has as yet not shown the promise of other sectors, though natural gas has been located offshore and in the Dollart estuary. On land, natural gas (worked since 1938) is found associated with oil as well as separately, with the largest occurrence in Zechstein rocks in the north and in Tertiary molasse deposits in the south, so that the Federal Republic covers over half its domestic needs. In The German Democratic Republic, the first natural gas was struck in 1907 at Langensalza; in 1930, natural gas and oil were found at Volkenroda in northwest Thuringia, followed later by more natural gas finds (notably at Salzwedel). Good quality oil was struck in 1964 at 2300 metres at Reinkenhagen southeast of Stralsund; later finds have been made at Grimmen and east of Greifswald, with small finds near Guben and near Forst; but these resources are inadequate for the republic's growing demand. Both states have resources of nuclear fuel minerals. The German Democratic Republic has particularly significant deposits in the Erzgebirge, first worked intensely after 1945 for the Soviet nuclear industry, while in more recent years mining has shifted to the Gera district. In the Federal Republic, a deposit has been worked in the Palatinate near Ellweiler, and other resources are known in the Baryrischer Wald.

Water power has been harnessed as an energy resource, although generally conditions are not very attractive. The major rivers are usually of too low a gradient, and those issuing from the Alps are small in volume. In many cases, generation of electricity is a by-product of barrages designed for other purposes (e.g., along the Mosel for navigation or in the central uplands for flood control and storage of water for industrial purposes). In the Federal Republic, hydro-electricity contributes 10 percent of total generation and in the G.D.R. only about 1 percent. Several hydro-electric plants (notably in the G.D.R.) are designed as pump storage works.

Deposits of metallic minerals are not only varied, but also widely scattered, although few are of a size and condition that warrants modern working unless world prices are exceptionally high. Iron ore deposits of various types are widely dispersed, though few are suitable for working under modern conditions even in times of high price, so that reserves of exploitable ore are limited. An important part in industrialization was played by the German control, from 1871–1918, of the large reserves of sedimentary 'minette' ores in Lorraine. The major contemporary German resources lie in the Ilsede-Peine area of Lower Saxony, the main mining area since 1945, supplying 70 percent of West German output, where important additional resources were found after the Second World War. Output of the Lahn-Dill and Siegerland-Wied districts has declined after activity in the interwar and postwar years, though these ores contain up to 6 percent manganese. The richest manganese-iron deposit (15–20 percent Mn) comes from Waldalgesheim near Bingen: others lie in the Weser Bergland and in the Saarland. Reserves of iron ore occur in South Germany – in the Sulzbach-Amberg area of Bavaria and in the Dogger ores of the Suabian and Franconian Alb, though prewar plans for extensive working never materialized. In the German Democratic Republic, modest resources are found near Schmiedefeld. Small deposits were held in Silesia until 1945. Tungsten (*wolfram*) is found in tin ores of the Erzgebirge, while nickel also occurs near Zwickau in the G.D.R., but small deposits in Lower Silesia were lost to Poland in 1945. Deposits in the Schwarzwald and Harz are also generally small. Some cobalt occurs in the Erzgebirge at Schneeberg, but deposits in the Riesengebirge were lost to Poland in 1945. In West Germany, the only workable resource is in the Kinzig Valley in the Black Forest.

Nonferrous metals are totally inadequate to cover domestic needs in both German states. Widespread lead and zinc deposits occur, notably in the Harz (particularly zinc) and in the Eifel, where at Maubach near Düren one of Europe's largest lead deposits has been found. Deposits also occur along the Lahn valley as well as in the Black Forest. Substantial zinc deposits in Silesia were partially lost to Poland after 1918 and fully surrendered after 1945. In the German Democratic Republic, lead occurs in the Erzgebirge and copper resources are small and localized with Mansfeld as the main producer, but workings also lie in the Erzgebirge. In West Germany, Rammelsberg in the Harz has lead-zinc ores containing meaningful amounts of copper. Since annexation by Poland, large copper resources – the richest in Europe – have been discovered in Lower Silesia near Liegnitz (Legnica) and Bunzlau (Bolesławiec). Tin deposits occur only in the Erzgebirge (G.D.R.), but are inadequate for domestic needs. Bauxite in small occurrences in the Vogelsberg in West Germany is poor in quality and difficult to work. Magnesium was found in Germany's prewar territory near Glatz (Kłodzko) in Lower Silesia. German territory is peculiarly rich in salt – sufficient could be produced to supply the world. In North and Central Germany, vast deposits of various potassium, sodium, and magnesium salts were laid down in the Permian Zech-stein sea, and the major salt basin surrounds the Harz; but salt dome structures and related forms stretch away to and under the North Sea, though these northwestern deposits are little surveyed. A small but valuable basin straddles the inter-German frontier in the upper Werra and Fulda valleys. Main producing centres are Helmstedt and Salzdethfurt in West Germany, with Bernburg, Langensalza, Halle/Saale, Erfurt, and the famous Stassfurt in the G.D.R. A promising but only partially used salt-bearing area lies on the lower Rhine (Moers, Rheinberg). In 1904 potash salts were discovered near Mülhausen (Mulhouse), in then German Alsace, and in 1912 on the right bank of the Rhine (Buggingen and Lahr). In the Salzburg Alps rock salt is found near Berchtesgaden and Reichenhall. Other deposits occur near Heilbronn, Kochendorf, Jagstfeld, Schwäbisch-Hall, and Rottweil. Until the loss of the Alsatian deposits to France in 1918, Germany had a world monopoly of potash salts, while it still retains a 40 percent share of world production.

A wide range of building materials exists, with local availability colouring building styles and the visual impact of town and village. The glaciated northern lands provide excellent brick clays, reflected in the distribution of the mediaeval brick Gothic (*Backsteingotik*) and more recent styles. Sands and gravels are dug widely in the glacial lands, but also in the major river valleys, where excavation has created large artificial lakes, commonly used recreationally. Volcanic powdered pumice for building blocks is typical of the middle Rhine, while basalt and other volcanic rocks are worked for building and ballast. Sandstone of various types is also popular building material, while forms of marble (e.g., from the Lahn valley) have been used for decorative work. Calcareous rocks form a basis for cement making, notably in Westphalia (Beckum, Lengerich), the Sauerland (Balve, Letmathe), the Neander Valley, the Voreifel, and in parts of South Germany. Rüdersdorf–Berlin, Bernburg, and Karsdorf are major cement works in the German Democratic Republic. Resources of high-grade sands for glass making are particularly important in the Upper Palatinate, Central and Upper Franconia, Thuringia, the northern Eifel, the Weser Hills, and Lusatia. Glass-making raw materials also occur in the Sudeten Mountains, though the German glass workers have been expelled from the Bohemian side of the border as well as from districts lost to Poland in 1945. Ceramic clays (often of high quality) are also widespread in the Westerwald (*Kannenbäcker Ländchen*), the Lower Rhine, the Saar, and Main valleys, as well as in the Upper Palatinate and in Saxony. Prewar Bunzlau (Bolesławiec) – now in Poland – was important.

Natural conditions for farming

Only in a few areas do conditions of relief, climate, or soil completely preclude farming, though over considerable areas a combination of adverse factors results in other land use, usually forestry. But extensive heath and moorland still exist, even though proportions of different land uses naturally change over time with changing economic and social conditions. With complex geological conditions, diverse local microclimates, and a varied relief, it is to be expected that soil conditions vary considerably, while the agricultural value of the various soils is conditioned by factors such as richness in nutrients, ease of working, moisture régime, the need for commercially available fertilizers. Flexibility of different soils to nourish crops is a significant factor from the farmer's point of view, who prefers to have a holding with several types of soils. Under German conditions, where variations in climate from one part of the country to another are small, the Dokuchayev view of soils as conditioned by climate is not readily applicable, so that parent material, hydrologic régime, and modification introduced by long tilling become important indicators.

The northern lowlands have soils conditioned by glacial clays and sands containing varying densities and sizes of stones and boulders. High rainfall and relatively low evaporation have tended to leach humus and valuable minerals, washing them well below the surface to form a hard cementlike layer (*Ortstein*), preventing drainage and encouraging waterlogging; and while such acidic and podzolic soils are not inviting to the farmer, expensive ploughing and liming can make them quite fertile. On the south of the plain and notably east of the Elbe, on younger glacial drift where there has been mixed or deciduous forest and parent materials rich in carbonate, so-called brown and grey-brown earths have formed, with a good humus content, generally richer in nutrient and with better physical characteristics. Around the North Sea coast, marsh soils formed in salt or brackish water are rich in nutrients and humus, with a crumbly structure, well suited to pasture.

A broad belt of *loess* along the southernmost flank of the lowlands and in broad

0   75km

Grey—brown soils partly podzolised

Predominantly podzolised soils

Acid brown forest soils

Humic brown forest soils

Mixed rendzina (carbonate) and podzolic soils

Humus carbonate soils

Black earths of various types

Moor soils

Barren rock and skeletal soils

Coastal and riverine marsh and meadow soils

Upland areas

Upland podzolic soils

Upland carbonate soils

Upland brown forest soils

Upland brown forest soils and mixed soils

Figure 1.4 Soils

The Two Germanies

embayments on the northern edge of the uplands provides a basis for rich and remarkably fertile soils of light texture. Where there is low rainfall in the rainshadow of the upland (e.g., in Saxony), a poorish black earth (formed possibly under parklike woodland) is found, but wherever the rainfall increases, rapid degrading occurs. The loessic soils attract some of the highest agricultural land values in Germany.

The Central Uplands have generally stony soils of widely different type, but most common are the brown soils developed under deciduous and mixed woodland on gentle or moderate slopes, with crystalline rocks commonly as parent material. These soils have suffered in general less leaching than the podzols, so that nutrient minerals and humus are present in the upper layers and a marked crumb structure renders them favourable. However, on shales and clays, they become heavy and need good drainage, but are much lighter in texture on limestone or patches of *loess*. The mineral-rich soils of the basalts need considerable amelioration, therefore often being left for forestry. In South Germany, there are areas – also found in the Central Uplands – of woodland soils of high carbonate content (*Terra Fusca* or *Rendzina*), heavy to work, stony, and dry, and liable to suffer seriously from erosion. Soils developed on the Lettenkohle, Keuper and Rhaetian beds are particularly hard to work, changing in quality according to their moisture content. Elsewhere in South Germany, podzolic and grey-brown soils are common, with modified forms occurring in the mountains, where they are usually thin and much leached, although large areas of calcareous rocks in the Alps largely condition the character of what soil exists.

The German lands in every way enjoy not only a central position within Europe, but are without great physical extremes, making them an attractive habitat for man. They are also reasonably endowed with natural resources that have conditioned in several respects their pattern of economic development.

Suggested further reading

Brinkmann, G.: Geographische Streifzüge durch Deutschland I + II, *rororotele* Pocketbooks 12 & 34, Hamburg, 1970.

Krebs, N. (ed): Landeskunde von Deutschland – I Der Nordwesten, II Der Nordosten, III Der Südwesten, Berlin, 1931–1935.

Passarge, S.: Die Deutsche Landschaft, Berlin, 1936.

Elkins, T. H., Yates, E.M.: The South German Scarplands in the Vicinity of Tübingen, *Geography* 58, 1963, pp.372–393.

Gellert, J. F.: Grundzüge der physischen Geographie Deutschlands, Berlin, 1958.

Hendl, M.: Grundriss einer Klimakunde der deutschen Landschaften, Leipzig, 1966.

Liedtke, H.: Die nordischen Vereisungen in Mitteleuropa *Forsch. z. deut. Landeskunde* 204, 1975.

Marcinek, J., Nitz, B.: Das Tiefland der Deutschen Demokratischen Republik, Leipzig, 1973.

Meynen, E.(ed): Handbuch der naturräumlichen Gliederung Deutschlands, *Bundesanstalt f. Landeskunde u. Raumforschung,* Bad Godesberg, 1953–1962.

Müller, S.: Böden unserer Heimat, Stuttgart, 1969.

Otremba, E.: Die natürlichen Grundlagen für die Entwicklung der deutschen Wirtschaft, Paderborn, 1962.

Schultze, J. H.: Die naturbedingten Landschaften der DDR, Gotha, 1955.

Semmel, A.: Geomorphologie der Bundesrepublik Deutschland, *Geog. Zeitschrift Beiheft* 30, 1972.

Wagner, G.: Einführung in die Erd- und Landschaftsgeschichte mit besonderer Berüksichtigung Süddeutschlands, 3rd ed, Öhringen, 1960.

Yates, E. M.: The Development of the Rhine, *Trans.I.B.G.* 32, 1963, pp.65–81.

CHAPTER 2

TERRITORIAL EVOLUTION FROM 1815

The French Revolution and new concepts of nationalism failed to shock the German lands into becoming a nation-state. The reorganization of the mediaeval patchwork of 360 German states begun by the French was largely upheld in the peace settlements at Vienna in 1815, though nevertheless Germany continued as little more than a 'geographical expression', for there remained 35 independent states and 4 free cities. All were secular states, for the ecclesiastical territories dissolved by the French were not reinstated; but over half the states were tiny in all dimensions and some even comprised several scattered parcels of territory.

North Germany was dominated by Prussia, which had come out of the war with considerable territorial gain, although Hannover (until 1837 headed by the king of England) lay as a wedge between Prussia's eastern and western territories, an apparent bar to their consolidation. There were also a number of smaller territories: the free cities of Bremen, Hamburg, and Lübeck, the scattered parcels of the territory of the Duchy of Brunswick, the Grand Duchy of Oldenburg, and the lands of Holstein and Lauenburg held by the king of Denmark. On the Baltic littoral lay the Grand Duchies of Mecklenburg-Schwerin and Mecklenburg-Strelitz, besides the other small territories scattered elsewhere among Prussian holdings. South Germany had a less confused pattern. Bavaria, Baden, and Württemberg had been preserved at Austrian insistence as a bulwark against France and Prussia, while they had also made some territorial gains in the general tidying up. Hohenzollern

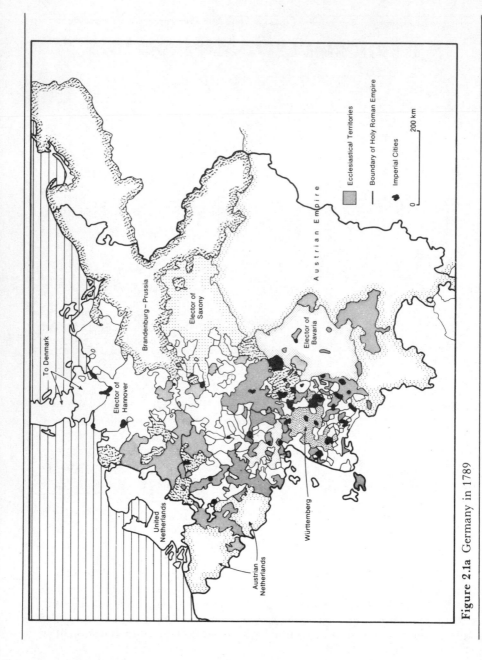

Figure 2.1a Germany in 1789

The Two Germanies

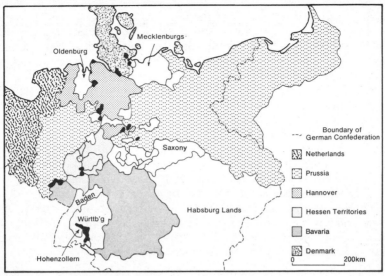

Figure 2.1b Germany in 1815

territory lay in the hands of the Franconian line of the family and only became a part of the Brandenburg line – consequently part of the Prussian state – in 1849. During the Napoleonic episode, Bavaria and Württemberg had been raised to the status of kingdoms and were determined to retain and (if possible) extend their rights and privileges.

Across the middle Rhine and Thuringia lay a shatterbelt of small states that the Vienna settlements failed to eradicate. In the Hunsrück lay Birkenfeld (held by Oldenburg), and Lichtenberg (ultimately to pass to Prussia), and Meisenheim, an outlier of the much fragmented Hessen, while Frankfurt was a free city. Wetzlar was held by Prussia, to which the Principality of Waldeck was to succumb later. The true *Kleinstaaterei* remained in Thuringia, where 8 petty states were subdivided into over 20 parcels of territory, among which were mixed pieces of Prussian territory. Although the elector had been raised to the rank of king, Saxony had lost territory and sought desperately to preserve its remaining privileges.

Struggle for leadership of the German princes

Austria and Prussia now struggled for leadership of the German states. The Austrian emperor believed that the centuries the House of Habsburg had provided Holy Roman emperors entitled it to leadership in preference to the upstart Prussian Hohenzollern. The Prussians, flushed with success (much at the expense of Austria), could not subordinate themselves to Austrian leadership, because they regarded the Austrians as inferior and feared subordination might undo the gains made. Neither the Austrian emperor nor the king of Prussia would sacrifice their position in the cause of German unity, and the stirrings of a national spirit awakened by the Napoleonic episode were everywhere stifled by local loyalties triumphing over the broader scene. The Congress of Vienna confirmed Prussian ownership of most of the important strategic territories taken in the Partitions of Poland, where the population was predominantly Slav, and Prussia was afraid that to take up the cause of German nationalism too enthusiastically might cause the ultimate loss of these valuable lands. Austria had also become a truly multinational state – the Slavs, Magyars, Rumans, and Italians outnumbered the German population, so that to survive, loyalty would have to be to the dynastic House of Habsburg, since national self-government would mean at best federation and at worst dissolution. Thus, both Austria and Prussia made their state-idea focus on the dynastic and not the national: for the ethnically German population, such a loyalty was not difficult to accept, for it generally held the commanding positions in the armed forces and in the administration.

The princes of the other German states were also cautious, because they feared that All-German unity would reduce their own authority. The middle-class element had little interest in changing the existing order, and in any case three-quarters of the population lived in the countryside, where almost feudal conditions still often prevailed. Even though emancipation had begun, many powerful landowners were able to dilute it to preserve to a substantial degree the old order. The active move to a liberal nationalism was the work of a minority: most people still identified themselves primarily by the state in which they lived, and only secondly as Germans in a broader context. The Congress of Vienna, where various drafts for 'Germany' were discussed, was essentially a princes' club intent on maintaining the old order. Although the Prussian minister Hardenberg sought at the start to get a constitution that would go at least some way towards the aspirations of German nationalism and German liberalism, the influence of Metternich, Austria's minister, to whom German unity was 'an infamous objective', triumphed.

The German Confederation
The Congress of Vienna created, however, a Federal Act that called into being a German Confederation, with permanent presidency going to Austria. Although this Act pledged rulers to give their people constitutions, no time limits were set, leaving only expectation. The Federal Diet in permanent session at Frankfurt am Main could pass legislation only if there were a unanimous vote from all 39 German states: it is hardly surprising that the Diet became a symbol of impotence and ineffectiveness. It was not even completely

German: the king of Denmark represented Holstein, the king of Holland acted for Luxemburg, and, until 1837, the king of England for Hannover. To preserve their independent sovereignty, Prussia and Austria purposefully kept considerable tracts of their own territories outside the Confederation.

Although a few South German states issued rather conservative constitutions, the old order was being restored within five years. The Karlsbad Decrees of 1819 effectively recognized Austrian leadership and put an end for thirty years to any real liberalization. The rebellious year of 1830 in Italy and Poland reverberated through Germany only to strengthen the states' stand against liberalism. The situation changed at the end of the decade, when French threats against the Rhineland marshalled a new enthusiasm for All-German unity, which continued to grow after the crisis had passed. The ineffectiveness of the Confederation was thrown into high relief by Danish threats to incorporate Schleswig and Holstein fully into Denmark: Holstein was a member of the Confederation, but Schleswig, though it was predominantly German in character was not.

The growing educated middle class in industry, commerce, and the professions was beginning to be restless against the political and social division of the country, while the growth of the economic horizon through the Zollverein, encouraged by Prussia, in the 1830s gave added impetus. In a rising tide of desire for national unity, many were, however, restrained by the fear of creating an All-German state without German Austria, faced by the choice between the Little German (*Kleindeutsch*) solution – without Austria – and the less practicable Greater German (*Grossdeutsch*) solution, in which the multinational character of the Habsburg empire raised serious problems. The weakness of Austria, rent by internal problems after 1835, made many Germans turn to Prussia (which was less ethnically diverse than the heterogeneous Habsburg empire and appeared to defend German interests against the Slavs in the east and the French on the Rhine) for leadership. While no less autocratic than the other states, it was generally more efficient and was becoming the leader in the economic sphere. Hopes were, however, dashed by the ambivalent attitude of the Prussian king.

As revolution began to break out all over Europe in the spring of 1848, pent-up German feeling of dissatisfaction with the achievements of the Confederation quickly became apparent, although the National Assembly in Frankfurt came close to achieving All-German unity. But it was weakened by the many shades of political opinion and by the rivalry between the states represented. It had no armed forces of its own, so its success in implementing decisions depended upon the willingness of the larger states – and to a lesser degree of the small states – to enforce them. The Assembly took the bold line of appointing a regent-general (Reichsverweser), and the state governments recognized his authority; but the king of Prussia refused to allow the Prussian army to swear allegiance to him. The Assembly continued to formulate a constitution, which ultimately provided for two houses (one representing the state governments and the other for the nation as a whole), an hereditary emperor, and a responsible ministry, with complete federal control over the army and foreign affairs, including the right to declare war, while taxes would have been levied to pay for federal activities. In early 1849, the Assembly tried to turn its deliberations into reality, accepting a *Little German* solution by offering the imperial crown to the king of Prussia, who unfortunately rejected it, believing that Austria should take the imperial role. At this failure, the states quickly began to withdraw their representatives from the Assembly, which fell apart as new revolts threatened.

The king of Prussia sought instead to impose his own solution and leadership in a union of the purely German states, and a perpetual alliance with Austria was proposed. In May, 1849, at a conference in Berlin, some states were ready to accept a conservative constitution recognizing Prussian leadership, but as the Austrian delegate withdrew on the first day and the Bavarian representative received no instructions, the meeting dissolved. Prussia was left with only a union of minor states, with renewed pressures to return to the old order. By autumn, 1850, an inner council of the old Federal Diet had again resumed its work in Frankfurt. Shortly afterwards in a serious constitutional conflict in Hessen-Kassel, the Federal Diet upheld the decision of the elector. This was acceptable to Austria, so that Prussia could not readily disagree: Hessen-Kassel was a member of the partially defunct Prussian Union and was crossed by important Prussian military highways. To reject the demand put Prussia in danger of war with Austria, which at first seemed likely: but, realizing that Austria was supported by Russia, Prussia climbed down and, at Olomouc (Olmütz), agreed to Austria's demands that the Prussian Union would be dissolved, and the outstanding problems in Schleswig-Holstein would be settled by a joint action. A conference was again called to discuss the organization of Germany and, when it eventually met in 1851, it recreated the old Federal Diet in the form of the relevant Acts of 1815 and 1820.

Schleswig-Holstein

The problem of Schleswig and Holstein likewise reflected the problem of German unity, as the personal union of two essentially German territories with the Danish crown was increasingly resented. Threats by Denmark to absorb these lands completely brought repeated attempts by Prussia (aided by other states) to liberate them. Each time, Prussia and its supporters were forced by Austrian and Russian pressure to leave the position unchanged, as the latter resented such 'national liberation', fearing similar movements among their own diverse ethnic groups, while they regarded territorial ownership as governed by dynastic and not ethnic-national considerations. Prussia was also unwilling to press liberation too far against the wishes of Russia and Austria, since their hostility could not be risked. When trouble flared up in 1849, Prussia and its supporters were victorious against the Danes, only to be forced to a truce by Russian and Austrian pressure, when the territories were put under the jurisdiction of an Austrian–Prussian commission. In 1852, the London Protocol, signed by Austria, Russia, Prussia, and Great Britain, recognized the integrity of the Danish crown and the right of the Danish crown prince to succession to the two territories. The Danes recognized that Schleswig and Holstein were united only by a personal union to Denmark and that they should enjoy special status in certain matters not common to the monarchy as a whole. Under Austrian pressure, the Federal Diet accepted the agreement: German public opinion was quite opposed to it, deepening the gulf between the people and their rulers, but contemporary society and its attitudes made any radical solution unthinkable.

By the late 1850s, Austria's international position was weakening, but the Habsburg were unwilling to relinquish their primacy in the German Confederation. Such a stand was increasingly resented in Prussia, whose strength was rapidly growing, and the issue precipitated the constitutional crisis of 1860–1862 that brought Otto von Bismarck to power as minister–president and foreign minister to deflect liberal-nationalism in Prussia to a national-liberalism on which the state's greatness and leadership in Germany were to be built. At the height of Prussia's troubles, Austria in 1863 invited all German princes to a meeting in Frankfurt to consider a reform of the Confederation favourable to its own position. This proved a damp squib, as the very limited proposals, though accepted, quickly dispelled popular enthusiasm, and the absence of Prussia made the resolutions worthless in the end. Instead, Prussia made counter-proposals: it was to have an equal place with Austria in the Federal Directorate in which there was to be a national assembly elected by the German states on the basis of population.

At this point, the new king of Denmark attempted to incorporate Schleswig fully into his kingdom, leaving Holstein, a member of the German Confederation, still only in personal union. This was an undeniable break with the London Protocol, and German public opinion began to clamour for a final separation of the territories from Denmark and incorporation into the German Confederation. When the Danish king refused to rescind the new constitution, Austria and Prussia took the provinces by force, under cover of the London Protocol but fundamentally mistrusting each other's motives. Diplomatic and political manoeuvre was as important as military operations, and Prussia manipulated events to leave an open-ended settlement in its hands. The other German states watched unhappily as they feared Prussian gains at the expense of All-German unity. In 1865, Prussia took Holstein and the Duchy of Lauen-

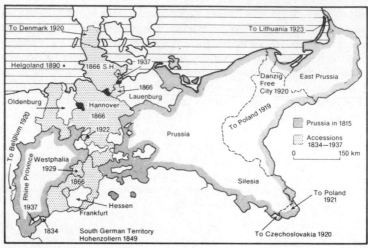

Figure 2.2 Growth of Prussia

burg (for 2.5 million Thaler), including the naval base of Kiel and the control
of military roads to Schleswig, which was held by Austria. Having succumbed
to Prussian demands and having abandoned some of the claims originally
supported, Austria had lost further face in Europe. Bismarck then secured
Italian and French neutrality and found an excuse to provoke Austria to war.

Unable to stand the cost of a long mobilization, Austria decided on a hard line
on Schleswig-Holstein in the hope of support from the other German states
against Prussia. As Bavaria, Saxony, Hannover, Württemberg, Baden, and
the Hessen states gave qualified support to Austria, the Prussians withdrew
from the German Confederation and war with Austria was a reality. The
Prussian armies, everywhere superior, decisively defeated Austria at
Königgratz (Sadowa) in Bohemia in a six weeks' war; but rather than provoke
the entry of other powers and prolong the war, Bismarck sought a moderate
peace. Prussia gained full control in the duchies of Schleswig and Holstein
(though a plebiscite to be held in the Danish-speaking areas was never carried
through). No further claims were made against Austria, while Saxony and the
southern states were left untouched, but Prussia annexed completely Hannover, Hessen-Kassel, Hessen-Nassau, and the free city of Frankfurt, adding
over 3350 square kilometres and 3.2 million people. Prussia was allowed to
create a North German Confederation (from which Austria was excluded,
though the South German states could freely decide their relation to it) and
was now in a commanding position in Germany, so that the new order was the
'Prussian model'.

The Two Germanies

The Franco-Prussian War

Prussia believed that victory over France was essential if absolute German unity was to be achieved. The creation of the North German Confederation was already a serious reverse for the French, since it represented a new and powerful force on France's eastern borders. During the Austro-Prussian conflict, the French emperor had claimed Mainz, the Saar, and the Palatinate in part as the price for neutrality, demands expectedly refused, by Prussia, which strengthened its position by treaties with the South German states, making its king commander-in-chief of all the German states' armies in case of war. The French unsuccessfully tried to get Prussian agreement to their annexation of Belgium and Luxemburg and then tried to buy Luxemburg from the king of Holland. (Since 1815 Prussia had by right garrisoned the territory, but, after a meeting in London, withdrew its garrison and the territory was declared neutral in 1867.) Austria was now removed from the struggle for German unity, because with the creation of the Dual Monarchy (1867), the Hungarians were no longer prepared to fight to renew Austrian primacy in German affairs. Russia, preoccupied in Balkan affairs, was anyway favourable to the still conservative régime in Prussia, while Britain had little sympathy for the French in view of their intrigue to annex Belgium, besides being too busy in its own imperial matters.

Warmongers in both France and Prussia used the candidature of a prince of Hohenzollern-Sigmaringen for the Spanish throne to excite tension, and the French fell for a Prussian diplomatic trap and declared war in 1870. Supported by Bavaria, Baden, and Württemberg, the Prussian armies in little more than six weeks decisively defeated France. The Prussians annexed Alsace and Lorraine – now declared a *Reichsland* (imperial territory) – and received a massive indemnity, with the right to occupy certain French eastern territory until it was paid in not more than four years. From the ruins of the Second French Empire arose the Second German *Reich*, declared in January, 1871, when, at the request of the German princes (without Austria), Wilhelm, *Landesherr von Preussen*, became *Kaiser* in the Hall of Mirrors at Versailles. For this *Little German* solution, Bismarck had skilfully given in to South German particularism in concessions more apparent than real to secure this 'request'.

Towards economic unity

The German states suffered economic depression after 1815, for the hothouse climate of the Napoleonic Continental System had collapsed, and new and wider trading horizons emerged, with consequent sharpened competition. Critical problems were the inadequacy of transport, the backward state of farming under old-fashioned social conditions in the countryside, and the disadvantages in the age of sail of the German North Sea ports compared to others in the Atlantic trade, while the old Baltic trade was now of secondary importance. Lack of financial resources also hampered investment. The political-geographical fragmentation, with its many customs barriers, conflicting fiscal systems, and the greed of petty rulers that kept taxes high, was also a serious hindrance. The Federal Act of 1815 had provided that members of the Confederation should deliberate to regulate commerce and transport between states, but the Diet in Frankfurt had done virtually nothing to organize German economic life.

In 1815, Prussia had gained underdeveloped but potentially great resources in the Rhineland and Westphalia, but the immediate problem was to overcome the difficulties presented by bad communications to welding the old and new provinces together. The Prussian state therefore took active steps to set matters right by building roads and improving navigation, as well as by gathering information on technical progress abroad, while trade treaties were also signed with neighbouring states. The new tariff laws of 1818 swept away many internal dues and collected customs at the frontiers, aimed at increasing trade between the two separate groups of provinces. While raw materials could be imported mostly duty free, only 10 percent on value was levied on manufactured goods and tropical produce paid 20–30 percent, rates that made smuggling unprofitable and did not offend important neighbours. Goods in transit across Prussia also paid a small levy, a valuable weapon against small but uncooperative neighbours. Indeed, the revival of commerce and industry with the new impetus given by stability and the expanding commercial horizons aroused by the industrial revolution in Britain made the existence of many independent tariff systems increasingly inconvenient. Several German states began to make moves to ease commercial relations and in 1828, three important unions came into being, incorporating the greater part of German territory. Prussia made a union with Hessen-Darmstadt on the same basis as arrangements with small enclaves under the tariff law of 1818; while Hannover, Brunswick, Oldenburg, and Saxony, along with other small central German states, formed another union, but without a common tariff and designed primarily to prevent Prussian control of main roads from the North Sea ports to the commercial foci of Frankfurt and Leipzig. Prussia countered this by its own road construction to ease movement north and south and by pressing the Dutch to reduce tolls on Rhine shipping. In the south, Bavaria and Württemberg came together in a shadow of the original concept of a grand South German Union.

In 1831, the Middle German Union collapsed when Hessen-Kassel joined the Prussian Union, so providing a through link between Prussia's eastern and western territories, and the Thuringian states and Saxony quickly followed suit. The major achievement came in 1834, when Bavaria and Württemberg joined the Prussian Union to form the *Zollverein*, covering over 23 million

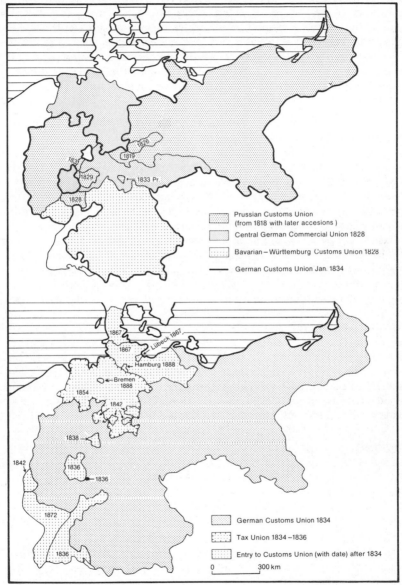

Figure 2.3 The *Zollverein*

people and an area of almost 422,000 square kilometres. In the next eight years, it was joined by Baden, Hessen-Nassau, Frankfurt, and Luxemburg; but until 1854 Hannover and Oldenburg remained outside to form their own Tax Union, though the various Brunswick territories had joined between 1837–1844. In 1867–1868 Schleswig-Holstein, Lübeck, Lauenburg, and the Mecklenburgs joined the *Zollverein*, while in 1872 the *Reichsland* Alsace and Lorraine was incorporated; but it was not until 1888 that the free cities of Bremen and Hamburg joined.

The growth of the *Zollverein* arose from the acceptance by many states of the idea that entry was the only way to alleviate their financial and economic problems. But they still guarded their political rights carefully to prevent Prussia gaining political advantage. The effects of the *Zollverein* took time to show, first being felt in financial advantages, since most smaller members drew more from the union than they took in dues. Its weaknesses were that it depended on a unanimous vote in its Congress which tended to hamper progress and that the treaties after eight years were renewed for fixed periods, so that the members with anti-Prussian sentiments could easily bring pressure to bear. Austria tried to get a broader union in an attempt to wrest economic and political supremacy from Prussia but, in 1862, to make a customs union with Austria impossible, Prussia signed a commercial treaty with France, well received in Saxony, but rejected by the South German states. The Austrians now seized the opportunity to try to establish a Greater German customs union, but Prussia impressed on the southern states that they must either accept the treaty with France or leave the *Zollverein*: they all renewed their *Zollverein* membership in 1864. The following year, Austria and Prussia came to terms on the basis of a vague future 'General German Customs Union', and a favoured-nation clause was introduced; but the war of 1866 left Prussia in an unquestioned position of economic and political supremacy in Germany that dominated further wrangling with Austria.

The monetary problem

At the formation of the Second *Reich* in 1871, Germany was divided into 7 separate currency districts, with 33 issuing banks, quite independent of each other and with different rules and regulations. Legal tender was silver, except in Bremen where gold was legal, and the states had various agreements on the relative parities of their currencies. In Prussia, the parity between gold and silver coins was legally defined, but elsewhere it was fluctuating. The new *Reich* accepted, however, a gold standard, and on 1 January, 1875, the Mark (= 100 Pfennig) became the currency in all the German states. However, it was not until 1935 that the last of the issuing banks had been squeezed out of existence. The German states also had a remarkable collection of measurements for various purposes: Prussia had sought to modernize the system in the late eighteenth century, but it was only in 1868 that the metric system was legally introduced in the North German Confederation and in 1871 throughout the *Reich*.

The years between 1871 and 1914 were used to secure Germany's world position, partly through elaborate treaty systems and partly through the efficient organization of its economic and military strength. Typical treaty systems were the *Dreikaiserbund* – Germany, Austria, and Russia – and the Triple Alliance – Germany, Austria, and Italy. At the same time, Central Europe as a German political force field was increasingly clearly defined. In the 1880s, the idea that Germany was a satiated power started to change and a scramble for colonial territory in Africa and the Pacific began: it was hoped that colonial ventures would deflect German migration from foreign destinations, mostly in North America. By the time (1890) Bismarck was dropped as pilot, the colonial empire was complete, although it was necessary to build an expensive navy to patrol it. One of the last acquisitions (1890) was Helgoland, British since 1807, exchanged in an agreement to recognize British rights in Zanzibar and Wituland.

The aftermath of the First World War

The First World War ended in 1918 with the Habsburg empire in ruins and Germany subject to stringent conditions laid down in the peace settlement of the Versailles *Diktat* that Germany resented as unjust and irrational. It stripped from the Second *Reich* about 70,000 square kilometres of territory and about 7.2 million people (58 percent ethnically German), representing 12.4 percent of its territory, 12 percent of the population, between 12–15 percent of its farming output, 10 percent of its manufacturing capacity, and almost three-quarters of its iron-ore production. The cession of all its overseas possessions swept Germany from the world map of colonial powers.

France sought retribution for the defeat of 1870. Germany had to cede Alsace and Lorraine, with their substantial textile and engineering industries, iron and steel plants, besides iron-ore and potash deposits, and oil resources. Culturally and linguistically a mixed area, neither France nor Germany had bothered to ascertain the true national and political wishes of its inhabitants, preferring to apply *force majeure* to the question. France sought and gained a long frontage on the Rhine: the Baden port of Kehl was joined to French Strasbourg for seven years (1919–1926) to allow the latter to be developed, while the Rhine Commission was reorganized to give France a major say and the seat moved from Mannheim to Strasbourg. The basin of the middle Saar, a completely German area, underlain by a valuable coalfield and enjoying a strategic importance covering the Lorraine Gateway, was claimed by France, having held it previously for brief periods. The Saargebiet carved from

Prussian and Bavarian territory (1890 square kilometres) was, however, put under League of Nations' administration for fifteen years, while the French were awarded ownership of its coalmines for the same period during the reconstruction of their devastated northern coalfield. In a plebiscite in 1935, as stipulated in the peace settlement, over 90 percent of the people voted for a return to Germany.

Under French pressure, Luxemburg left the German customs union and joined a close fiscal and customs relationship with Belgium. Claiming it could

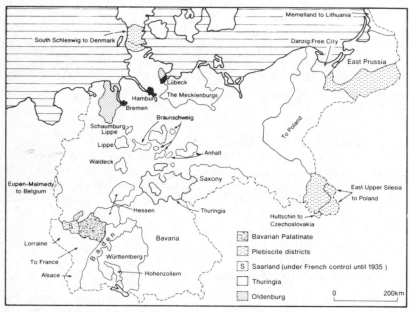

Figure 2.4 Germany after 1918

be threatened by the German hold of the western glacis of the Eifel, Belgium was awarded the small territories of Eupen (strongly German in character) and Malmédy (mostly Walloon) and the town of Moresnet, under international control since 1815. Aachen, an important industrial and railway town, now found itself on the German frontier, and great difficulty was experienced in the interwar years adjusting to the new situation. In the north, a plebiscite, long-promised but never honoured, was held in the Danish–German borderland. Despite the considerable ethnic changes since 1864 in German Schleswig (Danish = Sudslesvig), a plebiscite was held and some territory returned to Denmark. It was well organized and fair and, as far as possible, honour was satisfied in both parties, though transient economic and transport difficulties were created for the Germans.

In the east, the Polish state was resurrected to the cost of Germany, Austria, and Russia. The new state took all the Province of Posen (Poznań), where well over a third of the population before 1914 had been German; in the annexed lands of West Prussia the German element had been proportionally even higher, partly the result of Bismarck's Germanization policy. The latter territory was to form an access for Poland to the Baltic and included some areas still largely Slav (Kaschubian) in the Tucheler Heide (Tuchoła), making its acquisition easier to justify, but this Corridor had within it, in 1919, 439,000 Poles and 418,000 Germans. The Corridor proved a serious burden to Poland and to Germany. Flanked by German territory on both sides, it was too narrow to defend, and it irritated German feelings by restrictions placed on through railway traffic to the now physically separate province of East Prussia. The strongly German town of Danzig (Gdańsk) at the Vistula estuary was made a free city under administration of the League of Nations, though Poland enjoyed important extraterritorial rights. Failure to have full control over Danzig forced the Poles to build a new and unnecessary port on the virgin shore at Gdynia.

Many at the peace conference advocated that East Prussia should as a whole go to Poland, but the uncertainty of German reaction deterred such a decision. Instead, two areas with strong Slav minorities were put under an Inter-Allied plebiscite commission, around the town of Marienwerder (Kwidzyn) and the Masurian district in the south with its main centre at Allenstein (Olsztyn). The Masurians, though Slav in origin, regarded themselves not as Poles but as 'Old Prussians' (*Staroprusacy*). The predominantly Protestant population voted mostly for religious reasons to stay with Protestant Germany rather than go to Roman Catholic Poland, but there were also economic grounds for greater long-term faith in Germany. In the north, the long strip of coastal territory extending to the port of Memel, which was German in character but surrounded by Lithuanian countryside, was also under a plebiscite commission, but the territory was seized by Lithuanian irregulars and the Allied commission weakly withdrew.

Even more difficult was the territorial arrangement in industrial Upper Silesia, where there were important coal and zinc resources. Several proposals for the new boundary were put forward, but the Allied powers felt that to detach the whole industrial province would so weaken Germany that it might not be able to repay the reparations demanded, while the irredentist problem was also regarded as potentially dangerous. In this district, dialect and culture, as well as other criteria, were no guide to national sentiments. Despite the supposed predominance of Poles in the plebiscite area, the votes in 1921 showed 700,000 for Germany and 470,000 for Poland. Undoubtedly, economic considerations and a lack of trust in the future of Poland coloured some voters' minds, while accusations of unfair practice in the plebiscite have been made. The border, as finally decided, left 572,000 Poles in Germany and 350,000 Germans in Poland, besides disrupting the fabric of a closely knit industrial organism. Indeed, the repercussions of a nearly unworkable boundary were felt well into Central Germany, whose long-standing ties with the area were disrupted, while business confidence on both sides of the Upper Silesian border was shaken and the depression of 1929–1931 was felt particularly harshly. An agreement between Germany and Poland on the running of this problem area had over 600 articles, and its elaboration was such as to make implementation nearly impossible, so that throughout its supposed fifteen years of duration it was as much a burden as a help. Poland took 70 percent of the lead and zinc output and 53 out of 67 coalmines (24 million out of 31 million tons output). After the death of Piłsudski in 1935 and the rise to power of the Nazis, relations between the two countries deteriorated badly.

Only a small territory, the Hultschiner Ländchen (Hlučin) was lost to the new Czechoslovak state, but the fact that the 3 million Germans in Czechoslovakia were not allowed the right to say in what state they wished to live rankled badly in Germany. Fortunately, the minority laws were applied more liberally in Czechoslovakia than in most other succession states, at least until the mid-1930s. A major stabilizing effect in Central Europe which might later have helped to prevent the reestablishment of Prussian dominance was vetoed by the victorious powers – the economic union of the remains of Austria (so-called *Deutschösterreich*) with Germany. Economically more important to the Austrians than to the Germans, it would certainly have given much greater strength to the South German states. It was finally accomplished by the Nazi *Anschluss* in 1938.

The Second *Reich* was replaced by the Weimar Republic, named after the seat of the new government, with which came considerable internal change. There was, of course, an Allied occupation of the west bank of the Rhine (to be withdrawn in stages up to 1930) and, in a broad frontier strip round the country, new or changed defence works were prohibited. The old aristocratic states lost their particularism and became simply provinces of the new republic, whose law could override theirs. The Weimar constitution gave the opportunity to carry out a major territorial reorganization and many different schemes were put forward, based on various criteria. The Central Committee for Territorial Reorganization of the *Reich*, formed in 1920, achieved little and was dissolved in 1929, having failed to surmount the strong particularism lingering in the provinces that made compromise impossible. Nevertheless, some territorial adjustments were made, mostly eradicating irritating exclaves. Major achievements were the formation of the Land Thüringen, out of a mass of tiny Thuringian states in 1920, and of Greater Berlin. At the same time, against considerable opposition, a planning authority for the Ruhr coalfield was set up in the *Siedlungsverband Ruhrkohlenbezirk*. There was also a widespread modification of district and town boundaries in the late 1920s, while in 1929 Waldeck, a small territory near Kassel, was taken over by Prussia.

Further changes were made under the Nazi administration: in 1934, the two Mecklenburg states were united; in 1937 Birkenfeld in the Hunsrück was taken into Prussia: and there was a sorting out of territorial complexities in the Lower Elbe (including the creation of Greater Hamburg and the incorporation of Lübeck and Oldenburg-in-Holstein into Prussia). Preparations also began for major changes in the administrative system to prepare for the Thousand Year *Reich*, mostly through growing centralization and an attempt to create an efficient system of regional planning with particular reference to the solution of conflicts of land use. In 1935, a special commission was set up to regulate the land requirements of public bodies and, in 1936, the country was divided into 23 planning regions, with the Ruhr, Berlin, and Hamburg as special units and the rest agreeing closely to existing boundaries. The party organization was territorially arranged in *Gaue* (frequently cutting across existing provincial boundaries), which it was hoped would ultimately replace the traditional system.

The emergence of Grossdeutschland

The foremost objective of the Nazi administration was to create Greater Germany incorporating all the provinces taken from the Second *Reich* in the Versailles *Diktat*, as well as territories with German populations or minorities once part of the Habsburg empire. As a first step, the Third *Reich* was proclaimed on 30 January, 1933, while stronger contacts with the many German ethnic groups abroad were forged and Naumann's ideas of Mitteleuropa expanded into a great Pan-German dream of *Lebensraum*. In 1935, a plebiscite brought the Saar back to Germany as was to be expected; in 1936, remilitarization of the Rhineland began; and, despite an abortive *putsch* in 1934 and assurances in 1936 of the recognition of its full sovereignty, in 1938 Austria was incorporated into Germany as the *Ostmark*, adding a considerable economic and strategic potential. Next came a vociferous campaign against Czechoslovakia's treatment of the ethnic Germans in the 'Sudetenland', for this purpose extended far beyond its true geographical limits; and, under the threat of war in 1938, the British and French gave in to German incorporation of this industrially rich area, mortally mutilating the Czechoslovak state, which fell to a German takeover in March 1939. A few days later, Germany was again in possession of the Memelland. A similar campaign against Poland, culminating in a German invasion, precipitated the Second World War. Danzig and the old Prussian Polish provinces were reincorporated into

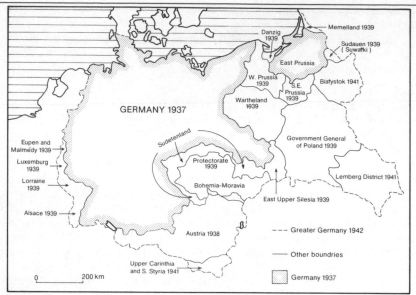

Figure 2.5 *Grossdeutschland*

the *Reich*, and the one-time Congress Poland made into a German-run Government General, with special status for strategic districts in northeast Poland. The 1940 campaign brought incorporation of Alsace and Lorraine, Luxemburg and Eupen-Malmédy: this was followed in 1941 by southern Steiermark and Oberkrain from Jugoslavia. In 1942, the term *Grossdeutschland* was adopted and the territory of this massive state – expressing the Pan-German *Lebensraum* concept – is shown in Figure 2.5.

Suggested further reading

Freund, M.: Deutsche Geschichte, Gütersloh, 1960.

Huttenlocher, F.: Die ehemaligen Territorien des Deutschen Reiches in ihrer kulturlandschaftlichen Bedeutung, *Erdkunde* 11, 1957, pp. 95–106.

Krebs, N.: Deutschland und Deutschlands Grenzen, Berlin, 1929.

Meyer, H. C.: Mitteleuropa in German Political Geography, *A.A.A.G.* 36, 1946, pp.178–194.

Müller-Sternberg, R.: Deutsche Ostsiedlung: eine Bilanz für Europa, Bielefeld, 1969.

Overbeck, H.: Raum und Politik in der deutschen Geschichte – Geopolitische Betrachtungen zum deutschen Lageschicksal, Gotha, 1929.

Sinnhuber K. A.: Central Europe-Mitteleuropa-Europe Centrale, *Trans. I.B.G.* 20, 1954, pp.15–39.

Taylor, A. J. P.: The Course of German History, London, 1948.

Vogel, W.: Deutsche Reichsgliederung und Reichsreform in Vergangenheit und Gegenwart, Berlin, 1932.

The Two Germanies

CHAPTER 3
ECONOMIC CHANGE

Mediaeval Germany had enjoyed considerable prosperity, but internal troubles after the sixteenth century had brought stagnation and decline, accentuated by the shift in commercial interest from Central Europe to the Atlantic periphery and the contacts with rich potential markets in the Americas, Africa, and even Asia. More stable conditions by the eighteenth century were marked, however, by a new stirring of commerce and industry, while during the Napoleonic Wars the blockade of Britain's trade further stimulated Rhenish and South German commerce and industry. Despite renewed competition from an even stronger industrial Britain after 1815, new moves towards political and territorial unity in the German lands fired a new impetus, enhanced by the spin off of technology generated in Britain.

The eighteenth-century stimulation of industry in the German states was mostly of luxury goods or equipment for their armies. Prussia particularly encouraged industry, both in Berlin and in its 'arsenal' of Silesia (after 1742). Reflecting the growth of luxury goods, the state Meissen porcelain works in Saxony opened in 1710: those in Nymphenburg in Bavaria in 1755; and the china works in Berlin in 1760; while at Pforzheim in 1775, Calvinist refugees started jewellery making. In Solingen the manufacture of special cutting steels (originally swords) expanded, with wire-drawing in Altena, Lüdenscheid, and Iserlohn. In 1727 metal working started in Central Germany at Lauchhammer, but expansion of metal production in several older areas, like the

Sauerland and Silesia, was hampered in the late eighteenth century by a growing shortage of charcoal, until the use of coke was introduced in 1789 in Silesia by a Scottish ironmaster. While calamine was used for brass making, the first metallic zinc was produced in Silesia in 1798. Problems were, however, many: for instance, mining in Silesia was brought to a halt about 1754 because the water table had been reached, and not until steam pumps became available could work again resume. The germ of a chemicals industry started with works such as that at Schweinfurt (1790) for the making of white lead and dyes. In the mid-eighteenth century, coal mining began in the Ruhr and Saar valleys on a renewed scale and, after 1770, spread in Upper Silesia. The iron industry in Silesia was already near the new coalmines, but iron making did not move to the Ruhr coalfield from the Sauerland, Berg, and Mark until the turn of the nineteenth century, forced by the difficulty of obtaining charcoal. The stimulus to industry through Napoleon's Continental System was followed after its collapse by difficult times from British competition. During the war years, the forerunner of the *Gutehoffnungshütte* in Oberhausen had been founded, while there was also the start of *Henschel's* engineering works in Kassel.

The basic railway network in Germany had been built by the time industrialization began its main phase of development, but railway construction (started 1835) was first covered by imported material, although a German industry soon began to develop and, in 1838, the first German locomotive had been built in Übigau. In 1841, Borsig in Berlin made his first locomotive; and the same year the *Maffei* works in München opened.

The puddling process for iron making was first used in 1824 in Aachen, followed by Neuwied and the Saar works, and in 1826 at Wetter on the Ruhr. The first successful application of cast steel was by Meyer at Essen in 1830 and in Bochum after 1840, though it was not until 1850 that its manufacture spread. In 1849, coke was first used to smelt ores at Mülheim on the Ruhr, and in 1855 there were more than 23 coke oven plants in the Ruhr, so that by 1860 the charcoal industry was virtually abandoned. The discovery of coal measure iron ore about 1820 was followed in the 1850s by an upsurge of smelting, though transport improvements soon made it cheaper to import ore as the better blackband ores quickly began to show exhaustion after the greatest output was reached in 1865, and by 1900 they were insignificant. Iron works had been established in the 1840s at Riesa in Saxony; in 1851 in the Upper Palatinate; in 1856 around Peine and Ilsede near Hannover; in 1866 at the *Georgsmarienhütte* near Osnabrück; and in 1872 at Unterwellenborn in Thuringia. A most important portent for the future had come in 1857 when iron ouput from the Ruhr exceeded Silesia, and by 1860 the Ruhr completely overshadowed the Sauerland and Siegerland, though the latter used modern methods, importing Ruhr coke. In 1850, Ruhr blast furnaces produced 11,500 tons, and by 1860 output was 160,000 tons, mostly from Oberhausen, Hattingen, Dortmund, and Laer.

In 1850, coal output from the 200 active mines of the Ruhr coalfield amounted to about 1.6 million tons, but most remained simple adits along the Ruhr valley, with some south of the river already nearing exhaustion. The concealed field, known from about 1820, had its first mine opened in 1837; and, once the move north had begun, the number of mines on the concealed field increased yearly, especially as cheap rail tariffs after 1861 gave a stimulus to wider distribution, though Ruhr coal still found it hard to compete against English coal in Northwest Germany, while Berlin derived its coal from Saxony and Silesia. Coal had moved from the Ruhr by water for a long period, and the construction of docks at Duisburg in 1820, which were enlarged in 1860, greatly helped the flow.

In Silesia, mining did not move to the concealed field until the mid-nineteenth century, and deep mining had begun only in 1823, with slow abandonment of the old open pits. Output came from a few large mines, but was retarded by the difficulties of transport and, even after the railway came, under 40 percent of the coal was sent away. Although mining conditions were easier, the poor coking quality (apart from the Waldenburg coal) was to hold back Silesian industry. The early promise of Upper Silesia as a metal producing district was not sustained after mid-century, when much of the output was in rails and similar products, but a serious problem was the relatively slow expansion of the market in the east compared to West Germany, while the efficiency of the plants also tended to decline relatively to the West.

Saar coal mining had a long history of working simple, shallow pits, though by 1830–1840 more elaborate adits were being sunk, and after 1840 deep mining became increasingly important; from 1860, output rose as railway transport replaced carts and river boats. Using local ores and charcoal, iron making is recorded in the fifteenth century in the Saar forests, but encouragement to use modern methods in the early nineteenth century came from the state ironworks, even though local coals were generally poor for metallurgical use. The transport of coal and coke from the Ruhr began on an increasing scale at this time, and import of ore also commenced, mostly from the Lahn-Dill district, brought by boat until the railways were built. Attempts were made unsuccessfully to use ore from Lorraine, while the Burbach works after 1857 used Luxemburg ore. The glass industry had grown in the 1790s, tied closely to the French market (e.g., making champagne bottles) and, like the iron industry, it drew closer to the railways of the Saar valley from the 1860s.

Although the coalfields were coming to dominate the industrial scene, there were other growing industries. Textiles, a long-established industry, began to change from a widespread distribution across the country, satisfying immediate local demand, to a more concentrated market-oriented pattern even before the eighteenth century, when the main manufacturing areas mostly lay near the great trading routes, for example, along the road from Augsburg to Nürnberg and through the Vogtland to Saxony and Silesia. The textile industries flourished under the Napoleonic Continental System, but once opened to English competition some of the older areas collapsed. Mechanization was the answer, at first with English machinery, until Hartmann's engineering works in Chemnitz opened in 1832. But for a long time German industry remained dependent on yarn imports from England.

In Silesia and Lusatia, the textile industry dates from the fifteenth century, particularly along the foreland of the Sudeten mountains; it was expanded by Protestant refugees during the Counter Reformation, while landlords had encouraged the linen industry by bringing in instructors. A new impetus to development came after Silesia fell to Prussia in 1742, although it was the spinning and weaving villages that benefited most. But new methods were not quickly accepted and the industry fell on hard times until the 1840s, after which new machinery and methods were more quickly adopted, while cotton replaced linen. With the change came a new distribution pattern and areas important in the past were deserted (for example, the Bober-Katzbach hills), while the newer factories came to be concentrated in the larger towns, and village industry died out.

The textile industry of Saxony grew in late mediaeval times to replace the declining mining and iron-making industry. From the upland areas where it had replaced other occupations, it spread into the basins of the Erzgebirge and the lower hills, partly as a response to rapid population growth. The change to mechanization was smoother than in Silesia, since the Saxons were less conservative and introduced cotton to replace linen (although cotton had been used even before mechanization on a greater scale than in Silesia). Similar trends also took place in Thuringia, where rather special forms developed, and in the Bavarian Vogtland around Hof.

Five distinct areas of textile manufacture emerged in the Rhineland and Westphalia from an early broad spread. The collapse of the old linen industry in the Ravensberger Land (Bielefeld) brought replacement industries closely connected with textiles, though a remnant remained. The Münsterland industry, widely spread along the Dutch frontier, came to concentrate on spinning, for which its humid climate made it suitable. Originally a linen area, it became one of the most important cotton textile areas. The textile districts of the Lower Rhine, around Aachen and Mönchen-Gladbach, were also originally linen areas, but Flemish influence brought an early turn to cotton. During the Napoleonic period, this area freed from the old guild system by liberal French policies made rapid progress, with entrepreneurs moving in

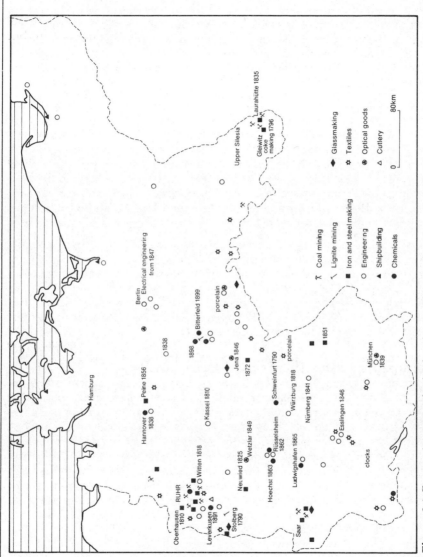

Figure 3.1 Economic geography in the nineteenth century

Economic Change

from guild towns east of the Rhine. By the 1840s, domestic and hand industry had become insignificant, with factories in Mönchen-Gladbach and Rheydt concentrating on cottons and in Aachen on woollens. Refugees in the Thirty Years' War had introduced silk working into the Krefeld district. The Elberfeld-Barmen area, using the clear hill water and valley meadows, was long known for its bleaching, with cloth brought from outside, and linen and cotton cloths were produced, though it could not easily compete with the western districts.

Southwest Germany was originally a linen-making district, though cotton was worked in Suabia, where textiles were made in the towns by craftsmen. Spinning and weaving tended to be concentrated in the north, while finishing was done in the south. Though division of inheritance in many areas provided labour for a rural textile industry, this was hampered by the animosity of the town guilds. The modern period introduced in the late eighteenth century came from Swiss entrepreneurs, taking advantage of cheap German labour, just as they also did in Upper Alsace; and, in the 1830s, South Baden became noted for the manufacure of silk cloths.

The optical goods industry, to become world famous in the late nineteenth century, was really founded with the opening of works in 1846 at Jena by Karl Zeiss, technician to the university, while the *Leitz* works in Wetzlar opened in 1849. Likewise, the chemicals industry also began to develop, when in 1861 the Stassfurt potash deposits began to produce for local works; and, in 1865, the *Badische Anilin- und Sodafabrik (BASF)* opened in Ludwigshafen, the core of the later chemicals industry on the upper Rhine.

The upsurge after the Franco-Prussian War

The Franco-Prussian War was followed by an upturn in economic development in Germany, because the war indemnity gave an injection of capital. The new-found sense of purpose in the new political unity of the Second *Reich*, the widening domestic market through the *Zollverein*, and a unified postal and consular service, all contributed to a vigorous growth, though not without ups and downs. The late upsurge also made possible avoidance of some mistakes made by others in earlier industrialization, while German plants came to have the most modern machinery. Despite the industrialization that had taken place, Germany was still a strongly agricultural country, but an increasing migration from country to town fed the new industries with labour. Alsace and Lorraine, taken from France, added an important textile industry (in Upper Alsace), but the phosporic minette ores were not usable until discovery of the Gilchirst-Thomas process (1879), while the large potash deposits were not used until 1909.

Coal and iron production rocketed ahead in the last quarter of the nineteenth century, but the growth in the Ruhr field was particularly impressive for both coal and iron output.

Table 3.1
Coal and iron output in the Ruhr coalfield

	No. of Mines	Coal Output	Iron Output
		– in '000 tons –	
1860	277	4,276	136.3
1870	215	11,571	360.8
1900	170	60,119	2,772.7

Source: various

The Ruhr increased its share of iron output from 5.5 percent in 1830 to 29.3 percent in 1870 and to over 36 percent in 1900; and the Rhine grew quickly as a route for imported ores after 1865. In 1869, the Siemens-Martin steel process was first used at Essen, employing Spanish ores, and by 1885 Germany was making well over half the world's basic steel. In 1880, works at Dortmund and in Ruhrort-Meiderich began to use the Gilchrist-Thomas process for the phosphoric ores from Lorraine. The attractions of ore import along the Rhine resulted in a growing concentration of the iron and steel industry at the western end around Duisburg, while innovation continued the trend to bigger but fewer plants. After 1890 imports of rich Swedish ore began (twice the iron content of the Lorraine ores), while completion of the Dortmund-Ems Canal in 1899 eased import of foreign ores through Emden.

Through the later nineteenth century, the Ruhr coalmines grew larger, deeper, and fewer, while at the same time they had moved further north onto the deeper concealed field. In 1850, the average mine had produced 8500 tons annually with 64 miners, but in 1900 the average mine had an output of about 280,000 tons and employed about 1400 miners. In the northerly movement, mines reached the Emscher and crossed it near Dortmund by 1869; by 1874, mines were being developed around Recklinghausen and west of the Rhine near Moers; by 1905, mines were working around Lünen and Werne on the Lippe and as far east as Hamm. Exports grew quickly: between 1885–1900, coal exports increased fourfold so that the port of Duisburg was further expanded, with three new basins added in 1908. In Silesia, coal export was also growing, not only to German markets but also to the Habsburg empire and to Russia. In 1868, 39 percent of the output had been exported, but this had risen to over 70 percent in 1901. The expansion was aided by the slow growth in other fields, notably Saxony and Waldenburg. The Silesian mines were, however, forced to seek new markets as the falling price differential between their coal and that of the Ruhr allowed the latter, whose quality was preferred,

Economic Change

to penetrate further into Central and Eastern German markets as railways were expanded. Nevertheless, after 1880 the value of coal in the economy of Upper Silesia exceeded that of iron and steel and nonferrous metals.

The Silesian lead-zinc industry remained strongly conservative, with its smelters only a few kilometres from the mines. With the use of oxidation of zinc from blende, quantities of sulphuric acid were produced and sold outside the region. During the 1870s, the industry saw a substantial growth, but in the 1880s German and Belgian producers agreed on a quota allocation that steadied output until the end of the century, after which a brief expansion followed until the First World War. After 1860 lead production also increased, but the relative importance of the two metals in the regional economy declined generally over the nineteenth century. The Silesian iron and steel industry also declined relatively in the overall German scene as coke smelting became more important, because the industry was slow to adopt new techniques. Most local ores were not phosphoric enough to make the best of the Thomas process, while it was hard to get enough local scrap from the poorly developed engineering industry for the openhearth process, and in general, puddling remained important longer than in the west. After 1880 local ores were supplemented by imports from Slovakia, Austria, and even Sweden, while the iron and steel works concentrated increasingly on the coalfield and near to railways.

The Saar coalfield and its industries received a stimulus from the incorporation into Germany of Alsace and Lorraine. Even before 1871, coalmining had been concentrating on the coking coal deposits and particularly on the more accessible parts of the Warndt district on the border with Lorraine, while mines had got larger and deeper. Output rose from 2.25 million tons in 1860 to 18.4 million tons in 1913. The best Saar coal was of mediocre coking quality, so increasing amounts of good Ruhr coal and coke were brought in by rail. Some works bought interests in Ruhr and Aachen coalmines, while they also took interests in 'minette' ore mines in Lorraine and Luxemburg (e.g., Burbach and Dillingen). By 1875, the small, old-fashioned ironworks of the 'Hochwald' away from the Saar valley had closed, though between 1881–1905 several new works were set up adjacent to minette ores in Lorraine.

Mining brown coal, carried on since mediaeval times, began around Bitterfeld on a large scale about 1840, but the main development came in the closing years of the century, linked to the growth of the Central German chemicals industry and to the growing domestic market (notably in Berlin). It was not until the 1880s that the Lusatian brown coalfield was being dug on any scale, while about the same time brown coal digging in the Ville west of Köln was expanded, though the first briquetting in Germany had been done at Brühl in 1877. Power stations burning brown coal were built to satisfy the rising demand for electricity – in 1913 the *Goldenbergwerk* power station in the

Rhenish brown coalfield was the largest in Europe, and in Central Germany similar stations were also built, notably the plant at Golpa-Zschornewitz with an overland line to Berlin, the start of regional electricity supply, inaugurated in 1915–1916.

Many famous names in the German engineering industry date from the last quarter of the nineteenth century. As an indication of the growing interest in electricity, the firms of *A.E.G.* and *Siemens-Halske* date from the 1880s, as does the contemporaneous *Bosch A.G.* in Stuttgart. In 1913, of 129 electrical engineering firms, 71 had been founded between 1890 and 1900. In 1880, the *Adler* bicycle works opened in Frankfurt and *Mercedes-Benz*, in 1901, at Stuttgart. In heavy engineering, *Blohm and Voss* in Hamburg was established in 1877, while the *Mannesmann* tube works were started in 1887. *Deutsche Babcock und Wilcox*, major boilermakers, began in 1898. Companies also grew larger: *Krupp* in Essen in 1873 employed 16,000 workers and by 1912, 68,300. Total employment in engineering in 1861 had been 51,000, rising to 356,000 in 1882 and to 1,120,000 in 1912.

Observers in the nineteenth century remarked on Germany's advances in the field of chemicals. In the 1860s, Prussia had 260 chemical works employing on average 16 to 18 operatives, but the major upsurge came particularly after 1880. Important items included mineral oils, alkalis, sulphuric acid, and soda; and the location of their production was dependent not only on raw materials but also on the distribution of industries using them (e.g., the textiles industry), though the close relationship between the chemicals and textiles industries in nineteenth-century Britain was not so pronounced in Germany. The smallness of German plants of the time is reflected in the fact that, in 1870, 3 of the 19 soda plants on the Tyne produced as much as all 20 German plants. The soda plants using the Leblanc process needed coal, but the more successful Solvay process was oriented towards suitable salt resources, first introduced in 1870 near Aachen, while in 1880 a second plant was opened at Wyhlen on the Upper Rhine; the main producer became Bernburg on the Saale (opened 1881), using brown coal and local salts. The decline of the Leblanc process left a considerable surplus sulphuric acid capacity for which plants making superphosphates were developed, requiring imported phosphates and pyrites. Consequently, sites on navigable rivers became important and, where possible, reasonably near to agricultural consumers (e.g., the Magdeburg plant lay near to the sugar beet growing area of the Börde). This development owed much to Liebig, who had established a works in 1857 at Henfeld in Upper Bavaria using North African phosphates, while the works in Stolberg used phonolite from the Volcanic Eifel and phosphates from the Lahn. With availability of Lorraine ores, basic slag (*Thomasmehl*) also began to be used as a fertilizer. The early twentieth century marked development of techniques to extract nitrogen from the air, and plants needed nearness to generous supplies of electricity, with the first opened at Magdeburg in 1905, followed by Knapsack on the brown coalfield west of Köln, in 1908 another plant using hydro-electricity opened in Upper Bavaria. Nitrogen substances were also produced in cokeries and gasworks, so plants were attracted to the coalfields, notably the Ruhr. In the early 1880s, Neckar salt was used at Heilbronn and Mannheim for making ammonia, but a major step was ammonia synthesis developed in 1913, first produced at Oppau (Ludwigshafen) and at Leuna, a strategic location near to lignite, allowing Germany to be independent of the Chilean nitrate monopoly.

Methods to extract a wide range of substances from coal beginning late last century were the basis of the German dyestuffs industry that was to attain almost a world monopoly. Synthetic dyestuffs that quickly replaced natural dyes after 1880 were important to Germany, whereas Britain and France could obtain natural dyestuffs from their colonies, and mineral dyes were first made at Stuttgart and tar dyestuffs at Ludwigshafen. A major contribution was made by *Bayer* from the Wiesdorf (Leverkusen) works taken over in 1891 (the original works dated from 1863), while production was supplemented during the First World War by the large Dormagen works. Other important producers were the *Hoechst* works (in 1913 able to offer 11,000 different dyes) and plants in Wiesbaden and Uerdingen, joined by *Casella* from Frankfurt. In 1897, the *Aktiengesellschaft für Anilinfabrikation* (better known as *AGFA*) was founded in Berlin-Treptow, opening the large Wolfen photographic materials works in 1909.

Using coal tar bases and related inorganic substances, *Hoechst* began pharmaceuticals manufacture in 1884 (also begun by *Bayer* while still in Elberfeld). The German plastics industry in 1908 developed the first phenol-formaldehyde combination (*Bakelite*) and manufacture began in 1910 near Berlin and shortly after at Dohna in Saxony. But experiments with polymerization produced few practical results before 1914. More important was the manufacture of artificial silk, though initially the process was dangerous, and only a small plant existed near Augsburg until large-scale manufacture began in 1899 near Aachen and from 1890 in Barmen. In 1904 a viscose yarn factory opened at Stettin, while for ladies' stockings artificial silk yarn was made in Barmen and in Dormagen. Explosives were first made in forest and heath lands away from towns but near to the coalfields, especially around the Ruhr. Nobel had begun production at Krümmel on the lower Elbe in 1856, but in 1886 significant producers opened in Köln-Troisdorf and Leverkusen-Schlebush.

The general growth of factory industry brought considerable change to the textile industry, which retreated from areas where there were more lucrative industries, as in parts of Berg and Mark; and the 1880s saw a rapid decline in domestic industry that had remained important far longer than in Britain, while the German industry was based primarily on the inland market, unlike the big export trade in Britain. The German cotton industry was considerably smaller than the British (in 1911, Germany had 10.2 million spindles compared to Britain's 53.8 million) and did not show the strong local specialization found in Britain. Strongly vertically organized, German writers claimed it was more resistant to crises than the British industry. A reason for the weaker regional specialization may have been that at a critical point in its growth during the Napoleonic Continental System there was a lack of political and

Table 3.2
Pig iron and coal production in Germany and the United Kingdom

	Pig Iron – '000 tons –		Coal – '000 tons –	
	U.K.	Germany	U.K.	Germany
1830	685	46	—	—
1850	2,228	215	49,000	6,700
1870	6,059	1,391	110,000	29,373
1890	8,031	4,658	184,500	70,238
1900	9,103	8,521	228,800	109,290
1913	10,424	19,309	292,000	190,100

Source: as below

Table 3.3
Occupational structure in Germany

	1907 %	1895 %	1882 %
Agriculture, inc. livestock raising, forestry and fishing	28.6	35.8	42.5
Industry, inc. mining and building	42.8	39.1	35.5
Trade and Transport, inc. hotel and licensed trades	13.4	11.5	10.0
Domestic service and variable paid employment	1.3	1.7	2.1
Public service and the professions	5.5	5.5	4.9
Occupation not stated or without occupation	8.4	6.4	5.0

Source: A. Sartorius von Waltershausen,
Deutsche Wirtschaftsgeschichte, 1815–1914,
Jena, 1923, p. 486.

economic unity in the German lands. Raw cotton imports, amounting to about 15,000–16,000 tons in 1840 and 67,000 tons in 1861, had risen to 116,000 tons in 1873 (little more than one-sixth of British consumption) and 375,000 tons in 1898. As late as 1880, two-thirds of all raw wool came from German sources, although this was insignificant by 1910.

After 1887 'Made in Germany' marked German entrance into world commerce and Germany had come to rival Britain as 'workshop of the world'.

Transport development

Mediaeval prosperity was hampered by the lack of good communications that arose from the lack of a strong central authority to maintain, regulate, or even build them. Little remained of the Roman roads and land movement was slow and cumbersome, while the rivers suffered from lack of effective regulation even though they were the main avenues of movement. From the sixteenth century until the mid-eighteenth century, there was considerable further decline in the already mediocre system. The revival of commerce in the more stable times of the eighteenth century stimulated states to undertake improvements and to begin some new construction, though political and strategic needs of the Napoleonic period were to give a particularly sharp stimulus. This trend was followed after 1815 by further commercial expansion, but also again by political needs, such as those of Prussia in joining together its separate eastern and western provinces. The most important feature of the early nineteenth century was, however, that industrialization did not really develop rapidly until the main outlines of the railway system had been built. In Britain, industrialization, in contrast, had generated the building of canals, and turnpike construction and railways had come only after the main spatial pattern of industry had been established.

Roads

The eighteenth century brought road building for military as much as for other needs when some states began piecemeal construction. Most new roads were made straight and narrow, lined by trees to give marching troops shade, on the French model, itself influenced by the rediscovery of the Roman tradition. These *'Kunststrassen'* were notably in South Germany, but there were also projects such as the Hamburg-Wesel-Venlo-Paris road. The first road with a proper foundation east of the Elbe was opened from Potsdam to Berlin only in 1793, and eighteenth-century travellers almost without exception remarked on the generally poor state of the roads, despite improvement from the seventeenth century onwards commonly associated with the needs of the postal service (especially the hereditary administration on behalf of the empire by the princes of Thurn and Taxis). An eighteenth-century postal coach seldom exceeded 30–40 kilometres for a day's journey and on the hillier routes

15–20 horses were needed to pull it. After the Napoleonic wars, Prussia had over half its metalled roads in the Rhineland and Westphalia, and construction was feverishly begun to join the eastern and western provinces, while in the Rhenish-Westphalian and Silesian industrial districts new roads were built to assist industrial development. The Prussian post also tried to accelerate links between the now far-flung corners of the state, and in 1824 the post coach run from Berlin to Magdeburg was cut from $2\frac{1}{2}$ days to 15 hours. Several small states also began road building to attract traffic from the Prussian routes, but the formation of the *Zollverein* reduced in importance some roads built as part of the commercial struggle between Prussia and the Middle German Customs Union as traffic quickly began to flow along the natural lines of movement.

The mid-nineteenth century was a time of road building throughout Germany. Whereas in Britain road building had proceded the railway-building period, in Germany road and railway building were undertaken simultaneously. But private turnpikes of the English type were unknown in Germany, where all roads were built with public funds, though tolls were levied for maintenance. In South Germany tolls were gradually abandoned between 1820–1840, but in North Germany they lingered until late in the nineteenth century and remained in Mecklenburg-Strelitz until 1915. The coaching traffic was run by the postal authorities instead of private companies as in Britain and in consequence did not feel railway competition severely until the 1880s. The Bavarian postal diligences, for example, especially in the Alps where tourism was growing, remained well patronized until this century. While the volume of goods and numbers employed in road haulage rose, the length of haul fell as railways and waterways captured long-distance traffic.

Waterways

Napoleonic French control of the Rhine broke the stifling hold on river traffic of the watermen's guilds and other restrictive mediaeval practices. As the roads had deteriorated in the sixteenth and seventeenth centuries, traffic had become increasingly dependent on waterways, and the Prussian kings had led the way for the future by building canals and improving navigation from the late seventeenth century. But progress had been modest.

The expanding economic horizons of the nineteenth century brought a new importance to waterways. The Rhine, one of the waterways to benefit most from these new demands, had long been the major artery of the western German lands, though in the Middle Ages movement had been hampered by the poorly maintained fairway and by the rapacious tolls levied along its course. Until the railways captured the more lucrative traffic, the river carried a wide range of goods that included slate and basalt, cloth, metalware, and coal. Timber was floated downstream from the Schwarzwald, often taking

15–20 weeks for the journey to Holland in rafts, some reputedly needing over 400 oarsmen and many highly skilled steersmen to guide them through the dangerous gorges. Until steam power came, boats were pulled upstream by horses and the maintenance of paths was a time-consuming local task; but there were also sailing boats, although the funnel effect of the valley in places demanded great skill in handling the vessels, and some vessels were even rowed.

The Congress of Vienna in 1815 decided that rivers running through more than one state or forming the frontier between states should be free to citizens of all the riparian states and that river dues should be reduced as much as possible. Agreements brought such an international status to the Rhine in 1831, but even when Nassau joined the *Zollverein* in 1836, it refused to reduce its tolls on its sections of the Rhine and Main. Likewise, Dutch tolls at the Rhine mouth remained high and the Köln-Antwerp railway (1843–1845) was an attempt to overcome them. Tolls were ultimately eliminated on the Rhine between 1851 and 1886 and on its tributaries between 1861 and 1863. Traffic made a marked upsurge in the 1830s and 1840s, before the railways became widespread and, to extend the range of the river, plans were formulated for a number of canals. In 1682 and in 1810 there had been abortive attempts to join the Rhine and Maas, but the major project, built from 1836 to 1846 on a totally inadequate scale, was the Main-Danube link (Ludwigskanal), which had 99 locks and could only take 120 ton barges and was soon eclipsed by the railway. The first steamship was introduced in 1816 on the Rhine, and by 1830 more than a dozen were regularly working on the river; in 1843 a Ruhr industrialist introduced the typical barge train that was to remain until the present day. River traffic was also increased before 1850 by railways built deliberately to feed traffic to it, though the railway soon became a serious competitor, taking over completely on sections difficult to navigate. After 1845, goods by river ceased to reach Basel and, after 1855, river traffic to Kehl (opposite Strasbourg) stopped, and for over fifty years Ludwigshafen-Mannheim was the effective head of navigation.

After 1871, a new interest was taken in the river, though the individual states and not the *Reich* controlled the river frontage. Between 1875 and 1910, the share of total German goods traffic carried by water rose from a fifth to a quarter, the substantial part of the increase on the Rhine, and there was a sixfold increase in shipping tonnage. The first modern harbour works date from 1830–1850 at Duisburg-Ruhrort, with major additions in 1868 and 1908; and major docks and quays were completed in most other river ports, often with considerable extensions later in the century. The Rhine Commission created in 1868 did much to encourage traffic by physical regulation of the river, since concerted action was now possible, with initial works designed to prevent flooding of villages and farmland. On the upper Rhine, the first

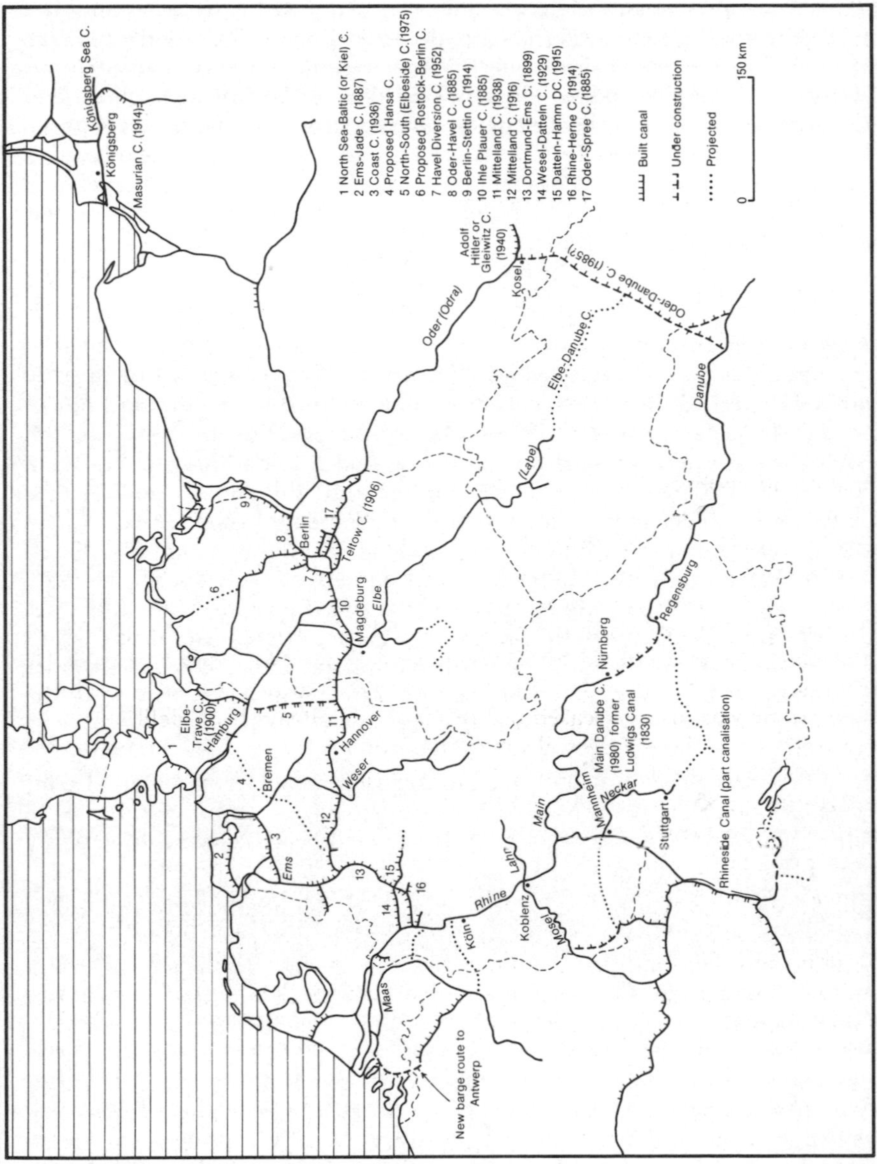
1 North Sea-Baltic (or Kiel) C.
2 Ems-Jade C. (1887)
3 Coast C. (1936)
4 Proposed Hansa C.
5 North-South (Elbeside) C.(1975)
6 Proposed Rostock-Berlin C.
7 Havel Diversion C. (1952)
8 Oder-Havel C. (1885)
9 Berlin-Stettin C. (1914)
10 Ihle Plauer C. (1885)
11 Mittelland C. (1938)
12 Mittelland C. (1916)
13 Dortmund-Ems C. (1899)
14 Wesel-Datteln C. (1929)
15 Datteln-Hamm DC. (1915)
16 Rhine-Herne C. (1914)
17 Oder-Spree C. (1885)
Built canal
Under construction
Projected
0
150 km
Königsberg Sea C.
Königsberg
Masurian C. (1914)
Oder (Odra)
Adolf Hitler or Gleiwitz C. (1940)
Kosel
Oder-Danube C. (1985?)
Elbe-Danube C.
Danube
(Labe)
Teltow C. (1906)
Berlin
Magdeburg
Elbe
Elbe-Trave C. (1900)
Hamburg
Hannover
Bremen
Weser
Ems
Main
Lahn
Rhine
Köln
Koblenz
Mosel
Maas
Mannheim
Neckar
Stuttgart
Nürnberg
Regensburg
Main Danube C. (1980) former Ludwigs Canal (1830)
Rhineside Canal (part canalisation)
New barge route to Antwerp

Figure 3.2 Canals and waterways

improvement had come shortly after 1815 by the simple expedient of cutting through meanders to straighten the channel; and to increase depth, groynes and training walls were built. The accelerated current made horse haulage difficult, one of the main causes of decline in navigation above Mannheim until powerful tugs were available. The down-cutting of the river became so bad that an emergent rock barrier at Istein prevented access to Basel except at the highest water, so that after 1919 the Grand Canal d'Alsace was constructed to overcome this hazard. In the particularly dangerous sections near Bingen and St. Goar, work had begun in 1830 to create a 2-metre channel at mid-water, though it was important not to deepen further the *Bingerloch*. By 1866, the first significant improvements in the channel were complete to Mannheim, and by 1914 the channel was being improved to Basel.

The growth of coal and ore movements in the Rhenish-Westphalian industrial area encouraged canal building. The Dortmund-Ems Canal, a link directly from the eastern Ruhr to Emden, was completed in 1899 (including 19 locks and the Henrichenburg ship lift) for 600-ton barges, but, by 1905, 800-ton vessels were allowed (present capacity, 1350-ton Europa barges). Traffic in 1900 was 400,000 tons; by 1913, 4 million tons and, in 1928, 8.74 million tons. A link from the Dortmund-Ems Canal to the Rhine was completed in 1914 with the opening of the Rhine-Herne Canal, and another route, the Wesel-Datteln Canal, across the Ruhr coalfield from east to west opened in 1929, while the capacity of the Ruhr had been increased as far as Mülheim in 1927. A waterway from the Rhine to the Elbe, suggested against opposition as early as 1856, was realized in the building of the Mittelland Canal – the Ems-Weser section completed in 1915 and from the Weser to Hannover in 1916, while the link to the Elbe at Magdeburg was opened only in 1938.

The Elbe forms a major waterway not only for Central Germany but also for Bohemia. Conditions in the Middle Ages seem to have been comparable to the Rhine, though traffic was not as great. In the eighteenth century, Elbe traffic seems to have greatly exceeded road traffic in its basin, with effort made to extend navigation in the river's basin: in 1743–1745 the Plauer Canal joined Magdeburg to Brandenburg and a voyage to the Oder was possible by the Havel-Finow Canal; between 1777–1785, a canal was built from the lower Elbe to the Baltic near Holtenau, in a sense a forerunner of the Kiel Canal; and between 1896–1900 the mediaeval Strecknitz Canal between the Elbe and Lübeck was enlarged for 1,000-ton vessels. In Brandenburg numerous improvements included the Oder-Spree Canal, an alternative route from the Oder to Elbe basins, which deflected some Silesian freights to Hamburg (coal, sugar, and zinc) at the expense of Stettin, and Berlin became a focus of waterways (some of quite small capacity) between the Elbe and Oder basins. Abolition of dues in 1863–1870 greatly encouraged traffic, despite railway competition, and the Elbe became a vital link for a large part of Central Europe to Hamburg, with a considerable part of Czechoslovak traffic flowing this way even after 1918, while through the Elbe flowed Silesian and, until 1920, Polish traffic. Downstream freights were Silesian coal and coke and chemicals from Saxony and Bohemia, as well as sugar beet, sugar, glassware, paper, salt, and even lignite. Upstream, wood pulp, petroleum, and chemical raw materials were despatched to Central German and Bohemian industry. The canalization in the last quarter of the nineteenth century of the Saale to Halle made possible despatch of paper and pulp for the Leipzig publishing trade. To increase capacity, the section above the Czech border near Děčín was canalized early in the twentieth century, while numerous groynes and other works were built on the German sector to improve the depth.

Eastern Germany was served by the Oder, usually navigated to Cosel (Koźle), though small boats could reach Mährisch Ostrau (Moravská Ostrava). In the 1870s, works were undertaken to improve Oder navigation, but it was later claimed that the course had been overstraightened, making run-off too quick. The Oder was linked to the Vistula by a canal system via the Warthe and Netze valleys, while between 1922–1928 an improved link to Berlin for medium-sized river vessels was established by the Stettin Ship Canal and the Hohenzollern Canal (including the Niederfinow Ship Lift).

Although the Danube is an ancient highway, it has been of relatively little modern importance to Germany, with the traditional head of navigation at Ulm seldom reached and the river notoriously unreliable and difficult to navigate; but below Regensburg its importance increased in the 1930s as German trade with the Danube lands and the Balkans grew, when upstream freights were notably bauxite and petroleum, while coal and coke and chemicals moved downstream.

The German ports
The German lands have long engaged in the trade of both the Baltic and the North Sea. Though in parts treacherous and liable to suffer from ice in winter, the circulation of the Baltic waters aided navigation by the simple sailing vessel, whereas the coast of the German Bight has always been notoriously hazardous for ships, with immense shallows and shifting channels of great danger in storms, beside Frisian communities that augmented a hard living by wrecking.

The Baltic ports
Lübeck lies on an oval-shaped island in the Trave. Founded in 1143, its prosperity came as leader of the *Hanse* in the thirteenth and fourteenth centuries, but the narrow estuary limited prospects as ships grew in size,

though the import of Swedish ore for the Ruhr in the nineteenth century brought back some life. Kiel, at the head of one of the drowned valleys that provide sheltered harbour sites on the Baltic, founded in the thirteenth century, became a member of the *Hanse*, but fell under Danish control that limited its growth. After the opening of the Kiel Canal (the Baltic–North Sea Canal) in 1895, it became one of the major German naval ports. Rostock, with a similar site and also a *Hanse* member, fell on hard times in the wars of the seventeenth and eighteenth centuries and suffered likewise from a nineteenth-century decline in Baltic trade, of which the same can be said of Stralsund. Another sheltered *Hanseatic* harbour at the mouth of one of the more important natural waterways leading to the Baltic is Stettin, which through improvement of access through the Swine and the building of the outport of Swinemünde late in the eighteenth century became a major port for Berlin, Silesia, and Central Germany, especially after the opening in 1914 of a barge canal to Berlin. It suffered sharply, however, from competition from Hamburg. Another *Hanseatic* port, Danzig, served as the outlet for much of central Poland and the Vistula basin, which came to overshadow ports such as Elbing. Changing ownership in later centuries resulted in it losing its position, although it remained an important exporter of grain and timber from the Polish lands. But its restricted harbour was a serious hindrance in the nineteenth century in competition with Stettin and Königsberg. Königsberg, a port of uncertain mediaeval fortunes, became a major port for the trade of Western Russia in the nineteenth century because, unlike the Russian Baltic ports, it remained ice-free, while Pillau was made the main German naval base in the eastern Baltic.

North Sea ports

Access to the ports of the North Sea coast has always been difficult: at low tide wide mud flats lie along the coast, while at both states of the tide entry to the ports is through tortuous, shifting channels, and the sites for ports are also fewer and less sheltered than in the Baltic, while several important ports developed well up the Weser and the Elbe. Access to Emden in the Dollart was made difficult by disagreements with the Dutch over the command of the estuary. Though the port flourished in mediaeval times, its importance really dates from 1866 when, taken over by Prussia, which began modern harbour works and especially canal building – the Jade-Ems Canal in 1877 and the major Dortmund-Ems Canal in 1899 – that made it a port handling foreign ores for the Ruhr. After 1900 it also became the main landfall for German ocean cables. Wilhelmshaven, founded by Prussia in 1854 through purchase from Oldenburg, became the major German naval base in the nineteenth century, well protected from interference by the difficult approach. After the First World War, it was depressed until rebuilding of the navy in the mid-1930s developed large U-Boat facilities. Bremen, a *Hanseatic* port, grew in the eighteenth century as the main importer of 'colonial' goods and also developed as a passenger port, active in the American emigrant traffic (the *Norddeutscher Lloyd* was founded here in 1857). By 1914 it controlled a quarter of the German merchant fleet. Its modern harbour was begun in 1830, but it suffered later from the restricted site as vessels grew in size. Several other ports lie on the Weser below Bremen: most important are Geestemünde (built by Hannover in 1847) and Bremen's outpost Bremerhaven (begun in 1830).

The dominant modern German port is Hamburg – 'Queen of the Elbe', where the many arms of the Elbe and the digging of artificial channels (*Fleete*) gave good shelter and anchorage. A major *Hanseatic* centre, the town's high level of political independence enabled its interest to be concentrated on commerce (free city from 1510); and the expansion of European trading horizons to the Americas and Africa was much to Hamburg's benefit so that it came to overshadow its former superiors of Lübeck and Danzig. Though avoiding the worst effects of the Thirty Years' War, Hamburg had to contend with Danish attempts to dominate Elbe traffic to the sea by making Altona a serious rival. The 'colonial trade' of the eighteenth century laid the foundation of nineteenth-century greatness and by the outbreak of the Napoleonic wars, Hamburg was importing about one-fifth of all British exports. Recovery after the wars came with widening economic horizons and the freeing of trade through the *Zollverein*. Though, like Bremen, Hamburg enjoyed a special position: full commital to the German customs union came only in 1881, in exchange for the right to remain a free port. The close ties established with the United States were reflected in the establishment of the *Hamburg-Amerika Reederei* in 1847, while Hamburg merchants were involved in several German colonial ventures. The late 1860s saw the beginning of modern harbour buildings, first on the north bank of the Elbe and then on the south, on land purchased a century earlier; and important extensions to the harbour continued into the interwar years. In the 1850s Hamburg handled about 1.5 million tons of shipping annually: by 1913 this had risen to well over 20 million tons, not only for Germany but also for a vast hinterland in Central Europe, a role that continued on a diminished scale after 1919.

The revolution in mobility – the railways

The particularist German states were perhaps drawn together more by the revolution in mobility provided by the railway than by anything else. Railways also greatly accentuated the significance of Germany's central position in Europe. Distances in the German lands are not extreme: from Flensburg to München, the north-south axis, is only 1000 kilometres, comparable in length to the east-west axis from Köln to Königsberg (London to Wick via Edinburgh and Perth is about 1200 kilometres). The railway network came to be remarkably evenly spread, and no large areas were left unserved after about

1875: this may be accounted for in some respects because the poorest areas economically offered the least physical obstacles to railway building which was thus comparatively cheap; on the other hand, the economically richest areas with a big demand for railway transport presented substantial physical obstacles, but promoters were prepared to pay to surmount these to tap the lucrative traffic offered. Some areas became essentially crossed by transit railways, linking together major traffic generating foci, whose spatial distribution was conducive to the evolution of a network geometry that spanned by necessity the more sparsely peopled and economically poorer areas that could not otherwise have generated their own network.

In 1807, a leading Bavarian civil servant, having studied mine tramroads in England, wanted to lay a 'road with iron ways' between the Rhine and the Danube, but the king preferred to resurrect the abortive *Fossa Carolingia* canal. In 1828, a Prussian minister proposed a railway linking the Lippe and Weser rivers, while the industrialist Harkort in 1833, with the support of the Westphalian *Landtag,* suggested a railway from Köln to Minden. At the same time, Köln was pressing for a railway to Antwerp, to avoid paying the extortionate Dutch Rhine tolls. From experience in America, Friedrich List, in a far-sighted paper in 1833, proposed an all-German railway system centred on Saxony but linking all the principal towns: for such vision, public opinion was just not prepared, and his proposals were ignored.

The first real railway was a modest 8-kilometre scheme linking Nürnberg to Fürth, following a survey having shown a daily average movement between the two towns of 1184 people on foot and 494 people in 185 carriages. The Bavarian Land Survey drew the trajectory across flat country between the towns, and 'English specialists' advised on the construction. The locomotive was bought at Stephenson's works in England, but the rails and chairs made at the Rasselstein works at Neuwied, because the Bavarian government would not allow their duty-free import from England. As an aside on comtemporary transport, the locomotive, packed in 19 crates and weighing 170 hundredweight, left Newcastle on 27 August, 1935, and arrived by sea at Rotterdam on 17 September, to reach Köln by river boat on 7 October. Loaded onto eight horse wagons, it got to Offenbach by 15 October, where the drivers refused to go further because of the state of their wagons' wheels and axles. Reloaded onto other wagons, it arrived in Nürnberg on 28 October. The English driver and mechanic erected it and then trained German drivers. The first steam-hauled train in Germany ran on 16 November, 1835, and on the official opening day (7 December, 1835) the locomotive drew a train of 200 passengers along the 8-kilometre line in nine minutes.

As a great commercial focus not on a navigable river, Leipzig more than any other town in Germany was interested in railway transport, since it was gravely concerned about its commercial future in the new upsurge of economic activity. Preliminary works on the Leipzig-Dresden railway began in 1835, when an English consultant advised against the original route suggested by List, because of the cost and difficulty of passing through the well-populated Mulde valley, so the route was changed to go through Riesa in the plains. The first 5-kilometre section, opened in 1837 from Leipzig to Althen, included the first German tunnel (512 metres) built by 380 Freiberg miners, and the continuation of the line demanded a substantial wood and stone bridge over the Elbe at Riesa, a deep cutting, and another major bridge at Röderau. The whole line, 115 kilometres long, built on the English model, opened in 1838, by which time other railways were also well advanced – Berlin-Potsdam, Braunschweig-Wolfenbüttel, and Düsseldorf-Erkrath, and in 1840, the Leipzig-Halle-Magdeburg line opened. In Baden, the construction of the Mannheim-Basel line began at a broad gauge (1600 mm – 5' 3") with the first section (Mannheim-Heidelberg) opened in 1840 and 485 kilometres of broad-gauge track were laid before ultimate conversion under outside pressure to standard gauge (1435 mm – 4' 8½") in 1854–1855. By 1841, the Köln-Aachen railway was open and, by 1843, there was through communication to Antwerp. A mild 'railway mania' had begun, though most projects were comparatively short lines, since the comtemporary mind boggled at the technical, organizational, and financial problems posed by major schemes.

By 1840, 500 kilometres of route in 10 short sections were open and much building was in progress, so that by 1845, route length had grown to over 2000 kilometres, three-quarters operated by private companies and the rest by the rapidly growing state railways. The first great trunk routes were beginning to emerge as short sections of line began to join up, while state governments were overcoming their suspicions of the railway and were more ready to issue concessions or even build themselves. By 1850, private enterprise using in part the state-owned railways had managed to link Berlin to the lower Rhine, so joining Prussia to its western territories. Berlin was also joined to Upper Silesia, making a through journey to Vienna via Oderberg possible, and only small gaps existed in the through routes from Berlin to Basel via Frankfurt and to München via Plauen. The politically powerful *Junkertum* had an early influence on railway policy in Prussia which contributed to the remarkable route length in the poorer agricultural eastern provinces. In North Germany, Hamburg was emerging as a railway centre, though the lines were not linked together because of political jealousies: one terminal in Hamburg served Berlin; in Harburg was a station for Hannover (no Elbe bridge existed until 1872); and in Altona, a station for the railway to Kiel, a German-sponsored line in then Danish territory. But Danish influence prevented completion of a north-south line in Schleswig-Holstein.

The higher construction costs in the more difficult terrain of South Germany were offset by the positive attitude of the South German states in financing railway building rather than wait for private initiative. The Württemberg state railway (Heilbronn-Stuttgart-Ulm-Friedrichshafen) had particularly difficult terrain to surmount in crossing the scarp of the Alb, where the 1:40 Geislinger Steige was ultimately built after various alternative routes and forms of traction had been discussed. The Württemberg railways were joined to those of Baden only in 1853 and to the Bavarian lines in 1854. At one stage there had been a chance that Württemberg would build to the Baden broad gauge but, nevertheless, Württemberg's practice was generally closer to the American than to the British model used on other German railways.

By 1855, 7400 kilometres of route were open – over twice as much as in France, but only 60 percent of the route in Britian. It was possible to travel (Figure 3.3) from Aachen on the west to Kattowitz on the east, while there was through railway communication from Stettin and Rostock to München via Nürnberg and via Frankfurt to Basel, and the main north-south line from Hamburg-Harburg to München was completed in 1856 via Kassel. Four years later, a serious gap was closed by the line along the west bank of the Rhine via Andernach and Koblenz to Mainz. The railways of Rheinhessen and the Bavarian Palatinate were still not linked to those on the east bank of the Rhine, while the crossing was made well into the nineteenth century by ferries rather than bridges. Although it was possible to travel from Berlin to Vienna via Prague, there was still no connection between Bavaria and Austria. On the east, Berlin was now joined to Danzig via Stettin, and completion of the Vistula bridge at Dirschau (Tczew) in 1857 opened through traffic to Königsberg.

The railway route length of 1860 amounted to 11,300 kilometres, with the main trunk routes now virtually complete, and the German railway system was quickly becoming a turntable for European railway traffic, even though the states still guarded their borders jealously and new routes had to take account of parochial and particularistic attitudes. One mainline of the period, the Berlin–Hamburg Railway, was not as straight as physical conditions would allow since the Hannoverians would only agree to it using their territory if the terminus was in Harburg and not Hamburg city, a condition its sponsors could not accept. It consequently ran across Mecklenburg's territory and through Hagenow so that it would be easier to lay a branchline to Schwerin, Mecklenburg's capital. The Berlin–Hamburg Railway became an exercise in diplomacy since it had to pass through the territory of the Duchy of Lauenburg, a possession of the king of Denmark. The town of Lauenburg was joined to the mainline at Büchen and all traffic between the two was carried free of charge, the so-called *Lauenburger Privileg*, agreed with the Danish king as part of the original concession. Honoured long after the Duchy passed to Germany, it ended only in 1937. In order to avoid crossing Hessian territory, the Hannover Southern Railway was built over the Dransfeld Plateau instead of through the

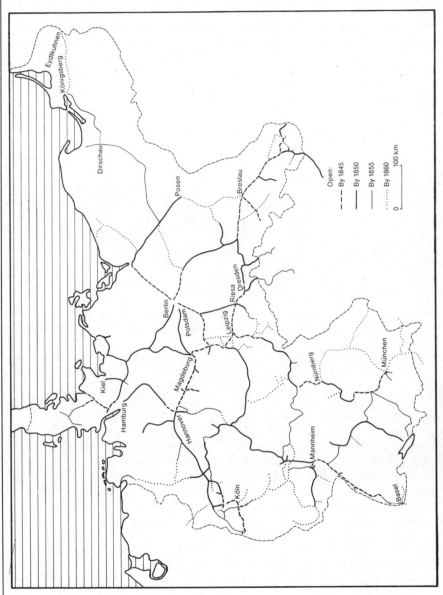

Figure 3.3a Growth of the railway system I

Economic Change

much easier Eichenberg Pass. The second main Prussian link from Berlin to the Rhineland also avoided unfriendly Hannover by making a long detour that needed heavy gradients and missed the then important towns of Einbeck and Detmold. Even until the Second World War, many expresses from Berlin to the south ran via Halle on the Saale instead of through the more important Leipzig, because this route was all Prussian track, rather than over the Saxon State Railway to Leipzig. In South Germany, Bavaria built a railway to Lindau across difficult terrain in its own panhandle of territory, rather than seek an easier route through Württemberg's territory. In 1869 Baden built the remarkable *Schwarzwaldbahn* to give a shorter approach from the Rhine valley to Konstanz and to avoid crossing Swiss territory at Basel and Schaffhausen; while the main north-south railway was not built through the industrial town of Lahr, because of its liberal views despised by the government. Because the Württemberg Railway from Ulm to Aalen had to cross Bavarian territory, Bavaria made it a condition that no expresses would use this section because of competition with its own routes; consequently, even into the 1930s, the Berlin-Nürnberg-Ulm-Friedrichshafen expresses ran as semifast trains between Ulm and Aalen. The Main-Neckar Railway from Frankfurt to Schwetzingen avoided both Mannheim and Heidelberg, because of local disagreements, and the station for the towns was built in open country at Friedrichsfeld, where junction was made with the Baden Railway's Mannheim-Heidelberg line.

Further major links were added between 1860 and 1870; for example, after 1865, the Flensburg-Hadersleben line formed a railway link to Denmark; Emden, Wilhelmshaven and Bremen were joined via Oldenburg; and important new lines built in Central Germany, notably the Göttingen-Nordhausen-Halle/Saale route. Berlin was joined to Görlitz via Cottbus and direct communication from Berlin via Frankfurt/Oder to Posen was completed. In East Prussia, the line to Eydtkuhnen (1860) from Königsberg provided a link to the Russian railways and the far northeast was joined by completion of the Tilsit-Insterburg line (1865), although ten years were to elapse before Memel was reached. Other important links also completed were Bebra-Fulda-Hanau, Würzburg-Ingolstadt-München, and the Köln-Gerolstein-Trier line, of military significance across the western Eifel, opened throughout in 1871. After 1871, using the French war indemnity, building continued (though several vital modern routes appeared piecemeal – for example, the link from the Ruhr to Hamburg via Bremen was completed in sections – from Hamm to Münster in 1848, from Haltern to Münster in 1870, from Münster to Osnabrück in 1871, from Osnabrück to Bremen in 1873). In 1872, Harburg had been joined by the Elbe bridge directly to Hamburg and, in 1874, the final link from Bremen to Hamburg was opened, part of the abortive Hamburg-Venlo (-Paris) Railway, of which the last section (Haltern-Wesel-Venlo) was opened in 1874 and abandoned in 1899. A new route of great importance was the Trier-Koblenz Railway along the Mosel Trog, linking the Rhine-Ruhr area by gentle gradients to the Saar coalfields, though it included numerous substantial bridges and Germany's longest tunnel (Kaiser Wilhelm Tunnel, 4.2 kilometres – 1879).

The decade 1865–1875 had added 13,200 kilometres of route, the highest for any corresponding period of any European railway system, although it included 840 kilometres of route by annexation in Alsace-Lorraine. The period was still dominated by private railways and influenced by jealousies between states, while railway policy was generally badly planned and uncertain, marked by opportunism. The states mostly only built strategic lines in which private enterprise did not show an interest. Many routes were opened as single track, for traffic was still generally light (compared to Britain), and civil engineering work was kept to a minimum. After 1875, new routes became essentially secondary track laid as inexpensively as possible, with many short but busy lines added in the rapidly growing industrial areas. Building of long, lightly constructed cross-country routes occurred particularly in the eastern districts – in Pomerania, Silesia, East and West Prussia, and Brandenburg, as well as in the North German countryside. A brief glory was enjoyed in West Germany by the North Brabant-German Railway, completed from Boxtel in Holland via Goch and Xanten to Wesel, opened in 1878, that carried through traffic at good speed from England via Vlissingen (Flushing) to North Germany and Berlin. After the First World War, this route – to the end a private company – lost importance as the Dutch and German state railways rerouted international traffic. It has been estimated that between 1880 and 1910, some 4000 kilometres of mainline and 22,000 kilometres of secondary (*Nebenbahn*) route was added.

Growing traffic density, higher speeds, and heavier trains gradually shifted the emphasis from new route to improving existing facilities by double-tracking, passing loops at closer intervals on single track, as well as on double-track routes with mixed fast and slow traffic, better bridges, and even avoiding lines at critical junctions. Urban railways also became important, notably in Berlin. A feature absent in Britain was the interest in railways taken by the General Staff, after their importance had been demonstrated by the wars of 1864 and 1866; and ample preparations were made for the role of railways in the war with France in 1870 and in the First World War. Besides directing railway building in frontier areas to handle a capacity greater than normal peacetime needs, there was planning of strategic routes across the country, with bridge building across the Rhine much influenced by military needs. Considerable attention was given to the so-called *Kanonenstrasse* from Königsberg via Central Germany, Kassel and the Lahn valley to Koblenz, and ultimately to Metz. Another strategic line was begun from Krefeld via Neuss and Rommeskirchen to the Ahr, allowing through traffic from Wesel to avoid the crowded lower

Rhine junctions, but it was never completed. The Prussian General Staff pressed hard for completion of the Berlin outer ring railway, and between 1875–1879 built a purely military railway from Berlin-Schöneberg via Zossen to Jüterbog.

The private and state railways, with different methods and standards, had agreed from an early date on standardized working to enable through traffic, but the growth of traffic demanded increasing coordination of operations. Although state control of railways was well developed early in South Germany, Prussia began to extend its control between 1881 and 1887 when nearly all the larger private railways were taken over. Bismarck, a strong supporter of state railways, had set his heart on the creation of an Imperial Railway (a name applied in practice only to the annexed lines of Alsace and Lorraine), and in 1873 a *Reichsbahnamt* was set up to supervise all German railways. In 1875 a single signalling code was agreed, and in 1877 a unified tariff system developed, with a series of operating codes formulated between 1871 and 1907, while in 1909 the major railways agreed on a common wagon pool.

Between 1870 and 1913, the railway network had grown over threefold, capital investment over fourfold, and the number of locomotives and rolling stock over fivefold, whereas passenger traffic had increased sixteenfold and goods traffic eightfold. By 1900, the railway scene was dominated by eight main state railways – the largest was the Prussian-Hessian system (united in 1896), but the Bavarian, Württemberg, Baden, and Saxon systems were also substantial, whereas the Oldenburg and Mecklenburg state railways were relatively small, though remarkably efficient. In 1909, the Palatinate Railway was taken into the Bavarian state system, while the lines in Alsace and Lorraine (where route length grew threefold after 1870) were administered directly by the *Reich*. The largest remaining private line was the Lübeck-Büchen Railway with a 136-kilometres route length.

Railway services – frequency and times
Early train services were light – a timetable of the Berlin–Hamburg Railway shows two through passenger trains each way daily, a through goods train, and a train that ran late in the day and stopped overnight at Wittenberge; in 1849, the Dortmund-Elberfeld line had only one daily through train and four others serving part of the route. Night trains began in 1847, first from Berlin to Köln and, by 1855, about one-ninth of all trains were 'expresses'. Until early this century, most international and the best internal trains were light, comprising only four or five coaches, while most ordinary expresses were comparatively slow and made numerous stops (often including lunch and dinner breaks). Sleeping compartments were introduced in 1851, but the first true sleeping cars began in 1873 from Berlin to Ostend, and dining cars followed in

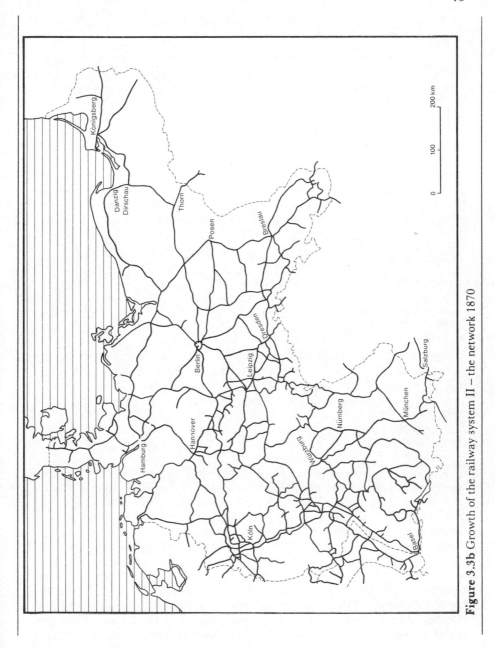

Figure 3.3b Growth of the railway system II – the network 1870

1880, usually run by the various railway companies, though a comprehensive system was organized in North Germany.

Although international railway connections had been established by the 1840s, international trains were slow to develop. But it was not until the 1870s that such traffic began to increase as internal through-running also grew. The development of the International Sleeping Car Company in the 1880s was an important factor in growth. Germany's own central position in Europe was reflected in the formation of the *Mitropa* Company in 1916 to serve both international and major internal links. Most first-rank international expresses between north and south, east and west in Europe crossed German territory at some point, with Berlin, Köln and Frankfurt/Main becoming key focal points. To ease Scandinavian traffic, train ferries were established – in 1903 from Warnemünde and in 1909 from Sassnitz (the through link much improved by completion of the bridge across the Strelasund in 1937).

Table 3.4
Typical journey times in Germany by railway

Route	1890	1914	1939	1975
		– hours and minutes –		
Berlin–Hamburg	4–32	3–18	2–33	5–04
Berlin–Breslau	10–00	5–48	3–05	7–42*
Köln–Mainz	3–46	3–30	2–12	1–43
Berlin–München	13–18	10–26	7–30	9–55
Essen–Dortmund	0–58	0–38	0–32	0–22
Hamburg–Kiel	2–06	2–00	2–02	1–03
Berlin–Leipzig	2–50	1–58	1–20	2–05*
Berlin–Köln	10–04	8–04	6–24	8–32
* = 1971				

Source: Timetables for respective years

With rising traffic and improved technology, trains became heavier, longer, and more frequent, while improvements were made in travel times. It was, however, not until the mid-1930s with the introduction of fast diesel railcar expresses that German trains collected laurels for speed. Among the best were also the light steam-hauled FD-trains and such prestige services as the *Rheingold* Holland–Switzerland link (after 1929). Tables 3.4 and 3.5 indicates the change in speed and frequency for selected routes and stations. A typical feature of German railways was the provision of numerous through carriages, which were often marshalled into three or four trains along various stages of

The Two Germanies

their journey, and demanded good timekeeping, careful control of rolling stock movements, and generous recovery times woven into schedules. Local services and secondary routes remained virtually unchanged in frequency and in timings between about 1910 and 1939. From the 1880s commuting grew around the principal cities, with an elaborate system developed in and around Berlin, and from the turn of the century electrification was carried out on many commuter lines (e.g., in Berlin and Hamburg). The Prussian railways sought to develop effective commuting services through the rationalization of the network originally created by three separate railway companies in the Ruhr industrial area, but plans for electrification and a special operational pattern were halted by the war and subsequent economic problems. However, in 1932 a system of fast steam-hauled trains with short halts sliced 30 percent off travel times, and diesel railcars were introduced just before the Second World War.

Table 3.5
Daily frequency of stopping trains in one direction for selected stations

Number of trains	1914	1939	1970
Diepholz	12	32	52
Gerolstein	10	12	19
Remagen	30	57	102
Rheda	13	42	53
Geislingen	30	44	74
Lahr	23	34	57
Ingolstadt	15	27	41
Bochum	71	138	154
Greifswald	13	16	18
Brandenburg	23	41	27
Waren	10	12	21
Eisenach	32	33	31
Döbeln	10	23	15
Fürstenwalde	15	34	18
Oschatz	17	35	18
Delitzsch	17	47	37

Source: Timetables for respective years

Beer was the first railway freight in Germany – carried on the Nürnberg-Fürth railway shortly after opening. Railways quickly began to see the opportunities for goods traffic, but its growth was slow at first until industrialization got underway in the 1860s, although through goods traffic between railways began about 1848. By the 1860s separate coal trains were being run, and as coal and lignite mining grew, so did the importance of these freights. Through

78

the nineteenth century, as in Britain, goods traffic was handled in small two-axled wagons, loose coupled in trains, although the capacity of the individual wagons rose slightly and Württemberg, influenced more by American practice, experimented with large bogie wagons. The absence of private owners' wagons on the scale that hampered technical progress in Britain allowed German railways to move more rapidly towards continuous braking

Table 3.6
Railway traffic in Germany per kilometre of track

	1868	1885	1903
Passenger/km	202,900	216,900	431,327
Ton/km	316,200	430,500	697,672

Source: Lotz, W., Verkehrsentwicklung in Deutschland 1800–1900, Berlin, 1906

on freight trains as well as towards the introduction of larger capacity wagons, especially between the World Wars. Goods trains were generally heavier than in Britain, and the Germans were more successful in getting full engine loads. Goods operations were also based on marshalling yard departure times (rather than destination arrival times as in Britain), which was claimed to speed freight movements. With fewer separate railways, particularly after the late nineteenth century, the small number of interchange sidings also speeded freight. Remodelling marshalling yards for greater capacity and speedier throughput began after 1910 and accelerated in the 1920s, creating highly effective installations like Hamm in Westphalia (a model for the L.N.E.R. yard at Whitemoor, March).

Coal and lignite were the main freights, though coal transport fell from 38 percent of the tonnage in Prussia in 1909 to 29 percent in 1937, when the six main industrial areas originated 40 percent of all freight (18 percent from the Rhine–Ruhr area alone), and all loaded more wagons than they emptied. Building materials, ores, and sugar beet were also major items. Rates were

Table 3.7
Development of the German railway system

	1870	1890	1913	1925	1930	1936
Operating length (km)	18,805	41,495	63,794	52,768*	53,844*	54,491*
Passenger (mill.)	113	421	1,834	2,106	1,829	1,611
Freight (mill.t.)	70	213	559	409	400	452
* = Plus about 4500 km. of private lines

Source: Stumpf, B., Kleine Geschichte der Deutschen Eisenbahnen, Mainz, 1954.

The Two Germanies

carefully designed to favour German ports, effectively extending their hinterlands, while special rates in the 1930s to encourage movement of selected items throughout the country or to promote regional development were also offered. Encouragement was given, even before 1914, to full-trainload shipments, chiefly to combat canal competition, while from the mid-1930s there were attempts to counter road competition.

The building of railways on a considerable scale before industrialization was properly underway meant a change in operation during the nineteenth century to a greater degree than in Britain. Even into the 1860s, railways were designed for low capacity and frequency operation in a predominantly rural countryside: between 1860 and 1880 a shift took place to a system, especially in Prussia and the Rhinelands, to deal with rapidly rising industrial traffics and a substantial growth in passenger traffic. This shift in emphasis as well as the organizational changes brought by rationalization into the states' railways and later a national system (*Reichsbahn*) saw important development work on the network and on its equipment well into the 1930s, a task complicated by the territorial changes after the First World War.

Industrial development between the World Wars

The territorial changes after 1918 (p. 43) brought considerable loss to the economic potential of the *Reich*, amounting to 14.6 percent of the agricultural area, 74.5 percent of the iron-ore resources, 68.1 percent of the zinc ores, and 26 percent of the coal output. Also lost were 500 power looms and 1.9 million spindles. The loss of the Alsatian potash deposits broke Germany's monopolistic position in Europe and the textile industry in Alsace turned into a major competitor. Loss of Lorraine and the exclusion of Luxemburg from the German customs union deprived the *Reich* of 2.5 million tons of pig iron and 1.3 million tons of steel (1913 figures). In Upper Silesia, 80 percent of the coal reserves went to Poland, and the consequent industrial disruption was a serious blow to the economy of Eastern Germany. The control of the Saar by France until 1935 and the military occupation of the Rhineland also raised difficulties. Nevertheless, despite reparations and the inflation of 1923, the second half of the 1920s until the Great Depression was relatively prosperous.

The country had emerged with an enlarged chemicals industry, developed to offset the problems of isolation during the war years, though many works had already been planned before 1914. Growth had been impressive in Central Germany: in 1916 the large Merseburg plant for nitrogen synthesis had been opened, and by 1926 synthetic petrol was being produced by the Leuna plant. Although Germany still retained over half the world's trade in dyestuffs, to fight competition the *Interessengemeinschaft der Deutschen Farbenindustrie (I. G. Farben)* was founded in 1926, a vast organization controlling the larger part of the chemicals industry, able to rationalize and develop along modern lines. The *Ruhrgas* Company was also formed (1926) to coordinate the use of coal for chemicals and rationalize industrial and domestic gas supplies.

In general, Lorraine remained more dependent on German coal and coke than Germany was on the now lost Lorraine ore. Ironworks were quickly adjusted to other supplies, though plans for a large steelworks on the middle Rhine near Koblenz, a break-even point between Ruhr coal and Lorraine ore, and canalization of the Mosel, were quietly dropped. Some of the pressure on the inland market was taken away by the Saar steelworks passing under French control and by the loss of some Upper Silesian capacity. The large quantities of scrap available from disused war equipment encouraged the development of electric and openhearth steels, and in German Upper Silesia plants used 75 percent scrap for their steel production. The formation of the *Vereinigte Stahlwerke* in 1926, controlling about one-third of all output, helped rationalization, but output of both pig iron and steel stayed well below prewar levels. Coal mining had been affected by the partial loss of the Upper Silesian field and French control until 1935 of the Saar, while in the Ruhr coalfield about 1923 a wave of closures of older and smaller pits marked the abandonment of the southern part of the coalfield. In 1922, brown coal production had exceeded bituminous coal production in tonnage and heating value for the first time, partly arising from an upsurge in electricity output, which also led to the building of hydro-electric generators (e.g. the Walchenseewerk [1918–1924] and the Kachlet station on the Danube [1927]). Between 1923 and 1928 an arterial 220-KV double transmission line linking Bludenz in Vorarlberg with Brauweiler near Köln was completed.

In 1920 the merchant fleet was 653,000 tons compared to 5.5 million tons in 1913, but by 1930 the prewar tonnage was nearly reached again (4.4 million tons), most new ships having come from German yards. Two new ships – the *Bremen* (1929, 51,700 tons) and the *Europa* (1930, 49,700 tons) were serious rivals in the still lucrative transatlantic traffic, for which a suitable terminal had been built in Bremerhaven (*Columbuskai*, 1925–1927). Railway engineering also flourished (though *Grafenstaden* in Alsace and *Ciegielski* in Posen had been lost by territorial change), for the state railway company, an amalgamation of the railways of the German states in 1920, sought to reequip with standardized equipment. As elsewhere in Western Europe, the motor car revolution began, notably with the introduction of a cheap small car by *Opel* in 1924; in 1930 *Ford* opened a works in Köln; while in 1928 *Opel* had become part of the American *General Motors Corporation*; and Saxony aided several small firms (*Horch, Wanderer, Audi, DKW*) to merge to combat competition in 1932. Despite restrictions by the Inter-Allied Control Commission, aircraft building flourished and by 1926 Germany had Europe's densest internal airways system. Well-known names were *Junker* in Dessau, *Messerschmidt* in Augsburg,

Klemm in Böblingen, *Zeppelin* (airships) at Friedrichshafen and Berlin-Staaken, and *Heinkel* in Warnemünde, Rostock, and Oranienburg, though small producers did not survive the great collapse of 1929.

The Third Reich
The National Socialists introduced policies that were to have considerable effect on the territorial distribution of industry, partly through changes with time and partly through conscious planning decisions. The worsening trade situation immediately after 1933 and a fear that Germany could become over-dependent on outside sources of raw materials and thus weaken its strategic situation, brought a move towards self-sufficiency, to be achieved partly by utilizing Germany's natural resources more intensely and partly by developing new synthetic substances. The four-year plan in 1936 stressed the need to raise synthetic petroleum production from around 7000 tons to 3 million tons yearly, annual synthetic rubber output from 'a few thousand tons' to 70,000–80,000 tons, and annual production of iron-ore from 2.5 to 7 million tons. Nevertheless, Germany was to remain dependent on iron-ore imports for two-thirds of its needs, with Sweden as major supplier, even though it was hoped ultimately to raise home ore production to 20–30 million tons annuallly. Even with expanded domestic synthetic and natural petroleum supplies at the then level of technology, it was not expected to be more than 50 percent self-sufficient. The peacetime demand for textiles could be expected to be covered only 40 percent by home raw materials, despite extensive use of synthetics and a general reduction in quality. At the outbreak of war, the *Reich* was still 80 percent dependent on imports for copper, 65 percent for petroleum and rubber, 45 percent for leather, and completely dependent for manganese, nickel, tungsten, chrome.

Partly through the growth of industry since 1914, but also through strategic considerations, a new concept arose of *Mitteldeutschland* as an economic-geographical unit, where the chemicals industry (with development of the new synthetic substances) had a strategic position in the Elbe-Saale basin well away from the dangerous peripheries of the country. On the western flanks, located in a countryside where labour was available and near to the Mittelland Canal, the Berlin–Ruhr motorway, and good rail links to bring in raw materials, the vast plant of *Volkswagen* arose (1938). Also for strategic reasons as well as availability of labour and local ores, a large new steelworks was built at Salzgitter with American help, where again good rail connections and a branch from the Mittelland Canal were to be used to bring in raw materials. It was to be supplied from large reserves of low-grade but relatively easily work-able sedimentary ore, but coal and coke were to come from the Ruhr. The plant, conceived as the main supplier for engineering industries in *Mitteldeutschland* and the Northwest, went into operation in 1937. Vast reserves of low-grade ore in South Germany were also considered for a similar large project in Franconia, which would also have helped the Saar to loosen its dependence on minette ore from France and Luxemburg. But after the *Anschluss* with Austria, where better ore supplies were available, plans switched to a Danube-side site at Linz, with high potential for the economic penetration of Southeast Europe. Coal was to have come from Czech Silesia by the never completed Oder-Danube Canal and via the then projected Main-Danube Canal from the Ruhr.

Besides expansion of existing chemical plants, new installations for the manufacture of synthetic substances were erected. In 1934, the *Braunkohle-Benzin A. G.* was formed to promote the production of synthetic petrol, with hydrogeneration plants at Böhlen, Zeitz, and Schwarzheide; in 1935 the Schkopau experimental plant started to use a technique first developed in 1927 to make synthetic rubber and the Leuna works also became a major producer of materials related to the manufacture of these substances. Another large synthetic rubber plant was built at Hüls near Recklinghausen (1940), forming part of a complex of chemicals plants in the northern and central Ruhr. Castrop-Rauxel became the centre for synthetic petroleum production, while between 1934–1937 tar distillation was doubled. Other synthetic petrol plants were built in Central Germany near Merseburg, on the Baltic coast near Stettin, and on the Rhine at Wesseling. In Silesia, whose strategic importance grew after the defeat of Poland, plants to make both synthetic petrol and rubber were opened in Heydebreck (Kędzierzyn) and (after 1940) at Auschwitz (Oświęcim) and at Most (Brux) in the Sudetenland.

After 1933 engineering was further developed, with Germany overtaking France as the main continental producer of motor vehicles, while standardization (e.g. the *Hanse*-ships) raised productivity. Important engineering plants were brought under direct German control through the *Anschluss* with Austria, the incorporation of the Sudetenland and the Protectorate of Bohemia-Moravia (e.g., *Škoda*, Pilsen, and *ČKD*, Prague). Some strategic dispersal of key industries also began after 1937, notably of electrical engineering firms from Berlin to South Germany; and aircraft production was decentralized, while a major rocket research station was built at Peenemünde on the Baltic, with assembly plants in Mecklenburg and Pomerania.

Improved techniques and expansion of existing plant as much as other factors raised iron and steel production to all-time records in 1938–1939, but thereafter air attack (steelworks were easily pinpointed) and difficulties in adjusting to wartime demands brought a slow fall in output, though the level of production remained well above the best general prewar level. Inland plant, less open to air attack, became increasingly important, particularly in Upper Silesia and Czech Silesia. After 1935 steel production had been augmented by

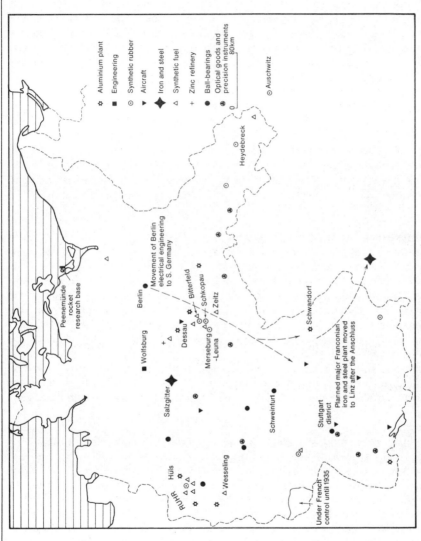

Figure 3.4 Economic geography of the Third *Reich*

Economic Change

the return of the Saar, though even before 1935 South Germany obtained much of its raw metal needs from Saar works, but from early 1939 to May, 1940, production in the Saar was stopped for strategic reasons. After 1938, capacity of special and alloy steel production had been increased by Austrian plants, though after 1941 efforts were made to conserve valuable alloy metals. Aluminium and aluminium alloy production had been developed to save expensive imports of other nonferrous metals and to supply the growing aircraft industry; and after 1925 the German–Hungarian *Bauxit-Trust A. G.* came to control many European sources of bauxite. In 1929 Germany had produced 1 percent of world aluminium, but by 1938 this had risen to 27 percent (U.S.A., 22 percent). The main plants were near large electricity generators in the Ruhr-Westphalian area (at Lünen, Grevenbroich, and Bergheim near Köln) and at Senftenberg and Bitterfeld in Central Germany, but also at Ludwigshafen, Schwandorf, and Rheinfelden in South Germany. At the outbreak of war, a large plant at Aken near Dessau in Central Germany was commissioned. The conquest of Norway provided additional large capacity.

Transport between the wars

Reparations and territorial loss caused considerable adjustment in transport in the Weimar period, but the main changes were to come under the Nazi administration. Most notable was the growth of motor traffic on the roads, with a big road-building programme begun to alleviate unemployment and to provide a fast, strategic system of highways. Equally, encouragement was given to air traffic, though even in the mid-1920s Germany had one of the most efficient civil air transport systems in Europe. After drastic reorganization, the railways were also modernized to provide another vital strategic system of transport, and not even canal building was neglected. Unfortunately, several of the grandiose schemes begun in the mid-1930s were still unfinished by the outbreak of the Second World War, as for example, the Rhine-Danube Canal.

Roads

For fifty years, road transport had been overshadowed by the railways, but after the First World War, the availability of surplus military motor vehicles gave a new impetus, though the volume of vehicles in relation to population remained below the United States and even the United Kingdom. Under the Weimar régime, some improvements were made to roads to deal with the growing number of motor cars: in 1921, the *AVUS*, a forerunner of the new motorway concept, was opened in Berlin between Grunewald and Nikolasee, while in 1928–1932 a private venture set out to build a super toll highway from Hamburg via Frankfurt to Basel (*HAFRABA*), though only the Bonn-Köln section was completed. From the mid-1920s onwards, motor bus services increased quickly, often displacing light railways and trams.

The National Socialist government, partly to reduce unemployment and partly for strategic needs, began one of the greatest modern road-building programmes in a system of super highways radiating from Berlin to all corners

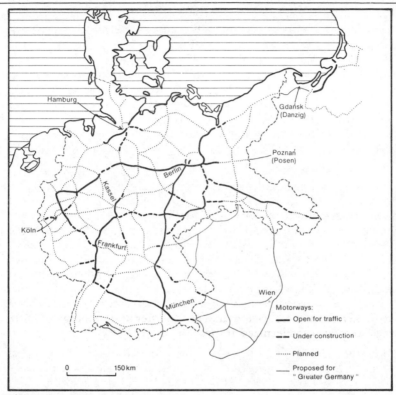

Figure 3.5 Hitler's motorways

of the *Reich* and with a number of strategic inter-regional links. The first section of *Autobahn* was opened between Frankfurt and Darmstadt in 1935. It was planned to build 1000 kilometres a year, and by the outbreak of war in 1939 some 4000 kilometres were open to traffic. The upsurge in cheap mass-produced cars was, as elsewhere in Europe, a considerable factor in the improvement of roads – in Germany, motor vehicles increased from 1.68 million in 1933 to 2.84 million in 1937.

The Railways
The German railways emerged badly run-down in 1919, with some 13 percent of the 1914 route length in annexed territories and much rolling stock sur-

rendered as reparations, while track had to be dismantled or reduced to single line in some border areas for strategic reasons. The creation of the Polish Corridor separating the province of East Prussia from the main body of Germany caused operating difficulties. Fortunately, the main Berlin-Königsberg line via Schneidemühl ran parallel to the new frontier for a long distance before crossing it, but onerous conditions were imposed on traffic across the short stretch of Polish territory. The division of the industrial district of Upper Silesia between Poland and Germany also made railway operations hard. On the west, the transfer of Eupen and Malmédy to Belgium put the Raeren to Kalterherberg railway (*Eifelbahn*) under Belgian administration even though it lay just inside German territory, so raising issues of extraterritoriality. With the loss of territory to Denmark in Schleswig, the old routes to the holiday island of Sylt were cut, and the Germans responded (1927) by building the railway across the Hindenburg Dam.

New construction was mainly improvement of existing routes and continued double-tracking, but financial stringency limited what could be done. New lines were mostly short: the Velbert-Kettwig and Witten-Wengern routes in the southern Ruhr, approved in 1911, were completed in 1926–1927, and the long needed Witten-Bommern-Schwelm freight line was opened in 1934. Of particular importance was the Münster-Lünen-Dortmund line, approved in 1913 and opened in 1928, avoiding the long way round through Hamm, but it has remained single track even after electrification in the 1960s. The opening in 1938 of the Celle-Langenhagen line provided a direct Hamburg–Hannover route, carrying from the start heavy, long-distance traffic, and the western ring route round Münster eased congestion and delay to freight traffic.

Although the Germans had pioneered electric railway traction, opposition from the General Staff hampered electrification of main lines. Before 1914, minor lines in Bavaria and Baden had been electrified; but after 1918 more progress was made, with the electrification of the Magdeburg-Bitterfeld-Leipzig line, some heavily graded routes in Silesia; and in South Germany, Salzburg to Stuttgart via München was electric by 1939 and also München-Weissenfels via Augsburg-Bamberg and via Regensburg, as well as the München-Kufstein line. In 1942, through working from München to Magdeburg with electric traction was opened, but the link to Berlin was never completed. Commuter line electrification helped compete against road transport in the late 1920s, while from 1933 the introduction of fast, long-distance diesel trains helped to compete with Germany's excellent domestic air services. On the local level, road competition was more critical: in 1935, it was estimated that 40 percent of all light railways (often narrow gauge) were uneconomic, with severe losses in passenger traffic.

In 1920, the several state railways had been grouped into a national system (*Deutsche Reichsbahn*) with unified management and standardized practices as required by the Weimar constitution, but there were few possibilities of rationalization of the network because route duplication, exchange sidings, or duplicated stations as in Britain were not nearly so evident. In fact, in Germany, competition between railways had never played much part in operation and had never been encouraged by the regulating authorities, as it had in Britain. The *Reichsbahn* was extended from the late 1930s by inclusion of the railways in annexed territories and during the 1939–1945 war also supplied personnel to run railways in other occupied territories, notably the immense *Ostbahn* in occupied Russia.

Waterways and ports
Much work on waterways was simply completion of projects begun before 1914, like the Mittelland Canal and canals in the Ruhr coalfield (p. 64). A large-scale improvement of Elbe navigation was begun in the mid-1930s, including proposed ship canals to avoid difficult sections, but the work was never completed. A small, significant improvement was the completion in 1940 of the Gleiwitz Canal from the Oder to the Upper Silesian coalfield to replace the old Klodnitz Canal (1788–1806). After the *Anschluss* with Austria and incorporation of Bohemia-Moravia, work began on the Oder-Danube Canal, whose initial works can still be seen near Vienna on this as yet incomplete project. The *Anschluss* also accelerated the slow pace of work on the Main-Danube Canal begun in 1919.

Territorial change after 1919 much affected ports. Danzig was lost to become a free city in competition with the new all-Polish port of Gdynia that also sought to lure traffic away from Königsberg and Stettin. Königsberg lost most of its Polish and Russian traffic and became the provincial port for the detached province of East Prussia, and because of the difficulty of rail links across the Polish Corridor to the main part of the *Reich,* developed a special shipping service with Stettin. Increased efforts were made to divert Rhenish and South German traffic from Rhine-Maas ports to North German Hamburg and Bremen, mostly by means of preferential railway tariffs.

The emergence of German agriculture
Economic and social conditions did not produce in Germany anything so forceful as the Improving and Enclosure Movements in Britain, while German agriculture was more protected than British against outside commercial influence in the critical years of the nineteenth century, and the peasant way of life was consequently preserved longer. The German lands witnessed an extensive mediaeval clearing of forest and draining of marsh in an inner colonization by peasants directed by the aristocracy, of which the settlement of the sparsely

settled Slav lands east of the Elbe was just a part. But the Black Death (1348–1350), the prelude to which had been bad harvests and rising grain prices, halted this colonization that never again had the same impetus: in fact, there was little increase in the cultivated area from the mid-fourteenth century until the early nineteenth century and the depression in agriculture in the fifteenth and sixteenth centuries, followed by wars in the seventeenth, resulted even in a retreat of settlement, with forest taking over the deserted villages.

Germany emerged from the Napoleonic Wars still predominantly agrarian – three-quarters of the 25 million people in 1816 lived in the countryside and engaged in farming, while many towns, particularly the smaller ones, had a villagelike appearance and the agrarian town (*Ackerbürgerstadt*) was common. In Prussia, in 1804 for example, 80 percent of the population was agricultural, but this had fallen to 64 percent in 1840 and 48 percent in 1867, and a similar pattern was followed in other large German states. Until well into the nineteenth century, the economy retained a considerable subsistence element and markets were essentially local, though some of the larger estates and more specialized farming areas engaged in trade. The old three-field system was still practised, but often only half the area was under cultivation at a time and manure was inadequate, with animals especially difficult to keep through the winter. Yield was low – in Pomerania and East Prussia, rye and barley seldom gave more than 6–7 quintals per hectare and the best farmers in Mark Brandenburg in the period 1816–1832 managed an average of only a five-fold gain of grain over seed. In places, attempts were made to improve conditions – Friedrich II in Prussia introduced the four-field rotation and fodder plants instead of fallow on several royal estates, giving every encouragement to the farmer who would farm 'English style'. By 1820, in the Goldene Aue and in Silesia, fallow had been reduced and crops such as potatoes, cabbage, legumes, and fodder plants were common, while in the period 1800–1820, real attempts had been made on some large estates in Brandenburg to break finally with the old three-field system – the nearness of the rapidly growing market of Berlin was incentive enough to increase productivity. Stall feeding was begun and immigrant Dutch introduced a dairy industry. In Saxony, older methods prevailed because many farmers depended on sheep for the wool trade, and the three-field system gave plenty of grazing for sheep, especially on the larger holdings and estates. In North Germany, where good arable was short, the distinctive two-field system was practised: potatoes, beets, and cabbage one year, grains – rye, oats, or barley – the next. In the poorest moor and heath – in the Emsland, for example – the ground was burnt and cultivated for 3–8 years and then left to recuperate for 10–20 years. In Holstein, there was rotation with grass and an important livestock economy developed, with similar trends in Mecklenburg, but the Baltic littoral for long remained a grain surplus area. Small areas had advanced systems of farming – along the Mosel, for example, a true rotational system not unlike the English Norfolk system was already in use. Observers usually suggested that farming in South Germany was behind the North, with the exceptions of such specialities as vines, hops, tobacco, and oil seeds: Baden was commonly mentioned as particularly advanced, with good fruit and vine cultivation, potatoes and tobacco, while use was made of clover in rotations, and its government looked after farmers and gave special encouragement to the middle-sized peasant farm.

The peasant class was clearly defined in German society and tightly tied to the soil; in the eastern parts from the sixteenth century, peasants had become increasingly dependent on their landlords. The death knell of this situation and the end of many feudal practices had been sounded by the French Revolution, though the first moves in a few places had preceded even this. Although some peasants in Brandenburg, Pomerania, and Silesia had been protected against landowners taking their land, the reforms of Freiherr vom Stein and of Hardenberg (1807–11) regulated relations between the peasant and the landowner, though not entirely to the benefit of the former except for the most able and wealthy, and it was still possible for the landed gentry to take land from small peasants and to extend the landless class. The reforms throughout the nineteenth century were invariably watered down by 'interpretive legislation', usually to the advantage of the landowners, and marking further dispossession of peasants to extend the great estates. The Russian peasant emancipation of 1807–1816 was paralleled in Bavaria by legislation in 1808, though the feudal ties were not finally swept away until 1848; in Prussia's eastern provinces, seignorial jurisdiction did not ultimately disappear until 1918. Emancipation came in 1812 in Nassau; in 1817 in Württemberg; in 1820 in Hessen-Darmstadt and in Baden; and in 1821 in Kurhessen. The emancipation came earliest to areas taken directly into Napoleonic France, as in the Rhineland, though some states like Hannover also had early legislation.

After the Napoleonic Wars, a crisis hit farming, but from 1830 onwards change accelerated. Important was an increasing scientific interest: Thaer stressed the value of enclosures and deep ploughing, improved crop rotation and better tools, but modern fertilizing techniques owe most to Justus Liebig. The older three- and four-field systems rapidly gave way in the 1840s to new rotations – red clover, potatoes, beets, and legumes replaced fallow. The westernmost districts generally made the greatest progress towards the new systems, but estates in the Baltic littoral and Prussia's eastern provinces were also known for better management and techniques, especially how to keep more livestock, while summer stall feeding became common, and improved breeds were developed. The first sugar beet factory had been unsuccessfully opened in Silesia in 1798, but renewed attempts had been made during the Napoleonic Continental System in Silesia and in the Magdeburger *Börde*. After 1815 cheap imported cane sugar ruined sugar beet cultivation until Prussian duties on

Economic Change

imported sugar gave home production another chance. Improvements in the sugar content of the beet and in its processing helped the industry to develop, while winter classes were provided to teach farmers about the crop. Stall feeding of cattle also demanded food, for which sugar beet waste was well suited. By the 1850s Saxony was the main centre of the industry – in 1851 it had 102 sugar factories, while in Silesia there were 47, with 21 in Anhalt and 8 in Brunswick. The demand for potatoes from the industrial towns in the second half of the nineteenth century was also to help many backward and less favoured areas, for example, the Eifel (the much prized *Oberländer*).

The reforms of the legal status of the rural population, beginning to show their effect in the 1840s, had clearly worked to the advantage of the large and medium farmers, whose diligence, orderliness, and thrift were rewarded. Fortunately, many small peasants who became landless labourers were able to find work in towns, but there was also growing purchase of land by townspeople, especially in years of agricultural depression. Particular difficulties arose in Southwest Germany, where division of inheritance was common and the country was becoming overpopulated as families struggled to live from dwarf holdings that not even potato cultivation made worthwhile, and particularly strong migration took place, notably in the 1840s to America. The growth of urban markets and ease of transport by railway made the scene increasingly competitive and the new economic trends encouraged money-conscious farming.

By the early nineteenth century, it had been realized that over wide areas real improvement in agriculture could only be achieved if the old field boundaries and patterns of holdings in a wide scatter of small parcels of ground could be reorganized into a more rational system and even consolidated holdings created. There was even a need to provide field paths in some places, as well as to improve the use of the common lands – meadow and forest alike – but at first all that could be hoped for was some reduction in the number and shape of parcels wherever possible, with the problem particularly critical in areas of divided inheritance, generally in the south and southwest. The first real attempt at reorganization (*Verkoppelung*) dated from 1829–1830 in Nassau, but most efforts came after the revolution of 1848 had swept away the last feudal vestiges: Baden in 1856, Hessen in 1857, Oldenburg in 1858, Bavaria and Württemberg in 1861 (and also the Prussian Rhine province). Efforts to get reorganization in Silesia had begun in the eighteenth century, followed by Hannover, while early progress had been made in Schleswig-Holstein, but the estates of the north and northeast had done much to help themselves. Progress in the north was generally better, because the political conditions and problems of ownership were less complex than in the south, but in the latter part of the nineteenth century the process speeded up as a fear spread that Germany would become, like Britain, too dependent on industry and imported foodstuffs. In Prussia between 1872 and 1914, some 50,000–60,000 hectares were reallocated annually.

German peasants had long been land reclaimers, although the Black Death slowed but did not halt the process: and in the sixteenth century there was widespread colonization in Southwest Germany, in the Rhön, and in the Weser basin, but especially on the coast of the German Bight where land was won back from that lost in the great mediaeval storms. Despite the troubles of the seventeenth century, in areas unaffected by war, reclamation and settlement went on, again notably on the coast of the German Bight, but the great period of reclamation was the eighteenth century. In Prussia, over 30,000 colonists were settled, mostly in the drained marshes of the Oder and Elbe basins (including many Dutch), but also in the forests of Silesia. The settlement of the peat moors of North Germany, begun in the sixteenth century, lasted well into the nineteenth century, strongly influenced by Dutch technique and experience, and the characteristic 'fen colonies' generally took 40 to 50 years to change from being primarily dependent on digging peat to being principally agricultural. Unfortunately, many not outstandingly successful became islands of poverty in the late nineteenth century, with some reclaimed moor ultimately turned to forest. South German colonization was generally on a smaller scale than in the north, though no less important, encouraged by the nobility who set out regularly planned villages. One of the main schemes was the reclamation of 19,000 hectares of the Donaumoos near München during the eighteenth century. Although the cultivated area went on expanding into the twentieth century, reclamation slowly turned from colonization to afforestation, with parts of the Lüneburger Heide planted in the late 1870s.

In the late nineteenth century, the inflow of cheap extra-European grain posed new problems, while railways made the German market accessible to grain from Austria–Hungary and Russia. The big grain farmers of Trans-Elbian Germany demanded protection, but at the same time began to switch to crops (potatoes, for example) and livestock that were finding a growing market in the expanding towns. There was an increasing tendency for food-processing industries (potato alcohol, sugar extraction, milling, butter and cheese making, etc.) to grow, often replacing activities once done on the farms. Despite protection by tariffs, agriculture sought to improve its performance by more intense cultivation of the best land with less fallow (and consequently fewer sheep) and abandonment of the poorest land (mostly to forestry), with increasing use of better techniques and fertilizing (made possible by the growth of the chemicals industry). The bigger farms and estates led the way. The small proprietor turned to cooperatives, notably the widespread *Raiffeisen* organization (established 1849). Education through agricultural schools and winter evening classes helped to improve production, while in general peasants devoted more time to farming and less to ancillary jobs. The drift of men from the land, however, increased the role of women. It was accepted that a large number of smallholdings were to be expected in an industrializing society, and in 1882 Bismarck praised them as preventing an extension of the proletariat. Though the general tendency for smallholdings was to increase slowly, they were mostly not in the hands of the agricultural population. Of the smallest holdings (below 0.5 hectares), 96 percent were secondary occupations and, in the 0.5–2 hectare group, 72 percent were in this category, producing largely for their cultivators. By the end of last century, migration from the countryside had such critical dimensions that several states sought to strengthen the social, legal, and economic position of the small and medium farmers and to make settlement on land easier. The largest – the great estates included – were felt, however, to be the most progressive and 'rentabel', though at the end of the nineteenth century they had begun to show critical financial weaknesses and to decline numerically. Considerable political opposition was aroused against the entailed estates, though they were often more careful and prudent of the long-term use of resources than the peasants; and in the eastern provinces the estates were seen as a defence against the spread of Polish influences.

Agriculture between the World Wars

After the First World War, there was a lack of suitable farm labour because many men had been killed or did not return to the land on demobilization. Wartime demands had reduced the amount of fertilizer and much slaughtered livestock had not been replaced. The economic crisis of 1929 revealed how deeply the farmers had indebted themselves to rehabilitate their holdings, but many weaknesses had been hidden by the strongly protectionist policy.

Before 1914 about three-quarters of the agriculturally used land was under the plough, but by 1937 this had fallen to 68 percent. Between 1928 and 1937, 1.4 million hectares had gone out of use, half to permanent grass and half to non-agricultural uses (proportionally less than in most other European countries). The expansion of root crops reflected attempts to intensify production, whereas the relatively small proportion of arable devoted to grass was accounted for by less suitable climatic conditions and sandier soils than in, say, France: only in the southwest, in Baden, were clover and lucerne grown on a significant scale, but generally crop rotations based on three course shifts had a strong grain element because of fiscal protection. In parts of South Germany, five grain crops were grown in succession and then the land was laid to grass for nine years. Between 1913 and 1938, oats and rye both declined in sown area, though the gain of wheat, limited to good soils, was only a quarter of the area lost to oats and rye (which nevertheless remained important, comprising a half of all grain used for bread). Barley, grown notably in South Germany, had been essentially for beer before 1913, when half the crop went to breweries, but this had fallen to a third in 1938 (reflecting a fall of nearly 50

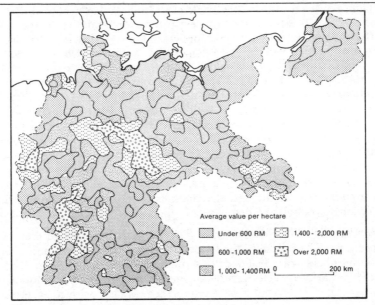

Figure 3.6a Farming between the wars I

percent in beer consumption between 1913 and 1938) and was increasingly grown as a home feeding stuff to replace imports. Oats had increased rapidly in area between 1875 and 1913 and then declined after 1933, as the number of horses fell and feed barley was substituted because of its better yield. In the 1930s cereals' yield had been at much the same level as in the United Kingdom, with Germany's poorer soils offset by more fertilizer and labour, though in the nineteenth century German yield had been below the United Kingdom.

Differences in performance could not be explained solely by the size of farm. The smaller farms were generally in the better soil and climatic conditions of Southwest Germany, but in any given district it was usually the larger farms that gave the best yield, since these were usually on the best local land. Sugar beet farms gave high grain yield, since beet put the land in good heart and could anyway only be grown on the best land. In many districts, the potato was important and in the more remote eastern districts had been used for starch and alcohol production or for livestock feed, the area sown having risen until 1914 and thereafter remaining static, while the Nazi administration encouraged surplus potatoes to be converted into dried flake under generous subsidy. Similar encouragement was given to sugar beet, usually grown on the

Economic Change

larger farms in Central Germany and Silesia. Yield was appreciably better than in the United Kingdom and all the beet was converted into sugar at home, where retail prices were among the highest in Europe. A critical problem in the 1930s was the supply of feeding stuffs, as the search for self-sufficiency forced restriction of imports. In 1909–1913, 5 million tons had been imported, and by the late 1920s this had risen to over 6 million tons (between a third and quarter of the total need), but by 1936 had fallen to only 1.6 million tons. There was a big rise in the use of silos, but their volume by 1939 was still inadequate. Attempts were made to raise the productivity of grassland and to develop varieties of maize which could ripen in North Germany and a soya bean that would ripen in South Germany. The use of fertilizers tended to increase between the wars, with the cultivation of the lighter soils made possible through the ready availability of potash-based substances, and there was also a substantial rise in the use of machinery, despite opposition during the depression years by the unemployed.

During the First World War, many cattle had been slaughtered and not replaced, partly because of the fodder shortage, so that not until 1928 were prewar numbers again reached (18.4 million), rising to over 20 million in the late 1930s. Various breeds were kept, though Frisians and Simmenthaler were most popular. Cattle were mostly kept on farms of less than 20 hectares where

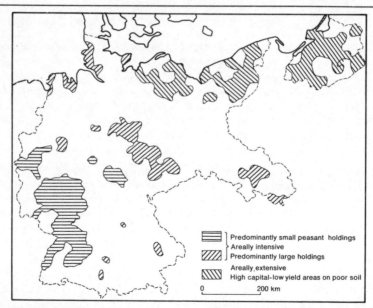

Figure 3.6b Farming between the wars II

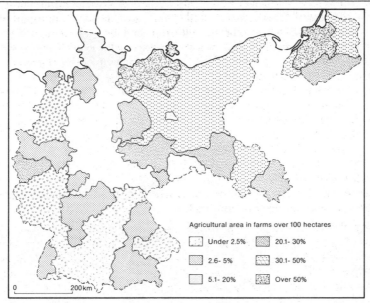

Agricultural area in farms over 100 hectares

☐	Under 2.5%	▦	20.1- 30%
▦	2.6- 5%	▦	30.1- 50%
☐	5.1- 20%	▦	Over 50%

0   200 km

Figure 3.6c Farming between the wars III

the necessary intensive care could be given, and they were also used for draught and work in the fields. The Nazi administration tried to improve livestock quality, while butter and cheese making were shifted increasingly to large-scale creameries and relatively little milk consumed in liquid form. By making butter available, import of oil seed for margarine was limited. The First World War also saw a corresponding slaughter of pigs, with prewar numbers reached by 1927 and some 26 million kept by the late 1930s. Farmers were compelled to switch from foreign imported feeding stuffs to potatoes, which by 1939 supplied at least half the fodder. When imported feeding stuffs were the main food, pigs were especially important in Oldenburg, Hannover, and Westphalia, but as the home-grown potato surplus was greatest east of the Elbe, pig farming later tended to move eastwards. In the 1870s there were over 25 million sheep in Germany, but by the late 1930s they numbered less than 4 million, usurped by imports of better Australian wool and by reclamation of their grazings. To reduce wool imports, the Nazi administration encouraged sheep rearing, though not with great success.

In 1920, a Prussian law allowed the state to reallocate land if asked to do so by a quarter of the owners of holdings in a community requiring *Flurbereinigung*, though in 1936 this legislation became law over the whole country and consent of the owners was no longer required. By 1930, however, reallocation had already been carried out on two-thirds of the farmland in Saxony and one-third in Bavaria and Württemberg, but very much less in Baden. The problem of the estates in North and Northeast Germany was tackled less resolutely, since the *Junker* landowners still formed a powerful political element, but settlement of peasants on estate lands in the east was carried on, particularly between 1930–1933 when many estates had got into financial difficulties.

Entail on estates had been abolished in 1919 and many had come on the market during the crisis years (though 800,000 hectares were in entail in 1939). The situation in the eastern provinces had become so serious that in 1931 the *Osthilfe* was instituted to help estates in difficulty, while this help was extended to the whole *Reich* in 1934.

Despite the Nazi view of the need of a strong peasant bulwark on the east against Slavdom and Bolshevism, peasant settlement slowed after 1933, due to less land becoming available because of rising land values and a growing reluctance to break up highly efficient farms into smaller, less efficient peasant units at a time when the country was aiming at a higher degree of self-sufficiency. About a third of the resettlers on the eastern estates came from western districts where farms were too small and families were large, though many would-be settlers were too poor to put down the necessary money. Peasant resettlement was useful in times of high unemployment, yet less desirable in times of labour shortage, but the aim was generally to stay the rural exodus rather than repopulate the countryside: between 1935–1939 it is estimated that 1 million people left the land. New farms established after 1937 were markedly larger than those of the early 1930s. In all, nearly 100,000 families were resettled on the land by this means, quite apart from the enlargement of existing small farms and holdings, during the interwar period.

The smallest holdings, nearly all part-time, were numerically large but relatively unimportant in their areal extent, and characteristic of Saxony, Württemberg, and Baden. The dwarf holdings were tending to disappear as people switched full time to other occupations, though many were run by the womenfolk. Three-fifths of farm output came from the farms of less than 20 hectares, while only holdings under 5 hectares sold less than four-fifths of their output. Size of holding was nevertheless affected by the difficulty of getting hired labour and the trend was towards solely family farms (ever since the 1880s when the labour shortage had become steadily more acute) despite legislation to hold labourers on the land between 1933 and 1936 (when the law was dropped as industrial labour became scarce).

The Nazi administration tightened its hold on the peasants as it sought to create an independent and largely self-sufficient farming community, since it was believed that the peasantry was the most stable element in national life,

Table 3.8
Farm holdings

Size of holding	% of holdings		
	1882	1907	1939
under 2 ha.	58.0	58.9	77.0
2–5	18.6	17.5	8.0
5–20	17.6	18.6	11.5
20–100	5.3	4.6	3.4
over 100	0.5	0.4	0.2
	% of agricultural land held by holdings in each category		
under 2 ha.	5.7	5.4	13.4
2–5	10.0	10.4	
5–20	28.7	32.7	39.7
20–100	31.0	29.3	30.1
over 100	24.4	22.2	16.8

Source: Various; A. Sartorius von Waltershausen, *Deutsche Wirtschaftsgeschichte, 1815–1914,* Jena 1923.

while it also sought to raise the standards in farming and in the countryside through the vigilance of the *Reichsnährstand.* Already stringent laws of inheritance (for example, in Prussia) were strengthened by the much disputed Laws for Hereditary Farms (*Reichserbhofgesetz*), which applied to all farms large enough to support a family (i.e., not less than 6 hectares) but not exceeding 125 hectares. These were entailed and the proprietor could not sell or mortgage them, but if he proved inefficient he could be deprived of his holding. Where holdings were only just adequate to support a family, peasants were forced to buy additional land to improve their position, consequently pushing up land values, and the general aim was to get rid of dwarf holdings, check further division, stop trading in farms and the accumulation of debt. The law affected 800,000 hectares, almost 50 percent of the farmed area. Certainly the size of holdings had increased from an average of 21 hectares in 1919–1921 to 48 hectares in 1937.

Self-sufficiency and the availability of large amounts of compulsory labour (*Reichsarbeitsdienst* and *Organisation Todt*) were the underlying factors in extended land reclamation in the Nazi period adding to the 2.8 million hectares reclaimed between 1919 and 1929. While the reclamation work included grandiose schemes on the North Frisian coast, much was concerned with improving field drainage, for it was reckoned that half the land was seriously in need of this.

The changing German forests

The great inner colonization in mediaeval Germany took place to a substantial degree by reclaiming and clearing land, the greater part wild and sombre forest. The travellers' impression of the German lands remains one of forest, reflecting the low agricultural value of much land, either because it is too steep or too poor. Richer in native tree species than Britain, especially conifers, forest would be the 'natural' vegetation of much of Germany if it were not for the interference of man, though existing forests bear a heavy imprint of long human action. Under natural conditions, predominant would be beech, Scots pine, and spruce. Beech is usually most successful on well-drained soils and is found from sea level up to 600 metres in the Harz and up to 1300 metres in the German Alps. Susceptible to late frost, it does not react well to a short and cool growing season, and consequently does not thrive in East Prussia, Brandenburg, and Silesia. The Scots pine comprised nearly a half of the nineteenth-century forest area of Germany, in some areas descended from the old natural forest, and remains most abundant in the northeast and in the lowlands, though found up to 1500 metres in the German Alps. Thriving on poorer and sandier soils than beech and withstanding more continental conditions, it is a naturally dominant species on all the lighter soils of central and eastern Germany. Extensive stands of spruce in central and southern Germany of a characteristic sombre and dark mantle (well reflected in the Schwarzwald), reflect extensive planting in the nineteenth century, often replacing less valuable trees or to cover wasteland, so comprising by the interwar years a fifth of the productive forest. As a native tree, spruce was restricted to the higher parts of the central and southern uplands, with small outliers in the Harz and in East Prussia. Unfortunately, spruce is commonly cut before it matures and forests seldom develop beyond the sombrely dense character of the younger trees. The attractive silver fir, a native of the mountains in central and southern Germany, is a warmth-loving tree compared to spruce. Only in the southwest, notably on the western slopes of the Black Forest, do extensive pure stands occur. Its altitudinal limits are much the same as for beech. Larch, native only in the Bavarian Alps and in the Sudeten mountains, usually between 450–1800 metres, occurs in pure stands near the limits of tree growth or at lower elevations in the presence of Arolla pine. Small mountain pines occur in the highest elevations in the mountains – in the Alps, Schwarzwald, and Bayrischer Wald, often as small semiprostrate shrub forming impenetrable thickets of *Krummholz*. Able to exist on extremely poor soil and withstand high wind, mountain pine has been used in afforesting sand dunes in North Germany. Under a tenth of German forest has been composed of oak, and pure stands are extremely rare, occurring mostly in association with birch in the northwest, with hornbeam in the west, and in the north and east with pine. The chief oak lands are west of the Rhine and in Silesia. The oak-birch forest of Northwest Germany is usually found on light sandy soils, frequently occurring in a clear ecological association with heathland, doubtless arising from grazing history. Wet lands attract alder, willows, and (often on wet peaty soils) poplars, so typical of the lower Rhine.

Thirteenth-century legislation put restrictions on further clearance of the forest and acts were passed to protect the interests of salt boilers, charcoal makers and huntsmen. The approximate present limits between farmland and forest had been reached by 1450 after a resurgence of forest over farmland in the devastation of the Black Death, although further modest clearing continued into the eighteenth century, mostly in South Germany and East Prussia. From the sixteenth century, ordinances regulating the use of the forest became common, though under the influence of Malthusian philosophy in the eighteenth century, some relaxation in their strictness was made. Until the eighteenth century, forests had been commonly misused: in times of war, peasants and defeated armies had fled to them for shelter, doing much damage, while they were sometimes burned to clear them of undesirables and there was overcutting and overgrazing. In the oak forests, much damage was done by the search for ships' timber, and wooden-framed houses also took a lot of wood. In the seventeenth and eighteenth centuries, to ape the French nobility, there was a tendency to overstock the forests with game, and hunting was carried out at the expense of the forest economy, but a rapidly emerging wood famine in the eighteenth century brought new conservation measures and the introduction of rapidly growing species, though these did not always prove most suitable. As transport improved and owners tried to maintain the financial profitability of forests, wood ceased to be a scarce commodity in the nineteenth century. In 1850, only 20–30 percent of the wood produced in state forests was for industrial use, with 70–80 percent taken for fuel, whereas by 1913, this ratio had been completely reversed and beech lost ground to more rapidly maturing species (pine and spruce). In many districts replacements of broad-leaved trees by conifers went too far, while attempts to establish 'monoculture' forest opened the stands to disease and pests, as well as to climatic elements. The last quarter of the nineteenth century saw a reversion to mixed age and type of trees and there arose the concept of *Dauerwald*, a long-term forest organism, swinging away from earlier clear-cutting policy that decimated broad-leaved forests.

After 1870 encouragement was given to afforestation, notably in heathland or other poor areas (e.g., in 1876, planting in the Lüneburger Heide). In 1938, 27 percent of the *Reich* area was forest-covered, with 71.2 percent of the forest consisting of conifers and 28.8 percent of broad-leaved trees. After 1918 there had been big gains in state ownership, which dated back to 1820 following earlier sales of state forest to raise money in the wake of the Napoleonic Wars. The Nazi administration, searching for self-sufficiency, tended to allow overcutting and wood was used widely as a substitute, while the use of producer gas cars in the war years accelerated the demand for wood. But there were also locational difficulties, such as an overconcentration of wood-using industries in Saxony or the production of mine timber east of Berlin, whereas the Ruhr sought cheaper spruce pit props from the uplands of the west that might have been better used as pulpwood.

The change from a predominantly rural landscape to an urban-industrial economy during the nineteenth century brought great change in the spatial pattern of the German lands, particularly marked by the emergence of great industrial districts associated with the coalfields. Though the main stream of this change began later than in Britain (after rather than before the growth of the main features of the railway system), it grew rapidly in the latter part of the century so that Germany overtook France economically and became a formidable competitor with Britain, which had already ceased to be truly the 'workshop of the world'. This upward surge was interrupted by the First World War; and, in the postwar years, territorial loss, reparations, and economic problems retarded the rebirth of expansion, although a remarkable fever pace with strong strategic undertones took place in the second half of the thirties under the National Socialists when emphasis was upon self-sufficiency. These patterns have been the basis upon which the post Second World War change and development have been formed.

Suggested further reading

Abel, W.: Die drei Epochen der deutschen Agrargeschichte, Hannover, 1962.
Benham, F.: The Iron and Steel Industry of Germany, France, Belgium, Luxembourg and the Saar, *London and Cambridge Economic Service Special Memo.* 39, London, 1934.
Bertsch, K.: Geschichte des deutschen Waldes, Jena, 1951.
Birkenfeld, W.: Der synthetische Treibstoff 1939–1945, Göttingen, 1964.
Borchardt, K.: Regionale Wachstumsdifferenzierung in Deutschland im 19 Jahrhundert, *Forsch. z. Sozial- und Wirtschaftsgeschichte* 10, Stuttgart, 1968.
Die industrielle Revolution in Deutschland, *Serie Piper* 40, München, 1972.
Busch, W.: Die Landbauzonen im deutschen Lebensraum, Stuttgart, 1936.
Clapham, J. H.: The Economic Development of France and Germany, Cambridge, 1955.
Ditt, H., Schöller, P.: Die Entwicklung des Eisenbahnnetzes in Nordwestdeutschland, *Westf. Forsch.* 8, 1955, pp.150–180.
Droege, G.: Deutsche Wirtschafts- und Sozialgeschichte, Frankfurt, 1973.
Erbe, R.: Die nationalsozialistische Wirtschaftspolitik 1933–1939 im Lichte der modernen Theorie, Zürich, 1958.
Farquharson, J. E.: The Plough and the Swastika, London, 1976.
Ferarius: Das deutsche Bahnnetz, *P.M. 57*, 1911, pp. 323–330.
Greiling, W.: The German Iron and Steel Industry, *London and Cambridge Economic Service Special Memo.* 11, London, 1925.
Hahn, H., Zorn, W.: Historische Wirtschaftskarte der Rheinlande um 1820, *Arb. Rhein. Landeskunde* 37, 1973.
Hartshorne, R.: The Upper Silesian industrial district, *Geog. Rev.* 24, 1934, pp. 423–438.

The Two Germanies

Heske, F.: German Forestry, New Haven, 1938.

Huppertz, B.: Räume und Schichten bäuerlichen Kulturformen in Deutschland, Bonn, 1939.

Kobschätzky, H.: Streckenatlas der deutschen Eisenbahnen 1835–1892, Düsseldorf, 1972.

Krzymowski, R.: Geschichte der deutschen Landwirtschaft, Ludwigshafen, 1951.

Laufenberger, H.: La nouvelle structure economique du Reich, Paris, 1938.

Müller, J.: Wirtschaftskunde von Deutschland, Leipzig, 1936.

Niehaus, H.: Agricultural conditions and regions in Germany, *Geog. Rev.* 23, 1933, pp. 23–47.

Niemeier, G.: Das Landschaftsbild des heutigen Ruhrreviers vor Beginn der grossindustriellen Entwicklung – Erläuterungen zu einer Karte der Zeit um 1840, *Westfäl.Forsch.* 5, 1942, pp. 79–114.

Pardé, M.: Les chemins de fer allemands, *Ann. de Géog.* 39, 1930, pp. 78–82.

Pounds, N. J. G.: The Upper Silesian Industrial Region, Bloomington, 1958. The spread of mining in the coal basin of Upper Silesia and northern Moravia, *A.A.A.G.* 48, 1958, pp. 149–163. Lorraine and the Ruhr, *Econ. Geog.* 33, 1957, pp. 149–162. The Ruhr: a Study in Historical and Economic Geography, London, 1952.

Reichsverkehrsministerium: Hundert Jahre Deutsche Eisenbahnen, Berlin, 1938.

Sartorius von Waltershausen, A.: Deutsche Wirtschaftsgeschichte 1815–1914, Jena, 1923.

Stöckl, F.: Die Eisenbahnen in Deutschland – Vom *Adler* zum *TEE*, Wien, 1969.

Stolper, G.: The German Economy – 1870 to the present, New York, 1967.

Stumpf, B.: Kleine Geschichte der Deutschen Eisenbahnen, Mainz, 1955.

Teubert, W.: Die Bedeutung der verschiedenen Verkehrsmittel in Deutschland, *Trans. 15 Internat. Geog. Congress*, Amsterdam, 1938, pp. 137–158.

von Geldern Crispendorf, G.: Die deutschen Textilindustriegebiete, *P. M. Ergänzungsheft* 214, 1932. Die deutschen Industriegebiete – ihre Entstehung und Entwicklung, Karlsruhe, 1933.

Wagenführ, R.: Die Industrie im Kriege 1939–1945, Berlin, 1963.

Wagner, J.: Deutsche Landwirtschaft auf dem Wege zur Nährfreiheit, *Zeitschrift für Erdkunde* 6, 1938, pp. 16–28.

Wiel, P.: Das Ruhrgebiet in Vergangenheit und Gegenwart, Essen, 1963. Wirtschaftsgeschichte des Ruhrgebietes, Essen, 1970.

CHAPTER 4

POPULATION AND ITS PROBLEMS
1815-1945

At the end of the Napoleonic Wars, the German states had about 22 million people, while France's population was about 27 million (it was moreover a united country unlike the fragmented and querulous German states). When bayonets were the primary index of national power, 'manpower' was the critical factor, and consequently in the mid-1850s a major shift in the European balance of power took place when the population of the German states, now moving towards unity, overtook that of France, and the gap

Table 4.1
Population of Germany*

Census date	Population Mill.	Population growth Percent
1816	21.9	
1834	27.1	23.1
1852	31.7	17.1
1871	36.3	14.6
1890	49.4	21.8
1910	64.9	32.2
1925	63.2	8.1
1933	66.0	4.5

* The *Reich* in its boundaries of 1934

Source: Von Borries, H. W. *Ökonomische Grundlagen der westdeutschen Siedlungsstruktur,* Hannover, 1969

widened quickly so that by 1870 Germany in the borders of that time had some 40.3 million people compared to little over 36 million in France. The creation of the Second *Reich* in 1871 further accentuated the power discrepancy and the growing economic contrast between France and Germany. By 1900, Germany contained well over 50 million people and France a meagre 39.2 million. Between 1870 and 1936, the population of Germany was to increase by over 29 million and that of France by a mere five million.

Recovery from the Napoleonic Wars, despite initial economic depression, was rapid, and between 1816 and 1834 Germany (within its 1937 boundaries) showed a population increase of 23 percent. The most rapidly growing districts at this time were the eastern provinces of Prussia, particularly East Prussia and Upper Silesia, but there was also considerable growth in the industrial parts of the Kingdom of Saxony, and in the southwestern provinces, notably the Saarland and Palatinate. Throughout these districts natural increase was the major cause of growth, though this was later offset by strong migration from rural areas. Migration overseas began to be significant in the 1850s, beginning in the Rhineland and spreading later to more easterly districts, while about this time were also the stirrings of internal migration to embryonic industrial areas.

Population development between 1870–1914

Although the future trend had begun to emerge in the 1860s, it was the industrial impetus after the Franco-Prussian War coupled to the new found political and economic unity of the Second *Reich* that stimulated population growth in towns and accelerated internal migration. Whereas the population upsurge of the industrial revolution in Britain came between 1800 and 1840, the corresponding phase was best seen in Germany after 1870. Forerunners in population growth were the ports of Hamburg and Bremen, followed by industrializing towns in the Kingdom of Saxony and Prussian Westphalia. In contrast, between 1850 and 1870 some areas, notably in South Germany, showed virtually no growth – here and in the Rhenish Palatinate, the small natural increase was largely offset by the rising tide of emigration.

Throughout the nineteenth century, whatever was happening to overall growth, there was an increasing tendency to agglomeration of population which reached its greatest intensity between 1870 and 1914, marked by the emergence of truly industrial districts and the growing strength of migration from the country to the towns. Consequently, the main growth foci between 1870 and 1914 were the provinces of Westphalia and the Rhineland, particularly the Ruhr coalfield and the industrial districts of the Lower Rhine and Aachen. Expansion in population numbers also marked the Saarland, where the coal and iron industry was growing, and rather slower growth was apparent in industrial Upper Silesia, while industrial Saxony also grew less quickly than the western industrial districts. Berlin, capital of the new *Reich*, with important political and economic functions, attracted substantial growth, chiefly through migration from the surrounding countryside, but also from the rest of the *Reich*, as chances of advancement for the ambitious were greatest here.

After the Franco-Prussian War, migration from the rural eastern provinces increased as many reservists had seen the better opportunities available in industrial Germany, while employers sent agents to the agricultural eastern districts to recruit labour. There was also migration elsewhere in both north

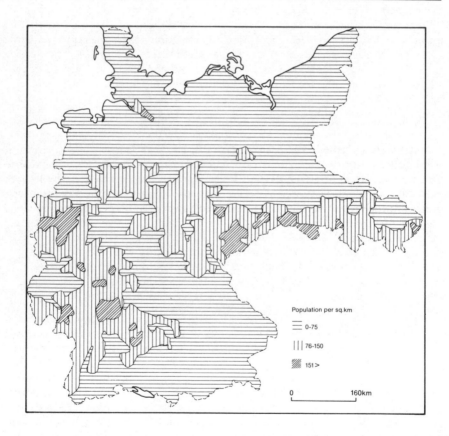

Population per sq.km

≡ 0-75

||| 76-150

▨ 151 >

0   160km

Figure 4.1 Population distribution about 1870

The Two Germanies

and south from most rural districts and, though the migrants usually came from the poorer districts, areas with better soils and prosperous farming near to growing industrial centres lost population as well. Migration to the Rhineland industries from South and Southwest Germany slowed after 1875 as South German industrialization began under the stimulus of the new *Reich*. Considerable migration took place within provinces: for example, people left upland Hessen to work in the towns of the Rhine-Main area, which also attracted workers from the Palatinate hills. In Westphalia, movement was from the Münsterland and the Sauerland to the Ruhr coalfield, which also drew metal-workers from the older industries of Berg and Mark. In South Germany, the new industrial towns of the Main and Danube basins, as well as old political centres such as München, attracted people just as industry drew people into the Neckar Basin. Much migration from the rural areas everywhere was concealed by continuing high rates of natural increase, but after 1885 some districts began to show population decline as emigration exceeded annual natural increase. In the 1890s, as public health and medical practice improved, there was a general slight rise in natural increase as birth rates remained high but death rates dropped, although continued migration of young folk away from the countryside tended to take away its future potential natural increase. Indeed, detailed examination shows that in the Westerwald, Eifel, and Palatinate over 40 percent of the *Gemeinden* were declining in population by the 1880s as the result of emigration. Some rural areas had a tradition of migration as, for example, in the Black Forest or Upper Bavaria, where inheritance passed farms to a son undivided and the unpropertied brothers usually sought employment elsewhere, or in the Westerwald, where pedalling local produce in other districts also encouraged permanent migration.

Until 1871, the annual rate of growth in western Germany (roughly the area of the modern Federal Republic) had been below the rest of the *Reich*, but thereafter the situation was reversed as industrialization drew in labour. Between 1900 and 1913 western Germany increased at an annual rate of 16.8 per 1000 inhabitants compared to 11.8 in the remaining territory. The importance of the industrial areas – in both east and west – as a focus of growth is reflected in the fact that between 1871 and 1933 Berlin, the ports of Bremen and Hamburg, the Rhenish-Westphalian and Silesian industrial areas, and Saxony claimed 62 percent of the total increase in population, though they comprised only one-fifth of the *Reich* territory. The trend was not so much a radical redistribution of population as a growing contrast between the major population axes and their foci and the rest of the country, which widened appreciably until the interwar years of the present century. Particularly important in this process was the appearance of marked population clusters associated with the coalfields and heavy industries, strung along the northern edge of the Central Uplands – from Aachen on the west through the Rhenish-

Westphalian coalfield to the varied industrial and lignite-mining districts of Saxony and eastwards to the coalfield of Upper Silesia. Along the Rhine axis, other agglomerations began to emerge – in Rhine-Main, in the Saar, and in the Neckar basin, quite apart from the growth along the river itself and in the basin around Neuwied. In the northern plains, amid relatively thinly populated country, there were clusters around the ports of Bremen and Hamburg, spreading downstream on the Weser and Elbe respectively, as well as around the rapidly growing Berlin. In the south, though less pronounced, the favoured nodal site of Nürnberg and the political importance of München also contributed to their growth as population nodes. By 1870 the basic features of the present population distribution pattern were clearly displayed, and a major east-west and a north-south axial belt, already present at the beginning of the century, were the dominant elements in the pattern.

Population development between the World Wars

The first postwar census in 1925 showed an appreciable slowing in the rate of population growth, while new and much more confused streams of migration were revealed. Despite Nazi attempts after 1933 to stimulate population increase, it was to remain well below the 1914 level, showing only a modest recovery in the late 1930s. That any natural increase took place at all was due to the substantial fall in the death rate: had this remained at the 1900 level, from 1924 onwards there would have been a strong natural *decline* in population. An important contributory factor to the fall in the overall national rate of growth was the surrender to Poland of eastern provinces that had shown some of the greatest natural increase before 1914. Nevertheless, East Germans tended to show a greater fertility and larger families, with higher natural increase than their compatriots in the western parts of the country.

About 1.2 million Germans from territories surrendered to Poland and to France and from German minority groups in East Central Europe entered the reduced territory of the *Reich* after 1918, though about 300,000–500,000 Poles working in Germany returned to Poland or went to work in French mines. After the First World War, the great migration from east to west, such a feature of the period 1871–1914, practically died away, largely through the decline in the economic fortunes of the Ruhr coalfield, though movement from the countryside to the towns continued on a substantially reduced scale. The proportion of people in rural *Gemeinden* had fallen from 40 percent in 1910 to 35.6 percent in 1925, and over the same period the proportion of total population in the towns with over 100,000 inhabitants rose from 21.3 percent to 26.8 percent. The low level of migration during the war was reflected in the fact that only 3.4 percent of the *Reich* population in 1925 had been living in another Prussian province or German state on 1 August, 1914. Where town populations were higher in 1925 than in the census of 1907, it is probably safe to assume that increase had taken place before about 1915, after which the deteriorating economy brought static conditions, but much of the modest increase in many Rhenish-Westphalian and Rhine towns resulted from relatively high natural increase concealing migration of men away from the area, whereas in contrast natural decline was more than offset by strong immigration in Berlin. The inflation of 1923 had also held many potential migrants in the countryside and even drove townspeople back to the countryside, while the French occupation

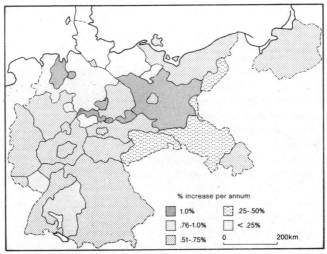

Figure 4.2 Population change in the 1930s

of the Ruhr certainly caused considerable temporary migration to other areas. But it was essentially the problems of heavy industry that underlay the virtually static population totals in the Ruhr towns, particularly in the older southern part of the field where mining was collapsing.

In the intercensal period 1925–1933 conditions were complicated by the economic depression and by an extensive reorganization of municipality boundaries in 1928. On the whole, population in country districts continued to grow by natural increase, though at a lower rate as the birth rate fell in the uncertain economic conditions; but the fall in migration from many of these districts was sufficient to give their local population growth a slight added push. Nevertheless, the population share in the smallest rural communities (those under 2000 inhabitants) continued to fall, reaching 32.8 percent in 1933. Emigration from much of Northwest Germany and North Germany still continued fairly vigorously, also a characteristic of the eastern provinces, notably through movement from depressed industrial German Upper Silesia, though it had gained some Germans from what had become Polish Upper Silesia and even from further east.

After 1933, Nazi policies put an emphasis on encouragement to people to stay in the countryside through the Nazi philosophy that gave new social status to the peasants and believed that the town generated all the social ills it sought to avoid. Consequently, substantial population increase was recorded between 1933 and 1939 in the more rural north, around Lüneburg and Osnabrück and in Oldenburg (where development of the naval port of Wilhelmshaven was important), while Schleswig-Holstein and the lower Elbe, as well as the Baltic littoral, Mecklenburg, and Brandenburg, also showed considerable growth. Other areas of marked increase were the environs of Berlin (mostly the result of suburban migration) and the less industrialized areas of the broad concept of *Mitteldeutschland*, notably Hannover-Braunschweig and the country around Magdeburg. Actual decrease of population was recorded in western Saxony, in the Zwickau and Chemnitz districts, where relatively low natural increase and painful economic adjustments, partly related to the exhaustion of mineral resources, were contributory factors. Eastern Saxony and the eastern provinces – notably eastern Pomerania and the Silesian lands, as well as southern East Prussia – were areas of low increase or even stagnation. In a broad belt along the Rhine from the Dutch frontier to Rhine-Hessen there was also only low growth in population (below 4 percent) and some big industrial towns lost population into new residential areas nearby. The areas with low population growth were generally marked by a strong emigration that cancelled much of their relatively high rate of natural increase and, with higher natural increase in the east than in the west, emigration from eastern rural districts could be generally stronger than in the west before it began to affect overall population growth. Likewise, in much of the north and centre, immigration strengthened natural increase to accentuate growth. Population growth in a particular region could, however, often be attributed to a few major projects; for example, the building of the *Volkswagen* plant at Wolfsburg; the erection of the Salzgitter steel plant; or the extension of the naval port of Wilhelmshaven and other military installations; and increases in population along the French and Belgian frontiers were doubtless also related to military works employing large numbers of civilian workers. After 1937 a decentralization of industry, particularly into South Germany, had also had some impact.

Age-sex structure

In 1910 the age-sex pyramid had had all the characteristics of rapid growth – a broad based structure without major irregularities and with a reasonably healthy biological structure. In 1925 – with 1.8 million war dead and the shortfall of births during the war years – the pyramid showed a marked contraction in the age groups born during the war years as well as the deep bite of

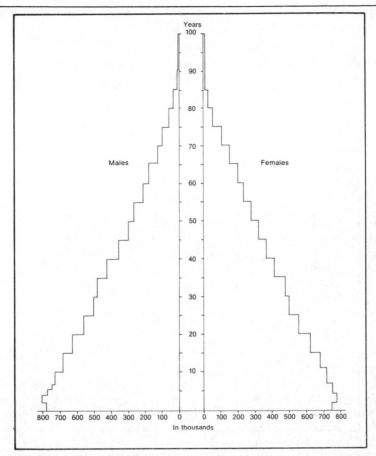

Years

Males

Females

In thousands

Figure 4.3 Age and sex structure – 1900

war dead into the male side of the 25–50 age group. Although by 1933 the upsurge in births immediately postwar was clear, the heavy bite into the male side and the wartime shortfall of births had simply moved up the scale. The population structure for 1939 reflected six years of Nazi policy to encourage population growth and the narrowing base of a pyramid of an imminently ageing population seen in 1933 had been given a broader base suggestive of new if modest growth. But of course the 'bottlenecks' of war losses had moved further up the pyramid. The small age group born in 1939 reflected the mobilization and war preparations begun in earnest in 1938. Between 1933 and 1939, there had, however, been some improvement in the net reproduction

Population and its Problems 1815–1945

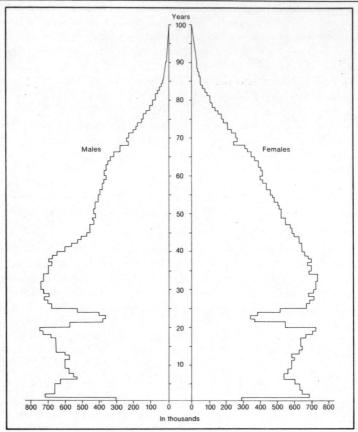

Figure 4.4 Age and sex structure – 1939

rate in Germany, unusual among European countries, but whose cause was a matter of speculation. Legislation controlled all forms of birth control and abortion and gave every incentive to marriage and increased family size, while for a time married women were excluded from a wide range of employment. But the success of marriage loans and other financial assistance to gain larger families withdrew too many women from a labour market desperately in need of their services and, in the end, economic and strategic needs won the day. It was also believed that keeping people in the country or getting people back into the country would also help to increase family size, and to this end the number of smallholdings available was increased.

The Two Germanies

The question of long-term population growth had become an important part of the argument for *Lebensraum* – living space – because computations in 1938 suggested that German population (including Austria but excluding the

Table 4.2
Numbers of births and deaths in the *Reich* – in millions

	1900	1922	1933	1936	1939	1942
Births	1.99	1.42	0.97	1.28	1.41	1.06
Deaths	1.24	0.89	0.74	0.79	0.85	0.84
Live births (per 1000 population)	35.6	23.0	14.7	19.0	20.4	n.a.

Sources: various statistical yearbooks

Sudetenland) would rise from 75.3 million in 1939 to 80.2 million in 1960, 80.5 million in 1970, and then fall from 79.7 million in 1980 to 77.0 million in the year 2000. Furthermore, it was demonstrated by this computation that the ageing population would become critical in the 1960s; consequently every effort should be made to increase fertility by 20 percent in order to maintain a healthy biological structure to the *Reich* population.

Population change and the settlement pattern

Towns have been one of the most important contributions of German culture to Central Europe and beyond, especially in a major phase of town foundation between the twelfth and fourteenth centuries. The Black Death brought the wave of new towns to a halt and thereafter activity waned, apart from some mining towns in the fifteenth and sixteenth centuries, when at least seven towns were founded in the Harz. There was also some foundation of towns for religious refugees, like Schönau and Frankental founded in 1560. In the seventeenth century a revitalization of town life began, and the design of towns was influenced conceptually by the Renaissance delight in order and symmetry, while baroque and rococo styles came to express the rediscovery of classical learning, with princes eager to follow French fashion active in 'modernizing' or laying out towns. Many commercial towns could not match this development in the uncertain atmosphere of the period and continued to stagnate well into the eighteenth century. The changes in warfare that made old mediaeval walls useless introduced new low profile defences of bastions and glacis in the style of Vauban, a noted French military engineer. Among the towns to receive the new defences were Mannheim, Berlin, Dresden, Gustavsburg, and Saarlouis. When these works were ultimately scrapped, the space left provided for broad boulevards and promenades.

The 'classic' baroque town is the remarkable radial pattern of Karlsruhe (1715), while earlier interesting examples are the incomplete square layout of Freudenstadt (1599), the rectilinearly planned Neuwied (1653), the Huguenot refugee town of Rastatt (1689), the grid pattern and the massive palace of Mannheim (1700–1710), the star-shaped Neustrelitz (1728) in Mecklenburg and Karlsruhe in Silesia (1743), as well as the twin foundation of Huguenot refugee town (1689) and princely seat (1708) in Erlangen. Magdeburg had been rebuilt after its sack (1631) and extensive rebuilding was conducted at various dates in Dresden which the Saxon kings made one of Europe's most elegant towns, especially after 1700; Bonn, Kassel, Düsseldorf, Koblenz, Tübingen, Trier, München (e.g., Nymphenburg, 1702–1704), and Hannover (e.g., Schloss Herrenhausen, 1698, and the treelined avenues to the town, 1726) were other towns that similarly benefited, whereas in Berlin, the Dorotheenstadt and the Friedrichstadt are among districts that date from this period.

The late mediaeval Holy Roman Empire (without the Netherlands) had had about 3300 towns, of which over 3000 had less than 2000 people, 250 were medium-sized, and some 25 were large towns of over 10,000 people that included Köln, Lübeck, Magdeburg, Frankfurt/Main, Nürnberg, and Regensburg. Town dwellers had seldom exceeded 10–15 percent of total population, except in favoured districts where they might rise to 20 percent. The stagnation in town life that culminated in the Thirty Years' War is reflected in the cathedral of Köln begun in 1248 but not completed until 1880; Dortmund, for example, had 8,000–10,000 inhabitants in the late fourteenth century, in 1618 only 6700–7000 people, while by 1700 it was an insignificant country town of 3000 people.

At the end of the Napoleonic Wars, apart from a few favoured princely or other seats and towns of later foundation, most towns were still within their mediaeval framework, a result of economic stagnation, the conservatism of the guilds, and the constraints of mediaeval legal systems, so that towns had changed little since the sixteenth century. The scene was dominated by small towns and even the largest were still modest by modern concepts – the large mediaeval town had had a population threshold of about 10,000 and few towns exceeded this even by 1750; by 1850 this threshold had risen to about 75,000 and to the present 100,000 by the mid-1870s. In the 1790s, Hamburg, then one of Europe's major ports, exceeded 100,000 and had 127,980 inhabitants in 1819; Berlin, the ebullient Prussian capital, with 198,000 inhabitants in 1816 (almost a quarter of the labour force then employed by the government or court) did not reach the million mark until the mid-1870s; Frankfurt, one of the greatest commercial centres, had 35,000 people in the late eighteenth century, about the same as contemporary Leipzig; whereas Köln, a town of mixed fortunes, had 56,000 people in 1819, smaller than Breslau (65,000) and

Dresden (62,000 in 1830); while the great mediaeval town of Nürnberg was little different in 1819 (26,800) than in 1500.

Table 4.3
Selected town growth in the nineteenth and twentieth centuries

	1819	1855	1890	1910
München	53,672	132,122	350,594	596,462
Nürnberg	26,854	56,398	142,590	333,142
Augsburg	29,809	40,695	75,629	123,015
Aschaffenburg	8,307	9,412	13,630	29,892

The revolution of 1848 cracked the power of the guilds and their social order that had become a drag against progress and growth in many towns, though it did not undermine the strong civic pride. The economic unity and widening horizons brought by the *Zollverein* were accentuated by the quickly expanding railway system of the 1850s that together stimulated town growth.

Table 4.4
Distribution of population by community size

	< 2,000	2,000–5,000	5,000–10,000	10,000–20,000	20,000–50,000	50,000–100,000	>100,000
	– percent of total population –
1871	63.9	12.4	6.2	4.9	3.6	4.1	4.8
1890	53.0	——19.4——		6.0	6.9	2.9	12.1
1910	40.0	11.2	7.6	6.5	7.9	5.4	21.3
1925	35.6	10.8	6.9	6.2	8.0	5.7	26.8
1933	32.9	10.6	7.1	6.2	7.7	5.2	30.4
1939	30.1	10.8	7.4	6.4	8.4	5.3	31.6

In the boundaries of the period, except 1939 in the boundaries of 1937.

Source: Statistisches Bundesamt, Wiesbaden.

While rural population in the German empire rose from 18 to 22 million between 1816 and 1925, the urban population rocketed from 6 to 40 million. Between 1871 and 1939, the *Gemeinden* with less than 2000 people had had their share of total population halved, but there had been less than a 25 percent decline in actual resident numbers. All other communities in the same period had seen a rise in both their share of total population and their resident numbers, though conditions had steadied after the First World War. The change was most marked in the towns of over 100,000 people, which rose in number from 8 to 59 and had increased their resident population tenfold and their share of national population sixfold. But a change became apparent between 1933 and 1939, when the small towns increased their population by 9.6 percent and the medium towns by 8.3 percent; but the growth of the big towns had slowed to a mere 2.6 percent, though numerically this was still sizeable.

It was the economic upsurge with industrialization from the 1860s that brought vigorous growth of towns, though the dwarf towns of South Germany were the last to be affected. One of the most powerful centres of town growth was the Ruhr coalfield through a strong current of immigration between 1870 and 1914 when the wave of growth had spread northwards as the 'frontier' of mining shifted. Several rapidly growing Ruhr towns were old market towns (Bochum, Recklinghausen, and Hattingen) and two (Essen and Dortmund) important mediaeval trading centres, but there were many entirely new growths – Oberhausen (chartered 1874) took its name from the local estate; Wanne-Eickel (chartered first in 1926) grew from a speculative station on the Köln-Minden railway; a cluster of mining communities came to form Gelsenkirchen (chartered 1875) and Castrop-Rauxel (eventually chartered in 1926); while Bottrop and Gladbeck (both chartered in 1919) grew from mining colonies. A major territorial-administrative change in 1928–1929 expanded the boundaries of several towns, Dortmund, for example, greatly increasing their population.

Table 4.5
Population growth in principal Ruhr towns

	1852	1871	1900	1910	1925	1939
			– in thousands –			
Bochum	5.8	21.2	65.6	136.9	211.2	305.5
Bottrop	0.5	5.4	24.8	47.2	77.3	83.4
Dortmund	13.5	44.4	142.7	214.2	321.7	542.3
Duisburg	—	64.7	160.7	229.5	272.8	434.6
Essen	10.5	51.5	118.9	194.7	470.5	670.8
Gelsenkirchen	0.8	7.8	36.9	169.5	208.5	317.7
Hagen	6.1	20.1	50.6	88.6	99.7	151.8
Herne	0.9	4.4	27.9	57.1	68.2	94.6
Mülheim/Ruhr	11.1	14.3	38.3	112.6	127.4	137.5
Oberhausen	—	12.8	42.2	89.9	105.4	191.8
Recklinghausen	4.0	4.9	34.0	53.7	84.5	86.3

Source: Statistisches Bundesamt

The towns of *Mitteldeutschland* were also stimulated by the widening nineteenth-century German economy, as late last century lignite mining began to expand and chemicals plants were built, though the main growth here in industry and towns alike came with the First World War. Industry was, however, generally more diffuse than in the Ruhr, and many workers lived in small towns and villages around the bigger plants. The railway was particularly important in the growth of Leipzig as the main commercial centre: in 1837, before the railway came, it had 41,000 people, but by 1870 it had reached 130,000, and in 1885 295,000,exceeded half a million early in the present century and reached almost three quarters of a million by 1939. The railway was also important in nearby Halle an der Saale – in 1850, it had 30,000 people and by 1870, 51,000, overstepping 100,000 people by 1890. Some Saxon industrial towns were retarded in growth by economic problems, for example, where the textile industry suffered severe English competition: the textile town of Chemnitz had 10,500 people in 1810 and no more than 23,000 in 1840, but thereafter the economic situation eased, and by 1880 it had over 95,000 inhabitants. But Central Germany was overshadowed by the rise of Berlin, whose point of take-off came with the creation of the Second *Reich* – in 1861, it had had 530,000 inhabitants but by 1881, 1,122,000, and it over-stepped the 2 million mark in 1905. Its population had fallen after the First World War until the creation of Greater Berlin in 1920 gave it a substantial boost – on 30 September, 1920, it had 1,902,000 people and on 1 October, 1920, 3,806,200.

Silesia was dominated commercially and administratively by Breslau, one of the most important of all Prussian towns, whose population rose from 68,000 in 1811 to over 100,000 in the early 1840s; by 1880, it reached 273,000 people and, by 1905, 471,000, though considerable latter growth was the result of boundary extensions. Local migration, including Poles from nearby Austrian

Table 4.6
Town growth in Upper Silesia

	1871	1910
	– thousands –	
Beuthen	16.0	68.0
Gleiwitz	13.0	67.0
Hindenburg	16.6	63.0
Kattowitz	8.1	42.4
Königshütte	19.5	72.2

and Russian territories, as well as officials and managers from Central Germany (particularly Saxony), played an important part in the rapid growth of the Upper Silesian industrial towns in the late nineteenth century, when several towns were chartered (e.g., Kattowitz, 1865). Nevertheless, Sosnowiec, just inside Russian Poland, rocketed from 6,500 people in 1870 to 44,000 in 1913, so quick growth was not restricted to the German part of the industrial area.

Cities important in mediaeval times along the Rhine had witnessed some of the earliest developments of modern industry. Köln, by far the most important, developed as a major railway junction and industrial centre, but towards the mid-nineteenth century its growth had been increasingly constricted by the ring of Prussian fortifications. While in the sixteenth century it had had about 37,000 people, in 1816 it could boast only 49,000; by 1823 it had risen to 55,000 but the 100,000 mark was passed by 1850, and with 372,000 people in 1900, it recorded some of the highest urban densities in Germany: in 1910 it exceeded 516,000 and, in 1939, population amounted to 777,200. Dismantling of the fortifications after 1919 helped growth, but its rise in population after 1883 had been largely achieved by incorporation of nearby communities, with Deutz absorbed in 1888 and Mülheim in 1914. A surge of commercial and industrial enterprise after the mid-century brought growth to the less distinguished Düsseldorf: from 10,000 inhabitants in 1810, it had risen to 26,100 in 1843 and, by 1850, to 110,000 inhabitants. By 1910 Düsseldorf had 358,700 people and 539,900 in 1939, though much growth came again through extending the boundaries. The growth of Rhine traffic and the railways, plus Baden's early membership of the *Zollverein*, stimulated Mannheim-Ludwigshafen, while further impetus was given by the chemicals industry after 1865. Mannheim was a fortress and *Residenzstadt* from the seventeenth century, but its Bavarian rival, Ludwigshafen, developed only from the 1840s. The splendid eighteenth-century *Residenzstadt* of Karlsruhe showed a more modest growth, though the commercial Frankfurt am Main, long one of the largest towns in western Germany, kept a steady growth, rising from 41,000 in 1816 to 91,000 in 1871, 179,000 in 1890, and 414,600 in 1910: by 1933 it reached 555,800, only to decline slightly thereafter, largely through population movement into surrounding towns and residential areas.

Table 4.7

	1816	1852	1871	1890	1900	1910	1939
				– thousands –			
Mannheim	18.7	24.3	39.6	79.1	141.1	193.9	285.7
Ludwigshafen	—	2.3	7.9	28.8	61.9	83.3	101.9

The role of migration in the rapid urbanization of last century is reflected in the movement of workers to the Ruhr coalfield. Initially, in the 1840s, workers came from the poorer districts of the Münsterland, Eifel, and Hunsrück, or even from the overpopulated wine districts of the Rhine and Mosel. Skilled metal workers from the Sauerland and Siegerland also joined the stream, and several Ruhr entrepreneurs were from the duchies of Berg and Mark. Unable to obtain sufficient labour from these areas for the feverish developments after 1870, recruiting spread to the Prussian eastern provinces and beyond into

Russian and Austrian Poland. The migrants, both Germans and Slavs, tended to go to the newer mines and iron and steel works, especially along the Emscher, where most 'colonial towns' with high migrant quotients were to be found, and by 1893, almost a quarter of the employees in the coalmines were, for example, from the Prussian eastern provinces. Movement was commonly from a particular province into a selected Ruhr town so that, for example, between 1865 and 1914, 160,000 East Prussians moved into Gelsenkirchen and Recklinghausen; Masurians went to Bochum; while Herne and Schalke attracted Polish settlement. Relatively few migrants went to the older, southern part of the field: in 1893, the mining district of Hattingen had under 9 percent of its workers from the eastern provinces, whereas Recklinghausen-West had 45 percent of its miners from the east. These migrants contributed much to the social character of the coalfield and in some districts came to out-number local people (as in the suburb of Erle in Gelsenkirchen).

Town growth between the World Wars

After the First World War, with town growth much reduced in uncertain economic conditions, some towns grew from incorporation of adjacent communities rather than from growth in the real sense. Under the Nazi administration, growth was strongest in the small and medium-sized towns and many of the largest towns showed little or no growth or even a small decline between 1933 and 1939, a tendency most marked in towns where industrial rather than administrative or commercial functions were strongest. The new towns of the period were in most instances simply communities given town status – for example, Freital (1921), Geesthacht (1924), Leverkusen (1930), Kornwestheim (1931), Idar-Oberstein (1933), Kamp-Lintfort (1934), Rheinhausen (1934), Garmisch-Partenkirchen (1935), and Herten (1936), while in 1929, Wuppertal was created by merging together six *Gemeinden*, including the towns of Elberfeld and Barmen.

Nazi ideas sought to strengthen rural against urban living styles, with an emphasis on colonies of small family houses set in gardens to give a 'rural' aspect, but new developments were nevertheless monumental in tone, with wide streets and imposing public buildings, ideas seen clearly in plans for München and for Berlin unrealized before the outbreak of war in 1939. The grandiose *Speer Plan* for Berlin envisaged a vast capital city in keeping with Nazi town-planning concepts that included an assembly hall for 1 million people and a projected population of 10 million. Two truly new towns were, however, created by the Nazi administration – in 1938, the town of Wolfsburg was planned (under the name of *Kraft-durch-Freude-Stadt*) for the Volkswagen plant, while in 1942 some twenty-odd communities were lumped together as Watenstadt-Salzgitter for the large Hermann Göring steelworks. A third new town would have appeared had the original intention to build a large iron and

118

steel complex in Franconia been carried through. Several towns received a stimulus through new economic developments like the expansion of aircraft construction in Dessau and the naval harbours at Kiel and Wilhelmshaven.

The village

The great upsurge in town population in the nineteenth century was at the expense of the countryside, from which the migrants came, so that, though the population of the *Reich* rose from 41 million in 1871 to 65 million in 1910, the population living in communities with less than 2000 people remained around 26 million and, as a proportion of total population, fell from 63.9 percent to 40.0 percent. There was marked change in the countryside, with considerable land reclamation and attempts to form more compact holdings, but the village remained the little altered dominant settlement unit in the countryside. Interest in peasant traditions last century brought close investigation of the village, with attempts to classify and describe different types, although it is unlikely the reasons for the different types will ever be adequately explained. The basic contrast is between the 'planted' villages of the Trans-Elbian lands and the 'organic' forms of the older German west. German classifications, usually based on morphology, are often diverse, but a basic system of village types may be described, in which forces of regional sentiment and territorial particularism, especially laws of inheritance, have played a major role.

The *Rundling* village, probably a Slav form from the early mediaeval march-lands, displays in its round form, usually much changed by later settlement, clearly defensive features, and is associated originally with a distinctly Slav field form. The most common 'planted' village east of the Elbe is a long regular street village (*Strassendorf*), later copied and modified in the Slav lands to the east; a variation is the village (*Angerdorf*) with a central elongated green reflecting a stronger defensive element. In the old German lands of the west there are varying degrees of nucleation and any element of planning is far less pronounced. Most common is the *Haufendorf*, found in many different sizes and degrees of nucleation, most pronounced on the loessic *Börde* country and in the tightly nucleated wine village (*Winzerdorf*) along the Rhine, Main, and Mosel. In Northwest Germany, small hamlets and scattered farms (*Einzelhof*) occur, notably in the Münsterland and in Lower Saxony, probably the ultimate disintegration of small villages. Small villages – the *Eschdorf* or *Drubbel* – also occur with their formerly common fields on patches of drier and more fertile ground in glaciated country. Hamlets (*Weiler*) in eastern Bavaria are frequently associated with late forest clearance, but they are also common in the poorer Rhenish uplands. The great mediaeval forest clearance in the Erzgebirge and Sudetenland produced long straggling villages along valleys, each house with its narrow feu stretching into the forest, but such *Waldhufendörfer* also occur in parts of Hessen and in the Thüringer Wald, and a

The Two Germanies

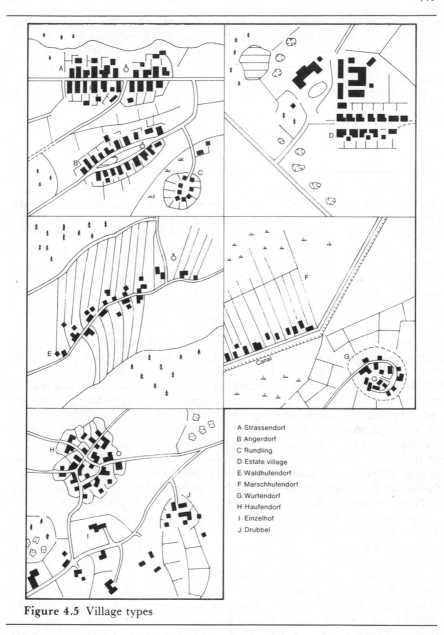

Figure 4.5 Village types

A Strassendorf
B Angerdorf
C Rundling
D Estate village
E Waldhufendorf
F Marschhufendorf
G Wurtendorf
H Haufendorf
I Einzelhof
J Drubbel

similar line of farms strung along a dyke with feus extending into marsh forms the *Marschhufendorf* of Northwest Germany, and such linear settlements in the moors are called *Vennkolonien* (of which Papenburg is the finest example). The earliest settlement in the North Sea coastal lowlands was the small raised mound with a cluster of houses (the *Terp* or *Wurt*), artificially built above the likely flood level, while the *Hallig* occurs on small, low islands (again with raised *Wurt*) of the North Frisian Islands.

In the Rhinelands, in the Main and Neckar basins, and in Central Germany, extending into the Thüringer Wald and the Erzgebirge, the larger villages have formed nuclei for industrial development or the home for industrial workers in nearby plants. In Central Germany, this tendency most probably slowed the mushroom growth of towns last century. In later times, especially as the Nazi administration tried to decentralize strategic industries, villages of 500–1500 people became sites for small industrial plants even in western and southern Germany, while village home industry has a long tradition in some poorer upland areas like the Black Forest, the Erzgebirge, the Spessart, or Westerwald.

Regional sentiment and religious patterns

It is difficult to appreciate Germany without some knowledge of the regional, social, and cultural distinctions of its people, the product of strong regional particularism that reached its peak in the territorial fragmentation of the seventeenth and eighteenth centuries. The Germans put great emphasis on local folk traditions and their regional distinctions. As a people, they can only be defined on a sociolinguistic basis and not on any unity of physical criteria. In physical anthropological terms, it is difficult to distinguish the Germans from their neighbours in many instances. The German tribes appear to have originated in the Baltic littoral and were in an expansive mood through the last millennium BC and well into post-Roman times. As Roman power crumbled, they spread deep into Gaul, Iberia, and even Italy itself, while others penetrated eastwards into eastern and southeastern Europe. The basis of the modern German people was laid in the great Frankish empire of Charles the Great (AD 768–814) that included almost all the German lands after the conquest of the Saxons and Bavarians in the late eighth century. After his death, repeated dynastic division came to separate the eastern and western Frankish kingdoms more clearly as French and German. Through the concept of the Holy Roman Empire of the German Nation and the continued use of Latin as a *lingua franca* that strengthened the dynastic concept of power, the ethnic pattern was overshadowed in state building. In the Roman provinces, the German tribes had begun to accept Christianity in the fourth and fifth centuries, with missionary work spreading east of the Rhine in the eighth century and in the Saxon and Bavarian lands in the ninth century.

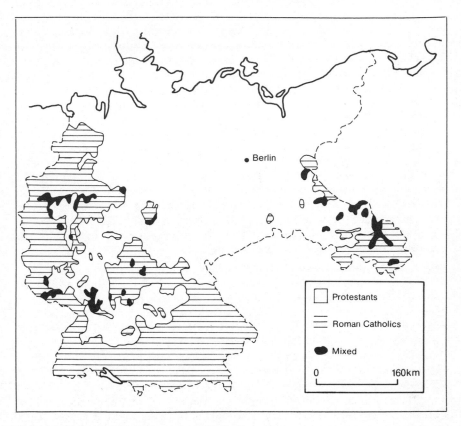

Figure 4.6 Religion and regionalism circa 1914

Threat of westwards infiltration by Slav tribes coupled to the Germans' missionary zeal, as well as the difficulty of further advance westwards or southwestwards, turned the still expansive Germans towards the east, where their domination was to go hand-in-hand with settlement as a slow but mostly peaceful advance through sparsely settled Slav country, establishing marcher lordships as they advanced (e.g., Altmark, Mittelmark, Neumark, Grenzmark), until halted by the Black Death. This impressive colonization, establishing villages and towns throughout the Trans-Elbian lands, underlies the modern landscapes, and in its advance absorbed many Slavs into the German political and cultural realm as witnessed by innumerable personal and place names. German settlers took the best lands, with two great eastern prongs – on the north along the Baltic littoral and on the south on the good lands of Silesia, leaving pockets of Slavs on poorer country in the Hannoverian Wendland, in Lusatia, and the Tucheler Heath on the lower Vistula. On a smaller scale, similar colonization took place into the Alps and into the outliers of the Danubian plains. Though the impetus of colonization was never regained after the Black Death, many groups did later settle in eastern Europe and the Russian lands, sometimes by invitation of local non-German princes, but also for social or religious reasons. The Habsburg encouraged German settlement in lands taken from the Turks in the eighteenth century (notably in the Banat and Bačka), though the Transylvanian Saxons (mostly from the Eifel, Rhineland, and Sauerland) had been established by the twelfth century as a defence against raids by steppe nomads. In the Baltic littoral, Slav princes invited the Teutonic orders of knights to help Christianize the Lithuanian and Borussian 'wilderness', while the Hanse too aided German settlement that in Kurland, Livland, and Estland provided townspeople and landlords. The German position was strengthened by immigration of Rhenish Jews as merchants, artisans, and professional people, making German and Yiddish an everyday language in east-central Europe.

The dynastic empires of Prussia and Austria encompassed the great majority of German colonists beyond the main belt of German settlement, so that as nationalism grew the Germans gained an increasingly privileged position and there is no doubt that many people described themselves as 'German' for material advantage. Acceptance of German language and culture was also spread by programmes of Germanization, notably in Prussia. The territorial changes after the First World War, nevertheless, were to leave several million Germans in the new succession states or under other foreign control. These 'Volksdeutsche' became one of the major interwar political problems, though many Germans in the former overseas colonies and in the new succession states chose to return to Germany. The Nazi authorities after 1933 encouraged Germans abroad to resist assimilation, but at the same time attracted home as many as possible, often under official resettlement programmes. Nevertheless, large numbers remained outside the *Reich* (Table 4.8) and were to become the key in a major reshaping of the ethnic map of Europe after 1945.

Local loyalty in mediaeval times contributed to the emergence of dialects and cultural connotations among the varied regional groups of Germans, while the religious pattern of denominations arose from the territorial fragmentation of Reformation times. These regional differences are nowadays jealously guarded and cherished. Every German sees him or herself as belonging to one or other of the main 'families' of the German people – *die deutschen Volksstämme* – conceived on a basis of common traits of language and religion, historical and geographical association. Each *Stamm* is spread across its own *Heimat* – its homeland – and distinguishes itself by elements such as folk costume, food, customs, and folklore, though many of these elements are of quite late origin and around the *Stämme* have been built music and literature cultivated by regional associations for their promotion (*Heimatvereine*). Some of the *Stämme* were recognizable by the eighth century AD, whereas others emerged only in the last century (*das Ruhrvolk*). Among the early groups were the Saxons and to their south the Franks, while in the southwest, the Alemans were early distinguished from the Bajuvarians (from whom later arose the Bavarians and Austrians). Other early groups were the Hessen, the Thuringians, and the Frisians. Later differentiation broke up some groups, for example, the division of the Alemans into Alsatians, German Swiss, and Suabians, while the Lower and Upper Saxons, the Eastphalians, and Westphalians emerged from the original Saxons. Colonization east of the Elbe generated further *Stämme*: the Prussians (taking their name from a non-German people), the Pomeranians, and Silesians among others, while Germans elsewhere in eastern Europe developed as *Stämme*, like the Baltic Germans, the Russian Germans, and the Transylvanian Saxons.

Table 4.8
Ethnic German population living beyond the boundaries of the *Reich* as at 31 December, 1937

Danzig	400,000	
Baltic States	300,000	(of whom 130,000 in the Memelland
Poland	1,000,000	
Czechoslavakia	3,500,000	(of whom 3,300,000 in Bohemia-Moravia)
Hungary	600,000	
Jugoslavia	700,000	
Romania	800,000	
Soviet Union	1,300,000	(estimate from 1926 census adjusted to mid-1930's)
Total	8,600,000	

Based on figures from *Verband der Landsmannschaften*, Bonn.

The *Stamm* and its distinctiveness (often with a legal connotation in early times) interacted to give particularism and regional sentiment its strength, fostered by the Romantic movement last century. This is not to say that *Stamm* territories are identifiable or coincident with political territories, though many can be related approximately to historical provinces. Bavaria, for example, contains both the *true* Bavarians south of Nürnberg and the Franks of Franconia, while Lower Saxony contains Low Saxons and Frisians. The *Stamm* has been given new life by federalism in West Germany since 1949, and even though the old Länder have been swept away in the G.D.R., old regional allegiances are frequently met in references.

The Holy Roman Empire had as its original mission the preservation and propagation of the Church of Rome, with which discontent flared into the open in Wittenberg in 1517. The Holy Roman Emperor, with neither the central control nor the time to deal with new ideas, took no firm stand until 1530, by which time the new Protestantism, with a firm hold in North Germany, was spreading steadily south until, in 1547, the army of the Protestant states was defeated by the emperor's forces. Agreement was difficult because of the deep mistrusts among the German princes, though in 1555 the emperor accepted a religious peace in the Treaty of Augsburg, ending the first stage of the Reformation. Each state was able to choose for itself (*cujus regio, ejus religio*) in the person of its prince. Unfortunately, the Protestants were split between the supporters of Luther and those of Calvin, the latter not being recognized by the Augsbúrg settlement. The Church of Rome mounted its own Counter-Reformation, when the Council of Trent (1545–1563) confirmed no doctrinal compromise, and this backlash managed to contain Protestantism and to eliminate it over much of South Germany and in Austria. The Thirty Years' War renewed fires of Protestantism in North Germany, but the Treaty of Westphalia (1648) fixed the religious map of central Europe that was to remain little changed until recent times. From this treaty arose 'Protestant' Prussia and 'Catholic' Austria as the major powers, with a complex denominational pattern among the other German states that was confused even more by industrialization and the growth of mobility, though there was a remarkable numerical balance between the membership of the two churches at the national level.

To describe nineteenth- and early twentieth-century Germany as a Protestant North and a Roman Catholic South is, however, a gross oversimplification. Most of North and Central Germany was and remains Protestant, though the eastern provinces of Prussia were largely Roman Catholic (notably from their Polish population), with patches of mixed denominational country. In East Prussia, the old Polish Ermland was Roman Catholic, but the remainder Protestant, including the Slav Masurians around Allenstein. Upper Silesia and parts of Lower Silesia were Roman Catholic, but there were also mixed areas. The lower Rhineland, Westphalia, and the Osnabrück area remain Roman Catholic, while Berg and Mark are chiefly Protestant, though migration to the Ruhr towns confused the pattern, and most large towns throughout Germany show mixed denominational structures. Complex confessional patterns still occur in the middle and upper Rhine and in Southwest Germany, though Bavaria and Baden are chiefly Roman Catholic, whereas Württemberg remains markedly Protestant. Until the Nazi period, considerable Jewish communities were found in towns of long-standing in the Rhineland, whereas Berlin, for example, had attracted many Jews from Eastern Europe, notably the Russian 'Pale' before 1914.

The Two Germanies

After a long period of stagnation, population increased considerably during the nineteenth century and until the outbreak of the First World War. Particularly the years 1870–1914 had seen rapid growth and powerful migration within the *Reich* as the pattern of modern industry had grown. Nevertheless, the extent of the German ethnic area had remained fairly stable from the early eighteenth century, despite Germanization programmes in the last century; but the first changes began to appear after 1919, heralding the dramatic shifts to follow in 1945. Within the *Reich*, the years after 1919 witnessed considerable change – the slowing of urban growth and of internal migration and a slackening in the rate of overall population increase, though by the late 1930s new policies designed to rectify the more serious demographic problems were to be blighted by the outbreak of war in 1939. It is nevertheless from this pattern with its different elements that the two postwar German states have had to build their new spatial and demographic structures of population.

Suggested further reading

Born, M.: Die ländlichen Siedlungesformen in Mitteleuropa, *Berichte z. deut. Landeskunde* 44, 1970 pp.143–154.

Czok, K.: Die Stadt, Leipzig, 1969.

Dickinson, R. E.: The Western European City, London, 1950.

Graafen, R.: Die Aus- und Abwanderung aus der Eifel in den Jahren 1815–1955, *Forsch. z. deut. Landeskunde* 127, 1961.

Die Bevölkerung im Kreise Neuwied und in der Koblenzer-Neuwieder Talweitung 1817–1965, *Forsch. z. deut. Landeskunde* 171, 1969.

Groon, H.: Zur Entwicklung der Städte im 19 und 20 Jahrhundert, *Studium Generale* 16, 1963, pp. 565–575.

Grote, L. (ed.): Die deutsche Stadt im 19 Jahrhundert – Stadtplanung und Baugestaltung im industriellen Zeitalter, *Studien zur Kunst des neunzehnten Jahrhunderts* 24, München, 1974.

Haufe, H.: Die Bevölkerung Europas – Stadt und and im 19–20 Jahrhundert, *Neue Deutsche Forschungen* 7, Berlin, 1936.

Keyser, E.: Bevölkerungsgeschichte Deutschlands, Leipzig, 1941.

Köllmann, E.: The Population of Germany in the age of Industrialism *in* Population Movements in Modern European History, pp.100–108, London, 1964.

Köllmann, E., Marschądek, P. (eds.): Bevölkerungsgeschichte, *Neue Wissenschaftliche Bibliothek* 54, Köln, 1972.

The process of urbanisation in Germany at the height of the industrialisation period, *Journ. of Contemporary History* 4, 1969, pp. 59–76.

Industrialisierung, Binnenwanderung und 'Soziale Frage' – zur Entstehungsgeschichte der deutschen Industriegroszstadt im 19 Jahrhundert, *Vj.-Schrift für Sozial- und Wirtschafts-geschichte* 46, 1959, pp. 45–70.

Radig, W.: Die Siedlungstypen in Deutschland, Berlin, 1955.

Schröder, K. H. Schwarz, G.: Die ländlichen Siedlungsformen in Mitteleuropa, *Forsch. z. deut. Landeskunde* 175, 1969.

CHAPTER 5

THE HARD YEARS 1945-1950

The Allied powers – Britain, the U.S.A., the Soviet Union, and junior partner France – had debated what should be done in the event of the 'unconditional surrender' of the Third *Reich* demanded at Casablanca in 1943. The drastic territorial reshuffle in Europe in 1919 would not be repeated, but any territorial adjustments were to be at the expense of Germany. The war-making potential of Germany was to be destroyed and the Germans were to pay for the damage and loss incurred by other European countries. It was agreed that Germany would be occupied by Allied forces for a considerable period, during which time it was hoped to create a new society through education. How these aims were to be achieved was far less clear. Numerous plans and proposals were made, some plainly unrealistic, some overtly selfish, few clear in their long-term effect on Europe as a whole. The ruthless Morgenthau Plan would have flooded German coalmines, carried off industry and reduced Germany to an economy like that of 1815: how the German population, let alone the large numbers of refugees from lost German territory and ethnic colonies in Eastern Europe, would have survived was not clear; nor was it clear how this could have been achieved without immeasurable damage to Europe as a whole. When the final German collapse came, the Allied powers seemed remarkably ill-prepared to deal with the task of occupation and administration. Even if they had unity of purpose, unity of policy was absent, and any solidarity possessed in battle quickly dispersed. From facing a common enemy they turned to being hostile to each other – the Western Allies facing the Soviet Union.

In dealing with the 'German Problem', each power displayed its own inclinations and aims, governed strongly by its long-term view taken of Germany's future and of Europe. The Soviet Union was clearly set on reducing its major likely rival in Europe to powerlessness and to sweeping away the political concept of *Mitteleuropa* that had long stood in the way of Russian ambitions. At the same time, it sought a fearsome link between the Russian resource base and the long-admired, if feared, German genius for industry and organization. America, while acutely aware of the advantages that could accrue to it from the new industrial and financial situation, sought to apply idealistic, if vague, policies to give the mystic blessings of the American way of life. It had been hoped that a comparatively speedy withdrawal of the American presence from Europe would be possible, but the Cold War with the Soviet Union quickly turned Germany into a forward defence zone for the United States. France was set on a traditional course – a Europe under French guidance if not leadership, and a France at least able to extend its '*limites naturelles*' in a Germany as weak and divided as in 1789. Britain approached its immediate tasks in Germany almost in the spirit of the Indian Civil Service and in the long term hoped to create its ideal Europe – a Europe that involved the minimum British involvement – though this quickly melted as relations between the United States and the Soviet Union cooled. Unfortunately, Britain's economic problems and the political tensions of the disintegrating Commonwealth denied it the chance to take the leadership that Churchill's 'Europeanism' could have given.

It had been decided that the occupation would require Germany to be divided into zones, each administered and garrisoned by one of the powers. The original discussions had been for three-power occupation, but ultimately it was decided to allow the French an occupation zone, carved from the British and American zones. The final scheme was for the British to hold the northwest (with special rights for the Americans in one major port); the Americans were to occupy South Germany; while the French were to have a zone on their own eastern borders; and Central Germany was to become the Soviet Zone (Figure 5.1). In step with the definition of these zones went a new territorial-administrative structure, because it had been decided that the country should be decentralized and the old German states in part should be resurrected as large new administrative units suitable for eventual federation. Prussia, for historical reasons, would be swept away. The revived states (*Länder*) were in part long-standing territories that had lost their autonomy progressively under the Second and Third *Reich* and the Weimar period, in part new creations on the basis of recognized regional associations, and in part former Prussian provinces or large cities elevated in status. Some of the new *Länder* can be traced back conceptually to the proposed territorial reforms of the 1920s. The *Länder* were grouped together to form the Occupation Zones.

The Occupation Zones

The British Zone comprised most of Northwest Germany. In the north, *Land* Schleswig-Holstein was a recognizable historical unit to which was added the former Hanseatic City of Lübeck and territory once part of Oldenburg that had passed to Prussia in 1937. Renewed agitation, with Danish support, for a realignment of the German–Danish border blew up: on the German side, it came from people who saw that incorporation into Denmark could bring a rapid improvement of living conditions compared to what could then be expected in Germany for many years ahead. Fortunately, the British and Danish governments did not give way to these 'Bacon Germans' and the agitation died away by the early 1950s. The two great ports of Hamburg and Bremen were made *Länder* in their own right, largely on historical grounds. While it was easy to justify Hamburg's status, that of the half-million city of Bremen was more debatable. Less damaged than Hamburg and a useful deep-water port with good passenger facilities at Bremerhaven, it became the main American port of entry with a special status making it effectively part of the American Zone.

In the territorial reforms of the 1920s and the planning concepts of the 1930s, a new unit with a distinct historical sociocultural identity appeared – Lower Saxony (Niedersachsen). This was confirmed in 1946 as a new *Land*, comprising basically the Grand Duchy of Oldenburg, the Duchy of Brunswick (Braunschweig), plus the former Kingdom of Hannover (annexed by Prussia in 1866), and the small territory of Schaumburg-Lippe. Another new *Land* was formed from the former Prussian province of Westphalia (Westfalen) and the three northern government districts of the one-time Prussian Rhine province and the small territory of Lippe-Detmold. Originally the whole Rhine province was to have been included, but creation of the French Zone made it necessary to allocate the southern government districts to that power. This new *Land* North Rhine-Westphalia was the most populous in Germany, but also the most devastated as it included the heavy industrial area of the Ruhr coalfield, for which a special international régime was instituted (1949–1951) to·rehabilitate production.

The United States Zone was formed of old German states with a long history of self-government. The largest and most important was Bavaria (Bayern), though the Lindau district was put into the French Zone. Its long tradition of self-government and the preservation of its administrative structure during the interwar years made it relatively easy for the Americans to get life going again. The core of the American Zone became the *Land* Hessen, an old name in a new form, since it was in fact 'Greater Hessen', lumping together the greater part of the Hessian states (the remainder went to form the French Zone). Originally the American Zone would have included all Württemberg and Baden, but in

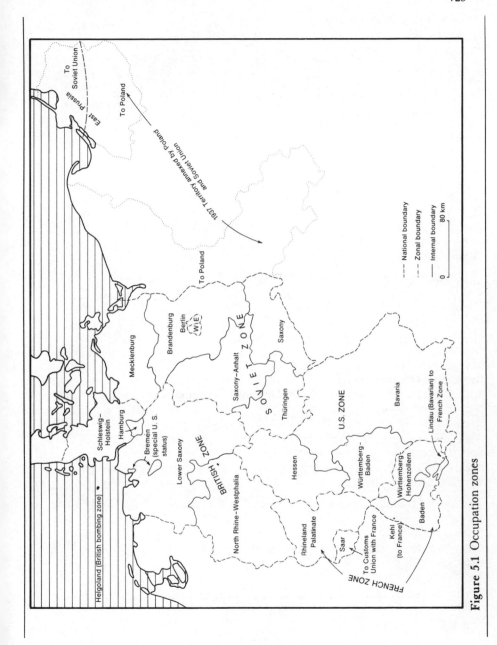

Figure 5.1 Occupation zones

130

order to give the French territory opposite their bank of the Rhine, part of Baden and Württemberg went to the French Zone.

The resultant French Zone thus comprised a northern part made up of the Bavarian Palatinate, the southern government districts of the Prussian Rhine province and some former Hessian territory, together to form a new *Land* Rhineland-Palatinate (Rheinland-Pfalz). The Saar was put under a special régime, though it was expanded in area compared to prewar, and quickly

Figure 5.2 Boundaries of the Saar

The Two Germanies

became closely integrated into the French economy. The southern part of the French Zone composed southern Baden and the southwestern part of Württemberg, and the Hohenzollern territory, regarded by the French as two states – Baden and Württemberg. Kehl, the important Rhine bridgehead opposite Strasbourg, was, however, closely integrated into France.

The Soviet Zone comprised the old Kingdom of Saxony (Sachsen), the *Land* Thüringen (formed from a collection of petty territories in 1920), and the two Prussian provinces of Saxony and Anhalt merged together as one *Land*. The central part was formed by the *Land* Brandenburg (another former Prussian province), and the Mecklenburg territories (joined in 1937) formed a new *Land* in the north. Remains of Silesian and Pomeranian territory left in Germany by the new boundary with Poland along the Oder and Görlitzer Neisse were incorporated into adjacent *Länder*, while along the western boundary, for ease of administration, some enclaves of Lower Saxon and Hessian territory were incorporated. The territory of the Soviet Zone did not represent the area initially captured by the Red Army since both British and American forces had advanced well into what had been assigned to the Soviet Zone.

Greater Berlin, with some small territorial adjustments to ease administration and to put Gatow airfield entirely in the western sectors, was placed under joint four-power administration, but some small parcels of territory entirely surrounded by the Soviet Zone were left under British and American control and became a dangerous flashpoint in later years. Most of the devastated centre with its strong historical associations was left in the Soviet sector. Access to Berlin for the Western Allied powers was by land and air along defined routes across the Soviet Occupation Zone, though their exact legal status seems never to have been other than most vaguely defined, resting on an assumption that the Western presence in West Berlin gave right of access.

Territorial Loss

Territories which had been part of *Grossdeutschland* before the capitulation, but had not been within the *Reich* on 31 December 1937, were lost: Alsace and Lorraine returned to France; Luxemburg, again autonomous, passed into the emergent Benelux customs union, while Belgium took back Eupen and Malmédy; the 'Sudetenland' returned to Czechoslovakia; and Austria again became independent. Helgoland (though remaining German) was evacuated and its military installations destroyed through its use as a British bombing range. Holland put forward claims to German territory along the Ems and on the lower Rhine and the most important concession was the temporary elimination of the *Selfkant*, a small salient off German territory near Geilenkirchen that dominated the Maastricht-Roermond-Nijmegen railway; otherwise the Dutch obtained only a few small modifications, some later

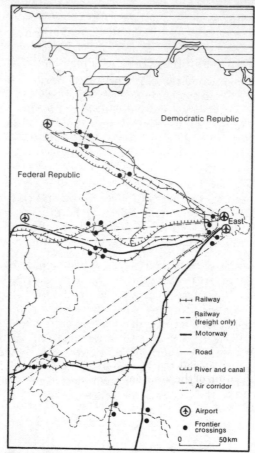

Figure 5.3 Access to Berlin – the initial situation

rescinded. Belgian and Luxemburg claims were also only modestly met, mostly by uninhabited territory on the Eifel flanks.

The major territorial change came, however, on the eastern border that had seen the greatest changes after the First World War. The Allies had agreed that Poland should be compensated with German territory for the loss of its own eastern territories to the Soviet Union. The original Western view seems to have been for the surrender by the Germans of East Prussia (the northern part going to the Soviet Union), Danzig, and the province of Upper Silesia, with small adjustments in favour of Poland along the rest of the German-Polish

The Two Germanies

border of 1937. Under Soviet pressure, the border was pushed westwards to the line of the Oder and western or Görlitzer Neisse, whereas there is evidence that Western statesmen, in agreeing to the *Neisse* as the boundary, were under the impression that this referred to the eastern or Schlesische Neisse, which would have left Breslau, Liegnitz, and the Waldenburg coalfield in Germany. At the Oder mouth, Poland was given the port of Stettin and the country around it on the west bank of the river as well as the exit to the open sea at Swinemünde. Later a further small adjustment in favour of the Poles was made by the German Democratic Republic at Stettin. These changes meant for Germany the loss of some of its best Baltic ports (including the valuable naval base of Pillau from which the eastern Baltic and the Gulfs of Finland and Bothnia could be commanded). The Upper Silesian coal, zinc, and lead deposits, and the coking coal of Waldenburg, went to Poland, which has since annexation of the territory discovered copper deposits in Lower Silesia claimed to be Europe's largest. The new frontier was pushed to within 50 kilometres of Berlin, while Zittau, Görlitz, Guben, and Frankfurt an der Oder have become frontier towns and Central Germany has lost its outlet through the port of Stettin. The loss was seen by many Germans at the time as a serious threat to their food supplies as this area was a major agricultural producer. The overwhelming part of the German population (estimated at almost 10 million in 1937) was expelled into the remaining part of Germany.

At the time, these territories were described as 'under Polish administration until a final German peace treaty', though this never seems to have been applied to the Soviet-annexed part of East Prussia (Kaliningrad *oblast*). This uncertainty undoubtedly left hopes on the German side of a possible ultimate favourable modification of the boundary, just as it created fear in Polish minds, leaving the territory as a potential bargaining counter as circumstance dictated. The German Democratic Republic, doubtless prompted by the Soviet Union, in the early 1950s recognized the Oder-Neisse line as a 'frontier of peace', but not until 1970 was agreement on its inviolability reached between the German Federal Republic and Poland.

Using the presence of the Slavonic Sorbs in Lusatia as a reason, both Poland and Czechoslovakia (as after the First World War) had tried to secure additional territory by claiming this community as members of their own people. No real idea existed of how extensive the Sorb settlement area was, nor how many people of Sorb affinity sought union with another Slav state.

Germany under occupation

Despite the original Allied intent to treat Germany as a unit for social, economic, and political purposes, the Occupation Zones quickly became small 'states' of their own, the result of the occupying powers applying their own systems to the running of their particular zone. Each zone had problems which were later to be passed in some form to the new German national states. The American Zone, comprising largely old German states with a tradition of autonomy and administrative experience, was able to get life back on the road to normality fairly quickly, aided because these states had escaped the worst of the air bombardment and ground fighting. The markedly light nature of much of industry in the south meant that the American Zone avoided the worst of dismantling for reparations. In contrast, the British Zone, covering much of Northwest Germany, had suffered some of the most intensive and destructive bombing, had also been fought over by ground forces, and included the Ruhr industrial area where there was severe dismantling for reparations. Whereas the inflow of refugees from the east into the American Zone had been absorbed fairly easily, the same inflow into the British Zone was particularly large in the poorest northern rural areas which already housed considerable numbers of evacuees from the bombed cities. The territory comprised largely former Prussian provinces without a strong local tradition of administration, which combined with economic structure and wartime damage to make the zone hard to rehabilitate.

The French Zone lay immediately adjacent to France, making the task of administration and organization easier than for the British and Americans, while the Saar became for all intents and purposes an integral part of France. Though the few heavy industrial towns had been attacked, the relatively poor French Zone escaped the worst of the bombing and dismantling for reparations, though it had suffered heavily in places from ground fighting, and the French claimed, as nonsignatories of the Potsdam Agreements, exemption from accepting refugees from the eastern territories. They were in a commanding position to dominate traffic on the middle and upper Rhine and especially to control movement along some of the main links between the British and American Zones, but attempts to reorient the traffic systems in their favour, especially to divert rail traffic through Alsace from Baden, brought considerable friction with the Americans.

The Soviet Zone was largely agricultural in the north, with large estates suitable for collectivization or state farming, whereas the south, with medium and small farms, had considerable engineering and chemicals industry. The Soviet authorities' task of introducing their own policies was eased, because industrial Saxony was traditionally a Socialist stronghold. Rehabilitation of the zone's economy was not only made difficult by extensive reparations dismantling and bomb damage in the industrial towns, but also because the zone was increasingly isolated by the split between the Allies from its usual raw and semifinished materials sources in western Germany and equally isolated by the new frontier with Poland from Upper Silesia. The greater part of the territory comprised former Prussian provinces with little experience of self-government, again slowing the process of recovery, while the expellee burden was particularly heavy.

The relations between the occupying powers and the German population varied considerably between the zones. The British applied their tradition of indirect rule through district officers and the Germans quickly received considerable rights of local government, while the army was unobtrusive. The Americans made a more direct approach, though the Germans again received responsibility for everyday administration quite soon after the occupation. The American armed forces were more in evidence and families were sometimes quartered in quite small places and took part in everyday life. The French infiltrated local government to a much lower level than either the British or Americans, while their personnel commonly lived among the German population, often with members of their families, including in-laws and grandparents brought from France, and the French military presence was also more obvious if less impressive. The Soviet Zone was quickly taken over for everyday running by German Communists or other sympathizers, whose influence was strong in sovietizing the zone, particularly the educational system. The Red Army, though present in great strength and living off the land to a greater degree than in the Western zones, was not generally obvious.

The economic and imperial problems of Britain quickly brought a union for economic purposes between the British and American Zones in the *Bizone* (January 1947), with a consequent widening of horizons and more concerted common policy in which American views tended by reason to predominate. Comparable pressures also forced the reluctant French into a similar relationship to create the *Trizone* from August, 1948, bringing further expansion of the horizons for the organization of German social and cultural life. Although apparent that four-power administration in Germany had effectively broken down, an unsuccessful attempt was made to get Russian agreement on a currency reform to give a sounder economic basis to the country. The Western powers decided to go ahead with their own currency reform and on 18 June, 1948, the *Deutschemark* replaced the grossly devalued *Reichsmark*, while a feared flood of worthless *Reichsmark* from the Western Zones into the Soviet Zone forced a reform there (19 June, 1948), though much less sophisticated in concept. In Berlin, two currencies were in use for a time, with East and West marks side by side. This situation was used by the Soviets not only to isolate their zone finally from the West, but also as a trial of strength by introducing restrictions on Western access to Berlin and effectively blockading the western sectors of the city. Through a massive airlift the Western powers maintained their position until the blockade was lifted in May, 1949, and won perhaps their greatest victory in the Cold War. The ultimate split in Berlin came in September, 1949, when Communist demonstrators forced the creation of two separate administrations and effectively two cities.

The Hard Years 1945–1950

The emergence of the two German states

This widening gap between Eastern and Western interests accelerated moves to give the Germans responsibility for the government of their country, and by late 1949 two separate German national states had appeared (Chapter 7), marking the end of Allied attempts to treat Germany as a political and economic unity. The Western powers sponsored the German Federal Republic, comprising the three western zones without the Saar but including West Berlin in a special relationship arising from the peculiarities of Allied agreements on the city's status. The Soviet Union quickly countered Western moves by creating the German Democratic Republic, which from the start incorporated East Berlin, an act claimed illegal by the Western powers. Emergence of two German states left the Berlin problem as the lynch pin in the East-West struggle and the Western powers felt they must under all circumstances maintain and constantly insist on their position in Berlin, stressing that their presence in the city was in its own right and not by grace of the Soviet Union. The several proposals on the German question in general made by the Soviet Union and the Western powers invariably foundered on Berlin's future. After the crisis of the blockade of 1948, the most serious situation arose in 1958 when Khrushchev called for a revision of the Berlin position, with the four powers giving up the occupation régime. He threatened to hand over all Soviet functions to the German Democratic Republic in Berlin, which he regarded as the legitimate capital of the latter state, and the Western powers would then have to negotiate their interest in the city with the G.D.R. government. The Soviet proposals suggested a Confederation of German States, while Berlin was to become a 'demilitarized free city' with the structure of the state within whose borders it lay but with its own government. A time ultimatum of six months for settlement was made. The Western powers in consultation with the Federal Republic rejected the proposals which they said were an 'ultimatum threatening unilateral action' and the Soviets countered by a draft peace treaty, to be signed in either Warsaw or Prague. Following further proposals and counter-proposals, a foreign ministers' conference was held in Geneva in 1959, but already Khrushchev had climbed down.

The Western proposals for German reunification were to start by unifying Berlin – in effect to return to the four-power status and one-city administration as it was before the 1948 blockade – in order to make ready for the city to become the capital of a united Germany. No progress could be made, because of the East *bloc* insistence on a 'free demilitarized city of Berlin', which the Western powers suspected as an attempt to dislodge them, with no guarantee of a unified Germany in the end. The West also felt that the Soviet proposals, particularly the rejection of free German elections, denied the essential element of self-determination for the Germans. In response, the Soviet government increased the tension by sealing off the western sectors of Berlin by the famous 'wall'; by challenging the Allies' rights to free use of their air corridors to Berlin; and by the resumption of nuclear tests. The sealing of the western sectors reduced the crossing points from 72 to 6, disrupted public transport, and prevented the continued employment of East Berliners in the western sectors, while West Berliners needed permits to enter East Berlin. The Western powers stressed that the existing ties with the Federal Republic were in no way incompatible with the four-power status of Berlin and rejected as inadmissible attempts by the Soviet Union and the German Democratic Republic to integrate East Berlin as capital into that republic's territory. As other pressure points in East-West relations emerged, the Berlin issue eased, and in 1964 the Soviet Union and the German Democratic Republic signed a treaty which, among other clauses, regarded West Berlin as an 'independent political unit'. It was agreed *inter alia* that 'the creation of a peace-loving united democratic German state can be achieved only through negotiations on an equal footing and on a basis of agreement between both sovereign German states'. The Western response to this agreement was that it in no way altered Soviet obligations to existing agreements, particularly on Berlin and access thereto. West Berlin was, in the Western view, not 'an independent political unit' but remained legally under quadripartite administration, irrespective of any unilateral Russian initiative. The Western powers did not recognize the *de jure* existence of the German Democratic Republic because they considered the only freely and legitimately constituted German government, entitled to speak for the German people in international affairs, was the German Federal Republic. The Western powers have constantly reiterated that 'the application in the whole of Germany of the principle of self-determination' remained 'a fundamental objective of the three governments'. They felt that the German Democratic Republic's treaty with the Soviet Union of 1964 did not change the international situation nor pose a threat to the Western position on West Berlin, and while boosting the morale of the G.D.R. government, it conveyed the Soviet view that it was intended to leave the Berlin position unchanged and not to press a separate peace treaty. After 1964 the situation stabilized and the *status quo*, albeit not very happy, remained for a number of years. From 1966 the Federal Government in Bonn dropped much of its intransigence towards its neighbour and sought closer and friendlier contacts, though the German Democratic Republic quickly revealed its fears of any *rapprochement*, a different stand to its early proposals for reunification. The new Federal *Ostpolitik* with Eastern European states considerably 'defused' the situation, but its disappointments were particularly in the failure of better relations with the German Democratic Republic, even though the Hallstein doctrine of no relations with states that recognized the G.D.R. was dropped. In 1971 a four-power agreement confirming the *status quo* in Berlin was signed with subsequent modest easing of the tension, and by 1973 easier relations between East and West led to Britain (among other Western countries) and the German Democratic Republic exchanging ambassadors.

Moves on German reunification now (1978) seem to have switched to the German level, since with the emergence of the Sino-Soviet disagreements and competition for leadership of the Communist world, Russia seems less interested in German matters. The United States has also become less inclined to push its interests in the German cause, so that on both sides the brinkmanship of the early 1960s has dissipated. Inter-German relations remain uncertain and problematical, with continued friction over Berlin: it is as though the old German particularism retains its virility and the struggle for unity has its age-long characteristics.

The inter-German border

The inter-German 'frontier' has become one of the most jealously guarded and tender in Europe, but its disruptive influence in Germany has been exceedingly great. What has become an international division originated as a boundary for administrative convenience between the Soviet and Anglo-American occupation zones, merely to define territorial responsibility of the occupying powers. It was therefore hastily defined using preexisting local government boundaries, simplified in a few places to make administration easier, but it took no consideration whatsoever of the economic and human landscape, disregarding land ownership and communications. The difficulties of such a situation, designed for an Allied policy which was to have treated Germany as a unit, at once became apparent when this policy was not implemented, especially as relations across the boundary deteriorated.

In the north, the presence of uncooperative G.D.R. authorities on the east bank of the Trave (Figure 5.4) makes navigation to the port of Lübeck difficult, especially as vessels can inadvertently sail into G.D.R. territorial waters. Development of Lübeck itself on the east is limited by the nearness of the frontier, while tensions are also present further south over access to the Ratzeburger See and the Schaalsee, both touched by the frontier. The common Elbe frontage between Büchen and Schnackenburg is also difficult to administer, especially cooperation over river works and barge traffic. Whenever tension rises, considerable disquiet is felt in the Lower Elbe as Hamburg lies only 30 kilometres from the new frontier.

The impact of the new frontier has been particularly harsh in the richer *Börde* country, cutting across the main east-west lines of movement between Magdeburg and Braunschweig. South of Helmstedt, the frontier disrupts several brown coal mines, while a new power station had to be built at Offleben on the western side to compensate for current formerly supplied from the G.D.R. Harbke power station. Another complex problem in the area around

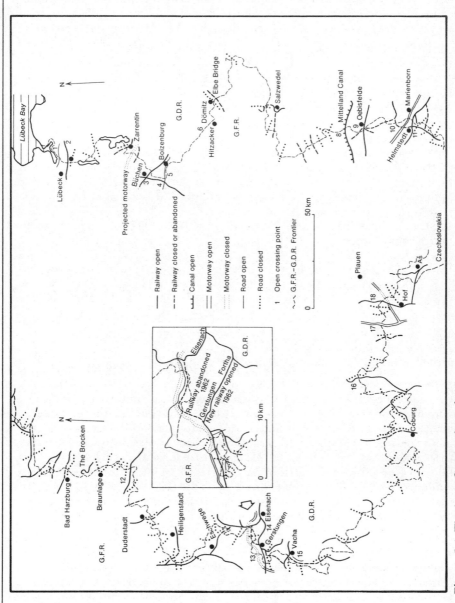

Figure 5.4 The inter-German boundary

Bebra and Eisenach arises from the frontier crossing and recrossing main railways and roads, so that the G.D.R. built a new section of railway entirely within its own territory The Eckertal dam near Bad Harzburg is bisected by the frontier with a barrier erected on the demarcation line halfway across, so hampering maintenance and operation.

Major disruption by the new frontier of closely knit textile, glass, and porcelain industries has occurred in the Upper Franconian and the Saxony-Thuringian industrial area, where the Coburg district has been cut from its usual railway access to North Germany and the Lower Rhine, requiring now a much longer and correspondingly more expensive journey. In *Landkreis* Kronach, Bavaria, the railway connection of the Tettau glass and porcelain industry has been cut by the new frontier and up to ten wagonloads daily have to be brought over ten kilometres on road rollers from the station at Steinbach am Wald, the additional costs being carried by the Federation. The brewery at Falkenstein, also in *Landkreis* Kronach, has lost 90 percent of its market area by the new frontier cutting it from Thuringia. On the eastern side of the border, the small and once prosperous resort of Blankenstein now has no tourist traffic because it lies in the 500 metre protective zone along the frontier. In all the new frontier has closed 32 railway crossings, 3 motorway crossings, 31 main highways, and over 140 other roads, besides innumerable tracks and paths. There remain open 8 railways, 5 roads and motorways, the Mittelland Canal and the Elbe.

The impact has been considerable on the German Democratic Republic side because of its extremely elaborate security system along the border. Villages and individual houses as well as trees and forest near to the border have been pulled down in a 275-metre-wide zone, with 4 barbed wire entanglements (including electrified sections, ploughed strips, and minefields, the whole dominated by watch towers and control points), and behind this lies a closely guarded 500-metre-wide belt and a 5-kilometre-wide restricted access zone along the whole 1381 kilometres of border. The total security area is larger than Luxemburg, while over 100,000 hectares of farmland and forest may not be used (three times the area of *Land* Bremen). West German farmers are denied access to 2000 hectares of farmland in the G.D.R. nominally theirs. In the 1950s, the population in the 26 border districts on the eastern side declined by 9 percent compared to a national average of 7 percent, while the population on the western side in the special border area (*Zonenrandgebiet*) increased by only 6 percent compared to 10.1 percent for the nation as a whole.

Territorial loss and a new territorial-administrative structure formed for Allied convenience were important elements in the spatial structure of two new German sovereign states that emerged as the outcome of the breakdown of original Allied intentions to treat Germany as a whole. These states have set the pattern of the new Central Europe for over a quarter of a century and seemingly into the foreseeable future, possibly beyond.

Suggested further reading

Brailsford, H. N.: Our Settlement with Germany, London, 1944.

Clay, L. D.: Decision in Germany, London, 1950.

Gollancz, V.: In Darkest Germany, London, 1947.

Merkl, P. H.: Die Entstehung der Bundesrepublik Deutschland, Stuttgart, 1965.

Mosely, P. E.: The Occupation of Germany – new Light on how the Zones were drawn, *Foreign Affairs* (NY) 28, 1950, pp. 508–604.

Pross, H., Hirsch, K.: Deutschlandpläne, München, 1967.

Ruhm von Oppen, B.: Documents on Germany under Occupation 1945–1954, London, 1955.

CHAPTER 6

ECONOMIC COLLAPSE AND RECONSTRUCTION
1945-1950

The general trend of industrial output for essential equipment had been upwards until about 1943, when growing British and American strategic air power had begun to spread destruction rapidly, although, because of a large element of 'area bombing' rather than 'precision bombing' of individually selected targets, destruction had fallen more heavily on residential accommodation than on industrial plants. In Köln, for example, 'thousand bomber' raids had obliterated much of the centre, including housing and commercial premises, but had missed major industrial installations on the outskirts. Certainly some critical industrial plants had been attacked, notably ball-bearings and vital synthetic petroleum and rubber plants. Iron and steelworks had also been bombed continually because they were almost impossible to conceal at night and lay from the opening of the war within bomber range from eastern England, following a relatively safe route across the Ijsselmeer or the Emsland. Naval ports (particularly U-boat bases) had also received much attention, as had railway junctions and inland waterways, harbours and bridges.

Initial surveys immediately after the ceasefire surprisingly revealed a remarkable part of industrial capacity operative if not undamaged, though of course the situation varied between branches. The loss of territories to Poland deprived Germany of about 17 percent of its 1939 coal output, as well as 40 percent of the lead and 75 percent of the zinc output, besides a considerable loss of iron and steel production and the synthetic chemicals produced in big plants like Heydebreck developed in the later 1930s. These territories also contained a substantial engineering industry (e.g., shipbuilding at Stettin and railway engineering at Breslau), not to mention textiles and pottery, and, in East Prussia, at Palmnicken, an annual production of 300–600 tons of amber now passed to the Soviet Union. The considerable investment made in Austrian industry after the *Anschluss* was also lost. Further loss for over a decade of industrial capacity arose when France incorporated into its own customs area the coal mining and iron and steelworks of the Saar, though this saved them from reparations dismantling.

The state of German industry in 1945–1946 was, however, to arise from factors other than just wartime destruction – these included collapse of the financial system, the inability to trade and obtain raw materials, as well as the breakdown in transport. Allied restrictions on industrial production and the reparations programme exacerbated the situation, while considerable reorganization of the spatial links of industry was demanded as the rift between the Eastern and Western occupying powers grew. For Germany and for Europe, the Allied authorities wisely chose not to apply the vindictive programme proposed by Morgenthau, though their policy was nevertheless rigorous; all industries of war-making potential were to be prohibited and destroyed – not only factories making military equipment, but also the ball and roller-bearing plants and works producing heavy machine tools, tractors (tanks) and synthetic petroleum, oils, rubber, and ammonia; also included were raw aluminium and magnesium production, the preparation of radioactive materials, and even parts of the iron and steel industry; while the building of seagoing ships, aircraft, and radio equipment was banned. The restrictions, if continued, would have prevented the development of synthetic substances that became everyday necessities in the 1950s. As the prohibitions were especially strict on installations built after 1936, it was foreseen that the modern and efficient sections of industry would disappear, while overall industrial production was not to exceed 70 percent of the 1936 level (equivalent roughly to the 1932 level). Compared to the productive capacity of 1938, the steel industry was to be reduced to 25 percent, basic chemicals to 32 percent, and other chemicals to 50 percent. Not more than 5.8 million tons of steel could be produced annually and all excess capacity over 7.5 million tons was to be dismantled. While the cement industry was to retain 53 percent of its 1938 capacity, aluminium, magnesium, and beryllium manufacture would entirely disappear. Germany's large electrical goods industry, along with shoe production, precision goods, and optical equipment were to be cut to half the 1938 level, but motor vehicle manufacture was pruned to a fifth of that level. Not more than 40,000 motor cars and as many lorries could be made annually, while only 10,000 motorcycles (not exceeding 250 cc.) were allowed. Machine tool manufacture was to be limited to only 11 percent and other heavy engineering to 31 percent. The restriction of the textile industry to 55 percent of its 1938 capacity seemed a little draconic. Despite immense damage to the railways and the surrender of equipment to other countries, no railway locomotives were to be built before 1950. Limits were even placed on the generation of electric current and on the level of foreign trade (three-fifths of the low level of 1936), but the limitations on steel production alone would have gravely limited the ability of other branches of industry to produce. The Potsdam Agreement not only forbade shipbuilding in Germany, but also virtually took away the right to own ships. Of 4.5 million gross registered tons of shipping in the merchant fleet in 1938, only 755,000 tons remained to pass into Allied hands (the Germans claim 1.4 million tons were taken): the Germans were left with 140 steamships under 1500 tons (average age over 45 years) and unable to exceed 12 knots, only fit for slow and limited coastal traffic. Participation in air transport, even gliding or ballooning, was completely forbidden.

Reparations, according to the views of the Western powers, were to be taken solely from existing capital equipment and German foreign assets, but the Soviet authorities interpreted the agreements to include 'current production'. The Soviet Union was to receive not only material from its own zone, but also from the western zones amounting to about 10 percent of the industrial capacity considered necessary for a peacetime economy, and additionally 15 percent of all dismantled equipment in the western zones was to be sent to the Soviet Union in exchange for raw materials such as coal and grain. The reparations story became one of vacillations and uncertainties: as disagreements between the Soviet Union and the Western authorities mounted, reparations for the former from the western zones were stopped. Dismantling was in general partial in any one plant and few plants were completely removed from the West, whereas in the Soviet Zone it was far more rigorous and even railway track and telegraph lines were removed. Dismantling in general proved unsuccessful because much machinery could not be used piecemeal elsewhere as it was designed as part of a whole plant for which, moreover, appropriately skilled labour was necessary. Certainly some German plants were successfully rebuilt and used: two synthetic petroleum plants were established in Siberia and the Soviet synthetic rubber industry owed much to German equipment and know-how at sites in European Russia, with the large numbers of German prisoners of war doubtless a great help in getting these works going. In the Baltic and the Black Sea, German shipyard equipment was used to extend yards; and the Moscow underground benefited from rolling stock from the Berlin system. Many German technicians were recruited to work in specialized fields in the Soviet Union, notably in aircraft production, rocket propulsion, and nuclear physics.

Soviet disappointment with attempts to rebuild and operate German plants in their own territory brought a scaling down of dismantling and the establish-

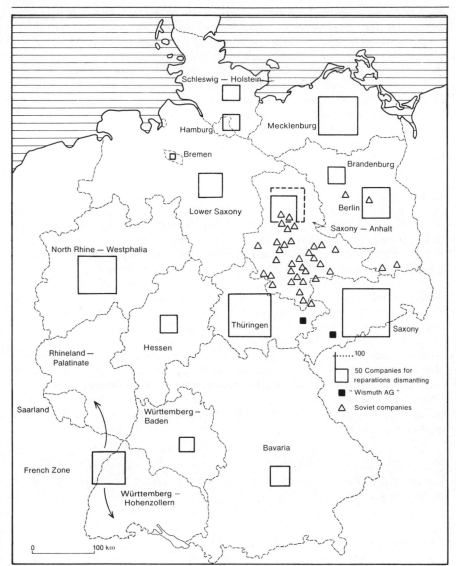

Figure 6.1 Reparations

Economic Collapse and Reconstruction 1945–1950

ment of Soviet companies to use plant *in situ* in Germany with German labour to produce goods which went entirely to the Soviet Union, quite apart from the reparations taken from current production of other German plants. Over 200 plants were taken over, comprising about 30 percent of the industrial capacity of the Soviet Zone, and by the early 1950s one-seventh of the labour force was working in these companies that held all the major chemicals plant, four-fifths of potash production and mining, and one-half the capacity of steel making, electrical goods, and vehicle building. About two-fifths of the capacity of heavy engineering, nonferrous metal processing, and energy production was also in Soviet hands. A major development was the mining of uranium ore, first in the Erzgebirge and later in the Gera district and the Vogtland where the Soviet *Wismut AG* employed about 150,000–200,000 Germans.

Whereas the Soviet authorities removed most of the *Zeiss* works from Jena as reparations, the American army had already taken to its own zone much of the most unusual and valuable equipment along with the technicians to operate it before the town was handed to the Russians. It is perhaps an irony of history that the British turned down the opportunity to have the *Volkswagen* plant as reparations. The French authorities, not having signed the Potsdam Agreement, felt free to take what they could from their zone, though it offered far less industrially than the other zones, from which they also received reparations. Nevertheless, the stream of reparations deliveries to France was so considerable that even in 1946, when German foreign trade was at its lowest ebb, Germany was fourth in volume in the French import trade. Most important for France was control of the Saar industrial area, though its incorporation in the French customs area was not well received by the other occupying powers. But it did prevent the considerable iron and steel industry from being dismantled, while the coalmines were quickly resuscitated. This territory grew with such vigour from this association that it quickly became a strong contrast to the rest of the languishing German economy.

Initially, the 1946 Western 'Levels of Industry Plan' would have taken some 1800 factories from the three western zones, either in full or partial demolition, but the rapid deterioration of relations with the Soviet Union (which would have received a considerable part of the dismantled equipment) and American disfavour with France, brought a change of attitude reinforced by a growing awareness that reparations and dismantling slowed rehabilitation of the shattered European economy. In the summer of 1947 a new plan contained only 858 plants, though it included three large shipyards and four major electricity works, while over a quarter of the named plants were in North Rhine-Westphalia. Industry in the British and American zones was now allowed to reach the level of 1938, a year distinguished by neither boom nor slump conditions, with production of 10 million tons of steel permitted, for which an adequate capacity was to be retained. In late 1949 the dismantling list was reduced to 697 plants, and West Berlin was removed entirely as a political consequence of the blockade. The *Thyssen* steelworks in Duisburg (which prewar produced about 10 percent of total German output) were reprieved, as well as the synthetic rubber works at Hüls near Recklinghausen, and synthetic petroleum plants such as the *Gelsenberg* installations and the Scholven hydrogenation works. Others included the synthetic petrol plant in Castrop-Rauxel and similar works in Wanne-Eickel, Bottrop, Oberhausen, and Dortmund. For some communities, the reprieve of their main plant (e.g, the Henrichshütte at Hattingen) brought new hope of survival, but a major omission was the steelworks at Salzgitter, the core of employment in a new town of about 100,000 people, where public pressure in the end brought a reprieve for this plant, which in 1951 finally brought dismantling to an end. At the same time, the gradual reduction of restrictions aided an amazing upsurge, notably in shipbuilding and synthetic chemicals production (though synthetic petrol and rubber were not to occupy the important position they had held before 1945).

The Ruhr became a focal area of rehabilitation as Western Europe depended for its revival on the coal industry to supply vital fuel, for none of the other fields could cover much more than local needs. As it was desired to break the power held by the industrial trusts and concerns, and at the same time to ease the Germans back into the European community, a special approach was made to the Ruhr. Early ideas of complete detachment of the Ruhr and Rhineland from Germany as a separate political unit had been quickly abandoned, despite French resentment, but in February, 1947, however, France put forward a plan to 'internationalize' the Ruhr and separate it in some measure from Germany, though any suggestion of permanence for the separation was clearly unacceptable, especially as it could well encourage irredentism. As rapprochement between Germany and the Western powers grew, so the French idea was emasculated, and in its place in 1948 an International Control Authority was established with an area rather larger than the old Ruhr planning authority and containing at the time 137 productive coalmines. Its task was to share out Ruhr coal and steel production reasonably equally among the Western European countries, but by 1952, with the creation of the European Coal and Steel Community, this authority was made unnecessary.

The terrible winter of 1946 brought home to Europe the interdependence of its national economies and highlighted how much had been lost through the slowness with which German industry had been revived, while the weakening financial position of Britain and the growing dependence of Germany on American aid strengthened the need to get German industry working again. Sweden felt the collapse of the German iron and steel industry through the loss of a valuable market for its ore, for German steel production had not even reached the low level of 5.8 million tons of the first Levels of Industry Plan (in

1946 output was only 2.5 million tons in the three western zones). With the British coal industry undergoing reorganization and barely able to satisfy home demands, Germany became a major continental source, with the Saar mines primarily satisfying French needs and those of Silesia lost to Poland. With labour shortage, transport problems, and lack of equipment, Ruhr coal output in 1945 was 5.1 million tons (West Germany including Saar, 5.6 million tons); by 1946 it had risen to 8.7 million tons (9.6 million tons) and in 1947 to 12.7 million tons (13.9). The fall in German trade meant that Rotterdam and Antwerp lay underused: in 1938 over 75 percent of the goods handled in Rotterdam had been sent to Germany, but in 1946 Rotterdam's traffic was less than a fifth of the prewar volume, while world tramp shipping suffered considerably through the absence of German trade. The disrupted railway system in Germany made communication between Scandinavia and France and the Low Countries difficult, while the inability of the damaged port of Hamburg to handle its traditional Baltic trade likewise acted detrimentally to Scandinavia.

An element of confusion was introduced by the decision at the Potsdam conference to break up all forms of syndicates, trusts, and cartels, or other practices that allowed 'excessive concentration of economic power': it is claimed that 6 banks and 70 industrial groups held two-thirds of German industry in 1938; 6 concerns held 98 percent of the iron production and 95 percent of the steel production in the Ruhr. The coalmines were now separated from steelmakers, steelmakers from steel users, and all came under Allied supervision, though the executive side remained in German hands. Prewar, the big firms had been streamlined, often with their own railway links between coalmines, cokeries, and steelworks, and this close integration was probably more efficient than had the units operated independently. In the chemicals industry, the massive *IG Farbenindustrie* was broken up, though the resulting units, like *Bayerwerke*, *Hoechst*, and *BASF* were in themselves large.

As the cleft between the Western Allies and the Soviet Union deepened, there was a move towards coordinated action in the three western zones, although the French tended to be odd-man out. Most significant was the creation in the summer of 1947 of the Combined Economic Area (Bizone), a fusion of the British and American Zones, which greatly speeded recovery, especially as the American Zone had tended to return towards normal conditions more quickly because its industry had been less damaged and contained less of the proscribed elements, while the important position held by farming in its economy could more readily feed its population. Part of this agricultural production was now available to feed the devastated towns of the British Zone where recovery was hampered by the vacillating overall policy on dismantling and reparations. At the same time, coal to drive the industries and railways of the American Zone could now be readily obtained from the Ruhr and Aachen coalfields, while ports of the British Zone provided access to the outer world.

The Two Germanies

The three western zones – the area of the Federal Republic – were left after the war with a more balanced economic structure than the Soviet Zone, though with several points of imbalance in the overall economic structure. They were still recovering from the extensive devastation of the main industrial districts well into the 1950s, even though the actual loss of industrial capacity had turned out less than the intensity of the bombing suggested. Recovery was plagued until the end of dismantling in 1951 by uncertainty in sectors like iron and steel and chemicals over the likelihood of plants being removed, while the various levels of industry plans also restricted expansion in most industries, though many fell short anyway of the allowed levels of production. Contemporary views of the future were, however, reasonably encouraging since the coal and iron and steel industries were the keys to satisfactory industrial structures of their period, especially as the Ruhr and Aachen coalfields were among the most important in Europe (even though the Saar coalmines had been monopolized by France), and with the loss of the Central German chemicals industry the plants in West Germany became all the more significant to the industrial structure of Western Europe. The engineering industry also remained viable even after dismantling and the restrictions placed on its product range, though heavy engineering showed undue predominance since prewar the lighter branches had been better represented in Central Germany. There were also structural imbalances in the textile industry, chiefly in the Rhineland and Westphalia and in Württemberg, but there were many refugees from the Sudetenland and Silesia with skills to develop the poorly represented sectors once capital became available. The weakness of the western zones was particularly in the shortage of raw materials either first through the absence of the ability to trade or later because of the poor bargaining position of an impoverished Germany. Home ore supplies, despite wartime development, were inadequate for more than a modest industry and there was dependence on foreign supplies of petroleum, though further development of deposits in the North German Plain seemed possible. But the production of synthetic petrol had been stopped by the occupying powers, even if the plants were neither damaged nor dismantled. Considerable alarm arose from the feeling that West Germany had suddenly become dependent on food imports and that it could not draw on the agricultural surfeit of Central and East Germany. But in 1946–1947 the main causes of food shortage were disruption of transport and the distribution system, and there was a substantial difference between the amount of food *officially* available and that hoarded by peasants and grown on allotments and gardens, though in the big towns it is true people suffered acute hunger. Transport was a critical bottleneck because not only were the railways badly damaged and the equipment in a poor state through overuse, but the system was dislocated by the division of the country and the consequent redirection of traffic flows. The inland waterways had also suffered damage, particularly severe to the Rhine fleet, where the river was strewn with debris and wrecks, and the few roadworthy motor vehicles were short of petrol. The main ports had all suffered serious damage that limited the possible throughput.

The real recovery came with the Currency Reform of 1948 (that gave an incentive to work for the new scarce money) and the generous aid extended by the Marshall Plan (April 1948 – February 1950), though with the new monetary economy unemployment rose sharply to remain serious into the early 1950s. Between early 1948 and late 1950, the real period of the *Wirtschaftswunder*, industrial production rose from 60 percent to 130 percent of the 1936 figure and the rebuilding of housing got properly underway, though it was not until a decade later that the backlog was truly surmounted, while the growth of industrial activity and the rebuilding of towns made possible a start on the spatial redistribution of the expellee burden. The rebirth of activity along the Rhine axis, into which expellees began to move to satisfy its growing labour demands, made the plight of the lands along the new border with the Soviet Zone stand out all the more clearly.

The division of the *Reich* had an entirely different appearance in the Soviet Zone, which in general had suffered less damage from air attack and ground fighting than West Germany, except in Berlin. Initially, despite the vicious dismantling programme and the disruption caused by sovietization, progress was quicker in many sectors than in West Germany, since the authoritarian administration acted speedily and decisively. According to German estimates of the existing industrial capacity in 1945, 45 percent was dismantled in the Soviet Zone, 33 percent in East Berlin, 67 percent in West Berlin (where many of the bigger factories lay) and only 8 percent in the three western zones. The biggest problems were to arise from the unbalanced economic structure of Central Germany. Prewar, the Saxon, Thuringian, and Berlin industries had depended for a considerable part of their raw metal supplies on the Ruhr and Upper Silesia, which had also sent nearly all the hard coal for the railways and industry; likewise, the textile industry had also depended on yarn from West German mills and the motor vehicle industry had taken many components from West German factories. On the other hand, the chemicals, opticals, and textiles goods had found a substantial part of their market in West Germany and in the capitalist world now closed to them. The territory of the Soviet Zone did, however, have useful natural resources for industry – notably lignite, potash salts, and some metals such as copper, besides formerly little regarded resources of uranium. The isolation of the Soviet Zone from the western zones, however, brought a need to reorganize the economy in relation to the new western, interzonal boundary, but adjustment was also needed to the new boundary with Poland. The Soviet authorities sought to integrate their zone economically into the Socialist *bloc* in terms of organization and close trading links, so that by the time the German Democratic Republic was formed, Soviet influence had already set the country on the way of its own thinking. An important element was national self-sufficiency, though few projects towards this end had been started before the foundation of the new republic. The formation of Soviet companies to work plants *in situ* with German labour was clearly an indication of the importance laid on the advanced Central German economy as a contributor to Soviet wealth, which has enabled the Democratic Republic to maintain favour with the Soviet Union. The wide changes in the economy and in society to come into line with Soviet ideas, as well as the failings through inadequate experience of centralized planning, made nevertheless for substantial wasted effort, but it was quickly labour that became the critical factor, even though the population was initially swollen by expellees.

The four occupying powers on the basis of earlier decisions were committed to a policy of land reform in Germany which was to be prepared by the German authorities or, in certain instances, to be carried through by the occupying powers. In the three western zones very little was done until 1947, when laws were published that led to a partial surrender of land against compensation. In the American Zone, where there had never been large holdings in significant numbers, surrender of land was to be on a rising scale for holdings over 100 hectares; in the British and French Zones an absolute maximum of 150 hectares was set for holdings, but in the end only part of the reform was carried out. There was, however, continuation of a policy pursued in prewar times that purchase of farm and forest land by nonagricultural interests required a permit. Events in the Soviet Zone were more radical for, in the autumn of 1945, all owners of more than 100 hectares had been deprived without compensation of their lands, while 4000 holdings under 100 hectares that belonged to 'war criminals and Nazis' were also taken and the sequestrated land passed to a land commission that redistributed it. At the end of 1948, another phase of land reform began, aimed at the small and middle-sized peasants from which only peasants with less than 20 hectares escaped relatively lightly; and the final stage of 'collectivization' was to come in the early 1950s, pushed through by the new republic. The serious disruption of agricultural production that these changes caused underlay critical problems of food supply that continued even into the mid-1950s.

Population in the early postwar years
The first indications of the effect of the war on population structure and its relation to economic conditions came in the census made late in 1946 in the four occupation zones and Berlin. The true aftermath of war could first be best assessed in the early 1950s when the diverging demographic trends between the two German states were becoming apparent. In 1939 Germany within its 1946 boundaries had contained a population of 59.75 million and the 1946

census showed that this population had risen to 65.98 millions, an increase of 10.5 percent, while Germany within its boundaries of 31 December, 1937, had in May 1939 contained a population only 5 percent greater than the total in the smaller area of 1946. The population in the 1946 area had increased by 6.27 million since 1939 but there were present some 9.68 million expellees in 1946: consequently, the actual resident population had fallen since 1939 by 3.41 million or 5.7 percent. In the period up to autumn, 1950, a further major inflow of expellees took place, notably into the newly formed western Federal Republic, where between 1947 and 1950 an absolute population increase of 3.8 million represented a net immigration of 2.6 million (including some 900,000 returned prisoners of war). Migration into the truncated 1946 area of Germany had thus been a major factor in population change.

In view of the large-scale immigration of expellees into Germany and the modest fall in the resident population, it may be asked what sort of overall war losses were experienced by the Germans. Table 6.1 is based on estimates made

Table 6.1
Population change in Germany, 1939–1947

Population (May 1939) including Danzig		69.7 millions
Territorial change	−9.2	
Births	+7.9	
'Normal' deaths	−6.3	
War losses	−4.2	
Population shifts		
inward	+7.5	
outward	−4.6	
Population, end of 1945		60.8 millions
Period 1946–1947		
Births	+1.8	
Deaths	−1.5	
Population shifts		
inward	+7.2	
outward	−0.6	
Population, end of 1947		67.7 millions

Source: Frumkin, G. *Population Changes in Europe since 1939*, Geneva, 1951, p. 81.

by Frumkin and widely accepted, but a later German estimate suggested that 'normal deaths' were higher and 'war deaths' lower than Frumkin's figures (Table 6.2).

Between 3 and 4 million appears to be the usual estimate of military war dead. Civilian war deaths, including foreign workers in the *Reich*, have been put as high as 550,000, of which possibly about 450,000 were German nationals: no

The Two Germanies

Table 6.2
German computation of war losses

'Normal' deaths	8.2 million
War losses – killed and missing	3.9 million
	12.1 million

estimate appears to have fallen below 350,000. There were considerable air-raid deaths in individual towns: 50,000 in Hamburg in July, 1943; 8,000 in Kassel in October, 1943; and at least 35,000 in Dresden in February, 1945. The number of Jews resident in Germany in May, 1939, was put at 200,000, of which 190,000 were to perish during the war years. If the *whole* German ethnic group is considered (including the large number of German ethnic settlements in Eastern Europe), then the official West German estimate exceeds 7 million people who perished in war and its aftermath, as indicated in Table 6.3.

Table 6.3
West German estimate of war losses to the German people

Losses to German armed forces	3.760 million
Losses of Volksdeutsche in armed forces	.432
Losses of civilian population in air raids in 1946 area of Germany	.430
Losses of German civilian population in eastern territories of *Reich* (incl. air raids and expulsion)	1.225
Losses of Volksdeutsche in expulsion	.886
Other losses	.300
Total losses	7.033 million

Source: Germany Reports – Press and Information Office of the Federal Government, Bonn, 1961.

The most significant element in the postwar population has been the expellees from German ethnic population beyond the 1937 boundaries of the *Reich* and also Germans expelled from German territories annexed by Poland and the Soviet Union (Figure 6.2). The total 1939 population so affected has been estimated at 16.9 million, to which should be added the Germans in the Soviet Union (given as 1.2 million in the Soviet census of 1926 and possibly 2 million by 1939). The population of these German groups between 1939 and 1945 had probably been increased by 660,000 through natural increase, though war losses were estimated at over 1 million. West German estimates suggest that between 1945 and 1960 some 11.73 million people were expelled into Germany and other Western countries, while 2.1 million perished in the expulsions and

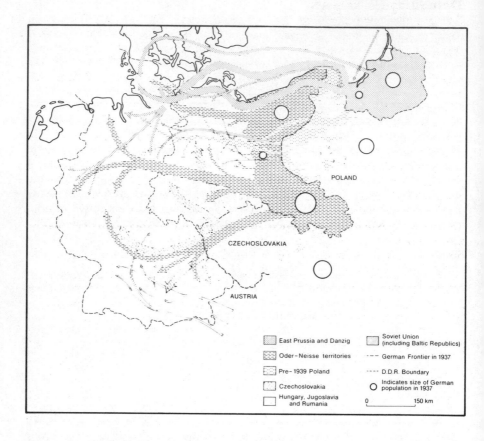

Figure 6.2 Flight of German refugees

some 2.72 million people remained in their homelands or are believed to be alive but not traced. The four-power census of 1946 revealed 5.963 million expellees in the three western zones, 120,000 in Berlin, and 3.605 million in the Soviet Zone. The 1950 census in the Federal Republic showed 7.876 million expellees, with a further 148,000 in West Berlin. Though no further direct figures of expellees were given for the G.D.R., estimates from the 1950 census suggest this highly mobile population had fallen to 2.212 million. All these figures include children born to expellees during or after flight. There was also a growing movement from the Soviet Zone into the three western zones, estimated at 1.55 million people by early 1950.

The Two Germanies

Demographic impact

The population pyramids in the two republics for 1950 diverged in detail rather than in degree. The lowest part of either structure revealed the small numbers of children born in and surviving from the difficult closing stages of the war and the early postwar period, though 1948 and 1949 had shown slightly larger cohorts. There were still visible in the respective parts of the pyramids the sharp bites taken by the small cohorts born during the First World War and the economic depression of 1929–1932. On the male side, the heavy inroads into the military age groups by war deaths in the First World War now extended down into the age groups affected by the second war and can be traced even to the 17–18 year olds called to the colours in the very last stages. Some of the youngest cohorts that served in the latter stages of the First World War had been still young enough to be called back to the colours in the Second World War and had consequently shown further losses. The effect of war losses on these age groups had greatly accentuated the imbalance between the proportions of men and women, though even in 1939 there had been higher than average proportions of women in the 35–40 age groups. In 1949 in the Soviet Zone, for example, there was already a substantial disproportion even

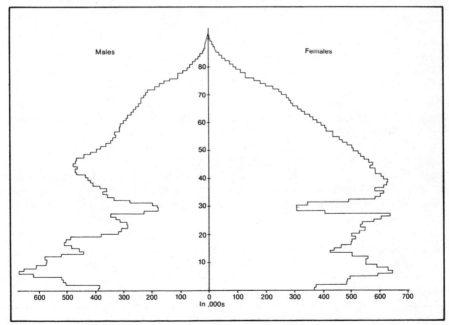

Figure 6.3 Age and sex structure – 1946

in the 18–21 age group, while between 21–35 there were thirteen women for every six men. The situation in the Soviet Zone in 1946 was more alarming than in the western zones, for an overall population increase of 14.2 percent represented an increase of women by 28.9 percent and a *decrease* of men by 1 percent. The corresponding figures for the western zones were an increase of 20.6 percent by women and an *increase* of 2.7 percent by men. Table 6.4 suggests that in 1950 the population of the German Democratic Republic was of a generally older structure than in the Federal Republic. Particularly important was the higher proportion of people aged 65 years and over, while the proportion over 45 years old amounted to 33.9 percent in West Germany compared to 38.1 percent in the Soviet Zone. The effect of migration of young people to the western republic was also reflected in the lower proportion of children under six years old in the Democratic Republic, since people had taken their children with them or delayed having a family until established in West Germany.

Table 6.4
Age and sex structure in the two German states, 1950

	Federal Republic		Democratic Republic	
	Total Pop.	Prop. Female	Total Pop.	Prop. Female
	– percent –			
Under 25	37.9	49.3	36.5	50.3
25 to under 45	28.2	56.6	25.4	60.8
45 to under 65	24.5	55.0	27.5	57.3
65 and over	9.4	55.3	10.6	57.1

Source: Die Bevölkerung des Sowjetischen Besatzungsgebietes – Bestands – und Strukturänderungen 1950–1957, Bonn, 1961.

Alarm about future population was expressed on the basis of projections in the immediate postwar years, though such studies appear to have been published only in West Germany. A projection made in 1949 by the American commission studying the expellee problem forecast a population of 48.6 million in West Germany in 1959, 50.6 million in 1969, and 52.1 million in 1979; but by 1959, the population was already 55.1 million and in 1969 it had risen to 61.2 million. The prognosis was for a steadily ageing population with a numerically constant labour force, though it was thought that the proportion of women would slowly decline, so that by 1969 there might be a slight surplus of males in all age groups up to about 40 years old and that in general the expellees would remain a younger and more male element in the population into the foreseeable future. With the prospects of a long military occupation and restriction on economic development, there was a feeling that Germany was overpopulated and that suitably controlled migration might be a correct policy and could also ease the problem of integrating the expellees. Churchill's supposition that the expellees would step into the places of war casualties was far from true. The economic improvement in West Germany following the currency reform of 1948 and the easing of restrictions on industry subsequent to the Korean War invalidated most gloomy forebodings. The Soviet Zone authorities, singularly uninformative on demographic questions, could not hide the trends that appeared in population statistics, especially the influence of the higher death and lower birth rate than in West Germany. Until 1949, population in the Soviet Zone had increased through the influx of expellees, but when this stopped, population began to decrease, especially as the stream of young, demographically and economically active people to West Germany grew.

Table 6.5
Birth and death rate in Germany, 1947–1950

	1947		1948		1949		1950	
	B.R.	D.R.	B.R.	D.R.	B.R.	D.R.	B.R.	D.R.
			– per 1,000 of population –					
Western Zones	16.4	12.1	16.5	10.5	16.8	10.4	16.2	10.5
Soviet Zone	13.1	19.0	12.8	15.2	14.5	13.4	16.5	11.9

Source: Statistical yearbooks of the two German republics

The greatly increased proportion of women to men meant that economically rewarding jobs would have to be found for women as the prospects of marriage diminished. Certainly, the traditional view of woman's concern with the 'three Ks' (*Kirche, Küche und Kinder*) would require liberal revision and, as the 'male vacuum' raised numerous fears, some observers suggested modifications of the accepted views of marriage and cohabitation to relieve social tensions. Equally clear was that the male labour force would suffer varying shortages as the war-torn age groups travelled up the pyramid and that it would take 70–80 years, even without any substantial future fluctuations, to eradicate the irregularities created by the two World Wars and their aftermath from the population pyramid.

Immediate postwar regional patterns and problems

Whatever the problems of overall change in population, change between the main regions of the truncated post-1945 German territory was particularly significant. In general, a close correlation between the percentage of expellees in the total population and the percentage change in the combined population can be seen in the results of the 1946 census, the only one that provided detailed information on expellees in all four zones. Figure 6.4 shows the large

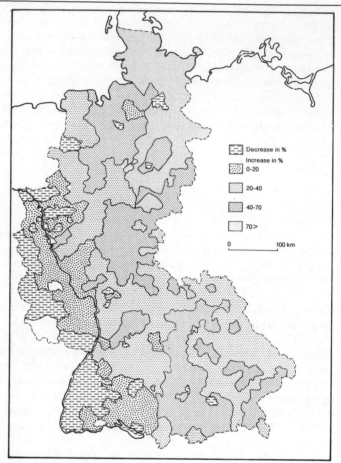

Figure 6.4 Population change 1939–1946

proportional changes in population in the countryside of Schleswig-Holstein and Mecklenburg, while a broad belt of considerable though more modest growth marked the countryside between the Elbe and the Weser, rural Hessen, and considerable parts of Franconia and Upper Bavaria. The growth in the countryside suggested a retreat into areas least affected by the advancing armies and an escape from the bombed towns: as a generalization, the more remote the district, the greater generally had been population growth. The frontier districts along the Rhine and in the path of the advancing Red Army in eastern Brandenburg as well as most of the industrial towns stood out as areas

The Two Germanies

of population loss. The industrial towns of the Ruhr and Lower Rhine had been continuously attacked, though some towns had suffered short intense attacks (often 'Baedeker' reprisal raids) or had got caught in ground fighting. Because of their distance from British and American airfields, the industrial towns of Saxony and Thuringia had in general suffered less bombing, as had towns in the lost eastern territories, for Russia had had little interest in strategic bombing. Nevertheless, substantial population growth had been witnessed in some quite badly damaged towns where air attack had been against industrial targets rather than 'blanket bombing' of residential districts.

The expellee population was strikingly important (Figure 6.5) in the countryside of North Germany: in Mecklenburg most districts had more than half their population composed of expellees. In Schleswig-Holstein and much of Lower Saxony between the Elbe and Weser, expellees formed more than 30 percent of the population. In South Germany, the proportions were less impressive and only in a few parts of eastern Bavaria did expellees reach more than one-third of the population. In many districts of Saxony, Saxony-Anhalt, and Baden-Württemberg, the expellees had been the sole element in population growth, even though they formed only a modest part of the total population, so that in several areas they had offset an otherwise substantial decline in resident population. As the expellees had come from lands on Germany's eastern borders, it is not surprising that they formed a relatively unimportant element in the Rhine basin: over much of Hessen, North-Rhine Westphalia, and the southwestern states they comprised less than one-fifth of the population and west of the Rhine generally less than one-tenth. France, not a signatory of the Potsdam Agreement, claimed exemption from its clauses, notably Article XIII on expellees, so that less than 4 percent of the population of the French Zone was expellee. In the Soviet Zone, all parts (except Berlin and industrial Saxony, where accommodation was limited), especially those adjacent to the new frontier with Poland and the border with the Sudetenland, had expellee population exceeding 20 percent of the total population. Few expellees had found accommodation in the countryside immediately around the bombed cities, for here evacuees from the towns had been quartered – well seen round Hamburg, Bremen, Berlin, the Saxon industrial towns, and München, while it also accounts for the low proportions in parts of the Westphalian countryside nearer the Ruhr and Rhine. Though often present in considerable numbers (usually through contacts with relatives), expellees formed generally no more than 3–5 percent of the total urban population, itself depleted compared to 1939.

The impact of the expellees

While the expellees have been carefully studied in West Germany and much done to ease their integration, the Soviet Zone and the later Democratic

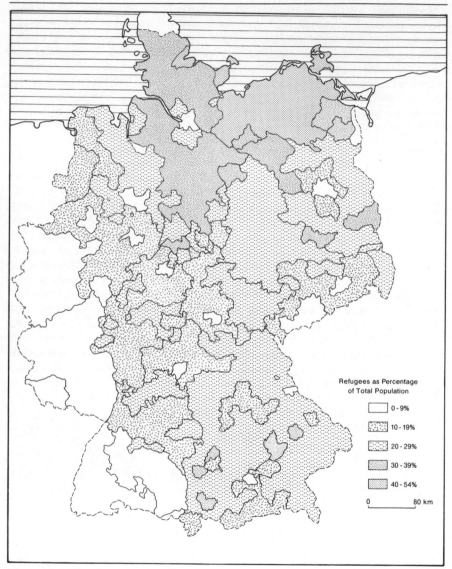

Figure 6.5 Distribution of expellees in Germany

Refugees as Percentage
of Total Population

0 - 9%

10 - 19%

20 - 29%

30 - 39%

40 - 54%

0   80 km

Republic have given them no special consideration, even though they were at first classed as 'resettlers', a name clearly chosen because it was politically undesirable that they should be regarded as having been 'expelled' from other members of the Socialist *bloc*. The proper regulation of the movement foreseen in the Potsdam Agreement never got underway and at first there was no standard definition of the status of 'expellee'. The incomers had to go wherever accommodation was available (consequently mostly to the poorer and remoter country districts), while movements were also strongly influenced by the disruption of transport.

Expellees tended to become grouped according to their homeland in different parts of the country (Figure 6.6). The location of these groupings was affected by such things as the routes taken by the various transports and trecks, as well as by existing interregional contacts or religious ties. East Prussian refugees who came along the Baltic coast or by sea from their homeland tended to settle in North Germany, like themselves predominantly Protestant. The Sudeten German refugees moved into eastern Bavaria and into Hessen, where the predominant Roman Catholic faith matched their own beliefs, whereas in Saxony they had to settle among folk of different faith, but the industrial pattern was more akin to their own homelands than in either Bavaria or Hessen. East Prussians and Silesians tried to reach the Ruhr district, for here many families had relatives who had settled there early in the century. The expellees from Pomerania and eastern Brandenburg found themselves in Protestant districts west of the new Polish frontier, and South Germany and Austria received most Danubian Germans from Hungary and Jugoslavia and limited numbers from Rumania (which treated its German minority quite liberally). German 'Balts' from Estonia and Latvia found their way, along with others from Galicia, Volhynia, and the Bukovina, into Northern and Central Germany.

Fortunately, the *Reichsdeutschen*, all residents of the *Reich* in 1939, predominated (58.3 percent) and resettled with relative ease, accustomed to life in Germany, so that small frictions have arisen only through local variations in habit and usage. On the other hand, the smaller groups from areas far from Germany's borders, long out of touch with the mainstream of German life, were more difficult to integrate. The Germans from Latvia and Estonia were traditionally professional people and landowners who acutely felt their 'declassed' position in the new homeland. Likewise, the parly de-Germanized *Volksdeutschen* from Volhynia, the Bukovina, or southern Russia found life in Germany strange, and some groups had suffered more than one such transfer since 1939. The smaller groups, for example those from Danzig or from Jugoslavia, were usually widely scattered and consequently more isolated than the larger groups, like the East Prussians or the Silesians, who maintained more of their own social cohesion.

The German churches did much to bridge the gap between the incomers and

Economic Collapse and Reconstruction 1945–1950

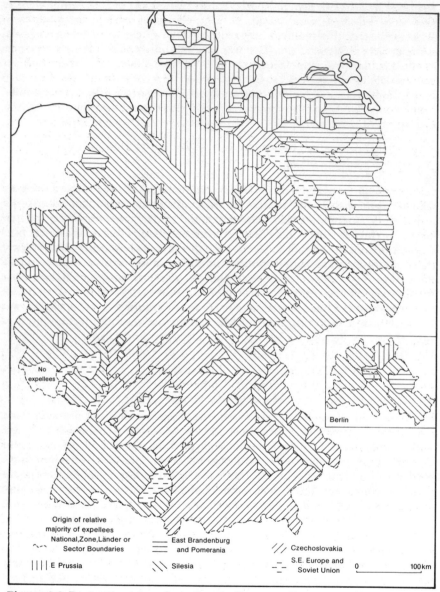

Figure 6.6 Regional origins of expellees in Germany

the local population, especially where a sudden inflow of expellees had upset delicately balanced social forces. A most successful force in the integration process was intermarriage, though marriages between expellee men and local women were more frequent than the reverse. Local girls often provided an opening into a local family business or job for the expellee male, while families encouraged their daughters to marry expellee men because the East Germans and *Volksdeutschen* had a reputation for being thrifty and hard-working, a good replacement for a lost son where a hard-won inheritance had to be handed on. On the other hand, expellee girls, without local connections and the dowry still commonly expected, were less favoured by local boys. Social standing *before* flight or expulsion was generally a more important factor than the class position in the new homeland.

Despite heavy war losses, the German labour market found itself with about 5 million more hands than in 1939, but no corresponding increase in job opportunities, made worse by three quarters of the expellees living in rural districts, though under half their number had occupations associated with country life. The proportion of labourers among expellees rose from 45 percent before flight to 85 percent afterwards, but the self-employed had fallen from 26 percent to 3 percent. Even where expellees managed to get back into their profession or trade, most initially had to take lower ranking jobs. One incentive to move to the town was that the expellee felt he faired better in impersonal urban life than in the parochial countryside.

After the currency reform of 1948 made it no longer worthwhile to work for food alone, increasing pressure for rewarding jobs arose among expellees, and in the years of high unemployment in West Germany running into the early fifties, the expellees had a disproportionately large share. One of the most difficult spheres in which to become reestablished was farming, because there were inadequate numbers of farms without heirs in which public funds could place expellee farmers and the well-settled West German countryside of small and medium-sized farms offered little scope for new holdings to be created through land reform. Possibilities of land reform in West Germany were estimated likely to yield about 500,000 hectares, mostly in the Emsbasin, the North Sea coast, and the Lüneburger Heide, while some observers suggested reducing the forest area (little of which was, however, suited to worthwhile farming), though the Reichswald had a number of families settled in clearings. In the Soviet Zone, extensive land reforms did, however, create smallholdings on dispossessed estates in the north and centre, where expellees received some of the new holdings, but further changes in agriculture quickly drew even these into state and collective farms. As restrictions on industry were lifted, the best employment prospects began to emerge in this sector in which a substantial part of the expellee population had originally been employed. In West Germany, the demand for coal quickly absorbed expellee miners from Silesia and even young expellee men without mining experience. Once able to recruit capital, the refugees from the Soviet Zone and expellees began to establish new firms in the West, with their entrepreneurial and technical skills important in the textile industry (for example, the large *Kunert* stocking firm from Warns-

Table 6.6
Expellees in the four Occupation Zones in Germany, 1946

Land	Expellees		Migrants from Soviet Union	
	Thousands	%*	Thousands	%*
Schleswig–Holstein	837.5	31.6	123.0	4.5
Lower Saxony	1,475.5	22.9	278.8	4.3
North Rhine–Westphalia	710.9	6.0	144.2	1.2
Hamburg	57.9	4.1	32.5	2.2
Bremen	25.3	5.2	10.9	2.2
Bavaria	1,657.8	18.4	168.4	2.0
Hessen	552.5	13.6	98.6	2.4
Württemberg–Baden	549.3	14.9	20.0	0.5
Rhineland–Palatinate	35.0	1.2	16.0	0.6
South Baden	24.3	2.0	14.8	1.2
Württemberg–Hohenzollern	35.8	3.2	14.4	1.3
Brandenburg	541.2	21.4	—	
Mecklenburg	910.1	42.5	—	
Saxony–Anhalt	905.6	21.8	—	
Thüringen	564.9	19.3	—	
Saxony	679.9	12.2	—	
Berlin	119.7	3.7	—	
* = percent of total population				

Source: Edding, F., *Das Deutsche Flüchtlingsproblem,* Kiel, 1949.

Table 6.7
Expellees in the Federal Republic, 1950

Land	Thousands	%*	Thousands	%*
Schleswig–Holstein	857.0	33.0	134.0	5.2
Hamburg	116.0	7.2	68.0	4.2
Lower Saxony	1,851.0	27.2	369.0	5.4
Bremen	48.0	8.6	21.0	3.8
North Rhine–Westphalia	1,332.0	10.1	379.0	2.9
Hessen	721.0	16.7	166.0	3.8
Rhineland–Palatinate	152.0	5.1	47.0	1.5
Baden–Württemberg	862.0	13.4	144.0	2.2
Bavaria	1,937.0	21.1	228.0	2.5
West Berlin	148.0	6.9	80.0	3.7

Source: Federal Statistical Office

The Two Germanies

dorf in northern Bohemia reopened in the Allgäu); while fine glass makers of world renown from Bohemia began to open plants in Bavaria and North Rhine-Westphalia; porcelain and pottery makers from Bohemia, Silesia (Bunzlau), and Saxony also started work in Bavaria and other *Länder*, often using their own workers. Artificial jewellery makers from northern Bohemia established a remarkably successful industry in Bavaria, while the famous *Zeiss* photographic tradition from Jena was reestablished with American assistance in Baden-Württemberg, and the British encouraged the reopening of the *Olympia* typewriter plant (originally in Erfurt in the Soviet Zone) in the depressed naval port of Wilhelmshaven. By the early 1950s some branches, like the musical instrument makers from southern Bohemia, were already employing half their prewar numbers. It is difficult to find similar cases in the Soviet Zone, where the centralized control of industry did not give the same encouragement to individual initiative, though expellees became an important element in the labour force.

Much of the harsh experience that befell expellees could have been avoided had the French and Soviet Zones agreed in 1946 to a more even distribution of the refugee burden, while such an action might have allowed more of the scarce resources then available to have been devoted to rehabilitation rather than to relief work.

Suggested further reading

Edding, F., Hornschu, H-E., Wander, H.: Das Deutsche Flüchtlingsproblem *Institut für Weltwirtschaft*, Kiel, 1949.

Frumkin, G.: Population Changes in Europe since 1939, *UNO-League of Nations*, Geneva, 1952.

Fuller, J. F. C.: The Second World War 1939–1945, Chapter 12, London, 1948.

Gassdorf, K. O., Gassdorf, M.: Kriegsfolgenkarte von Westdeutschland 1939–1950, Frankfurt, 1950.

Hasenack, W.: Bilanz der Demontage, Essen, 1948.

Klöss, E.: Der Luftkrieg über Deutschland 1939–1945, München, 1963.

Nette, J. P.: The Eastern Zone and Soviet Policy in Germany 1945–50, Oxford, 1951.

Reichelt, W. O.: Die Demontageliste, Hamburg, 1947.

Rupp, F.: Die Reparationsleistungen der sowjetischen Besatzungszone, *Bonner Berichte aus Mittel- und Ostdeutschland*, Bonn, 1951.

─── PART TWO ───
THE TWO GERMAN STATES OF THE 1970s

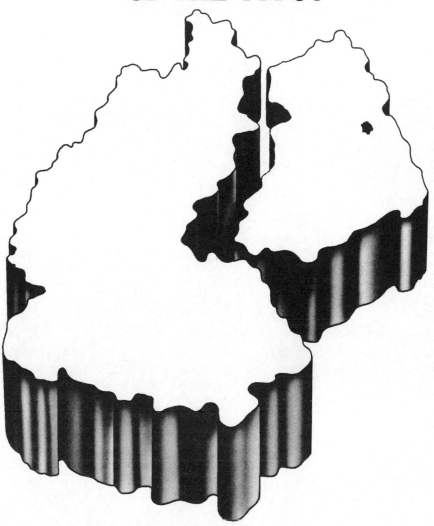

————————————CHAPTER 7————————————

THE TWO GERMAN STATES
SOME INTRODUCTORY COMPARISONS
AND CONTRASTS

Before examining the social and economic geography of the two German states, it is worth considering some of the basic differences in their political and social philosophies. The new states together occupy a little more than three-quarters of the *Reich* territory of 1937, but the Federal Republic alone contains just over half the prewar territory. Of the 69.3 million people living in the 1937 *Reich* territory at the census of 1939, 88 percent were within the territories held presently by the two German republics; in fact, 62 percent of the 1939 population was living in the territory now the German Federal Republic.

The return of responsibility to the Germans moved slowly at first, but once started it became in a sense competitive between East and West in the hope of winning German support for their own cause, though the pace was also conditioned by the need not to offend susceptibilities outside Germany. Even the Germans, certainly in the West, showed some hesitation to proceed to steps that might deepen the division of their country. Nevertheless, pressures on all parties in both East and West were such that during 1949 two new state organisms emerged, each cast in the political image of the *bloc* that sponsored it. Both states suffer from imperfections caused by the arbitrariness in the way they are put together territorially, as well as by the events and atmosphere of their formative years.

The German Federal Republic
The legal basis of the West German Federal Republic is the Basic Law, so named to imply that it would be replaced as soon as a constitution was agreed

for an All-German state. Several of its Articles are adapted from the Weimar Constitution. The West German state is not only a parliamentary democracy but also a federation, though in no way a *confederation*. The federal structure rests upon the ten *Länder* created at the end of the Second World War by the Allied authorities in a conscious attempt to decentralize Germany. Created hastily from different territorial origins, their wide disparity in size, economy, and population creates problems of drawing them together into concerted action in many different fields, while West Berlin's membership raises special difficulties. The question of a territorial adjustment to create a more equable balance between the *Länder* has been a serious but intractable problem, especially as the *Länder* were vested with considerable autonomy. But since the inception of the republic, the federal government has generally made inroads into their freedom of action, and at the same time there has been increasing recognition that joint action, formal or informal, between the *Länder* themselves and with the federal government is more desirable.

The federal government reserves to itself all rights to act for defence and foreign policy on behalf of the federation as a whole. Otherwise the *Länder* have their own ministerial (or in the city states, senatorial) officers for such things as education, economic affairs, finance, etc., and they also keep representatives in Bonn, the federal capital. In several fields, federal and state responsibility overlaps, particularly in important aspects like finance and planning (one of the later developments), though their respective spheres are usually carefully defined. While some sources of revenue (e.g., customs duties, commercial vehicle taxes, and certain specific financial duties) are wholly at the disposal of the federation, others go wholly to the *Länder* (e.g., beer revenue, casino taxes, certain road taxes), whereas some, like income tax, corporation tax, and VAT, are shared between the *Länder* and the federation on a variable relationship fixed periodically. Because of the different levels of revenue arising from the varying size and wealth of the *Länder*, an adjustment of revenues is undertaken in order to equalize the standard of services between the states. A frequent criticism of the federal system is the expense of maintaining a large and often duplicated administrative structure between the *Länder* and the federation. The supporters of federalism counter this by claiming that it is better able to reflect regional sentiment and also prevents central government becoming too powerful and too detached.

The Basic Law makes the federal principle inviolable: there must be a federal government as the central authority with *Länder* as federal members, though no *Land* as such has the right to exist *per se* nor to be within unalterable boundaries. The *Länder* must be states in their own right, however, and must, like the federal government, have legislative, executive, and judicial organs, as well as the right to make their own political decisions, so long as these are not to the detriment of the federation. At the same time, the *Länder* may not change

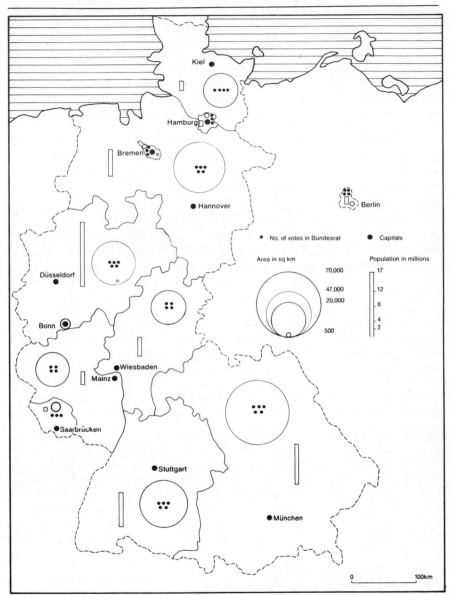

Figure 7.1 Representation of the *Länder* in the *Bundesrat*

their political system from that of a representative parliamentary democracy. Federal law has, however, precedence over *Land* law, while the federal government has the right to take adequate measures to ensure every *Land* fulfils its federal obligations and there is no right whatsoever of secession. The central government of the federation is expressed through its head-of-state, the Federal President, who represents the Federal Republic at home and abroad. The *Länder* have no formal head-of-state, though if such a function is to be performed, it is done by the Minister-President (or his equivalent) of the *Land*. The federal government as an organ of political leadership and direction is responsible for all spheres where the federation has sole competence, that is for foreign policy, defence, and security, and for monetary policy, and for such questions as nationality, customs and excise, as well as for the federal railways, air traffic, and postal communications.

The lower house of the federation (*Bundestag*), representing the electorate (i.e., all citizens over eighteen years of age) of the Federal Republic, has authority only over federal affairs: it has no authority over the *Länder* governments. It is the task of the *Bundestag* to act to secure unity of purpose and action between the members of the federation, to strengthen the democratic consciousness of its citizens, and to win and maintain support for the principle of democratic parliamentary government. The administrative function of the federation is in a complex relation to that of the *Länder*, except in those spheres where the federation has sole competence. The Office of the Federal Chancellor and the Federal Ministries are the supreme federal agencies, with special bodies serving the foreign service, the federal post, and railways and other means of communication, as well as those spheres of finance and customs and excise where the federation has sole competence; others include the Federal Cartel Office and administration of certain corporations and institutions like the Federal Bank. Federal legal jurisdiction is limited to the upper courts.

The *Länder* manage their own affairs within the legal and constitutional constraints outlined above, with a limited right to enact laws, which may be overridden by federal legislation, so that the bulk of the legal code in effect stems from the federal government. The elected parliaments of the *Länder* (*Landtage* or *Senate*) are restricted in competence to affairs within their own *Land*, but they maintain their own ministers (or their equivalent) and their officers and control the structure of local government through the *Regierungsbezirke* and *Kreise* (where such exist), while they also control various public corporations or institutions like universities and radio and TV stations, and look after education, police, and regional planning within their own territory. The *Länder* administer federal law for activities within their jurisdiction, such as building regulations, commercial laws, and environmental protection, but they also administer federal laws on behalf of the federation for activities within federal jurisdiction within their territory (e.g., federal highways, motorways, some

The Two Germanies

educational activities, etc.). With the exception of Schleswig-Holstein (which uses federal agencies), the *Länder* maintain their own constitutional courts for cases within their own territory and competence; but they must provide all facilities for the administration of the middle and lower levels of the law.

The original division of responsibility between the federation and the *Länder* agencies was redefined in 1969 with a bigger involvement of federal agencies. *Land* responsibilities that were also significant for conditions beyond an individual *Land*'s boundaries were made joint between the *Länder* and the federation, especially where such action could help to improve the quality of life (e.g., planning, environmental protection). Particularly significant in the new division was expansion or development of tertiary educational facilities, improvement of regional economic structures, or betterment of agricultural conditions, and the strengthening of coastal protection.

The link between the *Länder* and the federation is maintained by the Federal Council (*Bundesrat*), in a sense the upper house. Its primary objective is to draw the federal states into the central law-making organization by means of which the *Länder* may influence federal decisions. Each *Land* sends a prescribed number of representatives in relation to its population; these are not directly elected but nominated by the *Land* parliament from among its members, which binds them to vote as directed. Critics claim this system is less democratic than the American senatorial system, which gives each state the same number of senators, elected independently and not its nominees. Counter claims suggest that such a system simply duplicates the party political structure at the expense of regional interests, whereas because the members of the *Bundesrat* are senior members of their *Land* government, they are an effective counterweight to the federation and safeguard of regional interest. Creation of the *Bundesrat* in its existing form was one of the most hotly debated issues in the parliamentary council that drew up the Basic Law. The *Bundesrat* has no term of office: it is an ongoing organ, though after each *Landtag* election its personnel is usually at least in part changed to respond to new political trends. In the *Bundesrat*, voting by each *Land* must be unanimous, but much work is carried through not by the plenary sessions but by sectional committees. Decisions are valid only when more than half its members are present and a two-thirds majority is needed for laws changing the Basic Law (the *Bundesrat* possesses an absolute veto), whereas other laws require a simple majority.

In the governmental system of the Federal Republic, West Berlin is considered by its own authorities and by the federal authorities in Bonn as the eleventh *Land* – this is not accepted by the German Democratic Republic and by the Soviet Union, which reluctantly have accepted it as (in their terminology) 'an independent political unit', part of neither republic. The British, Americans, and French still regard Berlin as a whole under four-power control, and though accepting some activities of the federal government in West Berlin *de facto*, they do not accept West Berlin *de jure* as a federal *Land*. The twenty-two Berlin representatives in the *Bundestag* are not directly elected but chosen from the sitting members of the West Berlin parliament and their votes are separately recorded. Unlike other *Länder*, a federal law does not automatically become law in West Berlin, but must be ratified by the city parliament. Nevertheless, in *de facto* terms, West Berlin is very nearly fully integrated into the Federal Republic, though there has been some disagreement with the Allied authorities over how many and what federal functions may be operated from West Berlin. In the 1971 Quadripartite Agreement, the Soviet Union accepted the ties between West Berlin and the Federal Republic in several fields, though it rejects the federation's right to perform any official or constitutional acts that would suggest West Berlin is a part of the Federal Republic. The Federal Republic would not wish to alter the Western powers' attitude if this would in any way jeopardize retention of their garrisons in the city, the sole guarantors of West Berlin's security and existence.

The German Democratic Republic

Under strong Soviet influence, the German Democratic Republic has followed very different political lines to the Federal Republic, conditioned by the acceptance of Marxist-Leninist dogmata as applied to the typical Eastern European people's democracy. Initially divided into five *Länder*, the original draft of the constitution (implying duration unlike the Basic Law of the western republic) noted that the German Democratic Republic was composed of these *Länder*, but the federal principle was never effectively applied and their governmental responsibility and autonomy kept in a low key. The constitution stated that the republic decided all affairs significant for the existence and development of the German people and retained the right to all law making, rendering the *Länder* little better than ordinary organs of local government in contrast to their relatively high level of autonomy in the West. In 1952 the final break was made when the republic was reorganized into *Bezirke* modelled on Soviet ideas and the *Länder* were said to be 'an old system of administrative delineation stemming from the Kaiser's time that has become an impedance to new development'. The reforms of 1952 confirmed the German Democratic Republic as a highly centralized state in which a strong element stems from the political organization of the Socialist Unity Party that draws together all party activity under the leadership of the Communist Party and provides a single candidate list at elections. In the G.D.R. all political power is constitutionally exercised by the 'working people' (not by the people as a whole as in the Federal Republic's Basic Law) and thus corresponds to the Marxist-Leninist dictatorship of the proletariat. In all organization of the state, the accepted principle is 'democratic centralism' provided by the working people through the party, in which all organs of and within the state look to its leadership and its direction in planning. It is hoped that such a central focus will lead to the liquidation of local egoism and to the fullest possible mobilization of all the material and human resources within the state.

The supreme organ of the state is the *Volkskammer*, the People's Chamber, elected every four years on a single list of candidates and comprising some 500 deputies, of which 16 are nominated by the City Chamber of East Berlin and have only an advisory role. The *Volkskammer* is the sole body empowered to make laws and constitutional amendments, but much of the day-to-day work is conducted by the Presidium and by its committees, where much of the legislation originates for approval. The Ministerial Council serves as the executive organ of government, but its functions were taken over to a considerable extent by a State Council that replaced the office of President of the Republic after the death in 1960 of Wilhelm Pieck. Since 1971 the Ministerial Council has taken back many of its original functions as first defined in the constitution, leaving the State Council more as the international representative of the republic and as support for the work of the councils of the *Bezirke* and other local government. There has been a rather fluid relationship between the formally defined organs of government, suggesting that the real power lies in the hands of political figures irrespective of what title or position they hold on paper, while the Socialist Unity Party holds the dominant position by virtue of its majority in membership.

With the whole economy closely controlled and to a large part operated by government agencies, the powerful State Planning Commission is in fact the central organ of the Ministerial Council, charged particularly with the supervision of economic matters and supervision and control of planning commissions in the *Bezirke* and the *Kreise*.The omnipotent position of planning is reflected in local government, for the design of the *Bezirke* and their subordinate levels is related to territorial planning on the Soviet model. Just as all activities are regulated from the central government authorities responsible to the *Volkskammer*, so even at local level the *Bezirksrat* (regional council) and the *Bezirkstag* (regional Assembly) carry out not only those services and infrastructural operations considered a part of the function of local government in the West, but also regulate prices, other economic activities, and planning, all under direct supervision from central government.

Compared to the modest changes in society in the Federal Republic, mostly reflected in an increasing proportion of employees compared to the self-employed, policies adopted under Soviet guidance in the Democratic Republic have brought dramatic changes. The shift of ownership from the private to the public sector has been a major contrast with the Federal Republic, where private ownership on a wide front has been fostered. The early period was used to introduce new organizational concepts that inevitably led to full state ownership of the means of production, often in the process driving out elements from society (many private entrepreneurs and farmers) unable to accept the change. This period first brought the introduction of the idea of the 'Workers' and Peasants' State' where all power was vested in the hands of the working people (die Werktätigen), i.e., industrial workers, peasants in the socialist sector of farming, white collar workers, and the 'creative' intelligentsia. Consequently, the decrease in the proportion of the self-employed has been much steeper than in the Federal Republic, and the younger skilled workers have become the new élite. Socialism has brought a widening horizon of state participation in all working and leisure activities, and the importance of radio, television, the theatre, and the printed word in the battle for popular support is reflected in the generous allocation of resources to these media. A not dissimilar motive underlies the promotion of sport, particularly the value laid on high-level performances in international events as an indication of the advantages of the 'system'.

Contrasting economic philosophies in the two German states

The contrasts between the two German states are reenforced by differences in economic philosophy, basically the question of ownership and the degree of state participation and control. The Federal Republic has advocated the free 'social market' economy, with private ownership of and competition between the means of production recognized as fundamental. The Democratic Republic, following Marxist-Leninist dogmata, has become a fully centralized, planned, command economy common throughout the Socialist *bloc*.

In the immediate postwar years in the three western zones there was at first a strong lobby for a planned economy with powerful state participation, a view supported by both the Socialist and Christian Democratic parties. Particular support was forthcoming for the nationalization of heavy industry, as well as parts of the financial and credit mechanism. At the time, only the liberals felt private ownership and enterprise to be essential for a healthy economy. The British Labour government of the time expectedly gave support, though the rising influence of the Americans acted in the opposite direction, because for them German economy, with such things as state railways, was already relatively 'socialistic'. Several proposed *Länder* constitutions included public ownership of varying sectors of their economies, though these conditions were ultimately suppressed by the Allied authorities before ratification, but a clause allowing for such action where in the interest of the nation as a whole was included and ratified in the Basic Law (Article 15).

An important move came with the creation of the Bizonal Economic Council, especially after its powers were extended early in 1948 and after election of Dr.

Ludwig Erhard (against the wishes of the Socialists) to its Directorship Erhard, originally a nonparty expert elected to be Bavarian minister of economics, became a resolute protagonist of the social market economy, developed by the Freiburg school of economists. It was a notion of an economic and social order that was essentially free but, in contrast to the old liberalism, it rejected the view that the state should in no way interfere with the operation of the market forces. The state should not have the formal control seen in Eastern European socialist states, but it should legislate to secure the highest degree of economic freedom equiparate with the highest level of social justice: the state was to be the arbiter and to rectify imbalances and injustices that the free market forces were unable to influence or encompass. Freedom and support for private initiative and the stimulus to make wealth on one side was to be balanced by protection of the economic and socially weak on the other, and the aim was the greatest possible welfare for all. Orderly competition, with strict regulation of cartels and monopolies, and continual economic growth and full employment were regarded as vital, while freedom of foreign trade and free currency convertibility were to be assured, and all controls were to be lifted as soon as possible. The clearly felt betterment of the economic situation at this time (1948–1952) weakened opposition to Erhard's policies, though it is hard to know how far such change arose from these or from a response to events outside Germany. The urge to win back lost ground (in which expellees and refugees were a significant force) drew management and labour together, aided by codetermination in certain industries and works' councils in others. The generally improving level of life for all concealed until the 1960s the widening gap in private wealth between a small and numerically declining group of self-employed and the rising proportion of employees and pensioners. Criticism has grown of this phenomenon and of government inaction to push ahead socially desirable reforms.

From the structural crisis in the coal industry of the mid-1950s, government intervention in industry has grown, particularly through an active fiscal policy of direct or indirect tax concessions, subsidies, and loans, while the public and governmental acceptance of a growing planning component has been marked as it has become apparent that a pure social market economy has been unable to rectify many imbalances at regional and lesser level. This culminated in the 1975 federal regional planning programme ratified in agreement with the *Länder*. Likewise, in the shock of the 1967 recession, economic forecasting – until then regarded as the first step towards a socialist *bloc* style economy – was introduced in the Act to Promote Stability and Growth in the Economy, while the power of the federation in economic affairs was enhanced by the oil crisis of 1973.

The planned economy of the German Democratic Republic

A quite contrasting economic philosophy has been applied in the G.D.R., so that the economies of the German states became most divergent at the height of the Erhard social market economy and the rigorous Stalinistic centralism in the 1950s. During the sixties a slight freeing of the excessive centralism in the East and acceptance of a modicum of planning in the West narrowed what nevertheless remained a deep gap. In the G.D.R., the acceptance of Marxist-Leninist dogmata implied radical change in the ownership of the means of production and of property and the application of a rigorous central direction to the economy. The basic tenets were rational use of resources and the long-term view of their development, by which it was hoped to get full employment and to eliminate the cyclic nature of business and industry caused by the 'anarchy of the market'. The initial phase in the immediate postwar years was a wide-ranging reform movement denoted as 'anti-fascist democratic' when both land and industrial capacity were taken into an increasing public ownership, with a growing state participation in remaining private enterprises. An already elaborate planning structure was converted into a State Planning Commission on creation of the republic. Though its responsibilities were later modified on a number of occasions, it has nevertheless retained full responsibility for planning in association with the several industrial and other economic ministries supervised by the Ministerial Council.

The task of the State Planning Commission is to design plans for long-, medium-, or short-term objectives set by the *Volkskammer*, which in the 1968 version of the constitution defined the G.D.R. as having a 'socialist planned economy'. The planning content is influenced by the political aims of the Socialist Unity Party, the economic and social factors (e.g., potential labour force, degree of mechanization) conditioning development of the economy, the situation in relation to intra-German and international economic relations, especially with the Soviet Union and with COMECON, and finally the general overall situation at home and abroad particularly in strategic terms. Whereas in West Germany it is the market forces of supply and demand that regulate volume and price as well as the relative relationships between different activities, these are all formally fixed in advance in the G.D.R. as part of a plan to be fulfilled in a given period. Even profit levels and investment patterns of individual industries and plants are fixed by the state planners unlike the free movement of market forces under government surveillance in the Federal Republic. The broadest general aims are outlined in long-term perspective plans related to the longer term development of COMECON up to 1990, but the five-year plan is significant in laying down the growth objectives for the period and the strategies and means to achieve them. Detailed planning is on year-to-year basis, drawn up even for individual plants. Under the theme of 'socialist integration' introduced in the early 1970s in COMECON, coordination between the plans of the Eastern European countries has become a more significant element. The sophisticated economic basis from which planning began in the G.D.R. made necessary many detailed changes from Soviet experience and several other COMECON members where the economies were less complex and also often more self-sufficient.

While the Federal Republic's social market economy has shown numerous and as yet unsurmounted imperfections, the centrally planned economy in the G.D.R. has not been without its own structural weaknesses and bottlenecks. In any comprehensive system of planning, time-lag between collecting, collating, and analysing material is inevitable, though new computer techniques can improve the performance. But generally, for example, production figures have been three years out-of-date in published plans. There are also as yet unsolved difficulties in relating effectively branch and regional planning, while the rate of diversification and sophistication has generally been faster than planners have been able to take account of in their studies, and there is the continual problem in assessing future demand, patterns of choice, and even the effect of technological change and innovation. Demographic projections have been a serious constraint in longer term planning because of their notorious unreliability. There has been long debate over how far the economy should be regulated by introduction of a limited market mechanism or by modest decentralization, while Soviet uncertainty over whether planning should be principally by branch or by regional management has also influenced decisions. Regional planning (termed territorial planning in the G.D.R.) is closely related to overall economic and associated planning and is undertaken for every level of territorial-administrative unit. The *Bezirke* created in 1952 were specifically designed with this aim in mind. Every element of urban planning and industrial location is included, so giving the state absolute control over the ultimate spatial patterns of the economy. The implications for the geographer of this system compared to that of the Federal Republic require little comment.

The German republics and the broader European scene

Both republics have become members of broader formalized international communities in their respective political sphere. As a member of the European Community, the Federal Republic is within an avowedly supranational organization, whereas the Council for Mutual Economic Assistance to which the Democratic Republic belongs has expressed itself as purely international, though quite obviously dominated by the Soviet Union. Since the early 1970s, COMECON has, however, begun to show some supranational tendencies, while through it the G.D.R., like the other members, has had its economy closely linked to that of the Soviet Union. Every member undertakes to follow the socialist policies of the council, where the Soviet struggle against polycentrism has resulted in a fairly uniform approach to problems (except agriculture), though again this has tended to weaken since the early 1960s. Soviet pressures have undoubtedly forced members to accept policies unsuited to their resources and needs, like the search for self-sufficiency Soviet-style in the 1950s. COMECON has always claimed to respect the sovereignty of its members and emphasis, at least publicly, has been on cooperation, first through rather crude trade and barter mechanisms, later through a concept by which members 'specialized' in what they could do best and then exchanged products between themselves, while since the early 1970s the coordination of plans and development of multi-national production projects has been heralded. COMECON policies have never encouraged mobility of labour or other factors of production between members, while the respect of sovereignty explains why no aid is given to problem regions within countries. Most striking has been the absence of any policy comparable to that for agriculture in the European Community. By its sophisticated economy, the G.D.R., despite its poor natural endowment compared to other members, has been a favoured member, for it is able to strengthen several structural weaknesses within the Soviet economy.

The European Community to which the Federal Republic is attached was designed from the outset to have a growing supranational role, ultimately leading to common government, common law, common financial policy, and a withering of all constraints to intracommunity trade, and it has a clear policy in which members contribute financial assistance for problem regions. Every effort is made to free on a community basis the mobility of labour and the factors of production in the hope of closely integrating member economies, and these policies have already produced considerable regional shifts in patterns of economic activity. Some ambitious policies to equalize conditions, like that for agriculture, through a complex price adjustment system, have, however, foundered in ever deepening contradictions.

Nation and nationality in the two German states

In 1945 Germany was one nation and one nationality in legal terms. The Federal Republic has argued that it is the continuity of the German *Reich* within its territorial limits in 1937 and its constitutional definition before 1933, and this continuity can exist as such because the Allies expressly stated that they had no intention of *de jure* annexation of the *Reich*. The claim has involved the Federal Republic in acceptance of a considerable financial obligation to uphold the belief, paying out large damages to many victims of the Nazi period; and the Federal Republic has consequently also accepted commitments arising from the *Reich*'s foreign treaties and debts. Succession to the *Reich* tradition is exercised *de facto* in the territory of the Federal Republic, though *de jure* it has been claimed to extend over all German 1937 territory not within the republic. Originally this stand was matched by a view that rejected the existence of the German Democratic Republic, when the Hallstein Doctrine would accept no diplomatic relations with countries recognizing that state. Under the influence of Brandt in the late 1960s, a more conciliatory attitude to the G.D.R. recognized that another state did exist in 'the other part of Germany'. In 1972 a Fundamental Treaty was signed to regulate relations between them, though neither made any major concessions on vital issues such as nationality and nationhood.

The Federal Republic, stemming from its continuity claim, offers its German nationality to all Germans within the 1937 *Reich* territory, besides those of German ethnic affinity forced into the postwar territory of Germany because of the Second World War and its aftermath. Most important is the consequence that people from the German Democratic Republic entering the Federal Republic are not treated as 'foreign' in any sense. The present nationality laws of the Federal Republic are based essentially on *Reich* laws of 1913, and the Basic Law of the republic made it impossible for any *Land* to institute its own nationality, as had been the intention of Bavaria at an early stage.

The 1949 Constitution of the G.D.R. originally described the new state as a 'socialist state of the German nation', while the East German view supported by Russian legal judgements believed in the dismemberment of the *Reich* and consequently no continuity. In the early stages, the attitude to nationality was similar to the West German state – that one German nationality remained – but after 1967 a less liberal concept of a separate G.D.R. nationality developed. The response of the Federal Republic was to respect this G.D.R. citizenship as a specific form of a single German nationality.

Like the Federal Republic, the G.D.R. also began by accepting the idea of a single German nation that would be ultimately reunited and the contention of 'two states – one nation' was later to be used as part of his *Ostpolitik* by Brandt. In the 1968 Constitution of the G.D.R. it was described as a 'socialist German national state', but later (1974) this was altered to 'a socialist state of workers and peasants'. Any implication that the G.D.R. still regards an all-German dimension as essential has become muted, possibly in fear of the initiative towards this end taken by the Federal Republic, though by the mid-1970s there were indications that a return to the earlier view was impending, perhaps the result of the development of relations since the treaty between the two states of 1972. Official sources have spoken of 'citizenship – G.D.R.; nationality – German' and Honecker, Secretary of the Central Committee of the Socialist Unity Party, has said, 'we represent the socialist Germany' and 'the socialist state of the German Democratic Republic is of German nationality' , while G.D.R. sources have claimed that the ethnic character of the Germans is slowly adapting and adjusting itself to the 'socialist way-of-life'.

It is under the impact of two contrasting political, social, and economic systems that the landscape of the German lands in the broadest sense is changing. In the Federal Republic we see a landscape whose spatial pattern is the result of change under free market conditions with only a modicum of planning and state intervention, while in the Democratic Republic change has been the result of an all-embracing planning and direction, though even here the priorities and the approach have vacillated to leave unfinished patterns. The differences are most clearly seen in the urban setting and in the countryside, where the two systems have had perhaps their widest divergence in philosophy.

Suggested further reading

Erhard, L.: The Economics of Success, London, 1969.

Franke, E. (ed): Bericht der Bundesregierung und Materialien zur Lage der Nation 1971, *Bundesminister für Innerdeutsche Beziehungen*, Bonn, 1971.

Grosser, A.: Germany in Our Time, London, 1971.

Hallett, G.: The Social Economy of West Germany, London, 1973.

Heidenheimer, A. I.: The Government of Germany, New York, 1975.

Johnson, N.: Government in the Federal Republic of Germany, London, 1973.

Leonhardt, R. W.: This Germany – the story since the Third Reich, London, 1964.

Leptin, G.: Die deutsche Wirtschaft nach 1945 – ein Ost-West Vergleich, Opladen, 1970.

Ludz, P., et al.: DDR-Handbuch, *Bundesminister für Innerdeutsche Beziehungen*, Bonn, 1975.

Mitzscherling, P., et al.: DDR-Wirtschaft - eine Bestandsaufnahme, *Deutsches Inst. f. Wirtschaftsforschung*, Berlin, 1971.

Mohs, G.: Gesellschaft und Territorium im Sozialismus, *Geog. Berichte* 17, 1972, pp.166–173.

Payne, J. P. (ed.): Germany Today, London, 1971.

Schnitzer, M.: East and West Germany: A Comparative Economic Analysis, London, 1973.

Walton, H.: Germany, *Peoples and Places*, London, 1969.

CHAPTER 8

THE GERMAN FEDERAL REPUBLIC TERRITORY AND POPULATION

The German Federal Republic is the most populous state in Europe outside the Soviet Union, though not the largest in area (France). The richest European nation and usually ranked as third richest in the world, it has formed an amazing European success story, while in population, area, and wealth it overshadows the German Democratic Republic. Although there have been many modifications and realignments in its organization of space, the main features of economic and population geography which emerged in the hectic period before 1914 still remain significant. Federal policy has sought to prevent too great a separation from 'the other part of Germany', notably through generous aid to problem areas along the new international frontier, but, nevertheless, the contemporary geographical patterns of the Federal Republic show a clear alignment and attachment to the European Community, which itself has developed strongly Rhenish tendencies. Despite its apparent and real affluence, there are many problems to be solved as the age of coal and iron recedes, for the future natural resource base of the country is unpromising (Chapter 1) and the acute dependence on imported raw materials paid for in export markets makes the Federal Republic vulnerable to world changes. The republic suffers in its spatial organization from the 'particularism of federation' which arises not only from the differences in society between north and south, but also through variation in wealth and resources between the federal *Länder* vested with considerable autonomy (Chapter 7). Fortunately, despite considerable regional change in the balance of population over the twenty-five years of its existence, the foresight shown in the weightings of *Länder* representation according to population in the government upper chamber, the *Bundesrat,* has allowed these changes to take place so far without any redistribution of seats. In the *Bundesrat,* each *Land* has at least three votes; those with more than 2 million people, four votes; those with more than 6 million people, five votes. Nevertheless, it looks as though both Hessen and Baden-Württemberg will in the not so distant future warrant greater representation. At the same time, with a maximum allowance of votes, both Bavaria and North Rhine-Westphalia have populations well above that of the smallest state entitled by its population to the same number of votes. On the other hand, to have singled out these two large *Länder* for additional representation would have vested them with too great an influence in the federation, of which they are anyway frequently accused. On the other hand, the smallest states have not the voting power to defend themselves against a coalition of any two of the larger states. There is nevertheless a resultant regional lobby in the *Bundesrat* with a North German predominance, unless Hessen, the Rhineland-Palatinate, and the Saar side with the South German states. The split of Berlin into two administrations by the time the Federal Republic had been formed posed a special problem of West Berlin as a likely candidate for inclusion in the federation and it is in fact listed – as Greater Berlin – in the federal members in the Federal Basic Law. In 1950 the West Berlin administration produced its own constitution that defined it as a German *Land* and City within the Federal Republic and specified that the Basic Law was also valid in its territory; but because of Western Allied reservations concerning their position in the still valid if moribund four-power statutes, full incorporation of West Berlin into the Federal Republic was deferred, as explained in Chapter 7. Nevertheless, the Western powers recognized (1949) that the economic well-being of West Berlin is the responsibility of the Federal Republic, while in 1952 they allowed it full integration into the West German financial system.

The situation in Berlin clearly made it unsuitable for the capital of the new Federal Republic. On the other hand, the new state did not want to give an impression that it had ceased to recognize Berlin as the German capital. Consequently, a provisional capital had to be chosen, but, even if correctly located, a number of big cities were too heavily damaged to be considered, among them Düsseldorf and Köln, while others, even if they had not been damaged, were unsuitably located in the extremities of the country, like Hamburg and München. Some were too near the new border with the Soviet Zone, notably Hannover and Braunschweig, though Kassel was at one stage considered. Karlsruhe could have well served by its location and by its nature, but Frankfurt am Main, while well-situated, had become so closely identified with the American authorities that it might have been thought a capital of a puppet

Figure 8.1 *Länder* of the Federal Republic

state. It was the strong personal influence of Adenauer, so many observers feel, that led to Bonn, an insignificant university town, being selected, though it was conveniently located for all three zones, had strong traditions of Rhenish liberalism and lay on the border between 'North' and 'South' Germany. It was also obviously provisional, with some government offices initially housed in old museums and university buildings, and even now it must rank as the most uncapitallike capital in Europe.

The *Länder* had been created without reference to their inhabitants by the Western Allies in 1945–1946, and the Basic Law in Article 29, recognizing that these territories might not be in accordance with the wishes of the people, allowed for plebiscites to make changes. An investigating commission in the early 1950s looked at the problems of reorganization, but unfortunately its deliberations came too late and there were grave inhibitions about change without at the same time German reunification: even by the early 1950s normalization of life and the roots of the new *Länder* administrations had gone sufficiently far to make change difficult even if desirable. The commission rejected the formation of any new Northwest State, say, a union between Hamburg and Schleswig-Holstein. The border between Lower Saxony and North Rhine-Westphalia, particularly the question of the Osnabrück area and East Westphalia, one of the most hotly debated problems of the commission, should remain unchanged, unless other changes were made. These might be the dissolution of the *Land* Rhineland-Palatinate and the incorporation of the Trier and Koblenz districts into North Rhine-Westphalia, which might then become unreasonably large, so that it would require to be either divided up or reduced in area to preserve the balance among the other *Länder*. In the Sieg-Lahn-Dill area, the commission proposed a change in borders only if the Rhineland-Palatinate were to be dissolved: if this were to happen, then the

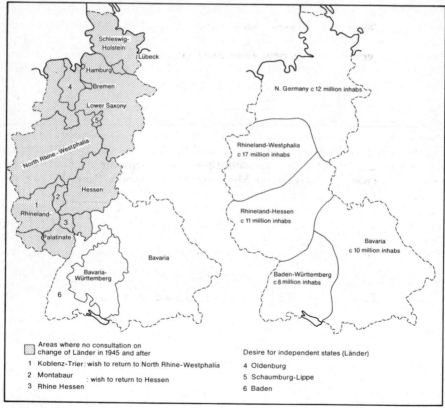

Figure 8.2 Territorial-administrative reform – some proposals

The Two Germanies

border should be altered in the Westerwald between North Rhine-Westphalia and Hessen to take account of the regional relationships of Limburg/Lahn. A small point was a regulation of the Württemberg-Bavarian boundary to prevent the separation of Ulm from Bavarian Neu-Ulm, while several local problems at Hannoversch-Münden, the Waldecker Upland, Aschaffenburg, Tauberbischofsheim, Lindau, and Wimpfen were recommended for no change. A major regional concept of *Mittelwestdeutschland* needed clearer definition by territorial-administrative reorganization: one such change might be an extended Rhineland-Palatinate, with perhaps the addition of the right bank areas around Mainz and Worms, the Rheingaukreis and even north Baden around Mannheim; alternatively, the Palatinate might return to Bavaria (as before 1945), while Rhine Hessen and the Montabaur district would go to Hessen and the Koblenz-Trier area to North Rhine-Westphalia (of which other variations were also proposed). The suggestion for a *Land Mittelwestdeutschland* was also made, either as an amalgamation of the Rhineland-Palatinate, Hessen, and North Baden, with or without the transference of the Trier and Koblenz districts to North Rhine-Westphalia. Another suggestion was a new *Land Pfalz* (Palatinate) by a union of the Rhenish Palatinate and North Baden, with transference of Trier and Koblenz to North Rhine-Westphalia and Montabaur to Hessen.

Because of uncertainty and possible upset, opposition to change was strong, while most of the federal *Länder* wished any reforms to be postponed until reunification of Germany. Five referenda did, however, take place with the requisite level of participation – these showed the desire for the reinstitution of the former Oldenburg and Schaumburg-Lippe as separate administrative *Länder*; there was also a wish in the Montabaur district and in Rhine Hessen to return to *Land* Hessen; while Trier and Koblenz sought their former place in the Rhine Province by voting for union with *Land* North Rhine-Westphalia; but insufficient votes were received in the Palatinate for union with either Bavaria or Baden-Württemberg. In 1951 the *Länder* Baden, Württemberg-Baden and Württemberg-Hohenzollern (so arranged for the convenience of defining the French Zone) were merged, however, into the *Southwest State*, shortly afterwards renamed Baden-Württemberg, though pressure for the recreation of a separate *Land* Baden has remained vociferous.

In 1973 the issue reopened and an expert commission recommended creation of five or six approximately equally sized *Länder* and drew up several possible variants. In 1975 voters in the Rhineland-Palatinate rejected any change, but in Lower Saxony voters sought independent status for two historic territories, and the problem of satisfactory solution now awaits a decision. The longer delay is allowed, the more difficult any voluntary or acceptable change in boundaries will become, especially as procedure for change is so complex.

The German Federal Republic: Territory and Population

In the early 1950s, as conditions in Germany began to catch up with and over-take living standards in France, a growing feeling in the Saar manifested itself for reunion with Germany, especially as the Federal Republic demonstrated a new sense of German unity. Attempts at first were unsuccessful through an unsympathetic French policy, though the *rapprochement* between Adenauer and de Gaulle encouraged a more liberal French approach. In 1955 the Saar people rejected by a two-thirds majority a European Statute for the Saarland. A rapid change in the political scene allowed an agreement in 1956 between France and Germany which brought the Saarland (in its extended boundaries) back into the Federal Republic on 1 January, 1957. France's interests were safeguarded by a transition period until 1959 to allow for the adjustment of economic interests and by the right to mine 66 million tons of coal in Germany, as well as to benefit from an agreement between itself, Germany, and Luxemburg to canalize the Mosel.

Population in the Federal Republic

The German Federal Republic is the largest state in population outside the Soviet Union (if that be counted as Europe) and, at the census of 1970, the tenth largest country in the world. Its constituent *Länder* are also in some instances equivalent in size to the medium and smaller nation states; for example, North Rhine-Westphalia with its 17 million people is as large as the German Democratic Republic and considerably larger than the Netherlands. Although not as densely peopled as the Low Countries, the overall density of population by the early 1970s exceeded the United Kingdom and lay well above France. The republic is also among the most highly urbanized countries of the world, though it is fortunately not dominated by one or two major cities far in excess of the rest.

The population of the republic since 1950 has shown a growth in absolute numbers at the upper end of the spectrum for Western Europe: population increased by over 11 million, compared to a little over 6 million in the United Kingdom. The immigration of Germans from the Soviet sphere of influence was an important element in growth until 1961, while substantial natural increase characterized population growth into the sixties until the 'pill' began to be commonly used as a contraceptive. In the late 1960s, the inflow of foreign workers (*Gastarbeiter*) also helped to maintain overall growth as natural increase fell. An important factor in growth was the relatively youthful character of the immigration from the German Democratic Republic and later from areas supplying the guest workers.

The strongest and most dramatic changes in population of the Federal Republic have been more than merely the 25 percent increase in population numbers since 1950: they have represented social and economic adjustments required by the new spatial organization of West Germany. The greater part of the inflow of expellees had already taken place, though the flow remained nevertheless quite formidable if declining – between 1949 and 1950 their number had risen by over 300,000, whereas between 1952 and 1953 they increased by little more than 130,000. There was also a powerful flow of

Table 8.1
Population of the *Länder* of the German Federal Republic

Land	Area Km²	Population (in thousands)				
		1939	1950	1961	1970	1975
Schleswig–Holstein	15,675.8	1,589.0	2,594.6	2,317.4	2,494.1	2,583.9
Hamburg	753.2	1,711.9	1,605.7	1,832.4	1,793.8	1,725.9
Lower Saxony	47,407.6	4,539.7	6,797.3	6.640.7	7,082.2	7,251.8
Bremen	403.8	562.9	558.6	706.4	722.7	721.1
North Rhine–Westphalia	34,044.1	11,945.1	13,207.0	15,911.8	16,914.1	17,177.4
Hessen	21,110.7	3,479.1	4,323.8	4,814.4	5,381.7	5,563.5
Rhineland–Palatinate	19,837.7	2,960.0	3,004.8	3,417.1	3,645.4	3,677.5
Baden–Württemberg	35,749.6	5,476.4	6,430.2	7,759.1	8,895.0	9,197.0
Bavaria	70,546.9	7,084.1	9,184.5	9,515.5	10,479.4	10,830.0
Saarland	2,567.5	909.6	955.4	1,072.6	1,119.7	1,100.2
Berlin (West)	480.1	2,750.5	2,147.0	2,197.4	2,122.3	2,004.0
Federal Republic	248,576.9	43,008.3	50.808.9	56,184.9	60,650.6	61,832.2

Source: Statistisches Jahrbuch der BRD, 1976, Wiesbaden.

refugees from the G.D.R. and, though the number of arrivals varied from year to year according to events in the other republic, it hit peaks of almost 200,000 in 1950, over 300,000 in 1953, and was around the 200,000 mark in the years following up to 1961. Thereafter the erection of the 'wall' and more rigid control reduced the flow to between 20,000 and 40,000 annually. By 1965 there were over 14 million refugees and expellees in the Federal Republic (over 22 percent of the total population), but because of people who did not register on entry, the real figure was probably 10–12 percent higher. The figure includes children born to parents after flight.

Immigration from beyond the boundaries of the Federal Republic generated the need to integrate the newcomers, while at the same time the rebuilding of the towns brought people back from temporary homes in the country. The consequence of these two processes and the spatial reorganization of the economy was a high level of internal migration, which continued into the 1960s. The steady rise in the demand for labour had been satisfied by the inflow of high quality workers from the German Democratic Republic, but when this supply was cut (1961), a serious potential situation developed whose solution was to encourage an inflow of labour from elsewhere in Europe, from which has come the problem of the 'guest worker'. Labour shortage also accelerated migration from the less prosperous rural areas into industrial districts.

The demographic situation

The population pyramid shows the ineradicable imprint of historical events on the age and sex structure. By the census of 1950 the return of most prisoners of war and the inflow of German groups from East Central Europe had corrected something of the drastic imbalance between the sexes in the military age groups shown by the census of 1946. Even by 1950 there was evidence of a return to more normal peacetime conditions in the fall of the death rate and a higher infant survival rate, whereas the encouragement of improving living conditions to people to have families was reflected in a slow recovery in the general index of fertility during the 1950s. But considerable fluctuations in the birth and death rate nevertheless took place. The increased number of births in the early 1950s is seen as partly the effect of children born to parents who had delayed having them because of war and its aftermath. It is also suggested that a tendency to earlier marriage in the latter 1950s was reflected in a rising birth rate; but also significant was the factor of large classes of 20–30 year olds, the product of the 'baby boom' of the mid-1930s. The sudden collapse of the birth rate in the late 1960s, while undoubtedly affected by changing social patterns (and the effect of birth control pills), has been partly the result of the sudden shrinkage of the 20–30-year-old groups, reflecting the lean years of the 1940s. The tendency for the death rate to rise in the late 1960s is not only the effect of recurrent influenza epidemics, but also the effect of the large classes born around the turn of the century having reached the threshold of 'three score years and ten', particularly on the female side, since the male side had been winnowed by the First World War. In the early 1970s, the slight natural decline in population, occasioned by a falling birth rate rather than a rising death rate, gave rise to some alarm, though thought to be a transient feature, again occasioned by disparity between the size of groups reaching critical economic and demographic thresholds. Whatever underlying causes these fluctuations have, the difficulties for manpower planning, whether in employment, education, or provision of social services, place a strain on German resources. An aspect that has created particular alarm is that the 4 percent of the population which is foreign-born has been the major contributor to the natural increase in population. Population decline in several large towns has clearly been moderated only through the high rate of immigration and natural increase among the guest workers. Almost 90 percent of the foreign born population is under 45 years old, whereas only 60 percent of the German population is under this age. Half the foreign-born population is in fact between

25–45 years old, whereas only a quarter of the German population falls into this group.

Though the birth rate has fallen throughout the republic, the greatest decline has been in areas where the birth rate has generally been highest – in the Emsland, in the western Eifel, the Sauerland, parts of Baden-Württemberg, and Bavaria, as well as the rural Saarland. Strongly urbanized areas like the Ruhr and the Saar, which had traditionally low birth rates, have shown less critical falls, resulting not only from the effect of smaller families and changes in the age structure of the population, but also from economic change such as pit closures and recession. In most cities the birth rate lies well below the death rate, especially in the largest towns, but this characteristic may also be found even in towns in rural areas (notably Celle, Straubing, Deggendorf, Landshut, Eichstätt, and Rothenburg ob der Tauber). The real cause of the large decline in the birth rate in rural areas does not seem to be fully understood.

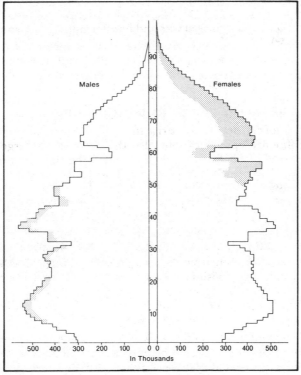

Figure 8.3 Age and sex structure – 1975

The German Federal Republic: Territory and Population

An important social change has been the reduction of the serious imbalance between the sexes that exceeded 120 women to 100 men in 1946. By 1950 this had fallen to 115 women per 100 men, and to 112 women per 100 men in the 1961 census. By 1974 it stood at 109 per 100 men, still above the 1939 level, which for the *Reich* had been 104 women per 100 men. Below 45 years of age, women form slightly less than half the population; but above this age (notably in the age groups around 50) the male cohorts most heavily decimated by the Second World War result in a serious imbalance between sexes. The problem of large numbers of single women remains a special social and economic question in Federal Germany. It is worth note that the ratio of male to female live births reached a peak of 1080 immediately postwar, but this ratio has now fallen to around 1050, characteristic of the greater part of the nineteenth century.

The prognosis of population development to the end of the century suggests that the distortions of the age-sex structure in the first half of the twentieth century will not be worked out until the early part of next century and that the general ageing will continue well into the 1980s, with a significant fall in the older classes thereafter, but with no major percentage increase in the classes below 15 years of age. On the basis of experience at the end of the 1960s, it is considered the population around AD 1990–2000 will be 64–66 million, but recent trends may result in an ultimately lower population.

Migration as a factor in population change

The federal government had to overcome the serious economic and social problems arising from the heavy burden of expellees in areas where expectancy of effective economic integration was poor. Various proposals for equalizing the burden between the *Länder* were discussed, but it was usually agreed that the best solution lay in resettlement which, based on a living standard similar to 1938–1939, required the movement of 2.29 million people, of which it was decided 600,000 would be expellees and refugees. These were to come from Schleswig-Holstein, Lower Saxony, and Bavaria, with the accepting areas being notably the *Länder* of the French Zone, North Rhine-Westphalia, and parts of the American Zone (Figure 8.4). Trends in the economy and changing patterns in living standards brought an upward revision in numbers, and between 1949 and 1965 the target of 1.03 million expellees resettled was achieved. The pattern of movement reflects the strong orientation towards the Rhine valley from the eastern areas along the border with the G.D.R.

By 1950, with the rebuilding of the bombed towns and industry reviving in the stimulus of the Korean crisis, a strong current back to the towns developed as accommodation became available, while many newcomers in overcrowded northern rural areas sought employment in the Rhine and Ruhr areas, which

The Two Germanies

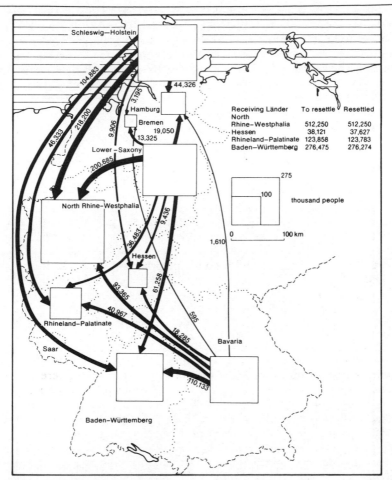

Figure 8.4 Expellee resettlement

became a focus as well for refugees arriving from the G.D.R. Within ten years, the effect of growing integration among the West European states was also making the Rhine valley increasingly attractive to industrial development, which in its turn attracted labour, and the structural crisis of the mid-1950s in the coal mining industry did little to affect the overall attractiveness, especially as new consumer-oriented industries grew in the middle and upper reaches and in the Neckar basin.

The German Federal Republic: Territory and Population

Figure 8.5 illustrates the pattern of change between 1950 and 1961 when the overall population of the republic had grown by 10 percent. Particularly striking is the decline in population in the eastern parts of the country, notably in eastern Lower Saxony and eastern Bavaria, but also in the far north, in Schleswig-Holstein. On the other hand, the Rhine basin showed a remarkable

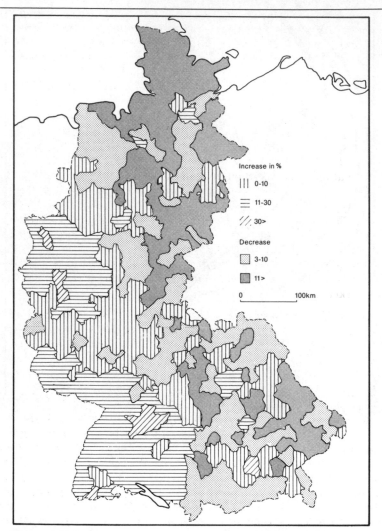

Figure 8.5 Population change 1950–1961

The Two Germanies

growth, though whatever the pattern of change, many districts on the east had populations still well above 1939, while in the west, others – despite growth – had not regained their 1939 levels. The revival of industry is, however, reflected in the islands of growth around the main towns even in the eastern parts of the country, while in the Rhine valley and the Neckar basin the towns themselves were among the areas to show the greatest growth. The economic growth points were well reflected in the pattern, like the rapid population increase in Wolfsburg, the main *Volkswagen* plant. The greater rewards of urban-industrial employment compared to farming also generated a drift from the land, so that decline in rural areas contained not only the movement away of the recent incomers, but also of local country folk. Even within some of the main population belts, low increase or even decrease marked rural areas where a shift from farming to industrial employment was beginning to take place, demonstrated in the Eifel and in parts of the Westerwald. After the mid-1950s, the growth of the larger towns began to slacken, with some, like the Ruhr coalfield towns, affected especially badly by the crises in the older sectors of industry. This trend became stronger in the 1960s, and the census of 1970 showed that many towns (though again notably in the older industrial areas) had begun to lose population, chiefly through a move away from residence in their central parts (Figure 8.6). The loss of the large towns was, however, the gain of the small and medium-sized towns and the countryside around them. If foreign population is discounted, the loss of population in many large towns is even more striking than global figures suggest, because the 'guest workers' have tended to congregate for cheap rents in poor quality older property and, in towns as different as Gelsenkirchen and Wetzlar, it is possible to define guest worker 'ghettoes'.

Until about 1967 the basic census unit, the *Gemeinde*, had remained fairly constant in number at about 24,300 – by 1973 this had fallen to 15,000 and by 1975 to 10,897. The gain in number, population, and area has been least in the largest *Gemeinden* (i.e., over 100,000 inhabitants), but greatest in those between 10,000–50,000 inhabitants (small to medium-sized towns). The most striking decline has come in *Gemeinden* with less than 2000 people, which by long-standing definition have been considered to be rural (*ländlich*). The favour shown to larger units has been backed by the desire to provide the requisite infrastructure considered necessary for modern life and most *Länder* plans foresee no communities (except in exceptional circumstances) below about 5000 inhabitants, though clearly the vigorous growth in the 'suburban' communities of this size and upwards adds further force to the plans. This trend must also be seen in relation to the *Verdichtungsräume* around the major towns, which now claim almost a half of the federal population on roughly 7 percent of the national area, for the greatest rate of population increase came between 1950 and 1970 in a belt up to 25 kilometres around major city centres, though the peak values occurred around 15 kilometres from such centres.

The regional pattern of change revealed by the census of 1970 showed several important contrasts to the period 1950–1961 when disparities and imbalances created by war were being adjusted to peacetime conditions. The most striking feature of the 1950–1961 period had been the contrast between the western,

Table 8.2
Population distribution by *Gemeinden* in the Federal Republic, 1950–1975

Size of *Gemeinde* by population	Percentage of total population resident			
	1950	1961	1970	1975
under 500	5.8	5.5	4.7	1.4
500–2,000	21.7	16.7	14.9	6.8
2,000–5,000	13.1	12.0	12.0	8.7
5,000–10,000	8.7	9.0	10.0	10.5
10,000–20,000	6.9	7.2	9.3	13.1
20,000–50,000	8.7	9.8	10.6	15.0
50,000–100,000	5.3	6.4	6.4	9.1
over 100,000	29.9	33.5	32.2	35.5
	100.0	100.0	100.0	100.0

Source: Statistisches Jarbuch der BRD, various years

Rhenish areas of substantial growth (notably in big towns) and the broad eastern belt of population decline. The period 1961–1970 showed that this clear gradient had been replaced by a general increase with a few patches of decline, though notably these were again mostly along the border with the G.D.R., where, for example, sheer inaccessability of a poor rural area brought marked decline in the *Kreis* Lüchow-Dannenberg, while in northeast Bavaria the declining fortunes of the textile industry around Hof and Naila were important in population loss. Elsewhere in the republic, rural areas of decline or near stagnation reflected the increasing drift from the land, especially where it was too far to commute to industrial employment or where local conditions precluded introduction of new employment possibilities as, for example, in the Eifel, northern Hessen, parts of middle Franconia, or the poor *geest* country of Lower Saxony and the lower Elbe.

Between 1961 and 1970, numerous towns had either virtually stagnated or even actually declined, particularly in the Ruhr coalfield. Where there had been building land within the town boundaries and either diversified industry or an important tertiary sector, the decline had been less than in towns whose area was already extensively built up or which depended heavily on coal mining or iron and steel making. The decline of coal mining had hit the small towns of the Saar coalfield heavily, while *Landkreise* where many miners lived had shown only modest growth. Though most other large towns – including Hamburg, Hannover, Düsseldorf, Frankfurt am Main, and Stuttgart – had shown a decline, the continuing strength of their economy was reflected in the considerable growth in the surrounding towns and rural districts, and even towns like Bremen, Köln, München, Bonn, Aachen, or Nürnberg that had shown some increase were also surrounded by a similar 'halo' of growth. Nevertheless, of 85 towns with over 60,000 people, 35 had lost population, while few towns with populations below this threshold demonstrated growth above the federal average.

The east-west gradient of population change, less marked than in the 1950s, is still recognizable between areas of decline along the eastern border and the growth prevailing along the Rhine axis, whose attractiveness remains, strengthened in parts through consolidation in the economic patterns of the European Community. The newest feature to emerge in the 1960s (and strengthened in the early 1970s) is the rising proportion of population growth absorbed by South Germany, represented by the *Länder* Baden-Württemberg and Bavaria: whereas South Germany (Table 8.3) had taken just over 30 percent in 1950–1961, its share had increased to 46 percent in 1961–1970 (in both periods Baden-Württemberg had accounted for around 24 percent). Between 1950 and 1961, almost half the total increase had been in North Germany (overwhelmingly in North Rhine-Westphalia), whereas between 1961 and 1970 only 35 percent had been in North Germany (North Rhine-Westphalia had contributed only 22 percent). An important factor in growth in South Germany has been immigration of foreign labour, notably into Baden-Württemberg, though this is also a significant factor in the Rhine-Main area, around München, and to a lesser degree in the Rhenish-Westphalian industrial districts. Bavaria and Baden-Württemberg contain 40 percent of the total foreign workers, while almost 30 percent are in North Rhine-Westphalia.

Before 1939 foreign labour in West Germany had been mostly from adjacent countries, notably the Low Countries, while Polish farm workers had been common in East Germany. Some 50,000 daily workers from across the West German frontiers are still employed. Lack of job opportunities in southern European countries in the early 1960s encouraged movement to West Germany which began to make immigration easier, with agreements signed with several southern European countries, and some specialized agreements (e.g., for miners) with more distant countries, but the inflow has varied according to West German economic conditions. In the early 1960s most workers came from Italy and other Economic Community countries or from Spain, but by the early 1970s Jugoslavs and Turks were the most numerous, and there has been a growing tendency to bring in dependants. While the total foreign pop-

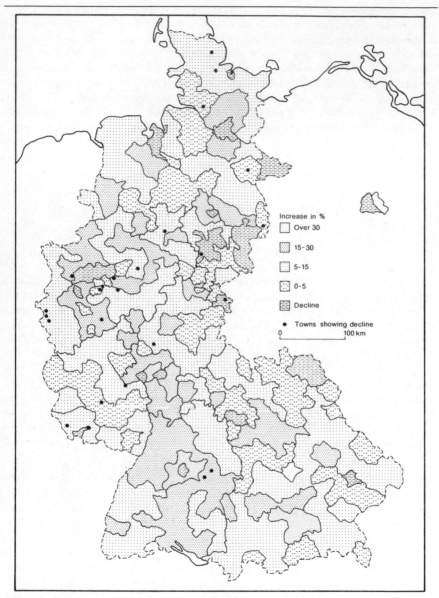

Figure 8.6 Population change 1961–1970

The Two Germanies

ulation is 4.09 million (1975), registered foreign workers number 2.07 million (over 10 percent of the labour force), somewhat below the maximum of 2.59 million in 1973.

Table 8.3
Population change in the German Federal Republic 1950–1961, 1961–1970

Land	Percentage change	
	1950–1961	1961–1970
North		
Schleswig–Holstein	−10.7	+ 7.6
Hamburg	+14.1	− 2.1
Bremen	+26.3	+ 2.1
Lower Saxony	− 2.3	+ 6.6
North Rhine–Westphalia	+20.5	+ 6.3
Centre		
Rhineland–Palatinate	+13.7	+ 6.7
Hessen	+11.3	+11.8
Saar	+12.3	+ 4.4
South		
Baden-Württemberg	+20.7	+14.6
Bavaria	+ 3.6	+10.1
West Berlin	+ 2.3	− 3.4

Of the total population change in the intercensal periods, the distribution between the North, Centre, and South was as follows:

North	49.96	35.14
Centre	19.27	18.53
South	30.77	46.33
	100.00%	100.00%

Source: Federal Statistical Office publications.

Although some foreigners (mostly from North America and other West European countries) occupy managerial, professional, and academic positions, the 'guest workers' are overwhelmingly employed in the lower paid and least attractive jobs: tedious work as in motor vehicle assembly (accounting for the striking concentration in Wolfsburg, the highest percentage of foreigners in North Germany); dangerous work (e.g., in asbestos works, coal mining); or in traditionally poorly paid jobs like hotel work. The guest workers have congregated rapidly wherever employment opportunities have been greatest, grouping themselves in colonies of fellow-countrymen, not only in towns but also in some parts occupying villages from which most German population has drifted away. In towns, the inflow of guest workers has been commonly offset by an outflow of Germans. Though mobile and transient, some guest workers learn German and gain trade qualifications, seeking to raise themselves in the economic and social scale, but the frustrations of their attempts to integrate themselves and move out of the 'ghettoes' raise difficult social problems.

Some regional patterns of guest workers have emerged (Figure 8.7), with them concentrated markedly in North Rhine-Westphalia and in Baden-Württemberg, each of which has over half a million, together over half the total in the country; another quarter of a million are found in each of Hessen and southern Bavaria. Within these *Länder* it has been the industrialized districts which have attracted most immigrants. In Baden-Württemberg they comprise over 16 percent of the total labour force (in some districts exceeding 20 percent), whereas in North Rhine-Westphalia, Hessen, and southern Bavaria they exceed the 10 percent national average in the labour force. In contrast, North Germany has in general only 5–7 percent of its labour force comprised of guest workers. Perhaps expectedly, the largest single concentrations are in the big cities and industrial towns, particularly where there are industries known for poor pay and working conditions shunned by German workers. Geographically the guest worker has been spreading, and groups gradually appear increasingly away from the main industrial concentrations and the original spread along the Rhine axis. The different nationalities also show regional patterns: Jugoslavs and Italians are particularly common as the dominant group in Baden-Württemberg; Italians are also significant in the Saarland, the Rhine-Main area, and in North Rhine-Westphalia outside the Ruhr; while Turks, everywhere common, are particularly important in the Ruhr (especially in coal mining and steel towns) and in southern Bavaria, but also in North Germany (heavy industry and assembly plants in Lower Saxony). Greeks are mostly in Franconia and in North Rhine-Westphalia. The pattern is influenced by gregarious national grouping, by local plants' preference for particular national groups (Turks in the Ford works at Köln), but some nationalities also seem to prefer certain occupations – Greeks and Spaniards in agriculture, forestry, or transport; Turks notably in mining and heavy industry but also assembly industries and textiles; and Jugoslavs in particular association with the building trades.

Population distribution in the Federal Republic

Population distribution in the German Federal Republic is marked by a range of density for *Kreise* (1970) from 41.9 persons/km² to 4653 persons/km², but it continues to be dominated by the two major belts with densities in excess of 100 persons/km² (prewar, 80 persons/km²). In any one district, such densities arise from a combination in various proportions between attractiveness to farming, suitability for industry (including occurrence of mineral resources), or nodal attractions on major routeways. The main west-east belt, part of a

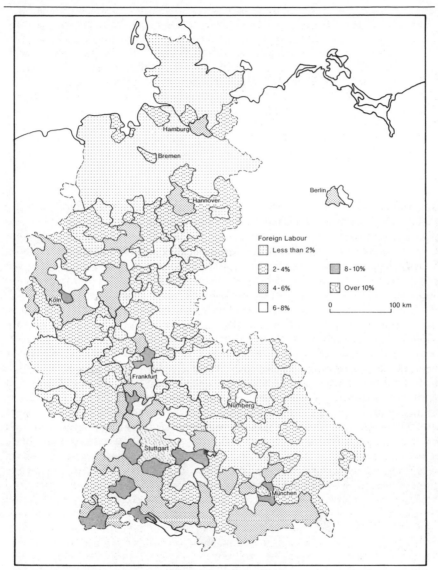

Figure 8.7 Foreign labour in the Federal Republic

The German Federal Republic: Territory and Population

broader feature of the population distribution of Western and Central Europe, extends from the Rhine-Maas-Scheldt estuaries across the northern edge and foreland of the Central Uplands, whereas the north-south belt also forms part of a broader European feature along the Rhine and into the Swiss Mittelland, with the merging of these two belts forming the important population agglomeration of the Rhenish-Westphalian and Lower Rhine industrial areas. Beyond these belts significant clusters of population also occur, both in North and South Germany, with densities considerably in excess of prewar. Of the ten main urban-cored clusters of population, four – Rhine-Ruhr, Hannover, Rhine-Main, and Rhine-Neckar – occur directly within the belts and two – the Saar and Stuttgart – lie in the periphery of the main north-south belt along the Rhine axis. The remaining four form significant clusters outside the main belts.

The industrial towns and surrounding spread of suburban settlement of the Rhenish-Westphalian coalfield, where densities are generally well above 300 persons/km^2, contains over 10 million people, five times greater than the next largest agglomeration. The core consists of large industrial towns, notably Essen (680,800), Dortmund (634,100) and Bochum (415,600), while the scattered communities formed into city districts (*Stadtkreise*) on the north are somewhat smaller – e.g., Recklinghausen (122,900) and Bottrop (198,400), but with 325,400 inhabitants, Gelsenkirchen is an exception, and there is also 'new town' development as in Marl (91,900). To north and south, densities are appreciably lower, and in the rural central Münsterland of scattered farm-steads and small towns, densities fall to under 150 persons/km^2, especially around Coesfeld and Warendorf. To the south of the Ruhr, numerous small industrial towns tend to keep densities high (around 200–300 persons/km^2). Eastwards, another area with densities substantially over 200 persons/km^2 is found around Bielefeld and Minden, where villages and small industrial towns are set in an agriculturally rewarding countryside: on the west, this belt extends towards industrial Osnabrück and the small Ibbenbüren coalfield. The belt continues eastwards through southern Lower Saxony, where densities well over 150 persons/km^2 are found on the better loessic soils, while mineral wealth – brown coal, formerly hard coal in a few small locations, and until recently iron ore – attracted industrial growth. It is a countryside of small industrial towns, large villages, and a few major urban centres, of which Hannover (557,000) is the core of an agglomeration of over 0.75 million people. Other important towns include Braunschweig (269,900), close to the border with the G.D.R., Hildesheim (106,000), and Salzgitter (119,000). To the south, this belt of higher density extends into the northern end of the Hessian Corridor around Kassel (207,800). The southeastern part of the belt lies along the border with the G.D.R. around the flanks of the Harz, where in the forested uplands densities drop below 80 persons/km^2.

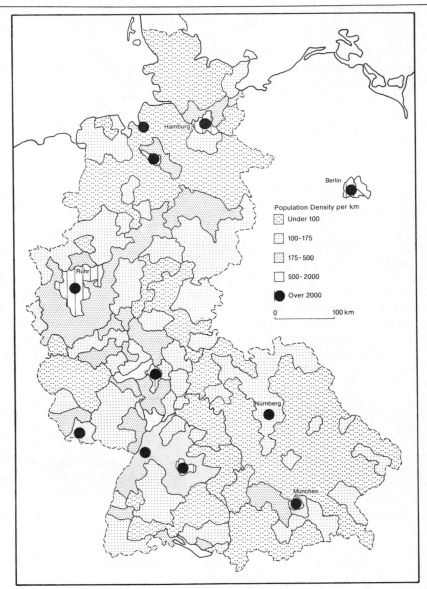

Figure 8.8 Distribution of population by density, 1970

The German Federal Republic: Territory and Population

204

The north-south belt reflects the economic and circulatory importance of the Rhine. On the north, it includes the western end of the Rhenish-Westphalian industrial area and the towns of the Lower Rhine around Krefeld and Mönchen-Gladbach (262,300), set in countryside of suburban development and industrial spread, as for example around Kamp-Lintfort (38,700) and Moers (101,700). Densities of well over 300 persons/km² extend westwards towards Aachen (241,900) and the Dutch frontier, with patches of country, especially near the Rhine where density rises to over 400 persons/km². The Rhine has become a focus of new industrial developments and is lined by important towns, from Duisburg (596,800) south to Düsseldorf (670,900) and Köln (1,017,200) whose boundaries have recently incorporated formerly independent communities. At the mouth of the Rhine gorge stands the Federal capital, Bonn, now a community of 284,000 after boundary extensions in the late 1960s. East of the river, densities are generally higher than on the west bank, particularly in the well-settled hilly country of Berg and Mark, where a group of towns lies around Wuppertal, forming together a cluster of around 0.75 million people, and another area with many small industrial towns and a dense rural settlement occurs in the Sieg valley.

On either side of the Rhine gorge, densities are reduced by large areas of forested upland, though many small towns and villages strung along the gorge floor and in the fertile basin around Neuwied and Koblenz locally raise densities to well above 300 persons/km². The uplands along the east bank – notably the Westerwald – are comparatively well settled, with iron ore of past importance and ceramic clays of continuing significance. In the poorer Eifel on the west, densities fall below 80 persons/km², notably towards the Belgian and Luxemburg borders.

One of the fastest growing areas has been the Rhine-Main agglomeration centred on Frankfurt am Main (645,600), but it also includes several other successful towns like Mainz (183,500) or the smaller Rüsselsheim (60,400) and is one of the most marked areas where the distinction between town and country is becoming blurred. The population agglomeration, numbering well over 2 million people, owes its importance in part to its commanding position at the junction between the Rhine corridor and that northwards towards Kassel, while from the west another routeway from the Saar and France comes along the Nahe depression. There is also well-settled countryside with rich farming, both to the north in the Wetterau and in the Rhine valley vine-growing areas around Mainz and the sunny south-facing slope of the Taunus (the Rheingau). Southwards, the main population belt becomes readily identifiable with the warm, fertile flat-floored Rift Valley, whose focus is the twin industrial towns of Mannheim-Ludwigshafen, together a population of almost 500,000. The many large villages (often with a strong commuting element of industrial workers) and vine-growing areas give rural densities of

The Two Germanies

around 300 persons/km², but again it is the east bank that has the higher densities and includes towns like Heidelberg (130,000) and the growing industrial district around Karlsruhe (281,700). In the more constricted valley towards Basel, despite some good fruit and vine country, densities tend to fall though remaining above 150 persons/km², and Freiburg (177,000) in the Breisgau is the main town. Densities on the German bank of the Rift are higher than on the French side and growth has come with completion of the motorway from Karlsruhe to Basel. Densities generally fall as the foothills of the Odenwald and Schwarzwald are reached, but the lower country of the Kraichgau is well settled. In the Neckar Basin, there are numerous small industrial towns, particularly grouped around Stuttgart (606,500) in an agglomeration with a combined population of over 2 million that has grown above the national average, especially through migration of both German and foreign workers.

The clusters of population outside the main belts are variable in character. Well over 2 million people live around the seaport of Hamburg (1,725,900 in the town itself) and suburban spread continues, though less markedly on the south bank of the Elbe. A million people comprise the smaller Bremen agglomeration (576,600 in Bremen itself), though population has declined downstream, notably in the poor west bank Wesermarsch district. The South German clusters are dominated by the agglomeration around the 'million city' of München (1,317,700), a focus of rapid growth of new consumer-oriented industries, in a cluster that forms the eastern end of a belt of better settled country, with density well above the general level of Upper Bavaria, that extends from Ulm and Augsburg on the west across the lower gravelly plateaus that form reasonable farming country. Standing amid well-settled country, despite not very promising conditions for farming, Nürnberg (503,900) is the centre of a cluster, including Fürth and Erlangen, of over 750,000 people in an increasingly suburbanized countryside marked by vigorous growth. Subsidiary clusters are the growing petroleum-refining centre of Ingolstadt and district and Franconian Würzburg, while a patch of countryside with densities of over 100 persons/km² lies right on the border with the G.D.R. in Upper Franconia, where several small textile towns comprise a critically depressed area showing a strong decline in population. In a southwestern corner of the Federal Republic, the Saar coalfield, a remarkable population cluster within a moderate to thinly settled upland area, is a landscape of small industrial towns separated by extensive workers' and miners' communities, farmland, and forest. Saarbrücken is the principal town (205,400) of an agglomeration of some 600,000 people, one of the slower growing areas where some towns have shown population decline.

Away from the main population belts and clusters, densities are well above prewar levels, though redistribution of the evacuees and expellees from overcrowded rural districts has tended to reduce the rate of growth and in some instances to contribute to actual decline from the early postwar years of grossly inflated populations. The Jutland peninsula in Schleswig-Holstein has a density in most *Kreise* of about 100–120 persons/km², with the lower densities towards the Danish frontier. In Lower Saxony rural population has been inflated by expellees and refugees, so that densities have been appreciably higher than before 1939. Densities are in places, however, comparatively low – e.g., *Kreis* Fallingbostel has only 68 persons/km², while in the poor country along the Dutch border and in Oldenburg there are under 80 persons/km² (*Kreis* Cloppenburg, 76 persons/km²), despite recent development from discoveries of natural gas and petroleum.

The higher and less hospitable parts of the Central Uplands stand out as the most sparsely settled parts of the republic, with a general tendency to population decline. In the Eifel, around Schleiden are only 78 persons/km², while the Prüm district has only 43 persons/km². Although the uplands of Berg and Mark, western Hessen and the Westerwald are well settled, there are in places sparsely settled areas, notably in the Rothaargebirge and Winterberg Plateau, the Kellerwald and the upper Eder valley. Were it not for the settlement in the valleys, densities would fall much below 80 persons/km². The hilly and forested country of eastern Bavaria along the Czech frontier is also sparsely settled by West German standards, with density seldom above 60 persons/km². Low densities also occur in the higher parts of the Suabian and Franconian Jura, but, on most population density maps based on the *Kreis* unit, these are concealed through the alignment of the administrative boundaries. Densities between 70 and 90 persons/km² are commonly found in much of rural Bavaria, even along the Alpine foot, where tourism has boosted the growth, but there are also large tracts of thinly peopled mountain country.

Suggested further reading

Dittrich, E.: Grundgedanken zu einem Bevölkerungsausgleich in der Bundesrepublik Deutschland, *Institut für Raumforschung*, Bonn, 1950.

Probleme der Umsiedlung in Westdeutschland, *Institut für Raumforschung*, Bonner Vorträge 2, Bonn, 1951.

Edding, F.: Die Flüchtlinge als Belastung und Antrieb der westdeutschen Wirtschaft, *Kieler Studien* 12, 1952.

Fürer, K. (ed.): Die Bundesrepublik Deutschland – Wirtschaftspartner der Welt, Oldenburg, 1968.

Inst. z. Förderung öffentlicher Angelegenheiten: Die Bundesländer: Beiträge zur Neugliederung der Bundesrepublik, *Wissenschaftliche Schriftenreihe* 9, Frankfurt, 1950.

Isenberg, G.: Die Ballungsgebiete in der Bundesrepublik, *Inst. für Raumforschung*, Vorträge 6, Bad Godesberg, 1957.

Riquet, P.: La Republique Fédérale Allemagne, Paris, 1970.

Sahner, W.: Aspekte der regionalen Differenzierung der Bevölkerungsentwicklung in der BRD von 1956–1961, *Informationen d. Inst. f. Raumforschung* 12, Bad Godesberg, 1962.

The Two Germanies

Salt, J., Clout, H. (eds.): Migration in Postwar Europe, Oxford, 1975.

Schöller, P. Neugliederung: Prinzipien und Probleme der politisch- geographischen Neuordnung, *Forsch. z. deut. Landeskunde* 150, 1965.

The Division of Germany – based on historical Geography?, *Erdkunde* 19, 1965, pp.161–164.

von Borries, H-W.: Ökonomische Grundlagen der westdeutschen Siedlungsstruktur, *Akad. f. Raumforschung und Landesplanung* 56, Hannover, 1969.

Wild, M. T.: Recent trends in the distribution of population in the Federal Republic of West Germany, *T.E.S.G.* 66, 1975, p.349–357.

CHAPTER 9

INDUSTRY IN THE FEDERAL REPUBLIC
ENERGY SUPPLY

The 'economic wonder' of the Federal Republic in the 1950s was based on a stable currency and generous American aid that provided money at low interest for industrial investment as well as vital foodstuffs and raw materials on which to rebuild the economy. There was also the urge of people at large to rebuild the losses of the war, with a particular drive coming from the dispossessed and socially declassed expellees. Rebuilding industry involved not just replacing old machines, but replacing them by an improved technology that enhanced productivity, to which there was little labour opposition. The substantially swollen population provided an ample labour force at the time when it was most needed. The postwar economic geography of the Federal Republic can, however, only be properly appreciated in the light of the prevailing neo-liberal social market economy. The fundamental attitude has been that there can be no political freedom without economic freedom. The concept of freedom is one in which the state is active in combatting crises on all scales, securing the stability of the currency, and in particular preventing monopoly and restrictive practice outside narrow limits. It is summed up in the motto – Competition as far as possible, planning as far as necessary.

A notable milestone was the Korean War, when the economic and political climate gave the republic a chance to win back a place in the trading community of Western nations. With British and American industrial capacity turned back to war production, new opportunities in export markets opened for West German goods. In 1950 West Germany also reached the important point where industrial output again attained the 1936 level, and the following year heavy deficits on overseas trade were turned to the surpluses that were to become a monotonous feature of subsequent financial success. After 1953 prewar standards of living were exceeded, and rising production, with an emphasis on export business, helped to mop up the serious unemployment that had appeared after the currency reform. By the late 1950s the steady inflow of refugees from the G.D.R. was taking the heat out of a growing shortage of labour in many sectors, but when in 1961 this inflow was cut, West Germany began to turn to foreign labour.

The creation (1953–1954) of the European Coal and Steel Community, the *Montan-Union*, set out to ease the flow of coal, coke, scrap, and iron and steel across the frontiers of Western Europe, a relatively easy task as these items were still in great demand and the Federal Republic, with its iron and steel industry rapidly recovering and a growing coal output, was well placed to benefit. Moreover, the E.C.S.C. could institute investment programmes of further benefit to German industry, but it also removed the last rigorous control on heavy industry by dissolving the International Ruhr Authority, on which Germany was by this time fully represented. It was quickly shown, however, that the model of the *Montan-Union* was not the way to European integration on a sector-by-sector basis, and proposals for such activities as electricity generation and farming were dropped; though the only other similar organization, EURATOM, helped reestablishment of German nuclear studies after years of proscription.

Far more influential on the spatial pattern of the West German economy has been the European Community created through the Treaty of Rome in March, 1957. The dismantling of fiscal barriers to trade has been relatively quick, while other agreements such as those on transport and mobility have had important repercussions in the Federal Republic, although the debatable Common Agricultural Policy further undermined an already unsatisfactory farming position. On the other hand, the Community has aided new regional concepts, like Saarlorlux and the Aachen-Maastricht area. Five of the original six members have close ties with the Rhine basin and the Community has developed a strong Rhenish orientation, which may be strengthened by British participation as a major industrial axis is linked across the North Sea from the Humber to the Rhine-Maas estuary. This has been particularly to the advantage of the Federal Republic, whose major growth areas have lain within the Rhine basin.

Restricted initially in a number of fields of high technology by Allied policy, West German industry became outstandingly successful in the high earners of the consumer durables (notably motor vehicles). Nevertheless, rising costs, especially for labour, have made some traditional labour-intensive industries

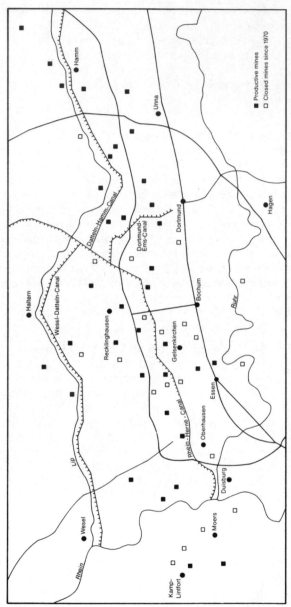

Figure 9.1 Coalfields – Rhenish-Westphalian (Rhur)

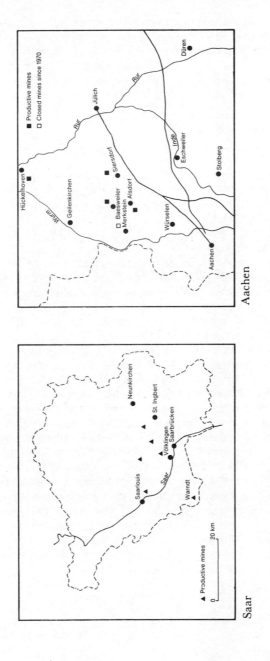

Figure 9.1 (continued) Coalfields

suffer severe competition from countries where labour costs are appreciably lower though skill little less. It is still too early to see what lasting major structural and spatial changes will come to the economy in the face of the energy crisis of the mid-1970s, whose true impact has been cushioned but not deflected by the financial success of the country's foreign trade.

The energy industries

A modern industrial structure depends massively on an adequate energy supply, whose type, quality, and cost markedly influence industrial infrastructure. Industrialization was based originally on the generous endowment with bituminous coals and lignite, but from the late 1950s there was a strong shift towards petroleum and natural gas. The energy crisis of 1973 checked this shift, and there has been debate on the possibility of moving to nuclear power or back to coal.

Bituminous coal mining

By 1950 coal production in the Federal Republic had climbed to 126 million tons and the last Allied industrial restrictions were lifted when the *Montan-Union* came into being. Coal output went on climbing until 1956, when it reached 152 million tons, but then the market collapsed, with large unsold stocks. In contrast, brown-coal mining has expanded through more modern equipment offering the fuel at a price attractive to the electric power industry. Although there has been consistently an export market in Europe, West German mines have not been able to push their productivity high enough to offset their costs compared to cheap imported American and Polish coal. Until the late 1950s, the Federal Republic had not had the financial resources or the technological capacity to take full advantage of petroleum, but the fall in prices and the improved German trading position brought a wave of conversion to oil. The free market economy that eschewed planning had initially only a weak and ineffectual policy to combat the rapidly worsening position of the coal industry. At first uncoordinated closures, near bankruptcies, and rising unemployment were softened little, but massive government subsidy and structural adjustments through new industries in the affected areas helped mining to undergo a sharp reduction in capacity between 1962 and 1969, though closures have continued. The greatest decline has been in the Saar coalfield, closely followed by the largest producer, the Ruhr; while Aachen, with a large element of foreign capital, has survived better as have small producers in Lower Saxony.

Compared to Britain, coal mining in West Germany is more concentrated: four fields produce all the coal, but 82 percent comes from one field, the Ruhr, where there has been a constant northwards shift of mining, with the southern exposed field largely abandoned in the 1920s, though two mines (Herbede and

Sprockhövel) survived until the early 1970s. Mine closures have been markedly along the so-called Hellweg line, leaving important mining towns like Bochum and Essen without any mines. Although the northern mines still generally work the tops of concealed saddles, the increasing amount of over-burden encourages the use of larger producing units, while the easier gradients of the more northern folds of the Coal Measures allowed a substantial increase in mechanization, which accounted for 16 percent of output in 1957 and 95 percent by 1972. At the same time, rationalization reduced the number of mining points underground from 2006 in 1957 to 297 in 1973 and yet output at each point rose from 204 tons to 1112 tons daily. In general, mine closures have been of the smaller, high-cost producers working limited concessions, though creation of the large holding company (*Ruhrkohle AG*) has freed future working from the restrictions placed by demarcated concession boundaries, so that already mergers between mines have become common. The axe has fallen heaviest on producers of the least-demanded coals (anthracite, semian-thracite, and some steam coals), reflected in mine closures in the southern part of the field. The surviving mines are particularly associated with the produc-tion of coking coals and occur notably along a line from Oberhausen-Hamm, as well as west of the Rhine around Moers and Kamp-Lintfort, and mining still dominates employment in Kamp-Lintfort, Rheinkamp, Bottrop, Castrop-Rauxel, Moers, Gladbeck, and Wanne-Eickel. *Ruhrkohle AG*, comprising 26 mining companies, controls 93 percent of the Ruhr output – at its inception only four mines (Westfalen, Auguste Viktoria, Erin, and Herbede) were not controlled by it. Observers have suggested 90 million tons as a realistic market for Ruhr coal, though some estimates had fallen as low as 60 million tons; but, since the crisis of late 1973, estimates have been generally upgraded.

French control of the Saar pushed coal production to its maximum, but its return to Germany coincided with the collapse of the market. France was

Table 9.1
Bituminous coal production 1950–1973

| Year | Coalfield | | | | – in thousand tons – | |
	Ruhr	Saar	Aachen	Lower Saxony	Federal Republic	Small pits
1950	103,329	14,985	5,457	1,969	125,740+	485
1956	124,627	16,956	7,208	2,572	151,363+	1,343
1962	115,898	14,919	8,050	2,269	141,136+	764
1968	91,050	11,261	7,299	2,402	112,012+	154
1973	79,883	9,175	5,970	2,311	97,339+	260
1975	75,856	8,975	5,749	1,812	92,392+	—

Source: Jahrbuch für Bergbau, Energie, Mineralöl und Chemie, 1974, Essen.

214

allowed to mine 66 million tons within 25 years from seams in the Warndt from shafts on French soil in Lorraine, and one-third of Saar output should by treaty go to industry and electricity works in Lorraine. A new company, *Saarbergwerke AG*, with the federation as majority shareholder, instituted a rationalization programme, reducing the number of mines from 18 to 6, though the original plan foresaw 8 remaining. Three small private mines produce about 250,000 tons a year. Output has fallen from 16 million tons in 1957 to a little under 9 million tons in 1975, though the *Saarbergwerke* mines are all in the million tons plus capacity. *Saarbergwerke* also rationalized electricity generation, concentrated in a few large modern units instead of the small generators attached to individual mines, while coking is now done at a central plant at Fürstenhausen of over 1 million tons capacity. (Saar coal does not coke well and must be mixed with Ruhr coal.) The company has also diversified its operations: the refinery at Klarenthal is supplied by pipeline with oil from Strasbourg and the by-products are sent to a chemicals plant on French soil, in turn associated with a German fertilizer factory at Perl on the Mosel. The company also has interests in an oil refinery at Emden in Friesland and in artificial fibre production.

The Aachen coalfield, supplying about 6 percent of West German production, is really part of a larger structure which extends into Holland near Maastricht (where mining has been largely abandoned) and into the Belgian

Table 9.2
Brown coal production 1950–1973

Year	Coalfield				– in thousand tons –	
	Rhineland	Helmstedt	Hessen	Bavaria	Rhineland Palatinate	Federal Republic
1950	63,677	7,598	2,909	1,672	92	75,948
1956	82,128	6,759	3,567	2,823	85	95,362
1962	85,369	6,862	3,760	5,260	—	101,251
1968	87,871	4,770	3,924	4,951	—	101,516
1973	101,733	5,981	3,583	7,361	—	118,658

Source: Jahrbuch für Bergbau, Energie, Mineralöl und Chemie, 1974, Essen.

Kempenland. The southern part of the German field in the Inde valley has been worked out and exploitation is now in the northern Wurm valley. Four mines are located around Baesweiler-Alsdorf, while the fifth at Hückelhoven (Sophia Jacoba), with strong Dutch interests, exploits anthracite in the Erkelenz horst. About 40 percent of annual output is coked locally, mostly for the ARBED plants in Luxemburg. Other uses are electricity generation and smokeless fuels (notably from Hückelhoven): about 54 percent of production is

The Two Germanies

eventually exported, largely to Benelux or France. The field's main problem is transport, for though it is well served by railways, it lacks cheap waterway transport to major markets.

Mining at Ibbenbüren near Osnabrück supplies a local market, though some coal goes to Benelux and France. Annual production is about 2 million tons. The field is regarded as a structural outlier of the Ruhr (though considerable change has taken place in the coal types) and covers an area of 6 by 15 kilometres, with mining down to over 800 metres. Unfortunately, in the

Table 9.3
Shift in regional refinery capacity

Federal Republic – throughput in '000 t.	1955 14,685	1960 40,463	1965 80,913	1970 115,093
Percentage from: Hamburg Schleswig–Holstein Bremen	44.7	27.1	20.4	15.6
Lower Saxony	12.1	14.1	9.6	7.9
North Rhine–Westphalia	42.8	58.8	39.9	34.4
Rhineland–Palatinate Saarland	0.3	—	2.5	3.6
Hessen Baden–Württemberg	0.1	—	13.9	20.4
Bavaria	—	—	14.2	18.1

Source: Daten zur Entwicklung der Energiewirtschaft in der Bundesrepublik Deutschland – Ausgabe 1970, Bonn.

northeast the seams dip to depths beyond current technological and economic limits. About 8 percent of output goes to the domestic market, 20 percent to briquette making and the rest for electricity generation. Mining near Hannover at Barsinghausen ceased in 1957. South Germany is poorly endowed with coal, though some small deposits were worked and the last, at Peissenberg, closed in 1970, lay on the northwest of a deposit between the Lech and the Inn. Coal went to the company's own electricity generator, though some was sold as domestic and industrial fuel in Upper Bavaria and Suabia. The shiny black *Pechkohle* had a good heating value.

Lignite mining

The Federal Republic is third world producer of lignite after the G.D.R. and the Soviet Union. German statistics usually accept that in heating value 3.7 tons of lignite are worth 1 ton of hard coal, but the ease with which it can be mined in opencast pits makes it an inexpensive fuel, notably for electricity generation, chemicals, and briquetting. Output has shown a generally upward trend, reaching over 120 million tons: 85 percent comes from the fields west of Köln, 5 percent from the Helmstedt district, 6 percent from Bavaria and 3 percent from scattered fields in Hessen. The Rhineland-Palatinate ceased its small production in 1960. Briquette production (90 percent from near Köln) has fallen sharply in response to household demand.

The brown coal field west of Köln lies in the horst structure of the Ville or Vorgebirge under a relatively light cover of sand and gravel between Greven-broich in the north and Brühl in the south. Another occurrence between Eschweiler and Düren is under heavier outburden, while some outliers (e.g., near Zülpich) have been worked out. Large reserves between the Rur and Erft rivers lie at considerable depths, too great for contemporary economic mining, towards the south. Seams between 20–100 metres thick are worked by opencast methods and a major improvement in output came after 1955 with the introduction of large bucket excavators. Consequently, larger but fewer opencast workings, often to greater depths, have reduced the pits from 13 to 7. In 1958, the deepest opencast pit was 120 metres, but by the 1980s working down to 250 metres is envisaged, though at such depths problems of the water table arise (the key factor in landscape restoration), which may be the long-term limiting factor. The southern part is already worked out and, around Liblar, restitution has created a recreational area for Köln as rigorous legal requirements enforce restoration of the landscape after abandonment of mining. The seams grow thinner towards the north, and the cost of mining rises as the ratio of overburden to coal increases. The low cost of lignite, despite high ash content and modest calorific value, makes it suitable for electricity generation and the field is the site of a number of large electric power stations served by a high capacity north-south railway of 100,000 tons daily capacity. Large reserves remain, but despite great improvements in opencast recovery techniques, a considerable proportion will not be exploitable at present cost levels: of 60 milliard tons remaining in the 3000 square-kilometre field, 8 milliard tons are presently regarded as economically worth working. Recent exploration suggests this is Europe's richest deposit.

The Helmstedt area has three pits, with that at Wülfersdorf cut by the frontier between the two German states. The Helmstedt pits now supply the Offleben power station built in 1952 to replace the Harbke plant on the eastern side of the border. Two seams of a total thickness of 20–25 metres under an over-burden of 25–60 metres occur here. Small workings occur in Hessen (around

Kassel, in the Rhenish Uplands and in the Wetterau) and in Bavaria, near Schwandorf, but a number of small pits closed in the early 1970s.

Petroleum and natural gas
The increasing shift to petroleum was slowed by the 1973 crisis. Home sources have been exceedingly modest and cover only about 5 percent of demand, so that increasing quantities of foreign crude have had to be imported, while as a result of reparations dismantling and the later cost advantage of natural crude, synthetically produced petroleum has ceased to play a role. Home resources of natural gas have been more generous, but rising demand has also increased the need to import – first from the Netherlands, and since the early 1970s, agreements have been signed to receive large quantities from Iran, the Soviet Union, and from the Norwegian Ekofisk North Sea field. Reserves of crude oil have been estimated at around 75 million tons; half west of the Ems and a quarter between the Weser and Ems. The natural gas reserves are put at 325 milliard m^3 (Vn), three-quarters lying between the Weser and Ems.

The most important oil producing area is the North German Plain, where five groups of fields occur: near Kiel, east of Hannover, west of Hannover, around Lingen in the Ems valley, and southeast of Hamburg. Deposits near Heide in Holstein are unimportant, while deposits around Wietze are exhausted. The main natural gas fields lie between the Ems and Weser, with Rheden and Hengstlage most important. Natural asphalt occurs at Holzminden. Small, scattered oil and gas deposits in the Rhine Rift Valley have already been partly exhausted: oil production now comes predominantly from Landau. In the Molasse basin of Bavaria, Alresried in the Iller basin is the main western oil producer, while a number of small gas and oil workings are producing between the Isar and the Inn, and hopes are pinned on deep boring. Exploration of the German sector of the North Sea, enlarged from its originally tightly drawn boundaries, has proved disappointing, although finds, none yet of major importance, have been made closely adjacent in the Dutch and Danish sectors.

Imports of crude petroleum come by sea directly to German ports or are received by pipeline from foreign ports (imports from foreign ports by river and railway have fallen sharply), though some refined petroleum products are still received not only direct to German ports but also by barge and train from adjacent countries. Shipments by barge and train are also made to the German Democratic Republic, Czechoslovakia, Austria, and Switzerland. Crude oil arriving in the Elbe estuary is refined locally and products distributed by road and rail: Hamburg, reached by tankers up to 80,000 tons, has four refineries; plans for a refinery at Stade have been mooted, while Brunsbüttel, reached by tankers up to 140,000 tons, has a small refinery with plans for a larger one. It sends crude to the small Heide refinery (also received from the Plön field near Kiel) which is joined to Brunsbüttel by a product and an ethylene line.

Tankers up to 50,000 tons can reach Bremen's refinery, but the main tanker terminal is the one-time naval port of Wilhelmshaven, open to vessels of 250,000 tons, where a refinery has been under construction. The crude is presently shipped by pipeline to the Rhine-Ruhr area and to the Hamburg refineries. Tankers up to 38,000 tons can reach the refinery at Emden. The oilfields of the Emsland feed the refinery at Lingen, which has pipeline access to the Rhine-Ruhr area, and there is a small refinery at Salzbergen. The oilfields of the Hannover area supply the small Misburg and Peine refineries by local pipelines.

A major pipeline focus is the Lower Rhine-Ruhr area, served from Rotterdam as well as from Wilhelmshaven. A product line also joins Rotterdam to the Ruhr, while an elaborate system of ethylene pipelines is being developed between the Ruhr, Lower Rhine, Rotterdam, Dutch Limburg, and Antwerp. Large refineries lie at Dinslaken and Gelsenkirchen, and smaller ones at Mühlheim and Duisburg, and there is a small plant at Essen, while a large refinery is planned at Rheinberg. An important refinery group lies in and around Köln (Monheim, Godorf) and the Wesseling refinery was originally built to make synthetic fuel.

The Raunheim refinery receives crude from Rotterdam by pipeline and is also joined to the Rhine-Ruhr area by a product and ethylene pipeline. It is similarly joined to the group of refineries that originally developed on Rhine transport at Mannheim, Speyer, Wörth, Jockgrim, and bkarlsruhe, to which a refinery at Germersheim will be added. These refineries, two of which have capacities exceeding 8 million tons, receive crude oil by pipeline from Marseille, and from Genoa and Triest via Ingolstadt. In the Saar, the Klarenthal refinery pipes crude also from Marseille and is joined to the French product and ethylene pipeline system. The main South German refinery group is at Ingolstadt which receives its crude by transalpine pipeline from Genoa and Triest. A refinery is being built nearby at Schwait, and there are refineries at Neustadt and Vohburg, while the Burghausen refinery has a product line to München.

The strategy of refinery location has produced four groups – North Germany, Lower Rhineland, Upper Rhineland, and South Germany – to serve the main consumption areas, and each major company has its refineries represented in at least three groups. There was a considerable change in the balance between the centres during the 1960s, notably the decline in the role of Hamburg as a refining centre, the growth in the Saarland and the Rhine, as well as the emergence of South Germany. The Upper Rhine and South Germany are associated especially with the growth of pipeline transport for large quantities of crude oil. The largest German refinery (11 million tons planned for the B.P. refinery at Hamburg) is modest compared to the largest of the Dutch

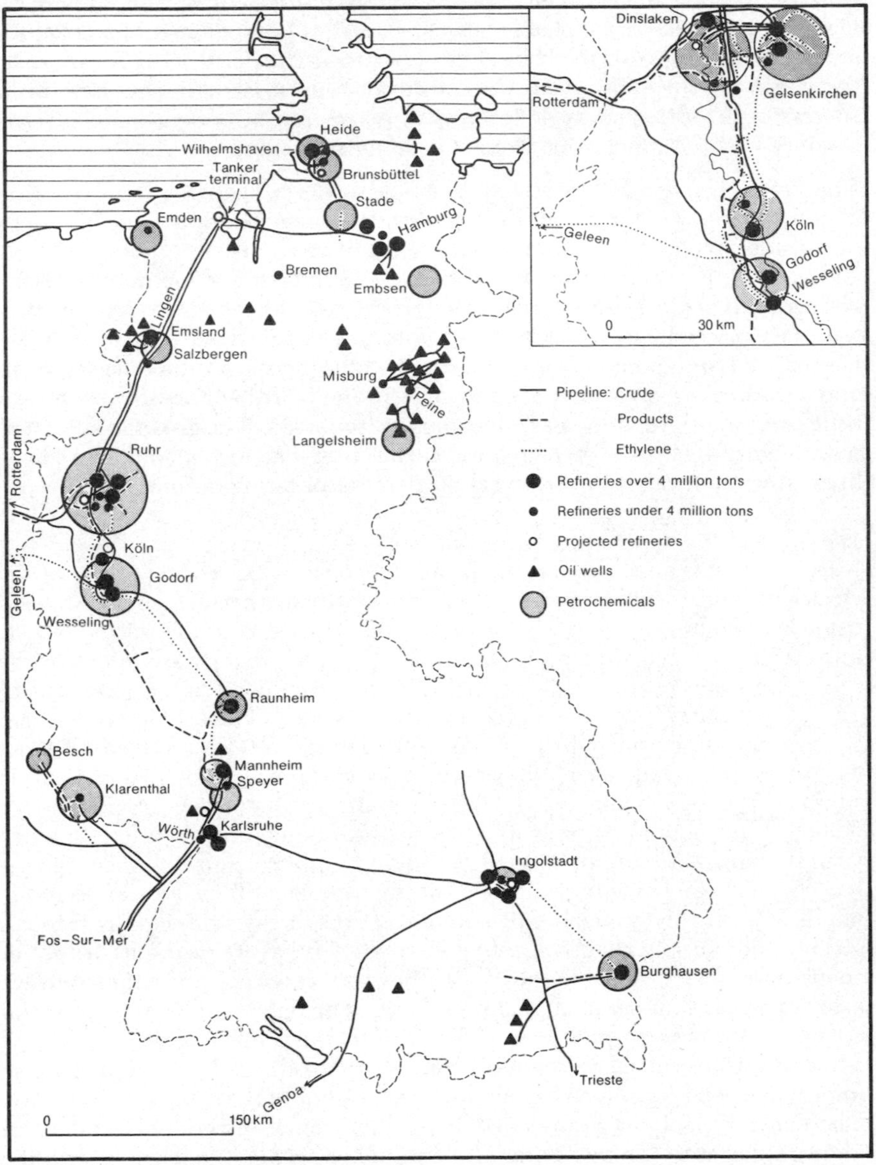

Dinslaken
Gelsenkirchen
Rotterdam
Geleen
Köln
Godorf
Wesseling
0
30 km
Heide
Wilhelmshaven
Tanker terminal
Brunsbüttel
Stade
Hamburg
Emden
Bremen
Embsen
Lingen
Emsland
Salzbergen
Misburg
Peine
Langelsheim
Ruhr
Rotterdam
Köln
Godorf
Geleen
Wesseling
Raunheim
Besch
Mannheim
Speyer
Klarenthal
Wörth
Karlsruhe
Ingolstadt
Fos-Sur-Mer
Burghausen
Trieste
Genoa
0
150 km
Pipeline: Crude
Products
Ethylene
Refineries over 4 million tons
Refineries under 4 million tons
Projected refineries
Oil wells
Petrochemicals

Figure 9.2 Oil refineries and pipelines

Europoort-Rotterdam group (26.5 million tons at the Shell refinery at Pernis). Discussions to receive supplies of Soviet petroleum by pipeline could introduce a new element in either the Hannover area (using the Polish-G.D.R. route) or the Nürnberg area (using the Czechoslovak route). Experiments have been successful in storing strategic reserves of petroleum in underground caverns produced by pumping brine from salt dome structures.

The 1960s also saw the rise of natural gas as a source of energy (now covering about 10 percent of the country's requirements) associated with the discovery of considerable quantities in the petroleum-bearing districts, notably North Germany. It is also imported from adjacent countries, and Germany and the Netherlands are in dispute over the Dollart deposits. It has been suggested that the high price demanded for Dutch gas has reduced its impact in West Germany. Large potential supplies can be obtained from the Soviet Union, and gas already flows via Czechoslovakia to the Nürnberg area. Currently, a little over one-third of the gas consumed is imported. The growing system of natural gas pipelines is replacing the earlier long-distance manufactured gas lines, since natural gas now covers 60 percent of total consumption.

Electric power generation and distribution
Much energy is consumed in the form of electricity. Over 90 percent of the electricity consumed is derived from conventional thermal power stations using a wide range of fuels – bituminous coal, lignite, peat, oil, various gases, and even refuse. A considerable additional thermal capacity was added by the reincorporation of the Saarland in 1957. Nuclear power, first generated in 1962, contributes just over 3 percent of the current, but development has met strong opposition from public opinion. Whereas in 1950 almost one-fifth of the electricity generated came from water power stations, lack of further suitable sites and the high capital cost retarded expansion, and it now supplies about one-tenth of the total current in a wet year and only one-twentieth in a dry year, though to use surplus off-peak energy, a number of pump storage stations have been or are being built. Public supply, though still in some areas in the hands of local generating and distribution authorities, is principally through seven major supply concerns, while West Berlin has its own authority, but cooperation exists among the supply authorities, as witnessed by the extensive grid system. A number of large power stations belong to individual industrial companies, whose surplus current is fed into the public supply system. As demand for electric current doubled in the 1960s, there has been a growing import of electricity, which is now twice the volume of the export of electricity. The Federal Republic draws current notably from Switzerland and Austria and supplies it to Denmark and Holland. There is also some trade with the G.D.R. Domestic consumers take about 20 percent of the total electricity, the metallurgical industries consume another 20 percent, the chemicals industries

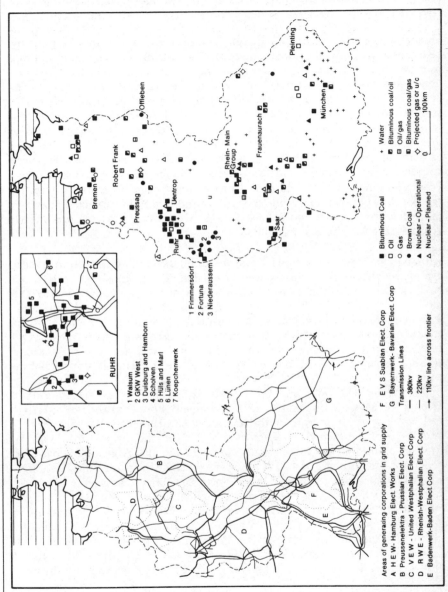

Figure 9.3 Power stations and electricity grid

Within the figure:

Pleinting

Offleben

Robert Frank

München

Bremen

Preussag

Uentrop

Frauenaurach

Rhein- Main Group

Ruhr

Saar

1 Frimmersdorf
2 Fortuna
3 Niederaussem

RUHR

1 Walsum
2 GKW West
3 Duisburg and Hamborn
4 Scholven
5 Hüls and Marl
6 Lünen
7 Koepchenwerk

Areas of generating corporations in grid supply
A H E W- Hamburg Elect. Works
B Preussenelektra - Prussian Elect. Corp
C V E W - United -Westphalian Elect. Corp
D R W E - Rhenish-Westphalian Elect. Corp
E Badenwerk-Baden Elect.Corp
F E V S Suabian Elect. Corp
G Bayernwerk- Bavarian Elect. Corp

Transmission Lines
— 380kv
— 220kv
→ 110kv line across frontier

■ Bituminous Coal
□ Oil
○ Gas
● Brown Coal
▲ Nuclear - Operational
△ Nuclear - Planned

+ Water
⊞ Bituminous coal/oil
⊡ Oil/gas
◨ Bituminous coal/gas
◇ Projected gas or u/c

0   100km

about 19 percent, and 18 percent is taken by remaining industry. The railways cover almost three-quarters of their needs from their own generating plants.

Half the thermally generated current comes from power stations fired by bituminous coal, while about one-third (and rising) comes from stations burning lignite. During the 1960s the amount of current derived from oil-fired generators rose from just over 1 percent to over 12 percent. Gas-fired generators contribute about 10 per cent of the current, but peat-fired power stations are insignificant. Though generation and distribution remains in the hands of private companies, considerable government aid is given, mostly directed at helping the coal and lignite industries to find new markets as demand from other sectors has fallen, so that financial aid for new power stations was offered in the mid-1960s if coal or lignite were used as a fuel for ten years. The high cost of coal has given the advantage to lignite, where the relationship between large power stations and highly mechanized opencast mines has grown closer and natural gas also becomes an attractive fuel on cost grounds, even in the Ruhr coalfield.

Although power stations fired by coal are found throughout the country, there are expectedly marked clusters on the coalfields, and those away from the coalfields are notably near to good waterway or railway connections: some have been developed to burn alternate fuels to cater for market fluctuations. The most marked concentration of coal-fired power stations is on the Ruhr coalfield. Some coalmines, particularly in the north of the field, are directly related to a particular power station: in the south, pit closures have left several stations dependent on rail-borne fuel. Among the largest plants are Scholven with a capacity of 1539 MW, Walsum 475 MW (a 700-MW station is being built), Herne 600 MW, and Westerholt 320 MW. Two power stations of around 150 MW operate on the Aachen coalfield. Four coal and one alternate fuel power stations operate on the Saar coalfield: three (St. Barbara, Fenne, and Weiher) are owned by *Saarbergwerke AG*, but the largest, the 540-MW Ensdorf plant, belongs to *Vereinigte Saarelektrizitäts-AG*. A group of coal-fired generators, including a 614-MW plant at Wedel, lie in and around Hamburg, where coal is imported by sea: other North German stations show a general waterside location (e.g., Kiel, Emden, Wilhelmshaven, Bremen), and the Salzgitter plant lies on the Mittelland Canal. Coal-fired power stations in South Germany lie along the lower Main, where water transport is available, in the Neckar basin, and on the Rhine itself, notably at Mannheim-Ludwigshafen and Karlsruhe, besides two large coal-fired stations at Nürnberg, while some small and medium-sized stations lie around München.

The lignite-fired power stations on the Ville field west of Köln are particularly large units – the Frimmersdorf plant has a capacity well over 2000 MW, while the Niederaussem power station also exceeds 2000-MW capacity, and Fortuna II and III have a joint capacity of 950 MW. The northern power stations lie in the present main area of mining, with modern mechanized pits, but the southern plants (where mining has declined or even been abandoned) are served by the special north-south high-capacity railway. Two stations with a capacity of 1350 MW operate on the lignite field at Weisweiler. Lignite-burning power stations (mostly small) are also found in Hessen, including a 356-MW generator at Borken. In Lower Saxony, the 770-MW Offleben plant was built in 1952 to replace Harbke now in the G.D.R. and burns Helmstedt lignite. In Bavaria, the 700-MW plant at Schwandorf uses local lignite and its current is primarily consumed by the local aluminium industry.

Oil- and natural gas-burning stations are mostly in North Germany. The two largest are the Robert Frank station (600 MW) west of Hannover and the Schilling station (375 MW) downriver from Hamburg, while a 400-MW station able to use coal, oil, and gas operates in Bremen. The Kirchlengern station (183 MW) near Minden burns only natural gas. An interesting gas-fired generator at Wiesmoor used peat until 1964 and its waste heat warmed a vast greenhouse complex. In South Germany, the Ingolstadt area is supplied by a 700-MW power station fired by oil and local refinery gas. Small oil-fired plants are also found at Pleinting on the Danube and at München-Süd

Water power has been used for generations mostly in the central and southern parts, where suitable resources are available. The hydro-electric stations are themselves small, though the Hotzenwaldwerk near Säckingen/Rhine is rated at 360 MW and the famous Walchenseewerk at 114 MW, and the 132-MW Jochenstein station on the Danube is shared with Austria. Several South German rivers like the Iller, Lech, Isar, and Inn have 'cascades' of small stations along them. A number of modest-sized stations lie along the French bank of the Rhine, associated with the Grand Canal d'Alsace, and another cascade has been built along the Mosel as part of measures to canalize the river for barge traffic. The physical character of the southern Schwarzwald provides numerous sites for hydro-electric power stations, with a group of generators each over 100-MW capacity associated with the Schluchsee and Schwarza. The Walchenseewerk has an elaborate system of water gathering and storage, including pump storage to use off-peak current. The Happurg station near Nürnberg is a large daily pump storage plant (160 MW). The hydro-electric power stations of Austrian Vorarlberg are important suppliers to the Federal Republic. In the Central Uplands and in the Harz, some reservoirs are used to generate small amounts of electric current, although primarily designed to supply industrial and domestic water (the largest is the 15-MW Bigge barrage). With large quantities of off-peak current from thermal stations, pump storage is important: the Koepchenwerk above the Ruhr valley near Herdecke has a capacity of 132 MW, the Rönkhausen plant on the upper

Lenne is rated at 140 MW, and the 220-MW Erzhausen pump storage plant uses water from the Lenne to fill up overnight. A similar plant (105 MW) has been built on the Elbe near Hamburg at Geesthacht and the Waldeck scheme in Hessen combines daily pump storage with a long-term reservoir.

Allied restrictions on possession of nuclear materials immediately after the war delayed research into nuclear generation, while the Federal government gave no encouragement because of its clear political implications and the electricity companies were reluctant to invest in nuclear power stations because of financial problems, so that nuclear-generated electricity accounts for only 4 percent of total generation. The United Kingdom derives about 12 percent of its current from this source and has twice as many plants operating as the Federal Republic, but by 1980 the West Germans plan to have about 27 nuclear power stations (1800 MW) supplying about 10 percent of the power requirements, though lack of truly isolated sites like those available in Britain has made public opposition in West Germany more resistant. Apart from five small experimental reactors, six plants with a total capacity of 2228 MW supply current to the public. The two largest are Würgassen on the Weser (640 MW) and Stade on the Elbe (630 MW). A large complex with an ultimate capacity exceeding 1000 MW is being built at Biblis near Mannheim, and a capacity over 2600 MW will be achieved by the Gundremmingen station when complete. A fast breeder reactor is under construction at Kalkar near the Dutch frontier, while a proposed plant at Uentrop will be close to the thickly populated Ruhr coalfield. Strong opposition has been faced by the BASF decision to build its own reactor at Ludwigshafen. Small experimental reactors at Geesthacht have been used to develop the nuclear ship *Otto Jahn*, a 150,000-ton ore carrier. An important locational factor is the need for vast quantities of cooling water.

The outline of a comprehensive grid had been laid in the interwar years, particularly after standardization of voltage in 1935. The basic national grid system was developed for 220 Kv, but the main trunks (still being extended) have been raised over much of the network to 380 Kv. The 380-Kv system forms the major north-south links, with the Rhine axis joining the thermal stations of the Ruhr and Lower Rhine to the hydro-power stations of South Germany. There is also a 380-Kv link to the Saar and similar links to Holland, France, and Switzerland, but the link to Austria is operated at 220 Kv. Links with the G.D.R. are made at 110 Kv (also used for local distribution). The grid system tends to focus on North Rhine-Westphalia, where almost half the national current is generated.

The Federal Republic has been negotiating to obtain electricity in bulk from a large thermal power station using Silesian coal in Poland, the building of which it would largely finance. Similar discussions have opened for a large nuclear power station in the Soviet Union in the Kaliningrad region (former German East Prussia), but the G.D.R. has been reluctant to allow the transmission lines to go through West Berlin, a point on which the West Germans have been insistent for political reasons.

CHAPTER 10
INDUSTRY IN THE FEDERAL REPUBLIC
IRON AND STEEL, OTHER METALS
AND CHEMICALS

The West German iron and steel industry now ranks fourth in world order, never having caught up with rising Soviet output after 1945 and having been eclipsed by Japan in the early 1960s, although its output now exceeds the whole output of the *Reich* before 1939. Allied policy decentralized the industry by breaking up the prewar *Konzerne*, but the European Coal and Steel Community (1953) provided the opening to regroup into larger units than original Allied policy had permitted. There has been resistance to mergers near the dimensions of such giants as the Steel Corporation of America, but it has been suggested that the whole West German industry may be ultimately concentrated into three groups – August Thyssen Hütte, Hoesch-Hoogovens (German–Dutch consortium), and Klöckner. Through financial tie-ups and technological change, the number of plants has been reduced by elimination of the least effective units. In the original community of the Six, West Germany produced 40 percent of the steel, more than France and Italy combined.

The industry is concentrated in North Rhine-Westphalia, especially on the Ruhr coalfield, though in some sectors (notably rolled goods) its proportion has fallen since the mid-1950s. In face of technological and economic changes, the Ruhr has been remarkably successful in holding its position, using locational advantages of local availability of excellent coke, dolomite, and limestone from the not-too-distant Sauerland, with splendid rail and water transport from ore importing harbours. The bulk of its products is sold within a radius of 100–150 kilometres, though again good communications make export attractive and feasible. The declining proportion of coke per ton of pig has loosened the tie with the coalfield – in the Ruhr, this ratio dropped from 941 kilograms in 1957 to about 500 kilograms in the mid-1970s, while concentration on high grade ore (as well as extensive enrichment) has eased the ore input in relation to pig output. The Federal Republic, one of the world's largest ore importers after the U.S.A. and Japan, is supplied from Scandinavia (about a quarter), Brazil (about a fifth), Liberia and Mauretania (about a

Table 10.1
Pig iron production

Federal Republic	1965	1969	1973	1975
– '000 tons –	26,990	33,764	36,828	30,100
	%	%	%	%
Schleswig–Holstein Lower Saxony Bremen	13.3	16.3	18.7	18.9
North Rhine-Westphalia	68.7	67.4	64.7	64.5
Hessen, Rhineland Palatinate Bavaria	4.4	2.7	3.1	3.0
Saar	13.6	13.6	13.5	13.6

Source: Statistisches Jahrbuch der Eisen – und Stahlindustrie, various years, Düsseldorf.

fifth), with a little under a tenth brought from Canada and a twentieth from Australia. Over half the manganese needed comes from South Africa. In the Saar, French Lorraine ores are important, though these amount to only 7 percent of overall West German consumption. Home ore now accounts for less than a tenth of overall consumption (in 1961 over a quarter) as the major cost savings from bulk ore carriers make imports of high-grade ores more attractive. The classic ore port, Emden, can accommodate vessels only up to 38,000 tons, though improvements make Bremen-Weserport accessible to ships up to 90,000 tons, but the largest vessels can use Rotterdam where, from a new ore terminal at Europoort, push tug trains up to 8000 tons can reach the Rhineside ironworks of the western Ruhr. Emden can send only 1350-ton barges along the Dortmund–Ems canal, mostly unloaded in Dortmund and the ore moved by rail to nearby ironworks, although 4000-ton railway freight trains carry ore from Emden to the Saar. Lübeck takes summer shipments from Swedish ports, though this once strategic connection has lost its importance.

New technology, rationalization, and the advantage of shipping through Rotterdam (all emphasized by the 1975–1976 recession) have tended to attract iron and steel making to the western Ruhr along the Rhine frontage, where Duisburg has become a major focus. Almost 60 percent of the total crude steel production now comes from the western Ruhr compared with only about a quarter from Dortmund, despite the western Ruhr having suffered more damage and reparations dismantling than the eastern end, which made a

Table 10.2
Blast furnaces

| | 1965 | | 1969 | | 1973 | |
	A	O	A	O	A	O
North Rhine–Westphalia	79	57	58	51	44	38
Schleswig–Holstein Lower Saxony Bremen	19	14	17	15	18	14
Hessen and Bavaria	12	10	8	6	7	7
Rhineland–Palatinate	6	3	1	1	—	—
Saarland	29	20	26	18	19	17
Federal Republic	145	104	110	96	88	76

A = available
O = operative

Source: Statistisches Jahrbuch der Eisen – und Stahlindustrie, various years, Düsseldorf.

somewhat quicker recovery immediately postwar. The largest producer in the Duisburg cluster is the *August Thyssen Hütte* group (ATH) which emerged by 1958 as the most dynamic and thrusting in the steel industry, having reconstituted itself after deconcentration by the Allied Control Commission. The trend towards smelting in fewer and larger units is reflected in the five closely integrated plants at Bruchhausen, Beeckerwerth, Ruhrort, Hamborn, and Meiderich, while a new modern plant has been built at the ore harbour at Schwelgern, and reorganization brought amalgamation and rationalization of once separate but contiguously adjacent plants. Ore is drawn from ATH holdings in Brazil, Liberia (where there is ore pelletization), Canada, and Mauretania, usually imported through Europoort, while flux comes from company quarries in the Bergische Land. Though its coalmines were handed over to *Ruhrkohle AG* in 1969, they still supply the plants, and there is an elaborate private works railway system and substantial holdings in the shippers handling its ore supply. Closely associated with ATH are the *Mannesmann* plants in Duisburg-Huckingen and Grossenbaum, which supply a number of tube and pipe mills in and beyond the Ruhr. *Mannesmann* steel making (other than for tube and pipe purposes) has been handed to ATH,

The Two Germanies

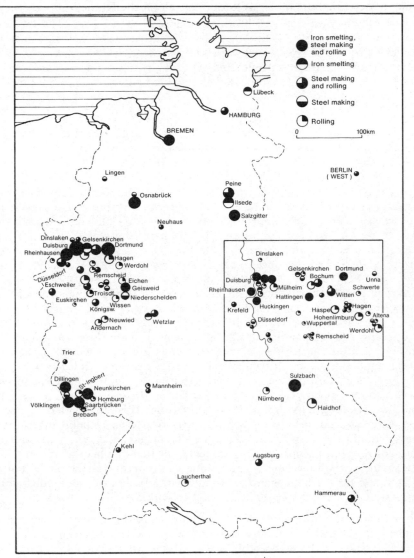

Figure 10.1 West German iron and steel industry

230

whereas the pipe and tube making of ATH at Phoenix-Ruhrort and Mülheim have been put under *Mannesmann* control. Concentration of blast furnaces closed two small works in Duisburg-Hochfeld, and in 1966 their steel-making sections also closed: they are now an integrated rod and bar producing unit. Also in Duisburg there is production of basic haematite pig iron and special low carbon pig as well as 'purple ore' for sinter plants. The importance of Duisburg is reflected in the fact that of the 80 blast furnaces in the Federal Republic, 36 (45 percent) lie in the Ruhr, 24 (30 percent) in the Duisburg area.

Closely associated with Duisburg is Oberhausen, where the one-time *Gutehoffnungshütte* (now *Hüttenwerke Oberhausen*) is a subsidiary of ATH (since 1967). Originally its blast furnaces used German or minette ores, but now mostly Swedish ore is brought via the Rhine harbour at Walsum or delivered from the Rhein-Herne Canal, with coal and coke from local mines. The blast furnaces at Oberhausen will be closed long term, but rolling and processing will remain (a new heavy plate mill has been built). Blast furnaces at Mülheim were closed in 1964 and rolling steel is supplied from Duisburg-Meiderich, though steel was made here until 1971. The *Schalker Verein* in Gelsenkirchen (part of *Rheinstahl*) produces coarse iron and foundry work. With the *Rheinstahl-ATH* merger, its future is uncertain as ATH and *Mannesmann* also own rolling mills at Gelsenkirchen. The *Henrichshütte* in Hattingen, dependent on expensive rail transport for its raw materials, also has an uncertain future, but it may survive as a rolling mill and for its continuous casting. Steelworks and rolling mills remain important in the central Ruhr, but iron smelting is now insignificant, where the major centre is Bochum with a 45,000-ton electric steel plant and hot and cold rolling mills. The former *Bochumer Verein* (now part of *Krupp*), once an iron smelter using railborne raw materials, now converts steel (annual capacity 1.3 million tons) and also has forging shops and rolling mills, with high-quality steel as a speciality. Since 1968, the fluid iron for steel has come in special 165-ton rail containers from the *Krupp* Rheinhausen plant, and about 50,000 tons are moved annually. There is also a plant making special steels, but the once famous production of bells has been abandoned. To the south, a small steelworks and rolling mill operates at Herbede, but at Witten special steels of world renown are made, as well as a substantial proportion of the LD-steel produced in the Ruhr.

The eastern Ruhr is dominated by Dortmund, where blast furnaces depend on ore brought by the Dortmund-Ems Canal or by the Rhine-Herne Canal. Coal and coke are available locally, while fluxing materials come from the Sauerland. Three companies formed by the Allied Control Commission had been reduced to two in 1951 by the merger between the *Dortmunder Hütte* and the *Dortmund-Hörder Union*: in 1966 the union of this merger with the *Hoesch* company put the industry under a single control. In 1972 *Hoesch* joined with the Dutch *Hoogovens* (there had been a working agreement since 1966), with a crude steel production of around 7 million tons per annum. Eighty percent of the steel produced in Dortmund is sold within a radius of 50–100 kilometres. Rationalization has sought to eliminate duplication of activities and facilities: in the *Hoesch* Phoenix works in Dortmund-Hörde, eleven Thomas steel converters were replaced by three 300-ton LD converters to make Europe's largest oxygen steel producer; while eight blast furnaces were replaced by three large modern units, reducing employment from 23,000 to 14,500, yet increasing crude steel output by 10 percent. As a consequence, the Thomas steel converters at the *Westfalenhütte* could be closed, but its rolling mills were extended and a galvanizing plant erected, and the works closely related to rolling mills at Hohenlimburg and pipeworks at Hamm. The *Hoesch-Hoogovens* merger has been seen as the basis for further rationalization by producing pig and crude steel at coastal works and carrying out the finishing (and possibly some steel conversion) in Germany. A coastal site would have distinct advantages of raw material assembly, while the finishing sectors in Germany would be well located in a strong market position.

In the Sauerland, one of the most important plants lies at Haspe, with three blast furnaces based on rail-borne coal and ore (originally from German domestic sources, but now largely foreign), and also steel making and rolling, but the owners, *Klöckner*, have preferred to expand iron making at their works in Bremen (an advantageous waterside site). Nearby Hagen is noted for stainless and special steel production. Throughout the Sauerland and Berg and Mark, there are numerous special steel plants, rolling mills, and other specialized producers, such as Hohenlimburg, Werdohl, and Neviges (rolled electric steels). Remscheid and Solingen specialize in cutting steels, stainless steels, and tubes, while at Wuppertal there is cold rolling of strip. Rationalization has reduced the small producers in and around Düsseldorf (notably associated with alloy steels, pipe and tube making, and strip rolling).

The main centre west of the Rhine is the large *Krupp* plant at Rheinhausen, with a capacity of over 3 million tons of pig iron and almost 4 million tons of steel as well as extensive rolling mills. In Krefeld, the *Deutsche Edelstahlwerke* produce a wide range of special steels in a large selection of forms, closely associated with the company's other plants. Eschweiler is a small electric steel centre, with strip produced at Breyell and ferro-alloys at Weisweiler and Knapsack.

A secondary iron- and steel-making centre is the Siegerland, where local ores and originally charcoal were the basis, while later Ruhr coal and coke were brought in by rail. Local ore mining has, however, declined substantially. The only blast furnace plant remains at Geisweid, making special cold blast pig iron, after the closure of several small blast furnaces. The industry has become increasingly dependent on special qualities of rolled steel and pipe making

(Eichen, Weidenau, Geisweid), though some steel conversion is still carried out. Galvanized ironware is made at Geisweid and high-quality welding is a speciality. In Hessen, Wetzlar produces pig iron and special alloy steels on a modest scale, while Burbach in North Rhine-Westphalia is a small smelting centre.

The Federal Republic's iron and steel capacity increased in 1957 on the return of the Saarland. Rationalization again reduced the number of plants: in the mid-1970s important full-cycle plants – smelting, steel making and rolling – were Dillingen, Völklingen, Saarbrücken, and Neunkirchen (rolling mills at Homburg). The Luxemburg *ARBED* company owns a full-cycle plant in Saarbrücken and rolling mills in St. Ingbert. There is steel conversion (French-owned) at Bous and smelting at Brebach (special pig). Though French and Luxemburg capital is substantial in the Saar, the Ruhr giants are not represented, while the Völklingen works long remained fully family-owned. In the immediate postwar years, the Saar enjoyed the inherent advantages conferred in the French market by membership of the French customs area, but since 1959 it has been exposed to the highly competitive West German market, cushioned a little by EEC legislation. The future of the Saar is uncertain, for the trend towards seawater locations undoubtedly poses problems for its industry, yet it is so far inland and serves such a special market that this may offset the advantages of the coastal sites. Nevertheless, transport forms an important key to its success and in this respect much is left to be desired. Already it has been helped by special railway rates, but the canaliz-ation of the Mosel has done little as the Saar river is still inadequate and there is little hope of a canal direct to the Rhine. The Saar industry feels under unnecessary pressure, since French heavy industry has received subventions not available to it and it does not enjoy the advantage of the Ruhr's cheaper and better coal and coke. The Saar has to use a mix of 60 percent local coal and 40 percent Ruhr, Aachen, or foreign coal to get an acceptable coke, though there has been growing cooperation between the ironworks and the coalmines to offset this problem: the survival of both is closely interlinked. Improved transport would also allow use of higher grade foreign ores at prices to compete with the low-grade, but inexpensive, Lorraine ore and yet realize considerable economies in coal and coke. Further modernization and rationalization could help: for example, the existing 19 blast furnaces could be replaced by 4 or 5 large modern furnaces, though use of LD steel converters has already begun. The industrial units are small by contemporary standards and a merger into a one-unit concern ('*Saarhütten AG*') has been suggested. The general trend has been to specialization, with closer cooperation with French and Luxemburg industry, whose problems are not dissimilar. Indeed, the regional concept of *Saarlorlux* embraces about a quarter of the iron and steel production of the original six-member community.

The Two Germanies

Distinctive iron and steel plants are scattered across North Germany. The Salzgitter works have emerged as the largest, still using considerable quantities of local ore (iron content 28–33 percent), but the attraction of foreign ore is increasing. Local ore has been restricted to nearby plants and has not been sent to the Ruhr since the early 1960s. Salzgitter remains largely dependent on Ruhr coal and coke brought along the Mittelland Canal, though foreign coal and coke imported through North German ports have become increasingly attractive pricewise. A related complex of iron smelting at Gross-Ilsede and steel making and rolling at Peine has similar raw materials, with ore mines at Lengede and Bülten. Iron and steel making and rolling on a small scale is found at Georgsmarienhütte and Osnabrück, though a tube works at Brackwede has closed. Another small iron and steel plant is Herrenwyk at Lübeck, using largely Swedish ores. The most significant coastal works is the *Klöckner* 'Idealplan' at Bremen on the site of a plant dismantled after the war, well-placed to receive seaborne shipments of ore and coal, with an ultimate capacity planned of 3–4 million tons per annum. Concentration is on plate and sheet steels important in North German motor car manufacture and ship-building. A small ferro-alloy plant at Hamburg has been augmented by a 'mini-steelworks' built by *Korf Industries* (who already operate a similar plant at Kehl on the Rhine) and another similar steelworks is operating at Lingen (Ems). Debate has taken place on the possibility of establishing a major iron and steel complex on the German North Sea coast, where a most likely site lies at the mouth of the Elbe on the low islands of Neuwerk and Scharhörn, though Stade has also been suggested. A discussed merger of all North German plants into a *Nordstahl* combine did not succeed.

Excellent communications provided by the Rhine valley have been important in the survival of metal processing long after the conditions for iron smelting disappeared. There is rolling at Schlebusch near Leverkusen and at Troisdorf, while rolling and steel making are carried on in a small way in Köln-Mülheim, with an even smaller plant at Königswinter. Important plants are the *Rasselstein* rolling mills at Neuwied and Andernach. The former rolls and galvanizes, while the latter is a cold sheet and plate rolling works producing over half the German output of tin plate, scheduled to have a full annual capacity of 1 million tons. The importance of sheet and plate rolling along the Rhine reflects the growth of the consumer durables and motor vehicles industries in the Rhine basin, while the tendency to develop mini-steel works with capacities up to 50,000 tons per annum, again serving special markets, is reflected in plants at Mannheim (where there is also rolling), at Trier and at Kehl.

The iron and steel industry of South Germany comprises plants whose long-term viability is uncertain. The largest at Sulzbach-Rosenberg has blast furnaces using up to 80 percent local ore, but the nearby *Luitpoldhütte* closed in

1968, while rolling mills operate at Haidhof and a foundry at Fronberg. The future lies in galvanizing, plastic coating of steel, heat resistant and other high quality tubes and railway rail. Steel finishing is carried on at Hammerau in Upper Bavaria, at Nürnberg, and at Laucherthal is also a rolling mill. A new mini-steelworks has been opened in Augsburg, with some rolling capacity. At Karlsruhe there is a ferro-alloy plant.

Table 10.3
Production of steel in ingot and foundry form

	In thousand tons	1966	1970	1973
North Rhine–Westphalia	Basic	5,436	697	—
	Open hearth	9,931	8,583	6,681
	Electric	2,456	3,132	3,019
	Oxygen	6,962	18,087	22,823
	Acid	13	10	4
Schleswig–Holstein,	Basic	—	—	—
Lower Saxony,	Open hearth	2,296	1,846	1,302
Hamburg, Bremen,	Electric	200	206	757
West Berlin	Oxygen	—	5,095	6,779
	Other steels	—	—	—
Hessen, Rhineland–	Basic	631	9	—
Palatinate, Baden–	Open hearth	525	561	507
Württemberg, Bavaria	Electric	202	621	1,028
	Oxygen	—	755	908
	Other steels	2	—	—
Saarland	Basic	2,921	2,934	1,729
	Open hearth	924	791	551
	Electric	210	452	457
	Oxygen	283	1,236	2,976
	Other steels	—	—	—

Source: *Statistisches Jahrbuch der Eisen – und Stahlindustrie*, various years, Düsseldorf.

Since the mid-1950s, great technological, economic, and political changes have affected Western European steel making. The creation of the European Community put German industry into a supranational setting in contrast to the watertight compartments of prewar economic nationalism: preferential treatment to home industry has become difficult, while the vastly widened market has introduced new producers like the Netherlands and Italy, but Japan has emerged as a most serious competitor to West German steel makers. Bulk carriers at sea have given the advantage to coastal steelworks and to larger producing units. The optimum size of an integrated iron and steelworks has risen from 1–2 million tons in the late 1940s to 4–5 million tons in the early

1960s and by the early 1970s to 10 million tons, a level not properly attained by the German plants. Not only does the per-ton capacity of the larger units cost less, but the large blast furnaces and oxygen steel techniques are also more economical and a given level of output can be attained with fewer units. Rationalization and modernization in West Germany has sought these ends. At the same time, there has been marked economy in the ratio of coal to ore in iron making: here the use of rich foreign ores has played an important part, while the *Hoesch-Hoogovens* link-up reflects the gains of marrying inland steel producers near to their markets to the coastal iron makers, taking advantage of cheap raw materials. The advantages of oxygen steel and electric steel in relation to the pattern of regional demand for special steels has led to the spread of the mini-steelworks of about 50,000-tons annual capacity, with a growing separation between ironmaking, steel converting and the finishing processes, where specialization and skill as well as market conditions are significant.

Nonferrous metals
Although mining of nonferrous metals has fluctuated according to world market conditions, the Federal Republic has an important smelting and processing industry, concentrated notably on the Ruhr coalfield and the Ville brown coalfield. Using the Rhine to import raw materials, Duisburg produces the greater part of West German output of pure tin, fine zinc, and other nonferrous metals. Other centres include Düsseldorf (lead, zinc), Dinslaken (zinc), Gelsenkirchen (brass), Essen (lead, zinc, magnesium), Stolberg (lead, zinc, brass), Aachen (zinc), and Lünen (uses nonferrous scrap for recovery). Originally using Westerwald ores, Braubach near Koblenz is an important lead producer; copper is worked at Kall (Schleiden/Eifel); lead at Rommeskirchen; and titanium at Krefeld. In the Siegerland, Dillenburg is a copper and nickel centre, Bad Homburg/Taunus works lead and zinc, and nearby Oberursel processes beryllium. Frankfurt is significant as commercial headquarters of important producers and brokers of nonferrous and precious metals. Hanau produces specialized metals, while Pforzheim, Fürth, Schweinfurt, and Augsburg work precious metals (including gold leaf and gold plating). Lead and tin are worked at Rastatt and there is various nonferrous metal processing in Stuttgart, Ulm, and Nürnberg. Mannheim and Bensheim specialize in nonferrous metals for electrical use and Lauchertal (Sigmaringen) is noted for bronze. Dachau and Traunstein handle molybdenum and tungsten.

A special position is held by aluminium, in which cheap electricity offers a strong locational pull, so consequently plants are either near thermal power stations or hydro-electric plants. Raw aluminium is made at Grevenbroich and Neuss near the brown coalfield; Bergheim/Erft produces aluminium substances; Düsseldorf-Mettmann processes aluminium; in the Ruhr, Lünen, like

Essen, is a raw aluminium producer; Unna and Voerde roll and draw; and Dortmund produces aluminium amalgams. On the Rhine, Koblenz rolls and draws, but Ludwigshafen produces raw aluminium, as does Rheinfelden, where plentiful electricity is available. Ulm and Singen also work aluminium. Schwandorf is a long-established alumina producer, but Töging on the Inn has become one of the largest producers in the south. More recently aluminium production has spread in North Germany: at Stade, where nuclear-generated electricity is available, and at Hamburg.

The chemicals industry

The West German chemicals industry uses raw materials available in the country – coal and lignite, salts of various types and limestone, as well as waste and by-products of a number of industries; notably, since the early 1950s, the by-products of petroleum refining have provided a wide range of petrochemicals. Nevertheless, there is also the substantial import of raw materials. Transport – both for raw materials supply and for distribution of produce – is an important locational factor, but others include adequate process water and energy, notably electricity. A large part of the industry still operates on prewar sites and has the imprint of the locational pattern impressed by the giant *IG Farbenindustrie*. Other factors have included the restrictions placed on 'war chemicals' by the Allied Control Commission until the early 1950s and the need to make in West Germany materials obtained prewar from the area of the G.D.R. There has also been development of new techniques and substances, particularly the wide range of artificial fibres and plastics.

The Rhine valley provides an excellent highway along which to receive raw materials or ship away finished products, as well as process water, though growing concern is being expressed about adding increasing quantities of warm-water effluents of a poisonous or saline nature to the river. An important cluster of plants occurs on the Ruhr coalfield, where coal has provided a raw material for the extraction of chemical substances, though in the last decade petrochemicals have penetrated the coalfield. The coal-based chemicals are particularly distinguished by the tars obtained from cokeries, from which chemists have separated over 160 substances. Some ten tar distillation plants provide raw materials for organic chemistry, pharmaceuticals, and aniline dyes. Benzol is another product of coal distillation, some going as additive in motor fuel, but most used for plastics manufacture. Benzol derivatives and synthetic resins are notably important in Herne, Wanne-Eickel, and Gelsenkirchen; ammonia substances come from Castrop Rauxel. Paraffins and alcohol are extracted from coal in Bergkamen and Wanne-Eickel, while cokeries in the western Ruhr are also major derivatives producers. Extraction of nitrogen from coke and cokery gas is significant in Oberhausen,

237

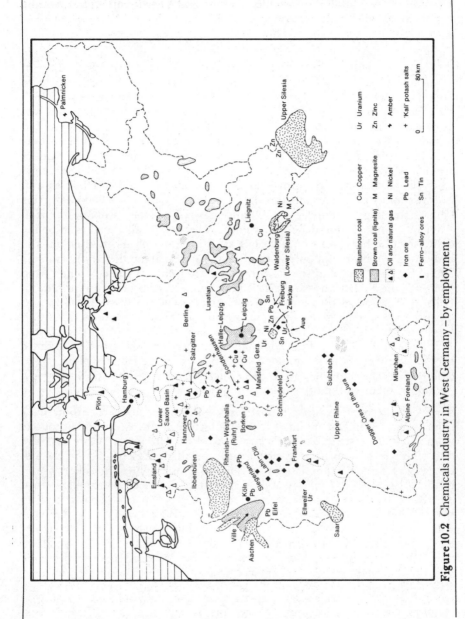

Figure 10.2 Chemicals industry in West Germany – by employment

Industry in the Federal Republic

238

Gelsenkirchen, Wanne-Eickel and Castrop Rauxel, which together supply about half the republic's needs.

The Allied ban on synthetic petroleum production and the subsequent cheap supplies of natural petroleum prevented redevelopment of synthetic fuels in the Ruhr coalfield, which had become important in the late 1930s. In place of plants badly damaged or dismantled have arisen refineries for natural crude. One of the largest contemporary plants stems from the development in 1938 of the Chemical Works Hüls near Marl on a then greenfield site. The plant was designed to use water from the Lippe, locally available electric current and 'waste' methane from a nearby hydrogenation plant. The original intent was to produce synthetic rubber, but when this was banned after 1945, the product range was diversified to a wide selection of 'harmless' plastics and detergents. The works belongs to a group of 21 associated plants, including refineries, and it draws all its raw materials through a pipeline system over 600-kilometres long (natural gas, refinery gas, liquid gas, propylene, propane, benzol, ethylene, butane, butadene, butylene), whereas it also makes pipeline deliveries to other works of materials such as cumarol and hydrogen. The associated works are not only in the Ruhr, but also along the Rhine as far as Köln (*Esso* refinery) and the *Bayerwerke* Leverkusen. Ethylene is piped from Geleen in the Netherlands and also from Raunheim near Frankfurt am Main. Hüls itself produces plastics and associated products, softeners, paint, and lacquer bases, detergents, raw materials for textiles manufacture, and products associated with rubber manufacture; the Buna Works (restarted 1958), the original core of the combine, uses acetylene and ethylene to make synthetic rubber (buna), butadene, and styrol; and the Houdry plant makes catalysts for the chemicals and petrochemicals industry, while a polyester yarn (*Vestan*) is made in the fibres plant.

The close interrelationship of industries is seen in the making of carbon black from cokery gas in Dortmund or the manufacture of zinc white and lithopone from zinc-rich waste in Europe's largest works at Homberg. Waste tin plate and other tin sources are converted into tin salts in Essen (used in the silk industry of Krefeld). The Duisburg Copperworks produces a wide range of chemical substances (notably soda compounds) besides nonferrous metals. The Ruhr coalfield is also a focus of sulphuric acid production, a basic requirement of the chemicals industry, with raw materials imported via the Rhine or from pyrites deposits within the country, but some plants are closely associated with nonferrous metal production by-products. Essen, Bochum, and Gelsenkirchen are among the main centres. Witten produces inorganic and organic materials for pharmaceuticals, soaps, and washing powders; Recklinghausen, Herne, Wanne-Eickel, Sterkrade, and Castrop-Rauxel are centres of ammonia and nitric acid production and a wide range of nitrates using limestone, soda ash, caustic soda, and potash as raw materials.

The Two Germanies

Elberfeld-Barmen remains a pharmaceuticals centre and in the Bergische Land are several centres, both large and small, making washing powders, soaps, paints, and related chemicals, with Solingen producing soda. Leverkusen, site of the large *Bayer* plant, is a chemicals giant that employs over 30,000 people, described as the 'Weltapotheke'. Dyes, chemicals for textile production, and a wide range of pharmaceuticals and pesticides are among the several thousand products, almost a half of which are exported to well over 100 countries, and also at Leverkusen are the *Agfa-Gevaert* photographic materials factories. *Bayer* owns the large Dormagen synthetic fibres plant, while the same complex manufactures sulphuric acid, synthetic rubber, and a range of plastics and pesticides.

An important raw materials base in the country around Köln is brown coal, and other raw materials are also brought along the Rhine, while petroleum refining has led to development of petrochemicals. On another scale, Köln is a major centre of the German cosmetics industry, with well-known international names represented, but most famous for its perfume, *Kölnisch Wasser* (Eau de Cologne). The pharmaceuticals industry has plants in Köln, Bad Godesberg, Eitorf, Bergisch-Gladbach, and Bensberg. Over 5000 people are employed in the artificial fibre industry in Köln-Weidenpesch and Siegburg. Köln-Kalk makes chloride associations, calcium associations, ammonia-based chemicals, and nitric substances among other basic chemicals. Other centres include Knapsack, where carbide is made as well as chlorine and sodium compounds; Wesseling, which produces a range of acids and salts; and Kalscheuren, a centre for carbon black – all characteristic producers associated with the brown coal field. Since the mid-1950s, an important olefin producer has operated in Wesseling on by-products from the nearby oil refinery. At Grefrath, silica carbide is made, and at Troisdorf, *Nobel AG* has a dynamite and plastics plant. The Aachen district was the first to make perlon in 1950 in the *Vereinigte Glanzstoff* factory, originally an artificial silk plant. In Aachen, there is production of caustic soda, chlorine, water glass, and super-phosphates. In Alsdorf, a plant reduces coal to tar oils, naphthalin, benzol, and toluol. Chemical stages of aluminium production are carried on at Düren, where late in the Second World War a large pharmaceuticals plant was built to become the largest penicillin producer in the Federal Republic. In Düren and in Eschweiler there is also paint and lacquer manufacture.

Düsseldorf has seen employment in the chemicals industry double since the interwar years, the bulk in the largest detergent works in the Federal Republic and one of the largest industrial undertakings in the city. In Hilden, there is a substantial paint and dyestuffs industry, while around Düsseldorf are numerous cosmetics, pharmaceuticals, and related plants. On the Lower Rhine, the chemicals industry shows a strong concentration on products for the textile industry. Krefeld and Neuss are makers of domestic soaps and washing media; Uerdingen produces heavy chemicals such as sulphuric acid, chrome-oxide and aniline dyes, and preparations for making perlon, plastics, synthetic resins and softeners, while Norwegian ilmenite is used notably in the manufacture of 'brilliant white' (titanium oxide). The one-time guano works in Krefeld now makes mineral fertilizers using raw phosphates imported via the Rhine, and there is a large nitrogen plant. Rheinberg produces plastics, caustic soda, and its compounds; near Moers, alcohol and paints are made; and Emmerich manufactures technical oils and inks.

The area around Frankfurt is dominated by the *Hoechst* plant in the town of that name: one of seven ammonia plants in the Federal Republic, it is best known as a manufacturer of pharmaceuticals. Since 1953 *Hoechst* has become an important producer of artificial fibres, but the company has a substantial holding in most other plants in the Rhein-Main area, including *Cassella* in Frankfurt, which originally specialized in dyes but had widened into plastics, artificial resins, and chemicals for agriculture. In Darmstadt, plexiglas-type materials and pharmaceuticals are made, which are also produced in Kassel, Wiesbaden, and Marburg. Mainz manufactures washing powders.

Situated on the Rhine for easy transport, Ludwigshafen (*BASF*) has become one of the largest complexes in the republic. Limestone and rock salt are easily available, while natural gas is drawn from deposits in the Rhine valley or by pipeline from the Netherlands. Coal gas is supplied from the Saar and there is access to the Lavera-Mannheim crude oil pipeline. Refinery products are also received by pipeline from the Karlsruhe refinery and from others in the north at Dinslaken and Godorf, while the plant's own generators provide most of its electricity. For the works, ammonia synthesis takes place at Oppau. Since the Second World War, besides the continued production of heavy chemicals and pharmaceuticals, there has been the development of a wide range of plastics among a production programme of over 5000 articles, including magnetized recording and computer tapes (mostly at the works at Wilstätt near Kehl). Ludwigshafen is now an important producer of caprolactum and organic acids. Domestic plastics (e.g., *Lupolen*) are made at the company plant at Godorf near Köln. *BASF* has over 280 associated companies throughout the Federal Republic.

The problems of heavy industry in the Saar in the long term have encouraged diversification. The fertilizer and urea plant at Perl is linked by pipeline to the ammonia works at St. Avold in France, from which it receives ammonia and carbon dioxide. The St. Avold works has a pipeline to the Saarland Klarenthal refinery at Fürstenhausen for shipment of naphtha, while the Fürstenhausen cokery produces ammonia, tars, and benzol. Near Neunkirchen, *Petrocarbona* makes special mineral oils and plastics; at Fenne there is an industrial oxygen plant, and there is a rubber factory at Büschfeld.

The main feature in South Germany is the so-called 'Chemicals Triangle' of Upper Bavaria, roughly centred around the valley of the Inn. Several plants date from the interwar years, using locally available hydro-electricity plus imported supplies of Ruhr coal, limestone from the Jurassic escarpments, and salt from the Neckar basin, though coal and limestone have been replaced by products from the Burghausen refinery, one of the first in Germany built primarily for the chemicals industry. Nevertheless, there has as yet been no appreciable shift of petrochemicals to South Germany, despite the building of several refineries. Trostberg has one of the largest plants making a wide range of inorganic materials, agricultural fertilizers, plastics, and associated materials. The chlorine works at Gensdorf in Upper Bavaria, opened just before the war, was dismantled but later rebuilt as a producer of plastics using raw materials shipped from Hüls, Burghausen (itself a plastics producer), and Ludwigshafen; on the Danube at Münchsmünster is an olefin plant; Aschau (Waldkraiburg) on the Inn makes explosives. At Kelheim on the Danube, the large sulphuric acid plant established on strategic grounds in 1941 was expanded in 1953 to include a superphosphate works, though it will not come to full capacity until after completion of the Main-Danube Canal. Using local salts, a group of works lies in the extreme southwest corner of the republic, taking advantage of local hydro-electricity to produce a wide range such as chlorine, sodium compounds, hydrogen, and carbides.

The North German plants lie either inland near the deposits of salts or near the coast where raw materials can be imported. Hamburg, a producer of considerable significance, uses its port for both import of raw materials and for distribution of finished products. Nevertheless, expansion of the industry has been hampered by the difficulties of waste disposal through pollution of the Elbe. Using imported pyrites, Hamburg produces about 8–10 percent of the sulphuric acid of the Federal Republic and is a supplier of carbon disulphide to the industries of the Rhine basin, besides producing pharmaceuticals, paints, and lacquers. There is also manufacture of dyes and preparations for the leather industry. It still retains its artificial fertilizer industry dating back to the last century as well as being the main supplier of borax and related compounds. There are fertilizer plants in Lübeck and in Nordenham. Although the focus of the petrochemicals industry has remained concentrated in the Rhine-Ruhr area, new developments have been made in the north, notably Stade and Brunsbüttel, using local refineries as a base. The problems of labour and other phenomena of 'locational saturation' in the Rhine-Ruhr and Rhine-Main areas have encouraged some firms to look more favourably on new locations in North Germany. Natural salts of the North German Plain, the Harz fringes, and the Werra basin give the character to the chemicals industry of Hannover and adjacent districts. An important share is held by *Kali-Chemie* of Hannover, though plants lie at several places such as Ronnenberg (potassium chloride), Salzdethfurth, and Heringen (Werra). There is also barytes from Bad Lauterberg in the Harz, besides common salt. Some plants, like that at Goslar producing zinc compounds and sulphuric acid, are associated with nonferrous metallurgy. Although the North German Plain has crude oil deposits and natural gas, the petrochemicals industry is as yet modestly represented, though there are some small fibre plants. Wilhelmshaven does, however, have production of inorganic chemicals. North Germany is an important centre of the rubber industry: Hannover has the large *Continental Rubber Company* works, and there is a strong representation of the industry at Hamburg, using mostly natural rubber.

CHAPTER 11

INDUSTRY IN THE FEDERAL REPUBLIC
ENGINEERING, TEXTILES AND
FOOD INDUSTRIES

Engineering covers an exceptionally wide range from delicate precision engineering to massive machinery, and some branches, like shipbuilding, have an almost completely separate identity. Labour is a key factor, constituting from 30–70 percent of the product cost, depending on the branch and, because skilled labour has generally not been migrationary, it has tended to hold certain branches in particular parts of the country. Consuming a widening range of raw materials – ferrous and nonferrous metals, plastics, other synthetic substances, rubber, and even wood and textiles – the volume of the final product may be between two and ten times greater than the volume of the original raw materials, while the added value may be ten to a hundred fold. In general, raw material supply has been less locationally significant than labour supply or even market orientation.

Although in terms of engineering employment and turnover, North Rhine-Westphalia dominates the scene, the value of output per inhabitant is greatest in Baden-Württemberg and least in Schleswig-Holstein and Lower Saxony. North Rhine-Westphalia accounts for nearly one-third of the employment and turnover, while the share of Baden-Württemberg is about one-fourth. Engineering is the largest single employer (over 13 percent of the employed population), but it shows a strong fragmentation into small firms – almost two-thirds employ less than 100 employees, though just over half the total employees are in firms employing more than 500 people. Firms over 500 employees provide 60 percent of the turnover, whereas those with less than 100 employees account for only 11 percent.

Readily definable distribution patterns for many branches are hard to find: factors such as personal experience of entrepreneurs, historical accident, diversification, and change of production lines, patterns of research and development, besides interlinkage of branches, play a significant role. The pattern is further confused by the large number of firms and the spread of industrial activity across the republic, especially with the broad spectrum of the market for engineering products and the excellent transport and distribution services for such high-value goods. The engineering industries of the coalfields show a large sector of heavier branches producing mining haulage gear, high capacity pumps, steam raising equipment, coal cutting and rock boring machinery, or equipment for steelworks such as rolling mills and forges. A close-market location is important since much machinery is specially designed for particular plants, while extensive research and development facilities as well as experimental institutes are also attractions. In the Ruhr, such branches are found in Essen, Oberhausen, Bochum, Dortmund, Lünen, and Gelsenkirchen, while Duisburg and Dinslaken are other centres. Product diversification has brought a wider production programme to many plants; for example, *Krupp* in Essen has spread to railway equipment, heavy process machinery, as well as machinery for the chemicals industry or most recently component manufacture for nuclear generators. Essen remains a research and development centre for *Krupp* plants in Bremen and Hamburg, while other firms provide such facilities for themselves and plants outside the Ruhr. Small and specialized markets may, however, exert a strong locational pull – brown coal mining and processing machinery is notably built near the Ville coalfield in Frechen, Grevenbroich, Köln, and Düsseldorf (the latter plant is a postwar migrant from Lauchhammer in Lusatia).

Textile engineering, while scattered through the republic (including refugee firms established after 1945 in North Germany), shows agglomeration in textile manufacturing districts, often reflecting local specialisms. Notable groups are found on the Lower Rhine around Mönchen-Gladbach (wide range of machinery), Krefeld (calico printing and jacquard equipment), and Viersen (silk and drapery machinery), while the textile industry east of the Rhine is reflected in the manufacture of cord- and tape-making machinery in Velbert, screen-printing machinery, special looms and ribbon-making machinery in Wuppertal. Herzogenrath and Aachen manufacture needles and needle-making machinery. Solingen and Remscheid, in keeping with traditional industries, make cutting and trimming machines for the textile and clothing trades. The South German textile industry is marked by the manufacture of knitting and hosiery machinery in towns such as Hechingen, Ingolstadt, and Stuttgart (also spinning, weaving machines, sewing machines, steam-processing machinery); Ottingen in Bavaria makes carpet looms; while looms and weaving frames are made in Reutlingen (including machinery for

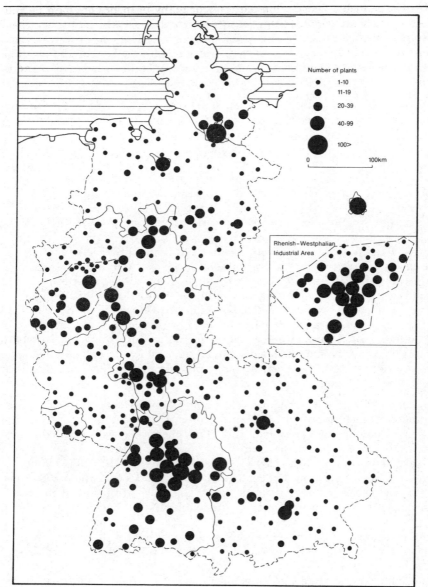

Figure 11.1 Engineering in the Federal Republic

plaiding and wire weaving). Manufactures in other districts include bleaching and finishing machinery in Sennestadt; Bielefeld and Karlsruhe are centres of sewing-machinery production, and Schauenstein (Hof) produces gathering and folding machinery. Textile engineering employs only about 5 percent of the labour force and accounts for about 6 percent of the turnover in engineering.

Manufacture of machine tools, automated process machinery, and items such as conveyor belts, counting, sorting and packaging or forming machinery is extremely widespread, and a similar wide scatter of the consumer durables industry has grown rapidly since the early 1950s. There seems little apparent reason for the pattern, in which opportunism may be a primary factor. Many products, like washing machines and refrigerators, result from assembly in a particular plant of components drawn from different manufacturers; but clusters of diverse branches are, however, typical of engineering as a whole. The major grouping lies in North Rhine-Westphalia, particularly in the Rhine valley, in Berg and Mark, around Bielefeld, and scattered through the Ruhr cities. Particularly rapid growth has marked the highly diverse engineering industry in Baden-Württemberg, founded on a long tradition of inherited skill, especially around Stuttgart, but also extending north into the Neckar basin to coalesce with the engineering towns of the Rhine-Main area. Important engineering centres lie scattered in Bavaria, with a cluster in the north around Hof and Coburg associated before 1945 with the similar industries of Thuringia and Saxony, whereas North Germany has significant clusters in Lower Saxony (Hannover-Braunschweig), and the North Sea ports. Despite its isolation, West Berlin remains a major producer of a wide range of small but highly valued labour-intensive articles.

In Baden-Württemberg, engineering is typified by the large electrical and car component factories of *Bosch* around Stuttgart; the making of clutches and other assemblies at Crailsheim and Heidenheim, as well as braking and transmission equipment at Heidelberg, or other centres like Geislingen, Dagersheim, and Eybach. There is widespread manufacture of machines for entertainment (e.g., in Baden Baden) and for food manufacture. The calcareous rocks characteristic of South Germany are reflected in several manufacturers of water-softening machinery. In Baden-Württemberg, particularly in the Neckar basin, almost every form of machine tool and automated process machinery building can be found: the diversity of many of the larger centres is well illustrated by Esslingen where there is the making of machine tools for screw and thread production, ramming and pressing machinery, perforating and punching machinery, die-forming machinery, scales and weighing machinery, planers, sewing machinery, ovens, drying and cleaning plant, and agricultural machinery.

North Rhine-Westphalia is no less diverse, but it is perhaps a reasonable generalization that a larger element of process machinery is found, particularly of the heavier type, often associated with local markets. Almost every town has one or more firms, often quite small, producing a fairly specialized range of machinery, whether it be for galvanizing or dust control, conveyor belt drives, or labelling machines. Solingen and Remscheid, for example, with a long tradition of making cutting steels, produce machinery for cutting and shearing; Ahlen has a large washing-machine manufacturer, while *Miele* domestic machines are made in Gütersloh; and there is a considerable agricultural-machinery industry, of which *International Harvester* at Neuss and *Claas* in Gütersloh are representative. The consumer society has brought demand for packaging machinery and several manufacturers are found in North Rhine-Westphalia, augmenting the considerable South German sector: Gevelsberg (where there is also lock making) and Ennepetal can serve as examples. Köln has a wide array of engineering plants and is the largest single employer in this sector among all the West German *Stadtkreise*. North Germany has a scatter of diverse engineering plants, some of refugee origin (including textile engineering). Rather special is the making of machinery for working peat (Delmenhorst, Meppen), but most characteristic is the large sector making components for ships, notably in Hamburg, Bremen, Kiel, and Lübeck.

Examined from the distribution of the production of given articles, the scatter for most products is widespread across the country, though some major branches – e.g., food-processing machinery – may show local specialization. Aachen manufactures, for example, special machines for its chocolate-making industry; the famous marzipan industry of Lübeck is supplied with machinery from local manufacturers (though there is also a manufacturer in Goslar); the cultivation of sugar beet in Lower Saxony is reflected in the manufacture of beet-handling and sugar-extracting machinery in Braunschweig. It is not unexpected that the typical port-located oil seed-crushing and flour-making industries are supplied from Hamburg, though other manufacturers are found in North Rhine-Westphalia and in Baden-Württemberg. Publishing centres like Frankfurt, Würzburg, Heidelberg, Bielefeld, and Stuttgart, with some subsidiary centres, produce printing and reprographic machinery. Office machinery is notably located in Frankfurt (*Adler*, *Torpedo*, *Burroughs*, and *Olivetti*), Nürnberg (*Triumph*), Stuttgart-Sindelfingen (*IBM*), and the 'refugee' plant of *Olympia* typewriters at Wilhelmshaven. Some of these firms, of course, have several plants scattered about the country: as an example of such dispersion, though refrigeration engineers are found in many towns, the firm of *Linde* in Wiesbaden has works in München, Köln, and Aschaffenburg for industrial installations, and in Mainz for domestic freezers.

Highly specialized clock, watch, and time-keeping machinery is notably concentrated in the Black Forest with a long Southwest German tradition of small domestic industry. *Junghans* has an important plant in Schramberg, *Kienzle* in Schwemmingen, and there is assembly in Triberg, though Berlin, München, and Pforzheim also make timing equipment. Camera and optical goods manufacture is found in Wetzlar (*Leitz*), Braunschweig (*Voigtländer* and *Rollei*), Giessen (*Minox*), Stuttgart (*Eumig* and *Kodak*), Wiesbaden (*Edixa*); Calmbach makes *Prontor* fittings; and *Braun* and *Paillard-Bolex* have plants in München. Düsseldorf is also a centre, with the German division of *Rank Xerox*, while *Zeiss* has been established as a 'refugee' industry in Oberkochen (other branches are at Heidenheim, Göttingen, Aalen, and Berlin). Japanese competition forced German camera makers to assemble overseas (e.g., *Rollei* in Singapore) to overcome the high-cost labour problem, though many firms have abandoned the cheap camera sector. Other specialisms include manufacture of precision measuring instruments in Aschaffenburg, drawing instruments in Pfronten and in Hamburg, and jewellers' machinery in the centre of the industry, Pforzheim.

Shipbuilding

Shipbuilding in West Germany provides both seagoing and inland waterways craft. Restrictions on shipbuilding in the immediate postwar years deprived the yards of skilled labour and know-how. In 1946 ships up to 1500 tons (the *Potsdam ships*) might be built, whereas from 1949 ships of any size might be built for foreign owners, but only up to 7200 tons for German owners. In 1951 all restrictions were swept away, and 1957–1961 was a boom period consequent on the Suez crisis. Shipbuilding output varies considerably from year to year, but since the 1960s West Germany has been in the top league, outstripping Britain in most years. Three centres for seagoing ships predominate: Kiel, with its deepwater inlet on the Baltic and long experience in building naval vessels; the deep water of the Elbe at Hamburg; and the more restricted Weser river at Bremerhaven and Bremen. Out of about 70 yards, 5 yards at these places provide two-thirds of the output by tonnage, including all forms of vessels and recently extended to oil rigs and platforms.

Howaldtswerke at Kiel, already one of the largest yards, is building a yard for ships up to 700,000 tons and has concentrated on large tankers and bulk carriers. A yard at Flensburg can build ships up to 40,000 tons; other medium-sized yards lie at Lübeck and Rendsburg (launching ships into a basin of the Kiel Canal). Yachts and fishing vessels are built at Arnis, Kappeln, Eckernförde, Niendorf, and Travemünde, and on the North Sea coast at Husum and Büsum.

Hamburg has a group of yards accessible by deep water to the main Elbe channel. Prewar *Blohm und Voss* dominated the scene, but the union in 1967 of *Howaldtswereke* and *Deutsche Werft* has now become most important. Extending along the Elbe waterfront in Steinwerder and Finkenwerder, the docks and slips can accommodate the largest vessels, including oil rigs, pipe-laying barges, and specialized ships. Of the medium-sized yards, the *Sietas Werft* is important and, of the smaller yards, *Norderwerft*, but there are also several small yards doing mostly repair work. Cuxhaven builds fishing vessels and tugs, whereas coasters are built at Elmshorn on the Krücken; Wewelsfleth and Wischhafen build small seagoing vessels; and upstream from Hamburg, Lauenburg builds small seagoing ships and river craft.

The *Weser AG* at Bremerhaven-Seebeck has a capacity for ships up to 650,000 tons; the company's yard at Bremen can also handle large ships. Together they employ 8000 people. At Bremerhaven there are two medium-sized yards for ships up to 6800 tons, and the *Norddeutscher Lloyd* yard does repair work, whereas the *Schichau* yard concentrates on tugs and special vessels. The yard at Vegesack can build superships up to 450,000 tons and employs 6500 people; nearby is the much smaller Lürssen yard; and the *Rolandwerft* in Bremen builds freighters up to 5000 tons. Other centres include Elsfleth on the Weser (up to 10,000 tons), Brake and Oldenburg on the Hunte (up to 4000 tons). Bardenfleth and Delmenhorst are among the yacht builders, also found at Wedel on the Elbe and on Nordeney. At Wilhelmshaven former naval yards do repair work. Emden has a large yard that can build superships; Leer and Oldersum build fishing vessels; but Papenburg has a yard for ships up to 160 metres long and 24 metres wide.

The light construction of inland waterway vessels makes the repair sector important. Using semiautomated production, vessels are usually launched broadside. Important yards along the Rhine include Walsum, Duisburg (a large centre), Wesseling, Köln-Deutz, Rheinbrohl, Lahnstein, Speyer, Germersheim, Mannheim, and Kehl. On the Weser, Minden, Lohnde, Hameln, Bodenwerder, Rinteln, and Vlotho have yards; along the Main there are builders at Erlenbach, Hassmersheim, Gustavsburg, and Würzburg; and on the Neckar, Neckarsteinach can build boats up to 1700 tons and Neckarsulm is also important. Regensburg is the main German yard on the Danube. Forty-nine percent of all river boats are built in North Rhine-Westphalia and 22 percent in the Rhineland-Palatinate. The main lakes, like the Bodensee and Chiemsee, have pleasure-boat builders (also found along the Rhine), whereas Berlin, with its many canals, has boatbuilding for pleasure and commerce, and Dortmund as a canal port has repair facilities.

Railway equipment

The Federal Republic, continuing the tradition of manufacture of railway equipment, has been an important exporter to world markets. Unlike Britain, railway equipment has never been built by the railways themselves, so many postwar builders are successors to well-known names. But the scatter still reflects a nearness to other engineering or early pioneers in developing railway nodes. The policy of railway electrification and the relatively small use of diesel traction has been reflected by the number of electric engineering firms (like *AEG*, *Brown-Boveri*, and *Siemens*) drawn into the railway market, often in cooperation with one-time steam locomotive builders, which include *Henschel* in Kassel, *Jung* at Jungenthal/Siegen, *Krupp* in Essen, *Krauss-Maffei* in München, as well as *Klöckner-Humboldt-Deutz* in Köln. Esslingen built steam locomotives until 1966, and *MAN* in Augsburg and Nürnberg was also active in the field. *MAK* in Kiel has been a postwar manufacturer of diesel locomotives, while *Linke-Hoffman-Busch* (formerly of Breslau) reopened in Salzgitter and the former Potsdam firm of *Orenstein and Koppel* has a plant at Dortmund.

Carriage and wagon building also flourishes widespread across the country, but no clear locational pattern exists among firms like *Talbot* in Aachen, *West Waggon* in Köln, *Henschel-Wegmann* in Kassel, *Hansa-Waggonbau* in Bremen, *Niedersächsische Waggonfabrik* in Elze near Hannover, *Credé* in Kassel, and the Uerdingen works. Others include *Waggon-Union* in Siegen and *Rathgeber* in München as well as *WMD* in Donauwörth. Railcars have been built in Nürnberg and Salzgitter, as well as in small numbers at Esslingen. Berlin still builds railway rolling stock, as does *Büssing* in Braunschweig, whereas Dortmund produces mine and field railway equipment near to a long-established fruitful market. Large repair railway workshops lie at strategic points in the network, though some face an uncertain future (e.g., Limburg/Lahn) through rationalization and the fall in the amount of rolling stock.

Motor vehicle industry
A main growth industry has been the making of motor vehicles, and during the 1960s the Federal Republic overtook Great Britain as the second world producer, only to be pushed into third place since 1967 by Japan; but since the middle 1950s, West Germany has held its place as a major exporter of motor vehicles. In 1973 it was estimated that one in seven of the West German industrial workforce was employed directly or indirectly in the production and maintenance of motor vehicles, while a whole range of industrial products depends upon the prosperity of the car and lorry plants. New firms and additional sites have been added to the prewar distribution pattern and the dispersion of the industry has greatly increased. In the early 1950s, a number of ephemeral firms emerged, but the industry has come to rest on the larger firms. As a markedly components assembly industry, good transport facilities and adequate labour are constant locational keys, while large flat spaces for assembly halls and storage yards are also significant.

The location of *Volkswagen* at Wolfsburg arises from the economic and strategic planning of the late 1930s. At its zenith, this plant employed 50,000 workers

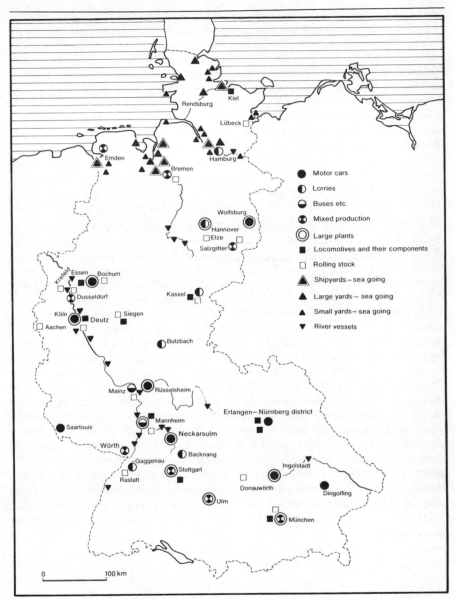

Figure 11.2 West German transport equipment plants

and, largely because of labour availability, spread to Hannover for commercial vehicle assembly; to Kassel-Baunatal, for engine and spare parts assembly (also in Braunschweig); and to Emden, for assembly of export vehicles. It was fortunate that the fortuitous element in all industrial location did not site the *Volkswagen* works a few kilometres further east, for it would then have fallen to the Soviet Zone in 1945. *Volkswagen* at one stage produced one-third of all German saloons and estate cars, but growth of its associated *Audi-NSU* and the agressive policies of *Ford* and *Opel* have since reduced this proportion. *Volkswagen* has important overseas plants (Mexico for North America and Brazil for South America); while export cars are assembled in Jugoslavia and Belgium and an assembly plant was planned at Richborough in Kent. Other North German plants include Hamburg, Hannover, and Bremen (producing commercial vehicles): a specialized producer of buses and lorries is *Büssing* at Salzgitter, while *Massey–Ferguson* has a plant in Kassel.

The Rhenish group is dominated by two American-owned firms, *Ford* established in Germany in 1930 and *Opel* taken over by *General Motors* in 1928. The main *Ford* plant is in Köln, but subsidiaries lie at Düren and Saarlouis, the latter well located for the French, Swiss, and Italian market. There is nevertheless close interchange maintained with other *Ford* plants, notably Dagenham and Halewood in Britain (design, engine building, and axles) and Genk in Belgium (wheels and related parts). Further expansion in Germany is unlikely as new plants seek low labour cost areas like Spain. *Opel* at Rüsselsheim owes its success to cheap small cars that attracted American interest. A prewar plant near Berlin was confiscated by the Soviet authorities in 1945. In 1962, *Opel* took advantage of the unemployment situation arising from the decline of Ruhr coal mining to establish large assembly plants in Bochum. More recently a plant for part assembly has been opened in Kaiserslautern, related to the *General Motors'* automatic transmission assembly plant at Strasbourg, and there are links to plants in Belgium. The drastic rationalization caused by the failing fortunes of *Krupp* of Essen demanded discontinuance of small-scale lorry building, but the plant was taken over by another manufacturer. Mainz has a small *Magirus* bus-building plant: *Daimler-Benz* have a small bus and lorry plant in Düsseldorf; at Erkrath, *Deutsche DAF* (*Volvo*) assemble from the parent firm at Eindhoven in the Netherlands; and Frankfurt and Dortmund have sections of *Kässbohrer*, the bus builders.

The South German plants are diverse, with the main concentration around Stuttgart. The principal firm is *Mercedes-Benz* (employment over 140,000), with plants in Sindelfingen and Untertürkheim, but there are also plants belonging to *Porsche* and *Auwärter*. *Mercedes* builds heavy vehicles at Wörth on the Rhine, Gaggenau, and Mannheim (buses) in Baden, while the company also has a plant in Berlin. München is the second main centre, where the

BMW plant (originally in Eisenach) has been reestablished: this firm also took over *Glas* in Dingolfing when production of the Goggomobile mini-cars ceased, and it has a plant in Landshut. In München, *MAN* assembles lorries and buses, and there is also the *Zündapp* plant, now subcontracting for other manufacturers. A postwar creation of importance is the merger of the Suabian *NSU* and the former Saxon *Audi* and *Auto-Union* now linked to *Volkswagen*. *Audi-NSU* plants lie at Neckarsulm, Heilbronn, Neuenstein, and Ingolstadt (12,400 workers), where there is also *Volkswagen* assembly. *NSU* was associated until 1959 at Heilbronn with *Deutsche Fiat*, closed in 1972 when all work was concentrated in Italy. Specialized lorry builders are *Kässbohrer* and *Magirus* in Ulm, *Faun* in Nürnberg, *Kaelble* in Backnang.

All the plants display good transport links by rail and motorway: it is difficult to argue that location is related to component makers, since this is a tremendously widespread industry, though certainly well-represented around the Hannover–Hildesheim area, in North Rhine-Westphalia, and in Baden-Württemberg. The North German plants are well placed for export, while the South German and Rhineland plants are fortunately placed to serve the large internal European Community market, though also provided with good transport links to the Rhine ports. Both South German and Rhineland plants have been significant in the growth of sheet and plate steel making in the Rhineland, while a similar trend may be discerned in North Germany. The German motorcycle industry enjoyed a brief growth in the immediate postwar years, but declined partly from growing Japanese competition, with 1972 production at little more than 10 percent of the level of the 1950s. Manufacturers include *BMW* in Berlin, *Vespa* in Haunstetten near Augsburg, *Zündapp* in München, and *Maico* in Tübingen.

Electrical engineering

Electrical engineering has been a major growth sector, closely linked to the rise in demand for consumer durables such as refrigerators, freezers, televisions, etc., so that not only have prewar branches grown, but new sectors have emerged, like electronics. This is a labour-intensive industry, consequently developing not only on its prewar sites, but also penetrating country towns where labour has been available. It has also taken advantage of the strong demand for jobs from women and has done much to adjust to working times suitable to the emancipated *Hausfrau*. While the industry shows a broad scatter throughout the Federal Republic, there is an impressive above-average employment in South Germany, along with West Berlin (an important prewar location). The Stuttgart area and the country around Ansbach (Mittelfranken), as well as Baden, Upper Bavaria, and the Upper Palatinate, are most significant. In general, it has tended to shift increasingly to South Germany: Baden-Württemberg and Bavaria together account for over half the total output by value. Other significant districts are southeastern Lower Saxony and western Hessen. There is considerable employment in North Rhine-Westphalia, but the industry does not have the commanding position it holds in other areas. Though this industry is dominated by a few large employers (e.g., *AEG-Telefunken*, 148,000; *Bosch*, 110,000; and *Siemens*, just over 300,000) with plants scattered at various places in the country, a vast number of small firms, often doing highly specialized or subcontracting work, also operate. There is also a strong American participation in electrical engineering, especially marked in the former U.S. Zone.

Berlin remains a focus of electrical engineering and firms in the western part employ over one-third of the industrial work force. Because of the transport problem to the West German market, firms producing high-value articles easy to despatch have succeeded best, though the important prewar cable, flex making, and manufacture of telephone equipment remain significant. Products include recording and sound equipment, electrical instruments, switch and control gear, and even household gadgets, medical, dental, and scientific equipment.

About one-fifth of output and employment come from North Rhine-Westphalia. The relatively small number of firms in the Ruhr towns concentrates on electrical equipment for the mining and iron and steel industries, but a very varied range of products comes from towns around Düsseldorf and Köln. Aachen has one of the larger *Philips* plants in Germany. Berg and Mark have a long-established electrical engineering industry, with some specialization in electrical cutting machines in Solingen and switchgear and cables among over 50 firms in Wuppertal. Hagen produces electrical ventilating and extractor systems, and Lüdenscheid makes electric cooking equipment. Altena has the *Graetz* radio and TV plant, and Neheim-Hüsten produces lighting equipment. Bielefeld district makes electrical cooking and baking equipment (notably for biscuit making), as well as electronic instruments. Lower Saxony contributes less than one-tenth of the output and employment in electrical engineering. Hildesheim has a radio and TV plant, and Hannover produces a wide array, including electrical counting and measuring instruments and batteries, whereas Göttingen produces electrical scientific instruments. The ports have a strong maritime bias, with radio, radar, and navigational equipment, and in Hamburg there are over 100 firms in the electrical engineering sector, including *DEBEG* for navigational equipment, *Elektrolux*, and *Philips*. Electrical and radar navigational equipment is also represented in Bremerhaven and Bremen, where the *Nordmende* radio and TV works employs more than 3000 people. Refugee firms have contributed substantially to the industry in North Germany.

With almost one-quarter of the employment and output in electrical engineering, Baden-Württemberg, especially the Neckar basin, is one of the major foci. A particular concentration is found in and around Stuttgart, including the large *Bosch* concern, the majority of whose 24 plants lie in the *Land*, and others include 'multinationals' like *IBM* (computers and electronic equipment) and *Standard-Electric-Lorenz*. At Mannheim, *Brown Boveri* (motors and machinery) has its main plant and there are several other significant producers in the town. Other towns have not only branch factories of the larger firms, but also their own local firms producing a wide spectrum of equipment. As examples, Bietigheim makes electrical components for motor cars, a particularly important branch in this part of Germany, and one of its plants employs 6000 people; a similar motor car component industry is found in Ellwangen; Böblingen has a domestic electrical equipment works founded in 1955, a typical date for many of the firms throughout the southwest. Highly specialized manufacture continuing in a new form an old tradition is reflected in Göppingen and Uhingen that make electric toys and models; while in the Black Forest and adjacent areas, the old clock and watch industry has established an electrical branch (Villingen and Schwenningen). Frankfurt produces electrical and electronic office machinery and domestic electrical appliances, radios, and television sets. Important companies are *Telefonbau und Normalzeit*, producer of all kinds of telephonic and related equipment (group employment 17,000), *VDO-Tachometerwerke* that produce all types of electrical measuring equipment (plants in Frankfurt and other centres employ some 10,000 people), and foreign firms such as *Honeywell* and *Sperry-Rand* (*Remington*). In Offenbach there is the large *Rowenta* domestic electrical appliance firm. The electrical industry of Mittelfranken is centred chiefly in towns like Nürnberg, Erlangen, and Fürth. *Grundig*, founded in 1945 and centred on Fürth, one of the greatest postwar German success stories, employs about 28,000 people to produce all types of recording, radio and television equipment. Three plants lie in Fürth, four are at Nürnberg and others in Augsburg, Bayreuth, Dachau, Georgensmünd, Karlsruhe, Kassel, Landau, Miesau, Vohenstrauss, Kenzingen, and there are also six small plants elsewhere. Nürnberg has over seventy firms whose varied products include electrical toys and musical instruments, equipment for aircraft, motors of various types, and cables and flex.

Since the Second World War, the head offices of *Siemens*, the largest electrical firm, have been in München instead of Berlin, a move made under some Allied pressure, but the original family has close connections with München, while the town and surrounding area offered a good and well-qualified labour force and the nearness to university research facilities. Now a considerable part of the labour force is foreign. For strategic reasons, *Siemens* had begun to decentralize their operations from Berlin in the late 1930s, and their plants in South Germany formed a nucleus for developments that spread quickly during the latter 1950s, while there are also *Siemens* plants in a number of the larger cities (Berlin, Augsburg, Braunschweig, Kiel, Speyer, etc.). As labour became scarcer in the latter 1950s, small plants were opened in country towns and even within the outer commuting ring of towns like München. In some instances, branch plants simply took over dissolved firms or sought towns with stagnating economies: the Regensburg plant (opened 1960) sought not only labour reserves in a stagnating economy, but also the prospect of the town becoming a university centre and its ultimate link to München by motorway.

Textiles

The textile industry has had to adjust to the division of Germany, with the loss of a considerable capacity to Poland. In common with other Western European textile industries, there has been strong competition from Eastern Europe and from outside Europe. Nevertheless, the Federal Republic has established itself as a major world producer of artificial fibres (usually ranking third). The textile-producing areas are all prewar locations and reflect the strong inertia to locational change that typifies this industry. Growth in North Germany has, however, come from refugee industries. Sixty percent of total employment is in Baden-Württemberg and North Rhine-Westphalia, and just over 20 percent in Bavaria. The textile industry is insignificant in Bremen, Hamburg, and the Saarland, though nearly 7 percent of employment is in Lower Saxony and almost 5 percent in Hessen. The Rhineland-Palatinate accounts for almost 3 percent and Schleswig-Holstein and Berlin have a little over 1 percent each. The textile industries in West Germany do not, however, show the local specialization marking these industries in Britain, probably because there was always a much higher degree of vertical organization than in the more horizontally organized British industries.

The Dutch-German borderland in the Ems basin remains a dominantly rural landscape across which are sprinkled numerous small towns where employment is heavily dependent on textiles – examples are Emsdetten, Greven, and Nordwalde, where more than three-quarters of the total employment is in the mills. Small and medium-sized factories in small groups produce mostly yarn and grey cloth and contain about one-quarter of all spindles and almost one-third of all looms in the republic. The main centres are Bocholt (weaving), Gronau (spinning), Rheine, Burgsteinfurt, Nordhorn, Greven, and Nordwalde. Other centres here include Bentheim, Bramsche, Osnabrück, Schüttorf, and Gildehaus. Emsdetten has considerable jute as well as cotton manufacture and the Münsterland has about half the total jute capacity which nevertheless has declined substantially through competition from synthetics. Knitwear and hosiery are found in Horstmar, Coesfeld, and Rheine, while Bocholt has one of the largest wadding factories in Europe. Effort has been made to diversify the industries of these centres, though some were badly hit by

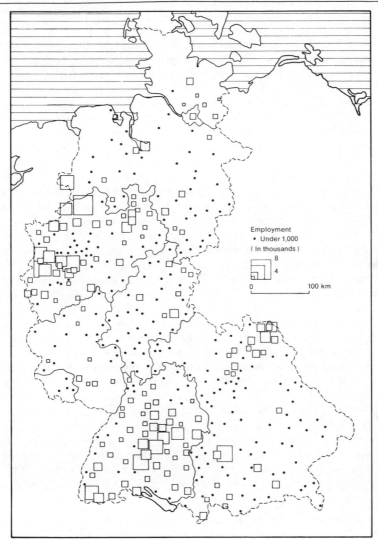

Figure 11.3 Employment in textiles in the Federal Republic

the depression of the early 1970s, having remained too dependent on textiles (e.g., Metelen).

The Lower Rhine textile industry is grouped around Aachen, Düren, Krefeld, Mönchen-Gladbach, Rheydt, and Viersen, with smaller centres such as Süchteln and Dülken. All produce from the range of cottons, calicoes, wool-cotton mixtures, gaberdines, and velours (Grefrath), while mills with mixed products occur in the *Landkreise* Kempen and Grevenbroich. Some centres have suffered through rationalization programmes (e.g., Kaldenkirchen and Wachtendonk), but the industry here shows both horizontal and vertical patterns of organization. Made-up clothing flourishes in Mönchen-Gladbach, dating from the industrialization of the Ruhr and Lower Rhine and the demand for cheap clothing in the 1860s. Krefeld is a centre for haberdashery. The silk and velvet industry on the Lower Rhine represents about one-half the total operatives in the Federal Republic. Three-quarters of the workers are in Krefeld, but also important are Rheydt, Süchteln, Dülken, Viersen, and some towns as far north as Goch, together supplying over one-third of silk cloth and over two-thirds of the velvet and plush. Rheydt produces over three-quarters of all German umbrella cloths (industrial and instrument-making cloths are also important). Carpeting, furnishing cloths, and curtains are made notably at Rheinberg. Cotton and wool cloths are concentrated in the Mönchen-Gladbach and Rheydt districts, with one-third of the heavy dress cloth, gabardine, and suiting industry in Mönchen-Gladbach, but also in Anrath, Jüchen, Kleinenbroich, Neeren, Oedt, Rheindahlen, Viersen, and Wickerath. The cotton goods, including mixtures with synthetics, cover a wide range of sheetings, moltons, Genoa cords and velveteens, poplins and shirtings as well as grey cloths for printed calicoes. The Mönchen-Gladbach area produces about 40 percent of all cotton sheetings and 45 percent of all cords and velveteens. Weaving is associated with spinning, thread and twine making, and there is also a substantial knitting, hosiery, and embroidery industry. In the finishing sections, 60 percent of the employees are in Krefeld and 40 percent in Mönchen-Gladbach-Rheydt. Krefeld has also taken up finishing woollen goods done previously in the Greiz-Gera districts of the G.D.R. The capacity of the finishing trades exceeds local needs, so cloth from other districts and even abroad is brought in.

The textile industry is one of the most important employers in Aachen and the immediately adjacent country, but also in Jülich, Düren, and Monschau. The cloths are high quality worsteds, tweeds, flannels, and cheviots. Most yarn is produced locally and there is a substantial felt (Düren – industrial felts) and carpet industry. Monschau is known for blankets and for velour for women's clothing. Near Wegburg and Wassenberg in the north are silk- and cotton-weaving sheds, while at Birgelen and Hückelhoven refugee industries now produce tights and stockings. There is a commensurate finishing industry.

Made-up clothing since the Second World War has been particularly marked in the Aachen area, notably in the smaller, less industrialized towns, including making up handkerchiefs by a Silesian refugee firm from Lauban.

Scattered textile factories are found in the districts of Berg and Mark. Wuppertal has a significant finishing industry (bleaching, dyeing, and printing), while calico printing is important in Herdecke, Hohenlimburg, and Hagen. Barmen (Wuppertal) is noted for tapes, ribbons, and elasticated cords, also made in Schwelm. Refugee activity opened a stocking factory in Menden and knitted goods in Iserlohn. The knitted goods and hosiery industry gained through the loss of the Saxon industry after 1945. Silk weaving is found in Wuppertal, Langenberg, Neviges, and Haan. Woollens and knitted goods are worked in southern Westphalia.

Bielefeld and Herford textile mills produce a great variety of yarns, though there has been specialization in crease-resistant and nonshrink textiles. Silk cloths, taffetas, and various light cloths are important, as well as corduroys, filter cloths, and even rope making. Textiles employ about one-quarter of the labour force in this district. Elsewhere in North Germany there are scattered centres – of particular importance are Hamburg (woollens, sailcloths) and Bremen (woollens), as well as Delmenhorst, Hannover, and Göttingen (knitted goods), but particularly renowned is the so-called 'carpet highway' (Hameln, Hessisch-Oldendorf, Einbeck, and Gehrden), while sisal is worked in a large plant at Grohn near Bremen. A new branch is curtain making, notably in Eystrup (Weser) and in the periphery of Hannover. Jute works lie at Delmenhorst and in Braunschweig, while Celle has a large silk works. Bedding is important in Osterode and Hannover. Neumünster is the main centre in Schleswig-Holstein (coarse cloths), with great diversification through small refugee firms, though since the latter 1950s the number of firms has declined as the remaining ones have grown larger. There has also been a vigorous growth of textiles (stockings, jerseys, furnishings, and industrial cloths) in West Berlin (a number of mills owned by West German firms), which now accounts for about 2 percent of the total textile production of the Federal Republic, but 15 percent of the output of jersey. Fashion wear is also an important product of the Berlin clothing trade.

In Württemberg the most important districts are the upper Neckar basin and the foot of the Alb, where towns produce a wide range of cotton and woollen goods as well as synthetic cloths: spinning, weaving, and finishing are well represented, and particularly important has been the upsurge in knitted cloths, of which Baden-Württemberg produces over 70 percent of the total output. Quite a few refugee firms are found, notably from Jena and the Vogtland. The main centres for knitted goods are Reutlingen, Tailfingen, Ebingen, Nürtingen, Stuttgart, Hechingen, and around the Bodensee.

Industry in the Federal Republic

Heilbronn produces industrial cloths, carpets, and sewing cotton; Ludwigsburg has printing and spinning mills (also in Backnang and Esslingen) and knitted goods; Göppingen weaves jacquards, tartans, and drills, and produces tapes and ribbons; at Mössingen there is making of tights and stockings, towelling, and knitted goods. Water shortage has been an important limitation on the growth of the textile industry in the southwest. Textile towns (e.g., Offenburg, Freiburg, Schopfheim, Lörrach, and Radolfzell) spread across Baden from the Black Forest to the Bodensee and show a strong element of spinning and weaving, sewing cotton as well as linen and hemp. Baden-Württemberg employs 65 percent female labour in its textile mills and, of the total labour force, 35 percent is foreign.

The textile industry of Bavaria is in four main groups: the Hof district of Upper Franconia; the towns along the Main valley; Augsburg; and München with southern Bavaria. The towns of the Hof district – for example, Schauenstein, Selbitz, Naila, and Münchberg – are a southern continuation in pattern of the Thuringian Vogtland districts now in the G.D.R. Hof has been hard hit by the new frontier because prewar its cotton spinning mills drew their raw materials from Bremen-Bremerhaven via the direct route across Thuringia and Saxony, but now must pay for a much longer rail haul from the North Sea ports, and much of their yarn went back to Saxony for weaving and finishing. Despite the adverse location and the difficulty of establishing new markets, the cotton mills have, with state help, concentrated on high-quality products for which satisfactory markets have been found. The towns along the Main are notably engaged in cotton spinning and weaving with a restricted finishing industry (mostly printing). There is a scattered knitted goods industry and stocking making (notably Forcheim and Erlangen); Kulmbach and Bayreuth make curtaining and industrial cloths; Bamberg weaves calicoes. One of the main Bavarian centres is Augsburg, dealing with mostly cotton and synthetic yarns, but with some worsted manufacture, but its spinning, weaving, and finishing works produce a wide range of fabrics and cords, carpets, and curtaining, as well as knitted goods (mostly jerseys and fancy knits).

The southern Bavarian centres include a number of refugee firms, notably the large *Kunert* stocking factory from Warnsdorf in the Sudetenland, which now has several plants in addition to its main works in Immenstadt. Kempten (Allgäu) has knitted goods firms from the eastern Sudetenland, while there are also weaving sheds for cotton goods and synthetics. Bad Aibling has a carpet industry, knitted goods (jerseys and velours), and special handweavers – also spread widely throughout the country for the substantial 'folk weave' market. Cotton spinning and weaving are also done at Kaufbeuren. München has a considerable knitted goods industry as well as sewing cottons, waddings, and lining cloths.

Food industries
One of the most widely scattered and diverse industries is the preparation of food and drink, which does, however, show some regional patterns. It is, nevertheless, one of the largest industrial sectors and ranks within the five major branches in employment and turnover terms in many parts of the country. In such a varied industry it is possible only to consider a few selected products.

Milling is characteristically distributed in the North German ports (Hamburg, Bremen) and along the Rhine (for example, in Duisburg and Ludwigshafen), with grain brought upstream from the estuarine ports and likewise along the canals (as in Dortmund, using the Dortmund-Ems Canal). Nevertheless, flour mills are also found in main inland centres, especially near some of the baking and biscuit-making towns (e.g., Hannover, Aachen). Flour milling, as a result of greater flexibility through the Economic Community's agricultural policy, has suffered overcapacity, with closure of some quite large mills (e.g., in Duisburg), while fall in bread consumption has also been a factor in the industry's problems. Margarine manufacture shows a relation to the oil mills, for example, along the Rhine (Neuss and Kleve) and in Hamburg; other centres are Coesfeld, Herford, and Bünde in Westphalia; Hilter and Dissen in Lower Saxony; Kiel and Elmshorn in Schleswig-Holstein; and also Bremen. In south Germany, Nürnberg and München are among the centres, while the Saar is served by St. Ingbert. Preparation of tea and coffee is particularly associated with Bremen, but Hamburg is a close rival, though many inland towns have coffee roasters of various sizes and *Nescafé* is made in Mainz. Tobacco processing also occurs in the main importing ports of Bremen and Hamburg, largely through association with the American trade, and in these ports there is also the making of cigarettes and cigars. Bielefeld and the Ravensberger Land (Bünde, Löhne and Vlotho) claim to be the oldest and most important centres for cigars. On the Rhine, Andernach has a considerable cigarette manufacturer, but others include Duisburg and Rees and, along the Dutch border in Aachen, Emmerich and Rheine; and in Hessen, cigar and cigarette manufacture is associated with Giessen, Wetzlar and Marburg. South German firms have depended more on Balkan tobacco, while German tobacco is most important around Karlsruhe and near Lahr. Most South German firms operate in small towns in Baden and Württemberg and a few large towns like München.

Most towns have slaughter houses, while butchers commonly prepare their own items like sausages. The larger meat processors usually employ between 80–200 employees, but the *Herta* plant at Herten in the Ruhr, with an aggressive export trade policy, employs 2500 people. Other large meat plants are Bünde and Oldenburg, but strong regional tastes and specialities are possibly significant in keeping the market fragmented and most plants small.

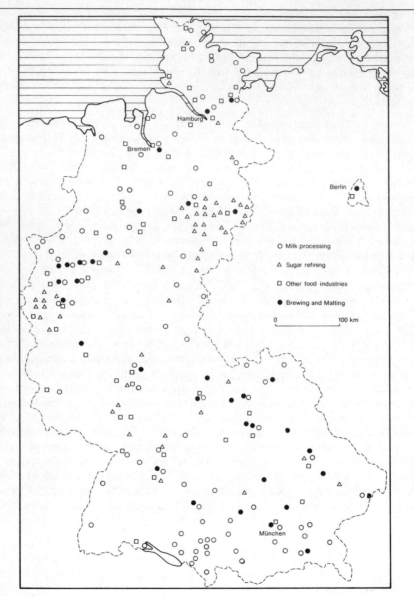

Figure 11.4 Food industries

Traditionally, fish has usually been consumed salted or pickled because of past problems of distribution; consequently, there is a large fish-processing industry in relation to the quantities landed, with canning nowadays important. The main centres are the principal fishing ports of Cuxhaven and Bremerhaven, but the industry is well represented in Hamburg, Bremen, and in Kiel on the Baltic. Some fish is also processed inland: for example, firms in Wesel and Hannover pack both meat and fish. Several North German towns smoke eel, though the traditional eel smoking of the Rhine has been abandoned through pollution ruining the eel catch. Fresh fish distribution is dominated by the *Nordsee* firm of Bremerhaven, which has over 300 retail outlets and 60 fish restaurants throughout the republic.

The jam industry, though formed by several important firms, is dominated by Bad Schwartau in Holstein (a good soft fruit area) and Aachen. Local specialities traditionally colour the production of sweetmeats, like *Aachener Printen* and *Nürnberger Lebkuchen* and even *Lübecker Marzipan*. Chocolate making is widespread; e.g., *Trumpf* and *Mauxion* of Aachen, *Sarotti* of Hattersheim (Main), *Sprengel* of Hannover, *Stollwerck* of Köln, *Waldbaur* of Stuttgart, and the Swiss firm of *Suchard* on the German side of the Rhine near Basel at Lörrach.

The Federal Republic contains over 1900 breweries, 80 percent of the total in the original Economic Community of the Six, with over 60 percent of the Community output, and is the world's second largest brewer after the United States and the second consumer (in litres per head) after Czechoslovakia. Large expanses of Triassic and related rocks provide an excellent source of water – 96 percent of the water consumed in breweries comes from wells and springs, and there is also a long tradition of hop cultivation, notably in South Germany in districts such as the Hallertau. Each hectolitre of beer requires about 180–220 grams of hops, but annual hop production commonly exceeds domestic requirements by a quarter, and there is consequently considerable export, but nevertheless import of hops with particular qualities is made, especially the highly regarded fragrant 'Saazer' (Žatec) hops from Bohemia. Barley is largely summer varieties and 40–77 percent of consumption is covered from home production, depending on the harvest, with any deficiency made good by imports from France and the G.D.R. For malt, home production covers 93–97 percent of the needs and each hectolitre of beer generally requires about 18 kilograms of malting barley.

Breweries are scattered throughout the country, but the output of the large number of small breweries in South Germany is offset by the production of the numerically fewer large breweries in the north. Breweries with over 200,000 hectolitres annual production form only 5 percent of the total plants, but account for 54 percent of the output. The number of breweries has tended to fall, though the degree of financial concentration remains much below the

United Kingdom. North German brewing is characteristically in a few large plants: one of the principal centres is Dortmund – the *Dortmunder Union* and *Dortmunder Actien Bier* are among the largest producers in West Germany and enjoy international renown. Other Ruhr towns with big breweries are Bochum with *Schlegel* and *Schultheiss*, Essen, Duisburg (*König Pilsener*), Recklinghausen, and Hamm; and Wuppertal is the centre of the *Wicküler* group, while important local breweries are also located in Düsseldorf. A particularly important centre is Hamburg – notable is the *Holsten Brauerei* (also in Kiel and Neumünster), but also the *Bill-Brauerei* and the *Elbschloss* concern, while the *Bavaria und St. Pauli-Brauerei* have plants in Harburg, Jever and Oldenburg.

Almost 70 percent of all German breweries are in Bavaria and 15 percent in Baden-Württemberg, overwhelmingly small units. The average production of breweries in Bavaria is 17,000 hectolitres annually and 39,000 hectolitres in Baden-Württemberg, whereas in the remaining states average production well exceeds 100,000 hectolitres. Several breweries are often found in a quite small town: Bamberg, with 74,000 people, has fifteen breweries. Most famous of all South German brewing centres is München with the famous *Löwenbräu* (sixth largest in the Federal Republic). The Bavarian state brewery in Freissing founded in AD 1040 typifies the long tradition of brewing. Würzburg and Kulmbach are other important Bavarian centres.

An interesting example of local resources is the mineral water industry, for, unlike the United Kingdom where mineral waters are produced almost entirely by artificial aeration, in Germany use is made of the widely occurring natural sparkling mineral waters, particularly in the Rhine valley and adjacent uplands (of which *Appolinaris* reached international status). Many of these natural waters require some treatment, such as removal of certain iron compounds or surplus carbon dioxide, while many are also sold with added flavour to give lemonade-type drinks. Despite their bulky nature and relatively low value, these are shipped over wide distances. The market has, however, been invaded by American-style *Coca-Cola* and its competitors.

Other branches include preparation of fruit juices, notably apple juice (widespread) or more recently grape juice (from wine districts). There is also some local specialization in spirits, though *Brennereien* are widely found: so for example from the Black Forest comes raspberry liqueur (*Himbeergeist*); but specially flavoured liqueurs are widely made in places as far apart as Berlin (*Mampe*) and Mainz (*Eckes*); and refugee firms produce specialities like *Bärenfang* (honey liqueur) from East Prussia and *Danziger Goldwasser*. *Schnaps* is a North German product: *Doornkaat* at Norden, *Schinkenhäger* Steinhagen, *Pott-Rumm* at Flensburg. Famous brandy centres are Rüdesheim (*Asbach Uralt*) and Bingen (*Scharlachberg*), while *Dujardin* has its distillery in Krefeld-Uerdingen.

265

Branntwein is widely made in the Upper Rhine. At Rheinberg is made the renowned 'tummy settler', *Underberg*.

In the producing districts, individual large growers market their own wines, but there are also various forms of cooperative action for small producers. At the same time large marketing firms exist that set quality and control long-established markets, like *Deinhard* of Koblenz. Particularly the sparkling wine sector is marked by firms of this type – *Deinhard, Kupferberg, Henkel,* and *Söhnlein*. Such wines are produced by some 84 firms in 43 locations, half in the Rhine-Main area, notably Eltville, Hochheim, Mainz, Wiesbaden, but Trier is also important on the upper Mosel.

Sugar refining is widespread throughout the areas of sugar beet cultivation, notably the loessic country of the Kölner Bucht, Lower Saxony, the Rhine rift valley and the Main around Würzburg. The main concentration of sugar refineries occurs on the loessic soils of Lower Saxony, but another important group is in the Lower Rhine, and large but scattered factories are found in South Germany. The bulk of sugar is produced from home-grown beet, but some cane sugar is imported.

Suggested further reading

Bergmann, W.: Unser Steinkohlenbergbau – Gestern, Heute und Morgen, *Gesamtverband des deutschen Steinkohlenbergbaues*, Essen, 1970.
Broich, F.: Die Petrochemie des Rhein-Ruhr-Gebiets, Essen, 1968.
Buchholz, H. J.: Darstellungen und Analysen des Strukturwandels an der Ruhr, *Westfäl. Forsch.* 24, 1972, p.195–211.
Dege, W.: Grossraum Ruhrgebiet, Düsseldorf, 1973.
Gansäuer, K. F.: Lagerung und Verflechtung der eisenschaffenden Industrie der Montanunionsländer in räumlicher Sicht, *Kölner Forsch. z. Wirtschafts- und Sozialgeog.* 1, 1964.
Grotewold, A.: West Germany's economic growth, *A.A.A.G.* 63, 1973, pp.353–365.
Hottes, K. H.: Die wirtschaftsgeographische Gliederung der BRD – eine geographisch-landeskundliche Bestandsaufnahme, *Forsch. z. deut. Landeskunde* 193, 1972.
Mayer, F.: Die Energiewirtschaft der BRD – Gegenwartsanalyse und Zukunftsperspektiven, *Geog. Rundschau* 26, 1974, pp.257–273.
Otremba, E.: Wirtschaftsräumliche Gliederung Deutschlands, *Berichte z. deut. Landeskunde* 18, 1957.
Standortsbedingungen und Verflechtungen in der BRD, Paderborn, 1973.
Schall, H.: Die chemische Industrie Deutschlands unter besonderer Berücksichtigung der Standortfrage, *Nürnberger Wirtschafts- und Sozialgeog. Arb.* 2, 1959.
Schniotalle, R.: Der Braunkohlenbergbau in der BRD – seine Stellung in Industrie und energiewirtschaftlichen Gefüge, *Kölner Forsch. z. Wirtschafts- u. Sozialgeog.* 14, 1971.
Weigt, E. (ed.): Wirtschaftsgeographischer Wandel in Deutschland, *Nürnberger Wirtschafts- u. Sozialgeog. Arb.* 1, 1957.

CHAPTER 12

THE TERTIARY SECTOR IN THE FEDERAL REPUBLIC

One striking feature of Western European countries since the Second World War has been the growth of the tertiary or service sector of their economies. Though development in the Federal Republic was slower than in some neighbouring countries, the pace has been accelerating. This sector, grouping all those activities that offer services rather than produce goods, has grown notably through the development and expansion of local and central government, education, and more sophisticated medical and social services, while it has received impetus from leisure activities made possible by greater affluence. It includes a wide range of banking and financial services, wholesale and retail trades as well as hotel and restaurant trades. Within this sector, German statistics also include transport, commerce, the service enterprises, and public and governmental activities: on this basis, in 1975, these branches included 46.9 percent of all employed persons and 49.6 percent of the gross national product. It is worth noting that the respective figures for manufacturing industry (including mining, energy supply, and building) were 45.9 percent and 47.8 percent. Though not quite comparable, the figures for 1950 were in employment almost 33 percent in the tertiary sector and nearly 43 percent in manufacturing industry, while of the gross national product almost 50 percent and little over 40 percent respectively.

Employment in the tertiary sector is significantly concentrated in towns and the great population agglomerations, but it is also important in the main holiday areas. In broad regional terms, employment shows its highest levels in

Northwest Germany and along the Rhine, while in the south it is particularly significant around München and in the German Alps. There is also a correlation between the distribution of higher order central places and the share of the tertiary sector in regional employment, though in view of such places' involvement in commerce, administration, and the various public services, that is perhaps not surprising. In Northwest Germany tertiary employment is notably in the city states of Hamburg and Bremen, and is particularly significant on the lower Rhine in such centres as Essen, Düsseldorf, Köln, and Bonn, as well as in the Rhine-Main area, with Wiesbaden, Frankfurt, Mainz, Offenbach, and Darmstadt. The relatively fewer important South German urban centres tend to reduce the apparent significance of the tertiary sector. München commands the South German scene rather than Stuttgart, which suffers through sharing some activities with Karlsruhe and Mannheim. The federal structure, with its separate *Länder* administrative systems, and the absence of a major capital city have been factors tending to encourage a wide dispersal of tertiary employment over many centres through the dispersion of the upper echelons of government. The loss of the capital role of Berlin after 1945 helped the postwar diffusion of commercial and financial activity: Bonn was not only unable to absorb all government offices because of its limited accommodation capacity but it was also undesirable to concentrate too much activity there in order to stress its provisional role.

There has been a steady growth in government and public service employment, and though such employment is found in virtually every town, these activities dominate Bonn and its immediate satellite communities. As federal capital, it houses all the principal ministries as well as the diplomatic missions of foreign countries, though some ministries have decentralized activities; for example, the Ministry of the Interior has branch departments in Wiesbaden (Federal Statistical Office), Köln, Koblenz, and West Berlin, while the Ministry of Economics and Finance has offices in Offenbach, Bad Homburg, Stadthagen, Karlsruhe, and Köln as well as Braunschweig, Frankfurt, and Berlin. The German Patent Office is in München, while several constitutional and legal functions are conducted in Karlsruhe, and the Ministry of Labour has departments in Nürnberg and district, decentralization quite feasible with modern means of communication. Each *Land* has its own capital with a wide range of its own ministries and legislature, and administration is an employer in the seats of the lower orders of local government – the *Regierungsbezirke* and *Kreise*, etc. Whereas local government reform has tended to reduce the number of territorial-administrative units and consequently the number of administrative centres, those remaining appear to have enlarged their administrative activities.

Related to this structure are the many welfare and labour or professional organizations that provide substantial activity in some towns: an example is the mining industry organization in Bochum with large administrative offices. Other towns with a strong representation of trade and professional associations are mostly larger regional centres (e.g., Frankfurt for motor vehicle builders, engineering, and the chemicals industry; Düsseldorf for the iron and steel industry, metalworking, and glass making; while Offenbach has associations for the leather and boot and shoe industries, and Köln is the seat of associations for the clothing trade, precision engineering, and optical goods). It is not always easy to relate the locations of these headquarters with the presence of the activities they represent.

The pattern of services such as health and education reenforce the pattern of government and administrative activities, while the level of these services is a useful indicator of the rank of towns as central places, for the more specialized the services, the higher the rank generally as a central place. Hospitals are operated by various local government, public and private organizations, though the level of provision in beds per 1000 of population varies considerably between the *Länder*. Facilities are generally largest and most specialized in university towns: Hamburg, Frankfurt, Köln, and München are notably important, but specialized facilities occur in the many spas and health resorts, while special hospitals are also maintained by some organizations, like the *Bergmannsheil* for miners' accidents and diseases in the Ruhr coalfield. The hierarchy of educational facilities is also a useful indicator of central place function, with present trends to gather the primary and secondary levels of schooling into larger units, especially in rural districts. Particularly important in the pattern of central places is the distribution of universities and equivalent institutions, with an explosion in tertiary education: university students rose from 180,000 in 1950 to well over 520,000 in 1974, while the number of universities rose from 17 before 1939 to 48 in 1976. The growth of tertiary sector employment in towns has left few truly 'university towns', though Giessen (12,800 students), Marburg (13,500), and Göttingen (18,200) still retain much of this air. The largest university populations are in the major regional centres – München (50,100), Hamburg (25,900), Köln (23,400), Frankfurt (21,600). Large in relation to the population of their towns are Münster in Westphalia (25,300 students) and Bonn (21,900), while the University (1962) of Bochum has 20,300 students. West Berlin has 49,200 students in its two universities and much encouragement has been given to study there as a boost for its virtual siege economy. Universities were created in the 1960s, not only to cater for rising demand for higher education, but also as an important tool in regional development. In the Ruhr, Bochum was chosen in the hope the university would diversify its economy and provide counterbalance to its declining coalmining, but Essen, Duisburg, and Dortmund have also received universities or their equivalent; the Medical Academy in Düsseldorf has formed the core of another; and a further one has been opened in Wuppertal. One of the first postwar universities was at Saarbrücken to provide opportunity for the young Saarländer unable to attend German or French universities, while Mainz University was founded to service the Rhineland-Palatinate. The new university at Regensburg proved an important attraction to new industry interested in using its research potential.

An important element in the designation of central places and their service areas is newspaper circulation, especially as the regional newspaper has remained more significant than the national daily. During the 1960s the number of papers decreased, often through grouping several together in joint editorial and printing facilities (sometimes original titles were retained and distinguished by a page of local news), but almost every regional centre retains one or more daily newspapers. In the Ruhr and Lower Rhine area, two papers appear daily in Dortmund, three in Essen, and two in Düsseldorf; other dailies come from Aachen (two owned by the same firm), Mönchen-Gladbach, Wuppertal, Köln, and Bonn. North Germany relies heavily on Hamburg papers, but Bremen, Oldenburg, and Hannover are independent centres, and despite a sparsely settled and relatively poor hinterland, Lüneburg supports its own paper. Flensburg is distinguished by its daily Danish-language newspaper besides a German-language one. In South Germany, the Rhine axis is not surprisingly lined by centres publishing daily papers, though the scene is dominated by Frankfurt. Stuttgart is important for the Neckar basin, and München, Regensburg, and Augsburg serve the far south, with Coburg, Bayreuth, Würzburg, and Nürnberg as secondary centres, while Saarbrücken is a distinct centre.

A number of national dailies emerged from the reorganization of the press after 1945, though the distribution of publishing centres is more dispersed than in Britain. The largest circulation is enjoyed by the inexpensive if sensational *Bild-Zeitung*, printed and distributed from a common matrix in nine regional editions. The other main dailies are *Die Welt* (Hamburg and Bonn), *Süddeutche Zeitung* (München), and the *Frankfurter Allgemeine Zeitung* (Frankfurt). The latter illustrates the pattern of sales – North Rhine-Westphalia accounts for almost 30 percent of copies sold, as do Hessen, Rhineland-Palatinate, and the Saar together, while little over 13 percent are sold in Baden-Württemberg and the same proportion in Lower Saxony, Schleswig-Holstein, and the Hanse cities, but in Bavaria only 10 percent and hardly 4 percent in Berlin. The economics of newspaper publishing have forced rising concentration, so that the dynamic *Axel Springer Verlag* has led to Hamburg becoming the press focus of Germany (*Bild Zeitung, Die Welt, Hamburger Abendblatt* and work for its other papers in Berlin). Hamburg has a 99 percent share of the restricted Sunday market (*Bild am Sonntag* and *Die Welt am Sonntag*) and produces over a quarter of the weekly illustrated magazines including the influential radio and TV paper, *Hör Zu*. Another major magazine publisher is *Burda* in Offenburg, with the largest share of the women's magazine market. Other centres include Gütersloh, Braunschweig, München, and Frankfurt.

Book publishing is dominated by a few centres, but again it is more dispersed than in Britain. Frankfurt has replaced Leipzig through its annual book fair and nearby Wiesbaden is also important. In the south, München has a strong contingent of publishing houses, whereas, in the north, Hamburg is the main centre, though significant firms operate from Kiel and Neumünster. *Westermann* in Braunschweig is a large scholastic publisher and has taken over the specialized prewar map and atlas trade from Gotha; other centres are Bielefeld, Hannover, Paderborn, Gütersloh, Köln and Düsseldorf, whereas Stuttgart has a large trade in children's and popular literature. University towns are expectedly seats of publishing houses, as for example in Freiburg, Tübingen, and Marburg.

Broadcasting and television are organized into nine regional corporations, the product of immediate postwar decentralization on the basis of the then occupation zones: West German Radio (Köln), North German Radio (Hamburg), Bavarian Radio (München), Radio Free Berlin, Hessen Radio (Frankfurt), Southwest Radio (Stuttgart), Radio Bremen, and Saarland Radio, but studios and transmitters for radio and television are scattered. In 1963 the Second German Television service began from Mainz. Together West German, North German, and Bavarian Radio command 62 percent of all licence holders. Apart from Mainz and Saarbrücken, the macroregional capitals notably stand out as the seat of these bodies.

The Federal Republic has become a significant European focus for fairs and exhibitions. Again, the major commercial towns stand out, all served by excellent transport links. West Berlin presents possibly some difficulty of access, but it has been developed for meetings of this kind in the hope of strengthening its economy. Hannover has its international trade fair, begun in 1949 as a successor to the Leipzig fair (until recently an essentially East *bloc* meeting). With an excellent central position for Western Europe, Köln is especially busy throughout the year, though both Düsseldorf and Frankfurt are also favoured, and South Germany is dominated by München. Other towns with international fairs are Nürnberg (toys), Hamburg (shipping topics), Offenbach (leather, shoes) and Stuttgart (wine processing). The number of events varies from year to year, but the participating towns hardly alter.

Financial operations
The success of the Federal German economy has brought a proliferation in all types of banking. A few financial focal points have arisen, with a markedly Rhenish distribution, though centres also lie in the north and southeast. The

present pattern is the outcome of the decentralization and deconcentration of economic activity after 1945 when the occupation zones became the basic framework of the country, but another influence arose from the prewar role of Berlin as a dominant financial centre and its special position after 1945. The Allied authorities broke up the large prewar banks and decreed that no bank should have branches outside its own *Land*. Until the creation of major regional banks in 1952, the *Land* central banks played the key role in financial operations, but in 1957 the major regional banks were merged into three big national banks, each with branches scattered across the country. With the creation of a federal central bank (*Bundesbank*) and the siting of federal financial agencies in Frankfurt, it has become the seat of the 3 largest banks and of over 100 lesser banks, besides the German giro and savings banks and the Trades Union *Bank für Gemeinwirtschaft*. Although Köln has a long banking tradition, the second most important centre has become Düsseldorf, where the largest banks maintain high-level management (for a time the *Commerzbank*, one of the big three, regarded it as its main base), but the head offices of the *Westfalenbank* are in Bochum and those of the *Volksbanken* (mainly concerned with agricultural and cooperative finance) in Bonn. The third important centre is Hamburg (again with a long tradition of banking, notably concerned with maritime operations and the financing of shipping; one of its main houses also maintains a presence in Mannheim to finance inland waterway shipping). South Germany is financially dominated by München which has its own distinctive banks, including some long-established merchant bankers and investment trusts, and Nürnberg and Stuttgart are subsidiary banking centres. Only München and Stuttgart have stock exchanges, whereas, in the north, Hamburg, Bremen, and Hannover have them, though the most important are Frankfurt and Düsseldorf, while Berlin has lost much importance.

Retailing

Rising labour costs and the problems of distribution are bringing numerous changes in established patterns of retailing in Western Europe, from which the Federal Republic has not escaped. Though employment has tended to fall in this sector, its turnover has been climbing. Obviously, the array of retail outlets in a town is an indicator of its role as a central place, and the value of retailing has been reflected in the efforts of many towns to develop shopping foci in competition with their neighbours. In the urban agglomerations considerable interurban shopping movements take place for small price differentials or for the range of goods offered.

Studies in several towns suggest that the number of shops is less than before the war, but that postwar shops are considerably larger. War-time damage and subsequent rebuilding has also often shifted the location of the main shopping streets slightly, while banks, insurance, and related offices are now a more prominent feature. Concentration has also been encouraged by pedestrianization in many central areas, with good examples in München, Dortmund, and Kassel, but also in smaller towns like Giessen and Andernach. Though the national multiple store is increasing, the German 'High Street' is still dominated by the individual shop or the branch of local chainstores, and the poor development of the major regional or national multiple possibly partly accounts for the interurban shopping movements noted above, while the specialist shop remains significant and can have considerable dimensions, like the multi-storied *Rasch* toyshop in Hamburg. The wave of clothes shops opened in the 1950s was followed by a spread of *Kunstgewerbe* – arts and crafts – shops, while during the 1960s a sign of the rising affluence was the multiplication of shops for electrical goods, car accessories, furnishings, sports and leisure activities, and even business equipment. Since the early 1970s the do-it-yourself shop has reflected escalating cost of labour in the home. These changes have gone along with the declining role of foodstores in the central shopping districts.

Like elsewhere in Western Europe, retailing, particularly for food, has become increasingly linked to the super- and hypermarket, of which the large out-of-town centre with copious car parking has become a marked feature, frightened away from the central town areas by exceptionally high land values. West Germany has more hypermarkets than its neighbours and these show a distinctly Rhenish location, though other clusters are around the *Hanse* cities and Hannover, and an increasing, if later, development has followed in the south. Though not among the largest individual units, there are over 400 in West Germany with floor areas exceeding 25,000 square metres and hypermarkets now claim well over 10 percent of total food sales, a powerful force in pressing individual food shops into marketing rings like *Spar*, *Edeka*, and *Coop*. The first large hypermarket was the Main-Taunus Centre, 11 kilometres from central Frankfurt, opened in 1964, subsequently developing as a regional shopping centre. The Ruhr Park Centre outside Bochum (opened 1964) illustrates the typical pattern of regional shopping centre development: the business area increased from 21,000 square metres at the outset to 70,000 square metres in 1974, while parking places were increased from 2500 to 6500 and employment from 1500 to 3500 with a growth in annual turnover from DM 78 million to 320 million. These centres mostly include a full range of shops, a post office, banks, a filling station, car wash, restaurants, and a free kindergarten. The typical number of cars (average three occupants) rises from 15,000 on weekdays to 30,000 on Saturdays and 80 percent of the customers arrive by car. The centres have had a wide influence on shopping patterns; for example, small shops up to 25 kilometres away around the Neuwied Basin complain of competition from the Rhine Centre outside Koblenz. In general, such centres are designed to have a hinterland of 100,000–150,000 people. A survey in 1972 showed that in towns of over 100,000 people, one-fifth of all households shopped at least once a month for food in a hypermarket.

Central places
As the service industries and related activities of the tertiary sector are predominantly urban in character, their spatial pattern is one of differential clusters in towns that act as a hierarchy of central focal points serving defined hinterlands. This structure, particularly clear in the long stable landscape of South Germany, led Christaller to develop the hierarchial concept, but in the densely settled industrial Rhineland, for example, the relationships are far less clear. Nevertheless, central places and their interconnecting axes have been favoured by postwar planners in the Federal Republic as a basis for spatial planning.

In reality, the interrelationships of administrative, medical, dental, educational, entertainment, sport, and even shopping functions in central places are complex and their service areas not always easy to define or necessarily coterminous. Figure 12.1 is an attempt to provide a meaningful generalization, but such patterns are by no means static and depend upon a balance between competing centres. Nevertheless, four main levels have been defined, a fact recognized and used in the designation of the federal postal code system. The lowest, fourth-order places are small towns of limited administrative responsibility, but there is usually a secondary school, various churches, a post office, and shops serving day-to-day needs, a bank or savings banks, while many have a small hospital with basic services (cottage hospital type), one or more G.P.s, a dentist and a chemist. In rural areas, they are commonly the seat of a farming, marketing, and purchasing association like *Raiffeisen*. The medium level, third-order centres cover more than just day-to-day shopping needs, having more specialized shops, several banks and savings banks, as well as cultural and entertainment or sport provisions. There is usually a wide provision for secondary and even tertiary education, a hospital with several specialist departments and appropriate medical staff. Solicitors, lawyers, and accountants, as well as other professional services, are represented and there is a considerable administrative function; altogether over 300 centres are in this category.

In the second order, centres serve as major shopping places, with large specialist shops and departmental stores, besides theatres, museums and art galleries. They have extensive hospital and special medical facilities, a full range of educational facilities with the tertiary sector well developed, as well as major administrative functions. Besides their extensive professional services (including banking), they are the seat of the higher echelons of the legal system and are distinguished by the range and importance of their commercial

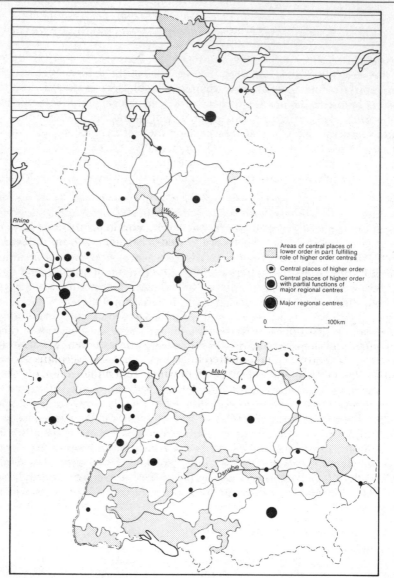

Figure 12.1 Federal Republic – central places

activities. About 42 towns belong to this category, but in the highest order are only four major cities that serve as macro-regional centres, with the highest-level national and regional administrative responsibility, a powerful commercial role, and offering the fullest range of specialist services in medicine and education. These centres are Hamburg for North Germany, Köln for the Rhineland and West Germany, Frankfurt for the Rhine-Main and West Central Germany, and München, the unchallenged centre for South Germany.

There are also about ten centres falling between the first and second order that have the full range of services and activities associated with the first order, but lack their macro-regional functions. This is usually because of proximity to competing centres, for example, the overlap between Düsseldorf and Essen or the downrating of Stuttgart through the proximity of Karlsruhe and Mannheim, which also lower Saarbrücken's regional function. Likewise, interplay between Hannover, Kassel, and Münster can be discerned. On the other hand, over thirty third-order places perform in part second-order functions – examples are Regensburg, Friedrichshafen, Düren, Lübeck, and Flensburg. Some act as centres for service areas not otherwise in the sphere of a second-order central place, though these special third-order places do not have such well-developed facilities nor so full a range of services as the true second-order centre.

Tourism and recreation

The West Germans have become possibly the world's greatest tourists, and the extent of this travel urge is reflected in 30.5 million West Germans taking 36.6 million holidays of five days or more, of which 18.6 million were outside Germany (since 1973 holidays outside Germany have exceeded those within). Financially, these tourists abroad spend almost DM 21,000 million, whereas only a third of this sum is spent by foreign tourists in the Federal Republic. Three-quarters of the bed-nights in hotels and other accommodation in Austria are provided by West German visitors, who also contribute over a third of the bed-nights in Italy and Jugoslavia. Of the foreign tourist traffic, much comprises transit movements across West Germany from Scandinavia, the Benelux countries, or Britain to Southern Europe – the average length of stay is about three days. The Rhine is particularly favoured by foreign visitors, while numbers swell for events such as the Oberammergau Passion Plays (notably British visitors). Certainly, the Netherlands, Britain, Belgium–Luxemburg, and France contribute most visitors, though there has been a growth in the number from America, Australia, and even Japan.

Expectedly, not all the country is equally attractive to holidaymakers, but two of the main attractions – scenically attractive landscapes and quaint mediaeval towns – commonly occur together, and there are also the major cities that lure visitors. The southern alpine landscapes are one of the most popular areas with both German and foreign tourists and with winter sports as well as summer attractions there is an all-the-year season. Principal centres are Berchtesgaden, Bad Reichenhall, Garmisch-Partenkirchen, Oberstdorf, while Oberammergau becomes a main focus in passion play years. This belt of holiday country also extends into the prealpine country to include the Bavarian lakes and the Bodensee on the west. Friedrichshafen and Lindau are the main centres on the Bodensee shore, while throughout this belt are several important spas. Towns and villages depend to a substantial degree on tourism, offering accommodation or making and selling souvenirs: many people have abandoned farming in favour of the more lucrative offer of *pension* in their attractive farmhouses. Another major South German tourist area is the Black Forest, whose fine forested landscapes and picturesque valleys draw considerable numbers of visitors. Less commercialized than the Alps, it has become much more accessible in the motor car age. Visitors come notably from South German industrial areas, but also from North Germany, and it is also popular with French, British, and Dutch holidaymakers. Particularly favoured is the high southern part around the Feldberg and the Titisee. A rather neglected area with tourist potential has been the endless rolling forest along the Czechoslovak border, though the closeness to the 'Iron Curtain' away from main roads and railways had deterred any but the venturesome, even though since the early 1970s substantial sums have been spent to provide more and better accommodation and to advertise it.

The Central Uplands, along whose flanks so many large urban agglomerations lie, have an extensive and developing tourist infrastructure. Characterized by rolling forest broken by farmed lands and cut by charming valleys lined by picturesque towns, these uplands draw visitors for longer stays as well as day visitors from nearby conurbations, and with a considerable proportion of the spas and health resorts, attract a large clientele. The drift of rural population away from these hill lands has also provided plentiful opportunity for city people to buy second homes, while people from the industrial agglomerations keep their holiday caravans on farms and caravan parks here for much of the year. Considerable investment has gone into developing gliding and water sports facilities, while the prewar Nürburgring racing circuit still draws big crowds. A great many visitors seek the valleys of the Ahr, Mosel, Lahn, and Rhine with their vineyards. The higher parts, like the Rothaargebirge and the Winterberg Plateau, offer good winter sports opportunities within easy weekend travelling of the major industrial districts. The Harz, with well-marked forest walks and quiet cleftlike valleys along its flanks, is still popular, despite division by the inter-German frontier that leaves the Brocken and its folklore on the G.D.R. side. Popular not only with Germans, it attracts many Dutch and Scandinavian visitors. Throughout the older upland country, even

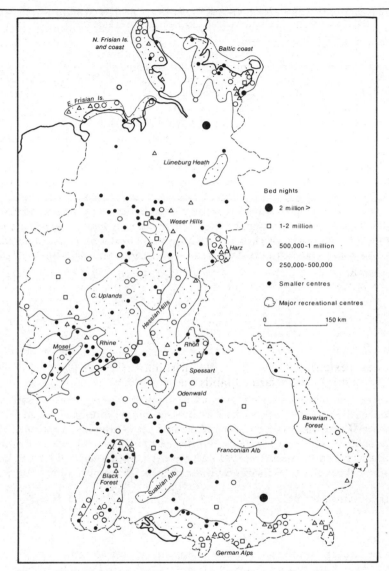

Figure 12.2 Tourism and recreation in the Federal Republic

in areas not commonly associated with being a tourist area in the accepted sense, there are few villages or small towns where a clear effort to attract and retain a tourist trade is not found.

A valuable tourist asset is formed by several German rivers, attracting longer stay visitors as well as those using them as routes to other destinations. Important, as already noted, are the Mosel, Ahr, and to a lesser extent the Lahn and Main, because of their vineyards. The small towns in the vineyard districts offer a great variety of cafés and restaurants that are busy throughout the year. The Danube is, however, far less used, largely because no major roads or railways follow it and apart from the attractive gorges near Beuron and Weltenburg-Kelheim, it is not particularly picturesque, though the tributary valley of the Altmühl has fine scenery. In North Germany, the Weser above the imposing *Porta Westfalica* is a tourist route of considerable charm, but apart from their opportunity for sailing, the shallow valleys of other North German rivers have little tourist attraction, except the Elbe downstream from Hamburg to Schulau that provides the interest of oceangoing shipping on the river and some delightful residential areas on the high north bank.

The Rhine, in a class by itself, is a highly commercialized world-famous tourist route, whose potential was first realized by English travellers on the nineteenth-century grand tours and later developed by the German Romantic movement. Excellent passenger boats maintain a daily service from March to October between Mainz and Düsseldorf and cruise ships join Basel to Rotterdam on 4–5 day voyages. Scenically the gorge sections between Bingen and Bad Godesberg are the most frequently visited, lined by picturesque small towns and vineyards and with many folklore associations.

Almost any patch of water has become a focus of watersports and sailing as affluence allows expensive variations on the long-standing German love of canoeing. Even the busiest lower reaches of the Rhine are used by private cruisers, and yachts abound on South German lakes like the Chiemsee, Starnberger See or Bodensee, while several modest North German lakes, including those of the Holstein Switzerland, are popular sailing venues.

In the German tradition, the seaside resort has played only a modest role. In Wilhelminian times, the attractive Baltic coast within easy reach of Berlin developed some formal resorts, but these have mainly fallen to the territory of the G.D.R. The Baltic coast is still popular in the Federal Republic: Grömitz has the largest number of visitors (including a considerable number from Scandinavia), but Travemünde (with its casino) and Timmendorfer Strand are also important. On the North Sea coast, Westerland and List on Sylt are well patronized, and holidays on the informal North Frisian islands such as Wyk, Amrum, and Pellworm are growing in popularity, as are centres on the mainland like St. Peter-Ording. The rebuilt facilities of Helgoland attract a rather distinct public, but the East Frisian Islands are especially popular, with formal Wilhelminian resorts like Norderney and informal communities like Juist. Some resorts offer health cures as marine spas (*Seeheilbäder*). All have a strikingly summer traffic, when the number of bed nights may be ten times that of the winter half of the year, while the clientele is over 95 percent German.

Nearly 60 percent of all holiday journeys are by private car (almost another 25 percent are by railway), and motorways are major arteries of movement so that along them are strung many camping and caravaning sites. An attempt to channel movement along certain routes began before 1939 with the designation of the German Wine Highway along the foot of the Haardt. Over thirty more routes have been added since 1945, mostly in the Rhineland and South Germany, and they are usually given some scenic or historical link – e.g., the German Coastal Highway in the north, the Romantic Highway from Würzburg to Füssen, or the Castle Highway from Heidelberg to Nürnberg.

While Nature Protection Areas of scientific interest have long been designated, the growing pressure on the countryside for recreation has posed special problems. In German forestry the rising emphasis is on amenity, especially in forests near to major towns, while near to large concentrations of population, local recreation areas have been designated and provided with facilities for boating or pony riding or marked paths for walking (sometimes with hurdles and climbing frames for the enthusiastic exerciser). A particularly interesting example is the reclaimed brown coalfield southwest of Köln. A considerable number of well-regulated Nature Parks have also been created in the Central Uplands and to a lesser degree in the north and more open south, where service provisions are concentrated at selected sites but effort made to attract people to recreational pursuits away from their cars.

The medical profession in Britain has neglected spas and hydropathic institutions, so popular in the eighteenth and nineteenth centries. The trend in Germany has been the opposite, with spas and health resorts becoming an integral part of the health service provision. The official *Calendar of Spas* lists 293 places, of which 198 have the official designation of spa (*Bad*) and whose names range from the famous Baden-Baden and Bad Ems to Wanne-Eickel in the Ruhr coalfield and the lesser known Senkelteich in the Weser Hills. Places usually offer relief for particular illnesses and the range covered is formidable: some resorts offer simply good air, others concentrate on various hydropathic cures, while still others have sophisticated heat and physiotherapy treatment. These health resorts and spas claim 44 percent of all overnight stays in the Federal Republic, and though expectedly busiest in the summer, there is a considerable public throughout the year and stays are usually for two to three weeks, most people claiming the expenses from the health insurance after an official recommendation by their doctor. The spas are notably concentrated in the Central Uplands, particularly where mineral springs occur: other areas are in the Weser Hills, the Harz, and the Black Forest, while there are also coastal spas, and several lie along the foot of the Alps.

The big cities also play a role in tourism, quite apart from their large number of German and foreign business visitors. The inflow varies from year-to-year according to the staging of particular festivals and exhibitions, but there are also annual events like the Beer Festival in München or Carneval in Köln. Many foreign tourists in the big cities are members of package tours and stays are usually brief, but they account in general for about one-fifth to one-third of all bed-nights. Some of the traffic arises from the transport function of the cities, i.e., the international airport at Frankfurt, Köln as a major railway junction, München as a motorway node, or Hamburg as a ferry terminal and seaport. Despite the problems of access, Berlin is remarkably successful in attracting tourists, offering them a wide range of cultural attractions.

The rapid growth of the tertiary sector has been one of the most distinct features of Western Europe and, though development in the Federal Republic was slower to start than in neighbouring countries, the subsequent expansion has been impressive. Whereas activities like banking, insurance, and tourism in several Western European countries, particularly Britain and Switzerland, add a significant dimension to their foreign currencies earnings, the tertiary sector in Federal Germany does just the reverse and in this respect contrasts with the role of manufacturing industry. It may be expected that growth of the tertiary sector will continue, because German planners and economists feel the Federal Republic is still over-industrialized in relation to comparable advanced countries.

Suggested further reading

Useful impressions of tourism and recreation can be built up from the guides and travel brochures available from German publishers.

Hahn, H.: Die Erholungsgebiete der Bundesrepublik Deutschland, *Bonner Geog. Abh.* 22, 1958.

Kloss, G.: West Germany – An Introduction, London, 1976.

Kluczka, G.: Zentrale Orte und zentralörtliche Bereiche mittlerer und höherer Stufe in der BRD, *Forsch. z. deut. Landeskunde* 194, 1970.

Riquet, P.: Approche géographique du secteur tertiaire – l'example de l'Allemagne Fédérale, *Ann. de Géog.* 85, 1976, pp.281–332.

Secteur tertiaire et métiers tertiaires – approche statistique des activités de service en Allemagne Fédérale, *Ann. de Géog.* 85, 1976, pp.1–33.

CHAPTER 13

FARMING AND FORESTRY IN THE FEDERAL REPUBLIC

Farmers in West Germany have not felt the shock of violent land reforms and new forms of farm organization like their compatriots in the German Democratic Republic. This is not to say that change has not taken place since the Second World War, brought by internal and external pressures, though government policy has generally tended to preserve existing patterns rather than bring about extensive restructuring. Farming in West Germany contributes slightly more (3.4 percent) to the gross national product than in the United Kingdom (2.8 percent), but this must be seen against the fact that agricultural employment (7.5 percent) is higher as a proportion of the national labour force than in the United Kingdom (3.3 percent). The numbers employed in farming in the Federal Republic are, however, only one-third the level of 1950 and yet agricultural output is twice as great. The Western Occupation Zones gave little scope for land reform; the relatively small number of estates and even large farms, as well as the very small size of many holdings, gave little opportunity for subdivision without displacing people from the land at a time when stagnation in industry and destruction in the towns made this both impossible and undesirable.

Initially there was a strong lobby for the preservation of the peasant way of life, though country life was becoming increasingly unfavourable when compared to the rising affluence of the urban-industrial population. This has been reflected in the declining social status of the peasant (*der Bauer*), with attempts to offset this by regarding him more as a 'farmer', by use of the term *Landwirt*.

Policy has, however, sought to preserve the family farm as the core of the agricultural system, adapting it in size and form to secure a standard of living for farmers comparable to the urban-industrial population. The long-term aim is to turn the countryside into a landscape of moderately sized holdings, with modern equipment and methods, and, wherever freely chosen, some form of cooperative action (e.g., *Raiffeisen*). Policy has also sought to increase agricultural output and productivity to help towards a reasonably priced food supply and a high level of self-sufficiency; and wherever natural and economic conditions have demanded, government support for farming has been forthcoming. Nevertheless, even if achieved, this ideal situation would still leave the one-time peasant at a social and economic level below what is conceptually seen fit for the British farmer.

Consolidation of holdings

It is untrue, however, that West German farming is a 'backward peasant community': in many respects it is technically advanced and effectively productive in relation to the labour input. The major hindrances arise from the laws of inheritance and the spatial pattern and size of holdings, notably the high degree of fragmentation in many districts, a problem reaching back to the eighteenth century. Holdings comprising scattered strips and parcels have been made worse in some districts by constant subdivision through inheritance: a holding of only 20 hectares may be divided into 200 or more small parcels of land scattered up to several kilometres from the farmer's home, most commonly in a village and not amidst the fields. Consolidation has become particularly needed since the mid-1950s, requiring not only tackling lands not previously consolidated, but also consideration of areas of former consolidation to bring them into line with modern requirements. Through the *Green Plans* begun in the early 1950s much progress has been made. Since 1945 some 5.5 million hectares have been consolidated, but 9.6 million hectares still await treatment (total area of farming, forestry, etc., 24.6 million hectares), though less than one-third is regarded as urgent. Before consolidation the average holding consisted of 15 parcels and 4 after treatment.

The area to be consolidated (including forests and other land) is notably in Lower Saxony (28.4 percent), Bavaria (17.7 percent), North Rhine-Westphalia (16.4 percent), and Baden-Württemberg (12.1 percent), whereas the Rhineland-Palatinate contains 8.4 percent of the area, Schleswig-Holstein 8.2 percent and Hessen 7.8 percent, but the Saarland has a mere 1 percent. The usual aim is a basic restructuring of the holdings and land parcels, as well as building new field roads, village amenities and even new farmsteads, often built in small groups to provide some element of neighbourliness for peasants used to living in a closed village community. At first, new farmsteads were built on the edge of the village lands, but recently it has been common to erect them

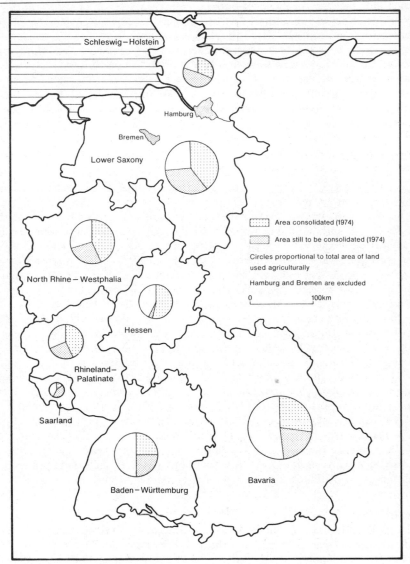

Figure 13.1 Farm consolidation in the Federal Republic

near the village, in the hope of better preserving a sense of community. In twenty years, over 22,000 new farmsteads have been built, some 26,000 old farmsteads improved, and 23,000 holdings substantially enlarged. Accelerated consolidation covering only rearrangement of the actual parcels of ground, without the ancillary operations to create a properly consolidated holding, has been done in some districts, while private exchange of land has been on a small scale and has generally tended to fall. Only about one-third of the new farmsteads have been associated with full land consolidation schemes, though the proportion has been higher in the north than in the south.

Major regional plans

Since 1955, the *Küstenplan* (Coastal Plan) in the North Sea *Länder* has sought to improve about 1 million hectares of farmland to reduce the development drag, especially acute in agriculture. Of particular importance has been effective drainage of low-lying areas, involving dike building, improvements of the sluices (*Siele*), and digging drainage ditches. The emphasis has changed from amelioration of the whole area to optimal productivity to a selection of the most promising areas for improvement. *Programm Nord* has also improved farming in Schleswig-Holstein since its inception in 1953 through land consolidation and related measures for a general betterment of the overall infrastructure. In 1950 a large programme (one of the earliest introduced by the *Bund*) began to reclaim waste land in the Ems basin through drainage but also improved soil quality, and much ground has been afforested. In South Germany, the *Alpenplan* (Alps Plan) emphasis has been on the protection of lower ground from floods, avalanches, and even mudflows. An important need has been an adequate supply of good drinking water, as well as efficient disposal of effluent. Particular attention has everywhere been given to areas with a high proportion of very small holdings: special programmes for this purpose in the eastern Upper Palatinate and in the Eifel-Mosel-Saar area have been instituted, while *Land* Baden-Württemberg has extended its so-called *Alb-Programm*. In these schemes, a major element constitutes the creation of industrial or commercial jobs, while there has also been a careful appraisal of soil quality to distinguish areas needing particular attention.

Farm size

Though West German farms remain generally small, there has been a marked shift in farm size since 1949 and the total number has fallen by almost 700,000, though the regional pattern varies considerably. Small holdings below 5 hectares predominate in the Saarland and comprise over half the total in Baden-Württemberg and the Rhineland-Palatinate. Large holdings – i.e., over 50 hectares – are most important in Schleswig-Holstein (about 6 percent) and in Lower Saxony (about 3 percent), whereas those between 20–50

Figure 13.2 Village change in West Germany – farm consolidation

hectares are most significant in North Germany, notably in North Rhine-Westphalia. The 10–20 hectares group make up a quarter of the total in Bavaria and holdings between 5–10 hectares form more than a fifth of the total in the Rhineland-Palatinate, Baden-Württemberg, and in Bavaria (over a quarter of the total). It is now considered that a holding of 20–50 hectares is the optimum for a balanced peasant holding, so that the first postwar holdings of 10–12 hectares created through *Flurbereinigung* are now considered too small and even the later 15–20 hectare farms have become inadequate.

Problems of inheritance

With farms predominantly owner-occupied (only about 8 percent are tenancies) change is often difficult because of the differing regional patterns of inheritance. There has been, however, a growing tendency to lease ground to enlarge holdings, especially as social fallow (*Sozialbrache* – see page 288) increases. Two basic forms exist: first, the inheritance by the eldest son or other traditional relative of the whole farm – land, buildings and stock – as a going concern, with a monetary settlement often for the other heirs; and second, the division of the holding among the heirs, with consequent fragmentation and reduction in the size of holdings over time (though this possibility of division is often avoided by various financial arrangements). In North Germany, the laws of agricultural inheritance are carefully codified and related to the size of the holding, whether or not it is a full-time undertaking; in South Germany much inheritance is by long-standing traditional usages; but, as a result of local variations, wide modifications to the two basic forms have arisen. Three main regions may be discerned: the North German and Southeast German closed inheritance and the Southwest German divided inheritance (though this is broken by enclaves of closed inheritance in the Odenwald and the Black Forest). Within these regions, however, there are complex patterns of local usages as well as of long-term change.

In Schleswig-Holstein closed inheritance of all sizes of farms is the dominant form, not only where legally binding under farm laws, though in the marsh of the west coast divided inheritance is still found. Mixed forms of inheritance have also found their way into the more industrialized areas along the Kiel Canal and around Hamburg. Similar effects of urban and industrial development can be seen in Lower Saxony, where traditional closed inheritance remains predominant over most northern districts, but around Hamburg, Hannover, Braunschweig, and Hildesheim there are some mixed forms. Divided inheritance remains otherwise only in small parts of the Weser marsh, in the Harz and its southwestern fringes and in the Leine Hills, though formerly more widespread in all these areas.

Two-thirds of North Rhine-Westphalia belong to the North German closed inheritance. The influence of industrialization has been to modify inheritance, so that some small pieces of ground are usually given to the junior heirs (particularly around the Ruhr and on the west bank of the Rhine). The *Land* contains, however, the main divide between closed and divided inheritance, with a distinct historical shift of the former southwards. Proper divided inheritance remains only in small parts of the Siegerland and the Eifel where junior heirs commonly rent their share to whoever continues to run the family farm, though this land is often later bought back.

Closed inheritance remains little altered in north Hessen and covers most of Bavaria. The traditional closed inheritance still predominates in the eastern Upper Palatinate, over all southern Bavaria (except some alpine parishes), the greater part of Middle Franconia, and eastern Württemberg. Mixed forms

287

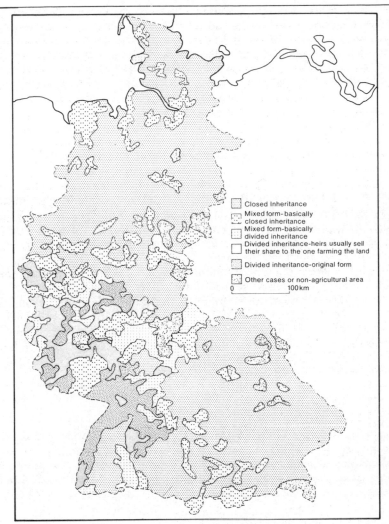

Figure 13.3 Types of farm inheritance in West Germany

occur in Suabia (around Ulm and Augsburg), but also in southeast Bavaria
(chiefly around München) where the smaller farms are mostly divided and
larger farms surrender small parcels of land to junior heirs. Closed inheritance
by an old tradition is found throughout most of the Black Forest and
Odenwald. In the Black Forest, the border between closed and divided

Farming and Forestry in the Federal Republic

inheritance is particularly sharp along the western edge, but in the northwest there has been a long tradition of divided inheritance. The sharp prewar distinction between the closed inheritance areas and those of divided inheritance has been blurred by legal changes and voluntary renunciation of extreme division. The once classical divided inheritance in the Saarland and the Rhineland-Palatinate has in particular changed since legislation in 1953, so that in the Hunsrück and the southwest Palatinate closed inheritance has appeared, but otherwise it is found only sporadically or in transitional forms (e.g., in the Gutland, the west Eifel, the North Palatinate Hills, the middle Rhine, and the lower Westerwald). Few districts remain dominated by true division of inheritance, still most common in the industrialized Saarland, in the eastern Eifel and Haardt, the poorest agrarian districts in Germany, but also in the Mosel valley, the Rhine plain around Ingelheim (elsewhere closed inheritance dominates the Rhine plain), and some intensively cultivated parishes of the pre-Palatinate lowlands. East of the Rhine, divided inheritance occurs throughout the Westerwald, though there is a balance between parishes with altered and unaltered forms. Influence of divided inheritance in Hessen is found mostly in the eastern Main plain, in the Taunus, and in the Rheingau (where industrial communities and vine growing are common). Divided inheritance exists in the southeastern districts of the Rhön, the northern Grabfeld and in the Main valley, the Markheidenfeld Plateau, and in the greater part of the Spessart, though usually strongly modified and transitional to closed inheritance. These forms have also penetrated much of the Neckar basin and the middle and northern Kraichgau. In Baden-Württemberg traditional divided inheritance is mostly associated with vine growing or other special cultures, or in industrialized areas where farming is not the main source of income.

Social fallow

Though the numbers employed in farming have fallen from about 5 million in 1950 to around 1.8 million in 1973, many who have left the land have not surrendered their holdings, fearing they might one day have to return to tilling the ground or hoping to sell for building development at inflated prices. These holdings therefore remain generally uncultivated or at best leased to some remaining farmer. Migration to work in industry has been greatest where demand is for semiskilled labour and where it has been possible to continue living in the village and commuting to work. The attraction of industry has also been greatest where holdings are inadequate to give a reasonable standard of living or where the ground is particularly poor. Social fallow has also increased in some districts as farmers have discovered that they make more from providing tourist accommodation than from farming. Regional policies that have helped labour-hungry industry to move into rural districts have also

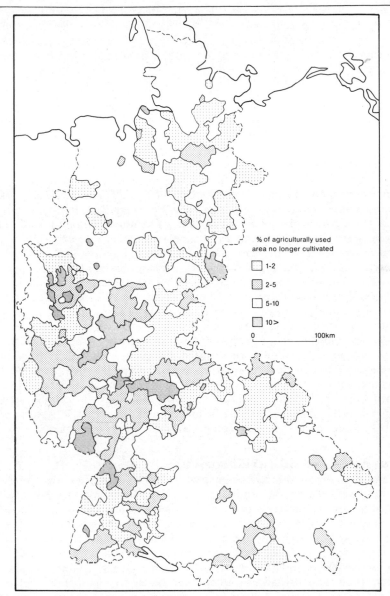

Figure 13.4 Social fallow in the Federal Republic

encouraged the drift from the land. Unfortunately, until those who have given up farming are prepared to surrender their land, many schemes of consolidation or the enlargement of holdings and the laying out of larger fields suited to modern machinery are hampered. The job of the remaining farmers is also made more difficult because weeds spread from the unkempt patches which become hideouts for pests.

Social fallow is unevenly distributed, but proportionally greatest in areas of very small holdings, of intense fragmentation of plots, of the poorest natural conditions, or sharpest competition for labour. It is most striking where there is notably poor farming in the Rhine Valley, in southern Westphalia, and adjacent Hessian districts, but it occurs also in Main-Franconia and the Rhine-Main areas of plentiful industrial employment. It is low in the Neckar basin (except along the foot of the Suabian Alb), where a tradition of working in industry and farming in spare time arose from small and fragmented holdings produced through divided inheritance. Though social fallow has tended to increase everywhere, there are a few exceptions usually explainable by local problems of structural unemployment, for example, in the Saarland through the decline of coal mining, or where it has been possible to take over social fallow and allocate it to other farmers or other uses. Many larger landowners (with 200–500 hectares) are beginning to cultivate their own land instead of renting it to small farmers, since so many of these are going out of farming. Particularly unrewarding areas for farming or areas with extensive social fallow might now be turned to amenity use through afforestation or landscaping. Related to social fallow is the rising importance of female labour: on holdings under 2.5 hectares, three-quarters of the known labour is female; while even on farms of 20 hectares, over one-third of the labour is female. Because women work on the family holding, the *real* labour force in farming may be larger than official figures suggest. It has been claimed that 40 percent of all West German households have some connection with the land.

Farming in an industrial society

Little of the new wealth has been spent on more food after the immediate postwar years when the demand rose sharply. In some respects, greater wealth has had an adverse effect: the decline in demand for potatoes has affected areas like the Eifel fringe as an important producer. Higher efficiency, especially on larger farms, has often lowered prices, so affecting adversely the smallest producer, and the growing sophistication of modern farming demands more complex machinery and its intensive use, which can be best achieved only with large fields and suitably large production units, criteria not met through much of West German farming. Likewise, cooperative action is important in obtaining contracts for mass supply to processing industries, such as canning and dairy plants. While improved social security benefits have attracted some of the older people from farming, it has suffered from loss of young people moving into industry or commerce. The buying out of farms with no heirs has been a policy of government in trying to bring back to the land expellee or refugee farmers or young people who had little hope of ever having their own farm. Nevertheless, if proposals of the European Community were to be put into operation, West German farming would have a long way to go to reach the ideal family farm, seen as a unit of 40–60 head of cattle for dairy farming, 80–120 hectares for arable crops and 150–200 head for stock farming.

Changes in cropping patterns
Compared to prewar times, there has been a distinct shift in the relative importance of several crops and marked rise in the importance of livestock. These changes have come about through increasing affluence affecting the demand patterns; by changes in farming itself; and through the Community Common Agricultural Policy. In general, high guaranteed prices encourage grain growing, attractive on the larger holdings that find difficulty in obtaining labour. Grains have generally occupied some 5 million hectares: until the latter 1960s, bread grains were most important, but were overtaken in output by fodder and industrial grains. Winter wheat and winter rye remain most important, though only in the 1960s has the area sown to winter wheat over-taken rye. Between 1935–1938 and 1968 the harvest of winter wheat rose by over 130 percent (largely through improved techniques and subsequent yield), whereas winter rye rose by a mere 3 percent, and rye is now largely regarded as a fodder grain. The increase in the area of winter wheat has been less than the decline in the area sown to rye, suggesting that cereal cultivation has been concentrated in areas with the most favourable conditions. On the moderately good soils, cultivation methods have improved, while on the poorer soils grain has been replaced by pasture. Summer bread grains, on account of the high summer precipitation, are of little significance, with yield commonly 10–15 percent below winter grain. Summer wheat accounts for only 11 percent of the total wheat area; summer rye is found only where there is competition from no other grain. Barley, commonly associated with sugar beet cultivation, is mostly a summer crop (winter barley accounts generally for only half the area sown to the crop) found on poorer soils as a fodder crop; though barley for brewing is now cultivated only on some of the richest soils. Oats and summer mixed grains are basically fodder crops, but oats has declined as the horse population has fallen. The much improved yield of grains on the best areas has more than offset the fall in sown area in the poorer districts such as the Central Uplands.

Over a million hectares are sown to root crops, about half taken by potatoes, though the total area has tended to decline in the past thirty years as yield has improved. Particularly marked has been the fall in the area sown to potatoes, which has been halved since 1935–1938 (only partly offset by higher yield), reflecting a change to more expensive foods and avoidance of undue starchiness. Early potatoes have suffered from cheap imports from early crop areas of Western Europe and the Mediterranean, but the market for later potatoes has held up. It is difficult to assess how far consumption has shifted from human use to fodder. For some years after the war, a serious deficit of seed potatoes existed, as these traditionally came from sandy soils in East Germany.

Sugar beet has been encouraged by high guaranteed prices in the Common Agricultural Policy, and compared to prewar the sown area has doubled and the harvest has trebled, concentrated notably on the loessic soils of the Braunschweig area, the plains of the Lower Rhine, the Upper Rhine, and around Würzburg, all well-located for processing plants, just as small areas of rising sugar beet production in Bavaria have likewise been associated with nearby processors. Most other crops, especially vegetables and fruit, have shown a modest increase in output as a result of higher yield from a smaller area. Apples and pears have experienced little increase in demand, though it has risen for table plums, peaches, and apricots; but German fruit growers have felt sharp competition from France, Italy, and even beyond the Economic Community, with imports more than doubled in the 1960s. The fruit growers in North Germany (notably cherries, red currants, etc.) have felt least the impact of imports, but in general an increased part of the vegetable and fruit harvest goes to canning and preserving.

From the nineteenth century phylloxera epidemic, the cultivation of the vine had been in decline, but after 1950 the vineyards began to expand in the more favoured districts, aided by various structural improvements such as easier access and cooperative handling of the crop (notably around the Kaiserstuhl) as well as through better promotion of regional wines (e.g., the Franconian *Bocksbeutel*). Productive vineyards rose from 67,137 hectares in 1962 to 86,436 hectares in 1974, but there were wide variations in the yield per hectare from 58.5 hectolitres in 1962 to 134.2 hectolitres in 1972 – bad years were 1965, 1966, 1971, and 1974. The area under grapes for white wines has risen more quickly since 1962 than for red wines (while there has also been some shift in the types cultivated), reversing the trend for more rapid growth in the much smaller area devoted to red wines than white wines apparent in the period 1900–1960. Despite increased competition from wines from other Community countries, German producers, by concentration on quality and their distinctive qualities, have held their position. There has also been a doubling in the area under hops, with a general improvement in yield. Nevertheless, the self-sufficiency level has fallen from 190 percent in the early 1950s to 105–135 percent in the 1970s. Over 70 percent of the total sown area and yield is in the Bavarian Hallertau.

Livestock farming

Most striking has been the fall in the number of horses – in the latter 1930s there were 1.5 million on the Federal Republic's area and by the early 1970s only 250,000, but this has since risen again as horse riding for leisure has grown in popularity. The old 'horse peasant' able to afford and use two horses has been replaced by the man with expensive and sophisticated farm machinery. In relation to the farmed area, the density of tractors is higher than in the United Kingdom, though many German tractors appear to be underutilized. It has been suggested that West German farming is heavily over-mechanized in many sectors, adding a substantial burden to its production costs.

Oxen for draught are now rarely seen, but in general the number of livestock in other categories has increased, with shifts in the age structure and use. There has been an impressive rise in the proportion of young cattle; though the extensive slaughter for food at the end of the war and the great loss in the abnormally dry summer of 1947, followed by subsequent epidemics, have taken a long time to rectify. The growth of cooperatives and interest in artificial insemination have also reduced the number of male animals held. The rising demand for milk and milk products brought a substantial rise in the holding of milk cows, though again fluctuations in the market have swung the producers in some years towards meat production. The emergence of overproduction, reflected in the butter, cheese, and milk 'mountains', produced structural problems through the as yet imperfect structure of the Common Agricultural Policy.

Pig keeping has not shown the same fluctuations and long-term changes, though the herd is now well over half as great again as prewar. Consumption of pig meat remains high, but the market now demands animals much younger than prewar. Sheep fell in number compared to prewar until 1965, though they are now increasingly used to control open grassland needed for recreational purposes (notably the small Lüneburg *Heideschnucken*) and where social fallow abounds as a means of keeping the land in good heart, with shepherds grazing extensive areas. The market for lamb and mutton is virtually nonexistent in West Germany. The reduced interest in allotment gardens has been a major factor in the catastrophic fall in the number of goats, and poultry keeping has switched increasingly to factory methods on the fringes of large urban markets or in districts where other types of farming have become unattractive. Despite an increase for a time in home production, there has been a serious challenge from imported poultry and its products from other Community countries.

Regional variations in agriculture

Spatially most widespread are the mixed enterprises, where no one element dominates – commercial and fodder crops, livestock and permanent crops (orchards, etc.) are reasonably balanced, so far as the farm's earnings are concerned. Commercial cropping (providing more than 50 percent of the earnings) predominates on loessic soil, notably in the sugar beet growing districts (Lower Saxony, the Lower Rhine, around Würzburg, the Rhine rift valley around Mannheim, and the Danube basin). Farms with a large element of fodder crops are marked in Northwest Germany, in Bavaria and Suabia south of the Danube (including the Allgäu), and in many parts of the Central Uplands, all readily identifiable with areas having large dairying or stock fattening elements in their economies. Equally prominent are the areas with vine cultivation (along the Rhine and Mosel, for example); hops (Hallertau); or fruit (southwest of Hamburg). In the poorer upland areas and wherever there is mixed agricultural-industrial employment, there occur enterprises with combinations of horticulture-agriculture or agriculture-forestry (Alpine areas) or even horticulture-forestry. In a few areas, there is concentration on pig rearing or poultry breeding in so-called *Veredlungsbetriebe*. Nevertheless, despite substantial changes in economic circumstance and even in organization, the regional variations have not changed radically from prewar times.

Northwest Germany is characterized by permanent and rotation grass and the keeping of cattle. Particularly valuable meadow lies along the coastal and riverine marshes, where the high water table, well-distributed rainfall and 'maritime' temperature régime favour the growth of grass. The summers tend, however, to be too moist for good hay making. Farming is clearly marked by the importance of livestock, fattening of young stock and beef cattle and the keeping of dairy herds (notably in Friesland). Sheep are mostly found on the grass on the landward side of the Frisian islands; on the *geest* 'islands' standing above the marsh; also on the salt marsh grasses on the outer side of coastal dikes, notably in summer, when geese are also kept there. These meadows are too soft for cattle, whose heavy tread would destroy the grass cover and allow high tides to wash away newly consolidated ground. On the newly diked *Kooge* (polders), wherever drainage is adequate, a rich arable farming can be pursued – wheat, beans, and rape. The farms are usually scattered among their compact fields or, in some older diked areas, strung along the old dikes, whose rich soil is now often used for farm gardens. As the older diked areas dry out, sinkage accentuates their drainage problem and the rising water table encourages a reversion to meadow, seen in the North Frisian marsh, the Elbe, Ems, and Weser marsh, and around the Jadebusen. Particularly on difficult wet soils in the old marsh along the edge of the *geest* grazings predominate. A few specialized districts distinguish the marsh belt, such as fruit growing (notably cherries) near Buxtehude or vegetable cultivation on the north bank of the Elbe.

The agricultural landscape of the *geest* is undergoing considerable change. Under population pressure since 1945, further reclamation has reduced the

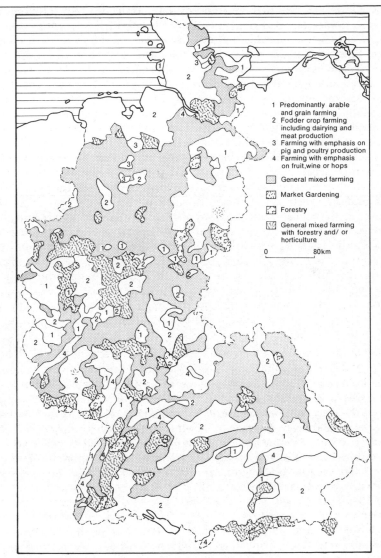

Figure 13.5 West German regional farming types

uncultivated land, but this nevertheless remains about half the total area, where forest has expanded at the expense of the heath and moor. The generally sandy or peaty soils need adequate fertilizer and the latter require good drainage and it is important to break the hard pan (*Ortstein*) if present. As areas of peat are skimmed, arable farming or forestry has developed, notably in the Ems basin on the Bourtanger Moor. At Wiesmoor, a new form of moor cultivation has been tried – instead of stripping the peat, this has been drained, deep ploughed, and limed. The results have been encouraging, but it needs considerable capital. In the sandy *geest* duststorms menace farmers in exceptionally dry weather. To improve the productivity of the *geest*, as for example in the more adversely located parts of northern Schleswig-Holstein, new drainage schemes have been built in the lower parts of the Scholmer Aue, Lecker Aue, and Treene depression, following work in the Eider depression begun under Danish supervision. Livestock is reared for meat or for dairy produce, though milk production becomes more important towards the south, nearer to consumers in industrial areas. Livestock raising is significant around Bremen and Hamburg which long enjoyed cheap imports of feeding stuffs. Arable crops are commonly used for fodder, and west of the Weser pigs are important, with rye, oats, and potatoes the most common crops. Modern market-oriented systems of cultivation contrast with the old smallholdings struggling to wrest a living from the poor skinned moor. New centres have concentrated on glasshouse and flower cultivation, though under increasing pressures from more favoured producers elsewhere in the Community. Also developed has been the cultivation of seed potatoes, formerly supplied from similar sandy soils in East Germany.

East of the Weser, the *geest* and marsh merge into the Lüneburg heathlands, a once heathy wilderness populated by flocks of the small sheep, *Heideschnucken*. Much of the heath has been afforested or reclaimed, and on its eastern flank it merges with the North German rye-potato region, where mixed farming is typical between the younger northern moraines and the loess-decked country to the south. The keeping of good permanent grass, apart from some of the moister valleys, is difficult, and the proportion of land devoted to arable (notably where there are ground moraine clays) is high, but forest covers 30–50 percent of the surface, especially on the sandiest soils. Rye and potatoes are traditional crops, the latter used for human consumption and for pig fodder, starch, and alcohol. Rye has tended to contract in competition with barley and increasingly with wheat, whereas sugar beet in contrast has expanded. The fall in consumption of the potato has made it liable to displacement by more rewarding crops, though seed potatoes are now significant. Livestock has become more important, especially in the westernmost districts, with consequent development of fodder crops. First introduced in the G.D.R., green maize for silage has also penetrated. Generous use of fertilizers is the key to keeping up productivity on the glacial soils with varying levels of podzolization and substantial increases in yield have taken place.

The younger morainic country around the Baltic littoral in the eastern part of Schleswig-Holstein is a hummocky region with thick glacial clays and sandy and gravelly material, with numerous marshy depressions and small lakes. The heavy, fertile soils encourage arable cultivation, but there is also forest. The main cereal has been rye, though wheat, cultivated on more favoured ground, has generally become more significant, whereas oats, always on the poorer ground, has declined. A considerable area is devoted to potatoes (mostly for livestock) and there is much rotation and permanent grass, despite climatic problems, so that beef and dairy production are major activities. Around Pinneberg are extensive tree nurseries (fruit and forest trees and garden shrubs). Schleswig-Holstein is characterized by large holdings and estates. The particularly fertile districts of eastern Holstein (Wagrien) are a landscape of hedged fields (*Knicklandschaft*), originated in the nineteenth century as more arable was turned to meadow and a clear demarcation between fields needed, but hedge planting has recently been encouraged to prevent sand and dust storms (e.g., spring, 1959) and the landscape has consequently a remarkable wooded appearance despite Schleswig-Holstein being one of the least forested parts of the republic. The large expellee population created a severe problem to provide employment and opportunity for the future. On the North Sea coast, measures to reclaim land from the sea (begun before 1939 by the *Reichsarbeitsdienst*) have been in operation, but inland the *Programm Nord* has tried to raise rural conditions in Germany to a level comparable to Denmark. Under this programme, a large central creamery has been built in Schleswig and attempts made to enlarge holdings and to rationalize the distribution of parcels of land.

A southerly extension of the agricultural systems with a strong grassland and livestock element occurs in the Münsterland and the Lower Rhine, where good pasturage exists in the valleys and in the moist depressions. Both in the Münsterland and on the Lower Rhine, sandy patches and *Stauchmoränen* (push moraines) tend to be extremely dry, suited only to heathland and forest, but some smaller islands of sand amid wetter meadows form arable ground. In this area, like much of the basin of the Ems and Ostfriesland, unusual in having scattered farmsteads rather than villages, holdings tend to be reasonably compact, with modestly sized fields in place of numerous strips. In the Münsterland, arable occurs chiefly where clayey or loamy soils overlie chalk or ground moraine, notably in the Baumberge and Beckumer Berge, with rye oats, potatoes, and fodder roots, while on the Lower Rhine arable is most important on the south and the role of cattle (for meat and milk) increases around Xanten and Kleve. Formerly the Lower Rhine and the Münsterland (around Warendorf) were noted for horse breeding. Fodder crops provide for pig rearing on a considerable scale.

Of particular agricultural importance are dark fertile soils developed over *loess* known as *Börde* – a landscape of wide vistas with little woodland and broken only by nucleated villages (often of considerable size) that extends discontinuously from the Köln Bay across into Central Germany, along the northern edge of the Central Uplands, penetrating deep into broad embayments along their northern face. On the north, the limit is generally a rapid thinning of the *loess* so essential to the formation of the dark coloured soils. Where this country lies in the lee of uplands, there is a tendency to drought. A high proportion of the *Börde* is arable, generally with large subdivided fields, and farms tend to be medium to large, with holdings of 200 hectares not uncommon in Lower Saxony. An insignificant part is played by pasture, except in moist hollows, although livestock is kept by stall feeding. Typical *Börde* occurs around Zülpich and Jülich, where wheat is particularly important, increasingly characteristic of this type of country. The large fields, the result of land consolidation begun early this century, allow effective use of machinery on a scale not commonly found. Another important crop is sugar beet, and its waste, a valuable stall feed for livestock, is supplied from the sugar works at Jülich. Vegetables are most typical out of the true *Börde*, on the gravel terraces of the Rhine (there is strong local specialization – for example, around Neuss cabbage for *Sauerkraut* is cultivated). The *Börde* country in the Weser Hills is broken by outliers of forested hills, while to the north the loessic mantle ends approximately along the line of the Mittelland Canal. This forms the core of farming in Lower Saxony, notably for winter wheat in contrast to the summer wheat grown in the moister areas nearer the coast. Brewing barley and some maize is grown, but sugar beet covers about a third of the area, and most of Lower Saxony's sugar factories are in this country, from whose waste milk cattle are fed. Peas and beans for fodder are grown, usually in association with grains and they are sometimes ploughed in. For almost all crops, yield in the *Börde* is consistently higher than elsewhere in Lower Saxony.

The broad rolling Central Uplands, broken by deeply incised valleys and wide basins, form a region of great agricultural diversity with three major elements, though everywhere elevation, angle of slope, and aspect are significant influences on farming patterns. The highest parts, usually bleak and moist, form grassland, with cattle keeping, broken by extensive forest; the basins and lower surfaces have essentially various mixed farming amid considerable forest, but some basins and valleys have specialized crops like fruit and the vine. These uplands are among the most problematical agricultural areas in the country, where even some of the more favoured basins and valleys are losing agricultural population. The uplands west of the Rhine are marked by greater moisture than further east, though high rainfall can be found on exposed western faces east of the river. In the Eifel, there is an unusually high proportion of grass, and livestock has been growing more important than arable farming, limited to oats and potatoes, for which demand has fallen sharply, and rotation grass has become everywhere more significant. Limited areas of calcareous soils give better returns for rye, oats, and potatoes, but on the skeletal soils of the highest surfaces, forestry has steadily taken over the poor arable and even meadowland. The Westerwald has on its higher slopes a moist, raw climate, while over large areas a heavy impervious soil is rich in plant food but hard to work. Despite strong rural depopulation, livestock fattening and dairying remain important, though there are large forests and arable is restricted to patches of more favoured ground. A family needs seven times as much ground in the High Westerwald as in the Rhine valley to maintain a comparable standard of living. The Sauerland is similar – though there is even more extensive forest, with livestock and arable still more limited. Soils are particularly unrewarding, except where there is a calcareous substratum. The western flanks of the Sauerland have the lower slopes dipping to the Rhine covered by *loess* on which good arable farming has developed. The high southern edge of the Rhenish Uplands, formed by the Hunsrück and Taunus, has a wide forest cover, with limited cultivation of rye and potatoes. The Hunsrück is a problem region, where too many still try to get a living from the soil, using backward methods.

The Rhenish Uplands are bisected by the narrow canyonlike gorge of the middle Rhine, with its tributary valleys and wider basin around Neuwied. Though liable to cold air drainage, with consequent early and late frosts, the valleys are known for the appearance of spring as much as four weeks earlier than on the surrounding uplands. The steep valley sides are either in long periods of shade or long periods of intense insolation; nowhere is aspect more significant in land use. The slatey soils of the valley sides, when terraced, give a well-drained foundation for grapes, while the constant air movement of the valleys generally prevents humidity reaching levels sufficient for mildew, and the long sunshine of late summer helps sugar formation without being strong enough to burn the grape. Being along the northern limits of vine growing, the wines are slow maturing and keep well. Vineyards line almost every available face where terraces can be built along the sunnier slopes of the Rhine gorge from Bingen to Koblenz and often extend up tributary valleys. In recent years roads have been built to cut out the need to carry everything up and down by hand from the vineyards, but abandoned terraces witness the decline of cultivation in the less rewarding areas. Along the Ahr, there has also been a marked contraction of vineyards once renowned for their 'burgundies'. Vineyards of no great renown exist along the narrow lower valley of the Lahn, but the upper Lahn flows through a rich farming basin, the Goldener Grund, favoured for grain cultivation. The Mosel vineyards are found on both banks of the meandering river. The wines, overwhelmingly white, mature relatively quickly and are variable in quality, with the best from around Bernkastel and Piesport. The wine villages are tightly nucleated and store rooms are often hollowed into the rock of the valley sides. On the gentler slopes near the rivers and in the broader parts of the valleys, there are orchards whose apples are made into ciderlike beverages for a local market. The Neuwied Basin is noted for its vegetable and fruit crops, but severe competition for land exists with the pumice mining industry. On the flanks of the Eifel around the basin, as in the Maifeld, there was formerly widespread cultivation of the *Oberländer* potato, now reduced through the fall in demand. Brewing barley is also grown.

Between the Hunsrück and the Rhine, with the French frontier on the south, a triangular area of rolling country of the Saar-Nahe basin and the Palatinate is similar agriculturally to the mixed farming of the Central Uplands, though in the Saar there has been a tradition of miners farming in their spare time. The wide spread of sandstone in the Palatinate is largely forest, but in the far west on the Luxemburg frontier there is an extension of the fertile *Gutland* around Bitburg. Vines are grown along the Saar, Nahe, and Ruwer.

A strikingly complex agricultural area lies in the Hessian Corridor and the upper reaches of the Weser, a hilly country with broad warm basins and ribs of bleaker upland, varied in geological conditions, so creating a wide range of farming conditions. Particularly good soils occur in pockets of *loess*, as in the Wetterau, and in basins and valleys, as for example in the Warburger *Börde*. In the lee of the Rhenish Uplands, the Hessian Corridor between Kassel and Ziegenhain has a moderate rainfall and an inclination towards drought. Mixed farming predominates in the basins and valleys, whereas on the higher areas, grassland with livestock and forestry on the steepest and bleakest slopes are typical. The most productive areas give good crops of wheat and sugar beet, and the higher surfaces yield mostly rye and oats. In the basins, livestock for meat and milk is stall-fed, for there is little pastureland, while the federal government has spent large sums trying to improve existing pasturage by drainage. Locally fruit cultivation is important and flax is grown around Fulda. The low rounded dome of the Vogelsberg is in the main area of pasture, with both sheep and cattle, where meadow has encroached on arable, but pasture has also been lost to forests on the highest parts. Last century arable was found up to 600 metres, but the modern limit is half that elevation.

The Harz, northern outlier of the Central Uplands, is an area where forestry has predominated and both pastoral and arable farming remain limited. It has been suggested that the importance of mining in the Harz until comparatively recent times gave particular importance to the preservation of forest at the expense of farming.

South Germany, marked on the north by the Main basin, reflects characteristics of farming in the Central Uplands, but also has its own character, derived in particular from the landscape of scarp and vale with broad warm basins, but there are also several cool, dry uplands. The diversity of lithology, soils, and hydrological conditions, as well as aspect, give rapidly changing character to farming over quite short distances. Much of the climatic advantage of greater warmth associated with a more southerly latitude and continental position is counterbalanced by the greater altitude compared to North Germany: the vine is a valuable indicator of climatic favouritism of the widely differentiated basins of South Germany. This is the countryside of the peasant and worker-peasant living in tightly nucleated villages, though the contrast between undivided inheritance over much of Bavaria and the divided inheritance of the southwest is important. There are, however, many fertile areas where even quite small holdings farmed intensively will give reasonable returns and the part-time farmer is also common.

Spring first arrives in the Rhine rift valley, where there is much sun and considerable summer warmth. Edged by steep warm slopes of the foothill belt, the

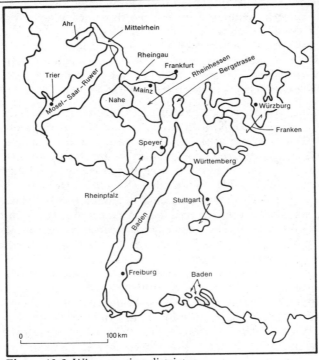

Figure 13.6 Wine-growing districts

302

valley floor comprises wide well-drained gravel terraces, in places decked by a cover of *loess*, whereas close to the river are moister meadows in the true flood plain (often in abandoned meanders). The foothills and lower slopes of the Black Forest, Odenwald, and the Palatinate hills are devoted to vineyards and orchards, like the rolling hills of the Kraichgau. Plums, peaches, apricots, the edible chestnut, and various nuts are grown, while cherries can be ripe by early June in a good year. Unfortunately, in parts of the rift valley fruit and vegetable growing has suffered through interference with the water table by works to improve Rhine navigation. The long warm summer and bright autumn are well suited to cereal cultivation, notably wheat and malting barley, while maize will ripen in good years, and sugar beet is grown; flax and various oilseeds have long been cultivated; and the rift valley supplies over a tenth of the German tobacco crop. The northern, wider part of the rift valley, with less troughlike character and gentle hills in Rhine Hessen, is one of the driest and least forested parts of West Germany, with extensive arable cultivation (including malting barley), but fruit and vegetables are also important (notably around Mainz). Renowned for its vineyards, some of the best German wines come from the sunny south-facing slopes of the Taunus (*Rheingau*), an area sheltered from cold north winds. Vineyards also extend southwards along the sunny slopes on both sides of the rift. On the west is the *Weinstrasse* along the well-drained slopes of the Haardt, while the western Odenwald on the east bank is the *Bergstrasse*. Rejuvenation of vine cultivation on the *loess*-covered remains of the old volcanic Kaiserstuhl near Freiburg/Breisgau has come through cooperative action.

An important farming area adjacent to the Rhine rift valley is the gently undulating *loess*-covered Kraichgau, a countryside remarkably free from forest, but with extensive areas of wheat, barley, and sugar beet as well as fodder crops. Hops, fruit, tobacco, and the vine are also grown. In the lee of the Black forest, the country has a climatic régime little less favourable than in the rift valley, but in places (like on the upper Nagold) there is no *loess* cover and the soil is rich in stones and not particularly productive. The clays are mostly used for grass or fruit growing and, where sandstone occurs on the caps of scarps, forest is common. The Liassic lands are mostly open farmland on *loess* over clays, though grass is more significant than in the Gäu landscape to the west where wheat and sugar beet are important. Fruit trees are common here, notably apples for a type of cider – while southeast of Stuttgart is known for its *Sauerkraut* cabbages. The scarps – notably the Suabian and Franconian Alb – have mostly grass and fruit trees on the foot slopes, while the steeper slopes are forested. The wide dip slope is usually dry and rolling, with evidence of arable given over to grass. An important activity is stall feeding of cattle for dairy purposes, while forest – mostly planted conifers in contrast to the natural beech woods – encroaches on the fields. Crops are found up to 900 metres with potatoes, barley, and oats, though *dinkel* and other older forms of grain were until recently widely planted. The Franconian Alb north of the Altmühl, wider, lower, and more plateaulike, is a bleak, dry, and sparsely settled country of little farming importance. Between the Suabian and Franconian Alb lies the sheltered and *loess*-covered Nördlinger Ries, a rich and flourishing farming landscape.

In the Neckar basin divided inheritance is a serious hindrance and has left holdings mostly too small to give a full-time occupation, while it has also created a situation of crops characteristically needing intensive labour (e.g., tobacco, hops, asparagus, vegetables). Wherever possible vineyards have been cultivated (notably on the lower part of many scarps), since a family can support itself from a vineyard only a third the size of an arable holding, so that consequently population in the vine areas is notably denser. The Main valley has extensive vineyards on south-facing slopes, but lower slopes by the river are used for fruit and vegetables. Some vineyards have fallen into a poor state through the parcels becoming of unworkably small proportions. The Rednitz basin is covered by poor infertile soils, though hop growing is of local importance.

South of the Danube there is undivided inheritance and less competition for labour from industry, both factors that favour farming. On the northern limits, grain and arable crops are mainstays, but along the alpine footslope, pasture and livestock become predominant. Around the Bodensee is a notable dairying area, but the warm slopes overlooking the lake, remarkably frost free, are mostly used for hops, vines, orchards, and vegetables, and the islands and peninsulas will support in many places near subtropical varieties of flower and fruit (Insel Mainau and the Insel Reichenau). Further east, extensive gravel terraces form a countryside of marsh and meadow on the valley floors, with arable cultivation on the middle terraces, mostly on the better, drier soils. The broad crescentic moraines are pasture covered, with forests on their dry gravel outwash. North of München, rough undulating hilly country has ill-drained wet meadows in the clayey valleys and arable fields on the slopes, especially where there is a sporadic cover of *loess*. The Tertiary hills are really the granary of Bavaria and Hallertau, the main German hop producing area.

The Alpine Foreland between the outermost moraines and the foot of the Alps is predominantly pastoral country. Towards the east, however, more continental climate allows arable cultivation, notably grains. In the Ramsau, wheat is found up to 1100 metres and in the inner valley of the Lech, it is cultivated up to 1320 metres. Alpine meadows reach up to 2300 metres. The high precipitation and moist air are important factors in the development of rich meadow, so that the German Alps have cattle raising and dairy production, with industries processing milk and cheese. The Allgäu is a major cheese-producing area, providing most German supplies of *Emmenthaler* and *Schweizer Käse*, and has large to medium-sized farms suited to livestock farming. Throughout the Alps, pastoral farming suffers from an acute shortage of labour in competition with tourism and industrial development, but population drift is greatest from the highest settlements, and transhumance, as elsewhere in the Alps, to the summer pastures of the *Almen* is in decay.

An exceptional agricultural area is the Black Forest, typified by farms mostly strung along the sunny side of valleys, with holdings of 500–1000-metres wide running down the valley sides. Permanent meadow marks the lower slopes, with patches of arable cultivation and rotation grass, whereas the upper slopes, often forest, provide summer pastures on which young stock is reared. Arable cultivation (oats, rye, and potatoes) is becoming increasingly uneconomic and specialized livestock rearing on permanent grass is dominating the scene. A considerable proportion of the farm population finds at least part-time employment in forestry or industry. The Black Forest has features in common with the morphologically similar Czech–German border country, where extensive forest is broken by cleared patches, with meadow or arable. Here the potato on some exposed parts will not flower until September and livestock is the mainstay of the farming economy.

The European Community and the peasant

The Common Agricultural Policy of the European Community has raised problems in all member states, no less so for the West Germans, since farming has been the Cinderella in an otherwise booming economy. The C.A.P. has widened the protective barrier from the national level to the Community level and it has been the dismantling of the national barrier that has caused the problems. The fiscal policies of the C.A.P. encouraging freeing of trade in agricultural produce mean that long-term considerable shifts in patterns of production should take place. Like other member states, the Federal Republic has been reluctant to allow this change to take place too rapidly in fear of losing confidence among the large peasant population. The widening gap between the rewards of farming and those of industrial employment has been exacerbated by the impact of the Community policy, so that structural improvement of farming has become an even more pressing priority. Unfortunately, the system of Community support that has made the C.A.P. almost unbearably expensive has fallen on the Germans heavily as major contributors, and they see the French as major beneficiaries making far less attempt to rectify weaknesses than themselves. The system of price support and free trade has not always worked as the Germans would like: in the late 1960s, the price support system designed to concentrate grain cultivation in the more suitable regions had the contrary effect and it rose in marginal areas, while in a number of sectors like dairying serious overproduction developed (e.g., the *Butterberg*), whereas in contrast severe competition arose for German producers of poultry, wine, and fruit. A very serious surplus of sugar beet arose for a time, adversely affecting the *Börde* lands that form some of the best and most prosperous farming areas. Finally, under the system of payments, fluctuations in currency parities can lower or raise the income from the support payments and, in the rising parity of the Deutschemark, the effect has been to lower this assistance to farmers.

The West Germans have committed themselves to support and foster the family farm, but this would be jeopardized if the proposals of the Community put forward by Commissioner Mansholt were applied. This would eliminate a large proportion of the German farmers, though it is argued that because three-quarters of the labour on the smallest farms is supplied by women members of the family the impact on the labour market would be less than envisaged. Nevertheless, so long as high industrial unemployment remains, it is unlikely such a change could be entertained. At the same time, much marginal land would go out of use, with particular infrastructural and social problems in the Central Uplands, the higher parts of the southern scarps, as well as the German Alps and large tracts of poorer country in the northern *geest* lands.

Forestry in the Federal Republic

With well over a quarter of its land under forest, the Federal Republic covers 60 percent of its domestic wood demand. Forests are nowadays regarded not only for their economic contribution, but also for their substantial amenity value. 'High forest' predominates and coppice of various types covers less than 5 percent. Of the high forest, 30.5 percent is broad-leaved and 69.5 percent is coniferous. The Federal Republic is one of the largest commercial coniferous timber producers in the European Community, but also one of the largest absolute wood importers (mostly topical hardwoods). The major forested areas lie in the south and in the Central Uplands. The North German Plain, apart from afforested areas like the Lüneburger Heide, has a relatively low proportion of forest.

The forests of the roughly dissected uplands present problems for extraction of timber and cutting has to be carefully controlled to avoid exposing unstable hillsides to erosion. The drastic clear-felling at the end of the Second World War had consequences that were salutory lessons to German foresters when *Kahlschlag* covered 12 percent of the Black Forest, 16 percent of the Harz, and 33 percent in the Lüneburger Heide. These areas have not yet been completely replanted, but massive cutting has been reduced everywhere, though the timber content of most forests is still not back to prewar levels.

Forest policy has sought four aims: to cover domestic demand for wood; to help conservation – notably shelter and water protection; to provide amenity; and to help socio-economic problems in areas of poor soils and declining farming. About 500,000 hectares of land for afforestation remain, despite an active postwar programme. Planting is usually on marginal lands that no longer give worthwhile returns from other uses or on lands falling to *social fallow*. There is also afforestation of industrial waste lands – notably on old coal, iron ore, and particularly lignite workings – while planting is also undertaken for shelter and water supply around towns. Urban development has, however, encroached on forests in many parts of the main conurbations.

Private ownership accounts for 44 percent of the forest area, but only one-fortieth of the private forest owners have more than 20 hectares. In contrast, state forests are usually of the order of 1000 hectares. Since 1965, creation of Nature Parks, 65 percent of whose area is forest, has helped conservation and management, but there is a great need for consolidation of the small private holdings into more workable units (some 800,000 hectares need such treatment). It is also desirable in many parts of the country to change coppice into high forest, to separate clearly forest and pasture, and to provide modern machinery and better forest roads. Only 13 percent of the private forests are purely forestry enterprises. The need is to improve the competitiveness of German forestry in the European Community. Legal support has been provided since 1970 for amalgamation of holdings and to help adjust annual production better to market needs.

Forest planting is of course a long-term operation: oak forest takes a rotational period of 140–180 years, beech 120–140 years, pine 100–120 years, and spruce 80–100 years. State forests contribute nearly 40 percent of the total timber harvest; the remainder is equally divided between private and communal forests. Hardwood and pine are cut in winter, but spruce is sometimes cut in summer to help spread the work load (summer felling is common in the mountains). Of the timber harvest, 6 percent is oak, 26 percent is beech (considerable overproduction), 54 percent is spruce, and 14 percent is pine. Spruce and pine are the main profit sources of most forest enterprises. An important by-product is 13 million Christmas trees, though a further 2 million are imported.

The once wide scatter of small sawmills is tending to change to a smaller number of larger units, drawing supplies from a wider area by the use of motor lorries. Sawmill capacity has tended to rise, though generally not fully utilized. In recent times, demand for hardwoods has tended to increase compared to softwoods, despite a marked overproduction of beech. Use of pitprops has fallen, while pulp and paper industries have felt strong competition from outside Germany. The upsurge in consumer spending has helped industries such as furniture making (main centres: Frankfurt-Hoechst, Stuttgart, Köln-

Bonn, Herford and Berlin), while the boom in building kept demand for timber going at a high rate.

Suggested further reading

Andreae, B.: Strukturen deutscher Agrarlandschaft: Landbaugebiete und Fruchtfolgensysteme in der BRD, *Forsch. z. deut. Landeskunde* 199, 1973.

Auswertungs- und Informationsdienst: Forestry and Wood Economy in the Federal Republic of Germany, Bad Godesberg, 1967.

Born, M.: Die Entwicklung der deutschen Agrarlandschaft, *Erträge der Forschung* 29, Darmstadt, 1974.

Bundesminister für Ernährung, Landwirtschaft und Forsten: Die Flurbereinigung in den Ländern der BRD, Bonn, 1960.

Die Forst- und Holzwirtschaft der BRD, Hiltrup, 1967.

Hallett, G.: Agricultural Policy in West Germany, *Journ. Agric. Economics* 19, 1968, pp.87–95.

Hartke, W.: Die 'Sozialbrache' als Phänomen der geographischen Differenzierung der Landschaft, *Erdkunde* 10, 1956, pp.257–269.

Mayhew, A.: Structural reform and the future of German agriculture, *Geog. Rev.* 60, 1970, pp.54–68.

Rural Settlement and Farming in Germany, London, 1973.

Otremba, E.: Die deutsche Agrarlandschaft, *Mitt. d. Inst. für Raumforschung* 30, 1956.

Die Deutsche Agrarlandschaft im Wirtschaftsgeschehen der Gegenwart, *Verh. Deut. Geographentages* 31, 1957, pp.327–334.

Die deutsche Agrarlandschaft, *Geog. Zeitschrift Beiheft* 3, 1961.

Der Agrarwirtschaftsraum der Bundesrepublik Deutschland, *Geog. Zeitschrift Beiheft* 24, 1970.

CHAPTER 14

TRANSPORT IN THE FEDERAL REPUBLIC

The transport system of the Federal Republic has been influenced in its orientation and development by the new alignments in the geography of Europe. The division of Germany, which split the prewar transport reticules, has meant a low level of contact with the transport system of the Democratic Republic and of the Socialist *bloc* as a whole. In contrast, the European Economic Community has brought closer contacts with the republic's western neighbours, emphasizing the Rhine axis compared to prewar times and tending to shift the orientation of the reticules to a north-south rather than an east-west axis.

Railway transport
By the time the Federal Republic was formed, the railways were back in working order and most routes reopened, though rolling stock and equipment as well as track were badly in need of renewal. The redirection of traffic to a predominantly north-south movement has been marked by the building of a few short sections of track to ease links and by redesigning junctions. The increase in north-south traffic has also been reflected, for example, by doubling sections of single line, and there has also been provision of a more direct route from Braunschweig to Hamburg. In the Ruhr area, a line has been built from Gelsenkirchen via the new town of Marl to the main route to the north at Haltern near Recklinghausen to provide a more direct north-south freight route. The loss of the ferry routes to Scandinavia via Warnemünde and

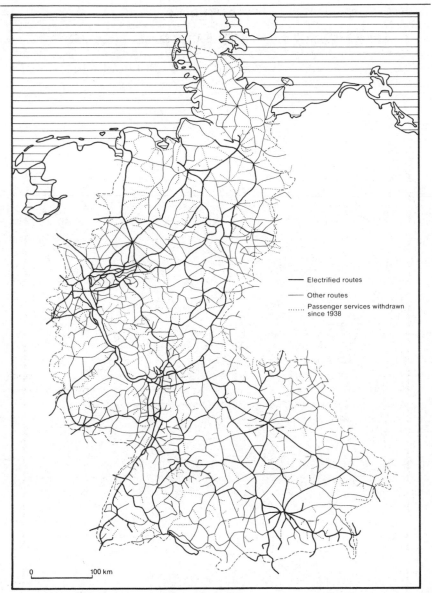

Figure 14.1 Railways in the Federal Republic

Transport in the Federal Republic

Stralsund in the G.D.R. forced West German–Scandinavian traffic on the long and circuitous route through Flensburg-Fredericia. A new ferry route was first developed from Grossenbrode to Gedser, but a more direct and quicker trajectory was opened in 1963 (*the Vogelfluglinie*) by bridging the Fehmarn Sound and building a new rail ferry terminal at Puttgarden to a Danish terminal at

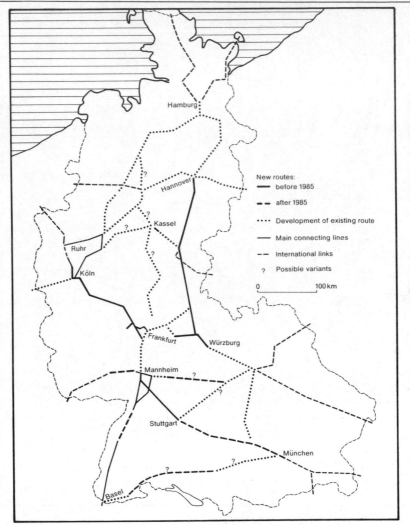

Figure 14.2 New railway trunklines in the Federal Republic

The Two Germanies

Rødbyhavn. There has also been building of new suburban railway systems, notably in München, Frankfurt am Main (including a line to the Rhine-Main Airport), Stuttgart, Köln, and Nürnberg, but by far the largest scheme has been to separate fast commuting services from freight and long-distance passenger traffic in the Ruhr area.

In 1971 a new plan for the development of the Federal Railways was outlined, optimistically based on an anticipated increase of 50 percent in freight and 100 percent in passenger traffic by 1985. As many existing trunk lines have reached the limit of their capacity, notably the Rhine valley routes, it was felt necessary to plan four new mainlines (total length 630 kilometres) capable of carrying 300 km.p.h. trains and to improve a number of existing main lines to carry similar traffic: the emphasis is entirely on improving north-south links in the first instance. The Hannover–Würzburg and Köln–Frankfurt lines will be new constructions, at least over the greater part of their length, and work has begun on the new direct line from Mannheim to Stuttgart, a serious bottleneck because of several awkward junctions.

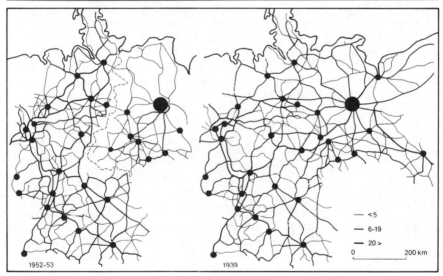

Figure 14.3 Railway passenger services 1939 and 1953 – fast trains daily

Figure 14.3 illustrates the shift in traffic by the early 1950s compared to prewar times. This shift has continued, accentuated by the establishment of the fast *Trans-Europ* international expresses, and the Federal Republic had a central place in a plan for long-term European rail services by the U.I.C. published in 1973. Internal traffic has been strengthened by a primarily north-south

Transport in the Federal Republic

oriented Inter-City express network, whereas several famous prewar expresses have been abandoned on east-west routes (for example, the Paris–Riga connection), though others have appeared, notably Soviet through sleeping coaches from Moscow across West Germany to Paris and Ostende. The growth in the number of Southeast European guest workers in the 1960s brought increased traffic with Jugoslavia and Greece, for which additional trains have been added, including through coaches Dortmund-Bar over the newly opened Jugoslav railway from Belgrade to Bar. The division of Germany has likewise affected railway freight traffic, though new international links have been established through the TEEM (*Trans-européene expresses marchandises*), as well as through the growing traffic between members of the European Community, notably to the Rhine-Scheldt ports and to the *Saarlorlux* region. Container traffic has helped North German ports to compete with the Dutch and Belgian ports, though Hamburg still has a considerable freight traffic by rail with the Democratic Republic and with Czechoslovakia. Conventional railway freight traffic has, however, tended to decline, though the share of railways is still higher than in the United Kingdom, helped by a higher proportion of longer hauls compared to Britain. Official policy has encouraged use of railways through such means as restricting weekend road haulage on motorways and by providing financial assistance with sidings to works and industrial estates. The decline of coal traffic has been a significant factor in the fall of freight tonnage in several coalfield traffic districts, while the growth of pipelines has limited the rise in tank wagon freights. Heavy bulk freights nevertheless remain important – the Ruhr traffic districts in general send out more than they receive, shipping away coal, coke, iron and steel semis, and heavy chemicals. An important movement into the Ruhr is still crude ore and scrap, though pit props have lost their significance as more locally made metal supports have been used. Duisburg, exceptional among the Ruhr traffic districts, receives more coal by rail than it ships away on the railway – this of course represents coal moving to the harbour of Duisburg-Ruhrort for shipment by Rhine barges. The Aachen and Saar coalfields both show large coal shipments to foreign countries – Aachen notably to Luxemburg and the Saar to France. The Saar receives ore shipments from Emden (in closed trainloads up to 4000 tons) and from France, as well as coal and coke from the Ruhr. Some special flows have also developed, such as motor vehicles from Southwest Germany and Lower Saxony to the North Sea ports for export.

While rural railways still carry a daily freight train, most passenger traffic has been switched to buses, at least during the quiet part of the day. The major share of rural bus traffic in vehicles owned by the railways or the post office demonstrates generally better intermedia coordination than in Britain. Experiments in the 1950s with road–rail vehicles were not successful, though battery driven railcars have been successfully used. Small nonstate railways, for instance the Westphalian *Land* Railway, have generally led in successful rationalization on lightly loaded lines. In passenger traffic, a conscious attempt has been made to compete with airlines on internal routes by providing a comprehensive system of fast, light express trains (*F-Züge* and *Inter-City*); and local systems of local fast trains (*Nahschnellverkehr*) for commuters and semifast trains over major routes have replaced the bulk of the former slow stopping trains, though many small stations have been eliminated, and a further wave of closure began in 1975. The local and semifast trains make a substantial loss, a chief factor in mounting financial deficits, partly because of obligations to carry concessionary traffic.

There has been a marked change in motive power since the mid-1950s, notably through the comprehensive electrification of mainlines, with much finance provided by the federal states, and showing a strong north-south orientation. Over 10,000 route kilometres were electrified by 1977 (compared to only 1700 kilometres in 1950), representing little more than one-third of the total route length and yet carrying over 80 percent of the total traffic. This network, when seen in relation to electrification in adjacent western countries, might be conceived as a system of Euro-trunklines. Electric traction has made possible much higher traffic densities: prewar plans to quadruple the west-bank Rhine route Köln-Koblenz-Mainz were replaced by electrification, and the double-track route now carries 326 trains a day compared to 199 in 1952 and 74 in 1938. Improved signalling and more passing loops have also helped to increase the capacity of several routes. Important links still not electrified are the Hamburg–Scandinavian routes, Köln-Trier, Bingen-Saarbrücken, besides links to Switzerland (e.g., Stuttgart-Konstanz), and to Austrian Vorarlberg (e.g., Ulm-Lindau-Bregenz).

Contraction in the railway reticule began immediately after the war as numerous short light railways, both narrow and standard gauge, mostly not part of the state railways, have been closed, notably in Lower Saxony and in the Lower Rhine, but also in Schleswig-Holstein. Some closures arose from damaged lines not being rebuilt. The state railways have also shed lightly loaded branches: by 1976 over 5200 kilometres of uneconomic route had been abandoned and a plan to prune unprofitable parts of the system proposed in 1975 is expected to reduce route length by 1980 from 29,000 kilometres to about 16,000 kilometres. Along the Rhine, primarily strategic bridges were not rebuilt after the war, notably at Remagen, Bingen and Wesel. The latter had carried the trunk route from Flushing (Vlissingen) via Boxtel and Xanten to Wesel of the one-time North Brabant-German Railway, little used after 1914, and the line from Wesel to the Dutch frontier has now been largely abandoned, while closure of the Straelen-Venlo Railway also ended the abortive Paris–Venlo–Hamburg Railway. The emergence of an international frontier between the two German states brought closure of thirty-five routes across it, so that now only five remain open to traffic. Whereas in 1937 there were fourteen daily expresses from Berlin to Hamm, thirty years later there were only four (six in summer). A number of routes that crisscrossed the frontier had to be closed entirely, while one section left completely isolated near Lüchow was dismantled.

Road transport

The Federal Republic revived motorway construction in the early 1950s, first completing links left unfinished by the war (though earthworks and bridges were often part finished) and then turning to new construction or to expanding the capacity of existing sections. New building has followed the prewar plans remarkably closely, but more emphasis has been put on links with Belgium, the Netherlands, and Austria, as well as Switzerland and France (whose own motorway development has been slow). Like the railway system, the most vigorous development has been of north-south links, though north of Hamburg, links to Scandinavia have been as yet poorly developed. Of particular note is the rapid growth of duplication of routes along the Rhine between the industrial areas of the Rhine-Ruhr and the Rhine-Main area, though motorway links across the river (except at Köln) are also sparse. Compared to prewar, more emphasis has been put on access (mostly still under construction) to the ports; and consideration has been given to motorway access to important tourist areas like the Black Forest. Motorways have been important elements in regional development; for example, along the Rhine from Freiburg to Basel as a means of opening a rather isolated district to new economic stimuli. Because of the restricted valley of the middle Rhine, already crowded by settlement and transport development, motorways skirt along the flanking uplands, where the Köln–Frankfurt motorway has demonstrated its importance in revitalizing the economies of rural districts through which it passes, like those around Montabaur and Limburg. Though reconstruction of the major classified roads other than motorways has been undertaken, it has not been so impressive in the general picture of road travel. Planning for roads has been based on the assumption that density of road traffic would double between 1958 and 1970 and would triple by 1985, though this rate of growth was slowed unexpectedly by the 1973 oil crisis and the assumption was being questioned in the mid-1970s, while a growing environmental lobby against new roads has become vociferous.

The 'consumer-society' has encouraged the growth of motor traffic, first through the growing distribution of goods best handled by road transport and second through the growth of personal ownership of motor cars. From 540,000 in 1950, motor cars increased to almost 18 million in 1976: in contrast, motorcycles fell from a maximum of 2.49 million in 1955 to a low of 198,000 in 1972. There is roughly one car to every four people, and it is estimated that

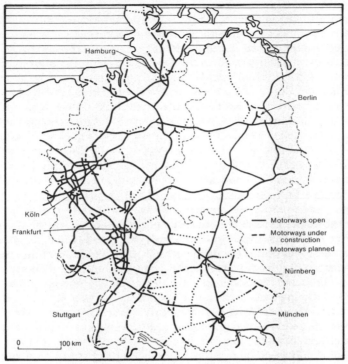

Figure 14.4 Motorways in the Federal Republic

between 75–80 percent of all journeys are now made by car. Commercial vehicles today comprise 14 percent of the total registered vehicle park; private cars, almost 85 percent. In 1950 commercial vehicles formed just over 27 percent and private cars not quite 27 percent, whereas motorcycles then comprised 46 percent of all registered vehicles. Most commercial haulage is done by firms in their own lorries and vans. Various means of fiscal and legal control have been made to restrict too rapid growth of road haulage in an attempt to get 30 million tons of goods off the roads. By far the most common items in road haulage are foodstuffs and building materials (cement, bricks, etc.), but chemicals and mineral oils are also significant elements. International road haulage traffic is dominated by movements to and from Holland (41.6 percent); France receives only 15.8 percent; Belgium, 9.4 percent; and Denmark, 11.4 percent. There is a growing road traffic with Southeastern Europe, with fruit and vegetables brought by Bulgarian, Romanian, Hungarian, and Jugoslavian lorries.

Transport in the Federal Republic

Inland waterways

An important part is still played by river and canal transport in the Federal Republic, dominated by the Rhine, whose role in the European Community has become superarterial. From the Rhine, access can be had to the canals of the Ruhr industrial area and via the Dortmund-Ems Canal to Emden or via the Mittelland Canal to the Hannover area, though this latter canal's importance has declined since the division of Germany cut its access to the middle Elbe basin. The North-South Canal (Elbe Lateral Canal) has been built to join the Mittelland Canal through West German territory to the Elbe just above Hamburg. Canalization of the Mosel to Thionville and beyond in France has, however, not been the success expected, and the Saar industrial area still presses for completion of a direct canal link to the Rhine. But the federal government will not accept the argument for the Saar-Palatinate Canal, preferring to canalize the Saar river. Canalization of the Neckar to Plochingen near Stuttgart opened up the industrially rich Württemberg, though the full benefits of the improvement of Main navigation will not come until after 1981 when the Main-Danube Canal is completed. There are fears, however, that the Main-Danube Canal will open West German waterways to severe competition from vessels of the Danube countries. Plans to make the Rhine navigable to the Bodensee have moved slowly (navigation is presently possible to Rheinfelden above Basel), and progress is also poor on the Trans-Helvetic Canal project from Koblenz/Aargau via Biel to the Lake of Geneva, while other links between the Rhine and Rhône have been proposed. Equally protracted are plans to join the Rhine and the Maas, while the one-time project of the Hansa-Canal from Osnabrück to Hamburg via Bremen has seemingly been shelved. One of the most important projects still under construction is the Rhine Parallel Canal (Grand Canal d'Alsace) on the French bank between Strasbourg and Basel that enables vessels to avoid this difficult section of the river.

River and canal traffic is nowadays dominated by the self-propelled diesel barge and efforts are being made to open almost all waterways up to the *Europa* ship of 1300/1500 tons capacity (length 85 metres, breadth 9.50 metres, and draught 2.70 metres). The tug-hauled barge train has been increasingly replaced by self-propelled barges or most recently by the push-tug introduced in 1957. Most economical in labour, it allows better manoevrability, with a payload up to 8000–10,000 tons. There are nevertheless too many vessels and an excess capacity that requires action on a Community scale.

Changes have taken place in Rhine traffic, with coal and brown coal shipments downstream from ports such as Wesseling and Duisburg-Ruhrort less important as the Netherlands has switched to oil and natural gas, but the substantial growth in upstream oil traffic in the 1950s has been pruned by the spread of pipelines. Upstream shipments of ore to Ruhr industry from

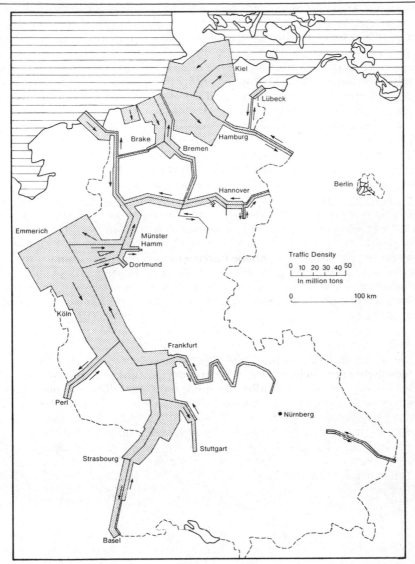

Figure 14.5 Traffic on West German waterways

Rotterdam have become more important, notably from the bulk handling ore terminal at Maasvlakte, but ore shipments are unimportant on other sections of the river. There is still substantial movement of mineral building materials downstream, while fertilizers and heavy chemicals remain significant cargoes. Upstream freights of coal and lignite have also grown, despite the strength of railway competition, partly through shipments up the Mosel to France moving on the Rhine from the Ruhr ports to Koblenz. Iron and steel goods move in both directions, though Ruhr shipments to Rotterdam–Europoort are particularly substantial. Total upstream traffic exceeds total downstream traffic, with the heaviest traffic between the Netherlands and Duisburg-Ruhrort, the largest Rhine port: Köln, Wesseling, and Mannheim are also major ports. The biggest tonnage passes in Dutch vessels, followed by German and Belgian boats. Coal, lignite, and metalware are the main upstream freights, along with some building materials and aggregate, on the Neckar and the Main, while coal and coke are the main goods sent up the Mosel. The Dortmund-Ems Canal carries ore, grain and timber to the Ruhr, while metal goods and even manufactured articles form return cargoes. Coal, metal, and ore are the chief items moving on the Mittelland Canal, and potash ores, heavy chemicals, and even lignite are sent by this route from the G.D.R., while similar items and timber come from as far afield as Poland. Complex local flows of ores, coal, coke, grain, cement, and timber move on the canal system of the Ruhr.

Sea transport and ports
Like all merchant fleets, the proportion of tanker tonnage has become increasingly significant in the German fleet, though trade is not handled solely by West German shipping or even by West German ports, with Rotterdam–Europoort and Antwerp particularly important. Growth of traffic in the last decade has been much slower in most West German ports (exceptions are Brake and Kiel) than in Rotterdam–Europoort, which has used its locational advantages compared to the German ports for the greater part of the West German market, particularly as regulations of the Economic Community have prevented the erection of protective fiscal systems to favour German trade passing through German ports. Two-thirds of the total turnover of West German ports is in imports of mineral oils and derivatives and some limited exports; one-tenth of the total turnover comprises imports of ores and raw materials; one-twentieth comprises imports of ores and raw materials; one-twentieth comprises imports and exports of coal and coke, with imports exceeding exports; three-tenths is in grain, where imports greatly exceed exports in most years; while a slightly smaller proportion is in iron and steel semis, where exports predominate. A little over one-fourth of the total turnover is in mixed cargoes, both in and out.

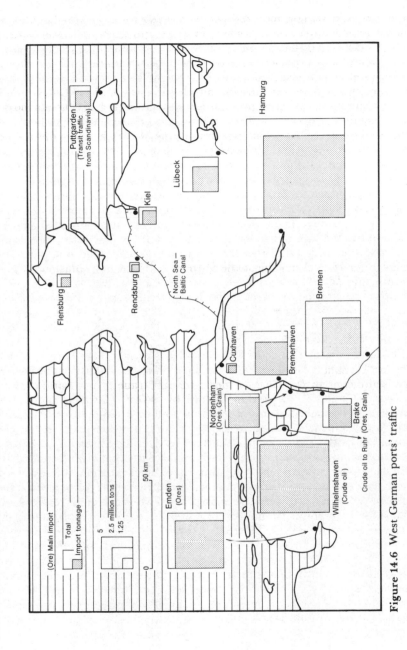

Figure 14.6 West German ports' traffic

The picture is dominated by Hamburg (where the dock area is to be extended along the Süderelbe), to which better motorway, rail, and canal access is being developed. In exchange for its original outport, Cuxhaven, Hamburg gained from Lower Saxony two islands, Neuwerk and Scharhörn, where it is proposed to build cargo handling facilities for very large bulk carriers. At present, fully laden vessels up to 95,000 tons can reach the port of Hamburg, over 130 kilometres from the mouth of the Elbe, whose channel it is planned to deepen to take vessels up to about 115,000 tons fully laden, but there is a wish to catch traffic in ships up to 300,000 or more tons at the Neuwerk outport. Hamburg feels itself better placed in the long term than Rotterdam to handle superships, because deep water comes nearer inshore than in the southern North Sea and navigational conditions are generally easier than in the restricted fairway of the English Channel. A pipeline has been constructed from Wilhelmshaven to Hamburg so that it can draw on the ability of tankers up to 250,000 tons to unload in the former. The postwar recovery of Hamburg was slow and not until 1960 did the turnover in the harbour exceed the best interwar years, a main reason for which has been the changed political geography of Europe that disrupted its traditional hinterland in the Elbe basin. Many goods which prewar would have moved from areas now in the Socialist *bloc* to Hamburg have been rerouted to G.D.R. or Polish harbours. Prewar, a quarter of Hamburg's trade was with the present area of the G.D.R. and very little has been recovered, though the volume of trade with Czechoslovakia has climbed back to roughly the prewar tonnage. The rules of the European Community to free mobility and prevent artificial traffic flows have affected Hamburg adversely because it is poorly placed to reach the most prosperous parts of the Federal Republic in competition with the Rhine delta ports, though its position may be improved by better transport links to the south. It also failed to seize the advantages of new forms of shipping, notably making a late start in container facilities, though there is now an excellent concentration point for general cargo in the large *Übersee-Zentrum*. Railway services have been improved by a new marshalling yard built on the southern outskirts that gives fast through-put of trains, and though motorway links have been extended, these are still lacking northwards to Scandinavia and westwards to the Elbe mouth. But Hamburg's position will be further improved when the new North-South Canal (Elbe Lateral Canal) makes direct bulk cargo transport possible to the Hannover–Salzgitter and Ruhr areas. Events held back industrial development in the port until the early 1960s, whereas Rotterdam had started in 1947. The building of atomic power stations on the lower Elbe augment available electric power, which has already attracted new style energy-intensive industries, especially as the port has been fortunate in having plenty of good waterside sites available for development. Shipbuilding remains important, though Hamburg's role as an oil-refining centre has been outstripped by inland sites.

The Two Germanies

The Bremen ports, the second major group, in general have been less affected by the division of the country, having traded only modestly with Central Germany before 1945. Both Bremen and Bremerhaven developed container facilities relatively early, largely through American encouragement. Bremerhaven has remained the main passenger port, changing to holiday cruises as the North Atlantic and other traffic declined, whereas Bremen remains notably a general cargo port, with 'colonial' products (cotton, wool, timber, tobacco, and coffee), though some specialist traffics have also developed, notably the export of motor vehicles, with substantial roll-on roll-off facilities, and Bremerhaven has developed a considerable ore import trade (which has outstripped Hamburg). Unlike in Hamburg, little oil is handled. Nordenham and Brake on the lower Weser remain chiefly coasting ports, though also engaged in a substantial grain trade, and fishing is still important though the scene is dominated by Cuxhaven on the Elbe. The Weser estuary has been deepened to take 100,000-ton vessels at Bremerhaven, though it is felt it would be imprudent to deepen it to take vessels over 140,000 tons because of the danger of the river banks collapsing into too deep a channel. The journey is slow and awkward for large vessels upstream to Bremen, but it can be reached by vessels not exceeding 9.6-metres draught. The Bremen ports suffer primarily from inadequate links with the interior of the country, particularly as traffic on the Weser is limited to boats under 1000 tons and upstream movement is very slow. Most bulk cargoes move by railway (including a good network of container trains) or by road over the greatly improved motorway system. About half the imports are used in local Bremen industries, notably foodstuffs, textile, and tobacco industries, whereas Lower Saxony and North Rhine-Westphalia remain the main hinterland for the Weser ports.

Though the tonnage handled at Wilhelmshaven is impressive, the port is essentially an oil-importing terminal open to very big tankers, with petroleum constituting over 90 percent of the turnover, totalling about a quarter of the crude oil imports used in the Federal Republic. An oil refinery has been built and pipelines extend to the Rhine. The Dollart estuary is restricted to ships of only 35,000 tons with little prospect of making it accessible to vessels larger than 40,000–45,000 tons, so limiting development at Emden, but a proposal has been made to offload 70,000-tonners into lighters at the island of Borkum. Iron ore and crude oil (local refining) form the main imports, though for a time considerable quantities of American coal were imported and it is a major motor vehicle exporting port, although exports form less than one-fifth of its total freight turnover. It is relatively well served with transport links, using the Dortmund-Ems Canal for ore shipments to the Ruhr, though again European Community legislation in stopping the former preferential tariffs for ore shipments to the Saar has limited growth of promising traffic.

Lübeck still has its traffic in ore from the Swedish Bothnian ports in summer, but otherwise is restricted to Baltic trade, and its position almost on the new frontier has created special problems as care must be taken in entering the Trave not to stray into G.D.R. territorial waters. Almost half Lübeck's traffic is ferry traffic to Scandinavia. Kiel, a revived naval port with shipbuilding and repairing, has its traffic largely restricted to Baltic trade. Expansion of the capacity of the Kiel Canal to enable larger vessels to reach the Baltic is unfortunately likely to have only a minimal effect on Kiel, although it has been developing as a ferry port for Scandinavia. Brunsbüttel at the Elbe end of the Kiel Canal is a largely oil-importing port.

Air transport

Civil aviation did not restart until 1955 and the state airline, *Lufthansa*, is now internationally well known. There are six charter carriers and over thirty air

Table 14.1
Share of traffic among different media

Originating passengers	1950	1956	1962	1968	1973
		– as percent of national total –			
Railway	17.8	10.7	6.5	4.5	3.7
Public road vehicles	46.2	35.6	33.2	25.5	22.8
Air	0.0	0.0	0.0	0.1	0.1
Private cars	35.1	53.0	59.2	68.8	72.2
Passenger traffic (P/km)					
Railway	37.7	24.5	13.9	8.4	7.1
Public road vehicles	28.9	23.4	18.1	12.7	11.4
Air	0.1	0.5	0.7	1.1	1.4
Private cars	33.8	51.3	67.0	77.4	79.9
Originating goods tonnage*					1976
Railway	61.5	50.9	43.9	36.9	32.3
Inland waterways	21.2	24.5	24.8	26.0	21.7
Roads	9.7	13.8	15.9	17.0	24.7
Pipelines	—	—	3.1	7.9	7.6
Sea	7.6	10.8	12.3	12.2	13.7
Goods traffic (T/km)†					
Railways	56.0	44.6	37.5	30.7	32.3
Inland waterways	23.7	27.5	26.9	25.0	23.9
Roads	20.3	27.9	32.6	36.9	36.1
Pipelines	—	—	3.0	7.4	7.7

* = without railways own traffic, air traffic, and local road haulage tonnages
† = without railways own traffic, air traffic, and sea shipping

Source: Verkehr in Zahlen, Bundesminster für Verkehr, Bonn, 1974.

The Two Germanies

Table 14.2
Growth in registered motor vehicles

	1950	1958	1966	1974	1975
			– in thousands –		
Motor vehicles of which:	2,368	6,787	13,147	20,424	21,011
private cars	598	3,097	10,302	17,341	17,899
motor cycles	1,150	2,254	552	230	250
buses and trolley buses	16	31	40	58	60
lorries	445	646	891	1,077	1,061

Source: Verkehr in Zahlen, Bundesminister für Verkehr, Bonn, 1974.

Table 14.3
Growth in merchant marine

	1950	1958	1966	1973	1974
Ships No.	1,737	2,736	2,661	2,333	2,202
'000 GRT of which:	770	4,443	6,024	7,850	8,713
Dry cargo No.	1,595	2,481	2,378	1,651	1,332
'000 GRT	645	3,723	4,751	5,907	5,419
Tanker No.	38	110	118	140	159
'000 GRT	80	512	1,092	1,821	2,787
Passenger No.	7	20	12	4	
'000 GRT	27	175	128	63	
Milliard t/km.	22	108	150	106	

Source: Verkehr in Zahlen, Bundesminister für Verkehr, Bonn, 1974.

Table 14.4
Road haulage – percentage share of commodities carried

	1950	1958	1966	1973
Agric. and forest products	9.4	9.1	6.3	5.5
Foodstuffs and animal feed	4.3	5.0	5.6	5.9
Coal	34.3	25.6	15.8	10.7
Crude oil	1.4	3.2	11.4	12.8
Mineral oil products	2.6	5.0	8.9	10.9
Ores and scrap	9.7	11.3	10.1	10.3
Iron, steel, NF metal	6.2	7.3	7.8	9.6
Stones, gravel, etc.	18.3	17.5	17.4	15.0
Fertilizer	3.1	3.7	3.1	2.4
Chemicals	2.7	3.3	4.3	5.3
Machinery, etc.	7.9	8.8	9.3	11.6

Source: Verkehr in Zahlen, Bundesminister für Verkehr, Bonn, 1974.

Transport in the Federal Republic

taxi and short haul operators. While international services are provided, a network of internal links has been built up, the busiest being to West Berlin (operated by non-German carriers) since flying overcomes the harassments practised by the East German authorities on rail and road traffic. The largest airport in traffic terms is Rhine-Main at Frankfurt, which owes its inception to American initiative in the early postwar years and is now one of the major European airports. München airport has been limited by short runways, until reconstructed in the early 1970s, and runway extension at Düsseldorf–Lohausen has also been necessary at one of the busiest of all German airports, with considerable charter traffic. Bonn, the federal capital, does not have the largest national airport at its doorstep, but rather the moderately important Köln-Bonn airport at Wahn. Hamburg–Fuhlsbüttel, the most important North German airport, is scheduled for extension and reconstruction, while a new airport is planned just outside the *Land*. Hannover–Wunsdorf has particularly traffic with West Berlin, providing the shortest flight distance, and was important in the 1950s in the movement of refugees out of West Berlin. Frankfurt, München, Düsseldorf, and Hamburg are the main freight airports, though air freight has not yet grown to the significance in German trade that it has taken in Britain, with only about one-half the air freight handled by special freight aircraft.

Suggested further reading

Despicht, N.: The Transport Policy of the European Communities, London, 1969.

John, G.: Die Verkehrsströme innerhalb der BRD nach Gütergruppen und Verkehrsarten, *Deut. Inst. für Wirtschaftsforsch. Beiträge zur Strukturforsch.* 3, Berlin, 1967.

Kroner, G.: Der Güterumschlag in den Binnenhäfen der BRD, *Inst. f. Raumforsch.* 11, 1967.

Schmitz, A.: Verkehrsgeographie – Textteil und Bildteil, *Eisenbahn–Lehrbücherei der Deutschen Bundesbahn* 91, Starnberg, 1968.

Seebohm, H. C.: Die Verkehrswege der Bundesrepublik Deutschland, München, 1964.

CHAPTER 15

THE LÄNDER AND THEIR REGIONAL PROBLEMS IN THE FEDERAL REPUBLIC

Regional problems in the Federal Republic arise not only from common spatial factors like differences in natural conditions, resources, remoteness, and inaccessibility, but also from socio-economic conditions creating regional disparities in wealth and the complicating factor of political geographic changes since 1945. The federal structure has given a new impetus to the long tradition of regional particularism, and local sentiment, strong and vociferous, has gained a new virility through substantial devolution. There is also the wider context of the liberalization and mobility brought by the European Community, which has drawn West Germany into close contact with its western neighbours, emphasizing a strong centripetalism to the Rhine-Rhône axis. Once neglected western frontier regions have found a new focal and bridging function, but greater mobility and circulation have generated new orientations and avenues of movement. While much effort has been devoted to defining workable functional planning regions inside the country, new planning units extending across international frontiers, like the Regio Basiliensis and Saarlorlux, have emerged. The ideological division of Europe has, however, left a deep impress along the dividing line between the two German states that cuts into several well-integrated prewar regions, and through its isolating effect makes a broad eastern strip of country a regional 'cul-de-sac', the 40 kilometre-wide *Zonenrandgebiet*.

Regional policy and planning have had a rather Cinderella-like existence in the Federal Republic, especially as the more radical exponents of the social market-economy in the 1950s felt that market forces would take care of possible imbalances and disequilibria. More tolerant views were nevertheless also wary, since 'planning' was a hallmark of Naziism and Communism. Both views spoilt the public image of planning, and there was little opposition when

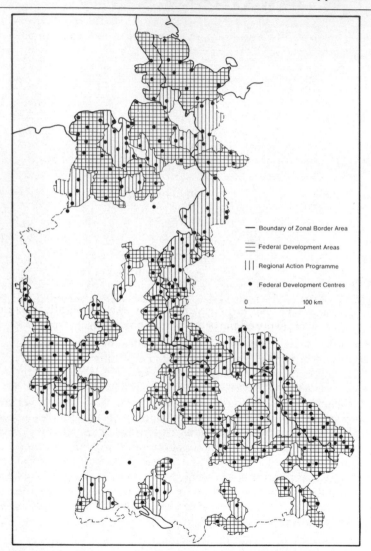

Figure 15.1 Development areas in the Federal Republic

The Two Germanies

regional policy was given a low key by both the federal and *Länder* authorities, with planning chiefly in the hands of the lowest rank of local government singularly ill-equipped to make anything but the most local decisions and unable to influence broader issues of land use and regional development. The attitude was well reflected in the rapid but relatively little coordinated rebuilding in towns in the 1950s when opportunities to replan were foregone by the claim that it was more important to get things rebuilt than to plan for an uncertain future.

The Länder and their problems

Regional problems in Northwest Germany – Schleswig-Holstein, Lower Saxony, and the 'city states' of Bremen and Hamburg – stem from the redrawing of the political map in 1945. Together these *Länder* contain roughly one-fifth of the Federal Republic's population and one-fourth of its area. Expellees and refugees after 1945 brought a large increase in population in most rural areas and in the smaller, less damaged towns, whereas air raid damage resulted in a marked fall in population in the major towns (notably Hamburg and Bremen) until they regained their populations in the 1950s, showing quite dramatic increases. Efforts to relieve the rural areas and small towns of the burden of expellees and refugees through resettlement elsewhere brought significant falls in their populations during the 1950s, despite a generally high if declining natural increase. From the mid-1960s, the largest towns again began to lose population as people sought pleasanter surroundings in the countryside around that brought growth of small towns where newly introduced industries also attracted people. Nevertheless, there has been generally a continued emigration to more favoured parts of the republic as the Northwest has failed to keep pace with general trends in the rise in wealth elsewhere less isolated from the mainstream of the European Community. The closeness of the 'Iron Curtain' to the Lower Elbe, leaving only a narrow corridor of movement from Scandinavia through Hamburg, has long given a feeling of insecurity in Northwest Germany.

Schleswig-Holstein has been covered by several development programmes where, because of its isolation and its long frontage on the Baltic, all the eastern part is included in the *Zonenrandgebiet*, while the rest falls under several federal development areas and regional action programmes, with the exception of *Kreis* Pinneberg whose close association with Hamburg has given strong growth tendencies, and there has been a spread of suburban settlement in a broad strip round the boundaries of Hamburg. The *Land* has well-developed agriculture (notably meat and dairy produce) likely to remain particularly significant in its economy in comparison to other *Länder*, but there is a need to increase the average size of holding from 20 hectares, though the territory is fortunate in having a higher than average share of large, well-managed estates.

The Länder and their Regional Problems in the Federal Republic

Unfortunately, increase in farm efficiency is generally not accompanied by a bigger demand for labour, so in the more agriculturally dependent parts of the north there is need to hold population in the countryside by providing a wider choice of jobs. In the west, notably in Dithmarschen and the Rendsburg area, as well as along the Elbe, the need is for better drainage and better farm roads as well as improvement in holdings both by size and in the distribution of parcels of ground, though fragmentation is not generally as bad as in South Germany. Under *Programm Nord* some 1800 hectares of reclamation and extensive afforestation on poor soils are planned, and along the west coast, as part of the *Küstenplan*, better protection from floods is still needed, though grandiose pre- and postwar plans for coastal land reclamation have been pruned. There

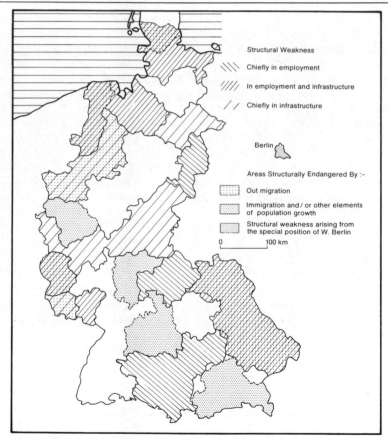

Figure 15.2 Federal Republic – problem areas

is much scope around Hamburg to extend special farming, such as tree nurseries and market gardening, with encouragement to process more farm produce in Schleswig-Holstein (a major development has been a central creamery at Schleswig). Tourist development is also included for the Holstein-Switzerland (Eutin-Plön), the Baltic coast, and the North Frisian Islands.

The only significant if limited natural resource is oil and natural gas and the disappointing German sector of the North Sea has failed to help. Industrial problems are associated with remoteness, though the *Land* is adjacent to the Scandinavian market. Kiel, a major shipbuilding centre, is dependent on trends in world markets and, although there is a small iron and steel plant at Lübeck-Herrenwyk based on Swedish ores, heavy industry is otherwise weakly represented and the modest textiles industries owe much to expellee initiative. Consequently diversification is regarded as an essential long-term objective.

Schleswig-Holstein performs a strong transit function, linking the Rhine Basin with Scandinavia, greatly strengthened in 1963 by the opening of the shortened rail–sea route to Denmark via Puttgarden. A new international airport just outside Hamburg at Kaltenkirchen will also improve accessibility, and electrification of the mainline railways radiating from Hamburg to Kiel, Lübeck, Puttgarden, and Flensburg is recommended. Roads need improvement, particularly by extending the existing motorway to Lübeck and to the ferry at Puttgarden, and by providing an axial motorway from Hamburg via Kiel to Flensburg, though the present main concern is to bypass the Hamburg bottleneck. While the Kiel Canal has been enlarged and the port of Rendsburg developed, completion of the Mittelland Canal-Elbe link will provide a reason to expand the Elbe-Lübeck Canal to take standard 1350–1500-ton barges. The disruption of circulation in eastern Holstein has been particularly critical, with Lübeck on the new frontier with the G.D.R. and cut from its former hinterland in western Mecklenburg. A similar isolation arises on the lower reaches of the Elbe where bridges, tunnels, or ferries are needed to improve contact across the river, and even the Kiel Canal acts as a barrier to easy circulation within the *Land*.

The area of reference of a joint planning body for the Lower Elbe (bringing together Hamburg, Schleswig-Holstein, and Lower Saxony) includes 200 square kilometres of Holstein in which four main development axes are proposed, radiating from Hamburg. While on one hand Danish entry into the European Community improved Schleswig-Holstein's position, since it is no longer the absolute margin of the Community, the situation is complicated on the other by the similarity between agriculture in Denmark and in the *Land*, bringing increased competition for the latter.

Hamburg is one of the two city *Länder*, but with a population of nearly 2 million it is a reasonably viable unit. It remains the Federal Republic's main port, but even though it handles almost a quarter more tonnage than prewar, its share of traffic of the twelve major ports in the European Community of the Six is only

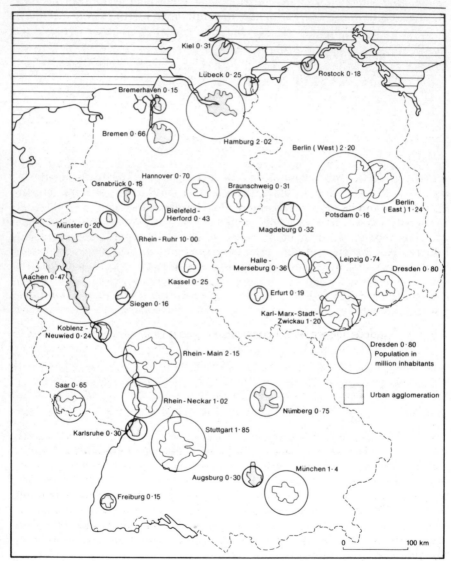

Figure 15.3 Urban agglomerations of Germany

The Two Germanies

half what it was in 1938, a combination of the disruption of its traditional hinterland in the Elbe basin and having to compete on open terms with Rotterdam and Antwerp, better placed to serve the growth foci of the Rhine basin. But completion of the canal joining the Rhine system to the Elbe through West German territory may hopefully increase the traffic moving to Hamburg. The Hanseatic City has bought Neuwerk and Scharhörn, islands off the mouth of the Elbe, for construction of a deepwater carrier terminal, a site reputedly with better long-term prospects than the congested waters of Rotterdam–Europoort–Antwerp, since deep water comes much closer inshore than in the southern North Sea and English Channel. New developments in the North Sea oil and gas industry are having a marked spinoff in Hamburg, intimately linked to the economic fortunes of 'North Sea Space', while as a free port it may benefit from greater interchange between oceanic and Baltic shipping in expanding East-West trade. The rising prosperity of Hamburg has put considerable pressure upon its own and surrounding territory of adjacent *Länder*, partly the result of the explosion of mobility provided by the motorcar. Loss of population raises serious questions in a federal state, since this weakens its position and its wealth, but an overflow has been inevitable and has been accepted in association with adjacent states, with new developments basically along the axis of the Lower Elbe rather than upstream towards the border with the German Democratic Republic. With the increasing filling of building space on the north (in Holstein), development emphasis is expected to shift to the Harburg district and to a southern axis running from the new industrial area around Stade through Buxtehude to Lüneberg, with an extension towards Buchholz.

Bremen's independence as a Federal *Land* was based on the criteria used to distinguish Hamburg, and similarly its trading relations are not primarily with the relatively poor country around it, but with interior Lower Saxony and the Rhine basin. Bremen and Bremerhaven have been notably dependent on road and rail traffic, perhaps one reason why they developed quickly in the 1960s compared to Hamburg as container ports. Bremen city, like Hamburg, has been outside the federal development plans, though Bremerhaven was included in the regional action programme for Northwest Lower Saxony. Nevertheless, Bremen has joined with Lower Saxony in a planning agency for the Lower Weser, another example of such bodies overcoming federal particularism. Interest has been directed to improvement of the Weser to take larger vessels up to Bremen, while preliminary planning includes a regional airport sited on Lower Saxon territory to replace the present Bremen airport in the 1980s. Coordinated development of Bremen and centres such as Oldenburg, Delmehorst, Brake, Nordenham, Syke, Verden, and Rotenburg (Wümme) is also proposed.

Lower Saxony, the largest of the northwest *Länder* and second largest in area in the republic, existed conceptually as a planning unit before 1939 but emerged only after 1945 as a territorial-administrative unit. The historical view of Lower Saxony as a cultural province is well understood, but the one-time political units comprising it – notably Oldenburg, Hannover, and Braunschweig – have not taken well to being compressed into the new body. Though it suffers less in the southern districts from remoteness than the rest of Northwest Germany, its northwestern districts had a comparatively marginal and remote location until bulk ocean transport began to impart a new attraction to coastal sites. It has suffered particularly through the division of Germany, because industrial areas in the southeast were in prewar times intimately linked to the industrial and economic structures of the Elbe-Saale basins.

Lower Saxony had a large influx of expellees and refugees, but during the 1950s much was done by resettlement or new developments to reduce the burden in rural districts, though the effect was not as dramatic as in Schleswig-Holstein. In the 1960s, the population of the countryside around the south of Hamburg increased only modestly, again in contrast to Schleswig-Holstein, since the poorly accessible Lower Saxon areas south of the Elbe were less attractive to commuters from Hamburg. In the 1960s, the bulk of population increase in Lower Saxony took place in the more industrialized south, with a notable increase around Hannover.

The greater part of Lower Saxony is included in one or other of the regional development schemes, but even areas excluded from these schemes around Osnabrück and Hannover are not without their problems, which in the case of Hannover led to the formation (1963) of a special planning body (*Verband Grossraum Hannover*). Lower Saxony has benefited under the *Küstenplan* (instituted after the flooding disaster of 1953), which though primarily aimed at coastal protection and drainage improvement, includes also better water supply for domestic and industrial use, land reclamation, and comprehensive rural improvement. Many poorer rural districts of northwest Lower Saxony were included in the system of federal development areas, and the whole area was later included in a regional action programme. In the zonal border area, quite apart from the disruption caused by the division of Germany, a number of districts have experienced structural economic problems, notably the decline of iron mining. The reasonably prosperous area around Salzgitter, Peine, and Northeim brought concentration of projects on the zonal border districts to north and south, particularly the difficult long, remote, and infertile salient around Uelzen and Lüchow-Dannenberg.

Since the late 1960s industrial employment prospects have improved considerably in the northwest as the growth of container shipping and bulk carriers in Emden (ore and containers), Wilhelmshaven (oil), and the lower

Weser have increased the attraction of coastal or riverside sites, while increased electricity generating capacity has brought substantial development around Stade, an important growth focus for the formerly problematical area between the Elbe and the Weser. Nordenham on the lower Weser has also received new industries, whereas new industries (e.g., *Monsanto Chemicals*) appeared in the Ems basin around Lingen, attracted by discoveries of natural gas, which along with oil and vast reserves of salt, provides an important resource base in Lower Saxony. Equally, the Hannover area has attracted new industries and extensions to existing industry, though the major problem has become infrastructural through the spread of settlement into the small towns and countryside around. It was growth industries of the 1960s like motor vehicle manufacture that eased the problems of the central part of the zonal border. Unfortunately, some of Lower Saxony's main natural resources lie adjacent to the border with the German Democratic Republic, notably brown coal mining near Helmstedt and nonferrous metals in the Harz.

Before 1945 southern Lower Saxony lay on the main axis of movement between West and Central Germany so the division of the country had a serious repercussion on the pattern of traffic flow through the loss of such a central position, though one of the principal north-south flows of traffic developed in the Federal Republic passes through the Hannover–Braunschweig area and another flows on a tangential course from Hamburg via Bremen to the Rhine-Ruhr area. A major feature of Northwest German plans is the importance laid on better rail (electrification) and road (motorway) links to and between ports. The opening of the North-South Canal, however, will benefit the poorer rural districts around Lüneburg and Uelzen while a need is to develop the Coastal Canal for 1350–1500-ton boats to join the Ems to the Lower Weser. Through encouraging Hamburg's plans for an offshore terminal at the Elbe mouth, the *Land* hopes to bring new activity to the fishing port of Cuxhaven, where present long-term prospects are regarded as unpromising.

North Rhine-Westphalia, though fourth largest in area, is clearly the largest in population of the federal *Länder* with over 17 million inhabitants. With over one-third of the national industrial turnover and a similar proportion of the value of export goods, it has almost 29 percent of the gross national product and much higher shares in several sectors of industry, commonly equivalent to Bavaria and Baden-Württemberg added together. Another product of the territorial realignments at the end of the Second World War, North Rhine-Westphalia is fortunate in its location straddling the lower Rhine between north and south, and with easy access to the excellent port facilities of Rotterdam–Europoort and Antwerp. The core of the *Land* is the great agglomeration of towns and suburban landscapes of the Rhine-Ruhr, containing over 10 million people, still centred on the Ruhr coalfield, a focal point of

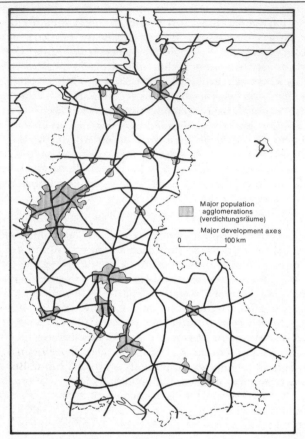

Figure 15.4 Federal development axes and growth areas

the transport system of Western Europe. The intersection of the two great population belts that run north to south and east to west emphasizes the nodality of this Rhine-Ruhr agglomeration, which is not only the largest single industrial area in the Federal Republic but also its major industrial problem area. The structural crisis in coal mining in the mid-1950s was reinforced by changes in the iron and steel industry generated by technological progress that marked increasing concentration on the most favoured sites during the 1960s. The changes in these industries and resultant slow economic growth resulted in a fall in population in several towns during the 1960s that had shown rapid growth in the previous decade, whereas in contrast, substantial increase in population marked adjacent districts with lighter and newer industries or with a more truly residential character. Though medium and small towns around the Ruhr fringe have generally grown, some new towns – like Wulfen – may not achieve their targets through the changes in heavy industry, reflecting the hazards of long-term planning projects. Attempts to bolster the stagnating economies of older industrial towns have introduced new activities like motor vehicle building, demanding extensive redeployment and retraining as well as new infrastructures. Educational facilities have been improved, notably by new universities in Bochum, Essen and Dortmund, Duisburg and Düsseldorf. Though major east-west routes are adequate, north-south links are weak and their expansion for the new flow patterns prominent in plans. Water supply is a constraint, particularly expansion of catchment areas: whereas in the republic industrial water consumption is four times domestic use, in the Ruhr this rises to 10:1. Pollution of both water and air has been tackled resolutely as part of improving amenities.

The Rhine-Ruhr agglomeration has suffered serious population pressure through immigration attracted by the almost insatiable labour market and the spread of urban development has produced a conflict in land use as housing and industry have spread onto good farmland. Examples are Hochdahl near Düsseldorf, the greatly expanded Leverkusen, and extensive dormitory development around Köln (like Bensberg) and north to Neuss. Spread of settlement along the northern edge of the Ruhr coalfield, for example in Marl, has been on poorer land. On the Ville lignite field, abandoned workings have been landscaped and the new town of Erftstadt developed, but the northern field of shifting workings and serious effluent pollution has required expensive resiting of settlements. Inadequately regulated growth around Bonn under the label of the 'provisionality' of the capital now challenges planners to unravel it.

The Rhine-Ruhr agglomeration has been affected by the wider contacts with the Benelux countries emerging through the European Community, with formerly neglected frontier areas around Kaldenkirchen and Aachen becoming zones of contact in contrast to prewar. The rising volume of transfrontier traffic has been reflected in the building of several motorway links, but the Rhine remains a barrier to east-west traffic despite additional bridges.

Relatively little of North Rhine-Westphalia has warranted inclusion in the various federal development plans, but in 1970 a regional action programme for southeast Westphalia was defined because of poor farming prospects and the need to expand industrial jobs through the several small industrial-commercial centres scattered in the area, while there were also good opportunities for recreation and tourism. Also included in an action programme was the north Eifel and Aachen area, where problems arise from the poor agricultural prospects in the south and structural industrial problems in the north, while later, the flagging textile and agricultural area of the north

Münsterland and the north Ruhr (with its structurally weakened coal mining area) were added. The north Münsterland was included in the special areas defined under the federal regional planning programme of 1974 as part of the Ems-Lower Rhine area of weakness in employment structure through growing difficulties in the textile industry.

Increasing international mobility as well as the often comparable problems on either side of an international frontier have evolved a number of transfrontier organizations. One of the first was the *Interessengemeinschaft Euregio*, an association of the German–Dutch textile region in the west Münsterland and Twente-Oost Gelderland, containing 1.5 million people and covering 7000 square kilometres, particularly significant as it lies between the major population agglomerations of the Rhine-Ruhr and the Randstad Holland. Another critical triangle of joint interest to Germany, Belgium, and Holland lies between the towns of Aachen-Maastricht-Liège, where structural problems associated with coal mining first gave common concern and there is also a joint Dutch–German commission watching developments along the frontier between Nijmegen and Maastricht. Cooperation with adjoining *Länder* has also become important, as for example with Hessen in the industrial problem areas of the Lahn-Dill and the Westphalian Siegerland, with their old iron working industries, or with the Rhineland-Palatinate in the Eifel and around Bonn.

The problems of the Rhineland-Palatinate, Hessen, and the Saarland have several features in common. The first state is a creation of the immediate postwar years that has needed to develop its own identity, while the Saarland was put in extended boundaries when joined in economic union with France, and Hessen is also a composite state of formerly separate members. The Rhine-Main confluence has emerged as a major growth region that laps on to the west bank of the Rhine between Mainz and Ludwigshafen. In contrast, the Saarland industries like coal mining and iron and steel suffer from structural and technological changes. Much of Hessen is, however, rural country with problems of farming, like the rural uplands of the Rhineland-Palatinate with poor farming country in close juxtaposition to the prosperity of the Rhine valley. The 'development axis' concept has proved particularly forceful in the Eifel and Westerwald where new motorways have attracted light, footloose industry into districts with good labour pools and have lured visitors to their recreational possibilities. In the Rhine and Mosel valleys, difficulties have arisen from the severe competition between industrial, agricultural, and tourist-recreational land uses.

These *Länder* which lie across the broad upland belt separating North Germany from South Germany that provides important natural routeways and transport infrastructure is consequently significant. The Hessian

Corridor on the axis Kassel–Frankfurt and the route along the Fulda into the Main basin comprise routeways with considerable potential for development, but in contrast the Rhine gorges, already crowded by railway and road links, leave no room for development, so that further movement axes are being developed on the higher ground above the river (the Köln–Frankfurt and Ludwigshafen-Bonn motorways) and the particularly busy railway route will be relieved by the proposed supertrunk railway from Köln to Frankfurt. The problem of the Saar is to maintain adequate transport links with the Rhine valley: the railway via Gerolstein to Köln has steep gradients, while the main links have been the Mosel line to Koblenz, the line to Bingen along the Saar-Nahe depression, and the route via Kaiserslautern to Ludwigshafen. French-inspired canalization of the Mosel, aimed mainly at easing contact from the Rhine to Lorraine, has not greatly helped the Saarland, which still presses for the direct Saar-Palatinate Canal. The Saarland, a focal point or 'turntable' in the communications between France and Germany, has been conceived in general planning as a west-east development axis across the international border between Metz-St.Avold-Saarbrücken, in which the Forbach *Centre Commercial Franco-Allemand* and a joint French–German *Saar-Lor-Chemie* combine are considered important elements. It is also proposed to provide a considerable area of new sites for industrial development to capitalize on the central position held in the Community by the *Saarlorlux* industrial triangle.

The Rhine-Main agglomeration, dominated by commercial Frankfurt and the spa town of Wiesbaden, has growth industries like motor vehicles, petroleum refining, petrochemicals, and precision engineering that have attracted strong migration, with population increase accommodated by the spread into small towns and rural areas, often at considerable distance from the place of work, though a number of satellite communities have been built. There has also been a spread across the Rhine around Mainz, but most markedly southwards along the Bergstrasse towards the lower Neckar, with commuting demanding improvement in communications, reflected in the emergence of a major motorway focus where the Rhine axis and the north-south circulation along the Hessian Corridor meet, whose focal function is enhanced by West Germany's main intercontinental airport, Rhine-Main. As this area spreads southwards it merges with the Ludwigshafen-Mannheim-Karlsruhe agglomeration and draws closer to the Stuttgart-mid Neckar agglomeration.

Baden-Württemberg and Bavaria form the long-standing South German states which even in the centralizing tendencies of the Second and Third *Reich* maintained much of their own ways. With a little under one-third of total pop-ulation, they make corresponding contributions to the national wealth (somewhat disproportionately concentrated in Baden-Württemberg). While marked differences exist in the economies of the two *Länder*, several regional problems arise from their relationships with adjacent countries. Bavaria has its eastern border with the German Democratic Republic and Czechoslovakia, and whereas before 1945 there was quite a lot of movement across the frontier, nowadays there is relatively little contact. The special border zone includes the industrial towns around Coburg and Hof whose position has become particularly isolated. The southern border with Austria has few legal and political constraints to transfrontier movement and, with Austrian trade closely linked to the Federal Republic, most problems of contact here are created by the mountainous physical environment. Baden-Württemberg has borders with two closely linked states: France, through the European Community, and Switzerland, through long traditions of commerce and movement. The Rhine frontier with France is intimately associated with German interests through navigation on the river. The Rhine and Bodensee also form a common interest with Switzerland, though here relations are complicated by territorial anomalies. The development of international trade and movement on these borders has led to the emergence of joint planning bodies, such as the Regio Basiliensis around Basel and CIMAB centred on Breisach-Neuf Brisach.

Both Bavaria and Baden-Württemberg have shown considerable growth of new industries since the Second World War. In Bavaria the marked development of electrical engineering in the late 1930s was expanded after 1950. The structural problems of the small prealpine coal-mining industry and the Franconian iron and steel industry have been offset by the successful growth of petroleum refining, petrochemicals, and other chemicals industries in the Upper Bavarian 'chemicals triangle'. Baden-Württemberg has flourished through the rapid expansion of consumer durables, including motor vehicles and electrical goods (especially in the Neckar basin), where the tradition of the 'farmer-peasant' provided a valuable source of skilled labour, though labour shortage has been the critical problem, leading to strong immigration, including a high proportion of 'guest workers'. The southwest corner of the *Land* has been much helped by improved road and rail accessibility, closely tied to the success of Swiss industry through industrial investment, while better Franco-German relations have helped Rhineside industry (including petroleum refining in Karlsruhe and expansion of chemicals in the Mannheim-Ludwigshafen conurbation). In a contrasting situation, eastern Bavaria has serious underemployment, with a considerable element of expellees contributing to the problem, though Bavaria has gained considerably elsewhere from new, highly skilled expellee industries (with high export quotients). There is usually no difficulty in attracting labour into South Germany, where the quality of living has a high popular image.

Bavaria does, however, enjoy relatively easy accessibility to all its territory, whereas the Schwarzwald and the Alb form formidable obstacles to intrastate communication in Baden-Württemberg, though these areas have a high tourist value. In Bavaria, the major focus is the Alpine belt, where tourism has become an increasingly important element in a local economy with few other attractions; but efforts have also been made to attract tourists to the pleasant landscapes of eastern Bavaria, little spoilt by outside intrusion.

Rural and urban problems
It is clear that the *Länder* share some problems, even if in different degree. These are particularly the increasing population pressure in areas of economic growth, and consequent continuing urbanization, and the growing gap in wealth, opportunity, and amenity between town and country. Within the West German economy, rural problem areas of stagnation have emerged, while economic change has begun to leave spots of urban distress. At the same time, a growing concern with environmental deterioration has emerged, in large part a product of the growing effluent and waste generated by an increasingly industrial and urban society.

One of the earliest postwar regional problems needing solution was the more even redistribution of the burden of expellees and refugees between the *Länder*. Programmes in the early 1950s foresaw the movement of over 1 million people and were virtually achieved by 1965. The basis was a theoretical 'carrying capacity' of each *Land*: those with a low excess were to take resettlers from those with heavy burdens, but much success in movement and rehousing was achieved through the remarkably rapid recovery of the economy that attracted people from overcrowded rural areas to centres with a rapidly growing labour demand and housing. Though the equalization of the burden of expellees and refugees was aided, the disparity in wealth and opportunity remained to make necessary help for depressed rural areas and towns. In 1953, a series of temporary redevelopment districts needing help was defined as areas of general economic weakness, areas with serious agricultural weakness, or rural areas affected by war damage. Included was the broad strip along the zonal border, while during the reintegration of the Saar in the late 1950s a peripheral area (*Saargrenzgürtel*) was also eligible. These were all areas where the free market forces were already having negative results, and some rectifying intervention from central government was necessary. By the late 1950s, events quickly showed that more distinct and positive developmental programmes were required. In the 1960s areas for economic and social promotion (*Fördergebiete*) were designated, using data on the gross product per head and also information on migration and demographic traits. Four kinds of problem area were identified: low income areas with satisfactory farming but little industry; areas with small and usually highly fragmented farms; special problem areas like the zonal border area; and new industrial problem areas. Even in many apparently successful industrial communities, living standards were not, however, keeping pace with the national trends – as for example, in

Wilhemshaven, Salzgitter, and several towns in Schleswig-Holstein – but some rural areas that had received aid in the 1950s were now excluded because of the substantial infrastructural improvements achieved.

The late 1950s had also seen a shift from blanket aid to selected foci through a central place programme of growth poles, in which ultimately 80 small communities of between 3,000–20,000 people were designated for the growth of industrial and tertiary employment. The growing federal involvement was emphasized and the developmental aspect of the programmes stressed, while federal development areas were defined for a minimum area of 500 square kilometres and a population of 100,000 people, achieved by grouping together *Kreise*, whereas smaller areas below this threshold were felt to be the responsibility of the *Land* in which they lay. The federal development areas spread over about 34 percent of the republic's area, but contained only about 13 percent of the population (a proportion less than in the United Kingdom, Italy, or France) and accounted for 5 percent of industrial employment and 7.6 percent of the gross domestic product.

To give closer coordination of development programmes and to deal better with special local problems, the federal development and promotion areas were grouped in 1969–1970 into larger regional action programmes, for which a joint planning effort over five years was to be made, with development focused on commercial and industrial centres with a hinterland of at least 20,000 people as crystallization points for the economic growth of a somewhat larger sphere of influence. Some action programme areas set a precedent by extending across more than one *Land*. Up to 20 percent (25 percent in the *Zonenrandgebiet*) of investment costs for new workplaces were covered and up to 10 percent of the cost of securing workplaces, with additional subventions for development of industrial sites and communal infrastructure. The extent of the programme brought up the total population living in development areas nearer to proportions for other West European states (i.e., over 30 percent), reflecting growing disparities in wealth.

The Basic Law empowered the federation to draw up regional policy guideline plans to apply nationwide, but the responsibility for planning legislation and execution had fallen squarely to the *Länder*. Some, like North Rhine-Westphalia, reactivated an honourable prewar tradition in planning; other states left planning almost untouched. A decision by the federal constitutional court in 1954 that 'planning cannot stop at the *Länder* boundaries' signalled more effective federal legislation and action and, after much difficult negotiation, though taking place in an atmosphere of changing public opinion, a federal planning law enacted in 1965 laid down the responsibilities and competence of the federal authorities, the *Länder*, and the lower echelons of local government. It stressed the need to develop a spatial structure allowing the greatest development of the community by creating the same level of amenity and environment throughout the republic and by building communities with an acceptable relationship between home and work that avoided creation of unhealthy social conditions. It emphasized the distinct nature of rural areas and the need to preserve them, but stressed that their living conditions should be in no way inferior to towns. Adequate social facilities should be developed in rural service centres, with sufficient nonagricultural employment to ensure a sound population structure and rewarding agricultural employment.

To create future confidence and to rectify the disorganization caused by the closed eastern frontier with the G.D.R. and Czechoslovakia, the zonal border district has been given particularly generous help, while it has also shown a remarkable continuity in planning thought since the early 1950s, even if the political motivation has changed. The 40-kilometre-wide strip from Flensburg to Passau covers one-fifth of the republic's territory and contains over 10 percent of its population, though innumerable problems in Schleswig-Holstein and the German-Czech borderland date from long before the Second World War. Other special programmes instituted to cover set objectives include, on the west, the *Emsland Programm* (1951, covering 5300 square kilometres in the Ems basin, to counter the Netherlands' territorial claim to border moorland) that put a major plan of land reclamation and amelioration into operation, with the work done by a corporation (*Emsland GmbH*). Discovery of oil and natural gas in the programme area has, however, altered its original nature. The *Programm Nord* in Schleswig-Holstein was designed to eliminate the contrast in living standards between German and Danish territory, largely to counter Danish-inspired agitation for a reopening of the *Sudslesvig* frontier question, whereas in contrast the *Küstenplan* and *Alpenplan* were designed for purely technical aims – coastal protection and reclamation in the first and flood protection in the second.

In 1975 a major policy document was approved in the Federal Regional Planning Programme (*Bundesraumordnungsprogramm*), to augment but not replace *Länder* plans, coordinating them for equalization of development in the provision of housing, jobs, and services throughout the country, while environmental problems in some areas have reached such proportions that they can no longer be surmounted by the responsible *Land* unaided. The programme defines 38 planning regions, claimed to be functionally balanced units, though they in no way prejudice territorial-administrative reforms or boundary changes in the *Länder*. Each unit contains at least one high-order central place or an area of marked concentration of living and working places (this core must have at least 100,000 people or the likelihood of such a population in the near future) as well as several medium-ranked central places; the minimum population in each unit must be 400,000 people. Every attempt has been made to avoid cutting across the spheres of influence of high-rank centres, so some units contain several overlapping centres. Areas lying far away from high-ranking central places may be defined as units, if they have at least 400,000 inhabitants or an area of at least 5000 square kilometres, one clearly defined centre or a marked population agglomeration. The borders are defined along existing *Kreis* boundaries, though *Länder* boundaries may be crossed by mutual agreement. As far as possible, the planning units within the *Länder* are respected, though the actual level of coincidence appears low. These planning units are expected to change areally over time through changes in settlement patterns, the spatial structure of the economy (including growing European integration), or the territorial-administrative pattern within the *Länder*; consequently they are to be constantly monitored.

The continued growth of urban population with the spread of built-up area creates extensive infrastructural problems, so that marked concentrations of urban and suburban development have been officially designated as *Verdichtungsräume*, and the mainstream of planning effort remains the reduction of the contrasts between these urbanized areas and the truly rural districts that came out forcibly in investigations in the 1960s. The problem is more critical when it is remembered that the officially defined *Verdichtungsräume* contain 45 percent of West German population on a mere 7 percent of the national area. There has been a gathering of wealth, economic potential, and population in clusters notably along the Rhine in the Lower Rhine, Rhine-Ruhr, Rhine-Main, and Neckar basin, but also on the Lower Elbe and in southern industrial Lower Saxony, as well as in Upper Bavaria around München. These *Verdichtungsräume* present special problems because of the strong immigration, with particular socio-economic difficulties generated by a large element of foreign workers, and effort has to be made to reduce the population pressure on their resources.

Within the urbanized landscapes of the *Verdichtungsräume*, planning effort is thus directed primarily to infrastructure problems – notably in the inner areas and along the development axes between the towns. Much has to be done to improve land ownership and land-use relationships irrationally developed during the postwar 'anti-planning' phase. There remains a continuing problem of providing a proper balance between housing, shopping, and schools, as well as facilities for effective public and other transport between workplaces and residential areas. A continuing dilemma is how far to develop private transport against provision of public transport structures. Increasing attention is given to amenity and recreation space as well as to green belts to prevent coalescence between towns. Every effort is being made to contain growth in the overtaxed agglomerations, though special problems have emerged in urban areas that have begun to stagnate economically. Whereas in the late 1950s planning started in the period of growth of big towns as postwar rebuilding drew back population, the shift has been to growth in smaller urban communities and to spread in rural areas around the large towns; and a broader spectrum of planning has been necessary to control effectively the location and form of new building in the main population agglomerations.

Rural areas become increasingly important as development has to be diffused from the overtaxed *Verdichtungsräume*, but rural development potential remains based on growth poles lying at the intersections of growth axes, of which a network covers the country, partly defined in the *Länder* plans and partly by a series of 'super-axes' in the 1975 *Bundesraumordnungsprogramm*. As West German population is expected to show little or no increase until well into the 1980s, it is particularly important to arrest movement from rural districts threatened by vigorous emigration. Of particular significance for the rural areas is the expectancy that employment in footloose industries will rise from 5.7 to 6.1 million as opposed to a decline from 2.0 to 1.1 million in locationally tied industries and a growth in the tertiary sector from 15.8 to 18.8 million jobs in the period 1970–1985. Though agricultural employment is expected to fall from 2.0 to 1.0 million in the period 1970–1985, every effort is now made to hold farming on the best soils, with the necessary changes to make it more effective employment, and a key to many rural problems is to surmount the difficulties caused by social fallow.

The problems of towns

The Federal Republic inherited towns still largely in ruins and, though rebuilding was pushed ahead quickly, the sheer volume of damage was immense (Figure 15.5). The emphasis was on housing, so bombed-out townspeople could move back from the countryside or undamaged small towns, where the new element of the expellees had intensified pressure on an already strained infrastructure. The upsurge in economic life gave a further impetus to reconstruction, with speed rather than planning for future needs as the major consideration. By the early 1960s, most 'rebuilding' had been completed and further building took the form of replacing outworn or provisional structures because an increasing proportion of the people ceased to be satisfied merely with a roof over their head and began to choose a residence governed by expectations of rising income. At the same time, the population, inflated by natural growth and the great immigration, required provision of an improved and expanded infrastructure of schools and other social amenities, though with more pressing tasks of economic reconstruction and stability, government was reluctant to spend money on public sector building that lagged behind adequacy. By the mid-1960s, the 'core towns' of the main agglomerations, which had demonstrated the most remarkable growth in the 1950s, began to grow more slowly, to stagnate, or even to lose population, although the latter was often more a sign of their affluence than economic failings, as people could afford to live out of town. Consequently much growth shifted into small and

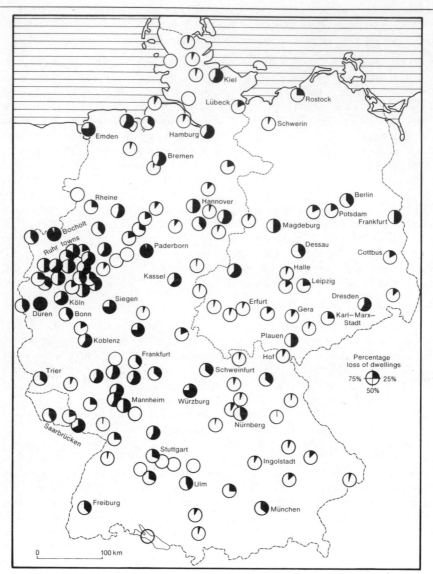

Figure 15.5 Wartime damage to towns in Germany

medium-sized towns within the major population agglomerations, where population in rural *Gemeinden* also rose and the process of 'suburbanization' reduced the distinction between town and country, while as urban and suburban land values spiralled, people began moving further out from the main towns.

The weakness of the planners' position prevented effective zonation and control, while the responsibility of the *Gemeinden* for planning permission was used by them to increase their wealth by allowing indiscriminate building. The federal fiscal system also helped the commuter, who could set the journey to work against tax, an immediate postwar measure that became rapidly more unrealistic in an affluent motorizing society. New towns were difficult to create and often a 'relief town' (*Entlastungsstadt*) emerged merely as an immense dormitory suburb, like Neu-Perlach near München, designed for 80,000 people in 25,000 dwellings on 1000 hectares of ground. Cities were left to deal with their own embarrassing local growth; examples are Nürnberg-Langwasser, Frankfurt–Nordweststadt, München-Hasenbergl and München-Freimann, Dortmund-Scharnhorst and, of the smaller ones, Bochum-Hustadt, while a most recent development is Köln-Chorweiler ('Neue Stadt'), designed for 87,000 people. True 'new towns' have been relatively few and several towns have been created simply by giving *Gemeinden* with growing populations the status of town. Most notable are the 'refugee towns' in former munitions works and army camps, where expellees from East Central Europe have brought their skills together in industries such as glass making, artificial jewellery, etc.; examples are Geretsried (17,500) and Waldkraiburg (18,500) in Bavaria, and Sennestadt (20,000) near Bielefeld. A true 'new town' sited between two motorways and with railway access is Hochdahl (17,900) near Düsseldorf, which is not simply a dormitory for its larger neighbour; in the northern Ruhr coalfield, the new town of Marl (77,000) is a combination of several small communities originally associated with local coalmines and the Hüls chemical works, whereas Wulfen, originally designed around two new coalmines, with an expected growth to 40,000 inhabitants, but poorly served by road and railway, has been slow to develop. More a residential overflow to Köln, Erftstadt (41,000) comprises a group of former brown coal mining communities (e.g., Liblar) around the country town of Lechenich, but it is scattered and incoherent, though with good recreational amenity.

The 'suburbanization' process has been accompanied by territorial-administrative change grouping together two or more *Gemeinden*, so consequently the former concept in German statistics of *Gemeinden* with more than 2000 inhabitants being regarded as urban (*städtisch*) is no longer suitable: the lower threshold of urban character now seems to be around 5000 people, though there are naturally exceptions in the more rural regions of the republic. Set against the pattern of national population increase, communities under

3000 inhabitants have shown a substantial decline and only a marginal increase between 3000–5000 whereas above the 5000 threshold all community sizes have shown substantial growth, especially towns in the 10,000–20,000 group, though the largest towns (i.e., over 100,000 inhabitants) have only increased marginally and in this latter group several towns have actually shown a decline or have virtually stagnated.

The morphology of the West German towns reflects the adjustments from interwar to postwar conditions. Efforts from 1946 until the mid1950s sought to create some semblence of normality quickly and emphasized rehousing people: extensive replanning was impossible with the financial means available, while public opinion favoured private enterprise. Piecemeal rebuilding on privately owned ground left ruins standing until ready for redevelopment; in contrast in the G.D.R., nationalization of all land brought the speedy clearing of ruins from large tracts then left open for many years. Public opinion in general also favoured a retention of well-known street patterns and features rather than radical new layouts. Some of the biggest changes in West German towns came in the 1960s when money became available for major schemes and there was speculation in real estate, but when planning had begun to play a bigger role. Restoring the old image was an important element in much rebuilding, but a special dilemma was the badly damaged historical town where to restore the destroyed fabric was often virtually impossible, either because of a lack of adequate records or because there was a large element of materials hard to copy. A number of towns sought through appropriate stylistic interpretations to recreate their former image – a successful venture is the *Prinzipalmarkt* in Münster in Westfalen. Often damage was too great other than to allow rebuilding of a few selected buildings of particular note (e.g., Frankfurt am Main). Fortunately, a great many small towns preserving a truly valuable mediaeval or baroque character were almost unscathed: here much has been done to maintain their character, including removal of the worst excesses of nineteenth-century romanticism. The main postwar changes have come in the town centres, though in few towns could it be called radical. In some instances, to have modified the street pattern, whatever its shortcomings, would have completely altered the town's character and it was consequently retained (e.g., in Mannheim). Large damaged public and commercial buildings were often left until their owners or others were able to rebuild them, but gutted houses and tenements could be readily cleared and consequently complexes of ruins in many instances became fixed points around which any new pattern was cast.

In central Köln, for example, the street pattern is easily recognizable from prewar maps, but some relocation of the central business district has taken place (even without planning intervention), and this phenomenon can be seen in several other towns. The cause has commonly been the inability of old business streets to redevelop, while fewer shops exist nowadays compared to prewar, partly the result of competition from large departmental stores (not necessarily members of national chains) and supermarkets since the early 1960s. Since the establishment of the first hypermarket in the Rhine-Main area in 1964, everywhere these new shopping complexes have resulted in change in local retail patterns because of their excellent car parking facilities and their common location in suburbanized sites between major towns.

An element of continuity with prewar town centres has been provided by public buildings, whose sites or even fabric often have historical associations, with some faithfully restored after damage (e.g., *Rathaus*, Münster in Westfalen), though many of little architectural note have been rebuilt in a modern idiom on the old site. Since the early 1960s large 'school centres' have been developed, containing several levels of education (e.g., Wilhelm-Röntgen-Realschule and Leibniz-Gymnasium in Dortmund) and sited near to residential catchment areas. New universities have required considerable infrastructural development: the new Ruhr University at Bochum has its own motorway and tram access, a shopping centre (with local government offices), and a big residential development (Hustadt). Special sites have been developed, for example, on the slopes above Würzburg or in the *Staatsforst* outside Saarbrücken. Much effort has been spent on rebuilding and re-creating museums, while the municipal theatre has been used to demonstrate a town's affluence and encouragement of the arts. Notable new buildings have been in Köln and Münster, while the new generously planned centre of Gelsenkirchen includes an imposing theatre, and Bremen has its remarkable *Stadthalle*. The wave of building elaborate and ornate cinemas that hit Britain in the late 1930s was absent in Germany and, consequently, though many destroyed in the war were not rebuilt, there was not the slaughter of cinemas that gripped Britain in the latter 1950s.

One of the important tasks following replacement of bombed housing has been replacement of dwellings of substandard type. Municipal housing has never played a big part in German towns in contrast to housing provided for workers by industrial companies – especially in the heavy industrial areas – or provided through various associations, often on a semioccupational basis. There has always been a large component of housing privately developed for rent, considered until recent years as one of the soundest investments on whatever scale it was undertaken, and home ownership financed through a building society has been encouraged. The first Federal Building Law (April 1950) charged local authorities at all levels to create 2 million dwellings by 1956 and there was a rapid rise to the building of over 500,000 dwellings annually, with considerable help and little constraint given to anybody willing and able to provide housing. Towards the town centres, much early postwar residential rebuilding was multi-purpose: shops or restaurants on the ground floor, with offices and residential accommodation above, while in the rear courts there were often small industries, because many entrepreneurs found such building a sound ancillary investment, though such residential accommodation has been encroached upon as the tertiary sector has expanded. Legislation anyhow favoured building of multiple accommodation rather than single family houses, while the substantial rewards from rents often changed building use, with former cinemas or industrial premises rebuilt as flats. Nevertheless many older residential areas passed to other uses in the enlarged city centres of the late 1950s, consequently substantially reducing population in many inner areas. After the main housing shortage had been overcome in the mid-1950s, building continued, but in the early 1960s building became more experimental and long street frontages gave way to blocks set at right angles or haphazardly arranged to give variety and lower residential densities. By the early 1960s, some 20,000–30,000 housing units (some even of immediate postwar construction) were being demolished or converted annually; by the end of the decade this had risen to over 100,000 units a year; and it is estimated that as many as 250,000 units could be replaced annually by the mid-1980s. This would amount to a virtual reconstruction of all cities inside forty years. By the early 1970s, 60 percent of all West German housing had been built since 1945.

In the replacement and expansion of the housing stock, a part has been played by large dormitory suburbs, built on the edge of large cities, with their provision of schools, shops and other amenities, and transport to places of work. These schemes tend to comprise mostly multi-storey blocks of flats, though the secret of their visual impression is how these buildings are arranged. They have sometimes had specific aims, like Dortmund-Scharnhorst (28,000) built to accommodate repatriates from Poland and Czechoslovakia. One of the largest schemes demonstrating some ambitious planning is Frankfurt–Nordweststadt, with some 8,000 households and 23,000 inhabitants destined to rise to over 50,000 people, forming an interesting contrast to the prewar Römerstadt nearby (built in 1927–1929). At Neue Vahr, Bremen, accommodation is available for 40,000 people, with a complete shopping centre and other amenities, as well as schools, dominated by a 22-storey block of dwellings; but Nürnberg-Langwasser, though better supplied with public transport, is too closely built of massive blocks of flats. These schemes are mostly built by non-profit-making associations like *Neue Heimat*, but as the public becomes more critical of mass-produced housing (best and most cheaply available through the associations), continued and satisfactory provision becomes more expensive, while weak planning controls have unfortunately in places been unable to prevent developments (often private speculations) of costly but crowded 'luxury' accommodation without adequate amenities (e.g., Frankfurt–Gravenbruch).

Since 1970 planning laws have been strengthened to allow better control of land speculation and permit land banks and more effective long-term plans to be formulated. The effect of weak planning control on urban development is well seen in Bonn, where for almost twenty years the republic sought to retain the atmosphere of 'provisionality' in this capital. Piecemeal but necessary developments have produced a remarkably incoherent mass of buildings, the antithesis of an affluent and well-organized state, arising from retention of restricted town boundaries surrounded by small communities, each with its own planning jurisdiction and a search for wealth. The outcome has been chaotic development of expensive properties along inadequate roads developed on the alignment of field tracks, problems hard to rectify even within the enlarged city boundaries since 1969. It is a comment on land speculation that everywhere the largest and most opulent house amid masses of boxlike flats or small flat-roofed villas usually belongs to the peasant who sold the land.

The great priority in the 1950s accorded the rehabilitation of industry did not permit extensive resiting, and numerous infrastructural aspects anyway held it to established sites, including water and electricity supply, transport and location in relation to cognate plants. Much new industry attracted to towns has been in the lighter sectors where transport is important, so it is not surprising that motorways and railways have held a key to its siting, especially as government financing of sidings has held plants closer to railways than in Britian. In attracting new industries there has been great competition among towns, which have often given industrial sites priority over other uses, with plants commonly located to the preference of the individual entrepreneur rather than in coherent industrial estates. In the decline of coal mining in the Ruhr, communities left without an adequate employment base have sought to diversify their industries, while extensive mine sites have been available for other uses. In Bochum, large *Opel* vehicle assembly plants established on open sites in the east and south have attracted new motorways and residential development; Wolfsburg in Lower Saxony has sought to diversify its employment structure because of overdependence on *Volkswagen*; whereas Kassel has seen the growth of the large southern industrial suburb of Baunatal around the *Volkswagen* plant; around München several new industrial areas have emerged; and large new industrial complexes have been established on the south bank of the Elbe at Hamburg.

Transport has been a vital postwar element in the West German town, as well as in the process of 'suburbanization', with immense expenditure on the road system and in the last decade on modernizing and expanding public transport. In several towns (e.g., Ludwigshafen, Braunschweig, and Heidelberg) completely new railway layouts have eliminated awkward terminal stations and removed obstacles to internal circulation. Whereas in Britain many towns have been generally hostile to the motor car, German towns have commonly accepted it, perhaps because the motor car revolution in postwar Britain was a gentle surge, whereas in West Germany it was a sudden explosion in the 1960s. At the same time, the taxation system, the price of motor vehicles in relation to other goods and their significance as status symbols, all contributed to their social acceptability. The need to improve the national road system to fit the new spatial pattern brought heavy investment in additional motorways, logically linked to motorway-type roads from the central areas of the towns (*Ausfallstrassen*). In the Rhenish towns, new Rhine bridges have been built in Köln, Düsseldorf, Koblenz, and Duisburg, and motorway rings have been built round large towns, notably Köln and Hamburg, and a major improvement in urban and interurban roads in the Ruhr undertaken. In contrast to Britain, the urban tramway routes have been extended in several towns, provided with reserved tracks and even underground routes in the town centres (e.g., in Köln). Tramways are being incorporated into new interurban *Stadtbahn* networks (for example, the network presently being built between the Ruhr towns) and other urban rapid transit systems have been built in Nürnberg, München, and Frankfurt, and expanded in Hamburg, with railways instrumental in 'suburbanization' by providing local fast services.

A marked feature of new city centre layouts has been pedestrianization: in some cases, this has been part of a major replanning of the shopping area (as in the most successful example, the *Treppenstrasse* of Kassel) or associated with redesigning of central traffic systems (the *Jan Willem Platz* in Düsseldorf), but in many instances it has been simply aimed at safety and convenience of shoppers, like the elaborate plan developed in central München associated with the building of the underground railway.

Failings and shortcomings in towns are concealed by the affluence of the growing ownership of cars, colour TV, or second homes. There is clearly concern over the results of the free market economy and a low-key planning approach demands more effective control to preserve the quality of the environment and particularly containment of the relentless 'suburbanization'. Private speculative housing ventures that have in many instances inherent failings have brought severe criticism. It is claimed more should have been done to develop effectively identifiable new towns with a real sense of community. Instead of spreading government aid over 300-odd towns, concentration on effective development of 50–60 key locations might have been better. It is also suggested that planning concentration on ranked central places and growth axes is too inflexible to allow for change in regional emphasis in the future.

Environmental deterioration and its problems
Like all advanced industrial countries, increasing concern has been expressed in West Germany over environmental deterioration. Recent federal legislation has sought to aid the *Länder* faced by problems too massive to handle alone, though the problems themselves have features common everywhere: air and

water pollution, eutrophic effects and the rising harassment of noise. One of the most serious difficulties is the maintenance of water supplies in the face of ever rising demand – domestic use per inhabitant daily has escalated from 85 l. in 1951 to 124 l. in 1974 and by AD 2000 will have exceeded 200 l., while industrial use has shown commensurate increases. At the same time, water pollution is becoming more serious. The rivers of the Rhine basin, with the heavy concentration of industry, are especially vulnerable, posing a serious threat to the water supply of over 20 million people, and factories continue to discharge contaminated noxious effluent into them. Particularly serious are various saline waters and those bearing heavy metals, but even relatively pure water if too warm can have deleterious effects, and large quantities of inadequately treated sewage are also fed in. The once valuable fisheries in the Rhine have suffered particularly seriously, with incidents that have poisoned thousands of fish at a time. In South Germany, the most serious effects have been in the Bodensee, where eutrophic 'blooming' has already been serious and the rising pollution poses a threat to this major source of water for industry in Baden-Württemberg. Few if any of the smaller lakes are free from deterioration (notably from eutrophic causes) and on some (e.g., those in Upper Bavaria) even recreational use is being restricted because of its deleterious effect.

Industrial plants and motor traffic are the main sources of air pollution which is worst in long periods of still air, when smog formation becomes a health and traffic hazard, unfortunately common on the Lower Rhine. A most serious case of air pollution has been the noxious fumes emitted from the Knapsack chemicals plant on the Köln brown coalfield at Hürth, where population has fallen from 4000 to 2500 by people moving away and where the remaining population is to receive government help to resettle in better air conditions. Experiments with exceptionally high chimneys are aimed to lift pollution above the usually habited levels, while it is hoped stricter regulations on exhaust disposal and types of permissible fuels will help traffic pollution. Even when air movement disperses polluting fumes from industrial districts, the effects may simply be transferred in diluted form elsewhere: in dry, high pressure conditions, dust from the Ruhr is carried into southern Lower Saxony and pollution from the Ruhr is claimed to contribute to rising acidity in Swedish lakes.

Among the consumer-oriented economies that generate rising amounts of waste, it is estimated that in the Federal Republic the volume of refuse will double every decade. Consequently, particular attention is being devoted to the location and planning of refuse tips and to more effective ways of waste disposal. Incineration is being increasingly employed, often producing electric current or building blocks as by-products, and reduction of appropriate waste to agricultural compost has also been developed. Disposal of harmful industrial waste also becomes more critical – for example, health damage has been recorded in children playing on waste lead tips in the Aachen area, while use of deep abandoned mine workings near Wolfenbüttel for burial of radioactive waste has not been without local resistance. Waste disposal in German offshore waters is also carefully monitored after several serious outbreaks of poisoning from eating contaminated fish, shrimps, etc.

The noise problem arises from industrial plants, motor traffic (in a few instances from rail or river traffic), and aircraft and airports, but a new source has been generated by leisure activities (e.g., motor boats, motor racing, etc.). Aircraft noise is particularly serious near built-up areas such as Frankfurt Rhine-Main, Düsseldorf-Lohausen, or Hamburg–Fuhlsbüttel, and the response has followed lines used in Britain and the United States. Experiments have shown that railway noise may be appreciably reduced by appropriate design of tracks and civil engineering features, principles which are being used on the new trunk routes planned for the 1980s. Environmental protection is a field in which a growing element of international cooperation has been developing.

The Federal Republic, having accepted the necessity of broad overall as well as detailed planning strategies, only at a late stage, now faces the unravelling of the many problems that largely unrestricted industrial and urban development generated until the late 1960s. These are now complicated by the growing public demand for attention to wider environmental issues that brimmed over in the early 1970s in public hostility to the building of nuclear power stations. The coordination of federal policy is made all the harder by the powerful influence of the regional interests of the *Länder*.

Suggested further reading

Boesler, K. A.: Beiträge zu einer Karte des Infrastruckturbedarfs in der BRD, *Abh. Akad. für Raumforschung und Landesplanung* 53, Hannover, 1969.

Boustedt, O., et al.: Die Stadtregionen in der Bundesrepublik Deutschland, *Forsch. u. Sitzungsberichte der Akad. für Raumforschung und Landesplanung* 14, Hannover, 1960.

Bundesminister für Raumordnung, Bauwesen und Städtebau: Raumordnungsprogramm für die grossräumige Entwicklung des Bundesgebietes, Bonn, 1975.

Clout, H. D. (ed.): Regional Development in Western Europe (Chapter 8 West Germany by Blacksell, M.), London, 1975.

Fuchs, G.: Die Bundesrepublik Deutschland, Stuttgart, 1977.

CHAPTER 16

THE GERMAN DEMOCRATIC REPUBLIC
THE STATE AND ITS POPULATION

With hardly one-third of the population of the German Federal Republic and a lower national income per head, the German Democratic Republic nevertheless remains one of the more important European states and ranks as one of the world's main industrial countries. It emerged from the pattern of military occupation zones after the Second World War to become a typical socialist *bloc* people's democracy with a rigorously centralized economy. The building of a Marxist-Leninist society and economy demanded far-reaching adjustments to the prewar pattern, radical changes made even more difficult in the early stages because of a slavish imitation of Soviet practice, seldom suited to Central European conditions. Its emergence may be dated from the foundation of the German Economic Commission (*Deutsche Wirtschaftskommission*) in the Soviet Zone in 1947, a counter-stroke to the Anglo-American Bizonal economic council, and the first real central administrative organism in the Soviet Zone. Two People's Congresses in 1947 and 1948 led to the election of a People's Council (*Volksrat*): the following year a constitution was formulated and the republic was formally declared. (Its nature is discussed in Chapter 7.)

The problems of the G.D.R. have, if anything, been greater than those of the German Federal Republic. Whereas the Federal Republic had to adjust only to a new eastern frontier, the G.D.R. has had new frontiers on both east and west, each equally disruptive of the existing cultural and economic landscape. Through isolation from Hamburg and Stettin (Szczecin), the G.D.R. has been cut from its prewar ports, while it is also isolated from West German and

Silesian industrial areas with which it had close prewar relations. The split of the Allied powers in Berlin left the difficulties of a completely isolated West Berlin to have its repercussions throughout the G.D.R.

Population in the G.D.R.

A serious constraint to the building of a new social and economic structure in the German Democratic Republic has been essentially demographic. Population had been swollen after 1945 by the influx of Germans from East Central Europe, but equally an outward flow of both the new immigrants and local residents to West Germany had begun and this westward flow out of the country continued long after the inflow from the east had fallen to a mere trickle. Population numbers reached their peak in 1948, and thereafter a steady decline took place through the interaction between migration and general demographic trends. Stopping further flight to West Germany in 1961 had by 1964 ended decline and initiated a period of virtual stagnation, though by the late 1960s a slight decline had again set in. By the 1970s both German states were among the world's countries with the lowest rates of natural increase, and in the G.D.R. there was no massive foreign labour influx to boost population as in West Germany.

Compared to the Federal Republic, the G.D.R. is essentially a smaller country: its population is only 28 percent of that of the Federal Republic and it is also less densely settled (Federal Republic, 244 persons/km² – G.D.R., 158 persons/km²), though it has a similar high level of urbanization. The distribution of population by size of communities is also similar in both states, though the medium-sized towns are more important and the large towns (i.e., over 100,000 people) less important than in the Federal Republic. The smallest communities also appear more significant in the G.D.R., but some of the contrast has to be related to the effects of territorial- administrative reform carried out in the Federal Republic. The population differences between the two states are to be explained not only in geographical contrasts of prewar origin, but also through the paths taken in the last thirty years in social and economic development.

The major characteristics of areal distribution of population in the G.D.R. remain little changed since prewar times, even though significant changes in detail have taken place. The northernmost parts – the former Mecklenburg, Brandenburg, and northern Saxony-Anhalt – are relatively sparsely settled, with densities seldom exceeding 50 persons/km², though a belt with as many as 100 persons/km² occurs along the Baltic coast, where economic development has attracted population. More densely settled country is also found around and east of Berlin, where many satellite towns are closely related to commuting into the city. The southern part of the republic forms part of the

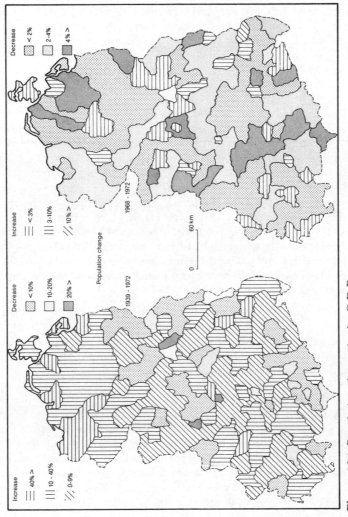

Figure 16.1 Population change in the G.D.R.

The German Democratic Republic: The State and its Population

main east-west belt of dense population across Central Europe. On the fertile loessic lowlands, a considerable element in population density can be ascribed to farming populations gathered in nucleated villages, though industry is also a factor in population agglomeration where lignite is mined. In the uplands and less fertile lowlands, industry has generated high local population density. Nevertheless, densities are modest compared to similar parts of West Germany. Over the predominantly loessic farming areas densities seldom exceed 100 persons/km^2 and similar densities are typical of the industrial uplands, though in the industrial areas of the Elbe-Saale basin (especially on the lignite fields) densities reach 150 persons/km^2 and even 250 persons/km^2 around Leipzig. Around Zwickau and Karl-Marx-Stadt in numerous small industrial towns as many as 300 persons/km^2 occur, though 150–250 persons/km^2 are typical of the country around Dresden. The small industrial settlements in the valleys of the Thüringer Wald and the Erzgebirge, reaching to remarkable elevations, contribute markedly to densities of around 150 persons/km^2, typical of the country near Gotha, Ilmenau, and Schmalkalden. Appreciably higher densities occur locally in the Erzgebirge around Aue, Schwarzenberg, and Annaberg-Buchholz. Densities of up to 100 persons/km^2 in the poorer farming country of Lower Lusatia are attributable to lignite mining and related industry in the *Bezirk* Cottbus. The bulk of urban population occurs in the south, where eight towns with over 100,000 (two – Dresden and Leipzig – with over 500,000) lie in contrast to only one 100,000-town – Rostock – in the north, while Berlin and Potsdam lie between the patterns of north and south.

The new republic inherited the great influx of expellees, spread unevenly throughout the territory, but particularly in the countryside least able to integrate the newcomers: in some *Gemeinden* in Mecklenburg between 1939 and 1946 population had increased by 50–80 percent compared to an average for the Soviet Occupation Zone of just over 14 percent. Large numbers of people had left the bombed towns, but their return was to be much slower than in the West. The 1950s were marked by steady decline in total population, numerically greatest in the industrial areas, though proportionally higher in rural areas. It was least significant from Brandenburg, notably from the satellite towns around Berlin, and the only *Bezirk* to gain population in the early 1950s was Frankfurt/Oder, where the building of Eisenhüttenstadt and other industrial developments attracted labour, while only a marginal loss occurred in *Bezirk* Cottbus, where expansion of lignite mining attracted workers. The development of Rostock as the main port also helped to stabilize population in the Baltic littoral. Decline was most drastic either in poorer rural areas with many expellees (e.g., *Bezirk* Schwerin) or in industrial areas particularly badly hit by dismantling (e.g., *Bezirk* Chemnitz/Karl-Marx-Stadt). The slow return to the towns arose from the low priority accorded rebuilding: population proportion in towns over 20,000 remained virtually constant throughout the 1950s, while some towns – notably Karl-Marx-Stadt, Erfurt, and Dresden – had fewer people at the end of the 1950s than at the beginning, and the only town to show appreciable growth was the port of Rostock. Two towns with over 100,000 people prewar – Dessau and Plauen – remained well below this level throughout the 1950s, while their position on the new frontier with Poland much reduced the populations of Frankfurt/Oder and Görlitz. About half the towns between 50,000–100,000 people had, however, managed to show a marginal growth in population during the 1950s.

By the mid-1960s, a small upswing in population reflected the stopping of migration to West Germany, as the low rate of natural increase was no longer swamped by emigration. In general, town population has gained by migration at the expense of the countryside and the medium-sized towns in particular have grown. Towns in predominantly rural areas have shown modest increase, partly through economic diversification of rural employment. *Gemeinden* with less than 10,000 people have generally lost population by migration, while the strongest immigration has been into towns between 20,000–100,000, though this needs some qualification. Over the greater part of the rural north, but also in the Lusatian countryside, the *Börde* country and the eastern Grabfeld, the population has remained virtually stagnant as low natural increase and modest out-migration have balanced, though throughout the 1960s internal mobility in the G.D.R. was well below the level in the Federal Republic. Modest decline took place in some older industrial districts, notably in the lignite-mining areas of Saxony (especially around Halle and Leipzig) and in industrial towns with problems of economic adjustment through large elements of low-priority consumer-oriented industry in *Bezirk* Karl-Marx-Stadt. Growth districts through migration formed only a small proportion of the total area, chiefly in the east along the Oder-Neisse rivers and in the newer lignite-mining areas of Lusatia (here lie the new socialist towns – Eisenhüttenstadt, Neu-Hoyerswerda, and the refinery town of Schwedt), but also in the new chemicals industry dormitory town of Halle-Neustadt. A marked feature of the new socialist towns has been the youthful structure of their population which has consequently shown an exceptionally healthy natural increase. Growth of substantial proportions for the G.D.R. has taken place around Berlin in both towns (e.g., Königs-Wusterhausen, Zossen, and Hennigsdorf) and on a more modest scale in the countryside. Much of this growth has been on the western flanks of the divided city as commuting around West Berlin to jobs in the eastern sector has grown to a large scale, made possible by improvements in the outer ring railway. Unlike the Federal Republic, migration into new residential areas around large and medium-sized towns has not been observable on any scale in the G.D.R., partly because of the lesser growth of affluence and partly because of the lack of private house building, while land use around and within the towns has been formally planned. Lesser towns where economic diversification has occurred have attracted people, even in the prevailing low level of internal migration. Although some urban agglomerations can be distinguished, they are generally of modest proportions, with the most extensive in Greater Berlin, in the Karl-Marx-Stadt-Zwickau group, and around Halle and Leipzig.

Demographic problems

The basic demographic features remain in essence similar to West Germany, but the detail has tended to diverge over time and the age and sex structure of the population has become increasingly problematical, with attempts to stimulate natural growth. The strong migration to West Germany up to 1961 was composed markedly of young people in the economically and demographically most productive age groups: this had an accentuated ageing effect on

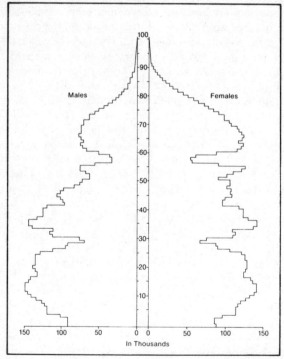

Figure 16.2 Age and sex structure in the G.D.R.

The Two Germanies

the population, but it was only in the late 1950s that the long-term seriousness had become apparent. The number of children fell with the departure of so many potential parents and there was a serious deficiency of men in the main working age groups adding to a deficit already generated by war losses, whereas people over fifty-five years of age were becoming an increasingly larger share of the total population. The effect was marked by a fall in the birth rate notably greater than in West Germany and a tendency for the death rate to increase. In both German states, marriage at a younger age has been accompanied by increased family planning, smaller families, and a tendency for married women to work longer after marriage. Better ante and postnatal care in the G.D.R. has secured, however, a somewhat lower level of infant mortality than in West Germany.

Problems of the G.D.R. space

In the German Democratic Republic, planning has aimed at fundamental change, both organizationally and spatially, whereas in the Federal Republic, planning (only effectively applied from the 1960s) has been to correct undesirable trends and imbalances arising from a largely unlimited free market economy.

As throughout the socialist *bloc* states of Eastern Europe, the whole concept of territorial planning and territorial-administrative organization in the G.D.R. has been influenced by and ultimately largely modelled on Soviet usage, despite the strikingly different stage of development and the contrasting spatial relationships. The traditional aim of Soviet planning has been to develop underdeveloped regions as quickly as possible and to eliminate the contrast between town and country. Because the Soviet state sought a high level of national self-sufficiency, these aims necessitated that high local autarky be established and such things as wasteful transport crossflows be eradicated (not unreasonable in the regional dimensions of the Soviet Union). These ideas, not wholly relevant or even applicable, were widely introduced into the entirely different spatial context of postwar Eastern Europe, first enforced with particular Stalinistic dogmatism. The problem of underdevelopment is a relative rather than a real concept in the remarkably sophisticated economic and social space of the G.D.R., while in a country of such small dimensions the question of transport effort becomes media selection rather than sheer economy of distance. Compared to Soviet experience, regional self-sufficiency in the German context also seems a minor question. The Soviet desire for regional self-sufficiency was reflected in attempts by planners to balance regional specialization against adequate development of other economic sectors: how far this should be carried in one direction or another has always generated debate in Soviet planning circles over the concepts of heterogenous and homogenous regions. The great diversity of the spatial economic structure inherited by the Democratic Republic from the former *Reich* meant that within any region, however defined, could be found both specialization and a high level of diversification. A local specialization might only form a small element in the local economy, but nevertheless constitute an important contribution to the overall national economy. A relatively simple major division could, however, be made between the more strongly agricultural economies of the northern areas (Brandenburg and Mecklenburg) and the southern lands (Saxony and Thuringia), where emphasis was clearly industrial.

An important element in the socialist *bloc* countries has been to equate living standards and opportunity between town and country, conceived within the framework of regional equalization. Consequently, in the G.D.R. industrial employment has been increased in the northern agricultural areas, along with considerable concentration on the development of urban settlement in lower ranked central places. In the industrial areas of the south, with large urban populations, there has been an attempt to diversify industrial employment, particularly in those districts with ailing, older industrial branches, or whose local natural resources, such as lignite, have faced exhaustion, or where industrial problems have arisen from the switch in priority in investment from consumer goods to capital goods.

Another facet of this problem has been attention to towns, since as proletarian centres they are the best diffusers of socialist dogmata and consequently become the favoured form of settlement, though at the same time, Marxist-Leninism has been strongly opposed to the giant town (Soviet success in controlling such growth has been mediocre). Rather like experience in the capitalist world, emphasis has been on urban planning at the expense of rural planning, with an equal lack of coordination and balance between the two sectors. The centrally planned economy has, however, allowed a closer control over urban development than generally found in the capitalist world. In the G.D.R. the task has not been simply to control further growth of towns and rectify their deficiencies, but to make major changes necessary to bring them into line with socialist society and economy. State ownership of all land, with prohibition of private building and land speculation, controlled town development more closely than in West Germany. Other factors contrasting with West Germany have been the different pattern of demographic development and a lower priority given to rebuilding war-damaged towns, while the absence of the 'motor car revolution' and the tighter control on land use have avoided the urban sprawl seen in West Germany. Several aspects have been aided by acceptance in the German Democratic Republic of higher housing densities and smaller allocations of space per person than in West Germany, but the task has been generally simplified by the absence of the large foreign-born population found in most West German towns.

The urban infrastructure has been at hand from the start in the G.D.R. as one of the most highly urbanized parts of Central Europe. According to Soviet tenets, towns should be 'national in form, socialist in content', and such a principle has been applied in new towns like Eisenhüttenstadt, though existing towns take much longer to remodel, but the central areas as rebuilt in many towns in the G.D.R. commonly exhibit this influence. A major contrast with West Germany is in the fewness of the shops, for the central area is essentially devoted to the threefold purpose of administration, political agitation, education and culture. Criticism of early rebuilding schemes was that shops were scattered too far apart: more recently the tendency has been to group them, but shops, hotels, and restaurants are planned by state monopolies in relation to likely demand and one of the most distinctive features of Leipzig is the generous provision of hotels to provide for the twice yearly Trade Fair. In several newly designed centres, streets have been replanned to allow for organized mass demonstrations (forcefully seen in the *Marx-Engels Platz* in East Berlin), but in replanning street patterns, however, lack of agreement exists over future needs, especially in relation to the growth of traffic and the increase in numbers of motor cars, despite a strong official policy to prevent an 'automobile explosion' on the American model. New town centres contain a mixture of office and residential accommodation to avoid the dead hearts of Western cities. Efforts have been made to organize towns on the basis of fully supporting neighbourhood units of 5,000–20,000 people, each with a planned quota of essential services and often related to local employment, so reducing the need to provide public transport for commuting within the towns.

Strong Soviet influence is seen in architectural style and in overall concept in the earlier schemes in a concentration on large blocks of buildings (commonly overhigh, strung along overwide streets to achieve, in Soviet terms, the 'big city effect'), while street plans were also rather geometric and had a marked uniformity. Preoccupation with the visual impact as an expression of the régime often resulted in overpowering appearances, like the ornate, monolithic Soviet-style buildings of Berlin's one-time *Stalinallee*, the *Georg Dmitroff Platz* in Leipzig, the earlier parts of Eisenhüttenstadt, while Rostock has a somewhat monumental interpretation of Baltic brick Gothic style. The slowness of rebuilding in the early 1950s saved most towns, however, from the worst excesses of Soviet-style buildings and planning. More successful recent development schemes include the *Strasse der Nationen* in Karl-Marx-Stadt, the newer parts of East Berlin, central Neubrandenburg, and the new town of Schwedt. Allocation of resources to house building remained inadequate until the 1960s, with time and resources wasted in the 'Fassadenkult' (the useless decoration of buildings). Mechanized building methods have brought monotony to many new residential schemes, but nevertheless the better quality of workmanship and finish sets the G.D.R. apart from the other socialist states.

The first socialist town, Stalinstadt (Eisenhüttenstadt), founded in 1951, illustrates the principles. The main road leads from the centre to the gate of its main industrial plant, while the town centre has the town hall, the House of the Party and accommodation for other mass organizations. Housing is in three- and four-storey blocks of flats with a few high rise blocks. Planned initially for 35,000–40,000 people, it was supposed to attain 50,000 by 1970. Almost before it was finished a second new socialist town at Neu-Hoyerswerda in Lusatia was begun as residential quarters for the large Schwarze Pumpe lignite *kombinat*, but in this instance focused around the existing town of Hoyerswerda, a practice followed later at Halle-Neustadt and Schwedt. Town planners in the G.D.R. have, however, expressed considerable concern at the overgenerous use of land in some schemes and emphasis is now on using smaller areas without loss of amenity, while as in the Federal Republic, it is now considered that truly 'urban' functions are found only in communities above 5000 people. Plans have selected areas for concentrated urban development – in the second plan, for example, seven areas were so designated: Halle-Leipzig, Cottbus-Spremberg-Hoyerswerda-Weisswasser, Vetschau-Lübbenau-Calau, Frankfurt/Oder-Eisenhüttenstadt-Guben, Pirna-Dresden-Meissen, Hettstedt-Eisleben-Sangerhausen, Gera-Sonneberg. Such a policy implies a selection of growth poles and long term could have considerable influence on the overall pattern of town distribution

The major organizational change in agriculture through creation of socialist-type collectives brought change and consequent planning problems in the countryside through the need to relocate and replan traditional settlements. The large farm units generally have raised problems of 'central places', either through the selection of small towns and large villages for development as their centres or through separation between residential and operational functions, so that the impact has been to alter the form of rural settlement to the advantage of larger villages or small agrarian towns.

New building in villages has introduced three- and four-storey blocks of flats besides elements usually associated with town life. There remains the imprint of the early land reforms, notably in Mecklenburg and Brandenburg, where the break-up of estates was accompanied by building small farmsteads on the outskirts of villages, creating new settlements, or expanding the original *Gutsdorf*. In the *Börde* country, traditional nucleation has helped the formation of collectives: but in the uplands, the many small, scattered settlements have presented organizational problems, and attempts to centralize settlement in a few larger units have been ruthlessly pursued. As elsewhere in Europe, changes in farming, whether economically or politically motivated, are bringing an end to the morphological patterns of villages little altered since mediaeval times. With the expressed intent that the ultimate unit of rural settlement should be the new socialist-style agrarian town (*Agrarstadt*, a version of the Soviet *agrogorod*), communities under a thousand people have already shown considerable decline. One of the new type is Ferdinandshof near Ueckermünde, and the choice of settlement for this role in any district seems to fall to the largest village or to the one with the best infrastructure and transport facilities. In parts of Mecklenburg and Brandenburg, existing traditional agricultural towns, where new industries have been hard to stimulate, have usually become the foci for conversion, but in rural areas where industrial employment has been created in small towns, workers have been moved from villages wherever possible into new residential accommodation nearby in order to reduce unprofitable commuting.

Territorial-administrative reform

The first major step towards effective centralized planning and the creation of the spatial structure for socialism was the sweeping away of the *Länder* and the institution in their place of fourteen *Bezirke* in 1952, each comprising about fifteen *Kreise* (whose area was reduced but whose number was increased); East Berlin was also given this status. They enjoy little independence and form organs of central government at the local level in a concept of 'democratic centralism'. Evidence is inconclusive as to whether or not an intentional relationship between the territorial-administrative pattern and the units of spatial economic planning was created (as had been done in the Soviet Union), though they do appear to be of roughly equal economic potential. In defining the *Bezirke*, conceived without relation to any existing or previously existing system, the principal of homogeneity seems to have been more pronounced than in the *oblasti* of the Soviet Union, on which they are modelled, and the *Bezirke* display several other qualities commonly seen in the Soviet *oblast* (though some observers claim such traits are more accidental than intentional). As in Soviet practice, each *Bezirk* is identified by its principal town, the largest and most important proletarian focus within its boundaries, though whether the *Bezirk* is conceived as the *Umland* of this centre (as is commonly claimed for the Soviet *oblasti* in the more loosely meshed settlement pattern of the U.S.S.R.) is less certain. Certainly the boundaries of the *Bezirke* have remained remarkably constant, without the fluidity shown by Soviet *oblasti* as economic relationships have changed.

East German writers have pointed to the desirability of agreement between the boundaries of administrative and economic planning units, which should be adjusted in response to regional economic needs. Nevertheless, suggestions that the existing boundaries need extensive revision to bring them into line with economic-geographical criteria have been ignored and the State Planning Commission and *Bezirk* planners have rejected any major realignment of boundaries in the foreseeable future. During the 1960s much study was devoted to defining economic planning units, usually by grouping together three or four *Kreise* (well below the general size of a *Bezirk*), though no comprehensive scheme has been published. There was general agreement that administrative and economic planning boundaries should form a unified system, though later it was felt that administrative boundaries might be left and economic planning units created by grouping together *Kreise* and *Gemeinden* into 'necessary and variable units' to form 'existing and objective territorial production complexes'. After 1968 renewed efforts were made to form economic planning units by merging the lower orders of administrative units together, so that in the northern *Bezirke* there was a considerable reduction in the number of *Gemeinden* through consolidation. An attempt was certainly made when designing the *Bezirke* to find an acceptable number for planning, statistical, and fiscal purposes, a problem commonly discussed in Soviet literature. While there have been critics of the haphazard way in which the congruence of administrative and economic functions in territorial organization has been pursued, there is nevertheless a conviction that territorial organization should be logically derived from the spatial pattern of production relationships in the new society.

Each *Bezirk* possesses a particular specialism – a natural resource or an economic activity – though in no case does this dominate the economic scene, largely because of the highly diverse pattern of activity in the republic. Though there is a considerable size range between the *Bezirke*, some attempt was clearly made to balance population, with the more thinly settled agricultural northern *Bezirke* areally larger than the southern industrial *Bezirke*, and possibly this difference is also related to the diversity and intensity of economic activity. One of the most clearly defined functional specialisms is seen in the *Bezirk* Rostock, the Baltic littoral, with a concentration of port facilities (Rostock, Warnemünde, Wismar, Stralsund, etc.) and related industries (e.g., shipbuilding). In contrast, *Bezirk* Cottbus demonstrates a considerable specialization in the mining and processing of lignite and is interesting inasmuch as it cuts across the territory occupied by the minority ethnic group of the Sorbs, so that some of their homeland falls to *Bezirk* Dresden. Here the important 'national principle' much respected in the Soviet Union appears to be violated. Lignite as a natural resource also plays an important role in *Bezirk* Halle, though the main specialism here is chemicals production, with over 40 percent of the total national capacity. Lignite mining, chemicals manufacture, and engineering are among the diverse industrial structure of *Bezirk* Leipzig, though its special contribution is the significant concentration of polygraphic industry and its commercial role through its trade fair. The main industrial contribution is, however, made proportionally by *Bezirk* Karl-Marx-Stadt: the main national producer of textiles (over 56 percent) and highly significant for heavy engineering, electrical engineering, precision engineering, and optical goods. Its most special contribution is from its small bituminous coalmines, the only ones in the German Democratic Republic, though these are expected to close by the 1980s. *Bezirk* Dresden, similar to Leipzig, Halle, and Karl-Marx-Stadt, has a special function as the leading scientific and technical research focus in the country. *Bezirk* Erfurt contributes the largest share of precision engineering and is the second main centre for motor vehicles besides the

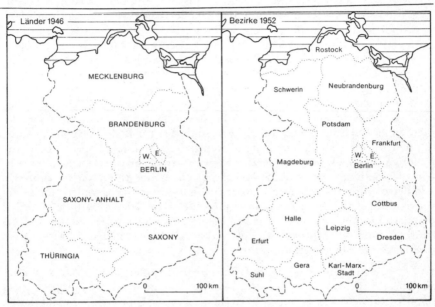

Figure 16.3 German Democratic Republic – *Bezirke* and *Länder*

importance of potash mining. *Bezirk* Frankfurt-an-der-Oder has emerged as the major heavy industrial focus in the east of the state, with the big heavy metallurgical complex at Eisenhüttenstadt and the oil refinery at Schwedt. An important concentration of light consumer industries and also potash mining is found in the smallest *Bezirk*, Suhl. *Bezirk* Magdeburg has an important position on the difficult western border, but it is also a main producer of heavy engineering goods and critical in COMECON as the largest producer of photographic gelatine. *Bezirk* Gera is industrially highly diverse, including the *Zeiss* plant at Jena (of importance to the whole socialist *bloc*), besides its role as a uranium producer. *Bezirk* Potsdam and East Berlin not only have an important industrial role, but also form a critical transport focus within the republic, while they occupy a very tender political-geographical position. In great contrast, the *Bezirke* Neubrandenburg and Schwerin are the only districts where industrial production accounts for less than 50 percent of the

The German Democratic Republic: The State and its Population

total output: farming, forestry, and food industries are the main activities.

The predominantly rural northern areas in the G.D.R. constitute a special problem of lagging social and economic standards where some form of framework of 'socialist development areas' has been proposed. Nevertheless, investigations suggest that investment in the main population concentrations (*Ballungsgebiete*) is attainable at greater cost effectiveness and lower capital cost than industrialization in the infrastructurally weak rural areas, especially through the need to recast their irrational settlement pattern. It now seems to be accepted that differences in living standards and in social and economic patterns between the *Bezirke* will never be completely overcome without consuming large amounts of scarce resources and that there are more pressing tasks. A special task, about which little has been said for strategic reasons, has been the 'disengagement' of the spatial structure of the economy and settlement inherited from the prewar *Reich* from that of the Federal Republic along the new frontier. Unlike the Federal Republic, which has a special planning region of the *Zonenrandgebiet*, no distinctive status is given to the frontier belt, with its acute disruption of the overall pattern of life, though in a belt over 5 kilometres wide residence and settlement is rigorously controlled (including the removal of all buildings wherever possible up to 300 metres from the actual demarcation line). Equally little has been said about the planning problems caused by the new frontier with Poland, though here engagement rather than disengagement has been important.

Following Soviet debates, the East European members of COMECON have considered the management of planning by the territorial approach as opposed to the branch approach. In the territorial approach, regional design becomes cardinal to the solution of problems, whereas in the branch approach planning is less dependent on territorial considerations, being done on a sectoral basis. Territorial planning, despite the apparent complexity of the economy, is easier than in the Soviet Union, because the size and number of individual planning units are more manageable than in the immensity of the U.S.S.R., where units of modest size become too numerous, and large units become too few to monitor developments truly (a Soviet complaint frequently made against the large planning regions, the *makrorayony*, while the ill-fated management planning units of the 1960s were too numerous, numbering between 47 and 109).

Suggested further reading
Gellert, J. F., Kramm, H-J.: DDR in Stichworten – Land, Volk, Wirtschaft, Kiel, 1976.
Jacob, G. (ed.): Beiträge zur territorialen Produktionsstruktur der DDR, *Wiss. Abh D. Geog. Gesell. d. DDR* 13, Berlin, 1976.

Zur Problematik der ökonomischen Rayonierung in der DDR, *Geog. Berichte* 7, 1961, pp.123–130.

Ludz, P., et al.: DDR-Handbuch, *Bundesministerium für Innerdeutsche Beziehungen,* Bonn, 1975.

Mitzscherling, P. et al.: DDR-Wirtschaft – eine Bestandsaufnahme, *Deutsches Inst. f. Wirtschaftsforschung,* Berlin, 1971.

Werner, F.: Zur Raumordnung in der DDR, Berlin, 1972.

---CHAPTER 17---
INDUSTRY IN THE GERMAN DEMOCRATIC REPUBLIC

As one of the world's present top ten industrial countries, in the carve-up of the economic organism of the Third *Reich* the subsequent adjustments required by the G.D.R. were in general greater than those in the Federal Republic: first, it was left with a more unbalanced economy and a poorer natural resources endowment (except for lignite and mineral salts); secondly, it had to adjust to an entirely new pattern and philosophy of economic and social organization; and thirdly, drawn into close ties with the socialist *bloc*, it had consequently to adapt to its needs. The G.D.R. has been turned into a centrally planned economy where limited decentralization began only in the declining 1960s and where effective mechanisms in the selection of correct economic priorities by plan evaluation have not yet been fully perfected, for centrally erected plan targets and steering of industrial development are liable to delay and disruption if policy or pace of development alter. Nevertheless, its economic development is closely related to COMECON which increasingly integrates its members' economies, even though without the supranational powers of the European Community, and whose changes in policy (reflecting changes in basic Soviet attitudes to planning, trade, and international cooperation) have considerable influence on policy in individual member countries. Early planning was influenced by Soviet ideas on self-sufficiency that left monuments like the Calbe ironworks and the Schwarze Pumpe lignite coke works to its passing. Later deficiencies were made good in bilateral trading, with specialization on products the G.D.R. was best fitted to produce, like chemicals, precision instruments, or even sugar beet handling machinery. When this did not prove efficacious enough, an attempt at closer international integration of plans with other members in COMECON socialist economic integration was involved, but the G.D.R. among other socialist countries has, however, forced acceptance by the Soviet Union of more sophisticated trade and financial mechanisms. Plans that currently foresee the formation of socialist *bloc* multinational companies will clearly further influence the spatial organization of the G.D.R. With COMECON, the G.D.R., as an advanced industrial economy, occupies a key position: it has only one-twentieth of the organization's total population, but in gross social product is third, with 8 percent of the organization's total (Soviet Union, 64 percent; Poland, 10 percent). Measured in terms of social product per head or per employee, it is one of the richest states, with a level 50 percent greater than the COMECON average.

The main elements of 'socialization' – forms of organization and concepts of labour on the Soviet model – had been extensively achieved by the time the new republic was formed, when banking, insurance, and all transport were in state hands. With the republic in a territorial framework conceived initially as an administrative convenience to simplify the task of occupation, an unbalanced economic structure expectedly resulted and, although the pre-1945 concept of *Mitteldeutschland* had fallen overwhelmingly to the G.D.R., this was far from self-sufficient as prewar it had depended heavily on the now inaccessible Rhenish-Westphalian and Upper Silesian industrial areas for bituminous coals and raw and semiprocessed metals, while Hamburg and Stettin – ports now denied it – had been its main outlets to the world. The early 1950s saw the building of an economy in line with Soviet views that emphasized self-sufficiency and capital goods industries but gave low priority to consumer goods. Iron and steel making, using imported socialist *bloc* raw materials, was given particular priority, while in the late 1950s, because of the poorly developed state of the Soviet chemicals industry, Russian encouragement was given to G.D.R. chemicals plants to expand and modernize. Despite heavy reparations dismantling, optical goods and precision engineering were also expanded because of their poor representation elsewhere in the COMECON countries. With consumer goods at a low priority, important industries of prewar times, like textiles, received little attempt to modernize or improve them.

In 1950 reparations deliveries to the Soviet Union had been substantially reduced, and in 1954 the Soviet limited companies (SAG), formed to help fulfil reparations deliveries, were transferred to German administration and their production added to the republic's economy, while the republic also agreed to COMECON plans for regional production specialization, of which one of the most important was expanded manufacture of synthetic fibres and resins.

Industry in the German Democratic Republic

Progress was not, however, dramatic, since the organizational change in the economy and failings in the process of planning made for considerable wasted effort, and labour shortage arising from the strong migration of people to West Germany, especially in the economically most productive groups, was beginning to be felt. Talk of importing foreign labour or of a transfer of the remaining German population in Poland and Czechoslovakia to the republic was not implemented, but the sealing of the borders with West Germany and particularly West Berlin (1961) helped to stem the loss. The demand from several COMECON countries in the 1960s for more sophisticated equipment worked to the advantage of the G.D.R. industries well able to cater for these needs, while continuing demand for capital goods has brought growth of heavy engineering, not strongly represented before 1945, whereas the large COMECON market for cheap quality textile goods attracted the Saxon textile industry in place of the higher quality market sought before 1939.

Energy supply

The G.D.R. is substantially dependent on imported energy sources, which have risen from 11 percent in 1960 to over 30 percent in the late 1970s (the Federal Republic is, however, over 50 percent dependent). Bituminous coal resources are modest (estimated at 200 million tons, of which only a small part is worth exploiting), with mining around Zwickau, Lugau-Oelsnitz, Freital, and Plötz. As coal output fell before 1939, processing and gas production had become increasingly dependent on Ruhr and Silesian coal; but attempts after 1945, when the Soviet Occupation Zone was cut off from its outside suppliers, to increase production were of limited success. Since the peak production of 3 million tons in 1951, output has fallen to below 1 million tons per year, though use of electric and diesel traction on the railways has reduced the demand, and it is expected that production will cease by 1980. The coals have a high ash content and only those from Zwickau have been suitable for coking. Exploration of the North European Plain, notably south of Berlin, has, however, revealed coal (reputedly of anthracite quality) at great depths beyond present technological and price limits. With an annual consumption of about 12 million tons of bituminous coal, the republic relies on supplies from the Soviet Union, Poland, Czechoslovakia, and even the German Federal Republic.

The German Democratic Republic mainly relies on lignite (brown coal), of which it is the world's largest producer, and in no other state does lignite play such a major role. Seams cover some 563,000 hectares, of which about 300,000 hectares are reputedly worth exploiting, with a total content of about 40 milliard tons of lignite, of which some 25 milliard tons are available by present methods of working. The largest exploitable reserves (15 milliard tons) lie east of the Elbe in Lusatia. The extensive opencast mining (92 percent of output) produces a serious land-use problem as the vast pits need careful landscape restoration after use in order to maintain the water table at an acceptable level, particularly in the Elbe-Saale basin, where serious water supply and effluent disposal difficulties exist. The lignites are classified by their chemical and physical properties according to their potential use. Those rich in bitumen are used for extraction of waxes, resins, and tars: in general the younger coals east of the Elbe tend to be less rich in bitumen than the older deposits west of the river, which unfortunately show an increasing measure of exhaustion, but greater use of natural petroleum is making them less important as a source of synthetic oils. Lignites west of the Elbe have most sulphur (usually even so below 2 percent) and sulphides (often of secondary origin) are a serious nuisance. Ash content varies between 6 and 25 percent, while salts, usually derived from nearby Zechstein deposits, may reach 35 percent by dry weight, especially in the lower seams, but true salt lignites, found only west of the Elbe, comprise only 6 percent of the reserves. Salt lowers the melting point of the ash and causes excessive clinkering, requiring specially designed grates and boilers. Coking lignites (mostly in Lower Lusatia) have low ash and sulphur content. Briquette lignites must not be too ashy nor too rich in tars, though sulphur content is unimportant, and they comprise 38 percent of total reserves, and where ash exceeds 15 percent and tars remain below 12 percent, lignites are suitable fuels for large thermal electric power stations (27 percent of reserves). Output of lignite rose to a maximum in 1964 (257 million tons), but growing use of petroleum and natural gas has since caused a slow decline and long term it will be used primarily for electricity generation. Use of larger and more powerful excavators has made possible economic removal of more over-burden as it has become necessary to get at the deeper seams. In 1964, one ton of lignite needed removal of 2.8 m^3 of overburden: in 1970 this had risen to 3.7 m^3 and by 1980 will reach 5.0 m^3. Although early postwar development was concentrated west of the Elbe, since 1950 increasing effort has gone to develop the reserves in Lusatia, notably around Cottbus, from where ultimately 60 percent of output will come. The high investment costs of modern machinery make mining only worthwhile where large exploitable reserves are assured.

In the Harz foreland, there has been little expansion, despite large reserves of salt lignites, and only a short future is seen for the lignite-processing plants of this area. Mining ceased with the end of shaft mining in the Köthen field in the 1950s. In the 1960s production grew substantially around Bitterfeld and further growth will take place after deflection of the river Mulde, with most output used in thermal power stations, and the briquetting industry will decline in the next few years. The Halle area has increased production, but the high rate of extraction in the Geiseltal will exhaust these rich reserves by the mid-1980s, though salt lignites may be exploited after this date around Halle. Mining has migrated eastwards in the Zeitz-Weissenfels area, but the field has become less important for gasification and chemical by-products. The districts of Borna and Meuselwitz-Rositz have doubled their prewar output to over 60 million tons. Particularly large opencast mines operate at Zwenkau and Espenhain, and new workings have opened around Borna, and there is a diverse processing industry.

Development east of the Elbe is dominated by the opencast pits around Cottbus. Production in 1936 was about 36 million tons, whereas by the early 1970s it had risen to over 134 million tons. Mining will move northwards to exploit the deeper, lower seam in areas where the upper seam has been removed in the past. An important district has developed around Spremberg in association with the Schwarze Pumpe chemicals and energy combine, and output is to expand at Weisswasser, where a large power station has been built at Boxberg to augment the Trattendorf plant. Other fields are in Upper Lusatia near Görlitz and Zittau, whose output goes primarily to the large power station at Berzdorf-Hagenwerder. Lignite mining near Frankfurt (Oder) ceased in the mid-1950s with closure of the main workings at Finkenheerd. Some power stations here (e.g., Hirschfelde) use Polish lignite from the pits at Turów.

Resources of petroleum and natural gas appear limited and finds have to date been meagre, usually occurring in Zechstein deposits, and this is disappointing since much of the area could be petroleum-bearing according to its geological character. Natural gas had been discovered in small quantities at Langensalza in 1907 and at Volkenroda in 1930; but search elsewhere in the Thuringian basin has brought only small finds of gas and no petroleum. On the northern Harz foreland, a small oilfield worked for several years until exhausted in 1967. Zechstein dolomite was the reservoir in which drillings with Rumanian and Soviet help in 1964 revealed petroleum at Reinkenhagen near Stralsund and later at Grimmen east of Greifswald. Seismic borings near Guben have also shown petroleum: other finds have been at Burg (Cottbus) and Forst. Recent encouraging natural gas finds have been near Salzwedel (Altmark) and immediately east of Berlin, while some gas and petroleum has been found on Usedom near Wolgast. Since 1963 the republic has been linked by pipeline from the soviet oilfields to Schwedt, the large new refinery on the Oder, though the share of soviet crude is falling as the republic obtains more from Arab trading partners. Schwedt is also joined by pipeline to the tanker import terminal at Rostock and to Leuna, around which are a number of small refineries (Bitterfeld, Böhlen, and Zeitz). A product line extends from Schwedt to East Berlin, and there are a number of local product lines in the Leuna-Bitterfeld chemicals region. A small refinery is located at Schwarzheide near Cottbus and at Lützkendorf (mostly lubricants), served by railway. Thirty percent of the petrol and 45 percent of the diesel oil used in the G.D.R. is supplied alone by Schwedt, whose annual capacity is to be raised to 8 million tons. There has been a substantial shift in the chemicals industry from lignite to petrol-based chemicals, with about 50 percent of the basic chemicals production now associated with petrochemicals, while synthetic petroleum production from lignite will be phased out.

Gas production in the G.D.R. has been based primarily on lignite, and natural gas has as yet played a far less important part than in West Germany, though its role is likely to increase, however, with bigger imports from the Soviet Union (by pipeline across Czechoslovakia) or through greater home produc-

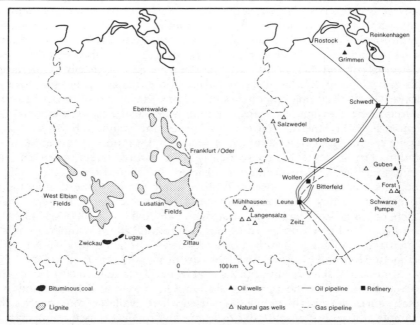

Figure 17.1 Lignite fields, refineries and pipelines in the G.D.R.

tion mostly from the Altmark of low-calorie gas. About four times as much coal gas is now produced as before the war (about 40 percent consumed by industry), nearly three-quarters of which is from lignite and about one-quarter from imported bituminous coal, a reversal of the position in the early 1960s. Production has been, as in West Germany, increasingly concentrated in big units and distributed through a grid system. The main lignite gas producers are around Cottbus (notably Lauchhammer and Schwarze Pumpe), which contribute about 25 percent of the national supply; another 11 percent comes from the lignite gas works at Böhlen (near Leipzig). Magdeburg, with coal brought along the Mittelland canal, remains a major producer from

Industry in the German Democratic Republic

bituminous coal (11 percent) and also turns out metallurgical coke. Bituminous coal (mostly Polish) is used in East Berlin to contribute another 11 percent of national output.

Wartime damage, heavy reparations dismantling, and dislocation of supply patterns created by the division of the country all held back expansion of electricity output until the mid and later 1950s; in fact, over half the present generating capacity has been erected since 1955, but it is barely sufficient to cover peak demand. The heavy dependence on lignite as a primary fuel and the general geographical distribution pattern of electricity generation remain remarkably similar to prewar, though output of electric current has roughly quadrupled, with a strong demand from electro-chemicals (where 40 percent of costs may represent energy) and electro-metallurgy. Before 1955 these industries covered their needs from their own generating plants, but demand has grown so rapidly that it has outstripped their capacity, forcing them to draw from the national supply system. The distribution of power stations reflects the importance of transport costs when using low-grade fuels like lignite: a 300-Mw thermal power station producing 2 milliard Kwh/p.a. using lignite requires four times as much fuel as a similar bituminous coal-burning station. The tendency has consequently been towards larger, more efficient lignite-burning units concentrated near to the opencast workings and to cooling water. In Lusatia, where cooling water has been short, abandoned opencast workings have been made into reservoirs. Large stations lie at Lübbenau and Vetschau in Lusatia, while at Boxberg a 3000-Mw plant is being built. Other important groupings are around Bitterfeld and Merseburg, Thierbach and Zeitz in Saxony. Lignite used away from the workings is mostly briquetted to stand transport, as in the case of Magdeburg, Peenemünde, and Merkers near Eisenach. Bituminous coal from Silesia remains the fuel at the prewar Berlin–Klingenberg power station. Oil is used at Schwedt, and in a small generator in Berlin, while gas is used where available from cokeries, for example at Eisenhüttenstadt and Zwickau. Hydro-electricity is unimportant, represented by six pump storage stations (5 percent of the total generating capacity), of which the largest are Hohenwarte (320 Mw) on the Saale, Niederwartha on the Elbe and Wendefurth in the southern Harz, but several small old-fashioned plants add local supplies in Saxony and Thuringia. A small nuclear power station at Rheinsberg north of Berlin is to be augmented by a larger plant at Lubmin near Greifswald and a much expanded capacity is foreseen for the future, including a large power station at Magdeburg. In 1980, 15 percent of all current is to be nuclear generated. The concentration of power stations on the lignite fields has made necessary extension of the prewar grid distribution system, with main generating centres linked to each other and to major consuming districts by 380-KV lines, while elsewhere 220-KV lines form the basic grid pattern. The two German republics are linked by a 220-KV

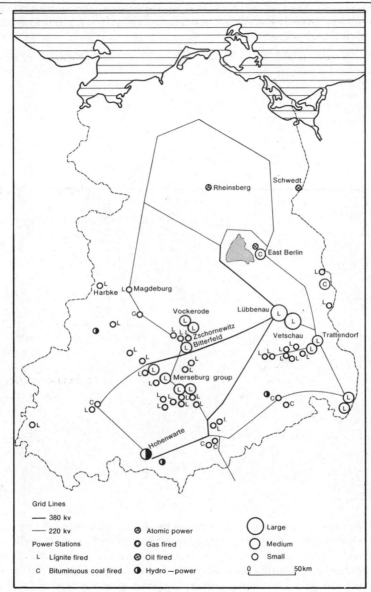

Figure 17.2 Electricity supply in the G.D.R.

line between the Harbke and Offleben power stations and also across the border in Thuringia, and similar links (part of the COMECON Peace grid) join the republic to power stations in Bohemia and to Poland, but power stations in West Berlin are no longer actively linked to the G.D.R. (even East Berlin).

Iron and steel industry

The alignment of the Occupation Zones disrupted prewar patterns of trade in iron and steel goods and left an extremely uneven distribution of capacity between the two German states. The large engineering industry in *Mitteldeutschland* had depended before 1945 for the major part of its raw metal needs on the Ruhr and Silesia, both areas now beyond G.D.R. territory. Iron and steel making capacity was decimated by reparations in the G.D.R. – 80 percent of raw steel making capacity, 85 percent of steel rolling capacity and over 50 percent of the casting capacity were removed. When dismantling ceased, a new start was made in the heavy metallurgical industry, especially as the intoduction of Soviet economic planning concepts demanded a high level of self-sufficiency in which iron and steel production played a significant part. Former works were rehabilitated and modernized while a number of new plants were built; but even if self-sufficiency in production could be attained, self-sufficiency in raw materials was impossible. Home ores (covering only 5 percent of the need) came from deposits with 20–35 percent iron (some with a trace of manganese), mostly from Schmiedefeld in the Thüringer Wald and Ramsdorf near Unterwellenborn, while mining (abandoned in 1926) was begun again in the Harz, and plans were formulated to mine ore in the Erzgebirge. Nevertheless, the overwhelming part of the ore needed had to be imported, notably from Sweden and particularly the U.S.S.R. The supply of coking coal and coke had also to be largely imported – from the Soviet Union, Czechoslovakia, Poland, and even the Federal Republic – but experiments to use lignite as coke were unsuccessful. As demand for iron and steel rises, an increasing proportion will be imported, particularly as COMECON policy has swung in favour of countries with an already substantial productive capacity expanding their output (e.g. Poland, Czechoslovakia, Soviet Union) and the G.D.R. will concentrate more on high-quality semi-finished products like precision-made pipes, tubes and plated sheet, and alloy and special steels.

The Maxhütte at Unterwellenborn makes pig from Schmiedefeld and foreign ore and imported scrap, while half its coke is from cokeries in the republic, half from Poland and Czechoslovakia. Its basic Bessemer steel capacity is being raised to over 250,000 tons annually. Built in 1950–1953, the Calbe plant (closed in 1970 when its ore sources in the Harz were exhausted) had been designed to use lignite coke and lean acidic ores in low, wide furnaces that allowed easy escape of the excessive slack and prevented crushing of the soft

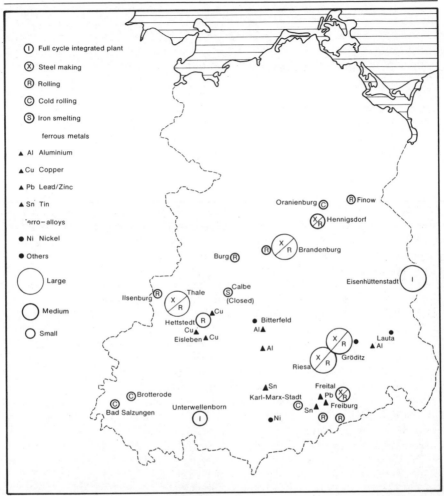

Figure 17.3 G.D.R. iron and steel industry

coke. Also of postwar origin (1951–1954), Eisenhüttenstadt (originally Stalinstadt) lies adjacent to the Oder-Spree canal, intermediate between its main market and main raw materials supply brought in by water. Most ore arrives from the Soviet Union in concentrate form along with high grade ore from nonsocialist *bloc* countries, while coke is from Poland, Czechoslovakia, and the Soviet Union. A large cold rolling plant using Soviet raw materials has been built and a steelworks is planned, but at present most pig iron goes to steelworks elsewhere in the republic. Steel comes mostly from works in Brandenburg, Hennigsdorf, Gröditz, Riesa (1 million tons per annum), and Freital, but concentration is on quality and special steels (except in Gröditz and Brandenburg, where general steels are produced). Scrap is particularly important in steel production, which is about twice the output of pig iron. Hot rolling is conducted at Finow, Kirchmöser, Burg, Ilsenburg, Olbernhau, and Hettstedt, whereas cold rolling (apart from Eisenhüttenstadt) is also done at Oranienburg, Bad Salzungen, and Brotterode, though a number of small rolling mills associated with other manufacturing plants also operate. Bitterfeld has a pipe and tube works A 'mini-steelworks' is being built at Ueckermünde.

Other metals

The critical supply problem for copper in the Soviet *bloc* brought efforts in the G.D.R. to increase output from the deposits of the Sangerhausen-Mansfeld area. Ore is refined at Eisleben and pure electrolytic copper rolled at Hettstedt, Berlin, and Aue. The industry has, however, to depend increasingly on imports of copper ore or part-refined copper (e.g., from Bulgaria), but output is well above prewar levels and though the copper content of the ores has fallen, they should last until AD 2000. Lead is mostly refined around Freiberg, where deposits have again been worked, but it is also a by-product from Mansfeld and much lead scrap is recovered. The annual output of about 30,000 tons is unlikely to increase. Zinc comes from the lead workings, from old waste tips around Freiberg, and from imported concentrates, while several trace metals produced in the refining process are recovered in Freiberg. Tin output from the Erzgebirge has also been increased, notably near Altenberg. The easy availability of generous supplies of electric current has encouraged expansion of aluminium production, mostly using Hungarian raw materials, with Lauta (being enlarged in 1977) and Bitterfeld as the main centres, while artificial cryolite is made in Dohna. The aluminium is used for further processing in the Saxon industrial towns and in Berlin. Magnesium production will commence in the 1980s using waste products from potash production and large amounts of electric current from planned nuclear power stations, but magnesium presently needed is imported from the Soviet Union.

Chemicals industry

The chemicals industry forms an exceptionally important branch making the G.D.R. one of the most significant producers in the whole COMECON group, while in terms of gross production it is second only to engineering, and between 1960–1976 growth was well above other industries. Chemicals have a high priority in the COMECON specialization plans for the republic, so that a large proportion of total production is exported: 80 percent of all photographic chemicals and films, 40 percent of all synthetic rubber, 35 percent of calcined

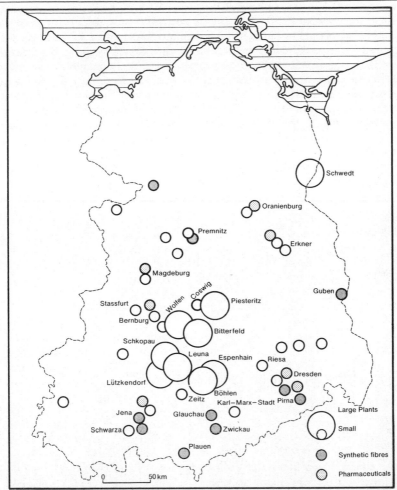

Large Plants

Small

Synthetic fibres

Pharmaceuticals

Schwedt

Oranienburg

Premnitz

Erkner

Magdeburg

Guben

Stassfurt

Bernburg

Wolfen

Coswig

Piesteritz

Schkopau

Bitterfeld

Leuna

Espenhain

Riesa

Dresden

Lützkendorf

Zeitz

Böhlen

Karl–Marx–Stadt

Pirna

Jena

Glauchau

Zwickau

Schwarza

Plauen

0   50 km

Figure 17.4 The Central German chemicals industry of the G.D.R.

soda, and 20 percent of synthetic fuel. The locational attractions, as valid now as prewar, of *Mitteldeutschland* to the chemicals industry include the process water of the Elbe-Saale basin; the availability of lignite as a fuel for electricity generation as well as for extraction of chemical substances; and the rich deposits of mineral salts around the flanks of the Harz; besides the excellent transport position within Central Europe; though an important pre-1939 generative factor had been strategic considerations. Though little damaged by

Industry in the German Democratic Republic

war, the industry suffered heavily from reparations dismantling, but formation of Soviet companies in some of the largest and most important plants like Leuna, Schkopau, Bitterfeld, Wolfen, Böhlen, Espenhain, and Schwarzheide kept them *in situ* and they were eventually handed back to German administration. The formation of a special commission for the chemicals industry within COMECON in 1956 (with its seat in East Berlin) gave a considerable impetus, further strengthened by the extensive Soviet chemicalization programme. The division of Germany had, however, left considerable imbalances: plants working phosphatic chemicals were deficient, while capacity to use the synthetic rubber made in Schkopau was also lacking, just as was an adequate pharmaceuticals industry, so that much effort has been devoted to removing the imbalances and to rebuilding sectors eliminated through dismantling; consequently about one-fifth of total investment has gone into chemicals.

The chemicals plants are markedly grouped in the eastern part of *Bezirk* Halle and the western part of *Bezirk* Leipzig, with almost 30 percent of the plants and 55 percent of the employment in this sector; while in *Bezirk* Dresden the plants, notably along the Elbe, number almost one-fifth of all plants in the republic and a little over one-tenth of the employment, and through the growth of petrochemicals at Schwedt, the *Bezirk* Frankfurt/Oder is emerging as a new centre. The total number of plants has declined through rationalization, but the remaining ones have become larger, though highly specialized small producers have generally been left and the highest level of concentration is in synthetic fibres, basic chemicals, liquid fuels, and tars. Nearly half the gross industrial production of *Bezirk* Halle is provided by the chemicals industry, with two main centres around Bitterfeld and Merseburg, near which lie four major plants: the Schkopau synthetic rubber plant (18,000 employees), also the largest plastics producer in the republic; the two large Leuna plants (30,000 employees), the main producers of ammonia compounds and large manufacturers of plastics and synthetic fibres; and the Lützkendorf mineral oil works (4,100 workers). The Bitterfeld district has an electro-chemicals combine (13,000 workers), the Wolfen dye plant (8,000 workers), the *ORWO* film and photographic chemicals plant (14,000 workers), and is important for production of sulphuric acid, chlorine chemicals, caustic soda, and related substances. Bitterfeld receives ammonia, methane, and some acids by pipeline from Leuna and also pipes products to Wolfen, while petroleum and natural gas are piped from Schwedt. Salt and brine are imported for neutralizing waste effluent and a pipeline is to carry brine from Angerdorf in Teutschental. While the plants have their own electric generators using local lignites, water is a critical constraint, especially as quality and purity are important. Difficulties in expanding the capacity of railways serving these works are also another restrictive element for future development. In *Bezirk* Leipzig two major plants are Böhlen and Espenhain with over 20,000 employees. The local bitumen-rich lignites provide a raw material for production of synthetic fuels, tars and phenols, etc., but long-term plans foresee crude petroleum and natural gas replacing lignite. As a petroleum base becomes more important in the chemicals industry, the *Bezirk* Frankfurt/Oder centred on Schwedt will become an even greater producer, chiefly for plastics and synthetic fibres.

Other chemicals plants, mostly of prewar origin and located in relation to then operative conditions, include the sulphuric acid plants at Magdeburg, Rudolstadt-Schwarza, Premnitz, and Salzwedel; and using local raw materials in the Mansfeld copper area, at Eisleben and at Freiberg, while Coswig uses local anhydrite from Nordhausen for greatly expanded production. Soda compounds are made in Bernburg, Stassfurt, and Buchenau near Eisenach, for whose production rock salt and limestone are readily available; ammonia is produced at Leuna and Schwedt; nitrogen compounds are associated with Piesteritz near Wittenberg. Apart from Wolfen, photochemicals are made in Berlin and Dresden and domestic chemicals and detergents are produced at Karl-Marx-Stadt and Wittenberg, but a considerable number of small scattered plants operate. Jena, Berlin, and Dresden, as well as Wolfen, Leuna, and Wittenberg-Piesteritz are the main pharmaceutical centres. Synthetic rubber covers three-quarters of the republic's needs, almost entirely from the Schkopau plant, whose production is worked in tyre plants at Riesa and Fürstenwalde and for other manufactures in Wittenberg and Walterhausen in Thüringen. Viscose fibres ('artificial silk') from a cellulose base are still made in Plauen, Elsterberg, Wittenberge, and Glauchau; copper-based artificial silk is produced in Pirna; and fully synthetic fibres are being rapidly expanded, notably at Guben, Premnitz, and Schwarza.

Water supply and effluent problems

The chemicals industry has critical problems of water supply, effluent disposal, and environmental pollution. Though in the early postwar period, many major plants found their water supply adequate, their own expansion or the building of new plants has produced a water shortage requiring solution on a national basis, especially as the industry takes well over a quarter of all industrial water for processing and for cooling. About 300 tons of water are needed to make a ton of synthetic rubber and 500–700 tons for a ton of artificial silk. Estimates suggest that 15 milliard m³ of water are available annually in the G.D.R. for all purposes, though this may rise to 30 milliard m³ in a wet year or fall to 6 milliard m³ in a dry year. Annually about 5 milliard m³ are recovered: about 3 percent from springs, 18 percent from ground water, 58 percent from rivers, and 6 percent from lakes, while 16 percent is taken from reservoirs. Well over three-quarters of this 5 milliard m³ is used by industry.

Industry in the German Democratic Republic

Unfortunately, demand occurs in areas where recovery cannot generally be easily increased, so that in dry years or even in dry summer months shortages quickly appear; for example, the Leuna works takes as much water daily from the Saale as it carries at low water. Water demand is expected to rise to 15 milliard m³ by the end of the century, when in dry years the deficit could mount to 9 milliard m³. Most branches produce large quantities of effluent requiring substantial treatment before safe disposal; for example, the synthetic rubber works at Schkopau produces effluent equivalent in volume to a population of 2.3 million people and feeds 900 kilograms of ammonia into the Saale hourly. The Lützkendorf plant's effluent is oily water with a considerable phenol content, and some 230 m³ of harmless waste is fed hourly into old opencast lignite workings. Special controls are necessary to make sure effluent is cooled below 30°C before disposal into streams. The Leuna plant is allowed to take up to 33,300 m³ of ground water per hour, Schkopau 20,000 m³/h, and Lützkendorf 1,565 m³/h, while the new refinery complex at Schwedt uses up to 200,000 m³ per day drawn from ground water and the Oder river, but it has a most modern processing plant for its effluent.

As far as possible water is recycled in cooling systems and every effort made to render effluent harmless, if not reusable, while production processes have also been sought that reduce the demand for water. Conservation of ground water, with attempts to increase its use to the maximum in relation to other interests, has become important, and additional storage reservoirs have been built, with efforts made to redistribute water from areas with surplus to high-demand areas by the construction of pipelines and conduits. For the Saxon industrial towns, reservoir capacity in the Erzgebirge has been increased; in Lusatia abandoned lignite workings are being used for storage; and in Thuringia a new reservoir system has been developed on the upper Unstrut and Helme. The industrial areas of Leipzig, Leuna, Halle, Bitterfeld, Dessau, and Magdeburg will be supplied by pipeline from gathering grounds in the ground water reserves of the Elbaue near Pretzsch, the Annaburger Heide near Torgau, and the Letzlinger Heide north of Magdeburg, while the Bodetal reservoir will also augment these supplies.

Effort to extract such things as fats, acids, and albumen from effluent has been made to render it harmless, so that it can be fed into the normal drainage system. Where this is not possible, a system of pipelines or canals to carry waste water to places of disposal has been suggested, using in particular suitable underground reservoirs in old mines or even natural 'retainers'. Discharge into the atmosphere of noxious waste gases has also been examined, especially in plants like that at Rudolstadt-Schwarza, where a valley or basin location demands special measures to dispose of fumes without damage to flora, fauna, or human living conditions.

Engineering

Engineering, more affected than any other sector by the division of Germany and by dismantling or wartime damage, employs about one-fourth of the labour force in the G.D.R. and is one of the mainstays of the republic's exports (80 percent going to other members of COMECON). It has shown certain different trends to West Germany, for in the G.D.R. there has been the development of a larger sector of heavy machine building compared to prewar in response to the strong capital goods orientation of the COMECON market, while motor vehicle building has been on a modest scale, though shipbuilding and railway goods have flourished. Precision engineering has prospered as one of the few well-developed producers of this type in COMECON, but the general trend has been to articles of robust but modest technical precision. Consumer durables have, however, played an increasing part since the late 1960s, with a considerable market for them in COMECON and as relatively inexpensive items in the mail-order business in West Germany. The *Bezirke* Karl-Marx-Stadt, Dresden, and Leipzig are the most important for engineering according to employment, followed by the *Bezirke* Halle, Magdeburg, and Erfurt. Rostock has an important group of engineering plants, as do Potsdam and Berlin, while plants with a strong local character are found in the *Bezirke* Suhl and Gera. Half the output of heavy engineering comes from the *Bezirke* Magdeburg, Halle, and Leipzig. Engineering works remain mostly in the big towns and urban agglomerations, which together account for nearly two-thirds of the total gross production; but because it is relatively footloose, engineering assembly has been an important industrial element dispersed into districts where there has been inadequate diverse employment, notably in the strongly agricultural areas of the north or where older industries have been declining, as in parts of the Saxon brown coalfields.

Magdeburg town is the most important single centre, with the largest single plant (Ernst Thälmann Works with 13,000 employees) which includes rolling mill equipment, chemical engineering machinery, and mining equipment in its wide range. Heavy engineering in the *Bezirk* Halle is widely scattered; characteristic centres are Dessau, making complete cement works for use in COMECON; Köthen, Aschersleben, and Wittenberg making mining equipment and cranes; Zeitz with a large plant manufacturing machinery for lignite mining and processing; and Halle and Gatersleben supplying machinery for the building industry and for making building materials. Chemicals machinery is made in Sangershausen, Reinsdorf, and Halle. Leipzig itself, the major centre in the *Bezirk*, produces a wide range of machinery for the mining and chemicals industries (as do Grimma and Wurzen), but also heavy transport and lifting equipment. Wurzen makes conveyor belts and bucket elevators, while chemical engineering is particularly important in Karl-Marx-Stadt. Gears are made in Penig, crushing and mixing machinery in Zwickau, lifting equipment in Mylau, and cooling and condensing equipment in Netzschkau. Electric-generating equipment is produced in Dresden, Pirna, and Görlitz. Conveyor belts and cranes with mostly hydraulic and pneumatic drive are built at Freital, Dresden (also drilling and boring machines), and Sebnitz, whereas Bautzen turns out endless belt systems and machinery for pottery making and for the building industry (also from Görlitz).

Machine tools and process machines are mostly made in the *Bezirke* Leipzig, Karl-Marx-Stadt, and Dresden. Leipzig manufactures machine tools, printing and reprographics machinery; meuselwitz has a large machine tool works; Altenburg is the location of a sewing machine works; Torgau and Döbeln make farm machinery; and Leising, textile machinery. Big plants in the Karl-Marx-Stadt area make planing and smoothing machinery, lathes, presses, and die-casting machinery, besides including one of the largest producers of machines for the plastics industry, and also has the largest textile engineering works. Plauen is important for machine tools; Limbach-Oberfrohna for special sewing and plaiding machinery; Aue manufactures machine tools and textile machinery; and there is a plant making plastics-forming machinery in Johanngeorgenstadt. Dresden itself has a very large machine tool works, and in Freital plastic injection machinery is made; but the *Bezirk* is the largest producer of farm machinery in the republic, notably from Lommatzsch and the big combine in Neustadt, besides numerous small producers. Printing and reprographics machinery is made in Radebeul, Heidenau, Bautzen, and Dresden, which also specializes in food-processing machinery and packaging equipment. Textile machinery is made at Dresden, Zittau, Neugersdorf, and Grossenhain.

The motor vehicle industry compared to West Germany is extremely small. With a limited domestic market, technically backward, and given a low priority, this is not surprising, while it was further inhibited by COMECON specialization plans that limited its range of vehicles produced. In the 1970s plans have been formulated to create a 'multi-national' industry between the G.D.R., Poland, and Czechoslovakia to achieve the necessary economies of scale and research and development facilities. One of the present largest motor vehicle plants is the *Wartburg* works at Eisenach, but Zwickau has the *Sachsenring* motor car works, and lorries are made in Karl-Marx-Stadt, Zittau, Ludwigsfelde, and, for special purposes, in Berlin, while small commercial vehicles come from Waltershausen. Zschopau and Suhl build motorcycles, with bicycles at Sangershausen and Karl-Marx-Stadt. Leipzig and Karl-Marx-Stadt make gearboxes, while Schönebeck (the only tractor works in the G.D.R.) and Karl-Marx-Stadt are important for vehicle diesel engines. Body builders are located at Aschersleben, Halle, Meerane, and Dresden. Some important prewar capacity was lost through dismantling and the republic produces now far less than the one-third of all German motor vehicles made in its territory in 1939, while it has had to develop several components branches poorly represented before 1945.

Part of the prewar railway equipment industry has turned to other products, but railway goods still remain significant, concentrated notably in the *Bezirke* Halle and Dresden. Halle-Ammendorf and Görlitz are the main railway passenger coach works (including change of gauge vehicles for through services to the Soviet Union). Refrigerator vans are made in Dessau for the COMECON market; Bautzen and Niesky make goods wagons and railcars; goods wagons are also made in Gotha; Hennigsdorf builds electric and light diesel locomotives. Potsdam-Babelsberg until recently produced mainline diesel locomotives, but these are now supplied from Lugansk in the Soviet Union. Ships over 10,000 tons are built at the Warnow yard in Warnemünde and up to 3,000 tons at the Neptune yard in Rostock. Wismar concentrates on passenger vessels and special ships, and Stralsund has developed a standardized freighter, whereas dredgers and other special vessels are made in Wolgast. Marine engines are made at Rostock, while derricks and lifting and winding gear are delivered from Schwerin. Boizenburg is the main yard for river vessels.

Over one-quarter of the prewar capacity of the German electrical engineering industry lay in the G.D.R., though in 1946 it produced only one-third of its prewar output as a result of reparations dismantling and destruction. This later became one of the fastest growing sectors of the economy, marked by emergence of an extensive electronics, communications, and data-processing equipment industry, especially important in relation to COMECON. The industry has tended to remain on prewar sites (where it has widened its product range) rather than spread to new locations; consequently Berlin (by far the most important), Dresden, Karl-Marx-Stadt, and Erfurt are the main foci. Nevertheless some attempt has been made to disperse assembly work to new plant in the less industralized parts of the republic, and *kombinate* that group together related plants have become characteristic. The dominant position of Berlin is reflected by its wide range of electrical goods, particularly cables and lamps of all types; television and radio equipment are also made on a substantial scale, besides the recently developed computer and calculating machine industry. Welding equipment, transformers, and current conversion machinery are made in Falkensee, with a large switchgear plant in Werder; Köpenick builds communications and measuring gear; Lichtenberg has a major plant for electrodes. Two-thirds of all high-tension equipment is made in Berlin, also most important for high voltage and power-generation installations, for which the republic has a special responsibility inside COMECON. Resistances and condensers are made in Berlin–Teltow, in Gonsdorf near Karl-Marx-Stadt, and in Gera. Dresden is also a major centre, with the manufacture of transformers, power-generating equipment, communications

Industry in the German Democratic Republic

and measuring installations. About one-third of the output of electric motors and generators comes from Dresden town (also nuclear equipment), but other centres are Niedersedlitz, Heidenau, Dessau, Wernigerode, Thurm near Zwickau, and Grünhain near Karl-Marx-Stadt. Power equipment for heavy industry is made at Halle. Karl-Marx-Stadt, besides manufacturing communications and measuring devices (including electrical components for motor vehicles), occupies first place for domestic electrical equipment, which is also made in subsidiary plants throughout the Bezirk and outside at Ruhla near Erfurt, Sonneberg near Suhl, and Berlin. A similar pattern of manufacturing is found in Leipzig and in Magdeburg, which is also a main manufacturer of radio and television goods. Rudolstadt produces valves and X-ray equipment; oscillographs and power equipment come from Erfurt. An important computer and electronics factory is situated at Radeberg, while Frankfurt an der Oder produces semiconductors (using female labour from the Polish side of the border). Schwerin is a new centre (cables and flex), the result of plants having been forced to decentralize because of labour problems. Other electrical engineering works include Plauen, Mühlhausen, Rochlitz, Cottbus, Pirna, Treuenbrietzen, Stralsund, Zittau, Mittweida, Rostock, and Meissen, as well as Vacha.

Optical goods and precision engineering
An industry whose importance to the economy of the G.D.R. far outstrips the numbers it employs is optical goods and precision engineering: this highly labour-intensive industry of world renown (with a major research and development component) gives the republic a particularly important place in COMECON. Two-thirds of the employment in this branch lie in the *Bezirke* Suhl, Erfurt, Gera, Karl-Marx-Stadt, and Dresden. Calculators are made in Zehla-Mehlis-Meiningen; fine measuring instruments come from Suhl, Beierfeld near Schwarzenberg, Radeberg, and Dresden; office machinery comes from Sömmerda and Erfurt (together 45 percent of the employment in this branch), but also from Karl-Marx-Stadt, Dresden, Berlin, and Leipzig. Clocks and timepieces are made in Ruhla, Weimar, and the Glashütte district. Precision engineering is also important in Rauenstein, Steinach, Ilmenau, and in Schmalkalden, Quedlinburg, Dessau, Magdeburg, and Bad Liebenwerda near Cottbus. Medical equipment is notably made in Leipzig, Dresden, and Berlin, but Suhl and Klingenthal are also significant centres. Rathenow is famous for spectacles and eye glasses. Cameras and optical instruments are particularly associated with Jena (*Zeiss* – 22,000 workers). Because of the difficulty of expanding high-quality labour in Jena, its plants have been decentralized to Saalfeld (3), Gera, Eisfeld, and Lommatzsch. Air pollution has also become a serious problem in Jena: in 1967 the nearby Göschwitz cement works was closed to ease the difficulties of the *Zeiss* works. Dresden has 60 percent of the total camera-making capacity grouped in the VEB *Pentacon*,

which has a large number of scattered small assembly shops and subcontractors.

Textiles

Textiles, the main branch of light industry and a third major industrial branch in the G.D.R., remain mostly in private or part-private operation, though large modern units have been developed by the state as plants are grouped together and automation introduced, with a growing input of synthetic and artificial fibres. The industry has problems of water supply and effluent disposal not unlike the chemicals industry. Prewar, the textile industry in the present territory of the G.D.R. produced about 40 percent of all German textiles, a much higher proportion of national output than any other branch, with the production of woollen and knitted goods and artificial cloths particularly important. In 1945, the republic contained 9 percent of total German spinning capacity (7 percent of fine spinning) and yet 29 percent of the cotton weaving capacity; 93 percent of the curtain and lace industry; 100 percent of the glove and stocking industry; and 55 percent of the cotton knitted goods industry. Consequently, major investment has gone into putting right the imbalance by building new spinning mills (Flöha, Venusberg, Burgstädt, Karl-Marx-Stadt, and Leinefelde).

Saxony and eastern Thuringia have traditionally contained a major part of the textile industry: nowadays 57 percent of all textile production and 36 percent of all clothing are produced in the *Bezirk* Karl-Marx-Stadt, which produces about half of all domestic textiles, knitted cotton articles, furnishings, and stockings. Typical small and medium-sized plants are found mostly in the northwest and southwest of the *Bezirk*. Making-up clothing and tailoring are widespread throughout the *Bezirk* Karl-Marx-Stadt, with considerable remaining domestic industry. In the *Bezirk* Gera, there is manufacture of worsteds and woollens (including the use of synthetics) and the lion's share of the carpet industry, besides there is also making-up of clothing. One of the main centres in *Bezirk* Dresden is the Zittau district, with its textile combine employing 6000 operatives concentrating on a wide range of cotton and woollen yarns and woven goods, as well as jute and rubberized cloths. Löbau and Zittau together produce most of the towelling made in the G.D.R. The cotton industry is also found in towns along the Czech border, often with plants related to the Zittau textile combine, but as elsewhere the cotton textile industry is undergoing a strong penetration by synthetics, notably the polyester fibres. There is a wide scatter of making-up clothing, with Bautzen concentrating on sportswear and Görlitz on woollens. The southern Brandenburg or Lower Lusatian textile area – mostly in *Bezirk* Cottbus – is noted particularly for woollens and worsteds, mainly around Cottbus, Forst, Guben, and Finsterwalde (fine cloths), but clothing is made in Lübben. Western

Thuringia has the main textile area around Mühlhausen (notably worsteds); knitted goods are made around Apolda and Worbis; Erfurt makes up clothing, which is also produced in Heiligenstadt and Mühlhausen; Leinefelde has a large new spinning mill. Leipzig, an isolated centre, is noted for spinning wool, cotton, and jute. Throughout, the textile industries have survived best where large reserves of female labour remain, whereas in other areas it has contracted before industries with higher priorities, such as electrical and electronic engineering.

Food industries

The shift from private enterprise to state participation in the food industries has brought larger producing units and a rationalization of location, but local specialities have been preserved by mixed part-state and part-private companies. The substantial organizational changes at first produced considerable dislocation, and low output made it necessary to ration foodstuffs until the mid-1950s. Rationalization phasing out small or old plants resulted in a slow decline in employment during the 1960s, though a high proportion of female labour remains and there is still (as in the sugar industry) strong seasonal employment. The industry is widely scattered, though it is more than proportionally important in the *Bezirke* Halle and Rostock. Many branches gravitate towards their raw materials, especially those with a heavy weight-loss component like sugar extraction. Wheat has become more important than rye in the milling industry, with the change taking place in the early 1960s. Some of the largest mills lie along rivers and canals where grain (including imports) can be received by barge, but only a quarter of the mills have a daily capacity greater than 10 tons. Baking is widespread, though small local bakeries are being replaced by large mechanical plants.

There is a wide scatter of sugar mills, though most have been associated with the traditional sugar beet growing areas on the richer soils of the *Börde* country (these mills are now old fashioned and require replacement). Magdeburg, one of the most important centres in prewar Germany, still remains a major district for sugar making, while the *Bezirk* Halle is also significant. Attempts have been made to establish sugar making in new growing districts in the northern farming areas (mills have been built in Güstrow and Schwerin). Confectionary is widely made, mostly in the big towns, but Berlin and Magdeburg are particularly important. The latter enjoys excellent transport facilities for distribution and remains a major centre for chocolate making.

Among the locations processing fruit and vegetables, Magdeburg, Stendal, Tangermünde, and Calbe, as well as Dresden and Berlin, are important, and in the Spreewald local industry processes gherkins. In the southern districts, most milk is processed for drinking or quick consumption in the form of soft cheese and butter, but in the northern districts, there are fewer but larger plants making hard cheese, dried and powdered milk and animal feeding stuffs. There has been a switch from small slaughterhouses and butcher's shops to meat combines, with the largest again in the north at Pasewalk, Teterow, Güstrow, and Ludwigslust, as well as Neubrandenburg, Demmin, and Perleberg. Halberstadt continues its long tradition of sausage making, and Erfurt has a major meat-processing combine. Fish from distant waters is handled in combines at Rostock, Stralsund, and Sassnitz, but there are also fishing collectives on Rügen and Usedom, while freshwater fish (notably carp) is raised in the Mecklenburg lakes, in the Spree and Havel, and in large ponds in Upper Lusatia.

Malting is done mostly in the Halle and Erfurt districts, though brewing is widespread in the main towns – Magdeburg, Dessau, Zerbst, and Köstritz, but also Berlin and Dresden. Hops are mostly imported from Czechoslovakia. Fruit wines are made in Werder and Klötze, while local grapes are used at Freyburg on the Unstrut, where there is a sparkling wine factory. Grapejuice and bulk wine are imported: at Radebeul imported raw materials are used for wine preparation. Spirits are produced in many small distilleries: Wilthen near Bautzen is an important centre, but Berlin, Halle, Magdeburg, Dresden, and Parchim are also well-known distillers, while distilling dates back to the sixteenth century at Nordhausen. Dresden, Nordhausen, and Mühlhausen have tobacco factories, using partly home production and partly imported Balkan leaves.

Suggested further reading

Bröll, W.: Die ökonomische Bedeutung der DDR für die RGW-Staaten, *Osteuropa-Wirtschaft* 14, 1969, pp.24–41.

Kohl, H.: Standortprobleme der Kaliindustrie der Deutschen Demokratischen Republik, *P.M.* 108, 1964, pp.15-90.

Ökonomische Geographie der Montanindustrie in der DDR, Leipzig, 1961.

Kohl, H.: et al.: Ökonomische Geographie DDR, Berlin, 1969, 2nd ed. 1976.

Leptin, G.: Die deutsche Wirtschaft nach 1945 – ein Ost-West Vergleich, Opladen, 1970.

Ludz, P. et al.: DDR-Handbuch, *Bundesminister für Innerdeutsche Beziehungen*, Bonn, 1975.

Scholz, D.: Die wirtschaftsräumliche Struktur der DDR, *Geog. Berichte* 16, 1971, pp.83–101.

Zur Methodik der wirtschaftsräumlichen Gliederung in der DDR, *P.M.* 112, 1968, pp.28–36.

CHAPTER 18

AGRICULTURE AND FORESTRY IN THE GERMAN DEMOCRATIC REPUBLIC

Agriculture has been the economic sector in the G.D.R. in which some of the most striking changes have taken place as the Marxist-Leninist principles of collectivization following Soviet models have been applied. With considerable regional variations in farm size and organization, regional differences in the response of the landscape to the new organization have been notable. One of the consistent features of the socialist *bloc* countries has been the continuing problems of socialization in agriculture, to which both farming by its nature as well as the deep-seated peasant tradition of independence are ill-adapted. This feature has been seen markedly in the G.D.R., where the highly disruptive effect of this policy lasted well into the 1950s and the poor performance of farming at this time attributed to it underlay the long continuation of food rationing. One of the most disruptive elements was land reform that vacillated considerably in the early stages and ultimately drove many efficient medium and large farmers from the land, leaving it in the hands of small peasants – former landless labourers or expellees – many of whom had neither experience to run their own farm nor the means to apply effective husbandry. Land reform was in itself merely part of a move towards a high level of collectivization, but after the shock of the first disruption, it was apparent that fully socialized agriculture could only be reached by moves whose effect did not threaten the whole economy. The reform of September, 1945, on the basis of Allied decisions to introduce land reform through all four occupation zones (in the western zones this did not come until 1947 in a much milder form and under careful legal formulation), was carried through under slogans such as 'Junkerland in Bauernhand' and was claimed to be an 'inevitable national, economic, and social necessity'. Holdings over 100 hectares, confiscated without compensation, were pooled in a land fund along with 4000 holdings each under 100 hectares belonging to reputed war criminals and Nazis, while on estates many mansion houses were pulled down or destroyed as 'symbols of feudalism'. The confiscated land was redistributed to 'new peasants', with some 209,000 holdings having been created by early 1949. The drastic changes of 1945 were followed by a pause to consolidate new farming organizations, such as the Association of Peasants' Mutual Aid, which sought to press official policy on the peasants without giving them any bargaining power. New agricultural cooperatives were at first welcomed by the peasants in the belief they would become like the nonpolitical pre-Nazi *Raiffeisen* cooperatives and similar hopes were entertained when the Soviet authorities in 1947 created the German Agricultural Association, but in all these new bodies it was quickly apparent that strong political undertones were powerfully dominant.

The years 1949–1951 marked a struggle to eliminate the medium and large peasant farm, despite the clear economic importance and efficiency of this type, and the reform now affected peasants with more than 20 hectares. From mid-1952 the socialist sector in farming began to appear more strongly, with creation of the *Landwirtschaftliche Produktionsgenossenschaft* (LPG) to intimidate independently minded peasants and as a step towards Soviet-type collectivization. Considerable control was exercised over the LPG through machinery being available only from Machine and Tractor Stations (later to become less important, following the trend in the Soviet Union). The LPGs brought much unfavourable reaction from the peasants and so many left the land that the process had to be slowed in 1953, with Machine and Tractor Stations allowed to help still independent peasants (who were declared indispensible for the economy), but nevertheless preferential treatment continued to be given to peasants who joined the LPG. Duress to collectivize remained, though in 1956–1957 the process was not pressed, but in spring 1960 a massive campaign was launched to pressurize peasants still outside the LPGs to join, and in little over three months almost as much cultivated land was added to the LPGs as in the years 1952–1959, so that by April 1960 the last district announced full socialization.

Three levels of LPG were defined, with the final stage close to the true Soviet-style collective, and membership at first limited to working peasants and landless labourers, but after 1955 the larger farmer was admitted. Complicated rules, less draconic than in the Soviet Union, regulate 'ownership' and the right to land in the LPG. On formation of an LPG the peasants were allowed to choose one of the three stages, though the first two are regarded as leading to the final, third stage. Type I LPGs have only the arable land in communal tillage; draught animals, machinery, and tools remain private but must be available to all users against compensation. Type II LPGs – now relatively unimportant – have not only the arable communally tilled, but also gardens, meadowland, and woods, and most of the tractive power, machinery, and tools in communal possession, while unused buildings can be placed at the LPGs disposal. The Type III LPGs have all arable, meadow, pastureland, and woodland, besides all livestock in communal use and, to achieve large scale production, there is extensive reorganization of the field boundaries. In Types II and III, each family may retain a few head of livestock as well as half a hectare of ground for private use, and these types control 94 percent of all agricultural land and comprise over 80 percent of all undertakings. The LPG may be adapted for special use (such as horticulture) on similar principles. The Soviet-style state farm is represented in the G.D.R. by the *Volkseigene Güter*, publicly owned estates, which serve as pace-setters and experimental farms, some originating from confiscated Junker estates, others from prewar research stations or plant and animal breeding farms. These 'cultural strongpoints of the countryside' have nevertheless been criticized for high annual deficits, footed by the state. Modelled on factory principles, the *Güter* are generally larger than the LPGs and more mechanized. The workers, allowed less ground and fewer animals than on an LPG, can buy food from the *Gut* at low prices.

The radical reorganization of farming resulted in over 40,000 farmers, many of the most able and successful, fleeing the republic to West Germany, and agricultural labour declined as industry became more attractive and the flight to the west created a growing labour shortage. Country people formerly with part-time or seasonal employment in industry now found themselves faced with a choice of full-time employment in either industry or farming. Between 1950 and 1970, agricultural labour input for every 100 hectares of farmed land was nearly halved, though a larger proportion of the total employed population remains on the land than in the Federal Republic, whose observers feel gross overmanning still remains in farming in the 'other part of Germany'. Ageing of the farming labour force, through loss of young workers to industry, is slowly undermining its productive capacity: by 1980 this process alone will have reduced the labour force at its 1970 level by 40–50 percent.

The reorganization also brought visible changes in the landscape – the narrow strips of cropland and patches of enclosed meadow have been replaced by larger fields, especially where machinery has been introduced on a large scale. On many northern estates, groups of small houses mark the homes of the *Neubauern* of the early land reforms, mostly on the edge of the village or in place of the park and the mansion (some have been made into clubs and schools); while villages are being slowly rebuilt, with small blocks of flats and complexes of buildings for animals, machinery, and stores erected on the village outskirts.

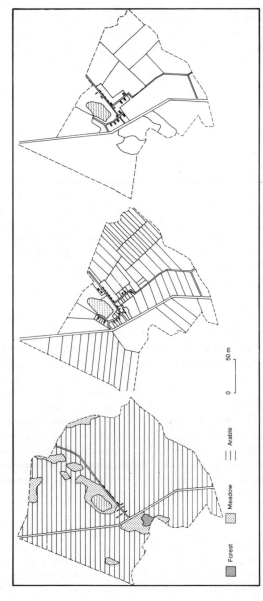

Figure 18.1 The new village and its lands in the G.D.R. On the left, the original estate in pre-1945 times; in the centre, the estate divided into small peasant holdings in the early post-1945 reforms; on the right, the estate after 1960 as a fully developed collective (LPG). The Laaske estate near Pritzwalk.

Agriculture and Forestry in the German Democratic Republic

394

The communal recreational buildings are often characterized by the banners and slogans so typical of the Soviet Union. Massive reorganization of farming has demanded substantial investment (though below the levels for industry), which has not been generally reflected in increased productivity of the land, largely the result of the long time needed to rectify the neglect of the war years. No substantial reserves of land suitable for agricultural use exist, and there is an annual loss of about 10,000 hectares to nonagricultural use, so that it has therefore been necessary to raise production through intensifying the use of land, with better yield per hectare against falling unit production costs. Farms have been grouped into land improvement units, investment made to improve farm land by better drainage, and other ameliorative works, though supply of fertilizers has been a bottleneck, partly because of the absence of adequate home resources of phosphatic minerals and partly because of the delay in reconstructing the chemicals industry after reparations dismantling; but use of some fertilizers in the 1960s caught up with (and in some instances overtook) the Federal Republic. To improve the use of fertilisers and pesticides, agro-chemical centres have been created to organize distribution and to arrange crop-spraying flights and other activities. Mechanization has been pressed but the apparent level is below the Federal Republic, though it is generally conceded that machinery in the G.D.R. is more intensively used and consequently more effective, attributed to the better size relationships and more appropriate organization of farms in the eastern state, though the radically different nature of farming makes comparison of limited validity.

The countryside is also being changed through the policy of concentration, specialization, and cooperation in agriculture. There is a growing division of LPGs between arable and livestock farming, with large farms dependent solely on pig or cattle raising, egg and poultry production, beginning to appear. Other processes such as drying green fodder, mixed fodder making, or pest control are also being separated from the LPGs. For the future, it is envisaged that these specialized undertakings will cooperate together and the units themselves will tend to increase in size and consequently become fewer in number, but the trend towards industrial methods in farming has encouraged closer links with food industries and commercial organizations. The reduction in number of LPGs through coalescence into larger units is expected to be greatest in the more densely settled southern districts, notably in the loessic *Börde*.

Land use and cropping
Compared to prewar and the immediate postwar years, there has been a small gain of pastureland at the expense of arable, though in both categories, land of marginal character used in the days of acute food shortage (1946–1950) has been abandoned: some has been afforested and the overall change has been

masked by modest land reclamation. Nevertheless, in population terms, there is a larger share of agriculturally used land per head in the G.D.R. (37.5 ha./100 inhabitants) than in the Federal Republic (24 ha/100 inhabitants), offset in part by the proportionally larger areas of poorer soils (notably light sandy glacial soils) and the less reliable climatic conditions (notably a tendency to drought) in the G.D.R. There has been some shift in the pattern of

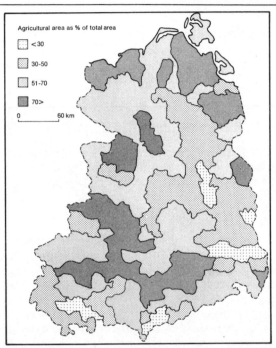

Figure 18.2 G.D.R. – Proportion of land used agriculturally

cropping, with cereals reduced in area compared to prewar and, in the late 1960s, rye conceded its dominant position to wheat. Potatoes have also declined in area, having reached their peak in the food shortage in the 1950s, whereas the emphasis on industrial crops has increased the importance of sugar beet, though it has tended to shift from the best loessic soils of the *Börde* into more northerly districts. The growing emphasis on livestock has tended to increase the sown area of fodder crops, especially for silage, though falling numbers of horses have been reflected in the decline of oats. Maize for green fodder has also become important following Soviet practices, though conditions are not always right. More attention has been given to oil-bearing crops

Agriculture and Forestry in the German Democratic Republic

to relieve a difficult position in the supply of fats. Whereas a critical structural problem in the agriculture of the European Community has been a tendency to overproduce, there has been a constant effort to increase production in the G.D.R., seeking a 90 percent level of self-sufficiency, with food imports limited to crops it cannot itself produce. Nevertheless, imports of grain, meat, fruit, and tobacco are still made from other COMECON members, and trade with developing countries has been used to augment food supplies.

Regional variations in farming

Regional differences in agriculture in the G.D.R. are marked by the proportion of land locally used for farming in contrast to forestry or mining; by local conditions of soil, climate, and relief that influence the relations between the proportions of arable, grass, or horticulture, as well as by the proportion of land remaining unused. Of the total area of the republic, almost 58 percent is used agriculturally and a little over 27 percent is forested, whereas buildings and transport facilities cover about 10 percent of the area. The proportion of land used agriculturally in any district varies considerably: in poor sandy areas, this may be less than 20 percent, but in the fertile loessic soils of the *Börde*, it may substantially exceed 75 percent. The major agricultural regions fit closely to the country's major landscapes. The northernmost region comprises the Baltic littoral and the northern morainic uplands extending south to the Prignitz and the Uckermark, characterized traditionally as a rye and potatoes region that has shifted towards wheat, sugar beet, and livestock. Much of the central part of the republic comprises a landscape of old meltwater channels and the southern heathlands associated with older morainic materials in the Fläming and Lower Lusatia: this is a region of livestock farming and dairying, with extensive forest and tracts of potato cultivation, though around Berlin special patterns are found. The most important region is clearly associated with the spread of loessic materials and related soil types across the southern part of the plain, lapping on to the footslope of the uplands and extending into the bays along the uplands' fretted northern edge. It is essentially arable *Börde* country of great wealth, but coinciding with some of the major industrial areas – notably lignite mining and chemicals. The southern uplands of very diverse character, including part of the great horst of the Harz, form a landscape of forested slopes, rolling upland pasture, with patches of arable and pasture in the valleys, though some wider basins and valleys support flourishing arable farming. Nevertheless, the uplands are basically livestock country, with sheep on the poorer parts.

The northern region of the younger morainic landscapes and the Baltic littoral has extensive patches of good brown forest soils, but also some poor sandy and wet soils, while the moister west and coastal belt is a weak contrast to the drier and cooler east. Prewar, this was a region with a large element of big estates,

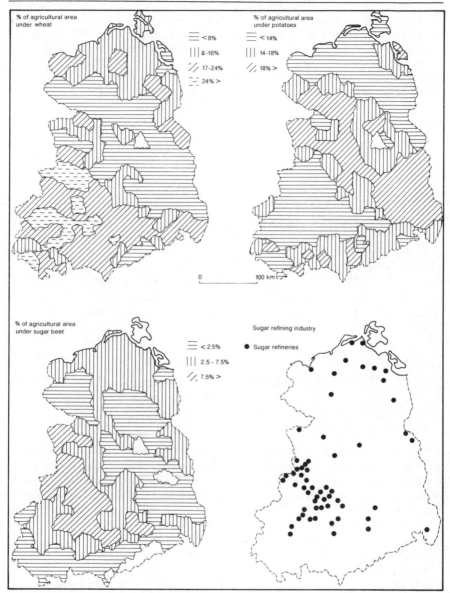

Figure 18.3 Areas of selected crops in the G.D.R.

but these have been divided among the peasants and collectivized or converted into state farms. The prewar estates were among the most efficient farms in the *Reich*, using considerable machinery and closely related to food processing industries (distilling, starch making, milling), thus, expectedly, some of the best state farms and several important research institutes, notably the centre for animal diseases on the island of Riems near Greifswald, lie in this region. Throughout this predominantly rural part attempts have been made to introduce new industries and reduce dependence on farming, especially in the small agricultural towns. The cropping pattern has changed from the strong prewar dependence on rye and potatoes, though these remain important, especially on the poorer soils; oats has also become less important, replaced by winter barley giving a much better yield, and is now found only in the moister coastal areas. Potatoes do well on the sandy soils that receive adequate summer precipitation, though the emphasis has shifted towards seed potatoes. They remain important around Pritzwalk, where pigs are also reared (there is everywhere some relation between potato production and pig rearing). Wheat, mostly summer varieties near the moister coast and winter wheat inland (for example, around Schwerin), has tended to replace rye. Sugar beet cultivation has also been encouraged, particularly (along with wheat) west of Wismar (other crops here include rape and oats) and in the broad morainic upland northwest-southeast of Neubrandenburg (where again wheat is important), while the Güstrow-Bützow area has become a major focus of sugar beet cultivation. Vegetable cultivation is mostly near the large towns, while winter rape is also a common crop (with one of the main areas near Schwerin), especially where there are heavy soils. Maize is particularly important around Neubrandenburg, where flax is grown as well. A general distinction can be made between the ground moraine on which most of the arable land occurs and the end moraines and their outwash that remain forest or heathland: gently undulating ground moraine allows use of machinery, for which the land parcels have been generally arranged.

In the undulating morainic country moist soil in hollows and along rivers provides good pastureland and meadows. To improve the more moist meadow, ameliorative works have been undertaken, notably near Pasewalk. Raising young stock is particularly important in the coastal meadows in the Darss and Fischland, while the Schwerin area is one of the most significant centres for pedigree cattle breeding. At Plau is one of the largest fur farms in the country (furriers are mostly concentrated in Berlin and Dresden), while Mecklenburg and Neuruppin continue as traditional horse breeding centres. In the east, the broad low meadows in the Peene and Ucker basins are especially significant cattle producers, and there is also much raising of geese; here have been established large new livestock producing units by grouping together LPGs.

The Two Germanies

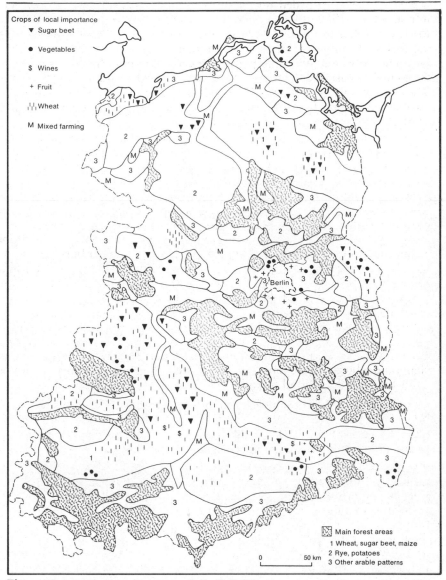

Crops of local importance
▼ Sugar beet
● Vegetables
$ Wines
+ Fruit
ıļı Wheat
M Mixed farming

Main forest areas
1 Wheat, sugar beet, maize
2 Rye, potatoes
3 Other arable patterns

0   50 km

Figure 18.4 Agricultural regions of the G.D.R.

Though the coastal area is in general one of the least forested parts of the republic, the end moraines inland carry extensive forest, mostly coniferous, though in the west – around Schwerin – there are stands of beech and oak. The Neubrandenburg area is the most heavily forested, particularly in the Ucker-mark. The many lakes and streams of the morainic plateau and the coastal belt provide an opportunity to farm fish (carp, pike, and trout) on a considerable scale.

The central agricultural region lies in the complex maze of channels, some used by modern drainage, others marshy and abandoned, of the meltwater system that converged around Berlin, and in the sandy heathlands and forests that stretch from Magdeburg to Cottbus. There is a good deal of standing water in lakes in the Mittelmark and broad moist depressions are typical of the Spreewald and the Havelland, while windblown sands from the meltwater streams lie along the interfluves, forming forested dune country. Before 1945, large holdings were common in this country and the emphasis on food produc-tion for the Berlin market had given an incentive to improve much ground. Rye, oats, and potatoes were long mainstays of farming, but wheat and sugar beet have become steadily more important, notably on the better soils of the ground moraine, while special cultures include hemp on the wet mineral soils of the Havelland and flax in Lusatia. The reclaimed land of the Oderbruch, east of Berlin, has wet mineral soils which, once effectively drained, are suited to wheat and sugar beet, and forms a major vegetable producing area, though glasshouses and irrigation are used to improve local climatic conditions. The Oder valley near Schwedt is one of the main tobacco producing areas, with the limited crop cured and processed locally. Cherries, apples, pears, and plums are grown around Berlin, though the Werder district near Potsdam is the most productive, with the fruit gardens gathered into LPGs and considerable rationalization of the crops undertaken; other vegetable and fruit districts are Fürstenberg and Oranienburg; Beelitz (Potsdam) has a long tradition of asparagus cultivation; Berlin's sewage fields remain productive; and the Spreewald grows in particular gherkins and pumpkins.

The meadows of the meltwater channels provide pasture for meat and dairy livestock, and the Potsdam district has been selected to concentrate on dairy produce for Berlin. Pig rearing is important around Frankfurt an der Oder and in the Fläming. In order to support an increased density of animals, emphasis has been on improving the yield of pasture rather than expanding the area under fodder crops, though fodder maize is common in *Bezirk* Frankfurt.

The extensive sands and dunes of the central region make it one of the most heavily forestered in the republic, so that in the *Bezirk* Potsdam about one-third of the area is under forest, mostly coniferous, but forest is particularly extensive in the sandy *Bezirk* Cottbus (42 percent of the area), with pine most common on afforested abandoned lignite pits. Extensive coniferous woodland occurs west of the Elbe in the Altmark, especially in the Letzlinger Heide, where otherwise pasture is common, and livestock is reared to be fattened in the southern *Börde* country. The Fläming, with its sands and rust-coloured woodland soils, is extensively forested as it is otherwise poor agricultural country devoted mostly to potatoes and rye, though a dusting of *loess* improves the soils in the east.

The broad belt of country running southeastwards from Magdeburg towards Dresden and its outliers in the Thuringian basin is the richest agricultural part of the G.D.R., whose extensive treeless plains with nucleated villages have best fitted the application of socialist-style mechanized agriculture, so that its many medium and small farmers early experienced the application of collectivization. The main problem of this belt, especially around Halle and Leipzig, is the clash between the needs of farming and those of the lignite-mining industry, though this is also a belt which contains other industries with considerable demands for space and which produce undesirable effluents or demand large quantities of process water. The best soils are the rich, dark earths developed in relatively dry lee situations over *loess*, but some good dark brown forest soils have also developed over *loess* where there is greater precipitation. Heavier moist mineral soils of the river valleys, though suited to arable cultivation, form in particular pasture because of the high water table and liability to flooding. The Magdeburger *Börde* is one of the most fertile farming areas of Central Europe, where sugar beet and winter wheat, both exceptionally demanding crops, flourish – in the *Kreise* Wanzleben and Oschersleben, 40 percent of the agricultural area is devoted to them. Summer barley is frequently associated with the winter wheat rotation. The light loessic soils, liable to drought in the lee of the uplands to the west and southwest, are readily subject to wind erosion, and through the 1960s, planting of shelter belts was undertaken, based on Soviet experience in the southern Ukraine. Eastwards, loessic patches and loamy soils are cultivated in the Lommatzscher Pflege for wheat, sugar beet, and for brewing barley (also grown near Artern, Sangershausen, and Querfurt on the west), while the Grossenhainer Pflege and the Klosterpflege (near Kamenz) are principally cultivated for rye and wheat; but sugar beet has been introduced between Kamenz and Bautzen through the LPGs, since previously the small Sorbian peasants' holdings were unsuitable for this crop. Sugar beat, a particularly significant crop, not only in the Magdeburger *Börde*, but also around Halle and Leipzig, suffers occurrence of endemic pests limiting its possibilities of expansion, so that, since the German Democratic Republic produces more sugar than it requires and also must accept some cane sugar in trade with Cuba, encouragement has been given to crops in which self-sufficiency is still to be attained; for example, grains in which the country is still only three-quarters self-sufficient. The

Thuringian Basin and the smaller Goldene Aue also count as part of this region and exhibit great fertility and, though liable to dryness in their lee position, are exceptionally good grain country, with long, dry, and warm late summers, but sugar beet, lucerne, and brewing barley are also widely cultivated. Hops have been introduced since 1945 by expellees from the Sudetenland, while the Goldene Aue is noted for its tobacco and the excellence of its grain for distilling.

Within the *Börde* region there is widespred cultivation of vegetables for the many industrial towns, particularly around the margins; and the Harz foreland is noted for its fruit. The *loess* covered basin near Zittau in the east is renowned for onions, cabbages, and cauliflowers, but other important centres are Halle, Aschersleben, Bernburg, and Quedlinburg (the latter for seeds and flowers). Erfurt has a particularly strong reputation for horticulture and is the seat of the COMECON International Horticultural Exhibition, a companion to the International Agricultural Exhibition at Markkleeberg near Leipzig. In the Unstrut valley and between Naumburg and Weissenfels in the Saale valley the vine flourishes, though its wines are not of outstanding quality: remains of a once more extensive vine-growing area are found along the Elbe around Meissen, Weinbühla, Radebeul, and Pillnitz; otherwise, the Elbe valley is known for its apples, pears, plums, and cherries.

Over wide areas of the *Börde*, pastureland is virtually absent, though nevertheless livestock farming is important. Green maize (and a little corn maize) is now commonly grown as fodder, for which rye and potatoes are also used, but the major source of fodder is the waste of sugar beet – leaves, roots, and factory waste – of which large amounts are available from October to April, when the factories fill the air with an unpleasant sweet aroma. Pigs are especially significant, now raised in large and specialized farm units, under which system poultry is also kept: a specialized pig farm with 24,000 animals and a poultry farm producing eggs from over 100,000 laying places are typical. Cattle are stall fed and few are seen except on the rich meadows along the rivers. Dairying (especially fresh milk production) is important for the industrial towns. Young stock is imported from northern areas. Large farming units are again typical.

The southern uplands and the Harz show agriculture influenced strongly by elevation, aspect, and slope, while micro-climatological features, such as cold-air drainage, also play a not insignificant part. Soils are equally variable, generally related closely to local lithological conditions. Forest is extensive and forms a mainstay of the local economy, whereas arable farming is secondary to livestock; but where it is carried on, fodder crops form a major element, though there are large proportions of rye and potatoes. South of the Thüringer Wald lies a small favoured area of most fertile country, an outlier of the Grabfeld, where wheat and oilseeds are raised, while there is some tobacco growing in the Werra valley. Intense fragmentation of holdings around Suhl, legacy of the old system of divided inheritance, raised special problems in organizing LPGs, which also faced the problem of a mixed peasant economy bringing together farming and domestic industry, but in general throughout the uplands the small size of settlements made organization of LPGs difficult, solved by moving people into the few larger centres with a better infrastructure. Angle of slope and the rough access to many patches of cultivation has made the reorganization of land parcels into larger units and introduction of mechanization especially problematical, yet, on the other hand, livestock farming has been easily put into the socialist pattern, with the formation of large LPGs closely tied to the food-processing industry. In the Erzgebirge, the emphasis has been on meat and milk production for the industrial towns to the north, but in the *Bezirk* Gera, poultry keeping and fish rearing (around Schleiz) have been developed, though dairying is also significant. A shift to livestock farming has been part of efforts made in the Erzgebirge to reduce unrewarding culture, like grains, practised by the old peasant system, and the altitudinal limit of arable farming has been considerably lowered. In the eastern part of the Thüringer Wald, sheep remain important, as they do on some other higher and poorer surfaces, but keeping goats has been discouraged. The Harz is extensively forested and has little arable farming, depending mostly on livestock raising.

Forestry

With forest covering more than one-fourth of the area of the G.D.R., its role in the economy is expectedly substantial, though it has been generally pushed to the poorer ground and, as in the West, forests have been shifting from purely economic production to amenity and conservation. Old usages, such as cattle and pig grazing in the forests, or charcoal making, have declined: it is no longer permitted to take pine needles and other floor deposits as bedding for stalls and the last remnants of beekeeping in the forests have disappeared. A little over 1 percent of the forest is classed as protective – mostly on steep slopes – while more than 25 percent is in the 'special' category (mostly of an amenity nature), and just over 75 percent is regarded as primarily wood-producing. Overcutting during the war and in the immediate postwar period has been offset by an active afforestation programme.

The main forests are in the uplands and on the rust-coloured forest soils or sands: the least forested areas are the loessic spreads and the riverine lands with a high water table (where the poplar is common). About 58 percent of the forest land is covered by pine, the least demanding of trees after birch, while some 22 percent is under spruce and fir: in all 80 percent of the forest area is coniferous. About 5 percent is under oak, a further 5 percent under birch and lime, and 10 percent under beech. Conifers predominate in the uplands, notably spruce, while fir is extensive in the lowlands. Deciduous trees are common on the better lands in the lowlands, notably in Mecklenburg, though towards the coast, where there is more precipitation, spruce is important. Lusatia and Brandenburg, with some very poor soils, have low-demanding conifers and large tracts of birch. Species have been influenced by past policy, notably the extensive stands of spruce in Saxony. In some parts, pollution has done substantial damage to woodlands – for example, sulphur dioxide emissions east of Bitterfeld, where experiments have been conducted to find more resistant species. Some of the largest continuous forest areas lie in the Fläming, in the Altmark, in Brandenburg, and in Lower Lusatia in the lowlands, but all the uplands carry large forests.

The main uses to which wood is put are for poles and planks (46 percent – notably conifers); cellulose and pulp (21 percent mostly spruce, fir, and beech); pit props (8 percent – particularly spruce); firewood (as much as 7 percent). Transport of wood is relatively short distance to a wide scatter of sawmills, though timber for pulping and veneers is carried over considerable distances. A major problem in the forests is the high average age of the labour force (which is ten years above the national average). Besides trying to improve yield by fertilizing and better drainage, access is also being improved by better forest roads, and mechanization has been introduced where possible.

Suggested further reading

Lendl, E.: Die mitteleuropäische Kulturlandschaft im Umbruch der Gegenwart, Marburg, 1951.

Ogrissek, R.: Dorf und Flur in der DDR, Leipzig, 1961.

Roubitschek, W.: Die regionale Differenzierung der agraren Bodennutzung 1935 im heutigen Gebiet der DDR, *P.M.* 103, 1959, pp.109–197.

Die regionale Struktur der pflanzlichen Bruttoproduktion in der DDR 1955 und ihre Veränderung gegenüber 1935, *P.M.* 108, 1964, pp.69–78.

Standortkräfte in der Landwirtschaft der DDR – Agrargeographische Gemeindetypen, Leipzig, 1969.

Stanek, I.: Landwirtschaft in Ost und West – ein Vergleich ausgewählter Agrarsysteme, Stuttgart, 1973.

————————————CHAPTER 19————————————

TRANSPORT AND THE TERTIARY SECTOR IN THE GERMAN DEMOCRATIC REPUBLIC

The creation of occupation zones in 1945 and the surrender of territory to Poland paid little attention to transport networks, and the G.D.R. thus found itself with two new international boundaries: on the east, the boundary with Poland ran along the Oder river, one of the main traffic waterways, and gave to Poland the port of Stettin; on the west, the new boundary cut across the road and railway system in one of its busiest and densest sections, severed the Elbe waterway to Hamburg, and left jagged ends of motorways hanging limp at the border. Deprived of easy access to its main prewar ports and not anxious to depend on its neighbours, a new main port had to be found. The division of Berlin, and the isolation of the western sectors, was accompanied by attempts by the G.D.R. to avoid using the transport links passing through West Berlin, so creating another problem in providing routes for new flows around it, a problem made no easier by the role of Berlin in prewar times as the major focus in North Germany that had resulted in a dense and complex system of routes. Furthermore, the association of the G.D.R. with the Soviet *bloc* put it in a group of states with a different transport mix and a different pattern of demand to that inherited from prewar Germany, so that consequently the development of the transport system has shown markedly different trends to that in the Federal Republic.

Railways
Following the other countries of the socialist *bloc*, the G.D.R. has placed the mainstay of its transport on the railways, brought increasingly into line

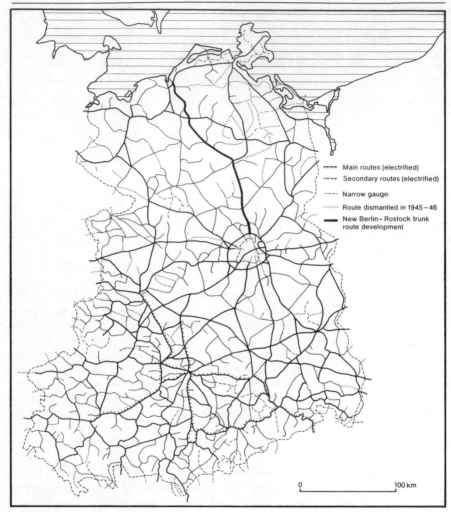

Figure 19.1 G.D.R. railway system

technically and operationally with those of Eastern Europe and the Soviet Union. Only in the latter 1960s has motor transport come to play a significant role in short-distance haulage of goods and passengers. The railway system was changed by the heavy dismantling – double track was reduced from 37 percent of the route to 10 percent and there was complete removal of the tracks from many northern cross country lines, though in the 1960s plans to redouble

The Two Germanies

some busy sections and rebuild some completely dismantled sections were formulated. Although mainline electrification equipment was completely removed in 1945, the reelectrification of mainlines began again in the late 1950s. But whereas prewar plans had been to electrify the mainlines radiating from Berlin to the principal provincial centres, postwar the aim has been to electrify only heavily laden goods routes (especially where there are serious gradients) in the Elbe-Saale basin and immediately adjacent areas (the so-called 'Saxon Ring'). Typical of many railway systems, 90 percent of all traffic is on less than 30 percent of the route length.

The new border with Poland caused considerable disruption, though the route from Görlitz to Zittau, an important freight link, along the Polish bank of the Oder is operated for the Germans by the Polish state railways. International freight and passenger traffic uses the frontier points of Frankfurt/Oder and Görlitz, and freight traffic runs from the G.D.R. to Stettin, now Polish. Railway access to Usedom has been cut by the new Polish boundary and the island railways can now only be reached by ferry at Wolgast. Along the border with Czechoslovakia, only two international lines operate, and the Germans have surrendered their prewar operating rights on the line through the salient of Czech territory near Aš (Asch). The overwhelming bulk of German–Czech traffic crosses at Bad Schandau and electrification is proposed for this Dresden-to-Prague route. Of over forty prewar routes across the border with the Federal Republic, only five remain open, not all for both goods and passengers. In order to avoid using the railways through West Berlin (only the main east-west international trunk route remains operative), the northern and final section of the Berlin outer ring line was completed in 1955. Using largely existing sections of railway (some only rural lines), a new trunk route from the Berlin area to the port of Rostock is being developed, but other new building has been limited to freight and commuter traffic routes in the Halle-Leipzig area.

Railway traffic
The railway directorates of Halle and Cottbus generate about 60 percent of all dispatched tonnage, but account for only 30 percent of the arrivals tonnage, reflecting big shipments from these directorates of lignite; but in the Halle area potash salts are also a major item, just as stone, gravel, and sand are important in Cottbus. The arrivals traffic is more scattered than dispatches, though Halle, Dresden (unloading 25 percent of all wagons), and Magdeburg directorates together account for 60 percent of all arrivals, mostly raw materials for manufacturing industry, fuels, and food supplies. Arrivals of fuel are especially important in the northern directorates of Schwerin and Greifswald. About 30 percent of all traffic moves within the same railway directorate. The majority of large marshalling yards lie in Saxony, but the

Magdeburg directorate is also important and the Berlin district handles the bulk of international transit and other traffic, mostly through the marshalling yard at Seddin to the southwest. It is estimated that 60 percent of all Swedish international railway transit traffic passes by rail ferries through the G.D.R., and a considerable transit traffic moves from Czechoslovakia and even Hungary to Rostock. The growing container traffic to Western Europe from Japan via the Trans-Siberian Railway largely finds its way westwards through the G.D.R. (about one-fifth of all traffic is containerized, but this is expected to rise to over 50 percent by the late 1970s).

Passenger traffic includes the main international links between Moscow and Warsaw and Western Europe and the north-south Scandinavian–Danubian axis (dependent on the Baltic ferries), while the G.D.R. is joined to the system of expresses linking together the capitals of the East *bloc* states. Despite an appreciable increase in the number of trains running between the two German states, through services remain a mere shadow of prewar densities; for example, in 1939, 21 trains a day passed the present zonal border at Büchen; in 1969, this figure had fallen to 3; and on the Bebra-Gerstungen section, the number had fallen from 33 to only 2. An important summer traffic is formed by tourist trains from the republic to such destinations as the Black Sea coast or to the various coastal and inland holiday places within the republic, while the twice yearly Leipzig Fair also creates a special traffic. Within the republic, there is a modest density of trains between the main towns, with commuter traffic in the southern industrial districts, but unlike West Germany the number of daily trains is still less than before 1939. Apart from the east-west international trains through Berlin and the trains joining West Berlin to the Federal Republic, the railway system of West Berlin since 1961 has been self-contained, with realigning of tracks where necessary.

Road haulage
Compared to the massive motorway investment in the Federal Republic, there has been a negligible addition to the road system in the G.D.R. Only in the early 1970s was the important Leipzig-Dresden motorway completed, while the northern part of the Berlin ring motorway still remains unfinished, largely because its prewar planned alignment would carry it through the northern tip of West Berlin and a new route must now be designed. Most likely to be carried out is the Berlin–Rostock motorway, giving access to the republic's main port, while another route (of less priority) is from Magdeburg to Halle, and plans for motorway access to Czechoslovakia have been discussed. By the mid-1960s the tonnage handled by road haulage exceeded that handled by the railways, though in traffic effort (t/km) the railways were still clearly predominant, with the average length of rail haul six times that of road haulage. But road haulage has taken over completely from railways on many lightly loaded routes. The

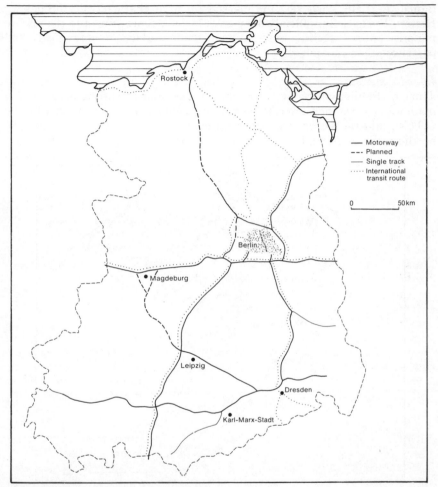

Figure 19.2 Motorways in the G.D.R.

main items in road haulage are building materials and foodstuffs, and most effort is in the south of the country: almost half the tonnage handled by lorries arises in the *Bezirke* of Karl-Marx-Stadt, Dresden, Leipzig, and Halle. The total number of passengers handled by buses has exceeded railways since 1962, and a wide network of buses has taken over increasingly from trains on lightly used cross-country routes, though journey length is short. The private motor car remains, however, much less important than in Western Europe,

Transport and the Tertiary Sector in the German Democratic Republic

410

though the late 1960s saw the marked upsurge characteristic throughout Eastern Europe. But official policy gives little encouragement to the private motorist. Most recently, international road haulage of both goods and passengers has expanded.

Inland waterways

Though the division of Germany created boundaries cutting across many main waterways, they nevertheless remain of considerable importance for the G.D.R., and the system has two main features: natural waterways provide north-south routes, while east-west links are provided by canals mostly follow-

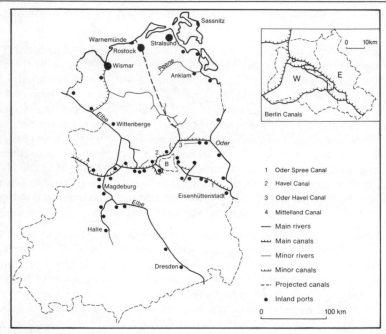

Figure 19.3 Inland waterways and ports of the G.D.R.

ing the natural depressions of the old meltwater channels. Although some 2519 kilometres are regarded as navigable, 1400 kilometres form the main waterway system, about 80 percent comprising natural watercourses. The main artery is the Elbe, which prewar was Germany's second most important waterway, but its general European importance has been reduced by being cut by the new inter-German frontier, so isolating the upstream sections from Hamburg at its mouth. Though the capacity of the Elbe in the republic is commonly given as 1350 ton barges, throughout the long period of summer low water it is possible to use barges of only 750 tons. The meandering Saale is used for navigation as far as Halle, despite long periods of both low and high water that make navigation impossible (750-ton barges can be used in general only for 170 days fully laden). The Havel, with several lakes along its course, has a more regular water level, but is important only from Zehdenick, while its use through West Berlin between Spandau and Potsdam is nowadays avoided and a 35-kilometre-long canal has been built to avoid barges going through West Berlin. The Oder, now the frontier with Poland, will carry 750-ton barges: for the Germans, it is most important between Eisenhüttenstadt and the entrance to the Oder-Havel Canal. Like all rivers in the G.D.R., it suffers more from ice than those in the Federal Republic, while it also has a long summer low water period, and the Poles claim navigation is hindered as a result of overstraightening last century.

Using the broad depressions of the old meltwater channels, the Oder and Elbe waterway systems are linked by the Elbe-Havel Canal that joins the Havel Canal around Berlin to the Oder-Havel Canal. The Spree-Oder Canals can be reached from the Elbe only via West Berlin. Access by the Rothensee ship lift on the Elbe near Magdeburg can be had to the Mittelland Canal that runs westwards into the Federal Republic, but prewar plans for an aqueduct across the river to give direct access to Berlin were never completed. These canals can all take vessels up to 1000 tons. Small navigable rivers and canals in Brandenburg and Mecklenburg are of no importance, while the Unstrut above Halle is no longer navigated. A major proposal has been a 150-kilometre-long canal to join the Elbe at Wittenberge to Rostock (or alternatively from this port to Berlin), while a better direct Elbe-Oder link has been suggested.

Limitations are placed on water transport because the estuarine ports of the Oder and Elbe do not lie within G.D.R. territory, while in general the waterways do not form major links between industry and its raw material sources. Some important industrial districts are anyway without waterway connections, while Rostock, now the main port, has no waterway as yet into the interior. The waterways could in general, however, take greater volumes of traffic: it is reckoned that the Saale carries only 10 percent of its possible potential. The busiest sections are the Oder-Elbe links and the middle Elbe, with Magdeburg one of the busiest inland ports, and over two-thirds of all waterborne traffic occurs between Magdeburg, Potsdam, Berlin, and Frankfurt/Oder. Lignite, building materials, and bulk chemicals (important upstream freight on the Elbe into Czechoslovakia), along with some iron goods, are the main cargoes. Passenger traffic is mostly on the Elbe (especially above Dresden), in and around Berlin, and on the lakes around Schwerin. There is some international traffic in freight from Poland to West Germany and the Netherlands, mostly in Polish vessels, while Czechoslovakian freight still operates to Hamburg.

Transport and the Tertiary Sector in the German Democratic Republic

The port problem

With the loss of Stettin to Poland and the political undesirability of using Hamburg in the Federal Republic, the G.D.R. found the need to develop its own major national port. The choice lay between Rostock, Stralsund, and Wismar, which together before the war had not handled more than 1 million tons of cargo. In 1957, a plan to develop Rostock was begun, but as the existing port lay 13 kilometres up the shallow Warnow, liable to silting and a difficult navigational entry, it was decided to build a new overseas port downstream at Rostock-Petersdorf, with ultimately an oil terminal in the sheltered basin of the Breitling. Unfortunately, there is little hope of expanding the port's facilities to handle ships much in excess of 35,000 tons. The port has been equipped for a rapid turnover of vessels and its railway and road links with the interior improved, while a railway ferry operates to Denmark from Rostock-Warnemünde. Nearly 90 percent of the cargo turnover is in imports (crude oil, apatite, bituminous coal, ores, phosphates, citrus fruits, and raw sugar). Cement, beet sugar, and industrial goods are exported. Oil comes mostly in medium-sized tankers which have loaded in Rotterdam from supertankers.

Wismar was the largest port until the opening of the overseas harbour at Rostock, but its harbour is less easy to dredge and navigation more difficult than at Rostock. Improvement of the railway and road links inland presented more problems, though the relatively little war damage had given it an initial advantage. Exports are mostly potash fertilizers, mineral oil products, and raw pig iron, while wood and grain are the chief imports. It is also a port for passenger traffic.

Stralsund on the protected strait of the Strelasund is relatively small and has only 6 metres of water at the quays while approach is difficult and more seriously affected by ice than either Rostock or Wismar. It is principally engaged in trade with small Baltic coastal vessels, and there has been a shift to a greater emphasis on exports, notably brown coal briquettes to Scandinavia, but salt and fertilizers are also important. Wood and ores are the main imports. Sassnitz, the railway ferry port for Sweden, is also a major fishing centre.

Air transport

With relatively short internal distances, air transport is unimportant, though the republic has a small airline – *Interflug* – which also carries out agricultural spraying and related work. Regular international flights began in 1956 from East Berlin to Warsaw, followed by flights to other Eastern European capitals and to Moscow, and from 1958 *Interflug* aircraft joined the service. The main airport is Berlin–Schönefeld, now with regular links to over 20 places in Europe, Africa, and Asia. Dresden also became an international airport in 1967 and serves as the diversionary field for Berlin and for the twice yearly

Leipzig Trade Fairs: it is the main freight airport in the republic. Leipzig-Schkeuditz also has international traffic, greatest at fair time, but Leipzig-Mockau, Erfurt, Barth (Ostsee), and Heringsdorf are of local importance, with summer services only from the latter.

Table 19.1

Transport – percentage shares of different media

Goods transport	1950	1956	1962	1968	1973
		– percent of national total –			
Railways T:	59.6	51.1	44.8	37.1	32.9
T/km:	81.0	81.6	62.8	38.5	32.3
Roads T:	38.6	45.6	52.8	58.6	61.3
T/km:	10.4	10.5	9.6	9.3	9.8
Inland waterways T:	4.4	3.3	2.0	1.9	1.5
T/km:	8.5	6.8	3.6	2.4	1.3
Maritime shipping T:	—	x	0.5	1.1	1.3
T/km:	—	1.2	24.0	49.0	54.1
Civil airlines T:	—	—	—	x	x
T/km:	—	—	—	x	x
Pipelines T:	—	—	—	1.3	2.9
T/km:	—	—	—	0.7	2.4

T   = Tonnage originating
T/km = Traffic in ton-kilometres
x   = Quantity too small to include

Passenger transport	1950	1960	1965	1970	1973
		– percent of national total –			
Railways P:	33.7	26.1	19.4	18.0	17.1
P/km:	68.2	54.6	45.2	41.5	42.8
Roads P:	3.9	19.1	27.1	32.7	33.8
P/km:	7.0	25.5	34.9	40.6	40.2
Urban transport P:	62.1	64.5	53.6	49.2	48.9
P/km:	24.2	18.9	18.1	14.8	14.1
Inland waterways P:	0.2	0.2	0.3	0.2	0.2
P/km:	0.6	0.5	0.6	0.5	0.5
Maritime shipping P:	—	x	x	x	x
P/km:	—	0.1	0.2	0.2	0.1
Civil airlines P:	—	x	x	x	x
P/km:	—	0.4	1.0	2.2	2.3

P   = Passengers originating
P/km = Traffic in passenger-kilometres
x   = Quantity too small to include

Source: Statistisches Jahrbuch der DDR, Berlin, 1974

Transport and the Tertiary Sector in the German Democratic Republic

The tertiary sector in the G.D.R.

Though the tertiary sector has become more important during the 1960s in the G.D.R., it still remains less significant than in the Federal Republic and displays a different character. Much of the difference can be attributed to the contrasts in the economic systems of the two states. Although the infrastructure inherited from prewar is still visible, it is being constantly changed through the central and planned direction of all economic and social activities. Planners in the G.D.R. accept the concept of central places as service centres and seek to plan their nature and distribution. The large bureaucratic structure of the centrally directed state means that governmental functions are particularly important in the towns that serve as seats for the *Bezirk* and *Kreis* administrations, but within the relatively small territorial framework of the state, Berlin as capital exerts an extremely strong influence. As the state controls all the retail outlets (apart from a few small private shops) and commercial functions like banking and insurance, competition is absent and these services can be planned to serve set populations, with any overlap between catchment areas eliminated. Similarly, the distribution of medical and educational services has been rationalized to the same pattern, with concentration into large units: exceptions are usually inherited situations of prewar institutions, like the universities of Jena and Greifwald or the mining academy at Freiberg. The distribution of central places in the hierarchy is expectedly denser in the more thickly settled industrial south than in the agricultural north, while for retail outlets the density and range is also greater in the wealthier industrial parts of Saxony and Berlin.

Provision of recreational and holiday facilities has been recognized as an important contribution to the efficiency of the state in the Eastern *bloc* countries, so that existing infrastructure has been carefully expanded along set lines. In the G.D.R., however, there has not been the explosion in this activity witnessed in the Federal Republic and again the character has been different, with state monopoly and planning predominant. Much of this branch is promoted by the labour organizations and by the state travel agency, with every encouragement for group travel. The independent motorized tourist is relatively unimportant still. Foreign visitors also form a greatly smaller element than in West Germany and anyway come mostly from COMECON states (especially Czechoslovakia, Poland, and the Soviet Union), just as East Germans mostly go to these countries (chiefly Czechoslovakia, Poland, and Bulgaria). Tourists from Western countries are relatively few, while impedances are still put in the way of movement between the two German states, just as movement between the Federal Republic and West Berlin across the G.D.R. is by strictly defined routes and somewhat uncertain.

The G.D.R. offers a wide range of tourist and recreational landscapes. The

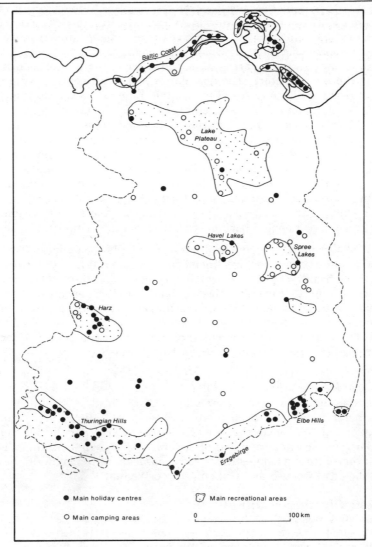

Figure 19.4 Tourism in the G.D.R.

Transport and the Tertiary Sector in the German Democratic Republic

Baltic coast has numerous pleasant resorts, notably Ahlbeck, Heringsdorf, Hiddensèe, Kühlungsborn, Prerow, and Graal-Müritz, mostly first developed in the latter nineteenth century. Attractive leisure activities are also possible in the Mecklenburg lake country, where over half the republic's camping places lie, and similar possibilities are available on waterways around Berlin, mostly used by short-stay visitors. The heathlands and forest country within easy reach of Berlin and the towns of the middle Elbe valley are also much frequented – the Fläming, Altmark, Dübener Heide, Schorfheide, and the so-called 'Märkische Schweiz'. The rolling forested country of the southern uplands is especially popular and is easily accessible to the main industrial towns. The chief districts are the Thüringer Wald, the Harz, and the Erzgebirge, while the combination of the river, unusual scenery and good communications makes the Elbe Sandstone Mountains (Saxon Switzerland) most attractive, with Bad Schandau, Bad Gottleuba, and Königstein the main centres. Oberhof and Brotterode in the Thüringer Wald and Oberwiesenthal in the Erzgebirge among other centres have a notable winter sports season.

As in West Germany, spas and health resorts still play a significant role, with long-stay guests sent for treatment and recuperation by factory and institutional health schemes. Several important spas, as in West Germany, lie on the coast; others are in the southern uplands; but there are also others in the central moor and heathlands. Mineral springs or particularly good bioclimatic conditions are important locational factors: of special interest is Radiumbad Brambach in the Vogtland where natural radioactive sources are harnessed. Nearly one-fifth of all spas lie in *Bezirk* Karl-Marx-Stadt.

The large cities attract many visitors: Leipzig has a special place with its spring and autumn trade fair and Berlin is a major focus for foreign visitors, with its museums and other monuments, like Dresden, several of whose architectural gems have been rebuilt. Potsdam is visited for its political associations of the Cecilienhof and Sans-Souci Palace. 'Political' sites are indeed stressed and large numbers of visitors pass through them annually, like the old concentration camp sites at Ravensbrück and Buchenwald, but also towns such as Eisenach and Guben or even Weimar.

Suggested further reading

Dörschel, W.: Verkehrsgeographie, *Lehrbuch für die Deutsche Reichsbahn* 4, Berlin, 1968.
Kohl, H. (ed.): Die Bezirke der Deutschen Demokratischen Republik, Berlin, 1974.
Kohl, H., et al.: Ökonomische Geographie DDR, Berlin, 1969, 2nd ed. 1976.

CHAPTER 20

BERLIN – THE DIVIDED CITY

The focal point of prewar Germany, Berlin is perhaps best considered in its present politically divided condition apart from the two German states. The origin of its present political status is discussed in Chapter 5; it is here the intention to examine the geographical problems that beset the divided city. The western part of the city under Western Allied administration is now a separate political entity, part of the Federal Republic with certain reservations; the Soviet sector of the city has become an integral part of the German Democratic Republic, which it serves as capital. West Berlin is completely isolated from the countryside around and to a large measure from East Berlin, though since 1970 this has been eased a little.

Reconstruction has consequently taken place under two contrasting régimes, with different concepts and under different pressures, though in both parts planning is under the strong influence of history – the need to maintain a belief in the ultimate reunification of Germany (and consequently Berlin) in some form or other. The early postwar 'Collective Plan' for all Berlin was cast in a linear pattern. The central business and administrative district was seen extending along an axis from the Silesian Station in the east to the Charlottenburg-Zoo area in the west. The main industrial zones were planned on the upper Spree (Rummelsburg-Schönweide-Wildau), on the lower part of the Spree, and along the Havel in Spandau, and it was hoped to parallel such areas of employment by residential districts separated by green belts, primarily in an attempt to restrict commuting. The chaotic prewar mixture of housing and industry was to be broken down into large coherent residential areas, with a maximum density of 250 persons per square kilometre. The main waterways and lakes, as well as the forests, were to be developed as amenity areas, while local and long-distance traffic were to be separated and prewar points of congestion eliminated. This plan, designed for a future population of 3.5 million people, was, however, dependent on Berlin remaining the capital of a united Germany, so retaining its high-level administrative and economic functions, while it was also to remain a major industrial centre, despite wartime decentralization.

West Berlin

Within five years of the end of the Second World War, the division of Berlin was complete: by 1961 the final isolation of the western sectors had come. For political reasons, a Western presence *had* to be kept in West Berlin which *had* to be seen as associated with the West German state, though within a strict legal interpretation of four-power agreements. It was, however, important to both sectors of the divided city that nothing should be done which could be seen as renouncing hope of one Germany, even if the aspiration seemed distant and unreal. In this political atmosphere and isolation, the need in West Berlin was to develop an economy and living space that allowed it to remain viable and to accept its isolation, though people sense the claustrophobic atmosphere. In many respects West Berlin is like an island nearly 200 kilometres from its mainland. Though the four-power agreement of 1970 brought hope for a détente in Berlin, its real effect has been limited and the hostility of the G.D.R. for West Berlin as an outlier of the Federal Republic remains.

West Berlin's population is likely to fall slowly and continuously to the end of the century, with natural decrease rising into the mid-1980s and easing a little thereafter, while at the same time there will be a slight fall in the number of employable persons, though their proportion in the total population will also increase a little towards the end of the century. Indeed, the considerably larger element of old people compared to the Federal Republic and even the G.D.R. has raised numerous social and economic problems, as have the lower proportion of children and the higher ratio of women to men. Decline would have been faster had it not been for modest immigration into West Berlin, though a large proportion of this has been transient foreign workers. Until 1961 West Berlin had benefited from a net inflow of refugees from the G.D.R. (many of them East Berliners), but there has been little attraction to migrate to West Berlin from the Federal Republic: it is no longer, as in prewar days, the centre for career advancement, and higher salaries do not offset the more expensive cost of living, besides the claustrophobia and long-term uncertainty of life there. Attempts to lure young people from West Germany attracted few permanent residents, so that by the latter 1960s many less attractive jobs could

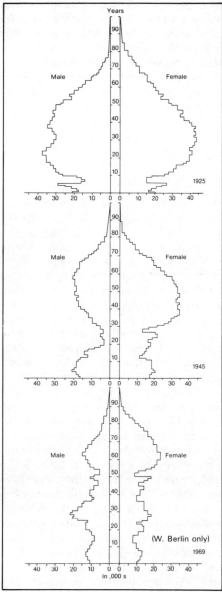

Figure 20.1 Age and sex structure of the Berlin population

only be filled by employing non-German guest workers, and the high proportion of young unmarried males also suggests a large itinerant population. Many young married couples in Berlin have migrated to the better security and employment in West Germany, so depriving the city of many children. The high proportion of old people in the city's population is further complicated by the high proportion of older women whose longer expectation of life aggravates the difficulties. The labour situation was particularly acute immediately after the raising of the Wall (1961) cut off 76,000 East Berliners who worked in the Western sector (the reverse flow was, however, only 13,000). The wisdom of introducing foreign labour into West Berlin has been questioned and policy is now to harness more of the local female population and even older people to suitable jobs (often part-time), which also helps to reduce the heavy social welfare costs.

The isolation of West Berlin has forced its redevelopment to make it independent of adjacent territories and to create an environment that does not leave an undue feeling of being beleaguered. Fortunately, in West Berlin there is a great deal of open space in its woods and lakes, but modern standards of housing demand more land for given numbers of people, though planners have been acutely aware of how careful land use must be in such an inelastic situation, even if the stagnant-to-declining population does reduce some pressure on land. Planning in West Berlin has sought to avoid recreating the massive prewar concentration of commuters into the city centre: there has been a distinct decentralization into several separate foci, which reputedly helps to reduce the claustrophobic feeling. In all quarters of the town, the aim has been to build new residential districts with a balanced social mix and approximately equal attractiveness and to provide them with greenery and recreational facilities. Among the more successful newer quarters are the Hansa Viertel (designed by international experts) and the improvements to the prewar Siemensstadt; but there are also some less successful schemes like the impersonal Märkisches Viertel. These residential areas and their shopping subcentres have been linked together by public transport and a system of urban motorways. Whereas the planners in East Berlin have planned the development of the old centre within their control for the functions of a capital city, the West Berlin planners have spread the former city functions through the inner districts. Around the remains of the Kaiser Wilhelm memorial church on the *Kurfürstendamm* there has, nevertheless, emerged the main hotel, entertainments, and shopping agglomeration, where many major companies, banks, and insurance firms have their Berlin offices. The city administration for West Berlin is in the old town hall in Schöneberg, with other branches nearby in Wilmersdorf, and the Western university is in new buildings at Dahlem, but a major higher educational focus has emerged around the *Ernst Reuter Platz* and the *Strasse des 17 Juni* that leads into the wooded *Tiergarten*. It

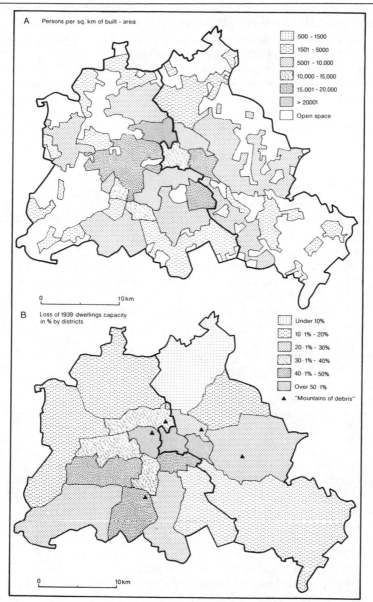

Figure 20.2 Wartime damage and population distribution in Berlin

Berlin – The Divided City

has been a central theme in West Berlin planning that only those functions remain in the old central city for which a central position is essential.

The pattern of population change has been decline in the innermost parts of the city, though densities still remain highest here, and growth has been in the outer suburbs into which industry and the tertiary sector have moved. In many outer districts, densities are relatively low, with extensive prewar estates of houses set in plentiful gardens. Every effort has been made to preserve the greenery of West Berlin and to spread it more evenly, replacing long street frontages and the airless courts of the old tenement blocks by blocks of flats with intervening open space, while interconnecting open space leads into the city margins, where new housing schemes have replaced extensive allotment gardens with small summer houses (*Laubenkolonien*). The close interweave of the old tenements and small industries has made redevelopment difficult, especially if the strong sense of community in such districts is to be preserved, while the close interlinkage of small industrial plants also complicates any relocation.

Energy and water supply present problems for isolated West Berlin, while waste disposal is also a difficulty, and the hostility of the G.D.R. authorities has encouraged development of a high-level self-sufficiency. Sufficient electricity is generated by six power stations in a local grid system in West Berlin, but fuel, both coal and oil, has to be imported across the G.D.R. The rich supply of ground water in the broad northwest-southeast *Urstromtal* across Berlin has been tapped to reduce dependence on the prewar waterworks outside the city, but waste and sewage still pass to treatment plants in G.D.R. territory. It is considered that the risk of epidemics which no political boundary could stop is adequate insurance against interference with West Berlin's waste disposal. Much garbage is, however, burned in Europe's largest incinerator and the ash used to make building blocks, so offsetting the import of expensive building materials from West Germany.

The disruption of the Wall in 1961 also divided the formerly integrated transport system in Berlin, so that only one through railway for long-distance international traffic from Western Europe to Warsaw and Moscow remains to join the two halves of the city. Local electric railways that ran out to adjacent towns have been cut, as has the Berlin inner ring railway, though some services between stations in West Berlin pass nonstop through the eastern sector: this also applies to the underground railway, though special conditions exist on the sections operated through the eastern sector. Plans to extend the underground railway are in hand. Road traffic is well catered for, though again access to the outside world is limited, with only two transit routes available to West Germany. Nevertheless, as a reminder of the 1948 airlift, West Berlin is served by three airfields – Tegel and Tempelhof and the military field at Gatow; air

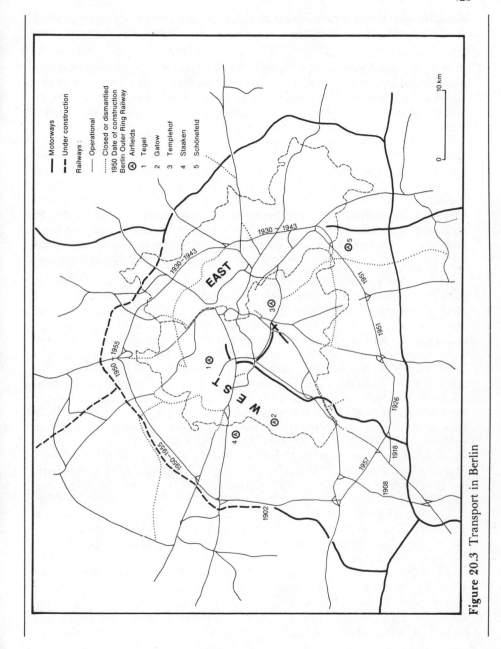

Figure 20.3 Transport in Berlin

Berlin – The Divided City

traffic for East Berlin uses Schönefeld on the southeast of the town. A considerable volume of traffic moves from West Germany to West Berlin by canal, but the return traffic is extremely limited.

West Berlin remains the largest industrial town in the Federal Republic and plays an important economic role in the federation. Over 40 percent of the labour force is industrially employed, with electrical engineering as the largest branch; food and drink manufacture and general and precision engineering are also significant. Food and drink industries are mostly small units for the local market or specialized markets in West Germany (notably drinks and chocolates). Though, measured in terms of firms and employment, textiles and clothing are well down the list, they are important earners, with about a quarter of all women's fashion wear in the Federal Republic made in West Berlin, and the clothing trade is an important employer of female labour. Electrical engineering has tended to decline because of transport difficulties in obtaining raw materials and shipping finished goods, as well as isolation from markets, so that major firms (*Siemens, AEG* and *Telefunken*) have shifted an increasing share of their development and production work to West Germany.

Attempts have been made to develop West Berlin as a cultural and entertainment centre of international standing, including film making and preparation of TV programmes: skill and creativity as raw materials present no transport problems and the finished articles are easily shipped by air freight. Equally, printing and publishing have remained important; West Berlin produces a wide range of government publications and a large part of the postage and fiscal stamps needed for the *Bundespost*. In contrast to prewar, commercial activity is less important, with little attraction now for banks and finance houses to have their head offices in West Berlin, and consultancy and research work has also dwindled, though some institutes (like the Institute for Nuclear Research in Wannsee) remain; in contrast, détente is encouraging firms engaged in East-West trade to open offices in West Berlin. The tertiary sector was a relatively more important employer than industry in West Berlin compared to East Berlin in 1939, but by 1960 the relationship had changed, with industry more important than administration in West Berlin and the reverse situation in East Berlin. West Berlin has nevertheless been maintained through massive aid from the Federal Republic, with generous tax concessions and other financial assistance offered to firms and to individuals moving to West Berlin. To attract firms to produce in West Berlin and also to buy from it, various incentives such as higher depreciation, easier credit, reduced VAT, and subsidized freight rates and postal charges are offered. Despite all these attractions, few firms have moved to the city, and though economic growth has been good, it has lagged behind the rest of the Federal Republic so that West Berlin occupies a declining position among the federal *Länder* and almost half its budget is from federal funds.

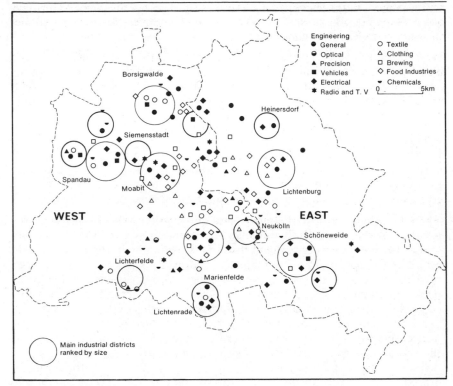

Figure 20.4 Berlin – economic geography

East Berlin

The Soviet sector of Berlin has emerged as the *de facto* capital of the G.D.R., whatever legal arguments may be made against this status. It has consequently had open access to the territory of the G.D.R. around it and has suffered none of the isolation and claustrophobia of West Berlin. Yet the division of Berlin has had severe consequences on the eastern part and has demanded many changes in its infrastructure and that of the surrounding countryside.

As the administrative focus of a highly centralized state, East Berlin has become a major attractive force, drawing to it all in the G.D.R. who seek advancement and promotion, and becoming the site of a large and elaborate bureaucracy. Consequently, its demographic situation is markedly different to West Berlin, with the proportion of the population of working age higher than the national average and higher than in any other *Bezirk*; on the other hand,

Berlin – The Divided City

children are a much lower proportion than the national average and form the lowest percentage of all *Bezirke*. In keeping with West Berlin, older age groups (pensioners, notably women) are also well above the national average. However, since 1950 there has been a general if slow rise in the proportion of children and old people in the East Berlin population, with a proportional fall in the working age groups. As in West Berlin, there is an imbalance in the sex structure – though less serious – which is expected to continue well after 1980. Labour is less difficult to obtain in East Berlin than in the western part because there is a strong commuting element from areas around, even from areas of the G.D.R. that require travel right round the periphery of West Berlin, and commuters, principally from the catchment area of the S-Bahn, form about 10 percent of the total labour force. Approximately half the labour force comprises women. Employment in administrative, commercial, and transport sectors has tended to increase proportionally at the expense of other sectors.

The rebuilding of East Berlin moved less quickly than West Berlin, where for political reasons considerable financial assistance was given to redevelopers. Only with the general upswing of the G.D.R. economy in the mid-1960s did rebuilding spread from a few major central projects to creation of a larger housing stock, with modernization and redevelopment in the outer suburbs. Redevelopment has been influenced by Soviet town planning concepts, which come close (if unintentionally) to the Nazi *Speer Plan* for Berlin. The street plan has been emphasized as a system of radial avenues, intersected by major 'tangential routes', that converge on a focal square (*Marx-Engels-Platz*), once the site of the royal palace. Emphasis was placed on development of a well-defined centre – the first part was the building of the monolithic blocks of Stalinist architecture in the *Stalin-Allee* (now *Karl-Marx-Alle*), though more recent development (e.g., *Alexander Platz*) has been of modern functional architecture and, in recent years, the bizarre Stalinist architecture has become an embarrassment as both parts of Berlin have increasingly become show windows of their respective economic and social systems. East Berlin planning has also sought to develop the neighbourhood unit principle (common in the socialist *bloc*) and to relate place of residence closely to place of work. The supply of land for development in East Berlin is less critical than in West Berlin, since not only is the population density considerably less, but development beyond the eastern city boundaries presents no major problem. Even so, some of the highest population densities in the whole of Berlin are found in the district of Prenzlauer Berg. In general, as in West Berlin, the old tenements, where they have survived, are being replaced by modern flats, mostly of factory-made sections giving a rather monotonous appearance.

East Berlin has few of the infrastructural problems of West Berlin, because with close and easy contact to the territory around, waste disposal, electricity, gas, or water supplies present few difficulties. Electricity from the Klingenberg plant is augmented by current drawn from the big power stations on the Saxon and Lusatian lignite fields (notably Vetschau and Lübbenau); gas is made in the city from bituminous coal imported from Polish and Czech Silesia; and water supply, as in West Berlin, is drawn from the ground water of the main Berlin *Urstromtal*. East Berlin accepts effluent from West Berlin onto its sewage farms, notably to the north and west of the city, so gaining a valuable agricultural asset.

The disruption of transport through the isolation of West Berlin has had its repercussions in East Berlin. Partly through reduction of traffic from lands beyond the Oder-Neisse rivers now in Poland or from West Germany, and partly through disruptions by the sector boundaries, a number of major prewar railway stations (e.g., *Lehrter Bahnhof*, *Görlitzer Bahnhof*) have been closed and trains now mostly start for G.D.R. destinations in Berlin–Lichtenberg or Berlin–Schöneweide, while Berlin *Ostbahnhof* is used for the few trains in east-west international traffic. In order to divert all trains from the western parts of the G.D.R. into East Berlin, it was necessary to complete the outer ring railway (begun before the First World War) in the mid and latter 1950s: this is also an important commuting line avoiding West Berlin. Parts of the existing line had been dismantled by the Russians, while other sections (involving some major civil engineering works) had to be realigned to avoid passing through West Berlin. Road access from the west to East Berlin was also cut by the isolation of West Berlin, though it is possible to use the southern ring Autobahn, while in the early 1970s work to complete the northern ring Autobahn began, though again realignment well out beyond West Berlin's boundaries compared to the proposed prewar trajectory has been necessary. Unlike in West Berlin, no urban motorways have been built.

Economic integration with the remaining G.D.R. territory is close. The central part of East Berlin is the administrative and organizational core of the republic, with between 25–30 percent of total employment in these sectors. The main focus of industry is the Ostkreuz area, with its good road, rail, and canal transport, extending to Schöneweide, with the main part of the East Berlin electrical engineering industry. Lichtenberg, also important for engineering, is a comparatively new industrial area, though there is much long-established industry, including metal working, ventilating, and refrigeration plants, and making electrodes; Weissensee has tool making, light chemicals (also in Adlershof and Schöneweide) and metal working, besides a large storage and distribution industry: Prenzlauer Berg has electrical engineering and a range of consumer-oriented industries. Johannistal-Adlershof has television studios and also research and development institutes, and in the northeast, at Berlin–Buch, a major medical centre, with hospitals, ancillary services, and research institutes. is being developed, a feature now common in much socialist *bloc* town planning. Industrially many comparisons can be made with West Berlin, notably in the importance of electrical engineering, but likewise also in consumer goods (particularly the clothing industry) similarities are apparent, even though these have been given a lower priority in the East.

Suggested further reading

Heineberg, H.: Berlin, Bochum, 1978.

Katsch, K. H.: Berlin – Struktur und Entwicklung, Wiesbaden, 1966.

Mander, J.: Berlin: Hostage for the West, London, 1962.

Richter, H. et al.: Berlin – die Hauptstadt der DDR und ihr Umland, Leipzig, 1969.

Schinz, A.: Berlin – Stadtschicksal und Städtebau, Braunschweig, 1964.

Stephan, H.: Rebuilding Berlin, *Town Plan. Rev.* 29, 1959, pp.207–226.

Zimm, A.: Zur Funktion der geographischen Lage West-Berlins, Gotha, 1969.

PROGNOSIS FOR THE FUTURE OF THE TWO GERMAN STATES

With so many imponderables, crystal-gazing in political geography is riddled with pitfalls, but it is worth suggesting some lines for the future that the two German states may follow. Arbitrarily cast, the two German sovereign states have existed for over twenty-five years, a product of division arising from the foundering of the original Allied intent to treat Germany as an economic and political whole. But from the moment of division, paradoxically, their ultimate reunification became the goal at least nominally supported by their opposing and ideologically incompatible sponsors. Reunification has, however, not always been viewed with enthusiasm by other European countries, an attitude not unexpected in the bitter light of history: even the opposing sponsors of the German states would also hardly wish for it unless the united Germany were to be firmly of their own persuasion.

While the Germans have been firmly conscious for many centuries of their identity within the bonds of Germandom, political unity eluded them, with a single German nation state more the exception than the rule. Parochial particularism was held together by Prussian power and dynamics in the Second *Reich* of 1871; the unity of the Weimar Republic held up only under outside pressures; while it was the effectiveness of Nazi centralization that clamped the Third *Reich* and transient *Grossdeutschland* firmly in political unity. Perhaps this explains how German indentity as a people and as a nation has been kept viable in the division between two remarkably contrasting states during the last quarter century.

Though hope has always been present, no progress towards reunification has been made: proposals and counter-proposals have always found implacable opposition or an inability to compromise on the vital key, wherever that has lain. Failure to move again towards one German nation state has come very much from external pressures through the inability of the major powers to find a formula acceptable to them, but even the two German governments, however much their electorate may yearn for reunification, have also displayed a lack of compromise and a rooted intransigence on tender issues no less acute than attitudes and events that coloured the same search in the first half of last century. Only in the 1970s have small concessions on minor issues been made as the direct participation between the two German governments has developed, though the Fundamental Treaty between them in 1972 virtually shelved the question of reunification for the foreseeable future. This is possibly a realization that the two states have grown so far apart that a long preparatory series of moves towards each other must first be made before such a delicate issue might even be mooted.

The legal basis of both German states recognizes that the Germans are one people and one nation: formal and overt rejection of this could generate political and popular pressures that neither state would find tolerable. Gloomy observers who claim that two German societies, with their own modes of speech and their own sets of values, are emerging are countered vociferously by reference to the traditional diversity among the *Volksstämme*, all of whom readily identify with Germandom. Yet nobody would deny that the longer division remains, the more difficult reunification becomes, both in the mechanics of recreating one state and in the political conditions needed. The spatial organization of both states grows continuously apart and diverges ever further from that inherited from the *Reich* in 1945, while the states themselves become increasingly absorbed into the matrix of the international economic and political systems to which they are attached. As a reunited Germany would be the economically most powerful and the most populous state outside the Soviet Union, its impact on a delicately balanced Europe would be formidable, coloured substantially by what sort of socio-economic conditions were to dominate in the new one-German state.

Relations between the two German states and any moves towards reconciliation, if not reunification, are coloured by the peculiar problem of Berlin. Continuation of the present situation accentuates all the social and economic problems of isolated West Berlin that tend to raise its dependence on subventions and aid from the Federal Republic – clearly any improvement in relations between the two states should give the reduction of the isolation of West Berlin high priority. Indeed, so long as division remains between the two German states, it is difficult to see what else may be achieved than to ease movement between West Berlin and East Berlin and the G.D.R.: any fundamental change in the *status quo* in Berlin directly involves the major powers and their own prestige. Even in a reunited Germany, Berlin would no longer be appropriately located to serve as capital, whatever historical arguments for or against this might be made.

Unless there is some most unlikely political upheaval in Europe, it looks as though in the foreseeable future the division of Germany into two sovereign states will continue, with reunification as the most improbable trend, even though the Germans will continue to profess their unity as a people and as a nation. The modest developments following the Fundamental Treaty of 1972 might well be used to lead slowly towards the establishment of a special relationship (which in certain respects already exists) between the two states, especially in fields such as trade and intra-German movement. Such a relationship could exist without impinging on the obviously incompatible spheres between the states, and many Germans on both sides would accept happily an easing of movement as an important step in the right direction. Yet, in the continuing aura of suspicion and incompatibility, any further progress would depend on a widening horizon of détente generally in Europe. In all dealings, however, the disparity in wealth and size between the two states puts the G.D.R. in a weak position and doubtless contributes to the inferiority complex it has shown in many negotiations; but on both sides there are many vested interests that put their own advantage before any appeal to such intangibles as nation and people. It remains patently obvious nevertheless that the health, wealth, and security of Europe are centred very much around the continuing story of the 'German Problem'.

BIBLIOGRAPHY

An immense geographical literature exists in German. Almost every university geography department produces a formidable array of monographs, while other institutions also have regular series, besides many well-known geographical periodicals such as *Erdkunde, Petermanns Geographische Mitteilungen, Geographische Rundschau, Geographische Zeitschrift, Geographische Berichte, Berichte zur deutschen Landeskunde* among others.

Abbreviations

A.A.A.G.	Annals of the Association of American Geographers
Forsch. z. deut. Landeskunde	Forschungen zur deutschen Landeskunde
Geog. Rev.	Geographical Review
Journ. T.P.I.	Journal of the (Royal) Town Planning Institute
K.N.A.G. Geog. Tijd.	Tijdschrift van het Koninklijk Nederlands Aardrijkskundig Genootschap
P.M.	Petermanns Geographische Mitteilungen
T.E.S.G.	Tijdschrift voor Economische en Sociale Geografie
Trans I.B.G.	Transactions of the Institute of British Geographers
Abh.:	Abhandlungen
Arb.:	Arbeiten
Gesell.:	Gesellschaft
Inst.:	Institut (e)
Mitt.:	Mitteilungen
Vj.:	Vierteljahr

I General texts

Barth, L.: Unsere Deutsche Demokratische Republik, Leipzig, 1966.

Basova, I. A., et al.: Federativnaya Respublika Germanii, Moscow, 1975.

Burtenshaw, D.: Economic Geography of West Germany, London, 1974.
Saar-Lorraine, *Problem Regions of Europe*, Oxford, 1976.

Clozier, R.: Géographie de l'Allemagne et des états alpestres, Paris, 1966.

Degn, C., Eggert, E., Kolb, A.: Deutschland, *Seydlitz für Gymnasien* 1, Kiel, 1966.
Deutschland – Probleme der Gegenwart, *Seydlitz für Gymnasien* 4, Kiel, 1971.

Dickinson, R. E.: The Economic Regions of Germany, *Geog. Rev.* 28, 1948, pp.609–626.
The German Lebensraum, London, 1943.
The Regions of Germany, London, 1945.
Germany – a General and Regional Geography, London, 1968.

Elkins, T. H.: Germany, 2nd ed. London, 1969.

Ernst, E.: Der Rhein – eine europäische Stromlandschaft im Luftbild, Bühl/Baden, 1972.

Fehn, H.: Zur Landeskunde Bayerns, *Zeitschr. f. bayer. Landesgeschichte* 15, München, 1949.

Fischer, G., et al.: Deutschland, Braunschweig, 1971.

George, P.: Géographie de l'Europe Centrale, Paris, 1964.

George, P., Tricart, J.: L'Europe Centrale, 2 vols, Paris, 1954.

Götz, W. (ed.): Rheinland-Pfalz – Heute und Morgen, Mainz, 1970.
Heidelberg und die Rhein-Neckar Lande, *Festschrift 34 Deutscher Geographentag* 1963, Heidelberg-München, 1963.

Gradmann, R.: Süddeutschland, 2 vols, Stuttgart, 1931 (*reissue* Darmstadt, 1968).

Grosser, A.: Deutschlandbilanz, München, 1970.

Hellen, J. A.: North Rhine-Westphalia, *Problem Regions of Europe*, Oxford, 1974.

Hübner, P.: Der Rhein – von den Quellen bis zu den Mündungen, Frankfurt, 1974.

Hüfner, W.: Hessen unter den Ländern der Bundesrepublik, Wiesbaden, 1970.

Huttenlocher, F.: Baden-Württemberg: kleine geographische Landeskunde, *Schriftenreihe d. Kommission f. geschichtliche Landeskunde*, Stuttgart, 1972.

Juillard, E.: L'Europe Rhénane, Paris, 1968.

Kayser, K., Kraus, T.: Köln und die Rheinlande, *Festschrift 33 Deutscher Geographentag* 1961, Wiesbaden, 1961.

Klute, F.: Das Deutsche Reich – Handbuch der geographischen Wissenschaften I & II, Potsdam, 1936–40.

Lenz, W., Richter, G.: Deutschland – das Land in dem wir leben, Gütersloh, 1966.

Meynen, E.: Deutschland und das Deutsche Reich, Berlin, 1935.
Die Mittelrheinlande, *Festschrift 36 Deutscher Geographentag* 1967, Wiesbaden, 1967.

Müller-Wille, W.: Westfalen – Landschaftliche Ordnung und Bildung eines Landes, Münster, 1952.

Naval Intelligence Division: *Geographical Handbook Series*, Germany 4 vols, London, 1944.

Nickel, A., Piepenstock, D.: Wirtschaftsgeographie – Teil I: Deutschland, Darmstadt, 1968.

Parker, G.: The Logic of Unity – An Economic Geography of the Common Market, London, 1969.

Partsch, J.: Central Europe, London, 1905.

Pounds, N. J. G.: The Economic Pattern of Modern Germany, London, 1963.

Reinhard, R.: Mitteldeutschland, *Geog. Zeitschrift* 42, 1936, pp.321–359.

Reital, F.: Les Allemagnes, Paris, 1974.

Rhode G.: Die Ostgebiete des Deutschen Reiches, Würzburg, 1956.

Sanders, H., Sanders, J.: Bundesrepublik Deutschland und die DDR, *Harms Arbeitsmappe Erdkunde*, München, 1975.

Scherzer, C.: Franken, 2 vols, Nürnberg, 1959–62.

Scheu, E.: Deutschlands Wirtschaftsgeographische Harmonie, Berlin, 1924.
Des Reiches wirtschaftliche Einheit, Berlin, 1924.

Schlenger, H., et al.: Schleswig-Holstein – ein geographisch-landeskundlicher Exkursionsführer, *Festschrift 37 Deutscher Geographentag 1969*, Kiel, 1969.

Schmidt-Renner, G., et al.: Wirtschaftsterritorium Deutsche Demokratische Republik, Berlin, 1962.

Schmitt, E., Gohl, D., Hagel, J.: Deutschland, *Harms Geographie*, München, 1976.

Singer, P., Fliedner, D.: Niedersachsen, München, 1970.

Sinnhuber, K.: Germany – Its Origins and its Growth, London, 1968.

Straszewicz, L.: Geografia ekonomiczna europejskich krajów socjalistycznych – Niemiecka Republika Demokratyczna, Warszawa, 1974.

Wagner, J.: Hessen – Eine Landeskunde, München, 1969.

II Physical setting

Backhaus, H.: Die Ostfriesischen Inseln und ihre Entwicklung, Oldenburg, 1943.

Behrmann, W. (ed.): Vierzig Blätter der Karte 1:100 000 ausgewählt für Unterrichtszwecke mit Erläuterungen, *Amtliche Anstalt für Kartographie und Kartendruck*, 4th ed., Berlin, 1951.

Bürgener, M. Die Landschaftsnamen Deutschlands, *Forsch. z. deut. Landeskunde* 16, 1968.

Flohn, H.: Witterung und Klima in Mitteleuropa, *Forsch. z. deut. Landeskunde* 78, 1954.

Frechen, J., et al.: Die Vulkanische Eifel, Bonn, no date.

Freitag, H.: Einführung in die Biogeographie von Mitteleuropa unter Berücksichtigung von Deutschland, Stuttgart, 1962.

Gohl, D.: Strukturen und Skulpturen der Landschaft – die Methodik der Darstellung am Beispiel einer Karte von Deutschland, *Forsch. z. deut. Landeskunde* 184, 1972.

Gurlitt, D.: Das Mittelrheintal – Form und Gestalt, *Forsch. z. deut. Landeskunde* 46, 1949.

Haarnagel, W.: Die Marschen im deutschen Küstengebiet der Nordsee und ihre Besiedlung, *Berichte z. deut. Landeskunde* 27, 1961, pp.203–219.

Haefke, F.: Physische Geographie Deutschlands, Berlin, 1959.

Kieler, R.: Natur und Wirtschaft im Wasserhaushalt der rheinischen Landschaften, *Forsch. z. deut. Landeskunde* 57, 1952.

Kietz, K.: Die Kohle in Mitteldeutschland, *Führer d. Aussenstelle d. Deut. Inst. f. Landeskunde in Leipzig*, Leipzig, 1949.

Knabe, W.: Zur Wiederurbarmachung im Braunkohlenbergbau, Berlin, 1959.

Krenkel, E.: Die Bodenschätze Deutschlands, Berlin, 1932.

Kukuk, P.: Unsere Kohlen, Leipzig, 1924.
Geologie des niederrheinisch-westfälischen Steinkohlengebietes, 2 vols., Berlin, 1938.

Louis, H., et al.: Landformen im Kartenbild (37 folios), Braunschweig, 1969–1976.

Meynen, E. (ed.): Deutsche Landschaften – geographisch-landeskundliche Erläuterungen zur Topographischen Karte 1:50 000 (4 folios), *Bundesanstalt für Landeskunde und Raumforschung*, Bad Godesberg, 1963–70.

Mordziol, C.: Der geologische Werdegang des Mittelrheintales, Bonn, 1958.

Müller-Miny, H.: Die naturräumliche Gliederung am Mittelrhein, *Berichte z. deut. Landeskunde* 21, 1959.

Quitzow, H. W., et al.: Die Entstehung des Rheintales vom Austritt des Flusses aus dem Bodensee bis zur Mündung, *Beiträge zur Rheinkunde* 14, Koblenz, 1962.

Rau, H.: Die Wasserversorgung des Ruhrgebietes in Abhängigkeit von den Naturverhältnissen, *Geog. Rundschau*, 1965, pp.147–155.

Ruger, L.: Deutschlands Erzvorkommen, *Geog. Zeitschrift* 40, 1934, pp.124–134.

Schott, C.: Die Naturlandschaften Schleswig-Holsteins, Neumünster, 1956.

III Territorial organization

Alexander, L. Recent Changes in the Benelux–German Boundary, *Geog. Rev.* 43, 1953, pp.69–76.

Bayrischer Staatsminister für Ernährung, Landwirtschaft und Forsten: Der Alpenplan – Schutz dem Bergland, München, 1969 et seq.

Bayrische Staatsregierung: Ein Programm für Bayern I & II, München, 1971.

Beck, H.: Bauland Prices and Raumordnung in the Federal Republic of Germany, Paper read at the IGU Conference, Montreal, 1972.

Boesler, K-A.: Kulturlandschaftswandel durch raumwirksame Staatstätigkeit, *Abh. Geog. Inst. der Freien Universität Berlin* 12, 1969.
Spatially-effective Government Actions and Regional Development in the Federal Republic of Germany, *T.E.S.G.* 65, 1974, pp.208–219.

Bundesminister für Gesamtdeutsche Fragen: Mitten in Deutschland – Mitten im 20 Jahrhundert: die Zonengrenze, Bonn, 1964.

Bundesminister des Innern: Informationsbriefe für Raumordnung, 115 topics, Wiesbaden, 1966 et seq.

Bundesminister für Wirtschaft: Regionale Aktionsprogramm 1970, Bonn, 1976.

Bundeszentrale für Politische Bildung: Raumordnung in der Bundesrepublik, *Informationen zur politischen Bildung* Folge 128, Bonn, 1968.

Burtenshaw, D.: Regional Renovation in the Saarland, *Geog. Rev.* 48, 1972, pp.1–12.

Dickinson, R. E.: City and Region, London, 1964.

Dittrich, E.: Grundfragen deutscher Raumordnung, *Mitt. d. Inst. für Raumforschung* 21, Bonn, 1955.

Ernst, W., Dittrich, E.: Raum und Ordnung: Probleme der Raumordnung in der Bundesrepublik, *Inst. f. Raumforschung*, Bonn, 1963.

Forst, H. T.: Zur Klassifizierung von Städten nach wirtschafts- und sozialstatistischen Strukturmerkmalen, *Arb. z. Angewandten Statistik* 17, Würzburg, 1974.

Franke, W.: Die deutsch-dänische Grenze in ihrem Einfluss auf die Differenzierung der Kulturlandschaft, *Forsch. z. deut. Landeskunde* 172, 1968.

Hartshorne, R.: Geographic and Political Boundaries in Upper Silesia, *A.A.A.G.* 23, 1933, pp.195–228.
The Franco-German Boundary of 1871, *World Politics* 11, 1950, pp.209–250.

Heiss, F., Ziegfeld, A. H.: Deutschland und der Korridor, Berlin, 1933.

Institut für Landeskunde: Raum und Ordnung – Probleme der Raumordnung in der Bundesrepublik Deutschland, Bad Godesberg, 1951.

Kirn, P.: Politische Geschichte der deutschen Grenzen, Leipzig, 1944.

Kluczka, G.: Zentrale Orte und zentralörtliche Bereiche mittlerer und höherer Stufe in der BRD, *Forsch. z. deut. Landeskunde* 194, 1970.

Körber, J. Planning Research in the Federal Republic of Germany with special reference to the Ruhr area, *Journ. T.P.I.* 52, 1966, pp.131–133.

Landesregierung Nordrhein-Westfalen: Nordrhein-Westfalen Programm 1975, Düsseldorf, 1970.

Marzian, H. G.: The German Frontier Problem: a Study in political Interdependence, Göttingen, 1969.

Münchheimer, W.: Die Neugliederung Deutschlands: Grundlagen – Kritik – Ziele und Pläne zur Reichsreform von 1919 bis 1945, *Frankfurter Geog. Hefte* 23, 1949.
Worum geht es bei der Neugliederung Deutschlands? *Frankfurter Geog. Hefte* 25, 1951.

Neff, E.: Das Problem der zentralen Orte, *P.M.* 94, 1950, pp.6–17.

Nelson, H.: Land and Power: British and Allied Policy on Germany's Frontiers 1916–1919, London, 1963.

Niessen, J.: Geschichtlicher Atlas der Deutschen Länder am Rhein, Köln, 1950.

Planungsgruppe beim Ministerpräsidenten des Saarlandes: Strukturprogramm Saarland, Saarbrücken, 1969.

Platt, R. S.: A Geographical Study of the Dutch–German Border, Münster, 1969.
The Saarland – An international Borderland, *Erdkunde* 15, 1961, pp.54–68

Robinson E. A. G.: Backward Areas in Advanced Countries, London, 1969.

Saute, G. W. (ed.): Geschichte der deutschen Länder, *Territorien Ploetz*, 4 vols, Würzburg, 1964 et seq.

Schat, P. A.: Veranderingen in de ekonomische planning in de DDR sinds 1961 – enige ekonomische verglijkingen met de BRD, *K.N.A.G. Geog. Tijd.* 9, 1975, pp.63–80.

Schwind, M.: Landschaft und Grenze – Geographische Betrachtungen zur deutsch-niederländischen Grenze, Bielefeld, 1950.

van den Bosch, H. M. J.: Ideologie en regionale Ontwikkeling in de DDR, *K.N.A.G. Geog. Tijd.* 9, 1973, pp.81–95.

Verband Grossraum Hannover: Verbandsplan 1967, Hannover, 1969.

Weigand. K.: Programm Nord – Wandel der Landschaft in Schleswig-Holstein, Kiel, 1970.

Wiek, K. D.: Regionale Schwerpunkte und Schwächezonen in der Bevölkerungs-, Erwerbs- und Infrastruktur Deutschlands, *Forsch. z. deut. Landeskunde* 169, 1967.

Wierling, L., Hötker, D.: Siedlungsverband Ruhrkohlenbezirk 1920–1970, Essen, 1971.

Wiskemann, E.: Germany's Eastern Neighbours, Oxford, 1956.

IV   Population and settlement

Abele, G., Leidlmaer, A.: Karlsruhe – Studien zur innerstädtischen Gliederung und Viertelsbildung, *Karlsruher Geog. Hefte* 3, 1972.

Ammann, G.: Mannheim-Ludwigshafen, *Geog. Helvetica* 15, 1960, pp.86–101.

Balon, E.: Altgablonz – Neugablonz, *Mitt. Geog. Gesell. in München* 38, 1953, pp.5–135.

Bartels, D.: Nachbarstädte – eine siedlungsgeographische Studie anhand ausgewählter Beispiele aus dem westlichen Deutschland, *Forsch. z. deut. Landeskunde* 120, 1960.

Bauer, W.: Das deutsche Bevölkerungsproblem in europäischer Sicht, *Europa-Archiv* 3, Frankfurt, 1948.

Beck, H. (ed.): Probleme der Bevölkerungsballung aufgezeigt am Beispiel des Raumes Nürnberg-Fürth, *Nürnberger Wirtschafts- und Sozialgeog. Arb.* 18, 1974.

Blacksell, M.: Recent Changes in the Morphology of West German Townscapes, *in* Urbanisation and its Problems – Essays in Honour of E. W. Gilbert, Oxford, 1968.

Blaschke, K.: Bevölkerungsgeschichte von Sachsen bis zur industriellen Revolution, Weimar, 1967.

Bose, G.: Entwicklungstendenzen der Binnenwanderung in der DDR im Zeitraum 1953–1965, *P.M.* 114, 1970, pp.117–131.

Boustedt, O.: Struktur und Funktion der städtischen Siedlungen im mittelfränkischen Wirtschaftsraum – Studien zum Problem der Trabantenstadt, *Forsch.- und Sitzungsberichte der Akad. f. Raumforschung und Landesplanung* 26, 1965, pp.117–156.

Braun, P.: Die sozialräumliche Gliederung Hamburgs, *Weltwirtschaftliche Studien* 10, Göttingen, 1968.

Brepohl, H.: Aufbau des Ruhrvolkes, Recklinghausen, 1948.
Industrievolk Ruhrgebiet, Tübingen, 1957.

Buchholz, H. J.: Formen städtischen Lebens im Ruhrgebiet – untersucht an sechs stadtgeographischen Beispielen, *Bochumer Geog. Arb.* 8, 1970.
Polyzentrisches Ballungsgebiet Ruhr, *Geog. Rundschau* 8, 1973, pp.297–307.

Büdel, J., et al.: Beiträge zur Geographie Frankens, *Festschrift 31 Deutscher Geographentag* 1957 – *Würzburger Geog. Arb.* 4–5, 1957.

Christaller, W.: Die Zentralen Orte in Süddeutschland, Jena, 1933. The Central Places of Southern Germany, (trs. Baskin) New York, 1966.

Dorfs, H-P.: Wesel – Vergleich zu anderen Festungsstädten, *forsch. z. deut. Landeskunde* 201, 1972.

Federal Minister of the Interior: Report of the Federal Republic of Germany on the Human Environment, *United Nations Conference on the Human Environment – Stockholm 1972*, Bonn, 1972

Fehn, K.: Räumliche Bevölkerungsbewegung im saarländischen Bergbau- und Industriegebiet während des 19 und früheren 20 Jahrhunderts, *Mitt. Geog. Gesell. München* 59, 1974, pp.57–73.

Förster, H.: Die funktionale und sozialgeographische Gliederung der Mainzer Innenstadt, *Bochumer Geog. Arb.* 4, 1969.

Franz, G. (ed.): Historische Raumforschung 1–9, *Akad. f. Raumforschung und Landesplanung*, Hannover, 1956–71.

Gorki, H. F.: Städte und 'Städte' in der Bundesrepublik Deutschland, *Geog. Zeitschrift* 62, 1974, pp.29–52.

Green, T.: West German City Reconstruction, *Sociological Review* 7, 1959, pp.231–244.

Grötzbach, E.: Geographische Untersuchung über die Kleinstadt der Gegenwart in Süddeutschland, *Münchner Geog. Hefte* 24, 1963.

Hall, P.: Rhine-Ruhr, *in* World Cities London, 1966, pp.122–157.

Holzner, L.: The role of history and tradition in the urban geography of West Germany, *A.A.A.G.* 60, 1970, pp.315–339.

Hottes, K-H.: Köln als Industriestadt, *in* Köln und die Rheinlande, Wiesbaden, 1961.

Ibeher, P.: Hauptstadt oder Hauptstädte? – die Machtverteilung zwischen den Grossstädten der BRD, Opladen, 1970.

Junghans, K.: Der deutsche Städtebau von 1848 bis 1945 im Überblick *Jahrbuch 1961 – Deutsche Bau-Akademie*, Berlin, 1962, pp.75–90.

Krenzlin, A.: Werden und Gefüge des rhein-mainischen Verstädterungsgebiets, *Frankfurter Geog. Hefte* 37, 1961, pp.311–387.

Kreuz, G., Stiebitz, W., Wiedner, C.: Städte und Stadtzentren in der DDR – Ergebnisse und reale Perspektiven des Städtebaus in der DDR, Berlin, 1969.

Kursawe, H-D.: Monheim – neue Stadtentwicklung zwischen den Grossstädten, *Kölner Geog. Arb.* 28, 1973.

Lemberg, W., Edding, F.: Die Vertriebenen in Deutschland, 3 vols, Kiel, 1959.

Lowinski, H.: Städtebildung in industriellen Entwicklungsräumen untersucht am Beispiel der Stadt und Amtes Marl, Recklinghausen, 1964.

Mackenroth, G.: Bevölkerungslehre, Berlin, 1951.

Mayr, A.: Ahlen in Westfalen, *Bochumer Geog. Arb.* 3, 1968.

Mellor, R. E. H.: A Minority Problem in Germany, *Scot. Geog. Mag.* 79, 1963, pp.49–53.

Merritt, R. L.: Infrastructural Changes in Berlin, *A.A.A.G.* 63, 1973, pp.58–70.

439

Mulzer, E.: Der Wiederaufbau der Altstadt von Nürnberg 1945–1970, *Mitt. d. Fränk. Geog. Gesell.* 19, 1972.

Neundörfer, L.: Können 47,5 Millionen Menschen in Westdeutschland leben? *Soziale Welt* 2, Dortmund, 1951, pp.389–398.

Niemeier, G.: Braunschweig – Soziale Schichtung und sozialräumliche Gliederung einer Grossstadt, Braunschweig, 1969.

Pehnt, W. (ed.): Die Stadt in der Bundesrepublik Deutschland – Lebensbedingungen, Aufgaben, Planung, Stuttgart, 1974.

Pfeiffer, G.: Nürnberg – Geschichte einer europäischen Stadt, München, 1970.

Richter, H. (ed.): Entwicklung der Siedlungsstruktur im Norden der DDR, *Wiss. Abh. d. Geog. Gesell. d. DDR* 12, Berlin, 1975.

Roewer, H.: Linksniederrheinische städtische Siedlungen, *Forsch. z. deut. Landeskunde* 83, 1955.

Rose, R. (ed.): Management of Urban Change in Britain and Germany, London, 1974.

Röthel, H. K.: Die Hansestädte, München, 1955.

Ruppert, H. R. P.: Bevölkerungsballungen – Analyse und Vergleich am Beispiel der Randstad Holland, der Rhein-Ruhr-Ballung und Rhein-Main-Neckar-Ballung, *Nürnberger Wirtschafts- und Sozialgeog. Arb.* 20, 1973.

Schliebe, K., Teske, H-D.: Verdichtungsräume in West- und Mitteldeutschland: ein innerdeutscher Vergleich, *Raumforschung und Raumordnung* 27, 1969, pp.145–156.

Schmidt-Renner, G.: Ursachen der Städtebildung, *P.M.* 109, 1965, pp.23–31.

Schneider, S.: Königswinter, *Berichte z. deut. Landeskunde* 26, 1961.

Schöller, P.: Allgemeine Stadtgeographie, *Wege der Forschung*, 81, Darmstadt, 1969.
Stalinstadt/Oder – Strukturtyp der neuen Stadt des Ostens, *Informationen vom Inst. f. Raumforschung* 25, 1953, pp.255–261.
Die Deutschen Städte, *Geog. Zeitschrift* Beiheft 17, 1967.
Veränderungen im Zentralitätsgefüge deutscher Städte – ein Vergleich der Entwicklungstendenzen in West und Ost, *Wiss. Abh. Deutschen Geographentages* 1967, pp.243–250.

Schrettenbrenner, H.: Gastarbeiter – ein europäisches Problem aus der Sicht der Herkunftsländer und der BRD, Frankfurt, 1971.

Schwarz, K.: Analyse der räumlichen Bevölkerungsbewegung, *Akad. f. Raumforschung und Landesplanung* 58, 1969.

Sonne, H. C. (ed.): The Integration of Refugees into German Life, *E.C.A. Technical Commission*, Bonn, 1951.

Stams, W.: Der Aufbau von Dresden – Planung einer sozialistischen Grossstadt, *Geog. Berichte* 13, 1968, pp.178–205.

Steinberg, H. G.: Die Sozialräumliche Entwicklung und Gliederung des Ruhrgebietes, *Forsch. z. deut. Landeskunde* 166, 1967.
Die Bevölkerungsentwicklung in den beiden Teilen Deutschlands nach dem zweiten Weltkrieg, *Geog. Rund.* 5, 1974, pp.169–179.

Temlitz, K.: Stadt und Stadtregion, Braunschweig, 1975.

Thomas, S., Tuppen, J.: Readjustment in the Ruhr – the case of Bochum, *Geog.* 62, 1977, pp.168–175.

Wagner, E., Ritter, G.: Zur Stadtgeographie von Duisburg, *Duisburger Hochschulbeiträge* I, Duisburg, 1968.

Welte, A.: Zur Entstehung der mainfränkischen Städte, *P.M.* 87, 1941, pp.233-250.

V Economic geography: agriculture

Franz, G. (ed.): Deutsche Agrargeschichte, 5 vols, Stuttgart, 1967 et seq.

Gaebe, W.: Die räumliche Differenzierung der Ernährungsformen in den Ländern der EWG, *Kölner Forsch. z. Wirtschafts- und Sozialgeog.* 5, 1969.

Häberle, D.: Die geographischen Bedingungen des deutschen Weinbaus, *Geog. Zeitschrift* 32, 1926, pp.405–430.

Hahn, H.: Die deutschen Weinbaugebiete – ihre historisch-geographische Entwicklung, *Bonner Geog. Arb.* 18, 1956.
Die deutschen Weinbaugebiete 1949–1960, *Erdkunde* 22, 1968, pp.128–145.

Haushofer, H.: Die Landwirtschaft im technischen Zeitalter, Stuttgart, 1968.

Immler, H.: Agrarpolitik in der DDR, Köln, 1971.

Jäger, H.: Zur Entstehung der heutigen grossen Forsten in Deutschland, *Berichte z. deut. Landeskunde* 13, 1955, pp.156–171.
Zur Geschichte der deutschen Kulturlandschaften, *Geog. Zeitschrift* 51, 1963, pp.90–143.

Jensch, G.: Das ländliche Jahr in der deutschen Agrarlandschaft, *Abh. Geog. Inst. d. Freien Universität Berlin* 3, 1957.

Kramer, M.: Die Landwirtschaft in der sowjetischen Besatzungszone: Produktions-möglichkeiten und Produktionsergebnisse, *Bonner Berichte aus Mittel- und Ostdeutschland*, 1951.

Meitzen, A.: Siedlung und Agrarwesen der Ost- und Westgermanen, der Kelten, Römer, Finnen und Slawen, Berlin, 1895.

Minister für Ernährung, Landwirtschaft, Weinbau und Forsten in Baden-Württemberg Albprogramm, Stuttgart, 1971.
Schwarzwaldprogramm, Stuttgart, 1973.

Pfeiffer, G.: The quality of peasant living in Central Europe, *in* W. L. Thomas (ed.): Man's Role in Changing the Face of the Earth, Chicago, 1956.

Röhm, H.: Geschlossene Vererbung und Realteilung in der BRD, *Verh. Deut. Geographentages* 33, 1961, pp.288–304.
Die westdeutsche Landwirtschaft, München, 1964.

Smit, J. G.: Ontwikkelingen in de landbouw van beide duitse staten, *K.N.A.G. Geog. Tijd* 9, 1975, pp.46–61.

Unseld, K.: Der Zuckerrübenanbau in der BRD, *Nürnberger Wirtschafts- und Sozialgeog. Arb.* 14, 1971.

VI Economic geography: mining and industry

Ahrens, T.: Standortprobleme der Eisen- und Stahlindustrie im Ruhrgebiet, Dortmund, 1962.

Baltsch, H. H. et al.: Blickpunkt Braunkohle, *Rheinische Braunkohlenwerke*, Köln, 1977.

Barr, J.: Planning for the Ruhr, *Geog. Mag.* 42, 1970, pp.280–289.

Baumgart, E. R.: Der Einfluss von Strukturveränderungen auf die Entwicklung der nordrhein-westfälischen Industrie seit 1950, *Deut. Inst. f. Wirtschaftsforschung* 70, Berlin, 1965.

Busch, P., et al.: Bochum und das mittlere Ruhrgebiet, *Bochumer Geog. Arb.* 1, 1965.

Childs, D.: Recent East German economic progress, *Geography* 51, 1966, pp.367–369.

Cordero, R., Serjeantson, R.: Iron and steelworks of the World, *Metal Bulletin*, London (irregularly).

Dittrich, E.: Die Wiedereingliederung der Flüchtlingsindustrien in die Wirtschaft der Bundesrepublik, *Inst. f. Raumforschung* Vorträge 1, Bonn, 1950.
Der Aufbau der Flüchtlingsindustrien in der BRD, *Weltwirtschaftliches Archiv* 67, Kiel, 1951, pp.327–360.

Elkins, T. H.: The Central German chemical industry, *Geography* 42, 1957, pp.183–186.
The brown coal industry of Germany, *Geography* 38, 1953, pp.18–28.

Fleming, D. K., Krumme, G.: The 'Royal' Hoesch Union, *T.E.S.G.* 48, 1968, pp.177–199.

Fleming, D. K.: Coastal steelworks in the Common Market countries, *Geog. Rev.* 57, 1967, pp.48–72.

Gebauer, K.: Das deutsche Erdöl, *Geog. Zeitschrift* 38, 1939, pp.449–466.

Geipel, R.: Industriegeographie als Einführung in die Arbeitswelt, Braunschweig, 1969.

Gesamtverband des Deutschen Steinkohlenbergbaues: Konzept zur längerfristigen Konsolidierung des Steinkohlenbergbaues, Essen, 1972.

Gesamtverband der Textilindustrie in der BRD.: Die Textilindustrie in der Bundesrepublik Deutschland, Frankfurt (irregularly).

Greipl, E.: Einkaufszentren in der BRD, *Schriftenreihe d. Ifo-Inst. für Wirtschaftsforschung* 79, Berlin, 1972.

Grésillon, M.: Les relations ville-industrie: le complexe de Halle, R.D.A., *Ann. de Géog.* 83, 1974, pp.260–283.

Grotewold, A., Sublett, M. D.: The effect of import restrictions on land use: United Kingdom and Germany compared, *Econ. Geog.* 43, 1967, pp.64–70.

Grotz, R.: Entwicklung, Struktur und Dynamik der Industrie im Wirtschaftsraum Stuttgart, *Stuttgarter Geog. Studien* 82, 1971.

Harders, F.: Die Hütte der Zukunft, *Werkzeitschrift der Hoesch AG 'Werk und Wir'* 3, Dortmund, 1971, pp.66–69.

Harris, A., Matzot, W.: Developments in the Aachen Coalfield, *Geography* 44, 1959, pp.122–124.

Held, C. C.: The New Saarland, *Geog. Rev.* 41, 1951, pp.590–605.

Helmrich, W.: Das Ruhrgebiet – Wirtschaft und Verflechtung, Münster, 1949.
Wirtschaftskunde des Landes Nordrhein-Westfalen, Düsseldorf, 1960.

Höhfeld, T. H.: Die Funktion der Steinkohlenreviere der BRD im westeuropäischen Wirtschaftsraum, *Kölner Forsch. Wirtschafts-und Sozialgeog.* 15, 1971. z.

Hommel, M.: Zentrenausrichtung in mehrkernigen Verdichtungsräumen an Beispielen aus dem rheinisch-westfälischen Industriegebiet, *Bochumer Geog. Arb.* 17, 1974.

Hottes, K. H.: Das Ruhrgebiet im Strukturwandel, *Berichte z. deut. Landeskunde* 38, 1967.

Illgen, K.: Geographie und territoriale Organisation des Binnenhandels, *Lehrbrief – Geographie* 5, *Hochschule für Binnenhandel*, Leipzig, 1966.

Institut für Raumforschung: Die Branchengliederung der Flüchtlingsindustrien in der Bundesrepublik, *Informationen* 1, Bonn, 1952.
Der Maschinenbau und Apparatebau in der sowjetischen Besatzungszone Deutschlands, *Mitteilungen* 5, Bonn, 1951.
Die Eisen- und Stahlerzeugende Industrie in der sowjetischen Besatzungszone Deutschlands, *Mitteilungen* 7, Bonn, 1951.
Industrielle Standortfragen als Problem der Wiedervereinigung Deutschlands, *Informationen* 44–45, Bonn, 1951.
Die Flüchtlingsbetriebe in der Bundesrepublik, *Information* 48–49, Bonn, 1951.

Jarecki, C.: Der neuzeitliche Strukturwandel an der Ruhr, *Marburger Geog. Schriften* 29, 1967.

Jurgons, R.: Die Hüttenstandorte Dünkirchen, Ijmuiden, Bremen und Lübeck – eine vergleichende Betrachtung, *Kölner Forsch. z. Wirtschafts-und Sozialgeog.* 7, 1969.

Kern, H.: Ein Modell für die wirtschaftliche Entwicklung der Region Unterelbe, Hamburg, 1971.

Knübel, H.: Die räumliche Gliederung des Ruhrgebietes, *Geog. Rundschau* 15, 1965, pp.180–190.

Köllmann, W.: Die Strukturelle Entwicklung des südwestfälischen Wirtschaftsraumes 1945–1967, Hagen, 1969.

Kozlov, I. D.: Zur Integration der DDR in der Energiewirtschaft der RGW-Länder, *P.M.* 117, 1973, pp.1–6.

Krümme, G.: The interregional corporation and the region, *T.E.S.G.* 61, 1970, pp.318–333.

Mareyen, H.: Die Edelstahlindustrie Deutschlands unter besonderer Berücksichtigung ihres Standortes, *Nürnberger Wirtschaft- u. Sozialgeog. Arb.* 11, 1970.

Mertins, G.: Die Kulturlandschaft des westlichen Ruhrgebiets: Mülheim-Oberhausen-Dinslaken, *Giessener Geog. Schriften* 4, 1964.

Meynen, E.: Die wirtschaftsräumliche Gliederung Deutschlands, *Berichte z. deut. Landeskunde* 15, 1955.

Mieth, W-H., Schenck, H.: Ermittlung des standortbedingten Kostenunterschiedes eines Hüttenwerkes – dargestellt am Beispiel Küste-Binnenland, *Stahl und Eisen* 10, 1970, pp.499–507.

Müller, H.: Die Ansiedlung der deutschböhmischen Glasveredlungsindustrie in Westdeutschland, *Forschung und Leben* 1, Bonn, 1951.

Orgeig, H. D.: Der Einzelhandel in den Cities von Duisburg, Düsseldorf, Köln und Bonn, *Kölner Forsch. z. Wirtschafts- u. Sozialgeog.* 17, 1972.
The localisation of the iron and steel industry in northwest Germany, *T.E.S.G.* 42, 1961, pp.174–181.

Pritzel, K.: Die wirtschaftliche Integration der sowjetischen Besatzungszone Deutschlands in den Ostblock, 2nd ed., Bonn, 1966.

Pruskil, W.: Die Auswirkungen staatsmonopolistischer Erdölpolitik auf die Standortverteilung der erdölverarbeitenden Industrie Westdeutschlands, *P.M.* 114, 1970, pp.195–204.
Geographie und staatsmonopolistischer Kapitalismus, *P.M.-Ergäzungsheft* 275, 1971.

Radzio, H.: Leben können an der Ruhr, Düsseldorf, 1970.

Reichsamt für Wehrwirtschaftliche Planung: Die deutsche Industrie, *Schriftenreihe* 1, Berlin, 1939.

Resch, W.: Die Wandlungen der Erzversorgung der Hüttenindustrie, Dortmund, 1968.

Ried, H.: Vom Montandreieck zur Saar-Lor-Lux-Industrieregion, *Themen zur Geographie und Gemeinschaftskunde*, Frankfurt, 1972.

Riguet, P.: Conversion industrielle et réutilisation de l'espace dans la Ruhr, *Ann. de Géog.* 81, 1972, pp.594–621.

Rinn, J.: Handbuch der Bergwirtschaft in der Bundesrepublik Deutschland, Essen, 1970.

Rugg, D. S.: Selected areal effects of planning processes on urban development in the Federal Republic of Germany, *Economic Geog.* 42, 1966, pp.326–335.

Salin, E., Stohler, J., Pawlowsky, P.: Notwendigkeit und Gefahr der wirtschaftlichen Konzentration in nationaler und internationaler Sicht, *Frankfurter Gespräche der List Gesell.* 62, 1969.

Sanke, H.: Entwicklung und gegenwärtige Probleme der politischen und ökonomischen Geographie der DDR, Berlin, 1962.

Schenck, H.: Strukturelle Merkmale der Eisenindustrie, *Stahl und Eisen* 25, 1968, pp.1394–1400.

Schmidt, U.: Methoden der Siedlungsstrukturplanung und -forschung in der DDR, *P.M.* 118, 1974, pp.261–266.

Schmidt-Renner, G.: Komplexe Entwicklung von Wirtschaftsgebieten, *P.M.* 107, 1963, pp.193–200.
Tendenzen der perspektivischen Standortverteilung der Industrie in der DDR, *Wiss. Abh. d. Geog. Gesell der DDR* 7, 1969.

Seraphim, P. H.: Industriekombinat Oberschlesien, Köln, 1953.

Siedlungsverband Ruhrkohlenbezirk: Gebietsentwicklungsplan, Essen, 1966.

Sinnhuber, K.: Eisenhüttenstadt and other new industrial locations in East Germany, *Festschrift für Leo Scheidl*, Wien, 1965.

Smotkine, H.: Un type de complexe industriel: le district de Karl-Marx-Stadt en RDA, *Ann. de. Géog.* 76, 1967, pp.154–167.

Sombart, W.: Die deutsche Volkswirtschaft im 19 und am Anfang des 20 Jahrhunderts, Berlin, 1921.

Spethmann, H.: Das Ruhrgebiet, 3 vols, Berlin, 1933.

Spilker, H.: Zukunftschancen des Wirtschaftsraumes 'Deutsche Küste', Hamburg, 1968.

Steinberg, H. G.: Die Entwicklung des Ruhrgebietes – eine wirtschafts- und sozialgeographische Studie, *Deutscher Gewerkschaftsbund*, Düsseldorf, 1967.

Thürauf, G.: Industriestandorte in der Region München, *Münchner Studien z. Sozial-u. Wirtschaftsgeog.* 16, 1975.

Treue, W.: Deutsche Wirtschaft und Politik 1933–1945, Stuttgart, 1962.
Die Feuer verlöschen nie – August Thyssen-Hütte 1890–1926, Düsseldorf, 1966.

Treue, W., Uebling, H.: Die Feuer verlöschen nie – August Thyssen-Hütte 1926–1966, Düsseldorf, 1969.

van der Rijst, A., van de Woestijne, W. J.: Veränderung der Einflussfaktoren für die Standortwahl von Hüttenwerken in Westeuropa, *Stahl und Eisen* 10, 1970, pp.493–499.

Voppel, G.: Die Aachener Bergbau- und Industrielandschaft, *Kölner Forsch. z. Wirtschafts-u. Sozialgeog.* 3, 1963.

Waller, P. P., Swain, H. S.: Changing patterns of oil transportation and refining in West Germany, *Econ. Geog.* 43, 1967, pp.143–156.

Warren, K.: The changing steel industry of the Common Market, *Econ. Geog.* 43, 1967, pp.314–332.

Weber, H-U.: Formen räumlicher Integration in der Textilindustrie der EWG, *Bochumer Geog. Arb.* 19, 1975.

Ziranka, J.: Die Auswirkungen von Zechenstillegungen und Rationalisierungen im Steinkohlenbergbau auf die Wirtschaftsstruktur ausgewählter Gemeinden im niederrheinisch-westfälischen Industriegebiet, *Forschungsberichte des Landes Nordrhein-Westfalen* 1311, Düsseldorf, 1964.

Zubkov, A. I.: Probleme der Standortsverteilung der Schwarzmetallindustrie im RGW, *P.M.* 114, 1970, pp.274–280.

VII   Economic geography: transport

Achilles, F. W.: Hafenstandorte und Hafenfunktionen im Rhein-Ruhrgebiet, *Bochumer Geog. Arb.* 2, 1967.

Bär, A.: Der Mittelland-Kanal, *Geog. Anzeiger* 27, 1926, pp.173–175.

Barrington, R.: The Hamburg 'outer port' project and related developments. *T.E.S.G.* 59, 1968, pp.106–108.

Breitenmoser, A. (ed.): Taschenbuch der Rheinschiffahrt Basel, 1974.

Buchholz, H. J.: Der Eisenbahnknotenpunkt Hamm (Westf.) – Entwicklung und Wandlung seiner Bedeutung, *Stadtverwaltung Hamm*, 1977.

Bundesminister für Verkehr: Verkehrspolitik 1949–1965, Hof, 1966.

Delacroix, R. et al.: L'allemagne – République Fédérale, Special Issue: *La Vie du Rail* 12, Paris, 1974.

Demangeon, A., Febrve, L.: Le Rhin, Paris, 1935.

Eckert, C.: Rheinschiffahrt im 19 Jahrhundert, *Staats- und Sozialwissenschaftliche Forsch.* 18, Leipzig, 1900.

Ende, H.: Die Verkehrsdichte des Deutschen Reiches, *Archiv für Eisenbahnwesen* Berlin, 1936.

Esselrügge, N.: Die Abhängigkeit des norddeutschen Eisenbahnnetzes von der Geländegestaltung, *Archiv für Eisenbahnwesen*, Berlin, 1933.

445

Freitag, U.: Verkehrsarten: Systematik und Methodik der kartographischen Darstellungen des Verkehrs mit Beispielen zur Verkehrsgeographie des mittleren Hessen, *Giessener Geog. Schriften* 8, 1966.

Fuchs, K.: Die Erschliessung des Siegerlandes durch die Eisenbahn, Wiesbaden, 1969.

Giese, K.: Die deutschen Städte und das Eisenbahnwesen, *Deutsche Eisenbahnen der Gegenwart*, Berlin, 1927.

Gothein, E.: Geschichtliche Entwicklung der Rheinschiffahrt im 19 Jahrhundert, *Die Schiffahrt der deutschen Ströme* 2, Leipzig, 1903.

Haufe, H.: Die geographische Struktur des deutschen Eisenbahnverkehrs, *Veröffentl. d. Geog. Seminar d. Univ. Leipzig* 2, 1931.

Hottes, K. H.: Verkehrsgeographischer Strukturwandel im Rhein-Ruhrgebiet, *Geog. Taschenbuch* 1970–1972, pp.102–114.

Hüttmann, E.: Verkehrsgeographische Probleme am Beispiel der Eisenbahnen Schleswig-Holsteins, Hamburg, 1949.

Jensen, W. (ed.): Der Nord-Ostsee-Kanal, *Wasser- und Schiffahrtsdirektion Kiel*, 1970.

Keller, E.: Die verkehrsgeographischen Grundlagen der deutschen Eisenbahnumwege, *Archiv für Eisenbahnwesen*, Berlin, 1929.

Laspeyres, R.: Rotterdam und das Ruhrgebiet, *Marburger Geog. Schriften* 41, 1969.

Lauth, W.: Die Standort- und geographische Leistungsstruktur der Unternehmungsformen in der Binnenschiffahrt der BRD, *Frankfurter Wirtschafts- und Sozialgeog. Schriften* 15, 1974.

Lütgens, R.: Die deutschen Seehäfen, Karlsruhe, 1934.

Mackinder, H. J.: The Rhine, London, 1908.

Maradon, J-C.: Der kombinierte Güterverkehr Schiene/Strasse in der BRD als Faktor der Industrieansiedlung, *Forschungsabteilung für Raumordnung – Geog. Inst. d. Ruhr-Universität Bochum* 6, 1973.

Marsden, W.: The Rhineland, London, 1973.

Martin, J. E.: Some effects of the canalisation of the Moselle, *Geog.* 59, 1974, pp.298–308.

Matznetter, J.: Grundfragen der Verkehrsgeographie, *Mitt. d. Geog. Gesell. Wien* 95, 1953, pp.109–124.

Meine, K-H.: Darstellung verkehrsgeographischer Sachverhalte: ein Beitrag zur thematischen Verkehrsgeographie, *Forsch. z. deut. Landeskunde* 136, 1967.

Mollowo, H-J.: Die Lokalbahnen im Steigerwald und in der Fränkischen Alb, *Mitt. Fränk. Geog. Gesell.* 19, 1972, pp.237–257.

Pirath, C.: Die Grundlagen der Verkehrswirtschaft, 2 ed., Berlin, 1949.

Predöhl, A.: Verkehrspolitik, *Grundriss der Sozialwissenschaft* 15, Göttingen, 1958.

Rauers, F.: Geschichte der alten Handelsstrassen in Deutschland, *P.M.* 52, 1906, pp.49–60.

Rees, G.: The Rhine, London, 1967.

Ritter, J.: Le Rhin, Paris, 1963.

Rössger, E., Rössger, A.: Die Bedeutung eines Flughafens für die Wirtschaft in seiner Umgebung, *Forschungsberichte des Landes Nordrhein-Westfalen* 2082, 1971.

Schliephake, K.: Geographische Erfassung des Verkehrs–ein Überblick über die Betrachtungsweisen des Verkehrs in der Geographie mit Beispielen aus dem mittleren Hessen, *Giessener Geog. Schriften* 28, 1969.

Schofield, G.: Canalisation of the Mosel, *Geog.* 50, 1965, pp.161–163.

Schroeder, K.: Der Stadtverkehr als Kriterium der Strukturwandlungen Berlins, *Erdkunde* 14, 1960, pp.29–34

Schultze-Rhondorf, F-C.: Die Verkehrsströme der Kohle im Raum der BRD zwischen 1913 und 1937, *Forsch. z. deut. Landeskunde* 146, 1964.

Siedentop, I.: Die Linienführung der Eisenbahnen, Strassen und Autobahnen in Mitteleuropa, Düsseldorf, n.d.

Stang, F.: Wasserstrassen, Häfen und Hinterland im Oberrheingebiet, *Forsch. z. deut. Landeskunde* 140, 1963.

Völker, W.: Die Entwicklung der Eisenbahnen im Ruhrgebiet, *Verkehrsprobleme in Ballungsräumen, Forsch. und Sitzungsberichte d. Akad. f. Raumforsch. u. Landesplanung* 12, Hannover, 1959, pp.101–123.

Voss, W.: Die langfristige Entwicklung des Eisenbahngüterverkehrs in Deutschland von 1880–1957, Hamburg, 1960.

VIII Statistical Sources

Bundesminister für Ernährung, Landwirtschaft und Forsten: Statistisches Jahrbuch, Bonn, annually.

Bundesminister für Wirtschaft: Leistung in Zahlen, Bonn, annually.

Deutscher Bäderverband: Deutscher Bäderkalender, Bonn, annually.

Deutscher Brauer-Bund: Statistischer Bericht, Bonn, annually.

Deutscher Gemeindetag: Statistisches Jahrbuch Deutscher Gemeinden, Braunschweig, annually.

Presse- und Informationsamt der Bundesregierung: Jahresbericht der Bundesregierung, Bonn, annually.

Staatliche Zentralverwaltung für Statistik: Statistisches Jahrbuch der Deutschen Demokratischen Republik, Bonn, annually.

Statistisches Bundesamt: Bevölkerung und Wirtschaft 1872–1972, Wiesbaden.
Statistisches Jahrbuch der Bundesrepublik Deutschland, Wiesbaden, annually.
(This Office also produces a wide range of statistical publications, including the weekly *Wirtschaft und Statistik*.)

Verband der Automobilindustrie: Tatsachen und Zahlen aus der Kraftverkehrswirtschaft, Frankfurt, annually.

Verband der Chemiewirtschaft: Chemiewirtschaft in Zahlen, Frankfurt, annually.

Verein Deutscher Maschinenbau-Anstalten: Statistisches Jahrbuch für den Maschinenbau, Frankfurt, annually.

Verlag Glückauf: Jahrbuch für Bergbau, Mineralöl und Chemie, Essen, annually.

Wirtschaftsvereinigung Eisen- und Stahlindustrie: Statistisches Jahrbuch der Eisen- und Stahlindustrie, Düsseldorf, annually.

Each *Land* publishes its own statistical yearbook besides a range of other statistical publications.

IX Atlases

Atlas der deutschen Agrarlandschaft: Otremba, E. (ed.), Wiesbaden, 1971 et seq.

Atlas der Deutschen Demokratischen Republik: Kohl, H. (ed.), Berlin, 1972 et seq.

Atlas des deutschen Lebensraumes in Mitteleuropa: Krebs, N. (ed.), Leipzig, 1937 et seq.

Atlas – Die Bundesrepublik in Karten: *Statistisches Bundesamt*, Wiesbaden 1965 et seq.

Atlas zur Geschichte der deutschen Ostsiedlung: Krallert, W., et al. (eds.), Bielefeld, 1958.

Atlas von Niedersachsen: Brüning, K. (ed.), Oldenburg, 1934 (2 ed. 1950).

Atlas Östliches Mitteleuropa: Kraus, T., et al, (eds.), Bielefeld, 1959.

Atlas zur Raumentwicklung: *Bundesanstalt für Landeskunde*, Bonn, 1976.

Das Saarland in Karte und Bild: Liedtke, H., et al. (eds.), Neumünster, 1974.

Der Deutsche Planungsatlas: in ten volumes, *Akademie für Raumforschung*, Hannover, 1960 et seq.

Die Landschaften Niedersachsens – Topographischer Atlas: Schrader, E. (ed.), Hannover, 1967.

Deutschland neu entdeckt: die Bundesrepublik in farbigen Senkrechtluftbildaufnahmen, Mainz, 1972.

Deutscher Landwirtschaftsatlas: *Statistisches Reichsamt*, Berlin, 1934.

Hessen in Karte und Luftbild, I & II: Neumünster, 1969 and Bielefeld, 1973.

Klima-Atlanten der Deutschen Bundesländer: *Zentralamt des Deutschen Wetterdienstes*, Offenbach, 1950 et seq.

Luftbildatlas Baden-Württemberg: Fezer, F., Muuss, U. (eds.), Neumünster, 1971.

Luftbildatlas Bayern: Fehn, H., Beckel, L. (eds.), München, 1973.

Luftbildatlas Deutschland: Muuss, U. (ed.), Neumünster, 1972.

Luftbildatlas Niedersachsen: Grotelüschen, W., Muuss, U. (eds.), Neumünster, 1967.

Luftbildatlas Nordrhein-Westfalen: Muuss, U., Schüttler, A. (eds.), Neumünster, 1969.

Luftbildatlas Rheinland-Pfalz, I & II: Sperling, W., Strunk, E. (eds.), Neumünster, 1971–1972.

Luftbildatlas von Schleswig-Holstein, I & II: Degn, C., Muuss, U. (eds.), Neumünster, 1965–1969.

Nordrhein-Westfalen Atlas: *Landesplanungsbehörde*, Düsseldorf, 1976.

Saar-Atlas: Overbeck, H., Sante, G. W. (eds.), Gotha, 1934.

Topographischer Atlas Bayern: Fehn, H., et al. (eds.), München, 1968.

Topographischer Atlas der Bundesrepublik Deutschland: Degn, C., Muuss, U. (eds.), Neumünster, 1977.

Topographischer Atlas von Niedersachsen und Bremen: Seedorf, H. (ed.), Hannover, 1976.

Topographischer Atlas Nordrhein-Westfalen: Schüttler, A. (ed.), Düsseldorf, 1968.

Topographischer Atlas Rheinland-Pfalz: Liedtke, H. (ed.), Neumünster, 1973.

Topographischer Atlas Schleswig-Holstein: Degn, C., Muuss, U. (eds.), Neumünster, 1963.

INDEX